Special Edition

USING
MICROSOFT®
EXCHANGE™
SERVER 5

J. WISHART
SYSTEMS SUPERVISOR
ISLAND PAPER MILLS
1010 DERWENT WAY
DELTA, B.C.
CANADA   V3M 5R1
(604) 527-2555   FAX: (604) 527-2592
E-MAIL: johnw@ebeddy.com

MAILING   PO BOX 2170
ADDRESS   NEW WESTMINSTER BC
             V3L 5A5

Special Edition

USING MICROSOFT® EXCHANGE™ SERVER 5

Written by Software Spectrum with

Kent Joshi • Tracy Bradley • Tito Del Prado • Neil Nelmida • Richard Romo • Intekhab "Inti" Shaikh • Robert Short • Valeno Valentino

and

Sal Collora • Mark Kapczynski • Ruben Perez • Ed Roberts

Special Edition Using Microsoft Exchange Server 5

Library of Congress Catalog No.: 97-65015

ISBN: 0-7897-1116-8

99 98 97   6 5 4 3 2

Interpretation of the printing code: the rightmost double-digit number is the year of the book's printing; the rightmost single-digit number, the number of the book's printing. For example, a printing code of 97-2 shows that the first printing of the book occurred in 1997.

Credits

PRESIDENT
Roland Elgey

PUBLISHER
Stacy Hiquet

PUBLISHING MANAGER
Fred Slone

SENIOR TITLE MANAGER
Bryan Gambrel

EDITORIAL SERVICES DIRECTOR
Elizabeth Keaffaber

DIRECTOR OF MARKETING
Lynn E. Zingraf

ACQUISITIONS EDITOR
Al Valvano

PRODUCTION EDITOR
Sherri L. Fugit

EDITOR
Kate Givens

PRODUCT MARKETING MANAGER
Kristine Ankney

ASSISTANT PRODUCT MARKETING MANAGERS
Karen Hagen
Christy M. Miller

STRATEGIC MARKETING MANAGER
Barry Pruett

TECHNICAL EDITORS
John Nelsen
Mark Streger

TECHNICAL SUPPORT SPECIALIST
Nadeem Muhammed

ACQUISITIONS COORDINATOR
Carmen Krikorian

SOFTWARE RELATIONS COORDINATOR
Susan D. Gallagher

EDITORIAL ASSISTANT
Andrea Duvall

BOOK DESIGNER
Ruth Harvey

COVER DESIGNER
Dan Armstrong

PRODUCTION TEAM
DiMonique Ford
Amy Gornik
Brian Grossman
Lisa Stumpf

INDEXER
Craig Small

Composed in *Century Old Style* and *ITC Franklin Gothic* by Que Corporation.

About the Authors

Neil Nelmida is a consultant for Software Spectrum-TSG Los Angeles. He is a Microsoft Certified Systems Engineer, specializing in Exchange, Mail, TCP/IP, and Windows NT.

Prior to joining Software Spectrum, he co-owned a private consulting firm, which was a Microsoft Solution Provider. There he designed and installed Windows NT based-networks with Exchange Server and connectivity to the Internet. He also provided training for network administrators to maintain their systems to run at optimum performance.

He has always had a love for computers. He majored in Computer Science at UCLA, where he developed a solid foundation for problem solving and programming. He also enjoys all multimedia games, especially golf.

Intekhab "Inti" Shaikh has over seven years of experience in the computer industry. Starting from the DOS 3.1 days to the present NT Server 4.0, Inti has all around experience with both Microsoft FrontOffice and BackOffice products. On the hardware side, Inti has upgraded a number of PC's, installed additional hardware components, and configured NIC cards. On the software side, Inti has a great deal of experience with Excel and Access. He has created full service payroll software within Excel that creates a payroll, calculates the federal and state tax liability, and builds payroll reports. He has also programmed spreadsheet applications that crunch formulas, run statistics, and automatically generate useful business reports.

Inti conducts training sessions on Excel, Word, and accounting software (payroll taxes in particular) for the CPA firms and small companies in the Los Angeles area. Inti owns and manages a payroll and bookkeeping company of his own. Additionally, Inti is a Microsoft Certified Professional and currently pursuing the Microsoft Systems Engineer certification. He also has multiple degrees from Cal State University and is a network consultant with Software Spectrum, Inc. in Los Angeles. Currently, he is working on deploying Microsoft Systems Manager Server in a 1,000 workstation client in Long Beach, California.

His passion is spending time with his family, Windows NT, reading technical books, keeping accounting books for his clients and spending time with a great team of consultants he works with at Software Spectrum's Los Angeles office. His e-mail is **ishaikh@swspectrum.com.** Inti owes his networking exposure to Kent Joshi, the primary author of this book, who is a good friend, and his mentor in this industry.

Richard Romo is a Principle Consultant and teacher for Software Spectrum. His experience has ranged from small to large corporations, and he has worked in the Southern California area for 13 years. Richard has a BA from the University of California at Santa Barbara in Economics. Richard has worked for a variety of accounts setting up UNIX Administration and TCP/IP networks. For three years he has been setting up NT networks, Exchange and SMS projects. Richard is an Accelerated Certified Engineer for Santa Cruz Operating System's UNIX and a certified teacher for Santa Cruz Operations. He also is a Microsoft Certified Trainer and is a specialist for Information Internet Server. Additionally, he has worked as a Senior Consultant for Grant Thornton, managing projects for NT and Microsoft SQL installation for Association and Professional Societies and has served as a director of a Microsoft

Authorized Training Educational Center in Orange County. He has extensive experience with Microsoft Exchange and System Management Server in some of the biggest companies in Southern California.

Tracy Bradley has been involved with Windows NT since the early BETAs of NT 3.1 in October of 1992 and the NT Inside Track Program of 1993. He has been a dedicated, avid NT and Microsoft supporter since then and travels to "Mecca" near Seattle every chance he gets. In addition to long term experience with NT, Tracy is a Lotus Notes Certified Specialist (LCNS) since 1994 with experience in administering and developing workgroup applications for several large corporations. Since joining Software Spectrum's Dallas office in 1995, Tracy not only completed MCSE certification, but has been involved with Exchange almost exclusively since BETA 1 of version 4.0 with extensive work with MS Mail as well.

Currently, Tracy is the Microsoft Messaging Team leader over a thriving business in the Dallas area and has worked with literally dozens of Fortune 1000 corporations across the nation in both design, implementation, and ongoing development surrounding Exchange. Tracy was a presenter at the first Exchange Deployment Conference in Austin, Texas in September 1996 and is in much demand for consulting engagements across the Software Spectrum realm.

When not jetting around the U.S. and abroad, Tracy enjoys time at home with his wife Sheryl and baby daughter Rebecca, without whom all of this work would be worthless. Not bad for a Music Education major from Hardin-Simmons University in Abilene, Texas, wouldn't you say?

Robert Short has over 12 years experience in the industry, and his skills range from Project Management to Infrastructure design.

He is a certified engineer with Microsoft, Novell, and Banyan and has implemented large cc:Mail, Beyond Mail WordPerfect Office/GroupWise messaging systems. He is currently an employee of Software Spectrum and is specializing in Microsoft Windows NT 4.0, Microsoft System Management, and Microsoft Exchange Servers. He designs and implements large Banyan Networks at sites like Litton Data Systems, Warner Bros. Records, and several agencies in the Los Angeles area. Bob has also installed a number of Novell 3.x and 4x Networks and has migrated Netware clients from Netware 3.x to Netware 4.x and Microsoft Windows NT. He has a strong background in System/Directory service design from his early days working with Banyan Vines StreetTalk. This knowledge makes the transition to Netware Directory Services a strong one and has helped with Microsoft Exchange designs.

Bob would like to thank his wife Kelly and his daughter Shayla for all their love and support.

Kent Joshi holds a B.S. degree in Finance from the University of Utah. Currently, he is the Microsoft Practice Manager for Software Spectrum Inc.'s Technology Services Group. He is responsible for all aspects of the consulting practice including financials, resource management, employee development, and maintaining a close relationship with Microsoft.

Previously, he owned and managed The Joshi Group, a technical consulting firm specializing in the design, deployment, and tuning of large corporate networks. The Joshi Group has recently joined Software Spectrum and Kent as well as his employees are now employed in their Los Angeles office.

Before managing his own company, he was employed at IBM Corporation, where he managed a team of consultants who installed and supported network systems for educational accounts.

Additionally, he has also worked for Microsoft Corporation, where he provided pre- and post-sales consulting for several Microsoft clients. In his role as systems engineer, he was recognized as the Outstanding Representative in the Western Region.

Feel free to reach Kent at **kjoshi@swspectrum.com**

Tito Del Prado has over nine years of Networking experience, having worked extensively with Novell Netware, Banyan Vines, and Microsoft Back Office. Tito is a Microsoft Certified Systems Engineer (MCSE), specializing in the Microsoft NT 4.0 operating system. He is a certified Netframe administrator and has a diploma in Computer Technology and Electronics from Computer Learning Center of Los Angeles. Tito is a Consultant at the Los Angeles office of the Technology Services Group of Software Spectrum, Inc.

Prior to working as a network consultant, Tito was a hardware engineer specializing in the legal arena. Having worked at most of the major law firms in the Los Angeles area, Tito has experience working with multiple platforms and applications as well as wide and local area networks. Tito also has experience working with many large government contractors such as Rockwell and TRW.

Aside from his various computer interests, Tito also enjoys spending time with his family, combing the beaches of Southern California for the perfect wave, and is an active member of his community coaching and organizing youth sports and activities. His e-mail address is **Tdelprado@swspectrum.com.**

Valeno Valentino has nine years of computer experience as a freelance programmer and five years of experience in networking infrastructure. Working for companies such as Paramount Pictures, GTE, Loma Linda Medical Center, Comp USA, and Kenneth Cole Shoes (just to name a few) has helped him become a seasoned computer professional. Database design and object oriented programming have probably been his claim to fame. On the networking side, he has implemented Windows NT 3.51 server with Workstation 4.0 clients on the LAN/WAN environment at Lawyers Title Insurance in Glendale, California. Troubleshooting DHCP and TCP/IP problems in the Los Angeles and San Fernando areas has made him a topnotch problem solver. He is now on the Software Spectrum Consulting Team where he happily coexists in the network infrastructure and application development worlds. He gives special acknowledgment to his mother, two sisters, nephew, and his girlfriend Lisa, without their support from the very beginning none of his accomplishments would have been posssible. He considers himself a dedicated and hardworking consultant who will be making his mark in the larger arena in the years to come. Drop him a line sometime at **vvalentino@swspectrum.com**

Acknowledgments

This book is for those who seek the new, but keep the best of the old.

First, I thank Noelani Rodriguez and Randy Newman for their silent patience. Although they sacrificed sleep and consulting income to ensure the first edition of this book was done right, they were never properly recognized. Thank you, my friends. The first edition would not have been complete without your contributions. Be sure to check out Noelani's book, *Using Microsoft SMS 1.2* published by Que.

Next, I thank Betty Dixon of Compaq and Ralph Smaldino of NEC for loaning us hubs and one incredible dual Pentium server. With the NEC server as our lab's heart and Compaq's hubs connecting to everything else, we turned a training room into a "virtual Software Spectrum." We simulated 11 Software Spectrum consulting sites across the world in one room complete with all the necessary connectors, protocols, and external mail systems.

I thank Software Spectrum for seeing value in this book and expending considerable time, money, and resources to ensure its success. Specifically, I thank Michelle Hollis, Site Manager for Software Spectrum's Technology Services Group (TSG) in Los Angeles for supporting me and helping me with my responsibilities so I could fully focus on authoring. You are a great mentor and a model manager. As you would say, "Thank you, thank you, thank you." I thank Dan Gardner, Director of Consulting West, whose warm personality and ultimate integrity continue to inspire me. I say thank you to Link Simpson, President of TSG. You are an outstanding example of leadership by principles. I also want to give a big Thank You to Phillip McCollough, Product Manager for Microsoft BackOffice Solutions who managed the marketing effort for this book from Software Spectrum's side and whose Microsoft contacts were key in taking this book to the next level. Also, thank you to Vic Clements, Principal Consultant, TSG-LA for assisting several authors in completing their chapters. Finally, I thank Judy Sims, Chairman, CEO, and President of Software Spectrum Inc. I have a deep respect for anyone who can successfully manage a company such as Software Spectrum.

I thank all of the Microsoft employees who helped make this book a reality. Thank you Elaine Sharp in Australia for all of your Exchange information and moral support and Brian Valentine for letting us use your quote to kick off Chapter 1. Also, thanks to Giuseppe Mascarella, Total Cost of Ownership Marketing Manager for your great assistance, and John Frederiksen and Len Wyatt in the Exchange Group in Redmond for answering all of our late night questions on Exchange 5.0 features and performance tuning. I thank Paula White for your Follow-up and coming all the way down to Los Angeles for our Microsoft Open House.

I thank Mario Santonastaso and everyone else at Campbell Hall School for their continued support and letting the team borrow a Macintosh for a key chapter. Mario, you're one heck of a client. Thank you from the bottom of my heart.

To the Fab Four, thank you for your tireless work. You know who you are.

Thanks to Mark Kapczynski for giving me an opportunity to participate in the first edition of this book.

I extend deep and loving thanks to my Mom, Miranda Lee, who supported me during the earliest phases of this book. Keep the faith, Mom.

I also send a big Thank You to Dad, Doe, and Dan in Ohio. You guys were always on my mind throughout the authoring of the book.

I also thank Al Valvano from Que Publishing for offering this book opportunity and working with me by taking calls at home and over the Christmas holidays. Thanks for being sensitive to our authoring schedule.

A loud and powerful thank you to Anthony Robbins. Although we only met briefly, your wisdom, energy level, and lifestyle continue to shape my life and the relationships around me. You were the difference that made a difference. I hope one day we can extend our meeting into a lunch. Live with Passion!

And finally, I extend thanks to someone I never had the pleasure of meeting. I thank Bill Gates whose company gave me my first technology job at the tender age of 18. One day, I'd like to meet and personally thank you for creating the company that started all this.

As I think about the amount of teamwork it took to complete this book, I'm reminded that with every accomplishment, there are always hidden heroes. If I've left anyone out, I truly appreciate your help, and I trust the book will somehow come back to reward you over the work you've put in.

Kent Joshi

Microsoft Practice Manager

Software Spectrum, Technology
Services Group (TSG), Los Angeles

kjoshi@swspectrum.com

We'd Like to Hear from You!

As part of our continuing effort to produce books of the highest possible quality, Que would like to hear your comments. To stay competitive, we *really* want you to let us know what you like or dislike most about this book or other Que products.

Please send your comments, ideas, and suggestions for improvement to:

The Expert User Team

Email: **euteam@que.mcp.com**

CompuServe: 72410,2077

Fax: (317) 581-4663

Our mailing address is:

Expert User Team

Que Corporation

201 West 103rd Street

Indianapolis, IN 46290-1097

You can also visit our team's home page on the World Wide Web:

http://www.mcp.com/que/developer_expert

Thank you in advance. Your comments will help us to continue publishing the best books available in today's market.

Thank you,

The Expert User Team

Contents at a Glance

Table of Contents

II | Installing and Migrating to Exchange

III | Exchange Administration and Configuration

12 Using the Administrator Program   225

13 Directory and System Attendant Configuration   247

IV | The Exchange Client

Introduction

Microsoft Exchange Server is one of the most scalable and feature-rich products from Microsoft. In a small office, it's a robust messaging and group scheduling system with Internet mail capability for any Exchange user to reach just about anyone on the Internet. In a large corporation, it's positioned to be the messaging backbone and a versatile groupware product. Using the Forms Designer, you can build custom workflow applications like a personnel profiles database. (See Chapter 34, "Developing Exchange Forms," for an actual personnel profile form application created from scratch.) Because larger companies usually have existing mail systems, Exchange provides several connectors, gateways, and migration/extraction tools for complete coexistence or migration to Exchange.

Plus, for any size environment, a single, intuitive Administration program manages your entire messaging environment. Exchange, in essence, becomes the heart of your messaging system. ■

The Key Features of Exchange

This section highlights both the new features from Exchange 5.0 and the original ones that make Exchange a robust messaging platform.

Who Should Use This Book?

This book addresses a wide audience. Managers, messaging specialists, and network administrators can count on this book as a complete resource.

How to Use This Book

Parts I and II give you an overview of Exchange and guide you through the planning process to deploy Exchange. Part III focuses on Exchange's core components, managing Exchange using the Administrator program, and connecting to non-Exchange e-mail systems. Part IV focuses on Outlook, Microsoft's premier e-mail client. Finally, Part V goes into the advanced features of Exchange such as EDI and developing Exchange Forms.

What Are the Key Features of Exchange?

Exchange is a vision into the future of messaging technology. Exchange provides revolutionary functionality at a low end-user cost. Now that you have an understanding of what Exchange is and how it's positioned for different types of companies, let's take a look at some of its features.

Outlook

Outlook is a next generation Exchange client. Positioned as an upgrade to the Microsoft Exchange Client and Schedule+, it was designed as Microsoft's premier e-mail client for 32-bit Windows-based systems. It is available with Exchange Server as a stand-alone product and as a component of Office97. Outlook operates with Microsoft Mail, Microsoft Exchange clients and Schedule+, enabling administrators to deploy their choice of client within a company. No matter what a company's decision, Microsoft will have a unified client architecture and logical upgrade paths from either client (Outlook or Exchange).

Combining the features of the Exchange Client (Inbox) and Schedule+, users can still manage e-mail, calendars, contacts, tasks, and to-do lists. However, Outlook enhances all of these previous features and adds enhanced views, journalizing capabilities, document management, and notes.

There is also e-mail functionality using a standard Web browser. Called Outlook Web View, remote users who do not have access to Outlook or have limited hardware resources (RAM, hard drive space) can easily retrieve messages from an Exchange Server using Internet Explorer.

N O T E You must have Microsoft's Internet Information Server (IIS) installed to provide e-mail access to Web View users. ▨

Built-on Internet Standards

Exchange supports several protocols, including SMTP (Simple Mail Transfer Protocol) and POP3 (Post Office Protocol) for e-mail, NNTP (Network News Transfer Protocol) for Internet newsgroups retrieval, LDAP (Lightweight Directory Access Protocol) for Exchange directory access, HTTP and HTML for Web access, and SSL for secure Internet transmission.

Any e-mail client that supports POP3 can be used to retrieve messages from a Microsoft Exchange Server, including the Microsoft Internet Explorer Mail client. Microsoft Exchange Internet Mail Service (IMS) provides a standard SMTP server for any POP3 client to submit their messages.

NNTP enables a full newsfeed of Internet newsgroups right into your company's public folders. Employees can post responses right into the public folder and the response is posted back to the appropriate newsgroup on the Internet.

LDAP is an Internet protocol that enables users to access Exchange's directory information. With the proper rights, clients can read, search, and browse Exchange's directory.

With HTTP and HTML, along with Internet Information server (IIS) and Active Server Components, users can access their private mailboxes using a standard Web browser such as Internet Explorer. Additionally, SSL is a supported, Internet-security protocol that protects data traveling on the Internet.

cc:Mail Connector

Exchange 5.0 also has a cc:Mail connector that provides complete e-mail connectivity to existing cc:Mail installations. Even e-mail with attachments may be sent to both messaging platforms. In addition, the connector enables you to rollout Exchange in phases instead of all at once.

Server-Based Message Rules

Exchange provides support for *server-based* rules, where users can configure rules to execute on their Exchange home servers to forward messages to particular individuals, reply with an "out of office" note to all incoming messages, and route messages to specific folders to manage messaging flow. Because the process runs on the Exchange Server, the user doesn't need to be logged in.

The server rules can apply to applications that are leveraging Exchange. Outside information stores, for example, will have a server agent configured from the client. The next time the user logs into the system, the server agent runs to retrieve information for the user.

Integrated with Microsoft Office

Microsoft provides tight integration between Office and Exchange. For example, you can send a document, spreadsheet, or presentation directly from any Office application to any Exchange mail user. Alternatively, you could also post the information directly into Exchange's public folders.

A new feature with Office and Outlook is enabling Word as your e-mail editor. Users who are comfortable with Word's layout and controls can have Outlook automatically use Word when creating a new mail message.

Delegated Access

Managers can delegate access to their information store and allow their assistants to access their messages. This is useful when managers travel out of town. Their assistants can retrieve their manager's mail, forward it, send replies on behalf of the manager, and so on. Assistants can perform all of these actions using their own Outlook client and without logging on as their manager.

Integrated with Windows NT Server

Exchange and NT are integrated in several areas. For example, Exchange ties directly into Windows NT Server's security. Users use a single log-in ID to access network and Exchange resources. Network administrators can create both a network ID and mailbox for the user using a single program. Also, Exchange administrators can take advantage of NT's log-on restrictions and password history control for tight messaging security.

Exchange and NT work together to support both roving and remote users. Users can move from workstation to workstation within their company and still have access to all of their Exchange related information (e-mail, calendar, journal, notes, and so on). Remote users can access their e-mail because NT's Remote Access Server (RAS) can support every standard dial-up package used by a Microsoft operating system. These dial-up packages include Shiva, used by DOS and 16-bit Windows, Dial-up Networking (DUN) used by Windows 95, RAS used by Windows for Workgroups and NT Workstation, and DUN from Windows 95 used by Internet Explorer. Note that Shiva is bundled with Exchange and not with DOS or the 16-bit Windows operating system.

Furthermore, the Exchange client is designed to sense line-connection speed and transfer less data over dial-up connections. This increases the efficiency of the connection. The client software downloads only mail message headers first on a remote connection. Then, message bodies are downloaded as needed.

Public Folders and Replication

Public folders are central repositories of common information. Exchange users can post messages, applications, forms, and so on into the public folders, which are replicated throughout the Exchange enterprise. Rather than sending a mail message out to many users, you can use public folders like an electronic bulletin board. Then, a user can post a reply into a folder creating a thread of responses.

Public folders can be replicated down to the client PC to facilitate off-line creation and reading. Permissions also can be set to restrict access to certain folder contents. The public folder replication is designed to minimize the amount of data to be replicated. Public folder contents are indexed and these indexes are available across the enterprise.

Exchange's Advanced Security

Exchange adds additional security over the C2 level security provided by NT Server. Exchange has a digital signature to verify the user sending the message is really the true sender. Exchange also offers message encryption to ensure only the sender and recipient can read a message's contents. New in Exchange 5.0 is Person to Person Key Exchange (PPKE). PPKE enables users to exchange digitally signed and encrypted messages over the Internet. Previously, this was only possible between users within an Exchange Organization.

Electronic Forms Designer

Exchange's Forms Designer is easy enough for end users to create basic forms and powerful enough for experienced developers to create form-based applications. These forms are meant to automate common requests such as time-off or an office supply order. Using public folders, you can multiply the effectiveness of forms by replicating the form and their information throughout your enterprise.

Multiple Language Support

Exchange will be supported in over 20 languages and provides many features for companies whose sites are spread throughout the world.

Single-Seat View for Administration

The Exchange Administrator is the central console managing all Exchange activity within an organization. This includes all servers, users, mailboxes, connectors, gateways, public folders, and sites.

On-line System Backup

Believe it or not, e-mail can grow in use to become a company's most mission-critical application. Especially in international firms, Exchange must be up 24 hours a day and seven days a week. Exchange enables you to perform backups of open messaging stores without shutting down the server or having users log out.

Support for 1984 and 1988 X.400 Standards

Exchange is the only Message Transfer Agent to support both 1984 and 1988 X.400 standards simultaneously, offering flexibility when designing an Exchange enterprise architecture.

Message Routing

Message routing provides multiple routes to transfer mail between sites. If one link for remote sites goes down, Exchange automatically reroutes mail using a secondary route. Exchange can also calculate the least costly route when all links are functional.

Migration Tools for non-Exchange Mail Systems

Microsoft realizes that many other systems are in use today. Therefore, Microsoft provides connectors, gateways, and migration/extraction tools to provide either complete coexistence with Exchange or a smooth migration path onto an Exchange platform.

Who Should Use This Book

This book is aimed at network and system administrators, as well as messaging specialists who are responsible for installing, configuring, and maintaining an Exchange system. Most of the examples in this book are geared for a large, international enterprise to draw out all of Exchange's features. MIS managers will be interested in using the information in this book to make key decisions about adopting and deploying Exchange. Finally, this book touches on application forms development. Although Exchange's Forms designer targets novice developers who may not have a strong a Visual Basic (VB) background, VB programmers can leverage their knowledge to make additional custom extensions.

How to Use This Book

This book is divided into five sections. The first two sections are intended for a general audience, and the last three sections depend on an understanding of the previous sections.

Part I Introduction to Microsoft Exchange

Part I welcomes you into the world of Microsoft Exchange. As described briefly in the preceding sections, Exchange is a completely revolutionary client/server messaging system. Part I presents a complete overview about how Exchange is integrated and used in your environment.

Chapter 1, "Overview of Microsoft Exchange," introduces the concepts of working with client/ server messaging, groupware, document management, and the universal Inbox. This chapter also discusses many new features available with Microsoft Exchange Server 5.0.

In Chapter 2, "Understanding Exchange's Organization and Sites," you'll learn about the different tiers in Exchange's messaging hierarchy.

Chapter 3, "Exchange's Integrated Server Components," provides a more in-depth look at Exchange's core components and how they operate with each other.

Chapter 4, "Integrating with Microsoft Windows NT Server," identifies the integration of Exchange into NT and Exchange NT dependencies.

Part II Installing and Migrating to Exchange

Part II is the core of the book. This collection of seven chapters spells out all of the planning essentials for migrating to or deploying a new Exchange architecture.

Chapter 5, "Designing Exchange Topology," introduces you to the planning process needed to design an Exchange architecture. Here you will analyze your company's messaging needs and infrastructure, and then design an Exchange architecture.

Chapter 6, "Installing Exchange Server," outlines the system requirements for Exchange, provides step-by-step installation instructions, and discusses adding additional Exchange servers into an existing Exchange Organization.

Chapters 7 through 11 provide information when your are working with non-Exchange mail systems. You'll be guided through connecting to or migrating from MS Mail, migrating from Lotus cc:Mail, installing Exchange in a NetWare environment, and migrating from external systems.

Part III Exchange Administration and Configuration

In Part III, you learn how to configure all of the Exchange services—connectors, message transfer agents, links to external systems, public folders, and address routing. This part also focuses on the administration of Exchange.

Chapters 12 through 15 discuss how to use the Exchange Administrator program, and the use of the core components in Exchange server.

Chapter 16, "Creating and Configuring Recipient," exemplifies how to create a mailbox and NT domain account for an Exchange user, which also includes distribution lists and foreign-mail system custom recipients.

Chapter 17, "Setting Up Site Connector and Dynamic RAS Connector," discusses how to install and configure a site and RAS connector.

In Chapter 18, "Using Directory Replication and Synchronization," you'll learn what directory replication is and how to configure Exchange's Directory Synchronization services.

Chapters 19 and 20 walk you through using the Microsoft Mail Connector for PC and AppleTalk networks. Exchange includes several custom features to support this integration.

Chapters 21 and 22 similarly discuss configuring X.400 and SMTP connections.

Chapter 23, "Setting Up NNTP," you learn what Network News Transfer Protocol (NNTP) is, and how to install, configure, and administer it.

The information in Chapter 24, "Exchange Performance Tuning and Capacity Planning," applies to all Exchange implementations. You learn how to use several performance tuning tools to detect and tune the most common Exchange bottlenecks. You also learn the techniques that answer the burning question, "How many users can one Exchange server support?"

Chapters 25 through 28 discuss managing and monitoring Exchange's operations day-to-day, as well as troubleshooting Exchange when problems occur. You'll also learn about Exchange's advanced security features in Chapter 27, "Exchange Security."

Part IV The Exchange Client

This part discusses the next generation Exchange client—Outlook. This includes several of Outlook's features like enhancing e-mail, effective scheduling, managing tasks, journals, organizing your contacts, and using notes to jot down important thoughts.

Chapter 29, "Installing and Configuring Outlook," describes the spectrum of setup methods and Outlook's system requirements.

Chapters 30 and 31 teach you how to use the common and advanced features of Outlook including printing, profiles and information services, and the Web Outlook view.

Part V Third-Party Integration and Application Development

Part V presents some other uses for the Exchange architecture. Chapter 32, "Implementing Third-Party Integration Tools," highlights several add-ons and enhancements from independent software vendors who are developing solutions for Exchange. It also describes consulting firms who are experts in developing, piloting, and deploying Exchange.

Chapter 33, "Using Electronic Data Interchange (EDI)," discusses how EDI applications can be designed by using the Exchange topology and support for industry standards. It also defines Exchange's role in EDI.

Chapter 34, "Developing Exchange Forms," teaches you to design custom forms using Exchange's Form Designer. This chapter discusses many of the programming issues associated with developing custom forms.

Conventions Used in This Book

Que has over a decade of experience writing and developing the most successful computer books available. With this experience, we learned which special features help readers the most. Look for these special features throughout the book to enhance your learning experience.

Several type and font conventions are used in this book to help make your reading easier.

- *Italic type* is used to emphasize the author's points or to introduce new terms.
- Screen messages, code listings, and command samples appear in `monospace typeface`.
- Code and other information that the user is asked to type appears in **`bold monospace type`**.

T I P Tips present short advice on a quick or often-overlooked procedure. These tips include shortcuts that will save you time.

N O T E Notes present interesting or useful information that isn't necessarily essential to the discussion. A Note is used to provide additional information that may help you avoid problems, or to offer advice that relates to the particular topic.

CAUTION

Cautions look like this and serve to warn you about potential problems that a procedure may cause, unexpected results, and mistakes to avoid.

Introduction to Microsoft Exchange

Overview of Microsoft Exchange

"**B**uild the world's fastest, most scalable, most reliable, easiest-to-administer messaging and groupware enterprise platform that can connect to the world."

> Brian Valentine, Microsoft General Manager,
> Exchange Group

That is Microsoft's compelling vision for Exchange since its conception in 1993.

But what exactly is Exchange? Microsoft Exchange Server is a messaging product for businesses integrating e-mail, group scheduling, electronic forms, and common groupware applications into one product that can be easily managed via a single administrator program. It facilitates collaboration within companies so teams can share the latest information obtained internally via intranets and externally from the Internet and newsgroups. It allows managers to schedule meetings with several people and manage resources through a common interface. Departments can set up information repositories (solution databases) for reference and discussion. Companies can create virtual knowledge bases with their business partners using an extranet. In short, Microsoft Exchange Server 5.0 is designed so you can communicate and collaborate with anyone, anywhere, anytime, easily. ■

The History of Microsoft Exchange

From host-based to shared-files messaging, Exchange represents the next level in messaging technology. Using a client/server architecture, Exchange overcomes the limitations of past messaging architectures.

The Key Components of Microsoft Exchange Server

Exchange has several features designed to meet the messaging needs from a small office to an international corporation. Plus, the new features in Exchange 5.0 enhance several areas including Internet connectivity and the client interface (Outlook).

Comparing Exchange with Lotus Notes

Both products were designed from scratch with different goals and thus have different database architectures. Overall, both products have strengths and weaknesses depending on their deployment.

Exchange Use Within Microsoft

Curious about how Microsoft uses its own product internally? Exchange is fully integrated into several of Microsoft's business lines from development to the tracking of Exchange's Early Adopter Program.

The History of Messaging

Electronic mail has been in existence for many years. The original electronic mail systems—including PROFS, SYSM, and Memo—resided on UNIX-based host computers or IBM mainframes. The single host, whether it was a mainframe or a minicomputer, was a centralized solution. These systems, many which are still running today, are text-based and provide enterprise-wide messaging.

Shared-File Messaging

However, PCs began to grow in capability and popularity. As their acceptance became widespread, their cost began to drop, prompting more purchases even in corporate America. More and more computing was taking place at the desktop instead of within a centralized machine. The PCs began communicating with each other via small workgroups and local area networks (LAN), extending their reach. It wasn't long that within the same company walls that housed the mainframe messaging solution, LAN-based messaging took root and grew.

LAN-based or *shared-file messaging* is where the client desktop initiates and controls all messaging activity. When a user composes and sends a message, it is the client software that sends the message to the server into a specific directory (or mailbox). Recipients retrieved their messages by accessing their specific directory (mailbox) on the server. The server is passive and primarily stores messages (see Figure 1.1).

FIG. 1.1

Message flow using shared-file messaging.

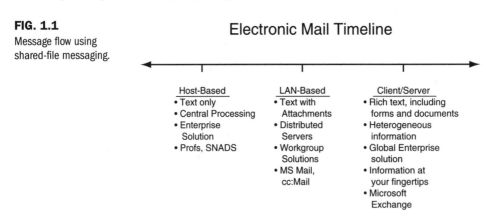

At the time, there were advantages to this architecture:

- *Reduced cost.* Server doesn't need to be high performance.
- *Simple design.* Relatively easy setup and administration.
- *Increased performance in some areas.* Application is running locally.

But there are weaknesses as well:

- *Inadequate security.* Each user needs full control (read/write) on the entire file system, including other users' mailboxes.

- *Increased network traffic.* Each client must constantly poll the server for new messages. In a small LAN or workgroup, the traffic can be manageable. In a large enterprise, it will grind things to a halt.

- *Limited scalability.* No matter how much hardware one adds to the server, there is a hard limit to the number of clients and number of messages that reasonably can be handled by the system, especially because bandwidth is the limiting factor.

Client/Server Messaging

To address these weaknesses, client/server messaging distributed messaging processing between the client and server, enabling each system to focus on tasks best suited for their role. For example, when a user composes and sends a message, the server places the message in the appropriate directory or forwards it to another server. The recipient receives the message without constantly polling the server. Microsoft Exchange was developed using client/server messaging architecture (see Figure 1.2).

FIG. 1.2
Message flow using client/server messaging.

One-to-One Communication

"Electronic mail"

Workstation   Workstation

It improves upon shared-file messaging in the following areas:

- *Better security.* Except for their own directory (*Inbox*), users have read-only rights for other Exchange areas.

- *Decreased network traffic.* Using *Remote Procedure Calls (RPCs)*, clients will connect and make messaging requests. The server will process the request and return only the requested information.

- *Extensibility.* Exchange runs on Windows NT, which easily scales when more memory or an additional processor is added. Also, there are several connectors, gateways, and Migration Wizards to extend your messaging reach. Exchange has evolved into a full-featured platform on which business solutions can be built, such as forms, work-flow charts, and document databases.

The Exchange client component on the recipient's PC receives information that is pushed to it from the creator or source. Exchange goes beyond the push model by providing a shared repository for storing information that is on call for the user. This repository enables users to pull information down to their workstations when they need that information. By providing both push and pull technology, corporations are not constrained by the distribution mechanism. Exchange provides a complete solution.

Overview of Exchange's Key Features

Now that you have historical perspective of messaging, let's discuss what Exchange key features are and how they can meet your messaging needs.

Key Definitions

You should become familiar with some key concepts and definitions that are used throughout this chapter:

- *Address Book*. A list of names, addresses, or other information. Names can include users, distribution lists, and public folders.

- *Custom Recipient*. A recipient outside your enterprise. For example, you would use a person's Internet address as the custom recipient when sending mail to them over the Internet.

- *Directory*. A hierarchical structure of objects that represent each component of the organization, such as the organization itself, recipients, and more.

- *Enterprise*. A corporate environment with a large electronic messaging infrastructure. A typical enterprise will have several thousand to tens of thousands of users on the mail system.

- *Information Store*. The back-end database that contains all messages and data located on the Microsoft Windows NT Server that houses the Exchange Server.

- *Microsoft Exchange Client/Viewer*. The program that a client uses to read, write, and manipulate the mailbox and folders.

- *MTA*. The Message Transfer Agent transfers and routes mail messages and attachments between servers.

- *Recipient*. The receiver of a message or form. A recipient can be a user, distribution list, or public folder.

- *Routing Table*. Table created by Exchange and used by the MTA to move messages between servers.

- *Security Descriptor*. Permissions information attached to every object under the Windows NT Server. Security descriptors tell the operating system who has access to a certain resource and whether that resource is a file, a service, or an application.

Universal Inbox for Information and Applications

The concept of the Universal Inbox has been around for years, but the capability to deliver such a product is revolutionary. Microsoft learned from its research that users want an integrated desktop environment (IDE) so they can be more organized and in control of their daily activities. A Universal Inbox interface makes it easy to organize personal, public (shared), or online information all in one place. A user can now view information in a variety of ways, and easily find information anywhere on the desktop. Future BackOffice products will seek to leverage this model.

The key to the Exchange Inbox is the fact that Microsoft provides the gateway to all your company information. Third-party software developers are leveraging or pursuing business opportunities on this foundation by building their applications on top of this technology; these applications appear as folders. The vision is to provide one standard location and interface for accessing information, regardless of format. Developers are even working on integrating voice-mail systems into Exchange. If you have a multimedia PC with an integrated sound system, you can access your e-mail as well as voice mail.

The Exchange Viewer or client interface embodies the concept of the Universal Inbox by providing a consistent look and feel across all the supported platforms and released versions.

The client also allows you to place filing, printing, viewing, deleting, and other functions on convenient button bars. These button bars keep the desktop uncluttered and yet allow the desktop to contain many pieces of information.

Folder Types

When you use the Exchange Viewer, you have control of several folders that are displayed off of the Microsoft Exchange root folder tree. These folders are very similar in layout to Windows Explorer, which ships with Windows 95, and to the File Manager in Windows 3.1 and Windows NT.

The three main folder types are:

- *Mailbox.* The Mailbox folder, listed first under the root, serves as the traditional inbox that most e-mail packages have. The main difference in Exchange, however, is that this folder holds much more than e-mail; it also can contain all the data types from several sources (for example, Dow Jones information). After reading the data, the user can move the data into several other folders or have it automatically moved to other folders based on certain rules.

- *Personal folders.* These folders enable the user great flexibility in organization. Some people like to organize documents by author, for example; others like to organize by subject. Personal folders also allow users to store the information on their hard disks for use offline. All mail in the mailbox is kept on the server until it is saved on the user's hard disk. Suppose that you're going on a trip. Before you leave, you log onto the Exchange Server and get all your documents from the server. You then save the documents to a private folder for reviewing offline. You can compose your replies, and when you connect to the Exchange Server the next time, those outgoing messages are sent on their way. In addition, the folder views are synchronized next time you log onto your Exchange Server.

- *Public folders.* Public folders facilitate the sharing of information. Each client who has access rights can read information stored in public folders. The administrator can assign read, write, and delete access to information contained in a public folder.

In addition, the creator of the information creates a view to standardize the look and feel of the information. For example, in many firms there exists a document on all the bulletin boards containing what job openings exist at the company. With Exchange, you could create an Access database that would hold standard information and simply create a form that resided in a public folder. People could then browse the information in a standard way, and all data would be updated whenever the database is updated.

Views

As mentioned earlier in this chapter, Exchange enables users to organize information according to their taste. Exchange provides some features to make this process much easier. Those features are described in the following sections.

A *view* is simply a way to order information. Information can be sorted by author, keyword, date, or subject.

Two kinds of views are available: folder views and common views. *Folder views* order information in individual folders. If you have a private folder called Peter that contains all mail from Peter, you can define a view that sorts all the objects in the folder by date. Then you could change the view for the folder to include a secondary sort criterion, such as subject. The data then would conform to the view only in that folder. *Common views* are views that can be applied to any folder. You can define a view called Date and apply it to many folders at the same time.

In addition, Exchange provides many predefined views, and Exchange is also flexible enough to enable you to create views on custom fields. If a public folder has a database element that contains a logical (Y or N) field, you can create a view that sorts all the Yes records before all the No records.

Rules and Auto-Assistants

Rules are a set of conditions that when met, organize incoming messages. For example, you can establish a rule that says `Sender= My Manager`, file the message in a folder called Urgent, and play a sound.

Auto-Assistants enable you to have rules in effect even when you aren't logged on. If you go away on vacation, you can have a generic message auto-replying to all messages saying you'll return in one week. If the message contains a certain keyword in the subject, you could have your mail forwarded to someone else to take care of it or to another e-mail account where you can review it.

Find

The Find feature is a powerful search engine that enables you to specify criteria for finding items in any or all of your folders. This feature is extremely useful when you remember either the subject or a keyword but can't remember who sent the message or what the actual content was. You can have the Find feature look for the message in all your folders.

The Find feature runs in the background and is treated like any other running program, enabling you to continue working while the search is under way.

Once you are presented with the objects that meet the specified criteria, any action you take on those objects takes effect in the actual folders the objects reside in. For example, you can use the Find feature to retrieve all messages 30 or more days old. As they are brought up in the Find window, you can select all of them and click the Delete button. They will all be removed from their respective folders.

Schedule+

With the proper permissions, you can view someone else's schedule to find the best time to have a meeting. The function, once in Schedule+, is now completely integrated into one client called Outlook. Read on for more information.

Application Development Tools

Exchange provides the *Forms Designer* to extend the functionality of Exchange. Exchange now becomes a platform product upon which business messaging solutions like document databases and groupware are built. The Forms Designer is targeted for the non-developer, but experienced developers can leverage their Visual Basic expertise to take Exchange's forms to the next level.

Forms Designer   The Forms Designer enables the administrator (and any other user when granted permission) to create custom forms that can replace paper forms. Most consulting companies have standard forms for consultants to describe their background for use in proposals. Why not create this form online, store it in a public folder, and allow the consultant to fill it out and send it to you for processing? In addition, you can create a Visual Basic program to take the data off the form and store it in an Access, FoxPro, or SQL Server database for later retrieval and manipulation.

Imagine putting office-supplies requisitions in an electronic form. You could tally the total cost of office supplies for a month quickly by using OLE to create an Excel table from the Exchange data.

Forms can be stored in three places: the Enterprise Forms Registry, the Personal Forms Registry, and the Folder Forms Registry. The following list describes these elements:

- *Enterprise Forms Registry*. This registry contains forms that are distributed across the enterprise—for example, office-supplies requisition forms. Most companies use a standard office-supplies vendor and a standard paper form. When you use an Exchange form, the paper form can be eliminated, and forms can be sent directly to the authorizing party or to the office-products vendor itself.

- *Personal Forms Registry*. This registry houses all the forms that the user needs to accomplish personalized tasks. If an Exchange user needs to send out meeting summaries that follow the same format and go to the same people, he or she can use a custom form that contains all the addressees and all the appropriate fields.

■ *Folder Forms Registry.* This registry contains forms that post data in public folders. This feature can be used between divisions and departments. In many organizations, a lack of communication exists between divisions. For example, Production may not be ready for some of Engineering's demands, due to lack of communication. By using custom forms, Engineering can keep Production informed by using a status form or action form to keep the entire company aware of what that division is working on. The form makes entering the data easy. The form can be customized to the user's liking.

By providing a simple graphical user interface, the Forms Designer enables users to create forms without the need for complex programming.

It may be difficult to believe, but the Forms Designer is a front end to Visual Basic. Simply drawing the fields in the form sends the proper commands to Visual Basic to create the executable form. You do not have to be a Visual Basic guru to create forms and to extend the functionality of Exchange beyond the transfer of messages.

> **CAUTION**
>
> Even with Outlook and Exchange 5.0, the Macintosh Exchange Client does not support the electronic forms of Exchange, due to the fact that the forms are Visual Basic executables. Microsoft does not have any immediate plans to directly support VB on the Macintosh platform.

Custom Application Programming with MAPI   Exchange Client applications aren't limited to those that ship with Exchange. Because Exchange uses *Messaging Application Programming Interface (MAPI)*, you can design applications that take advantage of Exchange's underlying folder architecture.

Custom applications can use MAPI to perform such tasks as open a public folder and drop in data, search data, delete items, and examine the contents of folders. All actions are subject to the permission that the application has for any given object. If the program is running with a certain user's permissions but that user doesn't have the capability to delete data, the application cannot delete any data.

MAPI also can be used to add functionality to a form created with the Forms Designer. You can write a program that takes data from a custom form, imports that data into Excel, performs some calculations, sends the user the compiled results in an e-mail message, and then faxes a copy to another recipient.

Group Information Sharing

Exchange allows the user to post information on an electronic bulletin board (public folder). For example, marketing representatives can track customer accounts from a shared contact-management database and access product information from a reference library.

Internet Support

In what used to be called the Internet Mail Connector (IMC) is a collection of new features and protocols. They are now grouped as the *Internet Mail Service (IMS)*. Included here are the current SMTP mail gateway between Exchange and the Internet for sending and receiving, as well as POP3 support for browser-based mail clients such as Internet Explorer or Mosiac. To facilitate easy directory access for these browser clients, *Lightweight Directory Access Protocol (LDAP)* has also been added. NNTP "news" feeds and function are supported. Finally, a rich environment for interfacing Microsoft's Internet Information Server (IIS) with Exchange to allow "publishing" and interaction with public folders within Exchange has been added collectively called *Active Server Components*. All of these help integrate a company's messaging enterprise into a much larger messaging system—the Internet. These are described in more detail later in the chapter.

Support for Remote Users

Exchange enables users to work offline. Users can use Exchange Client from their PCs via remote network access (dial-up connections) or while they are disconnected from the network. Exchange was designed to use RPC calls, which when coupled with dial-up connections are designed to sense the line speed and optimize performance.

Exchange can be used over asynchronous connections, including ISDN, PPP, PPTP, SLIP, X.25, and regular modem connections. This form of Exchange connectivity holds true for client-to-server connections as well as server-to-server connections. Additionally, security can be implemented when using NT's Remote Access Services (RAS) for dial-back and challenged dial-in via NT C2 security. Ultimately, increasing time or speed increases costs.

Administration

Microsoft Exchange Server administration is performed from a single location with a program called *Administrator*. This program gives the server administrator a graphical representation of all directory objects on any site for which he or she has permission.

This utility is used to define the hierarchical structure of organization's messaging infrastructure. You can define and set properties for elements such as connections to other mail systems, recipients, servers, and addressing templates.

The advantage of centralized administration is that it enables you to see the entire object tree or hierarchy of information and make any addition, move, or change in an easy, straightforward manner, regardless of the location of the server. If your company merges with another company that has a Microsoft Mail messaging infrastructure in place, for example, the Exchange administrator can add the Microsoft Mail Connector, and connectivity would be available to all specified users on all specified servers. The convenience of adding functionality from a central console is apparent in this case in size of enterprise.

Reliability

Many companies don't consider their messaging system to be a mission-critical application. However, the reality is that e-mail is one of the few applications that is on everyone's desktop and that most everyone relies upon. In order to keep your users happy, Exchange has a number of tools and features to prevent Exchange from becoming "unavailable" (see Table 1.1).

Table 1.1　Troubleshooting Tools and Features

Tool/Feature	Function
Link Monitor	Link Monitor watches for successful message connections between two points in an Exchange organization. They can also be configured to test connections to foreign messaging systems. Use this tool to determine if an Exchange server or network link is experiencing problems.
Server Manager	Server Manager can tell you whether any of a server's services has stopped and enables you to stop, start, or pause those services remotely (even across a WAN or telephone link).
Performance Monitor	Performance Monitor (PerfMon) enables you to monitor statistics for most software and hardware components (processor utilization, available memory). Installing Exchange adds several specific counters for detailed Exchange diagnostic work. PerfMon can be set up to page you if certain thresholds are exceeded, such as if the message queue has exceeded 1,000 messages.
Event Viewer	Event Viewer comes with Windows NT and logs system, security, and application events (including Exchange). Not all events are errors. For example, an event is logged when Exchange finishes recalculating the routing table. Use Event Viewer to determine the source of errors from Exchange.
Intelligent Rerouting	Exchange can have multiple connectors between servers to provide fault-tolerance. If one connection goes down, Exchange automatically reroutes traffic via another connection.

Tool/Feature	Function
Directory Service (DS)	Because the DS is like Exchange's telephone book, it must be protected. Not only is the DS replicated to every server in a site and synchronized, but it can recover from a catastrophic failure.
Fault Tolerant Store	Exchange uses a transaction-based logging system to ensure users never lose a message from the Information Store (IS). All transactions are written to a transaction log, then committed to the Store. In the event of power failure, all transactions can be completed using the transaction log.
Backup	Exchange provides an enhanced version, enabling the backup of open Exchange files.
Auditing	Auditing enables an administrator to log and view the full spectrum of security events—for example, someone attempting to use the Administrator ID or which user attempted to delete several mailboxes.

Messaging Security

As more people depend on e-mail for communication, the need for secure messaging grows. Exchange offers three levels of security and manages the user accounts and the Information Store activity. Exchange also hooks into the NT's C2-level security and incorporates several additional security mechanisms to protect the data stored on the server, on the client PC, and in transit.

Exchange provides for *RSA digital key encryption*, which is used to authenticate the user who is sending the message. When a user "signs" a message, the signature guarantees that the name associated with the message is the actual name of the author.

In addition to the digital signature, you can enable digital encryption of messages. Exchange uses an algorithm called CAST developed by Northern Telecom. Security is discussed further in Chapter 27, "Exchange Security."

Connectivity and Gateway Support

Exchange offers a wide variety of connectivity features. Through its connectors and gateways, Exchange enables users to exchange mail with external e-mail systems using different messaging protocols. This includes the host-based mail systems using SNA, Internet mail systems using SMTP, foreign host systems using X.400, and between Exchange sites using TCPIP, IPX, or NetBEUI. Exchange offers the following connectors:

- Microsoft Mail for PC Networks
- Microsoft Mail for AppleTalk Networks
- X.400

- SMTP
- cc:Mail
- RAS (dial-up connector)
- Site Connector

In addition to the aforementioned connectors, gateways for Exchange extend your reach. Exchange supports its own gateways and Microsoft Mail (PC) gateways as well. The following are just a few gateways that are available for Exchange from third parties:

- DEC All-in-One
- Fax
- PROFS/OfficeVision

- CompuServe
- MHS
- SNADS

Regardless of the origin of messages, all messages in a user's mailbox look exactly the same. The addition of any connectors and gateways is transparent to the user. That fact is a key advantage of Exchange. A user's data is collected and consistently formatted in the Universal Inbox.

Like incoming mail, outgoing mail routed through connectors and gateways is transparent to the user. The administrator creates custom recipients that reside in address books alongside regular Exchange recipients.

When a connector is installed to enable communication to the Microsoft Mail post office, for example, Exchange clients can immediately send and receive mail by addressing the message to the MS Mail user the same way they do when they send a message to another Exchange user. When Kent's boss says, "Please send a message to Dan Gardner at the Dallas office," Kent can start up his Exchange Client and send the message directly to Dan Gardner, because Dan's name is in Kent's address book in Exchange. Likewise, because Kent shows up in the MS Mail post office and Dan's address book, Dan easily can send Kent a reply.

Migration

When a connector or gateway solution isn't available, Exchange provides tools that are used to move data from one system to another:

- *Extraction tools.* These tools copy directory, message, and scheduling information from an existing system. For example, your cc:Mail post office MLANDATA, CLANDATA, and USR files would be run through the tool, dumping all the data into a file and keeping all pointers intact.
- *Migration tool.* This tool imports the data created with the extraction tools in Exchange. You would run the Migration tool on the file output by the extraction tools. The user information would go into the address books, and the data would be moved to the Information Store.
- *Administrator program.* You can use the import and export options in the main Administrator program in place of the preceding tools. These options enable you to use the tools with which you are most comfortable.

■ *Custom tools.* Exchange enables you to write custom command files that perform certain functions. These files can be tied in with the NT Server scheduling system to perform certain duties at certain times. If you have limited hardware capacity and want to import entries from a different messaging system over a certain number of days, you could write custom scripts that perform those tasks without overburdening your network or server. You also could write scripts that manipulate the extraction tools to feed only certain parts of the data to the Migration tool.

As you can see, Exchange provides the flexibility to be suitable for large and small environments, and the adaptability to import data from other messaging programs to provide integration with heterogeneous environments. Exchange is capable of providing messaging solutions for any size organization with any combination of existing mail systems.

Electronic Data Interchange

Another use of messaging is *Electronic Data Interchange (EDI)*. Most corporations use EDI applications to exchange messages that contain information about orders, sales, and inventory.

Third parties are providing support for financial transactions via Exchange. Microsoft's intent is to provide support for EDI domestically (with X.12) and internationally (with EDIfac). Exchange does not provide native X.435 support, but support in MAPI will provide X.435 functionality in the client.

Exchange provides a rich architecture for use in EDI transactions. Together with the integration with Microsoft SQL Server and other Microsoft application environments, Exchange will prove to be a very solid, useful, and cost-effective EDI solution.

FAX Routing

Third-party products from Right Fax and Integra provide a gateway for DID-supported fax boards, such as Brooktrout or GammaFax Boards. Faxes can be sent and received from a central location and routed to and from the Exchange client. This process eliminates the need to provide individual modems and phone lines at users' desktops or the need to print material and walk them to a manual fax machine. Significant cost savings can be found in reduced overhead for mail room efforts to deliver faxes and in overall reduced time for delivery.

Microsoft also supports its own fax gateway product for MS Mail 3.x. Moreover, the Exchange Client for Windows 95 can leverage the Windows 95 Microsoft Fax software, which is bundled with the operating system. This way, a user can leverage existing aliases and contact lists in the local directory to send e-mail and faxes from one location. Microsoft Fax for MS Mail 3.x also supports binary attachments.

Voice Mail

Several efforts are underway to integrate and unify electronic mail messaging and voice mail systems into a single architecture. Octel, the leader in voice mail solutions, has invested heavily in a product known as Unified Messenger that once installed into an Exchange site can actually replace a traditional voice mail system, if desired, with a completely PC-based solution. Benefits of such a system include ease of administration of both voice mail and e-mail from the Exchange Administrator program, reduced costs associated with PC hardware versus traditional proprietary voice mail systems, and enhanced client features such as the capability to listen to voice mail from the e-mail client or to play back the text portion of an e-mail from traditional voice mail access.

Workflow *Workflow technology* seeks to establish strict steps for a business process, with limited or no choice for individuals to change the business rules. Exchange with workflow goes beyond forms routing to address several workflow-application issues, such as status tracking, work management, deadline management, ad-hoc initiation of workflow processes, negotiation of dates, and autonomous reassignment of work.

Workflow has two parts: routing and true workflow. On the routing side, Exchange offers basic routing functionality via MAPI. On the workflow side, Exchange takes a modular approach, providing interfaces that enable workflow developers to design solutions that run with their database engines. Exchange is an ideal platform for workflow applications because of its MAPI foundation, directory services, and Information Store.

Imaging *Imaging* expands the capability to support multiple file types and provides a strong mechanism for reading, distributing, and annotating information. In the Exchange environment, you can integrate at the information viewer level in order to access public folder data objects from the client. With *Object Linking and Embedding (OLE)* support, you can drag and drop the actual image into the message. On the server, images are stored as objects in the Information Store.

Document Management *Document management* (also referred to as *document imaging*) consists of scanning documents into a system, archiving the images, and creating full-text indexes of the content. Document management now extends into the realm of multimedia and OLE objects.

Front Office Technologies offers a tightly integrated Exchange and NT document and information management solution that handles not only document management and archiving from a traditional PC DOCS or SAROS perspective but adds several new twists to leverage the replication, security, and administration of Exchange. Information gathering from the Internet and a "personal briefing" search-and-update agent greatly enhance the capability of Front Office to act as much more than a document management system.

What's New in Exchange 5.0

Now that you have an overview of Exchange's features, you can read about the specific changes and new additions in Exchange 5.0.

Outlook

Outlook, based upon the Universal Inbox, promotes not only communication (via e-mail within your enterprise), but also collaboration throughout your enterprise.

This is a new Exchange Server client for Windows-based 32-bit systems. It is available with Exchange Server as a stand-alone product and as a component of Office 97. Outlook interoperates with MS Mail, Microsoft Exchange clients, and Schedule+, enabling companies the choice in deploying the right client for its enterprise.

Outlook's basic philosophy builds upon Bill Gates' vision of "information at your fingertips." Today, most people experience information overload, especially with the popularity of the Internet. So the quantity of information isn't the problem, but organizing it so you can find what you need is still a challenge. Microsoft found that most people wanted a more integrated desktop. They started meeting this need as early as Windows 3.0's capability to cut and paste a graph from DOS-based Lotus into WordPerfect 4.1.

Then, Office 4.2 was developed to work as one application. Microsoft extends this vision with Outlook, giving it the capability to manage several types of information. These may include e-mail, calendars, contacts, tasks and to-do lists, documents or files on the hard drive, and Web links. Outlook also helps users share information by means of public folders, forms, and Internet connectivity (newsgroups). The following sections provide key features in Outlook. For more information, refer to the following chapters: Chapter 29, "Installing and Configuring Outlook," Chapter 30, "Using Outlook," and Chapter 31, "Using Advanced Outlook Features."

View   Outlook enables users to arrange information any way they want to see it. Outlook supports five types of views: Table, Calendar, Card, Icon, and Timeline. Users can customize these into an unlimited number of personal or shared views. Table, Calendar, and Icon views are probably familiar to most users. The Card view resembles a list of business cards or index cards that concisely displays key information, and the Timeline view arranges items chronologically on a horizontal time line.

WWW Access   Access your e-mail via World Wide Web. A browser, such as Internet Explorer, can retrieve e-mail via the Internet. Now, the users have more freedom to choose which operating system and platform (Internet Explorer for the Macintosh) is best suited for them. Microsoft has plans to enable scheduling and other Outlook features via a Web browser.

Full MAPI Client   Outlook is a full MAPI client, so it can work with all e-mail systems that support MAPI. Outlook is a full MAPI client application, and it works with any e-mail system that supports MAPI. Outlook includes drivers for MS Mail, MS Fax, Microsoft Exchange Server, Internet mail (SMTP/POP3), The Microsoft Network, and Lotus cc:Mail. Additional third-party MAPI drivers are either available or under development for America Online, CompuServe, Lotus Notes, Novell GroupWise, Hewlett-Packard OpenMail, and Digital's All-in-One.

Backwards Compatibility Outlook coexists with the Microsoft Exchange client and Schedule+ and works with earlier versions of Microsoft Mail, Microsoft Exchange client, or Schedule+. This allows a company to roll out Outlook in phases while enabling full communication between the old and new messaging system.

Message Recall If a user sends a message that is inaccurate or inappropriate, she can attempt to recall the message from the recipients. *Message Recall* can either delete or replace the original message. Message Recall works across servers and the Internet, but it will only recall the message if the recipient has not read or moved it and if the recipient is also running Outlook.

If the recipients are not users of Outlook, they will receive an e-mail message informing them that the sender would like to recall an earlier message.

N O T E If you want to replace a message, you must send a new one. If you do not send the new message, the original message is still recalled. ▓

Meeting Planner Outlook makes it easy to schedule group meetings and invite attendees by displaying the free and busy times. It will even automatically pick the next available time for attendees. See Figure 1.3 for an example.

Importing and Exporting You can import messaging information from several products including Schedule+, MS Mail, ACT, ECCO, Sidekick, and Timex Data Link watches. Some of these converters are on the ValuPack CD-ROM that comes with Office 97 or on the Microsoft Web site.

You can export Outlook data into comma- or tab-delimited files, as well as Outlook .PST files for moving large amounts of Outlook data.

> **CAUTION**
>
> Be careful not to confuse the Windows Messaging System client that currently ships with Windows 95 and NT Workstation 4.0. This client, while having many of the features of the "full" Exchange Client, cannot by default connect to an Exchange Server. Neither can the Windows Messaging System easily be upgraded to add the Exchange Server Service. Generally, an installation of the full Exchange Client or Outlook is required to enable access to an Exchange Server.

Lotus cc:Mail Connector

The *Microsoft Exchange Connector for Lotus cc:Mail* enables administrators to seamlessly integrate Microsoft Exchange into cc:Mail environments. Once installed, Exchange Server and cc:Mail systems can exchange messages and synchronize directories. The cc:Mail Connector supports both DB6 and DB8 cc:Mail post offices. By introducing Exchange Server into a cc:Mail environment, cc:Mail users benefit from Exchange Server's strong connectivity to the Internet and other systems. Also, customers can take a phased approach to migration that will cause minimal disruption with an organization.

FIG. 1.3
Using the Meeting
Planner in Outlook.

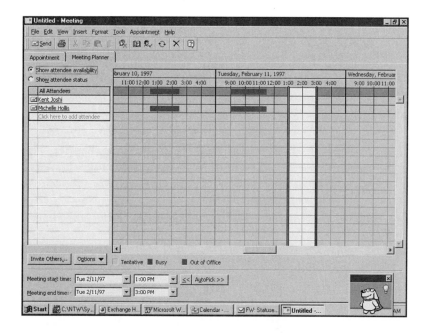

Messaging Security

New in Exchange 5.0 is *Person to Person Key Exchange*, which extends the functionality of the Key Management Server functionality provided in Exchange 4.0. Now, users from different organizations can exchange keys and certificates, which allows them to send signed and encrypted messages over the Internet.

Defense Messaging System (DMS)

Microsoft Exchange adds specific features to the commercial Exchange technology to comply with special specifications set by the U.S. Department of Defense. These specifications are called the *Defense Message System (DMS) Program*. This program was established by the Under Secretary of Defense (Acquisition) to facilitate and coordinate development of an integrated common-user message system for both non-classified and classified messages.
The program's primary goal is to provide a message system that satisfies writer-to-reader requirements while reducing cost and staffing levels. Its secondary goal is to improve functionality, security, survivability, and availability.

The Microsoft Exchange DMS technology is ideally suited for government enterprises and agencies that are required to use DMS-compliant products and companies doing business with the U.S. Government, especially in the defense area. For more details, see **www. microsoft.com_exchange_dms.html**.

POP3

Post office protocol version 3 (POP3) is an open Internet standard. Exchange 5.0 has implemented POP3 in compliance with RFC 1939 and 1734. As a result, any mail client that meets these standards can access and use Exchange as a mail server. Exchange handles inbound and outbound mail requests from these POP3 clients and either grants them access to their mailboxes on the Exchange server or routes their submitted message to appropriate Exchange users, or to the Internet as SMTP mail.

Furthering Exchange's flexibility, it's possible to switch between Outlook and POP3 clients seamlessly. All POP3 messages are stored on the Exchange Server, providing a single-message store. Additionally, all POP3 messages are protected via security from clear-text authentication to NT's Challenge/Response validation. *Secure Sockets Layer (SSL)* can be used in conjunction with clear-text authentication for encryption. See Figure 1.4 for the basic flow of POP3.

FIG. 1.4
Basic flow of POP3.

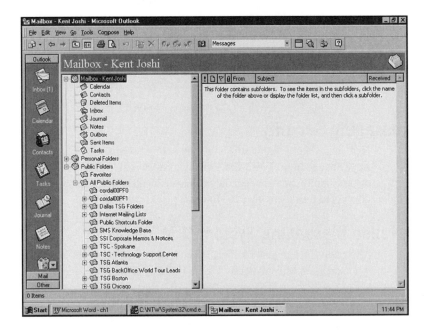

LDAP

To support directory access for these POP3 clients and other types of Internet-oriented applications, Exchange 5.0 adds Lightweight Directory Access Protocol (LDAP) support. LDAP is an adapted subset of the X.500 standard that has been developed for the Internet to ease mail addressing issues between various directory types that exist in various mail systems that touch the overall Internet. LDAP also will enable mail systems to more easily participate in directory synchronization as solutions are developed to facilitate this need. Microsoft Exchange supports any client that implements the LDAP version 3 specification, including future versions of Netscape Communicator, Internet Explorer, and current MAPI LDAP providers.

The indexing associated with LDAP conventions enables users to actually search for a user in the directory based on limited criteria, such as first name and department, when perhaps the last name is not known. An Exchange administrator can selectively lock out certain directory attributes to non-authenticated, anonymous users (such as home addresses or sensitive information). See Chapter 15, "Information Store Configuration," on securing directory attributes from non-authenticated, anonymous users. See Figure 1.5 for the basic operation of LDAP.

FIG. 1.5

LDAP basic operation.

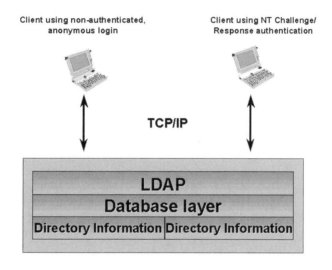

NNTP

NNTP (Network News Transfer Protocol) is an Internet standard protocol defined for distribution, inquiry, retrieval, and posting of news articles. Network News (Usenet) is a popular usage of NNTP. With NNTP, you can receive a Usenet newsfeed from a host or your Internet service provider (ISP) and place the newsgroups into Exchange's public folder for replication throughout your organization. Users posting to the public folders will have their posts put back into the specific Internet newsgroups. The same folders can be used to host your own Internet newsgroup for open discussion (see Figure 1.6). For both of these scenarios, Exchange also supports the use of NT's Remote Access Server (RAS) for scheduled transmissions of newsgroups. Outlook, a Web browser, or newsreader client can access Exchange's newsgroups.

All of Exchange's security options range from anonymous (non-authenticated) access, basic clear-text authentication, and Windows NT Challenge/Response. SSL can be used in conjunction with clear-text authentication to encrypt the data. Public folder access control lists give you complete control over which newsgroups each user can access. See Chapter 23, "Setting Up NNTP," for in-depth discussion on setting NNTP in Exchange.

FIG. 1.6
Basic flow of NNTP.

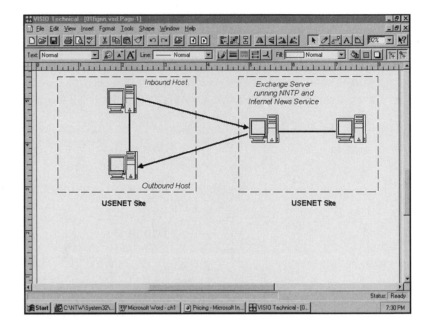

Active Server Components (HTTP)

Coupled with Internet Information Server (IIS), *Active Server components* give developers the building blocks to enrich Web sites with Exchange functionality, such as messaging, threaded discussion, and directory services. For example, Microsoft completed an Active Server application called Outlook Web View. *Web View* gives a user the capability to retrieve e-mail using a standard browser running on a wide range of platforms, including Macintosh, OS/2, and UNIX. Future functionality enabling users to access and modify scheduling and other Exchange features is planned after the initial release of Exchange.

Web View gives users more freedom to check e-mail wherever they are. With the advent of "Internet Cafés" and Internet kiosks, users can check their e-mail from anywhere in the world by simply logging onto their company's Web site. See Figure 1.7 for a basic flow of HTTP.

Message Flow

Message flow is the path a mail message takes as it moves from one recipient to another. Exchange determines whether the message will route inside of a server or between server by comparing the recipient's address with the addresses on the local site and those in the routing table. Messages will flow between servers if the address is in the routing table or within the same server if the address matches those in the local site. Before jumping into message flow, let's understand what MAPI is first.

FIG. 1.7
Basic flow of HTTP.

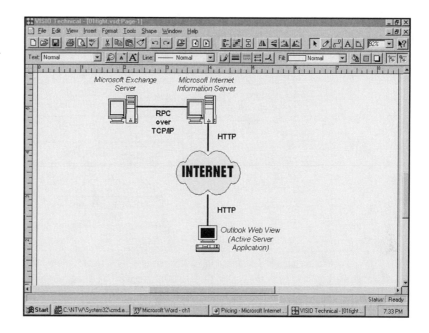

MAPI

MAPI (Messaging Application Programming Interface) is a set of functions that can be called by C, C++, and Visual Basic programs through Windows Dynamic Link Libraries (DLLs). MAPI enables custom programs that can control and manipulate Exchange objects (see Figure 1.8). MAPI is a powerful extension to Exchange that provides support for developers to enhance the core functionality built into Exchange.

MAPI has the following five components:

- Simple MAPI (sMAPI)
- MAPI
- Common Messaging Calls (CMC)
- MAPI service providers
- OLE Messaging

When the client application is using a function library, messaging services are processed by sMAPI or CMC. The *CMC interface* is an API layer defined by the X.400 API Association. CMC is similar to sMAPI but is specially designed to support cross-platform development. When MAPI objects are being accessed and manipulated, client requests are serviced by OLE messaging or MAPI itself. The OLE messaging component enables development by using tools such as Visual C, Visual C++, and Visual Basic; MAPI itself is a powerful, object-oriented C++ interface that enables complex manipulation of folders, forms, and messages. The MAPI service providers then perform the requested actions for the client and pass back action through the MAPI subsystem to the MAPI client.

FIG. 1.8
The MAPI framework
provides the map for
designing Exchange
applications.

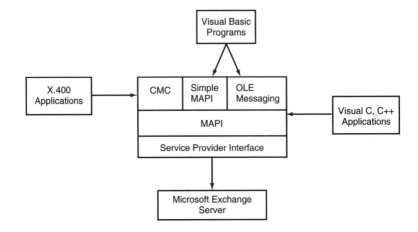

 In addition to the tools and sample applications provided by Microsoft, many utilities for Exchange are available from third-party companies. These utilities, which are discussed in Chapter 31, "Using Advanced Outlook Features," consist of gateways, connectors, Visual Basic custom controls, and administrative utilities.

Third-party developers, such as Lotus Development Corporation, have switched from proprietary messaging standards, such as Vendor Independent Messaging (VIM) to MAPI for designing messaging applications. This fact shows the strength of the MAPI standard of the multitude of development tools that will emerge for designing MAPI applications.

MAPI is the glue that enables client applications to converse with the server to build a robust communications architecture.

Message Flow Within One Server

Here are the basic steps a message goes through when the receiver is on the same server as the sender; this process is detailed in Chapter 2, "Understanding Exchange's Organization Sites:"

1. Using MAPI calls over a RPC connection, Client1 connects to the server and accesses the private IS where all mail messages are held. It sends the message to the IS.

2. The IS queries the directory to determine if the recipient (Client2) resides on the same server.

3. The directory identifies that the recipient (Client2) is on the same server.

4. The IS sends the recipient (Client2) a notice that a new message has arrived and Client2 receives the new message (see Figure 1.9).

FIG. 1.9
Message flow within
one server.

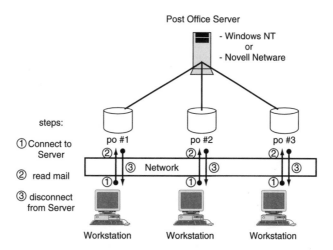

Shared-File LAN Electronic Mail

Post Office Server

- Windows NT
or
- Novell Netware

steps:

① Connect to
Server

② read mail

③ disconnect
from Server

po #1

po #2

po #3

② ②

② ③ Network ③ ③

① ① ①

Workstation   Workstation   Workstation

Message Flow Between Servers

Here are the basic steps a message goes through when the receiver is on a separate server;
this is detailed in Chapter 2, "Understanding Exchange's Organization Sites:"

1. Using MAPI calls over a RPC connection, client1 connects to the server and accesses the
   private IS where all mail messages are held. It sends the message to Server1.

2. The IS queries the directory and determines the recipient (Client2) resides on a
   different server. It then places the message in the MTA's queue.

3. Server1's MTA sends the message to Server2's MTA.

4. The MTA sends the message to the private IS.

5. The IS sends the recipient (Client2) a notice that a new message has arrived and Client2
   receives the new message (see Figure 1.10).

Exchange versus Lotus Notes

N O T E   Novell's GroupWise and Netscape's SuiteSpot are the two new contenders in the ring with
Lotus Notes. Due to the relatively short time GroupWise and SuiteSpot have been on the
market, comparative information is changing daily and should be retrieved from
www.microsoft.com.

On the other hand, Notes and Exchange have been old foes and the core differences between the two
products have been the same through recent versions. Thus, a section comparing Notes to Exchange
follows. Comparative information on Notes is still available at the same Microsoft Web address. ■

FIG. 1.10
Message flow between
servers.

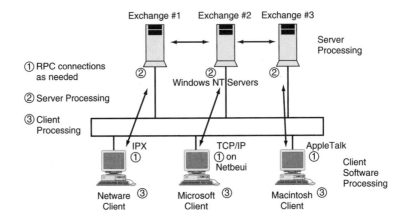

Client Server Exchange Mail System

Many critics attempt to compare Lotus Notes and Exchange, but no direct comparison can be made. Exchange has been designed from the ground up as an X.400/X.500-based enterprise messaging system. The MTA is designed to meet the exacting standards of 1984, 1988, and the proposed 1992 X.400 standards. The directory of Exchange is based on an extended version of X.500. Notes, on the other hand, began its life as a system of flat-file document databases that could replicate across multiple servers. Messaging was added as a way to enable additions to be "mailed in" to a database. Messaging has been enhanced in each version since 4.0 to approach the needs of an enterprise messaging system. Currently, the internal mail engine of Notes 4.5 is still based on Lotus proprietary standards, but Lotus offers a series of free "MTA" add-ins to handle X.400 mail, SMTP mail, and POP3 support with plans for LDAP support later.

The Notes directory itself is loosely based on X.500 standards and has been since Notes version 3.0. Provisions are included for all of the components of an X.500 naming scheme, and most of the fields associated with extended X.500 are included.

In terms of messaging, Exchange far exceeds the functionality of Notes version 3.x. Notes version 4.x has made significant strides in providing enhancements to messaging elements. Unlike MS Mail or cc:Mail, Notes has no legacy in shared file system mail. Notes has been essentially client/server from the beginning. Lotus recently has stated that Notes is the upgrade path from cc:Mail to a client/server messaging system. For many cc:Mail installations, this is potentially not desirable; thus, in Exchange version 5.0, Microsoft has included a cc:Mail Connector and the capability to perform directory synchronization with cc:Mail.

The two products can compete as groupware solutions, but Exchange provides an entire messaging infrastructure to connect with legacy systems and heterogeneous environments because Exchange bases all of its *workflow* on messaging. Both Exchange and Notes offer a "simple" forms and database development environment for basic users, and both offer several options for enhanced development with powerful programming environments. In Notes 4.x, Lotus has added a programming environment called *Lotus Script*, which is 95 percent compatible with Microsoft's Visual Basic. Lotus offers this tool as a way for Visual Basic programmers quickly to become productive developing Notes applications.

Exchange takes this extensibility several steps further with complete integration of Exchange with the full family of Microsoft development languages and tools. Now with the addition of Internet components and Web publishing via Exchange, all of the available Internet-oriented languages and environments are available for use.

> **N O T E** Several third-party developers offer gateway solutions to give Exchange tight connectivity with Notes. With proper implementation, Exchange and Notes can coexist effectively in your environment. ▓

Probably the biggest limitation of Notes that will not be corrected in the foreseen future is the basic flat-file design of a Notes database. Exchange is based on a relational database structure that lends itself to many traditional Relational Database Management System (RDBMS) programming concepts and features. Notes can attempt to address some of these limits with programming tricks and even replication to external SQL platforms, but the fundamental product that most clients will be working in do not take advantage of these workarounds.

Notes Advantages   Lotus Notes has a few advantages over Exchange when it is used as groupware. The product is mature, and Lotus has made several enhancements in it over the years. One exciting feature Lotus added first that Microsoft recognized and added in Exchange 5.0 is the World Wide Web "gateway." From a Web browser, you can access Notes databases. Likewise in Exchange 5.0, you can now access Exchange public folders.

In addition to Notes' base functionality of providing groupware solutions inside any enterprise, many organizations have adopted an information distribution channel by providing Notes databases of information or direct feeds from their product support. Companies such as SAP currently use Notes as a means to support their product.

Microsoft's Use of Exchange

When MS Mail was in production, interestingly Microsoft internally did not use its own shared-file e-mail system. Instead, it used its client interface on top of a proprietary UNIX-flavored system called *Xenix mail*.

To prove its commitment to the Exchange product, Microsoft has since moved all its internal mail systems to Exchange. At the time of this writing, Microsoft is on Exchange worldwide with 99 locations and 266 Exchange servers. The bulk of these servers are dedicated messaging servers, followed by dedicated public folder servers. They have more than 13,000 public folders in use with the majority of them used for development tracking purposes (build schedules, early adopter tracking).

On the client side, Microsoft has also moved to Outlook as the standard client browser to reinforce Microsoft's commitment to their own messaging platform.

Exchange's Momentum

Exchange has picked up considerable momentum since its first release.

There have been more than 750,000 Exchange seats deployed to date and around 65 percent of customers use Exchange for Internet Mail connectivity. Forty-five percent (more than one response could be marked) of them use Exchange for pieces of the company intranet. There are more than 125 companies actively developing applications and more than 12,000 professionals trained on the product.

From Here...

This chapter welcomed you to the world of Microsoft Exchange, introducing the key features of Exchange and providing an overview of the concepts of Exchange. For further information, read the following chapters:

- Chapter 3, "Exchange's Integrated Server Components," explains what makes up the Server and provides a basis for further understanding the administration of Exchange.
- Chapter 5, "Designing Exchange Topology," covers the entire planning process for Exchange within your enterprise.
- Chapter 6, "Installing Exchange Server," describes some concerns that you need to address before installing the software as well as step-by-step installation instructions.
- Chapters 29 through 31 describe in detail how to use Outlook.

CHAPTER 2

Understanding Exchange's Organization Sites

Microsoft Exchange Server is designed on a three-tiered model. The entire collection of Microsoft Exchange servers within a company is called the organization; i.e,. the root or starting point of the Exchange Server directory hierarchy. To facilitate administration and maximize performance, the organization is separated in distinct groups of servers called *sites*, which are one or more Microsoft Exchange Server computers connected together. Each site consists of what are called site resources, which are the individual Exchange servers themselves and the recipients who reside on those servers. Understanding this hierarchy and the underlying network architecture that supports it is crucial to the implementation of Exchange in any company. This chapter is designed to provide an overview of these concepts in order for you to start thinking about how each element applies in your specific situation. ∎

The Three Tiers of the Microsoft Exchange Server Hierarchy

The three-tier model consists of an Organization, a site, and Site Resources.

General Considerations in Linking Sites to Build an Organization

What is the current LAN/WAN traffic, how information is routed, and identifying connectors to use between sites.

General Naming Strategies to Consider When Building Your Own Exchange Enterprise

Good references on which to build is to follow company structure and geographical locations.

Exchange and a Company's Organization

The largest administrative unit in Microsoft Exchange is the organization. All Exchange servers in an association or company are included under the heading of organization. An Exchange organization can be a single-room office with a couple of servers or a huge, multinational facility with dozens of servers at great geographical distances (see Figure 2.1). Regardless of the situation, often there will be other types of messaging systems to which Exchange must communicate. These systems are not considered part of the Exchange organization, though they may play an integral part in your company's overall messaging scheme.

FIG. 2.1
A Sample Microsoft
Exchange Organization.

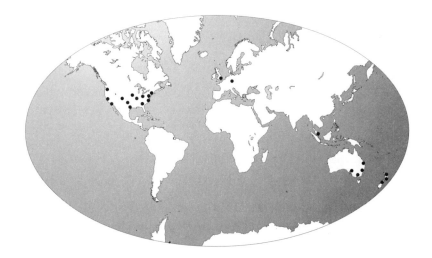

Exchange Server Sites

Sites are Exchange's second tier. They represent a logical grouping of several Microsoft Exchange Server computers. Servers in a site work together to provide messaging services to a set of users, unified administration, and communication services. Within a site, all servers can easily share information and can also be managed as a collection.

There are several other advantages to having multiple servers grouped into one site:

- Centralized administration. You do not need to log on to each server in order to perform administrative functions on any of the servers in a site.

- Directory information is automatically replicated between servers in a site. No additional connectors are required for this functionality.

- A user needs only to be added once to gain user access to resources on all servers within a site.

- Easier access to information resources. A user can access a relevant bulletin board without having to know its specific server location within a site.

Defining Site Boundaries

With all of these benefits, you might be inclined to put every Exchange server in one site. For several reasons, this is not always the best solution. Therefore, defining where one site ends and one site begins is worthy of some serious consideration (see Figure 2.2). Variables such as network bandwidth, physical links, protocols, network traffic, operating systems, and cost will affect where site lines are defined in your enterprise. Also, it is important to plan the number of sites and their boundaries well, because it is difficult to split or join other sites once they are created. Even moving users from one site to another in not a trivial task.

Part

I

Ch

2

FIG. 2.2

Sample site boundaries. These are also the actual U.S. offices used as examples throughout this book.

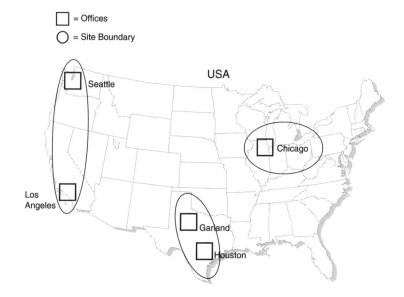

There are some general requirements that must be met by all servers within a site:

- All servers in a site must be able to communicate via Remote Procedure Calls (RPCs). RPC is a mechanism by which servers exchange messages and directory information. RPCs can communicate over the network by using the various Microsoft Windows NT-supported protocols, including TCP/IP, IPX, NetBEUI, and DLC. Generally, this means that all the servers must be on the same LAN or WAN. But if you do have a large network spanning geographical boundaries and that network connection supports communication via RPCs, then you could define those servers to all be within the same site (provided the other following requirements are met).

- High-bandwidth connections are required for server communication within a site. The definition of high bandwidth is somewhat arbitrary, but for our purposes we consider 128 Kb/s to be the absolute minimum bandwidth for reasonable intrasite communication.

Basically, the connection must be fast enough to allow efficient RPC connections between servers and handle the volume data, such as user messages, and Directory and Public folder replication. Of course, the bigger the pipe, the better the performance.

- The network connection must be permanent. The links between all servers in a site must be up at all times. Permanent connections include LAN, leased line, and other WAN links. Periodic connections (connections not available all the time) such as dial-ups are not a good choice.

- All servers must exist in the same Windows NT security context. This means all servers must be in the same Windows NT domain or within a trusted domain. Exchange servers in a site must be able to authenticate each other in order to share information.

There are many other elements to consider when planning Microsoft Exchange Server sites (administration schemes, number of users, integration of other messaging protocols, additional network traffic, and so on). Grouping users who work together on the same server and sites reduces network traffic and resource utilization. Chapter 10, "Installing Exchange in a Netware Environment," provides a much more in-depth look at such considerations.

Linking Sites

Once site boundaries are determined, further assessment is required to establish the network architecture that will join each one. Routing within a site requires little planning, however; routing between sites or to another e-mail system requires detailed planning and configuration. Again, this requires extensive study of messaging usage across your entire organization and any specific needs determined by your application of the technology.

The boundaries between sites will usually sustain a considerable amount of traffic due to the following types of information traversing site links:

- Standard messaging data (plus attachments)
- Directory replication data
- Public folder replication (or connections to public folders replication if not configured)

There are two primary Exchange components used to connect sites:

- Site connector
- X.400 connector

Site Connector   This connector is designed for sites located on the same LAN. A site connector is a Microsoft Exchange built-in connector to facilitate the transfer of messages between two Exchange servers. This connector is an integrated software component to the server. The site connectors use RPC calls to communicate with the other Exchange servers. Site connectors are unlike the Internet or X.400 connectors in that they will support any Microsoft networking protocol or any Exchange messaging address space or directory services. The key is that the Exchange servers have connectivity between the sites.

The site connector is the most efficient method of site interconnection, but the sites must be able to communicate at high bandwidth using remote procedure calls. Also, because the sites must authenticate each other during communication, they must belong to the same Windows NT domain (or be part of a trusted domain).

There are two major advantages to using a site connector instead of an X.400 connector:

■ Efficient communication between sites because messages do not need to be converted from the Exchange internal format.

■ Easy configuration since one does not need to define a network transport (RPC communications are transport independent) and you do not have to schedule connections.

X.400 Connector   Conditions often mandate the use of the X.400 connector for site links. X.400 connections are used for several reasons. One reason is that your enterprise has a connection to a Value Added network provider in order to send secure messages to a business partner. X.400 is the standard protocol for the VAN connections. The other reason is if your enterprise is quite large, you may configure Exchange to use the X.400 address space as the directory service for the messaging backbone. X.400 provides a standards-based address space, ensuring the longevity of the messaging system in the large enterprises. Microsoft itself uses Exchange with an X.400 backbone to support all 20,000 of its users. X.400 offers some advantages—you can define message size and schedule when connections happen, as well as the route the message takes. Some of the disadvantages are that X.400 is more complicated to configure and can be costly if there's a high volume of data. Generally, if any of the following conditions apply, you will need to opt for the X.400 connector:

■ Your remote site is not on the same logical LAN. This could mean you are using an asynchronous connection, X.25, or are connecting to a site at a different enterprise.

■ You want to use a public or private X.400 system as your messaging backbone.

■ You want all Exchange communications to fully comply with the 1984 or 1988 X.400 standards.

Messages routed through an X.400 connector must be converted to X.400 standard for messaging interchange. However, the wide range of connectivity options provided more than makes up for the slight loss in network efficiency.

Site Resources

Site resources are the third tier in the Microsoft Exchange hierarchy. This tier consists of two main elements:

■ Servers. The physical hardware and software package that operates Exchange.

■ Recipients. The elements toward which all messaging data is directed.

Servers

Server machines may wear many hats in an Exchange environment. An Exchange server can at the same time perform any number of the following tasks:

- Hold local users' mailboxes
- Hold public folders in a local information store
- Be a connection or gateway to other Exchange sites, MS Mail post offices or foreign systems
- Be a "bridgehead" server for directory replication between sites

Also, the server might hold the following additional Windows NT supporting tasks:

- Support dial-up users via remote access lines
- Be a Windows NT domain controller

To avoid overloading any one server, an optimal situation would be to have a dedicated server for each of the preceding tasks. However, in real-world situations this is often neither practical nor cost effective. A major goal in planning an Exchange hierarchy is to master the art of load balancing across several machines. Other load balancing factors include the number of Exchange servers, the type of platform number of disks, CPU speed, amount of memory, public folder replication, and type of mailbox rules. Subsequent chapters discuss load balancing in detail.

Recipients

It is important in a discussion of the Exchange hierarchy to consider the very entities of which directories are created. Recipients are the foundation of an Exchange messaging system. We are the reason that messaging technology exists in the first place. Microsoft Exchange server defines the following four types of recipients:

- Mailbox

  Called the "inbox." It is the most common type of recipient. One is usually assigned to each user. Mailboxes are recipients within the messaging site or local post office. They contain information about users, such as where that person fits in the organization, their name and phone numbers, and e-mail addresses.

- Custom recipient

  These are recipients outside the messaging site almost identical to mailboxes that contain information on users outside of Microsoft Exchange. One common custom recipient would be an Internet user with an SMTP e-mail address, such as **rshort@swspectrum(user@domain)**.

- Distribution list

  These are also known as aliases or groups in Microsoft Mail. This type of recipient is actually a group of other recipients (either mail boxes or custom recipients). Messages sent to a distribution list are delivered to each recipient on the list.

- Public folder

  A public folder is a recipient with the added functionality of allowing the received messages to be shared among many users in an enterprise. Created by the administrator with the Client interface, you can set access control and control the storage requirements.

- Hidden recipients

  Hidden recipients can send and receive mail, but they do not show up in the address book. Naturally, hidden recipients are not propagated in directory replication.

Each recipient is handled as an individual object by Microsoft Exchange Server during directory replication/synchronization. Each can be assigned individual trust levels (see discussion in Chapter 7, "Planning Connections to Microsoft Mail Systems") to determine whether its directory entry will be replicated to other sites in an organization.

Each recipient has many different properties and details which can be set by the administrator, but such discussion will occur somewhat later in this book (see Chapter 16, "Creating and Configuring Recipient").

Part

I

Ch

2

Exchange System Naming Conventions

A good naming strategy is crucial to the efficient operation of a Microsoft Exchange system. Each object in a Microsoft Exchange directory is identified by a unique name. This is called the Distinguished Name and it is set when the object is first built—when you create a new mail box, install a new server, add a new connector, and so on. With a good naming strategy that uses meaningful and logical names, you will be able to quickly pinpoint the object anywhere in your organization.

Good references on which to build names are traditionally as follows:

- Geographical locations (Garland, Los Angeles)
- Company structure (manufacturing, distribution)

Other things you should consider are whether you have to be compatible with another mail system or other applications, and whether your organization may someday expand beyond the country. Cute or comical names get old quickly and generally do not provide sufficient information for the widest possible range of personnel to understand your structure.

Microsoft Exchange Message Route

A well-designed Microsoft Exchange system within a reasonably large organization will reflect skillful interweaving of various messaging technologies. Message routing is the process through which a message eventually reaches its intended recipient. Because of Exchange's connector and gateway options, efficient message routing can and will be an intricate process throughout your enterprise. This section will cover basic routing concepts in order to start giving you a feel for how Exchange handles messages.

Fortunately for the end-user, the complex message routes are abstracted into the single inbox metaphor. As a system administrator, however, it is essential for you to understand all the possible instances of message routing in order to be able to create the most efficient routes in your Microsoft Exchange Organization.

The key elements involved in a routing process are as follows:

- Message Transfer Agent
- Directory Service
- Connectors and Gateways

How Routing Works

To route a message correctly to an intended recipient, Exchange needs to know not only the address of the intended recipient, but also information that describes the path to that destination. This is accomplished by two crucial pieces of addressing data:

1. Recipient Address

   The name of the specific mailbox toward which a message is intended. It must be in the standard of the recipient system, meaning a recipient on your Exchange system will be addressed following your naming standard, such as user first name and last name. An Internet SMTP address would be **rshort@swspectrum.com (user@domain)**.

2. Address Space

   Address space entries identify a certain type of message that a connector is responsible for routing. Typically, these entries are a subset of a complete address, identifying the route a certain message will take. Exchange takes each address space entry as a filter to determine whether a message should be sent through a connector or gateway.

Directory Names and X.400 Originator/Recipient Addresses

Microsoft Exchange uses a subset of the X.400 Originator/Recipient (O/R) to identify individual recipients. The X.400 O/R address is comprised of attributes that define a specific recipient by country, organization, common name, and a variety of other information.

A Routing Overview

Here is the step-by-step logic taken during routing of a message within an Exchange site:

1. MTA provides the engine for routing and transferring data to other servers. The routing process commences when an Exchange Server's MTA receives a message. The message can be derived from a user's mail box, a connector, or another MTA.

2. The MTA provides the addressing and routing information for sending messages and other information through the system. If the message's destination is specified by a Directory Name, then the MTA compares the site information of the message (part of the directory name) to the local site. If they do not match, then the recipient is on a different site and the message is routed by the process described in the following section.

If the message's destination is specified by an O/R address, then the MTA compares the site information of the message (part of the O/R address) to the local site. If they are not the same, then routing proceeds to another site (next section).

N O T E If the recipient is a distribution list, the list is separated into its component recipients. Each recipient then enters this routing process independently.

3. If the DN or the O/R address matches the local site, then delivery commences. For recipients on the local server, the MTA ensures delivery directly to the information store. For recipients on a different server in the site, the local MTA transfers the message to that server's MTA, which then ensures delivery to the information store.

If at any time an MTA encounters a connection problem with a connector, it will retry the transmission periodically until delivery is successful or until the time-out limit is exceeded. If the time-out limit is exceeded, then the message is returned as non-deliverable (NDR).

Part

I

Ch

2

Routing Between Microsoft Exchange Sites and Foreign Systems

Here is the step-by-step logic taken during routing of a message within an Exchange site:

1. MTA provides the engine for routing and transferring data to other servers. The routing process commences when an Exchange Server's MTA receives a message. The message can be derived from a user's mail box, a connector, or another MTA.

2. The recipient's address is compared to the local site. If they match, the message is delivered as in the previous list.

3. If the sites do not match, MTA will match the recipient's address space to an available connector or gateway.

   For example, if the recipient has an SMTP address, the MTA knows how to route it through an Internet Mail connector. If more than one such connection is available, then one is selected based on routing costs.

4. The MTA sends the message through the selected gateway.

5. The message is delivered according to the process of the receiving system. If the receiving system is an Exchange site, the message will be routed as noted in the previous list. Every other messaging system will have its own delivery methods.

N O T E Often there may be multiple message routes to a particular destination. In this case, the appropriate route is chosen by the routing cost of that destination.

Understanding Routing Tables

Routing tables contain all the information a message transfer agent needs to determine where to send messages. Every time you make a change that affects message routing, such as removing a site connector or site, you are prompted. The routing table will be rebuilt and saved. Routing tables also can be rebuilt manually through a button on the MTA property sheet, although in most cases, the routing tables are built dynamically.

Routing Attachments with Messages

Attachments are routed simultaneously with a message. All necessary file format conversions are handled by the appropriate MTAs through which the message passes. Exchange does have intelligent attachment handling when dealing with distribution lists. Only one instance of an attachment is sent to each mailbox. This eliminates wasted disk space to maintain exact duplicates of an attachment for several users in the same site.

Using Distribution Lists

Distribution Lists are groups of users that can be addressed as one by sending one message. For instance, sending a message addressed to a distribution list named "accounting" would be received by all members of that list. Lists are established and modified by the administrators and can be replicated across servers and sites allowing recipients with access privileges to see the members and the messages to them.

▶ **See** "Creating and Configuring Recipient," for more information on creating distribution lists, **p. 321**

An individual user can also join appropriate lists from within his or her Exchange Client. From the Exchange server standpoint, lists themselves are individual directory objects. This means they can each have specific properties attached to them and are replicated by directory replication and synchronization.

A message sent to a distribution list is treated as a single entity until it is split into its component recipients. When configuring a distribution list's properties, you define an expansion server where the list splits into its components.

Here is the process:

1. A user addresses and sends a message to a distribution list.
2. The message is routed as normal to its intended recipient (in this case, the distribution list).
3. The list object is routed to an Exchange server set as this list's Expansion server. At this point, the list is broken down into its component recipients.
4. Each message to the component recipients is routed individually.

Redundant Site Links, Routing Cost, and Load Balancing

For large organizations it is often efficient and safe to establish multiple links between certain sites. This not only increases the system's fault tolerance, but also can be used to balance messaging traffic between sites. Often there will be specific links which receive an extraordinary amount of large traffic. Message routing in this situation demands establishing a priority for whatever connections will receive the traffic. This will be discussed more in-depth in the site planning section of this book. There are some general considerations for situations where alternative routes should be established.

- Available Network Bandwidth. Links with more robust bandwidth will generally receive the bulk of messaging data between sites. An asynchronous modem link would usually be used as a backup, for example.
- Cost of Connections. Certain types of connections (such as the use of private X.400 connections) are less cost efficient and should be used only when other connections are overloaded or unavailable.

A variable called Routing Cost is assigned to each connection (in its property sheet) and used by Exchange message transfer agents to determine the path of a message. The cost of each route can be any number between 0 and 100. A route that costs 0 will always be used first if it is available, and a route that costs 100 will only be used if no other routes are available. Default value for all connectors is one. If two or more connections have the same routing cost, then messaging load will be roughly split equally among them.

In the Software Spectrum organization, for example, a number of connectors are set up to connect servers in the Los Angeles, California site, to the Garland, Texas site. In the connectors' property sheets we establish links between the following Microsoft Exchange servers:

1. A site connector over a T-1 line between servers Garland01 and LosAngeles01. We assign this link a routing cost of 1.

2. A site connector over the same T-1 line between servers GARLAND02andLOSANGELES02.

   We also assign this link a routing cost of 1.

3. An X.400 connector over a private network between server GARLAND02 andLOSANGELES02.

   We assign this link a routing cost of 2.

4. Finally, we have one last resort Dynamic RAS X.25 connection between GARLAND01and LOSANGELES02. We assign this link a routing cost of 100 due to its inherent monetary cost of message transfer and limited bandwidth.

Messages will normally traverse the first and second site connections. Their routing cost is equal, so Exchange will attempt to distribute message load across both connectors evenly. Under heavy message loads where message cues on both site connectors 1 and 2 are long,

Part

I

Ch

2

Exchange will commence to utilize connector number 3 (X.400). In the rare situation where all three above connectors are disabled (e.g., the T-1 link is down and the GARLAND03 is off-line for repair), Exchange will engage connection number 4 as a last resort.

Load Balancing is the fine art of crafting your system's connections to best handle your diverse system traffic. By considering the above and many other variables, you will able to design an efficient and fault-tolerant system for your enterprise.

Address List and Directory Management

A listing of all available recipients, such as a global address list, completes the corporate directory that contains the entire organization. Because the Global Address List is a list of individuals by name (not cryptic e-mail names), it is of great value to a user. From the standpoint of a network administrator, however, maintaining an accurate and timely address list can be one of the greatest challenges. Traditionally, Microsoft Mail has had a history of difficulties in implementing such functionality, and not since the arrival of Exchange has there been a bigger push for excellence in this area.

This section will overview the essential components of Exchange's directory architecture. Additionally, you will learn important concepts about directory synchronization that aid in planning and implementing Exchange in your enterprise.

The Directory Service is the primary component responsible for directory manipulation in Microsoft Exchange. The Directory Service uses Directory System Agents (DSAs) that are the subprograms responsible for executing specific changes to a directory structure.

Maintaining a useful, up-to-date directory involves managing user addresses within an Exchange site, between sites, and between your enterprise and the other systems with which you pass information. If, for example, a user is added on one server, you as the administrator need to decide which other site directories should reflect that change and configure appropriate connectors to facilitate the process. By administrating a combination of system processes you will be able to detail how directory information propagates through your system.

There are two principal Exchange operations that carry out directory management tasks:

- Directory Replication
- Directory Synchronization

Directory Replication

Directory replication is the process by which all the Microsoft Exchange servers in an enterprise share directory information. To maintain a useful user directory, updates must be accurate, timely, and available to all appropriate users.

Directory Replication Within a Site

Directory replication between servers in the same site is automatic (see Figure 2.3). Each server holds a local copy of the directory for that site. When you as the administrator modify a mailbox at one server, that change is automatically distributed to all servers in that site. Usually it takes about five minutes for new information to propagate across a site.

FIG. 2.3
Directory replication
within a site.

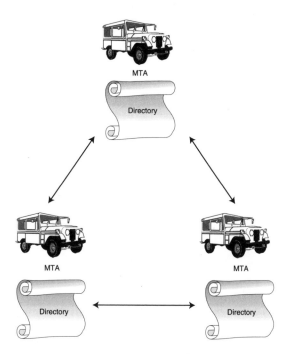

By default, all directory information is included in replication. This means an exact duplicate of each server's entire directory structure is exchanged during replication. This is efficient within a site due to the high bandwidth network connections typically found between servers. By the same token, network connections between sites are typically much lower bandwidth, so passing entire directory lists is not the most efficient method of maintaining timely address lists.

Directory Replication Between Sites

Directory replication between sites is not an automatic process. For two distinct sites to share directory information, there needs to be a specific connector established. This gives you the option to filter what data is actually replicated and what remains unique to that site.

Directory replication between sites can occur if the sites are on the same logical LAN, WAN links, or public and private messaging links (see Figure 2.4). Therefore, public X.400 systems, or even the Internet, can be the transport for your directory replication information between sites.

Directory replication across sites occurs asynchronously and is scheduled in the administrator program. Only one server in each site can be configured to either send or receive replication information. However, one server can be set up to both send and receive the data. Servers that act as the connection boundaries for directory replication are known as the "bridgehead servers."

There are two steps to resolve before directory replication occurs across site boundaries:

1. Decide what specific directory information you wish to exchange with other sites.

2. Act upon that decision and configure each site so only the desired information is replicated.

Replication Trust or Sensitivity Levels   Each directory object (such as mailboxes, public folders, or distribution lists) can be individually assigned a parameter called replication trust level or sensitivity level. These trust levels determine whether or not a certain object will be replicated to a certain site.

Example: The trust level for replication from the Boston site to the Los Angeles site is set to 50. You can create a user mailbox in Boston and set its trust level to 51 and information about that recipient will not be propagated to the Los Angeles site in the directory replication process.

FIG. 2.4

Directory replication
between sites.

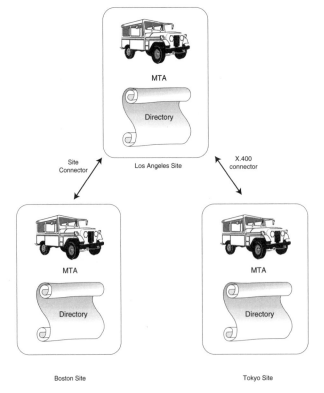

Directory Replication Tables

Directory replication tables are maps that describe the replication links between servers in a site. This is useful mainly when adding new servers. For instance, you bring up Server SEATTLE01 in a site, and then the directory replication tables are updated to include this server. The next time replication occurs, server SEATTLE01 can send and receive updates to all other servers in the site.

Directory replication tables also map links between servers in a site and the bridgehead server. This server is the one machine responsible for receiving directory updates from remote sites.

Directory Synchronization

Perhaps a greater challenge than replicating directory data between Exchange servers is synchronizing directory data with other messaging systems. Typically, this situation arises when linking Exchange to an existing Microsoft Mail network or to a foreign system through an external gateway. Exchange Server supports synchronization with any mail system that uses the Microsoft Mail for PC Networks version 3.x directory synchronization protocol.

Directory synchronization (dir-sync) is optional and it ensures that each directory (or post office for MS Mail) has an up-to-date address list. The dir-sync process is streamlined by propagating only the changes between systems and not the complete address lists.

Because Exchange's directory synchronization is based on the MS Mail dir-sync protocol, let us first examine the architecture of that system before proceeding (see Figure 2.5). MS Mail directory synchronization involves the following core components:

- Directory Synchronization Server—A single MS Mail post office assigned to the task of synchronizing directories.

- Directory Synchronization Requestor—Every other post office on the network that shares addresses with the dir-sync server.

- Server Address List—The master list of all users that is maintained on the dir-sync server.

- Dir-Sync Server—The directory synchronization server (there can be only one dir-sync server in a site) collects address list updates from requestors, updates the master directory list, and then sends out the resulting updates to each requestor.

- Dir-Sync Requestor—These systems send local directory updates to the designated dir-sync server (when the requestor is also a server it sends messages to itself). Requestors also obtain address updates from other requestors through the dir-sync server.

N O T E On a dir-sync server, the master address list is stored separately from local address information. Therefore, when a local address is changed on the machine operating as the dir-sync server, it communicates that change to itself as would any other requestor. ■

FIG. 2.5

Directory synchronization within a Microsoft Mail system.

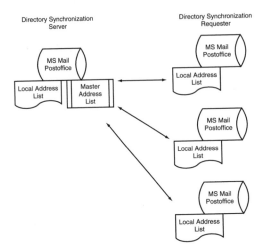

Microsoft Exchange server contains a component, the Microsoft directory synchronization agent (DXA), that can function in either the server or the requester role (see Figure 2.6). As with MS Mail networks, you can set up only one directory synchronization server in each Exchange site. Instead of having a server address list, Exchange uses its standard server directory.

> **N O T E** Microsoft Mail for AppleTalk networks can participate in directory synchronization with the Microsoft Exchange Connection Gateway installed on the appropriate MS Mail (AppleTalk) server. This connection includes a requester program that will function exactly as any other MS Mail requester. ▨

FIG. 2.6

Microsoft Exchange directory synchronization agent.

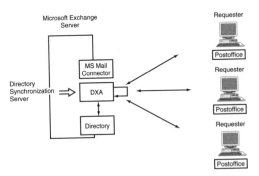

Directory Synchronization with Foreign Systems

Foreign mail systems can also participate in directory synchronization provided they can import and export addressing information using the Microsoft Mail 3.x directory synchronization protocol. In essence, the foreign system then becomes another requester and is seen as such by the directory synchronization server.

The following is a description of how a foreign requester participates in directory synchronization:

1. The foreign requester creates its own list of address updates and puts them into system messages.

2. The address updates are submitted to the dir-sync server via the appropriate gateway or transport.

3. The dir-sync server receives and incorporates the updates into its master directory list. A new message reflecting address changes is generated.

4. The message containing the updates is transmitted once again via the appropriate gateway to the foreign requester.

5. The foreign requester processes the changes into its local address list.

Consistency Checker

This tool is necessary for adjusting inconsistencies between the Directory and the Public Information Store. The challenge arises when there is a directory entry for a particular folder in the store, yet the folder no longer exists, or the opposite situation where a folder exists, but there is no corresponding directory entry. Typically, this is due to information restored from a backup that is out of sync with current records. The consistency checker is run by the system administrator to adjust such irregularities.

N O T E The consistency checker will create a directory entry only if a folder exists in the public information store. However, never will it create an entry in the public information store if an entry exists in the directory.

Understanding the X.500 Directory Service

Microsoft Exchange server directory architecture is based on the 1988 X.500 directory service recommendations. The X.500 directory structure outlines a logical directory object organization scheme, each object's attributes, and how they relate to one another. X.500 is a widely accepted standard, and with its application Exchange can participate in directory data sharing with many different systems.

Exchange defines additional object classes and attributes beyond X.500 standards in order to provide users more descriptive directory entries. For example, Exchange directories can support the following attributes that X.500 does not:

- Individual titles, such as president, MIS director
- Additional phone numbers
- Custom attributes defined by the administrator
- Organization charting information
- Alternate recipients

From Here...

This chapter has introduced you to some concepts surrounding the use of organizations and sites in Microsoft Exchange. These concepts included:

- Organizations, sites, and linking sites to one another
- Site resources such as servers and recipients
- Naming conventions
- Message Routing
- Redundancy
- Directory management functions such as synchronization, replication, and trusts

Grasping conceptual aspects of Exchange discussed in this chapter will help you understand the installation and configuration examples discussed in later chapters. The following chapters contain related information to some of the items in this chapter:

- Chapter 5, "Designing Exchange Topology," gives detailed information pertinent to the topics discussed in this chapter.
- Chapter 18, "Using Directory Replication and Synchronization," goes in-depth on those topics. Having read this chapter, you are better prepared to understand the configuration of these components.
- Chapter 27, "Exchange Security," discusses Exchange security features including data encryption and Person to Person Key Exchange.

CHAPTER 3

Exchange's Integrated Server Components

Exchange server comprises four fundamental system services that run under Windows NT server. Together, these services handle all basic client/server interaction, user lookups, message transmission, and storage of information in public and private folders. With these four core components, an Exchange server can function as a stand-alone unit. All other components are optional and are designed specifically to facilitate information transfer to other Exchange servers and other external information systems. ■

The Components of Exchange Server

Four basic components form the core of Exchange: The System Attendant, Directory Service, Information Store, and MTA.

How Components Communicate with Each Other

All of the services and components of Exchange are tightly coupled with the NT operating system and each other. This chapter will explore some of these interactions.

What Connectors Are and How They Work

Exchange 5.0 adds a new cc:Mail Connector to compliment the current MS Mail Connector and has added many new features to the renamed Internet Mail Service. We will review the basic interactions of connectors and older MS Mail gateways.

How Connectors Can Be Used in Various Exchange Environments

Exchange can continue to utilize MS Mail 3.x gateways as well as operate seamlessly in PROFS and UNIX environments.

Exchange's Four Central Components

This chapter is designed to provide an overview of the Exchange server's four central components and describe how they communicate with each other and with other optional components. The following are the integrated server components (see Figure 3.1):

- System Attendant
- Message Transfer Agent
- Information Store (public and private)
- Directory

FIG. 3.1
The Integrated Exchange Server performs all the functions needed in the Exchange environment.

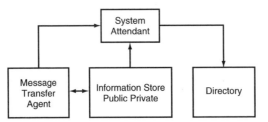

Introduction to System Attendant

▶ **See** "Directory and System Attendant Configuration," **p. 247**

This service performs general maintenance tasks. It functions much like the central nervous system for an Exchange server. Its operation is required in order for Microsoft Exchange processes to run. The System Attendant tasks are as follows:

- Monitor status of messaging connection between servers. This includes assisting in monitoring the state of links between servers in one site, two different sites, and between different systems.
- Gather information on each server in a site (such as what services are running) to assist in running messaging monitoring tools.
- Build routing tables in a site.
- Verify directory replication information and correct inconsistencies.
- Maintain information logs about sent messages for tracking purposes.
- Generate e-mail addresses for new message recipients you create. Default addresses created by the System Attendant are MS-Mail, X.400, and SMTP. Additionally, if you have any third-party gateways installed, the System Attendant will create appropriate addresses for those systems.

The principal reason for communication between the System Attendant and other Exchange components involves logging messaging activity. Message logs are kept for all messages arriving and departing from the Exchange server. The following are the components that make up the communication between Exchange services:

Agent	Function
Message Transfer Agent	The Message Transfer Agent notifies the System Attendant that it received or sent a message for delivery to other systems or sites.
Information Store	The Information Store communicates its messaging activity for logging by the System Attendant. This includes notice that it has received or sent a message for local delivery, i.e., on the same server.

Introduction to Message Transfer Agent

▶ **See** "Message Transfer Configuration," **p. 275**

The Message Transfer Agent (MTA) comprises the foundation of Exchange server's communication infrastructure. The MTA handles message transport to other servers, other sites, or foreign systems. In addition to being the transport vehicle for messaging information, it also maps addresses, routes them, and performs some message format conversion to other system's standards. (Other connectors and "gateways" installed on an Exchange server might also handle message format conversions, such as a PROFS connector.)

Being the principal message transport mechanism, the MTA communicates with all other Exchange components, as shown in the following mini-table:

Component	Communication
Directory	The MTA uses the directory to look up a user address. The directory instructs the MTA to submit mail from other sites' directories (to perform directory synchronization).
System attendant	The MTA tells the System Attendant (SA) to log each instance of a message transfer.
Administrator Program	From the Administrator Program, the MTA receives requests to manipulate messages in the queue.
Information Store	The Information Store (IS) submits messages for delivery to other systems and is notified to receive new mail by the MTA.
Microsoft Mail connector	The MTA is notified of new mail to handle.
Directory synchronization	The MTA is directed to send directory-related component messages from foreign systems.

Part

I

Ch

3

Introduction to the Information Store

▶ **See** "Information Store Configuration," **p. 287**

The Information Store (IS) is the end of the line for all messaging data transmitted successfully to an Exchange server. This includes both private messages sent to individual users and public information folders intended for viewing by many users. The IS maintains data in two distinct databases—the Private Information Store and the Public Information Store.

In addition to message storage, the IS handles local delivery of messages (when both sender and recipient are on the same server), replicates public folders, and enforces storage limits. The following is a list of the principal functions of the IS. The MTAs communicate with the following Exchange components.

Component	Communication
Message Transfer Agent	The IS contacts the MTA to accept new incoming mail, to deliver new outgoing mail, and to resolve addresses intended for gateways.
Exchange Clients	To the client the IS announces the arrival of new mail. Also, the IS accepts new mail submitted for delivery from the client.
Directory	The IS uses the directory to look up addresses, get user mailbox information, and create directory entries for public folders.
System Attendant	When the IS either receives or sends a message, it notifies the System Attendant so that a log entry is generated.
Administrator Program	The Administrator Program sends instructions to the IS to show statistics about connected users and other storage usage information, e.g., folder sizes. The Administrator Program connects to the IS to view information, logons, and resources.
Connectors / Gateways	IS communication to connectors/gateways involves the retrieval and delivery of messages to outside systems.

Introduction to Directory Service

▶ **See** "Directory and System Attendant Configuration," **p. 247**

The Directory Service (DS) keeps all the information about users and resources in an organization. This includes a structured view of all server names, mailboxes, and distribution lists in a site. Also, the directory keeps configuration information that other Exchange server components use when mapping addresses and routing messages.

In order to maintain consistency of addressing information across several Microsoft Exchange servers, directory data is automatically replicated among all servers in a site. This replication within a site is carried out by the MTA and administered by the Directory Service. The Directory Service also manages directory replication between sites on a scheduled basis (see Chapter 7, "Planning Connections to Microsoft Mail Systems," on directory synchronization/replication).

The directory classifies organization information (servers, mailboxes, and so on) as objects. Being objects, through the administrator program one can specify their characteristics, as well as determine who can use or change them.

▶ **See** "Configuring X.400 Connections," **p. 459**

The following is a list of components of the Directory Service and how they communicate with these Exchange services.

Component	Communication
Other Directories	Directories communicate with other Directory Services within the same site to replicate directory information.
Message Transfer Agent	The directory notifies the MTA in order to send mail to and receive mail from other directories (during directory replication). The MTA looks up addresses and configuration information from the Directory.
Administrator Program	The administrator program commands the directory to display and modify the address book, list of recipients, user properties, and directory objects (servers, monitors, connectors, and so on). Also, the administrator program can create objects in the directory.
Exchange Clients	Client programs call upon the directory to find a specific user's address and to display the address book, resolve an e-mail name to a full alias, and modify distribution list memberships.
Information Store	The IS uses the directory to look up address and configuration information, get information about mailboxes, and create directory entries for public folders.
System Attendant	The SA uses the directory to look up address and configuration information, build routing tables, generate e-mail addresses for new recipients, and verify consistency of directory information.
Directory synchronization	The directory synchronization component generates component requests to create, modify, and delete custom recipients. Also, it asks to look up recipients and configuration information.

Microsoft Mail Connector	The MS-Mail Connector looks up addresses from Microsoft Mail for PC networks and configuration information in the directory.
Connectors/Gateways	A connector/gateway uses the directory to replicate directory information and to look up address and configuration information.

The Administrator Program

The Administrator Program is the primary tool for administering Exchange. Though it is not an integrated server component, it does comprise an essential part of the Microsoft Exchange architecture. Further chapters will describe the multitude of functions provided by the administrator program, but this will present you with the basic description of its communication with a few integrated server components. The following is a list of programs controlled by the Exchange Administration program with their associated functions.

Program	Function
Directory	Through the administrator program one can display the address book, the main viewer, lists of recipients, properties of a user, and directory objects. Also, the administrator program allows you to create objects in the directory.
Message Transfer Agent	The administrator program allows you to manipulate messages in the various queues of the MTA.
Information Store	The administrator program enables you to create and delete mailboxes, as well as show statistics about information storage usage such as number of users logged on. It also provides information on the private and public information stores (connections, logons, re sources) and determines schedules for public folder replication.

Integrating Connectors in the Exchange Server

One of the big improvements Microsoft has made with Exchange is the integration of connectors into the server. For the most part, this feature eliminates the need for external boxes to establish connections to other mail systems. (Some exceptions might be fax or voice mail servers that may still require a dedicated machine.)

Connectors allow Microsoft Exchange to exchange information with various messaging systems. They provide tight integration with all the tools and utilities Exchange administrators will be using in the running of the server, such as the Performance Monitor, Link Monitor, and the Administrator Program.

This section will cover the following:

- What connectors and gateways are
- How connectors and gateways fit into the Exchange framework
- How gateways and connectors can be used to link sites
- What connectors and gateways are available

Using Exchange connectors will be an easy transition for anyone who has configured mail gateways for other mail systems. For example, the Simple Mail Transfer Protocol (SMTP) gateway for cc:Mail has many of the same configuration parameters as the Internet Mail Service.

N O T E In Exchange 4.0, the SMTP connector was called the Internet Mail Connector (IMC). This has been renamed in Exchange 5.0 to the Internet Mail Service to reflect the enhanced features that have been added. ▣

These include whether to act as inbound or outbound gateways or both, who acts as the administrator, where bounced and non-deliverable messages are delivered, and whether attachments are handled via Multimedia Internet Mail Extensions (MIME) compliance or UUENCODE. Being familiar with these terms as well as with Windows NT and 95 properties boxes facilitates configuration. By filling out properties sheets in the Administrator Program, as shown in Figure 3.2, you can be up and running without a lot of hassle.

Part

I

Ch

3

FIG. 3.2
The properties sheet for the Internet Mail Service gives the administrator many configuration options.

In addition, connectors can be used to link multiple mail system. For example, the Internet Mail Service can be used effectively in organizations where some departments choose to use Exchange, while others choose other platforms. Many of these organizations standardize on SMTP to transfer messages between departments because most LAN-based e-mail packages have some form of SMTP gateway since SMTP is a non-proprietary Internet standard. These kinds of uses will be explained in a little more detail later in this chapter.

The following connectors will be explained in this chapter:

- Microsoft Mail
- X.400
- Internet
- cc:Mail

The Microsoft Mail Connector

Connecting existing Microsoft Mail systems with Exchange is very common in a large enterprise during a migration and coexistence phase. With an installed user base of at least four million users, it makes sense that Exchange server would strongly support compatibility with MS Mail.

▶ **See** Chapters 19-20 for more information on configuring the MS Mail Connector.

Primarily, this compatibility comes in the form of the Microsoft Mail Connector. This component bridges the gap between standard MS Mail post offices and Exchange server. Essentially, Exchange emulates the functionality of an MS Mail post office so other MS Mail computers see it as just another member of the chain.

MS-Mail is a shared-file, LAN-based messaging system. Messages are sent to file servers hosting one or more post offices to which a user connects to retrieve messages. In order to integrate with this system, Exchange's MS Mail Connector presents a post office of its own to which any other post office can connect. This allows other Microsoft Mail post offices to continue normal operation—that is, of course, until they are migrated to Exchange as well.

The MS-Mail Connector (PC) consists of the following components:

- MS-Mail Connector Interchange. A system service that handles routing and message transfer between Exchange and the MS Mail connector post office.
- MS-Mail Connector post office (also called a shadow post office). A temporary information store for messages in transit to and from an MS-Mail system. It is often called a shadow post office because despite being structured very similarly to a standard MS Mail post office, it contains no local mailboxes and does not support direct installation of older MS Mail gateways.
- MS-Mail Connector (PC) Message Transfer Agent. A system service that handles message transport between the connector post office and the MS Mail post offices.

Similarly, the MS Mail connector can also establish communication with MS Mail for AppleTalk systems (see Figure 3.3). For connection to MS Mail for AppleTalk Networks, the Exchange Microsoft Mail connector also includes two additional components:

FIG. 3.3
The MS Mail Connector Architecture.

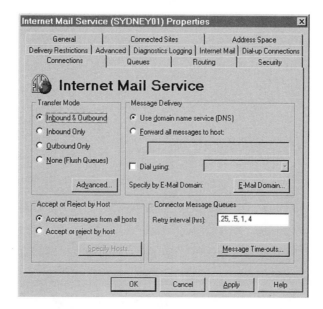

- MS-Mail Connector (AppleTalk) Message Transfer Agent is a system service that operates with the Microsoft Exchange Connection gateway to handle message transfer and translation between the MS-Mail Connector post office and MS-Mail (AppleTalk) systems (see Figure 3.4).

- Microsoft Exchange Connection. A gateway component installed separately on a Macintosh MS-Mail server. It allows that server to communicate with the Microsoft Mail Connector in Exchange.

LAN Connection to Post Offices

In this scenario, a Microsoft Exchange server with the Microsoft Mail Connector installed is connected to an MS Mail post office (see Figure 3.5).

The following is a typical example of message transfer between both systems:

1. Messages intended for MS-Mail recipients are picked up by the Microsoft Mail Connector Interchange from either the MTA or the IS.

2. There they are translated into MS-Mail format; any OLE or other attachments are converted as required and the message is placed into the connector post office.

3. The MS-Mail Connector (PC) MTA pulls the message from the connector post office and delivers it to the appropriate MS-Mail post office.

In the opposite situation, when a message originates from an MS-Mail user, the previous sequence is exactly reversed.

FIG. 3.4

The MS-Mail Connector (AppleTalk) Architecture.

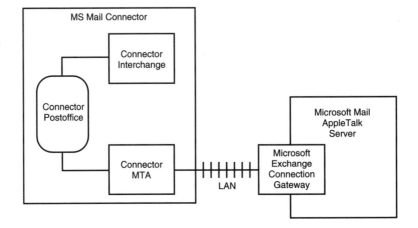

FIG. 3.5

MS-Mail connector.

Asynchronous Connection to Post Offices

Microsoft Mail networks not on the same logical LAN can also be bridged with the Microsoft Mail connector. Such connections are commonly established by modem or wide area X.25 links. Exchange's Microsoft Mail connector (PC) MTA can be configured to support asynchronous or X.25 connections (see Figure 3.6). However, a normal Microsoft Mail post office cannot alone handle this connection. There must be an MS-Mail 3.x External or Multitasking MTA program set up to provide the modem management and message transfer functions over a remote link.

FIG. 3.6

MS-Mail Connector MTA.

Part

I

Ch

3

Multiple MS-Mail Connector MTAs

A single Exchange server can run multiple instances of the MS-Mail connector MTAs (see Figure 3.7). Each MTA runs as a Windows NT system service that can be stopped and started independently of any other service. The best way to design such connections is to create one instance of the MTA for each type of network connection. Therefore, one MTA is dedicated to an X.25 link, while another can service a modem link, and still another can connect to a local LAN.

If your organization uses a large number of Microsoft Mail 3.x post offices or they are spread over a wide area, then you would perhaps want to set up multiple MS-Mail connectors within your organization and use Exchange as a "backbone" for these scattered post offices to ease administration and improve reliability of message transfer. It is not possible to "backbone" Exchange traffic over an MS-Mail network of post offices due to serial number restrictions in Exchange.

> **N O T E** It is important to realize that all MS-Mail connectors in a site will use the same e-mail address. From the MS-Mail perspective, each site will be seen as one large post office. As a result, it is not recommended that several Exchange servers in the same site pickup and deliver mail to a single MS Mail post office in order to prevent file contention on the MS Mail side. ▪

FIG. 3.7
Exchange server with multiple MS Mail connectors.

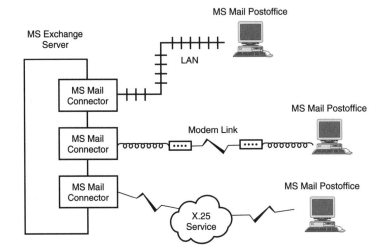

Understanding the X.400 Standard

Microsoft Exchange's use of the X.400 standard allows a broad interoperability with a wide range of messaging systems. X.400 is a standard set by the International Telephone Union (ITU), formerly known as the International Telegraph and Telephone Consultative Committee (CCITT). To date there have been three iterations of the X.400 standard (1984, 1988, 1992). The initial release version of Microsoft Exchange supports the 1984 and 1988 standards, with the 1992 version to be supported in later versions.

▶ **See** "Configuring X.400 Connections," **p. 459**

The X.400 standard defines the basic framework of a message handling system, the structure of the message and its components, and how messages are transferred. It is widely supported and used by most public e-mail carriers and telecommunication providers. Because of its widespread acceptance, many companies have already developed gateways to bridge their messaging systems with X.400. In real-world situations, where network, hardware, and communication standards are not strictly enforced, X.400 provides a common ground for interoperability between messaging systems. Microsoft has assured Exchange's strict conformance to government X.400 standards, which means that Exchange will be a reliable solution for the widest possible number of X.400 connections.

The Microsoft Exchange X.400 connector provides all essential connectivity with this standard. In this section, you will see the following:

- X.400 connector architecture
- X.400 Addressing
- Practical uses of X.400 with Exchange

X.400 Connector Architecture

The X.400 standard makes provisions for specific components of a Message Handling System (MHS), including a structure for message content and addressing. These components are as follows:

- Message Transfer Agents (MTA). Transport programs that execute message delivery
- Message Transfer System (MTS). Two or more MTAs working to transfer messages (sometimes called a *Reliable Transfer System* or RTS)
- Message Stores (MS). An intermediate message storage area between an MTA and a user agent
- User Agents (UA). A client program designed to send and retrieve messages from an MTA and an MS
- Access Units. Gateways to other messaging systems

Microsoft fulfills each element specified by the X.400 standard. In fact, the whole Message Transfer System design is the basis for Exchange's Server site and organization structure.

When referring to a Microsoft Exchange X.400 connector, one is really describing the use of a Microsoft Exchange MTA configured to connect to an X.400-based system. MS Exchange MTAs are compliant with other MTAs (in another Exchange server or an external system) that comply with the 1984 or 1988 X.400 standards. The Exchange MTA can be extensively configured to negotiate such connection over the standard X.400 network transports TP0, TP4, and TCP/IP.

▶ **See** "Message Transfer Configuration," **p. 275**

The Message Store requirement is met by Exchange's public and private information stores.

▶ **See** "Information Store Configuration," **p. 287**

The User Agents are realized as Microsoft Exchange Client programs currently available on several common platforms.

The Access Units are the many gateways currently available for use with Exchange (PROFS, SNADS, Fax, pager, and so on). Each provides a route into its particular system.

Part

I

Ch

3

X.400 Addressing in Exchange

Much like an Exchange address is identified by the user at site structure, X.400 addresses are distinguished by unique personal information and information about the system on which they receive messages. A typical X.400 address contains the following information:

> c=US; admd=MCI; prmd=Software Spectrum; o=Garland; ou1=Consulting; s=Bradley; g=Tracy;

Each element is described in Table 5.1.

Table 5.1   X.400 Addressing Elements

Element	Description
c=US	country
admd=MCI	Administrative Management Domain. Usually the name of your X.400 service carrier.
prmd=	Primary Management Domain. Usually equates to the name of your company or your Exchange enterprise.
o=	Organization. A sub-component of the X.400 prmd that to Exchange is the name of a site.
ou1=	Organizational Unit. The X.400 attribute which helps further identify the remote site. This component is by default not utilized in auto-generated Exchange naming conventions, but could be added.
s=	Surname. Usually a user's last name.
g=	Given name. Generally a user's first name.

NOTE   To appropriately route messages in a site or between sites, Microsoft Exchange uses what is called the X.400 global domain identifier (GDI) of the local site. In order for messages to be routed correctly, the GDI used for a Microsoft Exchange Server cannot be identical to the GDI of a connected foreign system. This will become an issue only when using Exchange to connect to foreign X.400 systems.

Adding Foreign X.400 Addresses into Exchange

As a system administrator, you can use Exchange's bulk import utility to merge a series of foreign addresses into Exchange's global address list. Additionally, the Exchange client's Personal or Outlook Address Book enables individual users to create user entries based on X.400 addresses via an X.400 template.

X.400 addresses for recipients on an Exchange server are automatically created when a new mailbox is created.

Application and Examples of the X.400 Connector

Connecting an Exchange Server site to a foreign X.400 system will be one of the primary uses of the X.400 connector. However, there are a number of connection possibilities afforded by the implementation of this versatile tool. Connections over X.400 between Exchange sites can be established to share directory information, replicate public folders, transmit standard messages, or all of the above. Figure 3.8 gives an example of possible usage.

FIG. 3.8
You can connect an existing MS-Mail server to a foreign X.400 system (through an Exchange server).

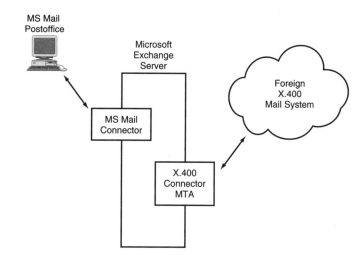

The Microsoft Exchange X.400 connector, in conjunction with the Microsoft Mail connector, can enable users on MS-Mail to access X.400 systems (see Figure 3.9).

Part
I

Ch
3

FIG. 3.9

You can connect an
Exchange Server site to
an MS-Mail post office.

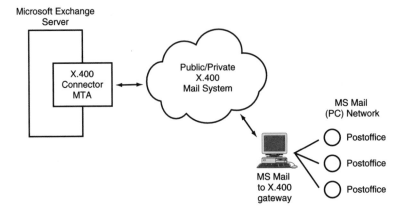

A common use of the X.400 connector in Exchange is bridging messaging systems that are
geographically dispersed. In this example, a Microsoft Exchange server is set up to transfer
messaging data with an MS-Mail system using an Exchange X.400 connector on one end and a
currently available MS-Mail X.400 gateway on the other (see Figure 3.10).

FIG. 3.10

You can connect two
Exchange Server sites.

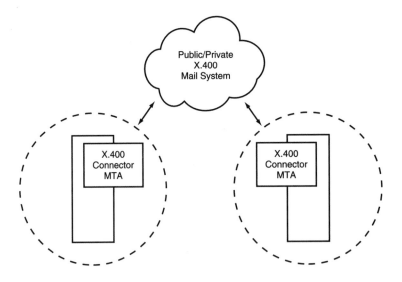

Two Microsoft Exchange Server sites can be linked via a public (or private) X.400 mail system. All that is required is one properly configured message transfer agent at either end. The same technique is applicable over a TCP/IP network, either intranet or Internet and might be desirable given possible bandwidth issues that prevent the use of the Exchange Site Connector.

The Internet Mail Service

As its name implies, the Internet Mail Service (which replaced the Internet Mail Connector (IMC) in Exchange 4.0) provides integrated, native SMTP connectivity to the Microsoft Exchange server along with other new features. In doing this, Microsoft has eliminated the need for the DOS-based SMTP gateway for Microsoft Mail 3.x that lacked robustness, had memory allocation problems, possessed little or no security, and needed an external HOST to send out SMTP mail.

The Internet Mail Service (IMS) solves those problems by providing a stable, proven, and secure platform with Windows NT Server. In addition, the Internet Mail Service can send and receive SMTP mail without the need for external hosts, is MIME-compliant, and provides robust performance.

Some of the new features added to Exchange 5.0 from version 4.0 include:

- Integrated Internet Mail Service and Remote Access Service (RAS)
- Route redirection for SMTP mail
- POP3 support
- Several options of enhanced security
- Improved message tracking facilities
- Support for SIZE and DSN SMTP Service Extensions (ESMTP)
- Support for Macintosh BinHex/AppleDouble file types
- Additional character set support
- Enhanced performance

▶ **See** "Setting Up SMTP Connections," **p. 479**

The following diagram (see Figure 3.11) shows how the Internet Connector fits into the Microsoft Exchange architecture.

In addition to providing Internet mail functions, the Internet Mail Service allows those users running TCP/IP over the backbone to connect Exchange sites to each other using the connector. As mentioned previously, decentralized organizations often give control of the mail system to the respective department. Many large universities and corporations operate this way. These organizations often choose SMTP as the way for disparate mail systems to communicate because it is an Internet standard. Microsoft has recognized that many companies route only TCP/IP over their WANs to maximize router throughput. A diagram showing how to link disparate Exchange sites by using the Internet Mail Service is shown in Figure 3.12.

Part

I

Ch

3

FIG. 3.11
Internet Connector
Architecture.

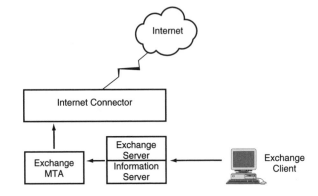

FIG. 3.12
Connecting Multiple
Exchange Sites Over
TCP/IP.

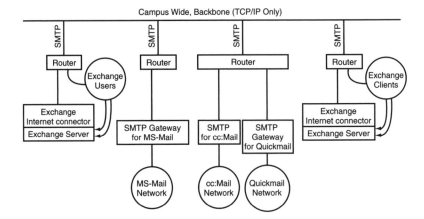

The Internet Mail Service provides for full integration into environments where security is a big concern. Many companies configure firewalls to protect internal data from hackers on the Internet. In addition to all the security components inherent to Exchange and Windows NT Server, the Internet Mail Service provides the ability to refuse messages from any specified hosts. This provides protection from many forms of hacking or "denial of service" attacks because many hackers use the e-mail system to carry out their work. For example, you might configure the connector to refuse mail from all hosts other than a certain mail relay. That means that a hacker could not send a message directly to your Exchange server or send commands directly to it. By refusing mail from certain hosts, Exchange is flexible enough to fit into existing company security policies. Any hacker would have to compromise the firewall in order to send a message directly to the Internet Mail Service.

Exchange can also be configured to enable only incoming or outgoing traffic through the connector. This is an important feature because one Windows NT server can only do so many things and complete so many tasks without taking a performance hit. Configuring the connector to only send out mail might be a good idea for a machine that is already overloaded. This configuration should not be cause for concern as long as there is an incoming Internet Mail Service elsewhere in the Exchange site or organization. For example, if you have the Internet Mail Service configured on two servers and configure one to receive-only and the other to send-only, the Exchange users' e-mail addresses will still be the same. Users will not know where the mail came in and don't really care. The connections are completely transparent. Figure 3.13 shows the properties screen where the administrator can configure security and transfer options.

FIG. 3.13
Internet Connector Connections Properties.

Part
I

Ch
3

Additional information about the functions and configuration of the Internet Mail Service can be found in Chapter 22, "Setting Up SMTP Connections."

Connecting to Lotus cc:Mail

The Microsoft Exchange Connector for Lotus cc:Mail provides seamless communication between Microsoft Exchange Server and Lotus' cc:Mail product. In the past year, Lotus has embraced the MAPI standard for messaging-enabled applications, switching from their previous Vendor Independent Messaging (VIM) standard. The cc:Mail Connector enables connectivity between Exchange and these cc:Mail post offices running Lotus cc:Mail Post Office Database Version 6, cc:Mail Import version 5.15 and Export version 5.14 or Lotus cc:Mail Post Office

Database version 8, and cc:Mail Import/Export Version 6.0. The cc:Mail Connector has many configuration variables enabling the use of the existing cc:Mail tools such as Import, Export, and ADE to enable robust, hassle-free connections to cc:Mail VIM post offices.

cc:Mail users are to be directly imported into the Microsoft Exchange Global Address Book and will appear just like any other Custom Recipient Exchange user.

Just as with the Microsoft Mail Connector, a cc:Mail post office is created on the Exchange server, resulting in Exchange server users appearing in the cc:Mail directory like all other cc:Mail users. This gives transparency to the cc:Mail user. As far as he or she is concerned, all users in the Global Address Book are local.

Exchange allows the administrator to set the paths to the standard Import and Export utilities that come with cc:Mail. These utilities are used to import and export directory and message data from the Exchange server to all other cc:Mail post offices in the cc:Mail network. Examples of the uses of this connector are shown in Figure 3.14.

FIG. 3.14

Architecture of the cc:Mail Connector.

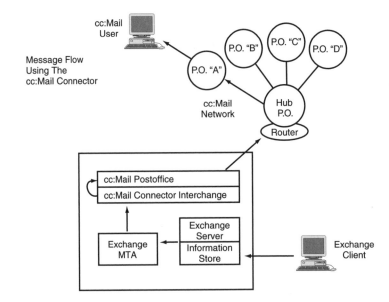

On the cc:Mail side, Exchange looks just like any other post office; by using Automatic Directory Exchange (ADE), all cc:Mail post offices, including the Exchange cc:Mail post office, can be kept up-to-date as users are added on both sides. Figure 3.15 illustrates some of the components involved.

FIG. 3.15
ADE Synchronization
between the cc:Mail
and Exchange.

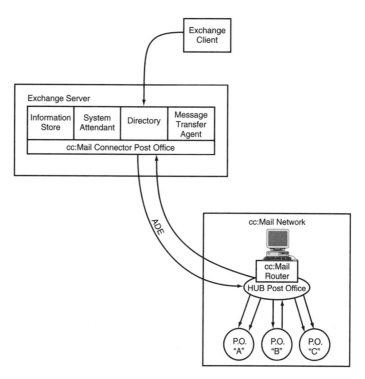

Microsoft realized that the cc:Mail is a large player in the LAN-based messaging market. By making the cc:Mail Connector available, it has leveraged this popularity. In some organizations, many dollars have been spent on training personnel to install and maintain cc:Mail, as well as hardware resources. Using Exchange means that your organization will not have to throw away existing mail systems to roll out a new one.

Understanding Gateways

Gateways provide a way for Exchange to integrate disparate information services into Microsoft's Universal Inbox, using the single Microsoft Exchange Viewer to organize all types of information. These include things such as voice mail, fax, paging, as well as e-mail from other vendors' systems.

Despite the variety of information services that snap into Exchange, the end user sees no difference. To him or her, the addressee is the addressee. A user can address a message and send it, and the addressee might get a page, fax, voice mail, or Internet message. The addressee may be using cc:Mail, PROFS, SNADS, or Microsoft Mail, and the user sending the message would never know because all he or she needs to know is the addressee's name in the Global Address Book.

Using Microsoft Mail Gateways

In addition to native Exchange gateways, Exchange can use standard Microsoft Mail 3.x gateways by using the Microsoft Mail Connector described earlier in this chapter. Each gateway uses the Microsoft Mail Connector to exchange data with foreign mail systems. This may be useful for sites with large Microsoft Mail installations that are migrating to Exchange slowly, but want to provide the core messaging functions first and add connectors and gateways later. In addition, some organizations are hesitant to sway from things that work. For example, if the Microsoft Mail gateway to PROFS has been working fine, some may be hesitant to roll out an Exchange PROFS connector or gateway because they haven't had the opportunity to test it and get their staff familiar with it. Figure 3.16 shows how Microsoft Mail gateways fit into the Exchange topology.

In the preceding case, the PROFS gateway for MS-Mail simply talks to the MS-Mail Connector post office. When configuring the PROFS gateway for MS-Mail, you simply point it at the MS-Mail Connector post office and the exchange of information becomes transparent.

With Exchange, Microsoft took those concerns into consideration and provided the flexibility to use legacy systems in the migration to a robust Exchange environment.

FIG. 3.16

Message flow of
Exchange to PROFS
using PROFS Gateway
for MS Mail.

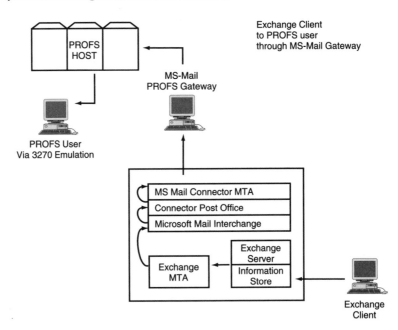

From Here...

Exchange has a powerful back-end architecture consisting of four components: the System Attendant, the Message Transfer Agent, Information Stores both public and private, and the Directory. In addition, connectors and gateways are integrated into the server to provide seamless connections to external systems.

Both connectors and gateways serve the following needs:

■ Integration of Exchange with existing messaging systems

■ Integration of Exchange with other information services like voice mail, fax, and paging

■ A slow migration path from other mail systems to a pure Exchange environment

■ Universal Inbox providing transparency for the client

The following chapters contain related information to some of the items discussed in this chapter:

■ Chapters 12-15 cover the detailed configuration of the four core components of the server.

■ Chapter 19, "Using the Microsoft Mail Connector for PC Networks," and Chapter 20, "Using the Microsoft Mail Connector for AppleTalk Networks," provide more information on how to plan the migration of your existing Microsoft Mail system to Exchange.

■ Chapter 21, "Configuring X.400 Connections," provides detailed information on the implementation of the X.400 Connector.

■ Chapter 22, "Setting Up SMTP Connections," will delve into how to connect SMTP systems to Exchange.

■ Chapter 24, "Exchange Performance Tuning and Capacity Planning," will explain the steps required to determine capacity requirements of your Exchange servers.

Integrating with Microsoft Windows NT Server

Microsoft Exchange Server is part of the BackOffice suite of server products that runs on top of the Windows NT operating system. Windows NT is a powerful 32-bit multithreaded, multitasking operating system. The Exchange Server can leverage this functionality by utilizing as many threads or application processes as needed to provide a robust messaging infrastructure.

You should now have an understanding of the core components and framework for the Microsoft Exchange server and client. This chapter helps you to understand the way Exchange integrates with the operating system. We also discuss how Exchange can leverage the NT platform to provide a robust and fault-tolerant messaging solution. ■

The Core Functionality of the Windows NT Operating System

Get an insight of the 32-bit, multithreaded, multitasking Windows NT operating system. Overview of the complete architecture of Windows NT, including multiple protocol support, security, and administrative tools.

Explanation of the Domain Architecture

Acquire a complete understanding of the domain architecture of Windows NT. Learn the different domain models NT has to offer and the need to create relationships among these domains for ease of centralized administration.

How Exchange Integrates with the Server

Learn how tightly Exchange is connected with the NT environment. Find out how Exchange leverages the NT operating system to exploit all the features of Windows NT server.

How Exchange Depends on the Server

Learn how tightly Exchange depends on NT server to exploit the offering of the NT services. Learn how closely Exchange works with NT services such as the single logon, user-defined permissions, client connectivity, Event Viewer, and the Performance Monitor.

The Core Functionality of Windows NT

Windows NT is a 32-bit operating system. It provides multitasking and multithreading capabilities. This means that the operating system can simultaneously process multiple requests or instances of an application.

NT is more that just an operating system. It is a framework to develop fault-tolerant client server applications. To enhance the operating system, NT provides a full set of Application Programming Interfaces (APIs) and Software Development Kits (SDKs). The operating system is more than a file and print server; it is an application server. Through the use of the APIs and SDKs, many applications can harness the power of the operating system.

The operating system runs on a variety of platforms including Intel, MIPS, Alpha, and the Power PC. This portable operating system has several key benefits. The following sections cover the benefits in detail.

Multiple Protocol Support

NT provides native support for the following protocols: TCP/IP, IPX, NetBEUI, AppleTalk, DLC, SNA, X.25, and X.400(TP/x). This enables the operating system to support a wide array of clients. NT can communicate with UNIX, Banyan Vines, DEC Pathworks, Netware, Apple Macintosh, and of course all of the Microsoft networking clients, including MS-DOS, Windows For Workgroups, Windows 95, and Windows NT Workstation.

This feature enables NT to interoperate in a heterogeneous environment. You will not be "bound" by implementing the NT operating system into one of these environments. NT can offer additional functionality in these situations. The alternative means provides native support which would be very costly or impossible.

For example, NT can be easily added to a Novell Netware environment to provide Remote Networking or Dial-in access. The NT operating system ships with a complete remote access server component integrated with the OS. With Netware, you would have to purchase an additional product known as "Netware Connect" to obtain this capability.

In the situation with Exchange, Netware clients can easily access an Exchange server running on NT with native IPX client software installed. Clients communicate with industry standards known as Remote Procedure Calls (RPC) using the Exchange server. NT supports every major communication protocol. Therefore, a client can connect to Exchange using RPCs over TCP/IP or IPX in a Netware environment.

▶ **See** "Installing Exchange in a Netware Environment," **p. 189**

In addition, Microsoft has released a standard for Remote Procedure Calls (RPCs) over AppleTalk, the Macintosh's native communications protocol. In order for a Macintosh workstation to connect to an NT Exchange server, it can make RPCs over TCP/IP or AppleTalk. This functionality shows Microsoft's firm commitment to a Macintosh operating system and recognizes that the Macintosh operating system has an important share in the marketplace (see Figure 4.1).

FIG. 4.1

NT supports most industry standard network protocols as seen in this OSI model.

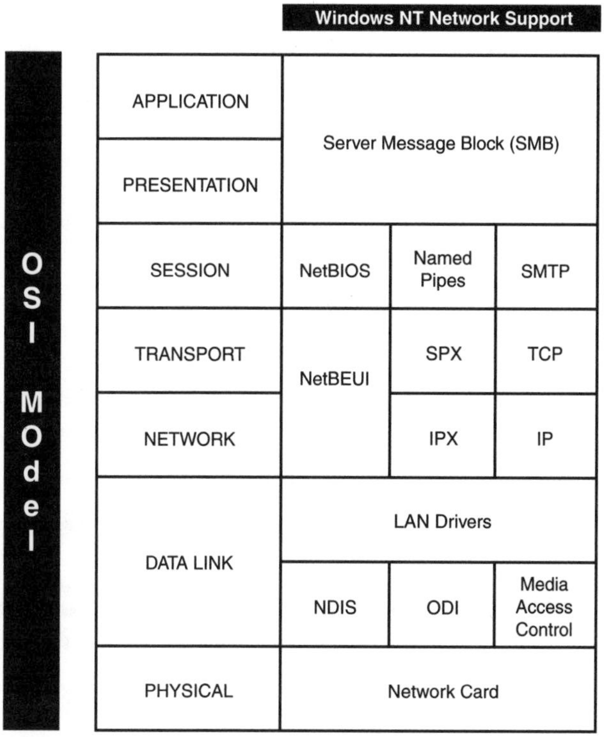

Windows NT Network Support

OSI Model				
APPLICATION	Server Message Block (SMB)			
PRESENTATION				
SESSION	NetBIOS	Named Pipes	SMTP	
TRANSPORT	NetBEUI	SPX	TCP	
NETWORK		IPX	IP	
DATA LINK	LAN Drivers			
	NDIS	ODI	Media Access Control	
PHYSICAL	Network Card			

C2 Level Security

Security is a key element of any messaging system. Users want to know that their message will get to its destination without someone intercepting it. Exchange expands upon the Class C2 Level of Security, which is at the heart of the NT operating system. The Department of Defense defines this level of security.

Class C2 requires a secure logon, discretionary access control, and full auditing capabilities. The secure logon requires that users identify themselves with a unique log-on identifier (user ID) and password. This logon must be validated prior to accessing any system resources.

The discretionary access control enables the owner of a resource, whether it is a file, sub-directory, or printer, to determine who can access the resource. This also defines the level of control the user has over the resource. The owner grants rights to a user or group of users.

Auditing is the capability to log the security information of each operating system transaction to a file based on user ID. This feature provides the capability to detect and record important security-related events or instances in which security was challenged.

C2 security has several other components to its matrix of functionality. However, the Exchange server leverages its core features. Not all aspects of C2 security are required for use with Exchange. You also do not have to use every feature of C2 security when working on or creating a network application operating system. The company using the C2 security system can determine the level of security required.

Integrated Administrator Tools

NT provides several tools to assist in managing the network, as well as the operating system. NT includes the Server Manager, the Event Viewer, and the User Manager to manage processes, define security privileges, provide auditing and security logging, and to create new users and groups, respectively.

The Server Manager (sgôRFigure 4.2) enables the administrator to view all of the servers from a single domain, multiple domains across the enterprise, or individual servers and workstations inside a domain. The functions that are available enable you to control the share or access points to the file systems of a server, and to stop and start application processes. Using these functions, you can also close user sessions and manage specialized access via AppleTalk, Netware Gateways, and the File Transfer Protocol (FTP).

FIG. 4.2
Windows NT Server Manager enables remote management of the network servers.

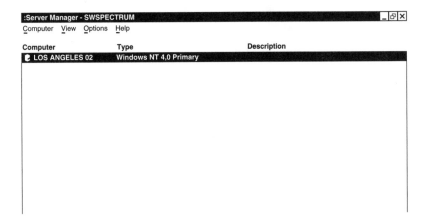

The Event Viewer, also known as the Event Log, is the centralized repository for system, application, and security information for a server or workstation. From a remote console an administrator can pull up the event viewer to see the entries of a network server. All Backoffice certified applications must write the events to the event viewer. Events can be informational (blue), cautionary (yellow), and serious (red) in nature. You will be able to tell whether your tape backup has finished properly and at what time of day it completed. From the system, you will see whether there have been any problems related to the operating system and the hardware. From the security log, you can view all of the information predetermined for auditing.

The event will store information related to the Exchange server and all of its gateways, connectors, and external processes. It will also store security information (see Figure 4.3). Exchange itself has a security log, which extends the basic functionality provided by the event log.

FIG. 4.3

Windows NT Event Viewer records systems, security, and application events from the operating system.

Date	Time	Source	Category	Event	User	Computer
1/16/97	6:26:50 PM	NETLOGON	None	5711	N/A	GARLAND01
1/16/97	6:26:46 PM	NETLOGON	None	5711	N/A	GARLAND01
1/16/97	6:21:48 PM	NETLOGON	None	5711	N/A	GARLAND01
1/16/97	6:21:47 PM	NETLOGON	None	5711	N/A	GARLAND01
1/16/97	6:21:46 PM	NETLOGON	None	5711	N/A	GARLAND01
1/16/97	6:16:48 PM	NETLOGON	None	5711	N/A	GARLAND01
1/16/97	6:01:46 PM	NETLOGON	None	5711	N/A	GARLAND01
1/16/97	5:56:47 PM	NETLOGON	None	5711	N/A	GARLAND01
1/16/97	5:51:47 PM	NETLOGON	None	5711	N/A	GARLAND01
1/16/97	4:40:02 PM	i8042prt	None	35	N/A	GARLAND01
1/16/97	2:03:38 PM	NETLOGON	None	5711	N/A	GARLAND01
1/16/97	2:01:37 PM	NETLOGON	None	5711	N/A	GARLAND01
1/16/97	2:51:45 PM	NETLOGON	None	5711	N/A	GARLAND01
1/16/97	1:46:44 PM	NETLOGON	None	5711	N/A	GARLAND01
1/16/97	1:41:46 PM	NETLOGON	None	5711	N/A	GARLAND01
1/16/97	1:32:01 PM	NETLOGON	None	5711	N/A	GARLAND01
1/16/97	1:30:17 PM	NETLOGON	None	5711	N/A	GARLAND01
1/16/97	1:26:43 PM	NETLOGON	None	5711	N/A	GARLAND01
1/16/97	1:24:35 PM	NETLOGON	None	5711	N/A	GARLAND01
1/16/97	12:12:23 PM	NETLOGON	None	5711	N/A	GARLAND01
1/16/97	12:10:41 PM	NETLOGON	None	5711	N/A	GARLAND01
1/16/97	12:07:38 PM	Wins	None	4097	N/A	GARLAND01
1/16/97	12:07:02 PM	DhcpServer	None	1024	N/A	GARLAND01
1/16/97	12:06:53 PM	EventLog	None	6000	N/A	GARLAND01
1/16/97	12:06:50 PM	BROWSER	None	8015	N/A	GARLAND01
1/16/97	12:05:50 PM	EventLog	None	6005	N/A	GARLAND01
1/16/97	11:06:50 PM	BROWSER	None	8015	N/A	GARLAND01
1/16/97	11:58:34 AM	BROWSER	None	8033	N/A	GARLAND01
1/16/97	11:58:33 AM	BROWSER	None	8033	N/A	GARLAND01
1/16/97	11:54:03 AM	NETLOGON	None	5722	N/A	GARLAND01
1/16/97	11:53:00 AM	NETLOGON	None	5722	N/A	GARLAND01
1/16/97	11:51:57 AM	NETLOGON	None	5722	N/A	GARLAND01
1/16/97	11:42:36 AM	EventLog	None	6000	N/A	GARLAND01
1/16/97	11:41:06 AM	Wins	None	4097	N/A	GARLAND01

The User Manager is a tool used by the security administrators or domain administrators to create the single domain logon user ID. This ID includes all of the user's application profiles, group memberships profile, and time and workstation restrictions. The User Manager helps you to define trust relationships among domains, define auditing functionality, and general domain user account functions.

From the User Menu, you can select to create a new user, a local group, or a global group. The user ID is the individual ID used in conjunction with the password to be authenticated by the domain to access network resources. Local groups are those residing within the single domain in which they were created. If the domain is referred to as "Dallas," all local groups created in this domain will only be able to access resources within the domain. Global groups, however, can be used to provide access to trusted domains. A local group can contain local user IDs, as well as global groups from both the local and trusted domains.

Exchange adds the functionality of creating a mailbox for users at the same time as assigning their domain logon ID (see Figure 4.4). This gives the mail, security, and domain administrators control over the same set of user accounts. In large organizations, this is the responsibility of a Network Security Group. This one group would be responsible for creating the user IDs, as well as the appropriate mailboxes.

FIG. 4.4

Windows NT User Manager enables you to create domain user IDs, including the Exchange mailbox.

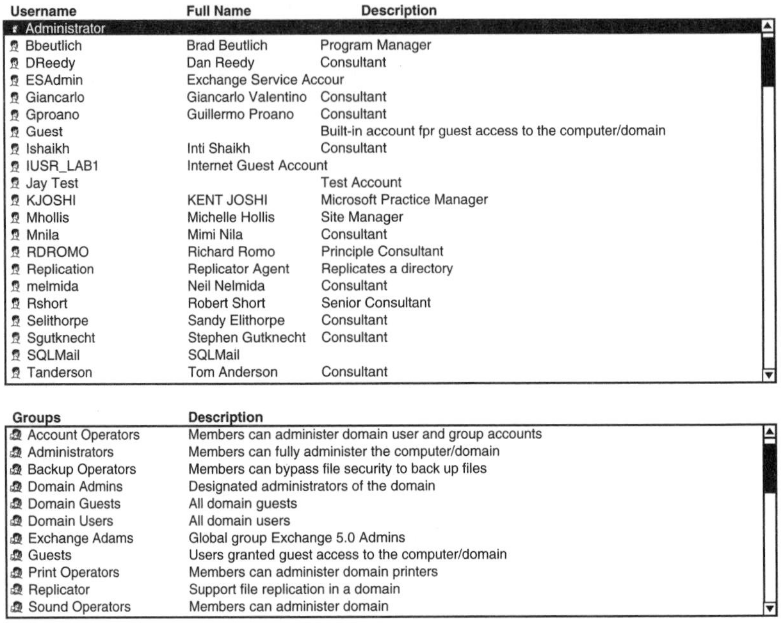

Username	Full Name	Description
Administrator		
Bbeutlich	Brad Beutlich	Program Manager
DReedy	Dan Reedy	Consultant
ESAdmin	Exchange Service Accour	
Giancarlo	Giancarlo Valentino	Consultant
Gproano	Guillermo Proano	Consultant
Guest		Built-in account fpr guest access to the computer/domain
Ishaikh	Inti Shaikh	Consultant
IUSR_LAB1	Internet Guest Account	
Jay Test		Test Account
KJOSHI	KENT JOSHI	Microsoft Practice Manager
Mhollis	Michelle Hollis	Site Manager
Mnila	Mimi Nila	Consultant
RDROMO	Richard Romo	Principle Consultant
Replication	Replicator Agent	Replicates a directory
melmida	Neil Nelmida	Consultant
Rshort	Robert Short	Senior Consultant
Selithorpe	Sandy Elithorpe	Consultant
Sgutknecht	Stephen Gutknecht	Consultant
SQLMail	SQLMail	
Tanderson	Tom Anderson	Consultant

Groups	Description
Account Operators	Members can administer domain user and group accounts
Administrators	Members can fully administer the computer/domain
Backup Operators	Members can bypass file security to back up files
Domain Admins	Designated administrators of the domain
Domain Guests	All domain guests
Domain Users	All domain users
Exchange Adams	Global group Exchange 5.0 Admins
Guests	Users granted guest access to the computer/domain
Print Operators	Members can administer domain printers
Replicator	Support file replication in a domain
Sound Operators	Members can administer domain

The functionality provided by these three tools is built into the NT operating system. These tools can be run on remote machines, 16-bit workstations, and from the Internet.

Introduction to the Windows NT Domain Architecture

At the heart of the Windows NT network operating system is the fundamental architecture of the Domain Model. A domain is a logical grouping of servers and workstations. One server in a domain must be the "Primary Domain Controller" (PDC) and subsequently have "Backup Domain Controllers" (BDCs). NT provides the capability to build servers as "name servers" which belong to the domain. These servers, however, are not responsible for replicating user account and security information throughout the domain. The PDC and BDCs remain synchronized by updating each other's user and security databases at regular intervals 24 hours a day, seven days a week.

The domain architecture consists initially of a single PDC of a single domain. From there, NT architecture can grow in any number of combinations that can include multiple BDCs in a single domain or a number of trusted domains with BDCs and member servers.

Trust Relationships Among Multiple Domains

Trust relationships can be created between multiple domains. Trusts enable users from one domain to be granted secure access to resources in a second domain. This maintains the concept of the single network logon. Users will see no change from a single domain to multiple domains.

Two types of trusts exist: one-way and two-way. One-way trusts are set up to enable users from the second, or "trusted" domain to access resources of the first or "trusting" domain. The second domain, however, has the freedom to create its user accounts and manage its own domain independently of the first domain. This can be illustrated using a distributed administration model in which certain divisions have their own network administration; however, there is a central domain providing corporate-wide resources. The divisional domains can completely administer their own domains without affecting the central domain. The central domain has the capability to enable the divisional domain to access the central resources. This is useful because full administrator privileges can be given out at the divisional level without administrative rights over the entire WAN.

Two-way trusts grant access and administrative functionality among all domains that are in them. This is also known as the Complete Trust Domain Model (see Figure 4.5).

FIG. 4.5

Establishing trust relationships between domains enables one domain to access the resources of another.

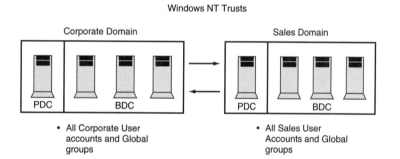

Windows NT Trusts

Single Domain Model

A domain is a logical grouping of servers that shares the same user accounts database and provides a single logon for all users to all the servers in the domain. As a comparison, on Novell Version 3.x networks, each server maintains its own user account database or "bindery." In this way, user accounts must be individually created on each server.

The concept of a domain is primarily used for centralized administration. All the servers in a domain are updated with a single action. Regardless of when the user ID is created or modified, all the servers maintain the single logon for the group of servers in the domain.

A single domain only consists of a PDC. For small organizations, additional BDCs can be added to validate user access rights. In the single domain, there are no trust relationships. Small organizations primarily use the single domain. These organizations do not have to be interconnected with other domains. Sometimes corporations use a single domain as a development domain. In this way, they do not affect the production domain. The server in the single domain can communicate with the other domains; however, additional user IDs will be necessary (see Figure 4.6).

Part

I

Ch

4

FIG. 4.6

Single Domain Model represents the simplest form of a Microsoft Windows NT network.

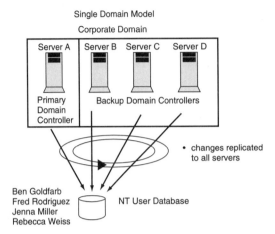

Master Domain Model

In an environment with multiple domains, you can create trust relationships between domains. As discussed previously, domains can be interconnected via one-way or two-way trust relationships. In the master domain model, there is a one-way trust between the divisional domains and the central domain. All users and global domain groups are defined in the master domain. All other domains trust the master domain. This model ensures centralized administration for all domains. Again, this model maintains the single network logon by establishing one user account for the enterprise.

For example, in a large organization, the MIS Division manages from a central point. Therefore, the same should hold with the domain architecture. From one location, all users and security are maintained. The master domain referred to as "Corporate" houses all users and global groups. The resource domains, "Sales," "Marketing," and "Legal," only maintain local groups. When a resource is needed from the Sales domain, a local group is created in Sales, and its members include a global domain group from Corporate.

One disadvantage to this model is that performance might decrease as the number of users and groups grows. For this reason, larger domains need to consider the next model (see Figure 4.7).

FIG. 4.7

The Master Domain Model puts global groups and users in the master domain. This Model also places resources in separate domains.

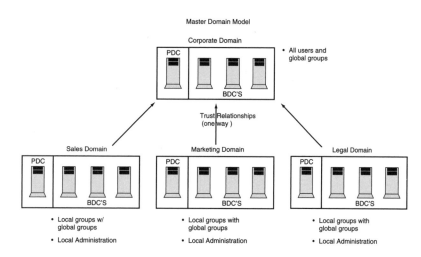

Multiple Master Domain Model

The multiple master domain extends the single master domain into a broader scope. This domain model is typically seen in very large organizations. If your organization has two major corporate headquarters, and many divisions, you might choose to implement the multiple master domain model.

Building on the previous example, the multiple master domain model has two tiers of domains (see Figure 4.8). The first tier interconnects the master domains. "Corporate" and "International" are the two domains. These two domains each house their respective users and global groups. These domains are then configured with a two-way trust. These domains trust each other. Therefore, only one copy of each user ID is needed.

The second tier of domains includes all of the resource domains. These domains each maintain a one-way trust to the two master domains. This model can be scaled to networks with any number of users. You can easily have upwards of 10,000 users supported with this model. The resource domains can then be grouped logically based on function and geographic location. The resource domains also provide for local administration at the divisional level. The disadvantage to this model is that there are more trust relationships to manage. Also, not all user accounts are located in one domain.

Part

I

Ch

4

FIG. 4.8

Multiple Master Domain Model provides the scaling capability needed in a large organization when the Master Domain Model is not sufficient.

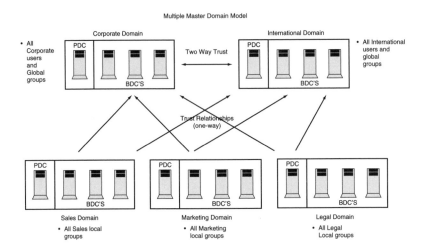

Multiple Master Domain Model

Complete Trust Domain Model

The final option available for an NT domain model is the Complete Trust. This model is best used in companies in which management of users and groups is distributed among different departments. Rather than being centralized, this model extends the administration down to the divisional level. Every domain trusts every other domain on the network. One immediate disadvantage to this model is that an administrator of one domain now has full rights over every other domain in the model. This can lead to security problems. If you are going to use this model, an auditing process could help manage who has made administrative changes on the various domains.

In this model (see Figure 4.9), the resources and the user accounts are grouped into divisions. Again, the only situation in which a Complete Trust is appropriate is when there is a lack of centralized management. This model is not practical for corporations with a large central department. The reason is that the model lacks the security needed for a large enterprise network.

Several options exist for an NT domain model. In Chapter 5, "Designing Exchange Topology," you are given the criteria for selecting which domain architecture to use when planning to deploy Exchange in your environment.

Microsoft also provides a tool through its BBS and Internet site to assist with planning a domain architecture. This tool is referred to as the "Domain Planner." It is a Visual Basic application that steps you through the options when choosing your domain and trust relationships.

FIG. 4.9
The Complete Trust Domain Model is intended for decentralized management and carries many security risks for an enterprise network.

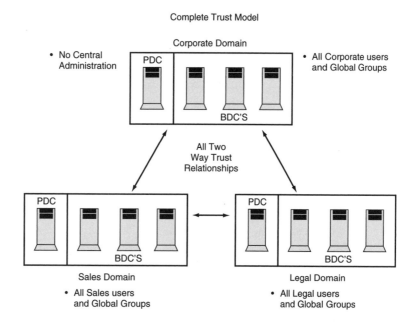

Complete Trust Model

Corporate Domain

- No Central Administration

PDC

BDC'S

- All Corporate users and Global Groups

All Two Way Trust Relationships

PDC

BDC'S

Sales Domain

- All Sales users and Global Groups

PDC

BDC'S

Legal Domain

- All Legal users and Global Groups

Part

I

Ch

4

Understanding Exchange and NT Operating System Integration

This section explains how Exchange leverages the NT operating system. Exchange has been created to exploit all the features of Windows NT Server, including all the tools. These tools include the single logon, permissions that can be user-defined, the User Manager for Domains, the Event Viewer, and the Performance Monitor.

Comparison of NT and Exchange Terminology

Exchange sits on top of the NT OS. However, it has hooks into the OS to provide a robust, high performance messaging system. Not all of the NT terminology applies or directly converts to Exchange terminology. The reason is that the messaging platform has its own architecture.

Exchange uses the concepts of Organizations and Sites, whereas NT uses domains. Organizations are at the top of the Exchange hierarchy. Typically, you find only one Organization name in the entire enterprise. Sites, on the other hand, can be geographic locations, divisions, or functional areas. Sites can also map one to one with domains.

Sites can span across multiple domains, provided that the domains are trusted. This is necessary because a server within a site must authenticate each user.

Both the NT domain model and the Exchange architecture use the term "server." Within NT, a server can be a PDC, a BDC, or a domain member server. Within Exchange, servers exist within a site. It is not necessary for the Exchange server to be either the PDC or a BDC of a domain. For performance reasons, it would be best for the Exchange server to simply be a member server. This way, the Exchange servers share the resources of a domain without having to continually replicate security information or validate user accesses to the network.

Integrated Features

Following is a list of Exchange's features that help the Exchange server to closely integrate with the NT Server.

  ▪ Exchange runs as an NT service

    Exchange is a 32-bit application written to integrate with the NT Server. Therefore, all the core components of Exchange run as services of the NT OS. This means that they will run in the background and do not require a user to manually execute their application components. A service is an application that the operating system is aware of and manages its execution. In addition, the service will log the activity of the process to the Event Viewer. From the performance monitor you can verify the impact the process has on the operating system. From the Server Manager, you can stop and start the processes.

    The 32-bit architecture of the executable enables Exchange to utilize the multithreaded, multitasking capabilities of the OS. Exchange runs in the background on the server. If a sudden burst of messages is passed to the Exchange server that needs to be forwarded, the executable can spawn more threads to effectively deal with the increased load.

    This integration is only one way in which Exchange leverages the NT operating system (see Figure 4.10).

  ▪ Additions to the User Manager for Domains

    Exchange adds functionality to the User Manager for Domains already discussed in this chapter. Exchange places an additional menu item with which you can administer user mailboxes from within the same consistent interface. Additionally, while you are creating users and assigning them group membership for NT file access, a dialog box pops up to add the users' mailbox to Exchange. The user can be added to any Exchange server across the enterprise as long as the administrator has permission to do so.

FIG. 4.10

The NT Service Manager enables you to start, stop, and pause services, as well as control their start-up properties.

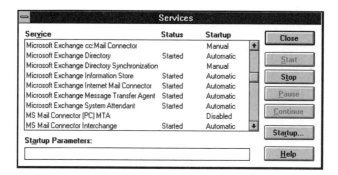

- Additions to the Performance Monitor

  Exchange extends the functionality of the Performance Monitor bundled within NT. This extensive monitoring tool enables you to observe both processor and disk space utilization, memory allocation, page faults, and over a thousand more counters.

  Exchange adds some specific counters to the performance monitor which enable the administrator to view statistics of critical elements of the Exchange processes. These include the number of open tables on the message store, cache hits, I/O performance on reads and writes, RPC packets per second, number of bytes sent and received, and more.

Exchange NT Dependencies

Exchange relies on the NT operating system for certain functionality. The major function is that you must create a user account in the operating system for Exchange to run its services. Exchange also can import and export names from the NT domain user database. This facilitates a quick migration to Exchange from your existing NT Network architecture.

Exchange relies on the connectivity that NT provides. Exchange enables all types of clients to connect to its servers. Novell Netware clients, Macintosh, UNIX, and all the Windows clients can connect to Exchange using their native protocols. This is made possible through NT's use of RPCs and multiple protocol support.

For remote access solutions, Exchange again relies on the NT OS. NT has an integrated remote access server as part of the operating system. The NT server running Exchange can be configured for a user to dial directly into the server and access Exchange, as well as any other network resources. For performance reasons, it might be more appropriate to set up the remote access server on a dedicated server.

Part

I

Ch

4

For WAN connections, NT supports X.25 and ISDN without any additional software. An Exchange server can be configured to use an X.25 or ISDN connection to bridge the message route. If WAN links are already in place, these dial-up solutions provide a second level of fault-tolerance and an additional message route, in an emergency.

System Service Account

The system service account enables Exchange servers to authenticate each other when transferring messages, updating the global address list, or performing directory synchronization. This account must be created with certain specifications.

It is important to carefully plan the implementation of this account. You must have a domain model that supports these user accounts. Whether you have trusted or untrusted domain, you must ensure that the Exchange services can be authenticated between servers. If this does not occur, mail will not be forwarded from one system to another.

Security Models

Exchange relies on the C2 level security of the operating system. Any user who attempts to access the system must first be authenticated by the domain. Exchange extends the single log-on ID. Therefore, the domain logon also validates users for accessing their Exchange mailbox. As mentioned previously, in the file-sharing mail systems, users had full access to the file system that comprised the post office. Exchange now manages the access to the post office based on the central domain user database.

Exchange itself provides three levels of security. The user accounts are leveraged from the NT user database. From within the Exchange Administrator Program, a user account can be specified as a complete administrator, a local administrator, or as a read-only administrator.

▶ **See** "Maintaining Exchange," for a detailed discussion on Exchange security, **p. 551**

There are many issues related to using Exchange on the NT operating system. NT provides connectivity to almost any other operating system used in the enterprise. NT should not be a point of concern when deploying Exchange. The NT OS interoperates more easily with your existing network operating systems and mail environments than some proprietary systems that communicate with themselves. This is the case with PROFS or OfficeVision. Exchange leverages the NT OS to provide a strong messaging backbone.

From Here...

In this chapter, you learned how Exchange integrates with the NT operating system. For more information, see the following chapters:

- Chapter 6, "Installing Exchange Server," helps you successfully install an Exchange Server System.

- Chapter 10, "Installing Exchange in a Netware Environment," helps you begin to plan your Exchange system.

- Chapter 12, "Using the Administrator Program," helps you manage and administer your Exchange System.

Part

I

Ch

4

Installing and Migrating to Exchange

CHAPTER 5

Designing Exchange Topology

A successful Exchange implementation requires planning for a proper fit into your organization. This chapter outlines an iterative, nine-step process that is scalable for all company sizes. Of course, smaller companies can choose a smaller, more appropriate set of steps, while larger, international companies will probably benefit from the entire process. However, many of the steps will provide value for all types of businesses. In addition, you may use this plan or create your own based upon another planning strategy. ■

Understanding Your Users' Messaging Needs

You must understand your users' messaging needs and how Exchange meets those requirements.

Understanding Your Network Type and Operating Structure

Your network topology and links have the greatest influence on Exchange's design.

Understanding Exchange Sites and E-Mail Addresses

Selecting an Exchange site depends heavily on your network topology and links. It's important to select the most universal e-mail addresses when connecting with foreign (non-Exchange) systems. Several systems may strip out letters from addresses that are too long or have non-standard characters.

Understanding Exchange Hardware Requirements

For general purpose Exchange servers, a good rule is to invest in memory and disk subsystems for performance and reliability.

Understanding Remote User Requirements

Remote or mobile users have special messaging needs, most of which can be met with the built-in communications software within Windows NT server and the client's desktop operating system.

N O T E The examples presented may not completely match your environment. It's extremely important you recognize your environment's unique elements, especially when installing and naming the organization, site, primary domain, and server. These names cannot be changed without reinstallation. ▨

Step 1   Understanding Your Users

The first step in designing your enterprise is identifying your users' messaging needs. Once identified, you can then match those needs to Exchange's features. This information also guides you when examining hardware purchases, training, network upgrades (due to increased traffic), increased support needs, and total cost of ownership. See Table 5.1 for an example of how one company met their messaging needs with Exchange.

Table 5.1   User Needs

Company Role	Needs	Exchange Function
All departments	Connectivity to other platforms; standard interface across heterogeneous desktops. Web Outlook View.	Share and organize information (e-mail, documents, schedules, images, reports, forms).
	Guarantee message confidentiality even when traveling.	Encryption and Person-to-Person key exchange. E-mail response.
	E-mail response when out of the office.	Out of Office Assistant.
	Reserve conference room.	Delegate feature.
Management	Enable secretary to respond to e-mail received by manager.	Send on behalf; delegate access.
	Distribute company report.	Public folder (such as an electronic bulletin board).
	Help Desk Solutions database.	Custom Solutions database.
	E-mail connectivity to Internet.	Internet Mail Service (IMS).
Field Sales	Remote e-mail access.	Remote connectivity. Web Outlook View.

Company Role	Needs	Exchange Function
Legal	Connectivity to existing mail system.	MS Mail and Lotus cc: connector.
Manufacturing	Migration from legacy mail system (e.g.,PROFS).	Source extractor and migration tools.
Engineering	Research latest technical developments.	NNTP to retrieve and post to live Internet newsgroups.

Step 2   Knowing Your Network

Your network topology has the greatest influence on Exchange's design. This step identifies the major characteristics of networks and maps some of Exchange's needs to your network's strengths. Contact your network administrator or architect and gather the following bulleted information regarding your network.

Each bulleted section will be described in detail and summarized on a table. If you are already familiar with networking concepts, you can reference the section entitled "Selecting Sites Based on Network Type" and Table 5.2, 5.3, and 5.4 before moving to the next step.

- Types and links
- Size
- Bandwidth
- Protocols

Network Types and Links

There are several types of networks and network links today. After understanding the Exchange features your company needs, you can determine if your existing network and links are sufficient. For example, one dial-up phone line probably isn't sufficient to move messages for thousands of users throughout your company.

- Dial-up phone line

  Phone lines are made of copper wire and mainly used for single users to remotely connect to existing LANs and WANs. They provide an inexpensive, but periodic, non-permanent connection.

- X.25

  X.25 lines are permanent, leased lines providing a connection between LAN segments (WANs). X.25 is an international standard for packet communication over public data networks.

- Frame Relay

  Frame relay is similar to X.25, but provides better performance than X.25 due to decreased overhead. Frame relay is a method to send packets over private and public data networks. Because frame relay can expand up to T-1 speeds, many companies use it to connect LAN segments, i.e., WANs.

Fractional T-1

Since T-1 lines can be divided into 24 separate lines or channels, fractional T-1 lines make connecting LAN segments, i.e., WANs, more affordable than using a full T-1. Bandwidth can be expanded all the way to a full T-1 by adding additional channels.

Integrated Services Digital Network (ISDN)

ISDN is digital communication over dial-up lines using the ISDN standard. ISDN eliminates the need for a voice digitizer (analog to digital conversion unit) in the telephone company's central office, thus allowing faster throughput than a modem over dial-up phone lines. Typically, ISDN is used by personal computer users at home and some LAN segment connections.

T-1

T-1 is a digital link carrying voice or data transmissions and is usually used to connect LAN segments. It also can be used to create private data and voice networks within a company.

Satellite Communication

Satellite communication is a wireless communication scheme that provides global data access. Typically used to interconnect LAN spread over a wide, geographic area and/or used to provide a redundant link when land-based lines are unavailable.

Microwave Communication

Microwave communication is a wireless link that uses microwaves to connect LANs that are typically on a business, campus, or industrial park.

ArcNet

ArcNet networks utilize a star or bus topology with a token-passing access scheme over coaxial cable (RG-62 or RG-59).

T-3

T-3 is similar to T-1, but has a higher bandwidth equal to 28 T-1 lines. Each of these channels can be divided and grouped into smaller portions. Typically, T-3s are used as high-speed WAN links.

Thin Ethernet

Thin Ethernet uses a linear bus topology with Carrier Sense Multiple Access with Collision Detection (CSMA/CD) over thin coaxial (10Base2) or twisted-pair (10BaseT) cable.

Thick Ethernet

Same topology and access method as thin Ethernet, but over thick coaxial cable (10Base5).

- Token Ring

  On a Token Ring network, all the computers are connected physically as a star and electrically as a ring. It uses a token-passing access scheme over shielded or unshielded twisted-pair (UTP) wire.

- 100BaseT Ethernet (Fast Ethernet)

  Fast Ethernet uses the CSMA-CD communication scheme and comes in two flavors (100BaseT4 and 100BaseTX) depending on the type of UTP cable in place. Stations connect to 100BaseT hubs in the same way they connect to 10BaseT hubs. Typically, Fast Ethernet is used in LANs and WANs.

- 100VG-AnyLAN

  Proposed by IBM and Hewlett-Packard, 100VG-AnyLAN uses the same Ethernet frame format but replaces CSMA-CD with a deterministic protocol called the Demand Priority Access Method (DPAM). DPAM is conceptually similar to the token-passing method in Token Ring networks. 100VG-AnyLAN is used in the same types of networks and linking as Fast Ethernet.

- Fiber Distributed Data Interface (FDDI)

  Communication over a fiber-optic cable usually uses the FDDI standard. This standard is similar to the token-passing technique of Token Ring but operates at a much higher speed. Typically, FDDI is used as a backbone interconnecting lower speed LAN, for example, Ethernet or Token Ring; connections to WANs; or to provide direct, high-speed attachments for routers and hosts.

- Synchronous Optical Network (SONET)

  SONET is a standard for high-speed communications over fiber-optic cable. It is a network transport (like Ethernet) and has a bandwidth equivalent to 48 T-3 lines. Like T-3, SONET is used to connect WANs together.

- Asynchronous Transfer Mode (ATM)

  From the standardization process of International Telecommunication Union (ITU) comes ATM, which was designed to handle voice, video, and data transmission over high-speed fiber-optic links. ATM's strength is that it can transport multiple data streams on virtual circuits operating at different data rates. Initially used as a LAN backbone (like FDDI), ATM is also being used to connect WANs over fiber-optic cable. ATM can use fractional T-1, T-1, T-3, and SONET as its physical medium.

Part II

Ch 5

Selecting Sites Based on Network Type

As a rule of thumb for the average organization, you'll want to design sites so Exchange servers can communicate over a class B (Table 5.3) or better (class C -Table 5.4).

Generally, links having 64Kbps or less of bandwidth have been classified by this book as class A (see Table 5.2). Class B links range up to 1.544 Mbps. All links with bandwidth over the 1.544 Mbps mark are considered class C.

Table 5.2   Class A Network Links

Type	Bandwidth
Dial-up phone lines	2.4 to 57.6 Kilobits per second (Kbps).
X.25	19.2, 56, and 64 Kbps.
Frame Relay	64 to 512 Kbps; newer implementations go to 1.544 Megabits per second (Mbps). At higher speeds, frame relay qualifies as a class B link.
Fractional T-1	Each channel is 64 Kbps. Additional channels can be added up to 24, which equals a full T-1 line. At higher speeds, a fractional T-1 qualifies as a class B link.

Table 5.3   Class B Network Links

Type	Bandwidth
Integrated Services Digital Network (ISDN)	64 to 150 Kbps
T-1	1.544 Mbps
Satellite Communication	128 Kbps to 1.544 Mbps
Microwave Communication	1.544 Mbps

Table 5.4   Class C Network Links

Type	Bandwidth
ArcNet	2.5 Mbps
T-3	44.148 Mbps
Thin Ethernet	10 Mbps
Thick Ethernet	10 Mbps
Token Ring	4 or 16 Mbps
100BaseT Ethernet (Fast Ethernet)	100 Mbps
100VG-AnyLAN	100 Mbps
Fiber Distributed Data Interface (FDDI)	10 to 100 Mbps

Type	Bandwidth
Synchronous Optical Network (SONET)	51.8 Mbps to 2.5 Gigabits per second (Gbps)
Asynchronous Transfer Mode (ATM)	100, 200, 400 Mbps up to 9.6 Gbps

In certain cases, you may want to examine a smaller bandwidth link over a larger one if reliability is a factor. For example, some high (class C) bandwidth links may not be as reliable as the low (class A) links. Because Exchange servers in the same site need a permanent link to communicate, it may be wiser to choose the more reliable class A link if messaging volume is light.

Keep in mind, this is only one piece of information in selecting a site. You will need to analyze other factors such as the number of users per server, message traffic, the volume of public folder replication, and so on. Review the appropriate sections of this guide to gather all necessary information before making your final site selection.

Network Size

Although this may seem obvious, it's important to determine if you have a small or large network. In basic terms, a small network consists of one or two servers, a few clients, and a single domain or site. A large network contains multiple servers, clients, domains, and sites (also records, if your sites are scattered throughout the U.S. or the world).

Second, it's important to know how quickly your network is growing and to what extent Exchange is being adopted. In many organizations, e-mail is the universal application that everyone seems to want. The need to exchange information, schedule meetings, and "to be in the loop" will overcome even the most technically stubborn user. Along the same lines, the quick adoption of e-mail will sometimes force a reluctant organization to grow its network to reach the needs of its users.

Given this information, it's helpful to draw up a low, medium, and high Exchange adoption or migration plan and include its impact on your network's current size. Manage to the medium, but prepare for the high.

Network Bandwidth

Through careful examination of the underlying physical network, you may determine that existing network connections and bandwidths appear adequate to meet your organization's needs. For the purposes of this design guide, network bandwidth is defined as the amount of data-per-second that can be transmitted over a communication link. However, it is crucial not only to take into account the size of your links, but also to carefully look at the link's utilization. You may find your network has very large and fast connections; however, they may already be inundated with other network traffic which impedes overall performance of the network link. This is called Net Available Bandwidth (NAB). If your NAB falls to the same speed as a class A network link, it may be necessary to increase bandwidth in areas of heavy network traffic.

Part

II

Ch

5

Another area to monitor is traffic bursts. Traffic bursts are short bursts of data transmission that utilize a majority of the bandwidth for short periods of time. You may find that some network links appear to have low overall utilization; however, during peak periods of the day these connections experience traffic bursts that impede performance.

Knowing or predicting network traffic patterns through a network link allows you to determine whether your link has enough NAB to support additional Exchange traffic.

To predict traffic patterns and prevent them from affecting your network, measure the network bandwidth utilization (how close a network link is to full capacity) and total packets-per-second (how close bridges and routers are to reaching full capacity).

Monitoring network traffic requires specialized tools such as dedicated network monitoring software like Microsoft System Management Server, packet sniffer, or NT's Performance Monitor. For more information on the specific Performance Monitor counters, please refer to Chapter 24, "Exchange Performance Tuning and Capacity Planning."

Network Protocols

For an effective Exchange design, you should know which network protocols are used on your network. Exchange offers several types of connectors, but each of them has unique requirements. For example, the X.400 connector requires the existence of TP0/X.25, TP4/CLNP, or TCP/IP. Another consideration is support for remote clients; for example, field sales needing remote e-mail access, for which Remote Access Server (RAS) or Dial-Up Networking (DUN) can be used. Both of these support the point-to-point (PPP) protocol that enables any client to use the TCP/IP, IPX, or NetBEUI protocol.

Step 3   Determining a Windows NT Domain Model

This step describes local and global groups, trust relationships, server roles, and domain models. A domain is a grouping of computers and users that eases administration of the computers and user accounts. Windows NT Advanced Servers all share a common user account and security database, thus enabling each user to have a single account that is recognized on all servers in the domain. The domain can also contain other Network Operating Systems (NOSs) such as LAN Manager 2.x and a variety of clients like DOS, Windows, Windows for Workgroups, Windows 95, and NT Workstation.

You can examine the following domain models to create your own domain or examine your existing one. Or you may use Microsoft's Domain Planner Wizard, which is available in the Resource Kit, or by calling Microsoft.

N O T E   Once a domain has been created, you will need to reinstall NT to make any changes. ■

Local and Global Groups

Similar in structure to user accounts, groups allow efficient assignment of access privileges to multiple users within the domain. The two classes of group accounts are:

- Local groups, which are not accessible outside the home domain, but may have global groups from the home as well as other domains as members.

- Global groups, which contain users from the home domain and can be assigned access to resources within the home domain as well as away domains.

Trust Relationships

Windows NT Server supports the ability for one domain to "trust" another domain, thus giving users of the trusted (or account) domain the ability to act as authorized users on the trusting (or resource) domain. It also allows users in the trusted domain to access resources in the trusting domain without re-creating their user ID and other security information a second time. Keep in mind that no matter where network resources are located, users will always log into their home (trusted) domain.

For example, let's say that you own a VCR and your neighbor would like to borrow it and watch a video of Bill Gates speaking about Exchange and the future of messaging technologies. You "trust" your neighbor (a user from a trusted domain) enough to allow him or her entry into your house (resource domain) to use your VCR (a network resource) without making a second key (re-creating security information).

In addition, trust is one-way and not transitive. If domain A trusts domain B, it does not imply domain B trusts domain A. This two-way trust must be explicitly established by a domain administrator. Also, if domain A trusts domain B and domain B trusts domain C, it does not imply that domain A trusts domain C.

While trust relationships are very useful capabilities, they also involve setup and maintenance. It is best to limit trust relationships to a number that satisfies the organization's requirements without creating unnecessary complexity.

N O T E   If an Exchange site spans multiple domains, there must be a trust relationship in place so that the servers can establish synchronous Remote Procedure Call (RPC) connections. ▓

Server Roles

A Windows NT Server computer can have one of three roles in the domain:

- Primary domain controller (PDC)

   The PDC maintains the original user accounts database. This database contains all the security information for the domain. The PDC should be physically attached to the most central and high-speed network segment possible. Because the PDC authenticates users and receives updates to the user accounts database, it should never be on an unreliable or periodic network link, such as a wireless network or dial-up line.

Part
II

Ch
5

- Backup domain controller (BDC)

   The BDCs receive a copy of the user accounts database from the PDC via replication. BDCs also authenticate users and can change their role to a PDC in case of PDC failure.

- Member server

   Member servers are not tasked with authenticating users, and thus are usually deployed as dedicated file, print, applications (such as SQL Server), communication (RAS server) or messaging (Exchange) machines. Depending on their function, member servers can be connected over all (class A to class C) links.

Exchange should be installed on a machine serving either a BDC or a member server role. You will not want to place Exchange on your PDC except in special circumstances. One example of this would be extremely small networks with very light mail volume.

Domain Models

Since Exchange needs a trust relationship to communicate between sites, you'll want to evaluate each domain model based on its implementation of trusts. If a domain model is already in place, evaluate its current trust capacity for an Exchange rollout. To monitor the status of your domain trusts, use the Domain Monitor for Windows NT.

- Single domain model

   This model doesn't use trust relationships. It contains a single PDC and can contain multiple BDCs and member servers. It's the easiest model to manage since user accounts and all groups (global and local) are centralized. Unfortunately, performance may suffer as the size grows toward the domain's theoretical capacity (around 26,000 users in NT Server 4.0) (see Figure 5.1).

FIG. 5.1

Single domain model.

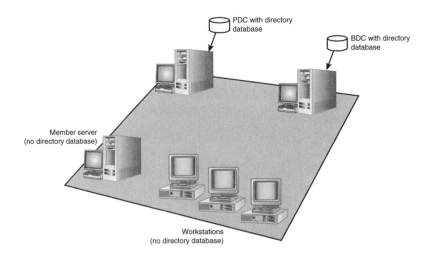

PDC with directory database

BDC with directory database

Member server (no directory database)

Workstations (no directory database)

■ Single domain with complete trust model

Here, each domain has a two-way trust relationship with every other domain in the enterprise. The total number of trust relationships that must be set up is equal to N*(N-1), where N is the number of domains. Each domain has its own user accounts and global groups.

For organizations that use distributed management or function without a central MIS, this model provides the best fit. Each department within a domain can effectively manage its home domain as well as other domains. However, as the network grows so does the administrative burden of adding additional domains and managing multiple trusts.

In Figure 5.2, a regional office of Software Spectrum has no central MIS and thus allows each functional department to manage its respective users and groups.

FIG. 5.2

Single domain with complete trust model.

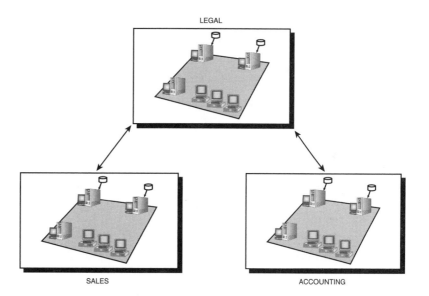

LEGAL

SALES   ACCOUNTING

■ Single master domain model

In this model, there are several domains but one serves as the central or master domain. All the other domains are resource domains that trust the master domain via a one-way trust. The resource domains do not trust each other. All user accounts and global groups are contained in the master domain, while the resource domains contain file, print, communication, and SQL servers as well as local groups.

Due to its centralized nature, this model allows a network administrator to manage all the organization's user ids from one domain, while the local administrators of each resource domain can manage their home domains. One disadvantage is that the single master domain can theoretically support networks of only up to 26,000 users and thus may not support explosive growth within an organization.

In Figure 5.3, Software Spectrum has centralized its user accounts and global groups within one master domain while organizing its resource domain along geographical locations.

FIG. 5.3

Single master domain model.

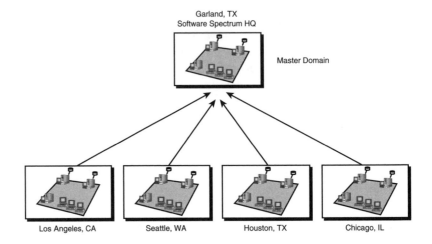

Resource Domains

- Multiple master domain model

    This model is organized into two tiers and combines the features from the second and third domain models already mentioned. There are two or more master domains on tier one. Each master domain has a two-way trust to all other master domains. Thus, a user need be defined only once. Each resource domain on the second tier trusts all master domains with a one-way trust. The second tier domains do not trust each other.

    The multiple master domain model scales easily to an organization's growth and works well when a company has a centralized MIS department. In addition, each master domain can theoretically support up to 26,000 users each. However, the administrative burden is heavier than the other models due to multiple trust relationships and user accounts dispersed through several master domains.

    In Figure 5.4, Software Spectrum has organized its first tier domain structure along geographically independent lines of business. It has offices in Tokyo, Los Angeles, Garland, and London. This strategy allows each office to administer its own security database while controlling access to the resource domains. Each of the resource domains is organized along functional departments allowing access to specific departmental resources.

FIG. 5.4
Multiple master domain model.

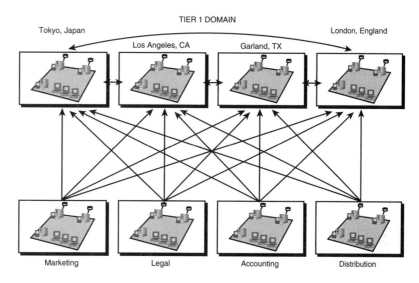

Microsoft Corporation uses this model with one special addition for Exchange. A special, global domain has been defined in the second tier. All Microsoft Exchange servers are located here allowing easy identification of messaging servers and providing consistently applied "global groups" to make server management easier.

Step 4   Selecting Your Sites

This step explains the difference between the critical and discretionary factors for a good Exchange site.

When determining which servers belong to which sites, you must consider two sets of qualifying factors. The first set includes permanent, RPC-compliant connections, plenty of NAB (Net Available Bandwidth), and proper security context. All of these factors must be present to group servers together in one site. Please refer to Table 5.5 for details.

The second set of factors are discretionary. They include connection cost, connection performance, replication, and company organization. Please refer to Table 5.6 for details.

N O T E   These examples may not completely apply to your environment. Please carefully consider all pertinent factors before selecting a site and choosing site boundaries. Any changes will require a reinstallation. ▨

Part
II

Ch
5

Table 5.5 Necessary Site Factors

Factor	Requirements
Permanent, RPC-compliant connection	Servers within a site must communicate over a permanent network link that supports synchronous RPC.
Proper security context	Within a site, all Exchange servers must run under the same security environment. Because all Exchange servers' services use the service account, they must either share the same domain or belong to domains that have the proper trust relationships set up.
NAB (Net Available Bandwidth)	The NAB must be equal to or exceed a class A network link (>64 Kbps). In certain cases, you may want to examine a smaller bandwidth link over a larger one if reliability is a factor. For example, some high (class C) bandwidth links may not be as reliable as the low (class A) links. Because Exchange servers in the same site need a permanent link to communicate, it may be wiser to choose the more reliable class A link if messaging volume is light.

Table 5.6 Discretionary Site Factors

Factor	Requirements
Consider large sites	Because Exchange will automatically replicate all changes within a site, consider making your site as large as possible to ease the administrative burden. Remember: It is easier to split than to merge.
Directory Replication	Network bandwidth is higher within a site than between separate sites—replication will automatically occur more often inside sites. If you wish to manually control replication, place the servers in separate sites.
Performance	If you have a group of servers connected at the same bandwidth, you should consider grouping those servers together in a common site. Place servers connected at a slower bandwidth in separate sites.
Company organization	Naturally, you'll want to group users in the same department or functional unit together. This provides a more effective use of network and Exchange resources.
Cost	If any of your servers are connected via a link that charges by the data amount or time, consider placing them in separate sites.

Step 5   Selecting a Site-Mapping Strategy

Now that network structure has been outlined and you've identified your critical site factors, it's time to choose a site mapping strategy. This step describes the major mapping strategies, basing them on several domain and network examples.

During Exchange's setup, the install program creates several services that start and run based on the context of a user account called the service account. This account is created on the first computer within a site. Other computers within the site are validated by the service account and thus are given access to Exchange's services. All Exchange computers within the same site must use the same service account.

If you have one domain and one site, you'll want service accounts created in the only domain. For multiple domains within a single site, create the service account in the account domain or whichever domain is handling your administrative domain functions. In a master or multiple-master domain model, the master domain would contain the service account (see Figure 5.5). In a single domain with complete trust model, any domain can contain the service account because it's accessible to all the other domains (see Figure 5.6—the grayed computer contains the Exchange service account).

FIG. 5.5

Single domain using a one-to-one mapping.

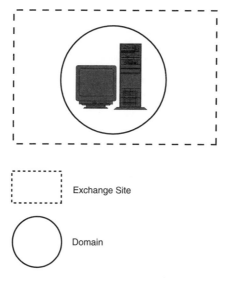

Exchange Site

Domain

Part

II

Ch

5

If two sites are in separate domains, one service account can be used for both domains if they trust each other. If they do not, you can use a site connector to serve as a link. In this case, you must set up the site connector to connect to the untrusted domain's service account. For example, let's say Exchange Site 1 uses a service account called Service1 and Exchange Site 2 uses Service2. Site 2 must connect to Site 1 with Service1's account name and password. Likewise, Site 1 connects to Site 2 with Service2 (see Figure 5.7).

FIG. 5.6

Single domain with complete trust using a one-to-one mapping.

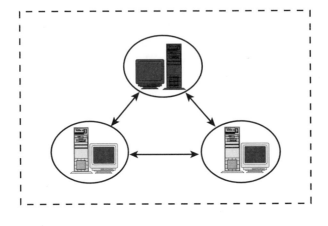

FIG. 5.7

Two single domain with no trusts using a one-to-one mapping.

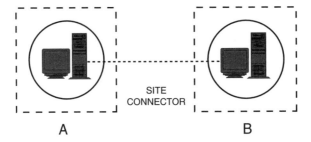

When laying a site framework over your existing network foundation, consider the following mappings:

- One-to-One Mapping

  For a small organization, consider a one site to one domain approach. This means there is one site within every untrusted domain. A one-to-one mapping is similar to the single domain model. One advantage with the one-to-one approach is that it's one of the easiest to configure and manage. In addition, everything is centralized in one site and one domain. However, it is difficult to increase the number of servers per site unless you create additional domains/sites and use site connectors. Usually, as an organization grows or plans to rapidly grow, its mapping strategy moves toward a one-to-many technique.

- Many-to-One Mapping

  Another mapping you may consider is mapping many sites into one domain. This is useful when you want group servers with similar bandwidths utilization together. Although easy to configure, this strategy may have more management overhead if you choose to connect the sites via one of Exchange's site connectors.

- One-to-Many Mapping

  Larger organizations should consider moving to a one-site-for-many-domains mapping. This is equivalent to moving from a single domain to a single master or from a single master to a multiple master domain model. Since Exchange will replicate all changes to properly trusted domains, a one-to-many mapping is fairly easy to administer and removes the overhead of managing site connectors between untrusted domains.

Overall:

- It is not necessary to map all sites to all domains.
- It is best to consider a large site over a small one when mapping sites to domains.
- Only domains containing the Exchange service account need to be mapped.

Review Tables 5.7 and 5.8 to determine the best mapping for your organization.

Table 5.7   Effective Site Mapping

Domain Model	Mapping Strategy	Description
Single	One-to-One	All servers within the site have access to the service account.
Single with complete trust	One-to-One	All domains and servers can access the service account (see Figure 5.6—the grayed computer contains the Exchange service account).
Two Single	One-to-One	Servers in the single Domain Model can access the service account in domain B via a properly configured site connector.
Single	Many-to-One	Each site can use its own service account or the service accounts in the other site via a properly configured site connector (see Figure 5.8).
Single Master	One-to-Many	With the proper trusts in place, both servers can use the service account because it's located in master domain A (see Figure 5.9).
Multiple Master	One-to-Many	As with the previous mapping, the trust relationships allow all first and second tier servers to access the service account (see Figure 5.10).
Two Single Masters	One-to-Many	The mapping here allows the servers in the second tier to access the service account defined in their local master domains .With a site connector, both untrusted domains' service accounts are linked together (see Figure 5.11).

Part

II

Ch

5

FIG. 5.8

Single domain using a many-to-one mapping.

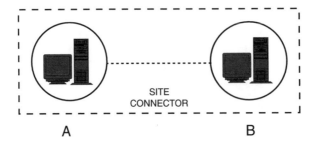

FIG. 5.9

Single master using a one-to-many mapping.

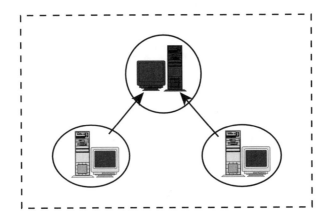

FIG. 5.10

Multiple master using a one-to-many mapping.

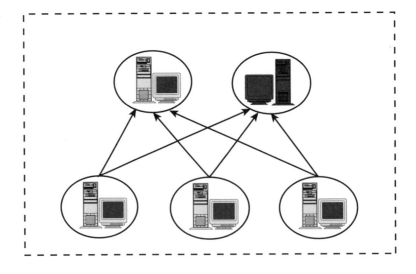

FIG. 5.11
Two single master
models with no trusts
using a one-to-many
mapping.

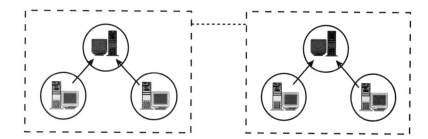

Step 6   Selecting a Naming Strategy

This step will describe the format, use, and restrictions of e-mail addresses within Exchange. Just as external messaging standards are necessary for different mail systems to communicate and share information, internal naming standards are just as vital to building a well-run, easily administered mail system. As with many items in this chapter, you must thoroughly plan before implementing a naming strategy because some changes will require reinstallation.

There are three elements of a sound naming strategy:

- It is not affected by a company's natural growth and reorganization. For example, base your naming conventions on geographic location, building numbers, and permanent floor locations. Avoid choosing company attributes that may change over time.

- It is easy to add additional items like sites, servers, users, and other directory objects.

- It is easy to use and administer the system.

Keep these elements in mind as you progress through the different mail systems and standards that follow.

Organization Names

An organization name should comprise your entire company and will be part of the directory names of all directory objects such as mailboxes, public folders, and distribution lists. Organization names can contain up to 64 characters, must be unique, and cannot be changed. When choosing an organization name, be aware that it can be used to generate e-mail addresses for non-Exchange systems, so it's recommended to limit the name to ten characters for compatibility.

Site Names

A site name can be based on function (sales, distribution), geography (countries, regions, cities), or physical location (building). Site names can contain up to 64 characters, must be unique, and cannot be changed. In addition, they are used by Exchange when generating non-Exchange e-mail addresses.

Part
II

Ch
5

Server Names

A network uses the server name to identify a particular NT machine. Server names must be unique, can contain up to 15 characters, and cannot include any of the following characters: bullet (·), currency sign ($), broken vertical bar or pipe (|), section sign (§), or end of paragraph sign (¶). In addition, do not put spaces in the server names on domain controllers if log-on scripts are part of your environment.

Mailbox Names

A mailbox name should be easy to identify and similar in form to your organization's internal phone lists. Because mailbox names are listed in Exchange's address book, you may want to create mailbox names that sort properly when displayed. Review Table 5.8 for a breakdown of mailbox names.

Table 5.8   Guidelines and Restrictions for Mailbox Names

Field	Guideline	Restrictions
First Name	User's first name	Up to 16 characters, can be changed.
Last Name	User's last name	Up to 40 characters, can be changed.
Alias Name	To route messages to non-Exchange systems, an alias name is used. Identify the external mail systems within your organization (and so on) PROFS, MHS, MCI Mail, AT&T Mail, and determine their unique requirements (for example, PROFS can accept up to eight characters for an e-mail address). For best results, the alias name should bear a recognizable resemblance to the original name—Kent Joshi becomes KJOSHI.	Up to 64 characters, can be changed.
Display Name	Base this name on how you want to display it in the Address book and Administrator window. Be sure to consistently use the same format for all names, for example, Last Name, First Name.	Up to 256 characters, can be changed.

Field	Guideline	Restrictions
Directory Name	Exchange uses this name to route mail messages. This is an internal name and is not displayed to users or administrators. Exchange will set this to the first alias name specified, but you can use another.	Up to 64 characters, must be unique, can't be changed.

E-Mail Addresses

When Exchange communicates with other (or foreign) mail systems, like the Internet, it must have a valid address format the other mail system understands. A foreign user whose address exists both on a foreign network as well as in the Exchange directory is referred to as a custom recipient. Exchange recipients (including mailboxes, custom recipients, distribution lists, and public folders) that have addresses on foreign mail systems are known as foreign e-mail addresses.

Exchange automatically generates an e-mail address for the following mail systems: X.500, X.400, MS Mail (PC), and the Internet (SMTP). Exchange does this to provide the widest possible compatibility with other messaging systems. Keep in mind that other addresses may be generated if there is a PROFS or another third-party gateway installed.

X.500 Addresses   X.500 was designed to provide an international standard for enterprise-wide directory service access. The 1988 X.500 directory service guidelines form the basis of Exchange's directory service. It is in the directory that Exchange stores all X.500 object classes in an X.500 schema.

The directory objects are organized in a hierarchical structure known as the Directory Information Tree (DIT) and they are identified by a unique item called a distinguished name.

Table 5.9 shows how the X.500 object name maps to an Exchange object.

Table 5.9   Mapping X.500 Names to Exchange Objects

X.500 Name	Attribute	Exchange Server Object
Country	c=	Country
Organization	o=	Organization
Organizational Unit	ou=	Site Name
Common Name	cn=	Exchange Server Recipient Container
Common Name	cn=	Exchange Server Recipient or directory name

Part
II

Ch
5

For example, the distinguished name for Kent Joshi who has a mailbox in Los Angeles within the Software Spectrum organization would be o=SWS/ou=LosAngeles/cn=recipients/cn=KJOSHI. When you remove the naming labels, you receive the form that Exchange uses: SWS/LosAngeles/recipients/KJOSHI.

Because X.500 doesn't support all object classes and attributes, Exchange also includes support for titles, organization charting information (who reports to whom in an organization), additional phone numbers, arbitrary attributes created by the administrator, and alternate recipients.

X.400 Addresses   X.400 is a widely recognized and accepted international standard by the messaging industry. Exchange's compliance with the X.400 standard is important for organizations that want to use e-mail with heterogeneous mail systems as well as those who want to communicate with external companies via public carriers.

X.400 addresses can contain all of the upper- and lowercase letters, all numbers (0—9), a space, left and right parentheses, the plus and equal signs, the comma and the period, the hyphen and the forward slash or solidus (/), and the colon and question mark. In addition, X.400 addresses can contain the following attributes which are listed in hierarchical order in Table 5.10.

Table 5.10   X.400 Attributes

Description	Attribute
Country	c=
Administrative Management Domain (ADMD)	a=
Private Management Domain (PRMD) (Exchange organization)	p=
Organization (Exchange server site)	o=
Organizational units	ou1=; ou2=; ou3=; and ou4=;
Common name	cn=
Generation qualifier	q=
Initials	i=
Surname (last name)	s=
Given name (first name)	g=

For example, a valid X.400 address for Kent Joshi who has a mailbox in Los Angeles within the Software Spectrum organization would be:

```
g=Kent;s=Joshi;o=Los-Angeles;p=SWS;a=mci;c=us;
```

This address also represents the minimum information you need to receive e-mail from someone else.

Microsoft Mail Addresses   If you will connect to Microsoft Mail for PC Networks or Microsoft Mail for AppleTalk Networks systems, character restrictions are:

Microsoft Mail network name	10
Post office name	8
Mailbox name	8

A valid MS Mail address for Kent Joshi who has a mailbox in Los Angeles within the Software Spectrum organization would be SWS/LSANGLES/KJOSHI. For more information on connecting to MS Mail, please see Chapter 7, "Planning Connections to Microsoft Mail Systems." For information on migration from MS Mail to Exchange, please see Chapter 8, "Migrating from Microsoft Mail Systems."

SMTP Addresses   Exchange's SMTP connector is a dependable way to exchange mail transparently with SMTP users as well as with Mail users on other LANs over an SMTP backbone. It also enables Mail users to easily access mail networks such as UUCP, BITNET, and Internet.

When communicating with the Internet or other SMTP systems, look at their particular character or addressing limitations. In general, SMTP addresses can include all upper- and lowercase letters (A—Z), all numbers (0—9), and the hyphen (-). However, spaces are not permitted.

A valid SMTP address for Kent Joshi who has a mailbox in Los Angeles within the Software Spectrum organization would be KJOSHI@LOS-ANGELES.SWS.COM.

External System Addresses   If your organization has other mail systems (PROFS, SNADS, and so on), you will want to examine any conditions they place on usable characters and addressing. This way you can properly configure the Alias Name field (see the Mailbox Names section earlier in this chapter) for your particular mail system.

Part

II

Ch

5

Step 7   Linking Your Sites

Now that you have your sites laid out and the proper e-mail address to share information, the next question is: How do I link my sites? This step explains the methods you can use to link your sites, and discusses the pros and cons of different connectors and how this affects the Microsoft Exchange Server.

Site Connector

The site connector is the most efficient way to connect two sites if they are on the same logical LAN. It also offers the greatest performance because it uses RPC for communication.

Listed in Table 5.11 are the pros and cons when using the site connector.

Table 5.11   Pros and Cons of Using the Site Connector

Pros	Cons
Provides automatic load balancing and fault tolerance.	Requires a permanent, high bandwidth connection of at least 56 Kbps or higher (class B or C link).
Easiest site connection option to configure and manage, because a site network transport isn't involved.	Transmits more frequently than other connection options. If you are charged for network traffic, e.g., frame relay or packets, you may want to examine another site connection option.
Messages don't need to be translated between sites.	Cannot control message size.
Configures both sides of the connection at the same time.	Cannot schedule connections.
Messages take fewer hops to reach their destination.	Can overwhelm network links when multiple Exchange servers use the same link.

RAS Connector

The RAS connector is useful where there is no permanent LAN or WAN connection, but you can link up to another site remotely. This is usually the case with small branch offices where permanent links are expensive or not available.

You can also use the RAS Connector to provide a redundant connection for sites using one of the other site connection options. For example, you can configure the RAS connector to handle message routing in cases where the primary connector link becomes unavailable.

Table 5.12 reveals the pros and cons when using the RAS connector.

Table 5.12   Pros and Cons of Using the RAS Connector

Pros	Cons
Connections can be scheduled.	Transfer is limited by speed of modem.
Can link sites over an asynchronous, periodic connection.	Link saturation is more likely since all site message traffic is flowing through one dial-up link.

X.400 Connector

The X.400 connector is useful where you are connecting to other sites via slow network links or on private or public packet networks. In addition, the X.400 connector provides compatibility with 1984, 1988, and future MTAs. This means you can communicate via X.400 with companies that are at different stages of implementing X.400 technology.

Microsoft Exchange Server supports X.400 over these OSI transports: TP0/X.25, TP4/ (CLNP), and TP0/RFC 1006 to TCP/IP. After configuring to a transport, Exchange routes the message with standard X.400 messaging protocols.

Table 5.13 reveals the pros and cons when using the X.400 connector.

Table 5.13   Pros and Cons of Using the X.400 Connector

Pros	Cons
Connects to foreign, non-Exchange systems that support X.400 standard.	Must configure network transports.
Can schedule connections.	Bottlenecks may appear since all mail traffic is flowing through one central server.
Can determine messaging.	Must verify that the existing routing through Exchange's network infrastructure topology (bridges, routers) can support the required protocols.
Message size can be controlled.	

Internet Mail Service

Although the Internet Mail Service can link two sites, its main purpose is to connect to the Internet using the SMTP (Simple Mail Transfer Protocol). Most UNIX systems and any mail systems supporting plain text-RFC 822, MIME (Multipurpose Internet Mail Extensions)-RFC 1521, MS Mail server format, or Uuencode/Uudecode standards can be linked, too.

Part
II

Ch
5

Listed in Table 5.14 are the benefits and drawbacks when using the Internet mail Service.

Table 5.14   Pros and Cons of Using the Internet Mail Service

Pros	Cons
Can forward all mail to a single host.	Must configure a network transport (TCP/IP).
Can be configured to accept or reject host connections.	Connections cannot be scheduled.
Can be configured to receive inbound or outbound messages or both.	

Microsoft Mail Connector

The Microsoft Mail connector provides seamless connectivity to Microsoft Mail for PC Networks, Microsoft Mail for AppleTalk-Networks, and Microsoft Mail for PC Networks gateways (PROFS, SNADS, NetWare, MHS, and FAX). It uses a "shadow" post office that is structured like a Microsoft Mail 3.x post office.

The Microsoft Mail connector runs over the following transports: TCP/IP, IPX/SPX, NetBEUI, X.25, Asynchronous, and Remote Access Service (RAS).

Table 5.15 lists the benefits and drawbacks when using the Microsoft Mail connector.

Table 5.15   Pros and Cons of Using the Microsoft Mail Connector

Pros	Cons
Can connect directly to another Microsoft Mail post office, allowing you to replace it without additional software.	In most cases, a network transport must be configured.
Allows you to migrate your MS Mail network in phases instead of all at once.	Must verify that the existing network infrastructure (bridges, routers) can support the required protocols.

Lotus cc:Mail Connector

The Microsoft Exchange Connector for Lotus cc:Mail enables you to tightly integrate Microsoft Exchange into existing cc:Mail environments. Once installed, Exchange Server and cc:Mail systems can exchange messages and synchronize directories. The cc:Mail Connector supports both DB6 and DB8 cc:Mail post offices. Like the MS Mail connector, you can take a phased approach to migration that causes minimal disruption with an organization.

Listed in the Table 5.16 are the benefits and drawbacks when using the Lotus cc:Mail connector.

Table 5.16   Pros and Cons of Using the Lotus cc:Mail Connector

Pros	Cons
Can connect directly to another cc:Mail post office, allowing you to replace it without additional software.	In most cases, a network transport must be configured.
Allows you to migrate from cc:Mail network in non-disruptive phases, instead of all at once.	Must verify that the existing network infrastructure (bridges, routers) can support the required protocols.

Step 8   Other Considerations

This step discusses other issues when planning for Exchange. This step is optional because it discusses advanced-planning items. You may want to fully complete all the other steps before beginning Step 8.

Estimating Hardware Requirements

Because Exchange is a transaction-based database, the proper server hardware is critical for a good Exchange system. This means that the Exchange components (information store) will first record a transaction, or create a message into a log file. During idle times, Exchange will commit those changes into the proper component (information store). If the Exchange server fails, it uses the log file to complete any missed transactions. Furthermore, Exchange uses RAM heavily to retain frequently accessed memory and address requests. A good rule of thumb is to invest in both additional memory and disk subsystem (hard drive, controller, RAID/striping technology) for a high performance general-purpose Exchange server. Because every company has variables that may utilize hardware differently, use Performance Monitor to be certain your hardware investment is providing the most value.

Part
II

Ch
5

Also, dedicating an Exchange server (as a gateway, public folder, NNTP server, and so on) will require more testing for the best hardware mix. You also have the option of adding non-Exchange services like RAS, SQL, and domain controller roles onto an Exchange server. For the best performance, however, it's best to place Exchange functions onto their own server.

Remote Users

With a little planning, mobile or remote users' needs can be met with the default communication packages delivered with Exchange or the operating system.

Client Requirements   To connect remotely to Exchange, all you need is the default communication package delivered with the Exchange client or your particular operating system. The Exchange client will automatically detect the communication software and connect and disconnect as needed.

In Table 5.17, you'll find the default communication package included with different Microsoft desktop operating systems.

Table 5.17   Client Requirements When Connecting Remotely to Exchange

Operating System or Browser	Default Communication Package
MS-DOS, Windows (16-bit)	Shiva (included with Exchange client).
Windows for Workgroups, NT Workstation	Remote Access Server (RAS) included with operating system.
Windows 95 Web Browser (Internet Explorer)	Dial-Up Networking (DUN) included operating system. Active messaging using Internet Service Provider (ISP) or DUN.

Server requirements   The Remote Access Server service (RAS) included in NT Server supports all the previously mentioned communication packages, including Shiva. Furthermore, you can use a modem, null-modem cable, X.25 (via the network or using PAD), ISDN, or security hosts and switches as connection methods. Note that you will need to estimate the number of users dialing in and plan phone lines accordingly.

Step 9   Reviewing Your Plan

Congratulations! You have all the necessary pieces to build a successful Exchange design that meets your organization's needs.

Keep in mind that every time you expand your network or Exchange site, you will need to enter a design phase again to create and implement a plan. Prepare for it by recording any important changes that may occur in the areas described.

From Here...

This chapter has provided a model for designing an Exchange topology. Depending on your current phase of implementation, you may want to proceed to the following chapters:

- Chapter 6, "Installing Exchange Server," provides step-by-step instructions on installing Exchange in your environment.
- Chapter 29, "Installing and Configuring Outlook," will lead you through the installation steps to set up Outlook.

Installing Exchange Server

Before proceeding with the Microsoft Exchange Server installation, you should make sure the machine(s) you use has the basic resources available to accomplish the task. This chapter concentrates on what you need and how to use it. The following lists show you the minimum hardware and software requirements necessary for installing the Exchange Server.

▬ **System Requirements for Exchange Server**

CPU speed, RAM, and Hard Disk Space should be addressed before installing Exchange Server 5.0.

▬ **How to Prepare to Install Exchange Sites**

Assessment of your organization from both a technical and business standpoint, is a must prior to installing Exchange sites.

▬ **Installation Procedures for Exchange**

The first Exchange 5.0 server installed in a new site is the most important.

▬ **Installation of Additional Exchange Servers in an Organization**

Gathering information about existing Exchange servers is the first thing that must be done before adding any additional Exchange Servers.

Required Hardware

For Intel and compatible systems:

Minimum

- 486-66MHz processor
- 24 MB of RAM
- 250MB of free hard disk space after NT 4.0 Server has been installed

Recommended

- System with an Intel Pentium 60 or faster processor; Pentium 133 recommended or supported RISC-based microprocessor, such as the Digital Alpha AXP or PowerPC
- 48MB of RAM
- 300MB—500MB of available hard disk space after NT 4.0 Server has been installed

N O T E Microsoft has announced it will no longer support the MIPS Platform.

Required Software:

- Microsoft Windows NT Server version 3.51 with Service Pack 5 (SP5) or later.
- Windows NT Server 4.0 with Service Pack 2 (SP2) or later.
- A Network Protocol (TCP/IP, NW-LINK, or NetBEUI).

Microsoft Windows NT Server is the base network operating system. You should install the appropriate Service Pack on the NT Server to be used before you begin the Microsoft Exchange Server installation.

If you want access from a Novell NetWare 3.XX or 4.XX File Server, the Windows NT NW-LINK and the NW-LINK NetBIOS protocol services need to be loaded on the Windows NT Server. This is a widely used protocol because unlike NetBEUI, it is routable.

When a new or existing Mail system will be using the Microsoft Exchange Server to transfer messages over the Internet, the Internet Mail Connector will be used. A necessity for the use of Internet Mail Connector is the Windows NT TCP/IP protocol. It must be installed and configured.

Optional Components and Services

- Internet Information Server (IIS) 3.0
- Windows NT Services for Macintosh (SFM)

Microsoft Internet Information Server version 3.0 is required to use Active Server Components. These allow you to access mailboxes, discussion groups, and the directory on Microsoft Exchange using any Web browser.

Macintosh Services will be necessary for MS Mail AppleTalk clients to access the Microsoft Mail Connector, which is the liaison between the AppleTalk clients and the Microsoft Exchange Server.

N O T E The Microsoft Exchange 5.0 Client for Macintosh now includes Schedule+. ▒

The preceding are the typical requirements. To enhance the performance of the system running the Microsoft NT Server and the Microsoft Exchange Server, at least a 90MHz processor with 64M of RAM should be used. For busy sites, you should use 1GB of hard disk space. This disk space requirement does not allow for user mail message stores on the server. Depending on the number of users, you may need to add additional server hard drive storage. ■

Preparing for Server and Site Setups

Before installing the Microsoft Exchange Server, you should gather some relevant information about the business or organization. This should include the number of users, usage patterns of e-mail, geographic locations, managerial style of the IS departments (central or distributed management), and more. You want to discern how the Microsoft Exchange Servers fit into the overall company plan.

The following are areas of reference you should review to help you design and install the Microsoft Exchange Server message system:

▓ Chapter 2, "Understanding Exchange's Organization Sites," teaches you what is required for designing single and multiple site Microsoft Exchange Servers.

▓ Chapter 5, "Designing Exchange Topology," and Chapter 6, "Installing Exchange Server," help you understand the issues pertaining to the setup, connection, and migration techniques involved in planning Exchange installations.

Gathering Information Used During the Installation

During the setup process, you are asked to answer questions regarding your organization and the Microsoft Exchange Server. Since some of the information can only be changed by reinstalling the Exchange Server, review the naming schemes that will be used for the message system and confirm they are set.

You should have the following information before you begin the installation process:

▓ An organization name

▓ The Microsoft Exchange Server Site name

▓ What role the Microsoft Exchange Server you are installing will play in the organization: making a new site or joining an existing one

▓ The Microsoft Windows NT Server Administrator account name and password

▓ The name of the Microsoft Exchange Server Administrators Group

When designing the naming scheme for the Microsoft Exchange Server Message system, use logical names with relative information to the end users and IS administrators. Because of the nature of Mail system standards, these names are also case sensitive. To avoid confusion, check each name entered before continuing; these names are used throughout the entire message system.

Setting Up a Single Server

The first Microsoft Exchange Server to be installed in a new site is the most important. All other Microsoft Exchange Server installations within the same site refer to this Exchange Server for configuration information.

The following list has steps for completing the first or only Microsoft Exchange Server in a site or organization:

1. Create the Service Account
2. Configure the Exchange Server Administrators Group
3. Install the Exchange Server software
4. Grant the Exchange Server administrators permissions for the site

Creating the Service Account

The Microsoft Exchange Server uses the Service Account to run its services on the given Microsoft NT Server. The account is granted the "Log on as a service" right. When creating and joining a new Microsoft Exchange Server within the same site, the Service Account name and password are required to continue with the installation. Microsoft Exchange Server Setup uses this account to transfer the configuration files to the new Microsoft Exchange Server. Furthermore, this account is also used by all Microsoft Exchange Servers in the same site to communicate with one another.

The following steps help you to create the Service Account:

1. Log on the Windows NT Server as the Domain Administrator or equivalent.

N O T E You must log in to the same Domain that holds the system for which you plan to create the account. ■

2. Click the start button and select programs, open Administrative Tools. Then, open User Manager for Domains.
3. From the User menu, choose New User.
4. Enter the information you have listed for the Service Account.
5. Check the box titled User Cannot Change Password.
6. Check the box for Password Never Expires.
7. Clear the box that says User Must Change Password at Next Logon.

8. Clear the box that says Account Disabled.

9. Choose Add (see Figure 6.1).

10. Choose Close.

FIG. 6.1

You can add the
Service Account.

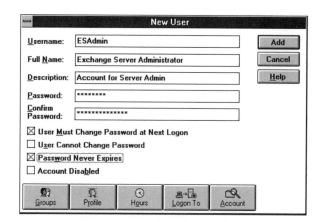

Creating the Exchange Administrators Group

The Exchange Administrators Group should consist of all the users permitted to administer Exchange. This group is a Global Group. Keep in mind that all users who become a member of this group have full control of Exchange and all of its features.

The following steps help you create the Exchange Administrators group:

1. Log on as a Domain Administrator to the Microsoft NT Server that is in the same domain as the Microsoft Exchange Server. This Microsoft NT Server will be the central location for the administrative functions of Microsoft Exchange.

2. Click the start button and select programs, open Administrative Tools. Then, open User Manager for Domains.

3. From the User menu, choose New Global Group. The New Global Group dialog box appears (see Figure 6.2).

4. Type the name and a brief description of the newly created group.

N O T E You will be required to know this group account name later in the installation and setup of the Microsoft Exchange Server. ▒

FIG. 6.2

Creating the Exchange Administrators group.

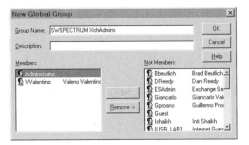

Installing the Exchange Server Software

Before beginning the actual installation, you should verify the following:

- Be sure that the PDC (Primary Domain Controller) is connected and operating.
- Review the proposed Microsoft Exchange Server naming scheme and design layout.
- Check that there is a working CD-ROM drive available as a resource on the Windows NT Server. You will use this drive during the installation process.

The following steps help you to install the Microsoft Exchange Server:

1. Log on to the Microsoft NT Server as the Local Administrator.
2. Load the Microsoft Exchange Server CD-ROM into the CD-ROM drive.
3. Double-click the My Computer icon; then, the CD-ROM icon.
4. Scan through and become familiar with the directory structure on the Microsoft Exchange CD-ROM.
5. Locate and change directories to the Setup directory.
6. Locate and change directories to one of the computer types (Alpha, i386). For example: d:\SETUP\i386.
7. Choose SETUP.EXE; then, press OK to continue past the Welcome dialog box.

N O T E If you plan to use Server Components, which will enable you to access mailboxes, discussion groups, and the directory on Microsoft Exchange using any Web browser, you must first install Internet Information Server 3.0. When installing Exchange you must run the Complete/ Custom install option and be sure that the Active Server Components box is checked.

8. An Installation Options box appears (see Figure 6.3). Select the desired type of installation and the location to which the files should be copied. The following are the installation options from which you can select:

   - *Typical*. Microsoft Exchange Server will be installed with the most common options.
   - *Custom/Complete*. Microsoft Exchange Server will be installed with only the options you select.

- *Minimum.* Microsoft Exchange Server will be installed with the minimum required options to run.

N O T E One of the selections in the preceding list might not appear on-screen. The reason is that there is not enough disk space for that particular option. Choose another type of installation or a different file location on another volume that has enough disk space to handle the installation.

FIG. 6.3

You can select from the Installation Options Box when setting up the Microsoft Exchange Server.

If you select the Complete/Custom type of installation, the next screen to appear is the Microsoft Exchange Server component selection screen. Each component can be selected by checking the box pertaining to the component, or clearing the box if that selection is not desired, depending on the given installation. The following lists the different components and their subcomponents available for selection during installation:

- Microsoft Exchange Server—The default location for installation of component files is C:\EXCHSRVR. This can be modified by choosing Change Location of Files. If all Server components are to be installed, approximately 100MB of disk space is required.

- Microsoft Mail Connector—Connects a Microsoft Exchange Server to MS Mail 3.x PC and AppleTalk Networks. This component requires 7KB of disk space.

- Internet mail is not transferred during the upgrade. If you have specific routing set up before upgrading, the routing information is not transferred from the registry to the directory.

To reset routing information:

1. Find the path for the ExtensionDLL parameter under the following registry value.HKEY LOCAL MACHINE\SYSTEM\CurrentControlSet\Services\MSExchangeIMC\parameters.

Part

II

Ch

6

2. In the Administrator program, choose the Configuration container for the site, and then choose Connections.

3. Select the Internet Mail Service.

4. From the File menu, choose Properties, and then select the Routing tab.

5. Select instead of the table, use this custom routing program, and enter the path from the ExtensionDLL parameter:

   - X.400 Connector—Connects a Microsoft Exchange Server to X.400 compatible systems. This component requires no disk space.

   - Microsoft Exchange Server Administrator application—The default directory path for installation of the Administrator components is C:\EXCHSRVR\BIN. You can change the directory path if you want a different location. The Administrator software component has no subcomponents that are selectable. This component has 15KB of local hard disk space.

N O T E If a Complete Install is executed, it will require a minimum of 140,114K of disk space. This does not include disk space for user mailboxes, just the Exchange system files. ▨

6. The Choose Licensing Mode dialog box appears. Select the type of licensing desired. Select I Agree; then, choose OK. The following shows the types of licensing modes from which you can select:

   - *Per Server Licensing*—Enter the number of Client Access Licenses that have been purchased. For concurrent connections, the number entered must be a value greater than zero. Otherwise, Microsoft Exchange Clients will not be able to connect to the Microsoft Exchange Server system.

   - *Per Client Licensing*—This type of access is based on the valid ownership of MS Mail 3.x client software and Microsoft Exchange Client.

7. Choose Create a New Site when the Organization and Site dialog box appears (see Figure 6.4). Enter the Organization Name and Site Name. Entering these names is mandatory. Choose continue.

8. A dialog box appears asking, "Are you sure you want to create a new site?" Choose Yes.

9. Next, the Site Services Account box appears asking you to choose the Service account (see Figure 6.5). Enter the Service account name and password created at the beginning of this chapter. Alternatively, you can choose Browse. Then, you can choose the account from the list provided. Choose add; then, click OK.

10. The dialog box appears confirming that the rights have been granted (see Figure 6.6). Choose OK.

FIG. 6.4

Creating a new
Exchange site.

11. To complete the installation, choose OK from the next dialog box. Microsoft Exchange
    Server Setup then copies the Microsoft Exchange Server files and installs the Services
    to the selected Microsoft Windows NT Server.

12. The next screen that appears is asking to which Windows NT Program Group the
    Microsoft Exchange Servers application icons should be installed. The default is
    Microsoft Exchange Server. Accept the default Program Group; then, enter a new
    Program Group name. Alternatively, you can select an existing Program. Then, choose
    continue.

FIG. 6.5

You can enter the
Services account name
and the appropriate
password.

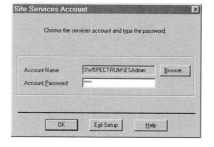

13. Finally, once the installation is completed, a dialog box appears asking whether the
    Performance Optimizer Wizard should be run (see Figure 6.7). Select Run Optimizer to
    have the Performance Optimizer Wizard analyze your hardware configuration. Run
    Optimizer also arranges files on the Microsoft Windows NT Server for optimum
    performance.

N O T E Running the Optimizer is critical to the efficient operation of the Microsoft Exchange Server.
The Performance Optimizer Wizard does not have to run at this time. However, it should be
run before Exchange is rolled out to live users. ▪

Part

II

Ch

6

FIG. 6.6

You should verify that the proper rights have been granted.

FIG. 6.7

Completing the Setup and Performance Optimizer option will get the Exchange Server up and running.

14. The Microsoft Windows NT Server needs to be rebooted to verify that the Microsoft Exchange Server services that were just installed have taken effect.

This completes the procedures for installing the first or only Microsoft Exchange Server in a single site.

Granting the Administrators Group Permissions for the Site

In order for the Microsoft Exchange Server to be administered, permissions have to be granted to the Administrators Group. The following steps provide a description of procedures for completing this task:

1. Click the start button and select the Programs Icon. Then, select the Microsoft Exchange icon followed by the Microsoft Exchange Administration icon. (This will start Exchange Server).

2. Connect to the new Microsoft Exchange Server.

3. Select the File menu and choose Properties. Then, choose the Permissions tab. You will see the Permissions Property page (see Figure 6.8). A list of Microsoft Windows NT user accounts for this site appears.

4. Select the Microsoft Windows NT Domain that you want.

5. Select the User(s) or group(s) that are to be added to the Administrators Group from the given list (see Figure 6.9). Alternatively, you can enter manually the User and Group names by typing the Domain Name followed by a backslash. Then, you can type the User account and Group names into the Add Name box, for example, **Domain1\User1**.

6. To continue to designate additional properties, choose Apply to activate the entered properties. Alternatively, you can return to the Administrators window by choosing OK to close the Permissions property sheet. Choosing OK applies the changes as well.

The Administrators Group has now been granted the correct permissions for accomplishing administrative needs.

FIG. 6.8

The Permissions page shows Microsoft Windows NT user accounts for this site.

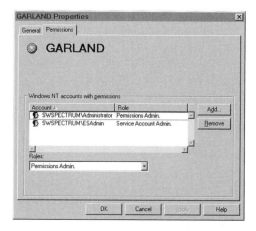

FIG. 6.9

You can choose users and groups that are to be added to the Administrators Group.

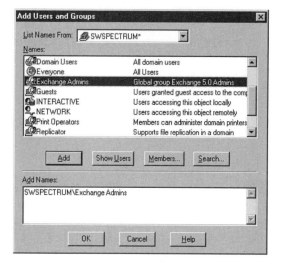

Part

II

Ch

6

Setting Up Additional Servers at the Same Location

The procedures for setting up additional Microsoft Exchange Servers at the same site are similar to the steps taken to create the first or only Microsoft Exchange Server. The major difference between setting up the first and a second Microsoft Exchange Server occurs at step 10 of the directions pertaining to the creation of a new Microsoft Exchange Server site.

When step 10 is reached, and the Exchange Site dialog box appears, choose the Join An Existing Site selection. Then, enter the name of an available Microsoft Exchange Server system. Choose OK. This new server will be added to the existing site. It will receive its configuration file from the existing Microsoft Exchange Server. You should continue through step 12 of the process to create a new Microsoft Exchange Server.

Adding Additional Microsoft Exchange Server Sites Within an Organization

If the Organization that you are designing and creating has multiple Microsoft Exchange Server sites, you need to remember the following (see Figure 6.10):

■ You need one Microsoft Windows NT Server to have an initial Microsoft Exchange Server created and set up at the site. You must use the steps described earlier in this chapter.

■ The existing site must have a Site Connector installed.

■ Installation of a Site Connector at the new site is required.

FIG. 6.10

Creating a new Exchange server to join an existing site.

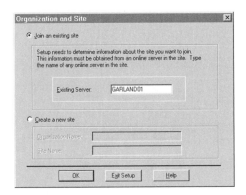

From Here...

The initial installation of the Microsoft Exchange Server is now complete. The following lists the different chapter references to help you further configure and enhance the performance of the Microsoft Exchange Server.

■ Chapter 13, "Directory and System Attendant Configuration," explains how to configure your information store and manage Exchange Server processes.

■ Chapter 15, "Information Store Configuration," explains how to manage and setup your information store.

■ Chapter 17, "Setting Up the Site Connector and Dynamic RAS Connector," provides information on site to site communication.

■ Chapter 18, "Using Directory Replication and Synchronization," provides setup for directory replication of user information.

CHAPTER 7

Planning Connections to Microsoft Mail Systems

Microsoft Exchange Server Mail Connector

Description of the major components that make up the Microsoft Exchange Server Microsoft Mail Connector.

Microsoft Mail Major Components

Description of the major components that make up MS Mail 3.x.

Integrating Microsoft Exchange

How to integrate Microsoft Exchange Server into an existing MS Mail 3.x mail environment.

Microsoft Exchange Server Directory Replication

Overview of Directory Replication between Microsoft Exchange Server sites.

Directory Synchronization

How Microsoft Exchange Server sites and MS Mail 3.x mail systems sychronize.

By coupling the functions of a Gateway Post Office and the External program, the Microsoft Mail Connector bundled within Microsoft Exchange Server becomes the primary link between Microsoft Exchange Server and Microsoft Mail 3.x (PC and Appletalk). It also provides the connectivity link that ties Microsoft Exchange Gateways and MS Mail 3.x Gateways. This Connector enables Microsoft Exchange Server to route and transfer messages to one or more MS Mail 3.x(PC) systems over LAN, Asynchronous, or X.25 connections.

You can configure Microsoft Mail Connector for message transfer and routing by using components provided with Microsoft Exchange Server. The components built into the Microsoft Mail Connector are comparable to the components in the MS Mail 3.x Post Office and External message transfer programs. The Microsoft Mail Connector components run as services on a Windows NT operating system, which allows for better error logging, memory management, and performance monitoring of the entire messaging system. Integration of an existing MS Mail 3.x system, using the External or the Multitasking MTA programs with Microsoft Exchange Server, can be easily configured to enable a common coexistence of both messaging systems on the same LAN. ■

Microsoft Mail Connector Components

The following three components are located within Microsoft Mail Connector and work in conjunction with each other transparently to transfer and route messages to and from MS Mail Post Offices (see Figure 7.1):

- Microsoft Mail Connector Interchange
- Microsoft Mail Connector Post Office
- Microsoft Mail Connector (PC) Message Transfer Agent (MTA)

Microsoft Mail Connector Interchange

The Microsoft Mail Connector Interchange is a Windows NT service that converts the message from or to MS Mail 3.x format, then routes and transfers messages between Microsoft Exchange Server and the Microsoft Mail Connector Post Office. This process is completely transparent to the users and completed in the background. Configuring the Microsoft Mail Connector Interchange must be done for LAN, asynchronous, and X.25 transport connections. Configuration requires using the Administrator program in the Interchange tab to create and set up an Administrator Mailbox for receiving delivery status messages, to establish a primary language used by the majority of the Post Offices using the Connector, and if MS Mail 3.x clients wish to view or save OLE documents received from Microsoft Exchange Clients, the Maximize MS Mail 3.x Compatibility item must be selected.

Microsoft Mail Connector Post Office

The Microsoft Mail Connector Post Office is a temporary information store for messages in transit. The Connector Post Office is sometimes referred to as a *gateway post office* because it is dedicated to message transfer and has no local mailboxes. The Microsoft Mail Connector Post Office sits between the Microsoft Mail Connector Interchange and the Microsoft Mail Connector MTA. Because this Post Office works with messages being transferred both ways through its information store, it temporarily holds messages that have been converted and are waiting to be routed to MS Mail 3.x clients or messages that have been sent from MS Mail 3.x clients waiting to be converted.

Microsoft Mail Connector (PC) Message Transfer Agent (MTA)

The Microsoft Mail Connector Message Transfer Agent is a Windows NT service that connects to and transfers mail between the Microsoft Mail Connector Post Office and one or more MS Mail (PC) Post Offices. It can execute most of the same operations of the MS Mail 3.x External and Multitasking MTA programs, including message distribution and delivery to users on MS Mail Post Offices. The MTA contains the information for which the direct and indirect connection routing of mail messages occurs between MS Mail 3.x Post Offices. The information is read from a list that is configured through the Microsoft Mail Connector section of the Administrator program.

Once again, all of the preceding components can be configured in the Administrator program, under the Microsoft Mail Connector within the individual component tab.

FIG. 7.1
Microsoft Mail
Connector compo-
nents.

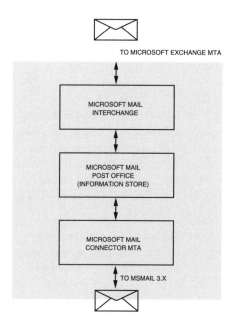

In an MS Mail 3.x environment, the External MTA and the Multitasking MTA (MMTA) programs transfer and route messages between MS Mail Post Offices. The programs do not have all of the same advanced features as the Microsoft Mail Connector. However, any existing MS Mail 3.x system using External and the Multitasking MTA programs to transfer and route messages can easily be integrated with a Microsoft Exchange Server directly with the help of the Microsoft Mail Connector.

The Microsoft Mail Connector MTA does not completely handle all of the functions of the MS Mail 3.x External or Multitasking MTA. In some cases, the messaging system may still require some of the functions found in the External program.

For example, when MS Mail 3.x Remote users dial in for their messages, they dial into the MS Mail MTA (External), which handles message transfer between Remote users and the MS Mail 3.x Post Offices. With users still using the MS Mail Remote client program, the MS Mail MTA (External) cannot be replaced by the Microsoft Mail Connector. The continued use of the External program will need to be maintained, as well as the Microsoft Mail Connector.

Another perspective is when you use the MS Mail MTA (External), the MTA administers to modem setup and the dial-out process. It also requires its own separate dial-in infrastructure. If other remote applications require dial-out access also, another separate dial-in infrastructure will be needed. This requires quite a bit of communications equipment.

Part
II

Ch
7

Microsoft Exchange uses Microsoft NT Server's standard remote network hardware that supports standard protocols such as the following:

- PPP
- TCP/IP
- IPX/SPX
- NetBIOS
- AppleTalk

Microsoft Exchange profits from the use of these standard protocols by making it possible to implement and integrate a single dial-in infrastructure to handle all remote communications services provided by the Microsoft NT Server. A multitude of remote access servers can be used by your Remote mail users to gain access to the mail system. For example, the Microsoft Exchange Client remote users can make use of the built-in Remote Access in Microsoft NT Server. This capability enables remote users to dial directly into Microsoft Mail Connector MTA through the Microsoft Exchange Server.

When both Microsoft Exchange and MS Mail 3.x Post Offices reside on the same LAN, you can configure the Microsoft Mail Connector to transfer route messages from the Microsoft Exchange Server MTA, convert the message, and deliver the message to the correct recipient on the MS Mail 3.x Post Office.

When you send a message to a Microsoft Exchange Server destined for an MS Mail 3.x recipient located on the same LAN, the message is received by the Microsoft Exchange MTA. Then, the message is routed by the Microsoft Exchange MTA to the Microsoft Mail Connector Interchange. Here, the message and any OLE attachments are converted to MS Mail 3.x format. The converted message is then sent to the Microsoft Mail Connector Post Office (Information Store) where it is held until the Microsoft Mail Connector MTA picks it up and delivers it to the appropriate MS Mail 3.x Post Office (see Figure 7.2).

MS Mail 3.x message delivery can be performed only over a Direct LAN connection. The Microsoft Mail Connector, External MTA, and Multitasking MTA determine their routing information between Microsoft Exchange Server and MS Mail 3.x by the information that is entered into the Address Space. The *address space* is defined as a set of MS Mail 3.x Post Office names, to which mail messages will be routed by the Microsoft Mail Connector. This entry in the address space is also known as an *instance*.

When connecting MS Mail 3.x over X.25 or Asynchronous services, the External MTA or Multitasking MTA program at the Remote Post Office location will also have to be configured with an instance in the address space of the MTA to connect with the Microsoft Mail Connector (see Figure 7.3).

FIG. 7.2
The message transfer process from Exchange Server MTA to MS Mail 3.x.

FIG. 7.3
Basic MS Mail 3.x External (or Multi-tasking MTA) layout.

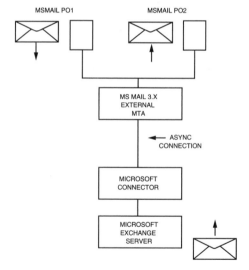

Configuring LAN Connections to Existing Post Offices

The LAN connection happens to be the easiest and one of the simplest types of connections in terms of setup and administration. In this particular case, you don't have to use the External or Multitasking MTA programs at all. Instead, you can use the Administrator program in Microsoft Exchange Server to configure the majority of the message routing and transfer between the Microsoft Mail Connector and the MS Mail 3.x Post Offices.

MS Mail 3.x Post Office

If you have multiple MS Mail 3.x Post Offices on the same LAN, a way to increase the performance of the Microsoft Exchange Server is to configure one of the MS Mail 3.x Post Offices as the direct connection Post Office. This MS Mail 3.x Post Office will be the recipient and sender of messages transferred to and from the Microsoft Exchange Server Microsoft Mail Connector. The Microsoft Mail Connector contains an instance in its address space to route messages to the MS Mail 3.x direct connection Post Office. Additionally, the address space of the Microsoft Mail Connector also specifies instances for all of the other MS Mail 3.x Post Offices located on the LAN as indirect connections. The MS Mail 3.x Post Offices configured as indirect connections transfer messages to and from the MS Mail 3.x direct connection Post Office.

Similarly, the address space of the MS Mail 3.x Post Office that is configured as the direct connection Post Office will also contain entries of indirect connection instances that describe the remaining MS Mail 3.x Post Offices located on the LAN (see Figure 7.4).

FIG. 7.4
Basic LAN connection with direct and indirect route configuration.

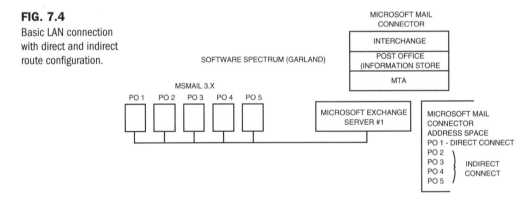

To transfer and route messages correctly, the Microsoft Mail Connector must know about each of the remote Post Offices. Microsoft Mail Connector has an integrated feature that automatically extracts Indirect Routing information from an MS Mail 3.x Post Office. This feature means there is no need to manually configure the routing information for each of the MS Mail 3.x Post Offices connected indirectly to the Microsoft Mail Connector. The only requirement for the automatic upload of routing information is a LAN Connection.

Unfortunately, if the MS Mail 3.x Post Office you are trying to connect to is over an Asynchronous or X.25 service, the indirect routing information will have to be input manually through the Microsoft Mail Connector property pages.

Asynchronous and X.25 Connections for Remote Post Offices

You need two components to connect Microsoft Exchange Server and an MS Mail 3.x Post Office over an X.25 or Asynchronous service. The first is the Microsoft Mail Connector MTA, the main routing component of the Microsoft Mail Connector included within the Microsoft Exchange Server. It runs as a service on the Microsoft NT Server. When configured, it contains the routing information in the address space that will be used to route messages to and from the MS Mail 3.x Mail systems.

The second is the MS Mail 3.x External or Multitasking MTA program provided with MS Mail 3.x Server. This program provides the message transfer and modem management functions necessary to communicate over a remote connection within an MS Mail 3.x system. If the MS Mail 3.x External MTA will reside on a DOS computer, this will need to be a dedicated computer. DOS will not allow multiple sessions, or executables, to occur at the same time. Setting up the Multitasking MTA on a Microsoft Windows NT Workstation would allow multiple MTAs to reside and route messages on a single computer. The Multitasking MTA can also reside on a separate Microsoft Windows NT Server if desired. I recommend using the Microsoft Windows NT Workstation because it doesn't require passwords.

If a Direct Asynchronous or X.25 route is desired, MS Mail 3.x External or Multitasking MTA must be located on the same LAN as the Post Office.

When a message destined for an MS Mail 3.x Post Office is sent from a Microsoft Exchange client, the message is stored temporarily in the Microsoft Mail Connector Post Office. If the message is not picked up by the Microsoft Mail Connector MTA and routed to its destination, the message will remain in the Connector Post Office until it times out and is returned to the sender, or it gets picked up and delivered by a LAN connected instance of the MS Mail 3.x External or Multitasking MTA or Gateway.

Using Multiple Microsoft Mail Connectors (PC) MTAs

Each Microsoft Mail MTA instance reacts differently depending on the type of connection it uses.

NOTE Each instance is named and registered as a Windows NT service on the Microsoft Exchange Server computer on which it was created and can be started or stopped independently of any other service. ■

Each instance has a primary connection type, although all instances can service LAN-Connected Post Offices. Depending on the number of Post Offices and what their connection types are, it might be more efficient to group the same connection types in the same instance. If the connection types are diverse, multiple instances should be created.

For example, if your network contains 10 LAN-connected MS Mail 3.x Post Offices and five Asynchronous-connected MS Mail 3.x Post Offices, it would be more efficient to create an instance on the Microsoft Mail Connector MTA for servicing only the LAN-connected Post Offices and another instance for connecting to and servicing the Asynchronous Post Offices.

If there are only two Asynchronous-connected MS Mail 3.x Post Offices and 10 LAN-connected MS Mail 3.x Post Offices, only one instance needs to be created on the Microsoft Mail Connector MTA for the Asynchronous connected Post Offices. Because all instances can service LAN connected Post Offices, the LAN connected Post Offices can then be added to the same instance.

Using Multiple Microsoft Mail Connectors

If your organization contains a large number of MS Mail 3.x Post Offices, you might need multiple Microsoft Mail Connector MTAs for message connectivity between MS Mail 3.x and Microsoft Exchange recipients. Since the same MS Mail E-Mail address is used by every Microsoft Exchange Server in the site, MS Mail essentially views each of the Microsoft Exchange sites as one large MS Mail Post Office. Therefore, it is recommended for routing purposes that one Microsoft Mail Connector MTA should be used for every Microsoft Exchange Server Site, which subsequently means multiple instances.

Additional Routing Considerations

If you are going to use Multiple Microsoft Mail Connector MTAs, make sure each Microsoft Exchange Server has its own Microsoft Mail Connector MTA. Also, use duplicate address entries in two or more Microsoft Mail Connectors to route messages based on cost. This is useful for redundancy and load balancing traffic across connections and between servers.

Using Exchange Server as a Backbone to MS Mail (PC)

Multiple MS Mail 3.x Sites and individual MS Mail 3.x Post Offices can be coupled into a single messaging system using Microsoft Exchange Server as a Backbone to the existing MS Mail 3.x messaging system. To make this connection, message transfer should first be set up between each of the Microsoft Exchange Server sites and a MS Mail 3.x Post Office. Make sure that each of the MS Mail 3.x Post Offices correctly routes the messages to its destination through the Microsoft Mail Connector. When connected through a Microsoft Exchange Server, this will allow each of the MS Mail 3.x Post Offices to see the other MS Mail 3.x Post Offices as connected indirectly through one or more other Post Offices.

If Directory Synchronization has been set up between any of the sites and the MS Mail 3.x Post Offices, all of the new information added to the Microsoft Exchange Server while setting up the message transfer between the sites and the MS Mail 3.x Post Offices will be replicated to each of the connected Post Offices and the information shared by all (see Figure 7.5).

FIG. 7.5

Basic site-to-site backbone configuration.

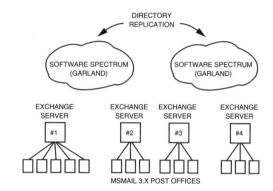

Using Existing MS Mail (PC) Gateways

Microsoft Exchange Server supports a wide variety of MS Mail (PC) Gateways, which grant messaging services to other messaging systems. Supported MS Mail (PC) Gateways include the following:

- AT&T Easylink
- Fax
- IBM PROFS and OfficeVision
- MHS
- SNADS
- MCI Mail Gateway (M-Bridge for Microsoft Mail for PC (Networks)

All of these Gateway programs come enclosed with Microsoft Mail Server 3.x on an options diskette included with the software. Each of the Gateway programs will require a short installation and configuration process. They are menu driven and easy to follow.

There are two ways Microsoft Exchange Clients can pass information through an existing MS Mail 3.x mail system gateway. First, a typical gateway scenario in an existing MS Mail 3.x environment would find the MS Mail 3.x Gateway software running on a dedicated computer. An MS Mail 3.x Post Office will need to be selected as the Gateway Post Office. All messages destined for the foreign mail system will pass through this gateway Post Office, and vice versa. In order for Microsoft Exchange clients to access the actual Gateway and pass messages to the

Part

II

Ch

7

foreign mail system, the Microsoft Exchange Connector Post Office needs to have the MS Mail 3.x Gateway Access Component installed on it (see Figure 7.6). Secondly, if a Microsoft Exchange Server is selected as the Gateway Post Office, the MS Mail 3.x Post Offices will then be required to hold a Gateway Access component. Either way will integrate a Microsoft Exchange Server into an existing MS Mail 3.x Gateway scenario (see Figure 7.7).

FIG. 7.6

Basic MS Mail 3.x Gateway Layout.

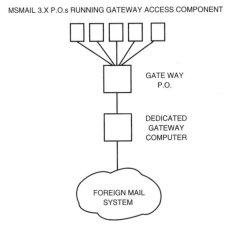

MSMAIL 3.X P.O.s RUNNING GATEWAY ACCESS COMPONENT

GATE WAY P.O.

DEDICATED GATEWAY COMPUTER

FOREIGN MAIL SYSTEM

FIG. 7.7

A typical gateway scenario.

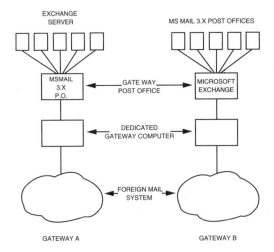

EXCHANGE SERVER

MS MAIL 3.X POST OFFICES

MSMAIL 3.X P.O.

GATE WAY POST OFFICE

MICROSOFT EXCHANGE

DEDICATED GATEWAY COMPUTER

FOREIGN MAIL SYSTEM

GATEWAY A

GATEWAY B

Using Exchange Connectors as Gateways

If you decide on using Microsoft Exchange for your Gateway needs, Microsoft Exchange X.400 Connector or Internet Mail Connector or both will need to be installed on the Microsoft Exchange Server. The MS Mail 3.x Post Office that's given access to the foreign mail service needs to be connected to the Exchange Server via the Microsoft Mail Connector and must have a gateway access component installed on it. One benefit to using Microsoft Exchange as a gateway is the capability to alleviate the need for a dedicated computer running the gateway (see Figure 7.8).

FIG. 7.8
Using Microsoft
Exchange as a
gateway.

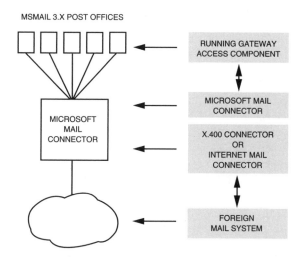

When a mail message is sent from an MS Mail 3.x Post Office destined for the foreign mail service, the message is sent to the Microsoft Mail Connector, which passes it to either the Microsoft Exchange X.400 Connector and/or the Internet Mail Connector. The selected connector will then pass the message to the foreign mail service. For a message traveling from a foreign mail system, reverse the procedure.

Directory Replication and Synchronization

Directory Replication is the automatic process of replicating the Directory information between Microsoft Exchange Servers within a site. The information that is replicated includes all the information available about an organization's resources and users, including mailboxes, public folders, distribution lists, servers, and more. Other components use the directory to

Part
II

Ch

7

map addresses and route messages. Replication can also be configured to automatically replicate all or only the desired amount of the directory information between multiple Microsoft Exchange sites.

Directory Synchronization is the process of keeping a Microsoft Exchange Server directory synchronized with directories from MS Mail (PC) and MS Mail (AppleTalk) systems. This is accomplished by the MS Mail 3.x DISPATCH program included with the MS Mail 3.x Server. Like Directory Replication between Microsoft Exchange Server sites, only the desired information will be transferred.

In order for a Microsoft Exchange Server to accomplish Directory Synchronization with a MS Mail 3.x mail system, the Microsoft Exchange Server must be running the MS Mail 3.x Directory Synchronization Agent. The Directory Synchronization Agent on a Microsoft Exchange Server plays one of two roles depending on the mail system environment: DIRSYNC Server or DIRSYNC Requester (see Figure 7.9). On an existing MS Mail 3.x system, the Microsoft Exchange server can be configured as either a DIRSYNC Server or Requestor (see Figure 7.10). However, the Microsoft Exchange Server cannot be configured as both a Server and a Requestor simultaneously. On a MS Mail 3.x mail system, there can only be one DIRSYNC Server. All of the rest of the MS Mail 3.x Post Offices can be configured as DIRSYNC Requestors. If the Microsoft Exchange Server is configured as the DIRSYNC Server, it can synchronize all other MS Mail 3.x Post Offices setup as DIRSYNC Requestors. Once again, integration into an existing MS Mail 3.x system is entirely conceivable and not difficult.

FIG. 7.9

Using Microsoft Exchange as a DIRSYNCH server on an existing MS Mail system.

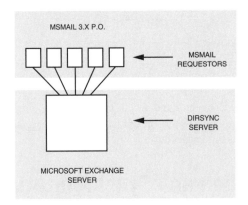

FIG. 7.10
Using Microsoft
Exchange as a
DIRSYNCH Requestor
on an existing MS
Mail system.

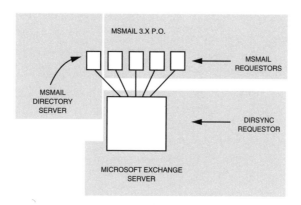

From Here...

This chapter has addressed the topic of planning your Microsoft Mail Connector. For more information, refer to the following:

- Chapter 8, "Migrating from Microsoft Mail Systems," which details the migration process, including the use of the Migration Wizard.

- Chapter 11, " Migrating from External Systems," which describes other mail systems that can communicate with Exchange.

- Chapter 20, "Using the Microsoft Mail Connector for AppleTalk Networks," which explains how to connect Exchange to an existing AppleTalk network.

Part
II

Ch
7

CHAPTER 8

Migrating from Microsoft Mail Systems

Migration is the act of moving users from one messaging system to another. This can include mailboxes, mail, addresses, and schedule information from your existing system.

In the past, mail migration was not considered something for the cautious. However, Microsoft Exchange is packed with migration features that support multiple scenarios for interconnecting to other Mail systems. Tools such as Migration Wizard simplify the migration process and ensure a smooth transition to Microsoft Exchange. ■

The Migration Elements

These include Migration Assistant and Source Extractor, Connectors, MTA, DXA.

A Sample Migration

Three-Phase Model of a sample migration.

Connecting Exchange Clients to MS Mail Post Office

How Microsoft Exchange clients are connected to MS Mail Post Offices.

Connecting Exchange Clients to Exchange Server

Decribes how to connect Exchange Clients to Microsoft Exchange Server.

Microsoft Exchange Server and Mail Clients

Use Exchange Server with MS Mail clients.

Exchange and Mail Clients

Using Exchange Server with Mail and Exchange clients.

Exchange Clients

Using Exchange Server with Exchange clients.

Using the Migration Wizard

Migration Wizard simplifies migration.

Migration Strategy and Planning

Microsoft Exchange Server has many migration tools to be used with Microsoft Mail (PC). As you plan your migration you need to consider the following:

- What level of migration coexistence, mailbox migration, mailbox creation, or a combination of these will be best for your organization?
- Should all users be migrated, or only a subset of users?
- Do users have all the hardware necessary or will migration occur in phases?
- What connectivity issues need to be addressed?
- Which users should migrate first?

Migration Levels from Full Migration to Coexistence

There are three levels of migration: coexistence, mailbox creation, and mailbox migration. The type you choose depends on how much data you want to move from your existing system to Microsoft Exchange:

- Establish coexistence with an existing system.

  This level enables users on both MS Mail and Exchange to exchange mail. You have a chance to test connections between the two systems; Addresses are extracted from the existing system and added as custom recipients in Microsoft Exchange. This provides a foundation for migrating users to Microsoft Exchange, usually before actual migration.

- Create new Microsoft Exchange Server mailboxes without data.

  At this level, only user account information is copied from the existing system. This will create empty mailboxes and, as an option, Windows NT accounts. This approach is used to migrate users without migrating their data, either with a plan to migrate their data later, or to skip migrating the data altogether.

- Migrate mailbox contents.

  At this level, mailbox contents are copied (not moved) from the MS Mail to Microsoft Exchange Server mailboxes. The contents include messages, attachments, and calendars. This enables the user to use Microsoft Exchange without any data loss. This can follow coexistence and mailbox creation, or it can be combined with those steps for a quick migration.

You can use one of these three migration levels exclusively, or you can use all three as part of your migration plan. For example, after you install your first new Exchange server, you can migrate addresses from MS Mail. For a test run, you can create new mailboxes without data. Once your testing is complete, you can migrate the mailbox contents to the new mailboxes and have the users upgrade their clients to Microsoft Exchange-based clients.

N O T E In this chapter, all references to the Exchange Client include both Outlook and the Exchange Client 5.0/Schedule+ 7.5. Client architecture and your organization's functional preferences will determine which product will be implemented.

The following list describes issues associated with a migration from MS Mail to Exchange:

- Migration testing shows that high volumes of data can take weeks or even months to migrate.
- Hardware used for the existing system needs to be freed up in early phases for redeployment during later phases.
- Existing messaging applications are needed in some departments until they can be replaced with Microsoft Exchange public folders and custom form functionality.
- Not all departments have the budget to upgrade at the same time.
- The group in charge of Microsoft Exchange implementation is small and can't afford to bring in extra resources for a quick migration.
- The help desk group is small and can't handle the short burst of requests a quick migration is likely to create.
- Some departments don't have the hardware or system software to upgrade now.
- Microsoft Exchange is being tested in a pilot stage first.
- Microsoft Exchange clients are not available for all platforms or networks.

The following is a list of the types or levels of migration from MS Mail to Exchange. You should choose the proper phase for your organization:

Single-phase migration. Gives users some of the enhanced features before migration, while you are planning and testing the enterprise design.

Multi-phase migration. Gives all users a common user interface as you migrate mailboxes in stages.

Multi-phase migration with dual access. Enables users to retrieve mail from their old mailboxes after their mailboxes have been migrated to Microsoft Exchange Server.

Taking into consideration the previous two lists, you should be developing an idea of the migration strategy for your organization. As you plan your organization's new messaging infrastructure, you'll probably want to break down the project into steps. The major steps of the migration process can be divided as follows:

- Connect Microsoft Exchange Client to existing systems
- Create directory and mailbox entries
- Extract and load accounts
- Set up directory synchronization
- Set up connectivity with gateway

- Migrate server contents
- Move user's data
- Update the directory

Now that you are aware of the issues, phases, and steps to migrating MS mail to Exchange, keep in mind the effect of these items on your organization. The next section takes the previous lists and applies them to an actual organization.

Introduction to the Three-Phase Method

Large organizations might consider phased migrations, concentrating on more challenging sites prior to the major Exchange roll-out. There may also be longer periods of coexistence with legacy mail. Smaller organizations by contrast would most likely be able to do a very quick migration—almost instantaneous.

If you belong to a large organization, your migration plan will probably take place in three basic phases:

- Installing Exchange Server centrally
- Migrating users or branch offices and coexisting with legacy systems, like MS Mail.
- Completing migration in remote locations

Sample Migration with a Three-Phase Method

A three-phased approach is used to simplify the task of migration. Inside each phase may be numerous individual tasks. On a high level, these three phases will apply to any organization. The following sample will be used to walk you through the migration process for an actual organization.

Software Spectrum has its headquarters in Garland, Texas, and offices in Los Angeles, California and London, England (see Figure 8.1). The two American offices are connected over a T1 line. The Headquarters and London office are connected over a T3 line network that uses X.400 services.

Its e-mail system consists of ten MS Mail post offices: five in Garland, two in Los Angeles, and three in London. In this example, all the PCs are using the Microsoft Mail driver and the Microsoft Windows 95 operating system. This enables it to use the Microsoft Exchange client with its existing MS Mail post offices.

FIG. 8.1

A sample migration—
using the three-phase
method.

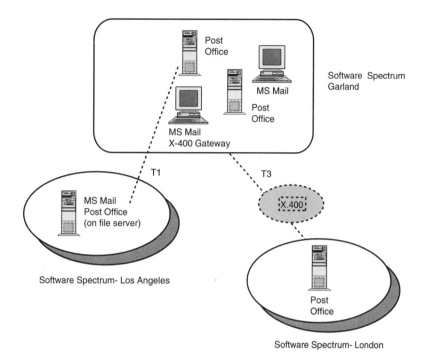

Phase One: Migrating Headquarters to Microsoft Exchange

Headquarters installs a Windows NT-based server with Microsoft Exchange Server on an existing Novell network. Then, using the built-in Migration tool, the company migrates its Microsoft Mail post offices at headquarters to Microsoft Exchange.

The Migration tool converts Microsoft Mail messages, Personal Address Book data, attachments, private folders, and meeting requests to the Microsoft Exchange format and creates new accounts on the Microsoft Exchange system. Microsoft Schedule+ 1.0 calendar files are automatically updated by the Microsoft Exchange group scheduling function. Because the X.400 gateway is integrated into Microsoft Exchange, this capacity is automatically installed with the initial setup.

At headquarters, they simultaneously start installing the Microsoft Exchange Server driver on each of the Windows 95-based workstations to access the Microsoft Exchange Server. Those still using the Mail 3.x driver can continue to communicate with other users of Microsoft Mail and Microsoft Exchange, but without the enhanced functionality provided by Microsoft Exchange. (See Table 8.1 for a comparison of Mail client versus Exchange client functionality.)

Installing Exchange Server consolidates the functions of three machines—the two Microsoft Mail post offices and the X.400 gateway—onto one machine. It also adds one stop administration, connection monitoring, and performance monitoring. Microsoft Exchange users can use Microsoft Mail 3.x gateways, and Microsoft Mail users can use the Microsoft Exchange gateways.

After the Microsoft Exchange driver is installed on all workstations, users in the Garland office have access to the complete functionality of Microsoft Exchange, including:

- Sending multiple messages to the same recipient
- Rich text formatting and OLE
- Information-sharing capabilities through public folders
- Flexible views
- Easy-to-use forms
- Improved group scheduling and task management
- Searching tools to save time locating addresses

Microsoft Exchange users in Garland can continue to communicate with their counterparts in Los Angeles and London. This enables the company to migrate in stages while still enabling all users to:

- Exchange mail messages with attached files and embedded objects
- Exchange meeting requests and free/busy information
- Take advantage of improved group scheduling and task management capabilities

Table 8.1   Client Feature Comparison After Phases of Migration

Feature	A	B	C
Rich text support	x	x	x
Auto reply	x	x	
Access to public folders		x	
Flexible views		x	x
Delegate access		x	
Remote functionality	x	x	x
Rich searches	x	x	
Group scheduling	x	x	x
Easy-to-use forms	x	x	x
Central forms registry	x		
OLE 2.0	x	x	

A—Microsoft Mail 3.x client/Microsoft Mail post office
B—Microsoft Exchange client/Microsoft Mail 3.x post office
C—Microsoft Exchange client/Microsoft Exchange Server

Phase Two: Coexistence

Next, the company installs Microsoft Exchange Server in the Garland office, and combines existing users of the two Microsoft Mail post offices on that server.

The organization still uses MS Mail post offices at the remote locations. Using the Microsoft Exchange Server as an MTA between the Microsoft Exchange Servers and the MS Mail post offices offers different advantages:

- *Auto routing.* The server automatically configures itself for efficient routing.

- *Load balancing.* If one communication link fails, the MTA will automatically reconfigure itself to balance the load over the remaining communication links.

- *Least-cost routing.* Enables administrators to assign costs to communications lines so the MTAs can intelligently route information over the line with the lowest cost. Combined with load-balancing, this provides the highest availability of lines at the lowest cost.

Software Spectrum also installs Microsoft Exchange drivers on all PCs at headquarters to access the Microsoft Exchange Server. At the end of phase two, all users in Garland and Los Angeles have access to the complete functionality of the Microsoft Exchange system. They can also continue to exchange messages with users in London via the X.400 connector through a "pass-through gateway." Mail Connector manages the directory exchange between Microsoft Exchange and Microsoft Mail during this coexistence phase.

Phase Three: Completing the Migration

In the final migration phase, the London office installs NT Server and Microsoft Exchange on both the server and the workstations. This consolidates the Microsoft Mail 3.x post office and Mail gateway onto one server. Now, users across the enterprise have full use of Microsoft Exchange's rich functionality and are able to share information with everyone else in their organization at any time.

The company has realized the cost savings of consolidating the functions of nine machines into three and has condensed the administration for all three offices onto one Windows NT-based workstation. They have a consistent enterprise-wide messaging and information exchange system with the features catalogued in the following list and can install additional Microsoft Exchange gateways to extend these capabilities beyond the enterprise:

- AutoSignature
- Blind carbon copy (BCC)
- Universal inbox in Windows 95
- Rich text
- Views
- Schedule+ 7.5/Outlook
- Built-in remote client

Implementing Client Migration

The Microsoft Exchange Windows clients can be used as clients for Microsoft Mail (PC) post offices. This is done by adding the Microsoft Mail service provider to the profile. This can be done before migration or before and during phased migration to move users to the new client while retaining the post office infrastructure.

Even if only the clients are migrated to Exchange, they will enjoy all the benefits listed at the end of the previous section. With this strategy, all users will also have a consistent user interface.

To install Microsoft Exchange client, users need the Profile Wizard, included with the client setup software. The Profile Wizard pulls default information for connecting to the post office from the MSMAIL.INI file.

N O T E To use the MS Mail post office, also called the MS Mail provider, you will need to make the Microsoft Mail (PC) provider the default for the client profile; for this you use the Setup Editor. The Setup Editor allows complete configuration of the Exchange client prior to installation on the user's PC. This is also true for installing the Microsoft Exchange provider. ■

After the client software is installed on the user's PC, the user then imports the contents of the Microsoft Mail Message File (MMF) file into the Exchange inbox format. If the MMF file is in the post office the user should first move the MMF file to the local disk or a viewable network share before importing the contents. If the MMF file is left on the post office, the contents will be migrated to Microsoft Exchange when the mailbox is migrated.

Once a user begins using Microsoft Exchange client, there is no easy way to migrate the messages they receive to an MMF or mailbag file. He or she can copy the messages to a shared folder and then retrieve them with the old client, but this does not guarantee privacy of the messages.

When you migrate the user's mailbox to Microsoft Exchange Server, you have two options:

■ Switch the profile over to connect only to Microsoft Exchange (single provider).
■ Switch the profile to connect to Microsoft Exchange and the old post office (dual provider).

Implementing Server Migration

The Mail Server or Exchange Server is the "provider." A single provider option is full migration from one messaging server to another. A dual provider strategy is one in which both messaging systems coexist and two servers or providers are used.

One-Step Migration

Depending on the size of your organization and your human resources, you may be able to do a one-step migration. This can happen overnight, on a weekend, or on company shutdown time. If your organization can't tolerate the downtime or doesn't have the resources to migrate everyone in a weekend, phased migration is the best choice.

Instant migration may be better for your organization if:

- There is little or no existing data to move from the old system.
- You have the human resources to migrate everyone in a night, weekend, or during a traditional downtime.
- All hardware and system software are in place.

One-step migration takes extra planning in the areas of:

- Replacing existing workflow applications
- User and help desk training
- Preparing for rollout and resource needs
- Preparing for contingencies

Should you choose to go with a single mail provider, like Exchange Server, the single provider option provides for these scenarios:

- Every mailbox on the post office is migrated.
- Only some mailboxes on a post office migrate, and their addresses change.

Update the global address list and the directory. Mail sent to the old addresses from the personal address books and personal address lists will be returned as non-deliverable (if you delete the old mailbox) or pile up in the old mailbox.

With a multi-phase migration, you have two "providers," MS Mail Post office and Exchange server, for instance. A dual provider provides for these scenarios:

- All mailboxes are migrated and addresses are changed.

  The users can still connect to the old post office and get mail that is sent to their old address, but as the global address list gets updated, new messages sent to them are routed to their Microsoft Exchange Server mailbox.
- Some mailboxes are migrated and addresses are not changed.

  Routing on the Microsoft Mail connector is not updated so that mail sent to these users from Microsoft Mail users still arrives at their old mailbox, but messages sent from Microsoft Exchange Server users are delivered to the new mailbox. The users can now send mail from their Microsoft Exchange Server mailboxes and use Microsoft Exchange Server public folders.

The drawback of these options is that the profile must be edited three times: first when the client is installed, again when the Microsoft Exchange Server provider is added, and again when the Microsoft Mail (PC) provider is removed.

When configured for dual providers, the use of the MS Mail provider should be limited to retrieving mail for the old mailbox. Mail addressed with the MS Mail address book will be delivered and can be replied to. Choose the Reply to All option on mail messages addressed to both Microsoft Mail mailboxes (not as Microsoft Exchange custom recipients) and Microsoft Exchange mailboxes will fail to reach the Microsoft Exchange mailboxes.

If the message is sent to Microsoft Mail mailboxes as custom recipients, the client transfers the message to the Microsoft Exchange server. The Microsoft Exchange server updates the Microsoft Exchange mailbox addresses when it transfers the message to the MS Mail Connector so they can be replied to by Microsoft Mail recipients.

Upgrading to Microsoft Exchange and the MS Mail Provider

Now that the one method for migration to Exchange has been discussed, now migrating the MMF files from MS Mail into the Exchange format is discussed. In addition, issues associated with upgrading from Schedule+ v1.0 clients to Exchange Schedule+ v7.0 clients are tackled.

Migrating MMF Files from Microsoft Mail for PC Networks 3.5   Microsoft Exchange client users must migrate their mail message files to a personal folder file. When MMFs are stored on a post office, you can use the MMFClean utility to manage their size and the age of messages (how long a message will be kept on file before it is automatically deleted). Personal folder files should not be stored on the post office.

The MMF Migration tool does not delete the MMF when it creates the personal folder file, move MMF files locally, or delete them after their contents are migrated to personal folder files.

Schedule+ Coexistence with the MS Mail Provider   Users who switch to the Microsoft Exchange client must also switch from Schedule+ 1.0 to Schedule+ 7.5. When they run Schedule+ 7.5 for the first time, it will migrate their CAL (Schedule+ 1.0 calendar format) file to SCD (Schedule+ 7.5 calendar format) file.

Schedule+ 7.5 can read CAL, POF (Schedule+ 1.0 post office free/busy times), and SCD files, but Schedule+ 1.0 can only read CAL and POF files. If your users make heavy use of Schedule+, switch everyone over to the new client at the same time. If some people switch to Schedule+ 7.5, the rest will not be able to view their calendars or act as their coworkers' delegate.

Migrating Partial Post Offices   Migrating everyone off a post office at the same time is not always possible. Some users are waiting for hardware upgrades. The migration might be a pilot test or a limited rollout. When migrating partial post offices, the following considerations are necessary:

   ■ Routing to old post offices must be maintained so that the remaining users continue to receive mail.

- Mail sent to migrated mailboxes that passes through Microsoft Mail (PC) gateways will be delivered to the Microsoft Mail (PC) mailbox, or returned as undeliverable.

- Directories in Microsoft Mail (PC) and with Microsoft Mail (PC) gateways that have the old mailbox address have to be updated immediately—the old address is invalid.

- For users who are still on Microsoft Mail (PC), any mail they received in the past from a migrated user can be replied to, but the reply will be delivered to the Microsoft Mail (PC) mailbox or returned as undeliverable.

- For users who are still on Microsoft Mail (PC), any Personal Address Book or Personal Address List entries they have for migrated mailboxes are invalid.

N O T E No routing changes are required or allowed when doing a partial post office migration. The mailboxes remaining on the post office need mail addressed to them to continue to be delivered.

Part of your migration plan needs to include how many mailboxes at a time will migrate to Microsoft Exchange servers. As a general rule, migrating the whole post office (every mailbox) will be easier to plan for, implement, and maintain than migrating a partial post office. Migrating a partial post office is more likely to occur during a pilot or limited rollout, when the number of users is small and the issues are easier to solve or work around. The following section explains why this is so, and gives examples of each of these scenarios.

Migrating Whole Post Offices If you migrate every mailbox on a post office, you can maintain original Network/post office/Mailbox Microsoft Mail address for each old mailbox as one of the proxy or e-mail addresses of the new mailbox. This has many advantages:

- With limited routing changes, mail continues to be delivered without interruption.

- Mail sent to migration mailboxes that passes through Microsoft Mail (PC) gateways will be delivered.

- Directories in Microsoft Mail (PC) post offices and foreign systems connected to them with Microsoft Mail (PC) gateways that have the old mailbox address do not have to be updated immediately—the old address is still valid.

- For users who are still on Microsoft Mail (PC), any mail they received in the past from a migrated user can be replied to.

- For users who are still on Microsoft Mail (PC), any Personal Address Book or Personal Address List entries they have for migrated mailboxes are still valid.

PC Mail Pass-Through Retaining the original e-mail address provides for pass-through from Microsoft Mail (PC) gateways. The Microsoft Mail connector post office must have an access component for the gateway installed. Because the Microsoft Mail type addresses for migrated mailboxes have not changed, the mail will be routed from the gateway to the Microsoft Mail connector, and from there to the Microsoft Exchange mailbox.

Personal Address Books for Users Who Haven't Migrated Personal Address Book entries function similarly to replies. For Microsoft Mail (PC) users, their Personal Address Book addresses continue to work for migrated mailboxes because the addresses are the same.

Migrated Personal Address Book entries will work for Microsoft Mail (PC) mailboxes that have not migrated. This means that if you do not update your Personal Address Book with the new Exchange e-mail addresses, some e-mail will still be directed to MS Mail mailboxes that no longer exist. Mail addressed to mailboxes that have since migrated will get routed to the Microsoft Mail connector. The Microsoft Mail connector does not have a post office configured with that address and will return the mail as undeliverable. This undeliverable mail can be readdressed from the Microsoft Exchange server global address list and be delivered normally.

There is no tool that updates the user's Personal Address Book entries as changes are made in the Microsoft Exchange server global address list. To prevent undeliverable mail, users can remove all personal entries of the MS type from their Personal Address Book after the entries are migrated to Microsoft Exchange mailboxes.

The Migration Package Elements

The following sections cover the main elements of Microsoft Exchange's Migration package. This package allows you to implement Exchange into environments with legacy mail systems. These tools assist with the extraction of e-mail addresses from the legacy systems and import them into Exchange.

The Migration Tools

There are several tools that assist with the migration from MS Mail to Exchange. These tools include the functionality to extract mailbox information from the legacy system. In addition, there is a server component called an MS Mail "server" post office. This post office resides on the Exchange server and can only be accessed by the Exchange and MS Mail MTAs.

The Source Extractor   There is a Source Extractor for every system such as MS Mail, PROFS, and the like. The Source Extractor extracts users, inboxes, folders, and address books from the source mail systems.

The following list is the components of the source extraction tool used to convert extracted addresses into the Exchange format and provide support information for the migration process. Other components include the directory agent to facilitate the dirsync process via the Exchange MS Mail server post office. Several other components include the free/busy connector to allow for group scheduling information and the pass-through connectivity to interconnect with Exchange.

- *Migration Assistant.* The Migration Assistant converts all extracted data from the source system to Microsoft Exchange.
- *Migration Wizard.* Microsoft Exchange includes a Migration Wizard to guide administrators through migration. There is an option included for one-step migration.

The Microsoft Mail Connector   The term *Connector* has taken the place of the Microsoft Mail Transfer Agent (MMTA) in MS Mail. The Connector is the main link between users of Exchange and Microsoft Mail (PC), as well as MS Mail gateways and Exchange gateways. There are three components to the Microsoft Mail Connector:

- *Connector MTA.* Connector MTA is a message transfer agent, similar to the MTA. It routes mail between a Microsoft Mail post office and the Connector post office, a Microsoft Mail gateway and the Microsoft Exchange server.
- *Connector Post Office.* Connector post office is the data file structure used to store messages in transit between users of Microsoft Exchange, Microsoft Mail, and gateways.
- *Microsoft Mail (PC) Interchange.* MS Mail (PC) Interchange manages the transfer and translation of messages stored in the Connector post office to the Microsoft Exchange MTA and vice versa.

Together, these components make up the Mail Connector, allowing Microsoft Exchange users to transparently send and receive messages and files, meeting requests, and free/busy information with users on MS Mail.

Directory Exchange Agent   The Directory Exchange Agent (DXA) in Microsoft Exchange enhances directory synchronization with flexible scheduling, better time zone management, and update scheduling. Its multithreaded design improves throughput. Because the DXA includes multiple server support, the directory synchronization load is distributed across multiple "dirsync" servers for increased reliability and faster response. This reduces address list maintenance, increases security, and assures that updates occur more promptly.

Microsoft Schedule+ Free and Busy Gateway   The Microsoft Schedule+ Free and Busy Gateway enables users who remain on Schedule+ version 1.0 using MS Mail 3.x servers to see free/busy information in the planner view of users who are on the new release of Schedule+ on the Microsoft Exchange Server computer, and vice-versa. The data from each server platform is replicated across the connector to appear to users on the other platform.

Pass Through Connectivity   Microsoft Exchange Server offers group distribution list support and enables MS Mail users to send messages to X.400 and SMTP environments through the Microsoft Mail Connector. Messages sent from the MS Mail 3.x users through the Microsoft Exchange Server computer can use the Microsoft Exchange X.400 Connector and the Internet Mail Connector to interchange messages with these environments. Alternatively, Microsoft Exchange users can send messages through any of the Microsoft Mail gateways, through the Microsoft Mail Connector.

Using the Migration Wizard

You can use the Migration Wizard to migrate one or more mailboxes on a Microsoft Mail for PC Networks post office. When each mailbox on the post office is migrated, you have a choice of what information to migrate.

The following is a list of available components to migrate into the Exchange environment. The list covers the components from the actual mailbox containing data to the Schedule+ file and then the group or shared folders and the personal address book entries on a user's local PC:

- Messages, attachments, private folders, and contents of mail message files (MMF)
- Schedule+ data
- Shared and group folders
- Personal Address Book entries

N O T E Make sure there is no mail activity during migration. ▓

The following preparations are recommended before migrating in order to ensure safe migration of data:

- The Migration Wizard and necessary files are installed with the Administrator program.
- Install the Microsoft Exchange Administrator program on a Windows NT computer with the Setup program.
- Compare free hard drive space on the server to the post office volume.

  The server should have plenty of available space, at least twice as much as the post office volume. If free hard disk space is less than twice the post office volume, you should watch available space with the Performance Monitor during migration. Stop migration if free space reaches less than 5M.

- Shut down the Microsoft Exchange server MTA, connector, and gateway services.

  Modify or shut down any server monitors that would restart these services. If these services are running while using the Migration Wizard and you need to restore your Microsoft Exchange server from backup, any mail they delivered during the failed migration attempt is lost.

- Shut down any MTA, external, or gateway programs that connect to this post office.

  MTA and external programs can be restarted after modifying their .INI file or command line options so they do not connect to this post office. The Migration Wizard requires that no mail be delivered to mailboxes during migration.

- Disconnect the clients.

  All users on both the post office and the Microsoft Exchange server must exit and log off their client programs. Use your network software with Microsoft Mail (PC) to check for connections to the post office share. Use the Administrator program on the Microsoft Exchange server to check Mailbox Logons and Public Folder Logons property sheets in the server's private and public information store properties, respectively.

  - If you are copying the post office to the Microsoft Exchange server for migration, copy it now. Once the copying is finished, you can restore MTA, external, gateway, and client connections.

■ Back up the Exchange server information store and directory.

Back up the post office. However, this is not a requirement because data on the post office is read, not deleted. You need read and write access to the post office because a datestamp is modified in each MMF as it is migrated.

To create the user list from a Microsoft Mail (PC) post office:

1. (Optional) Map a drive letter or connect to a file server where the post office resides. You need read and write access to the share or volume and have the name and password of the administrator.

2. Choose Programs with the taskbar, then select the Microsoft Exchange folder.

3. In the Microsoft Exchange folder, choose Microsoft Exchange Migration Wizard.

4. Select Migrate from Microsoft Mail for PC Networks, and choose the Next button.

5. Read the informational screen and choose the Next button.

6. In the Path to MS Mail Post office box, type the path to the post office.

   or

   Choose the Browse button to specify the path to the post office.

7. In the Account Name box, type the mailbox name of an administrator on the post office.

8. In the Password box, type the password for this mailbox and choose the Next button.

9. Select Two Step Migration and choose the Next button.

10. Select Extract a User List File and in the User List to Be Created box, type the path and file name of the new user list.

    or

    Choose the Browse button to specify the path and file name.

11. Choose the Next button.

12. In the Select Which Accounts You Would Like to Migrate box, choose the mailboxes you want to migrate.

    or

    Choose the Select All button to select all mailboxes.

13. Choose the Next button to create the user list file.

You can make changes as needed in the user list file. If you need to change the directory name of a mailbox, do it before the mailbox is created. Other fields can be changed now or later in this text file. To change them now, follow the process as outlined in the following paragraphs. To change them later, use the Administrator program to change them one at a time, or use the Directory Import command to change them in a batch mode.

To modify the user list file:

1. Make a backup copy of the user list file. You will need it later.

2. Open the user list file with a text editor.

3. Delete the first two lines that have post office information and save the file as text.

4. Open the modified user list file with a database program. The file is text, comma delimited, and the first row contains field names.

   The fields in Table 8.2 are in the user list. (The first two fields can't be changed, and the first six need to be kept in the same order.)

Table 8.2   User List Fields

Field	Contents
SFS_UserName	The mailbox name or alias of this mailbox in the post office. Do not change this.
SFS_FullName	The full or display name of this mailbox in the post office. Do not change this.
MigrateUser	Should be "Y" if mailbox is to be migrated and "N" if the mailbox should not be migrated.
Obj-Class	This field should be `mailbox`. Other valid values are `remote` for custom recipients and `dl` for distribution list.
Mode	Describes what should be done with this object—`create`, `modify`, and `delete` are valid options. The default is `create`.
Common-Name	The directory name of the mailbox. This can't be changed later without deleting the mailbox and re-creating it, so change it now to match your naming convention.
Display-Name	The display or friendly name as seen in the address book.
Given-Name	The first or given name of the mailbox's user.
Surname	The surname or last name of the mailbox's user.
Home-Server	The home server of the mailbox. You can move a mailbox within the site later without difficulty, but you should decide where each group of mailboxes is to be created.
Comment	This is the address book comment. It can be used to distinguish between two people with the same or similar names, or for notes about contacts for Schedule+ resources.
Assoc Windows-NT Account	Each mailbox needs an associated Windows NT account that has user access. On a Schedule+ resource account this can be a Windows NT group or account that is responsible for managing the resource, or the administrator who is going to sign into the account once to set up forwarding rules and Schedule+ access permissions.

* You can add additional directory import fields after Assoc-NT-Account.

5. After it is modified, export the file in CSV format.

6. Open the modified file and the backup file with a text editor. Copy the two lines from the backup file to the top of the modified file. Save the file as text.

After creating the user list and modifying it, you can migrate mailboxes from the post office to your site. This does not delete the mailboxes or remove mail, it only copies the information to the Microsoft Exchange servers where the new mailboxes are created.

To migrate mailboxes from a post office to a Microsoft Exchange server with a user list, follow these steps:

1. (Optional) Map a drive letter or connect to a file server where the post office resides. You need read and write access to the share or volume and have the name and password of the administrator.

2. Choose Programs with the taskbar, then select the Microsoft Exchange folder.

3. In the Microsoft Exchange folder, choose Microsoft Exchange Migration Wizard.

4. Select Migrate from Microsoft Mail for PC Networks, and choose the Next button.

5. Read the informational screen and choose the Next button.

6. In the Path to MS Mail Post office box, type the path to the post office.

   or

   Choose the Browse button to specify the path to the post office.

7. In the Account Name box, type the mailbox name of an administrator on the post office.

8. In the Password box, type the password for this mailbox and choose the Next button.

9. Select Two Step Migration and choose the Next button.

10. Select Use a User List File to Do a Migration and in the Existing User List File box, type the path and file name of the modified user list.

    or

    Choose the Browse button to select the file.

11. Choose the Next button.

12. Select the import options based on your needs (see Table 8.3).

Table 8.3 Import Options

Option	Description
Information to Create Mailboxes	Create mailboxes for the selected users in the user list file.
Personal E-Mail Messages	Copy messages and folders from the selected users mailbox and server-based MMF. You can select all messages or set a date range.

continues

Table 8.3 Continued

Option	Description
Shared Folders	Copy all shared folders to the public folder server.
Personal Address Books	Copy PAB entries in the MMFs and put them into the selected user's inbox in a special message.
Schedule Information	Copy calendar files from the CAL directory on the post office to a special message in the selected user's inbox.

13. Choose the Next button.

14. In the Enter a Server Name box, type the name of the destination Microsoft Exchange Server computer. Choose the Next button.

15. Select the directory container for the new mailboxes.

N O T E You cannot move a mailbox from one directory container to another after the mailbox has been created. ■

16. If you are using a mailbox template to reduce the work of setting up new mailboxes, choose the Browse button and select the template mailbox from the address list.

17. Choose the Next button.

18. In For Users That Don't Have Windows NT Accounts, choose one of the options (see Table 8.4).

Table 8.4 Options for Users Without NT Accounts

Option	Description
Create Accounts and Generate Random Passwords	Accounts are created with names that match the alias and random passwords. The passwords are written to the file BIMPORT.PSW in the working directory of the Migration Wizard. For users to log on to Windows NT, distribute these passwords to them.
Create Accounts and Use Alias as Password	Accounts are created with names and passwords that match the alias.
Don't Create Windows NT Accounts	No accounts are created and the mailboxes can't be used by anyone until an account is assigned later.

19. In the Choose a Windows NT Domain for New Accounts box, select the domain where the user's Windows NT accounts are to be located or created.

20. Choose the Next button to begin the migration process.

To migrate in one step from a Microsoft Mail (PC) post office, follow these steps:

1. (Optional) Map a drive letter or connect to a file server where the post office resides. You need read and write access to the share or volume and have the name and password of the administrator.

2. Choose Programs with the taskbar, then select the Microsoft Exchange folder.

3. In the Microsoft Exchange folder, choose Microsoft Exchange Migration Wizard.

4. Select Migrate from MS Mail for PC Networks, and choose the Next button.

5. Read the informational screen and choose the Next button.

6. In the Path to MS Mail Post office box, type the path to the post office.

   or

   Choose the Browse button to specify the path to the post office.

7. In the Account Name box, type the mailbox name of an administrator on the post office.

8. In the Password box, type the password for this mailbox and choose the Next button.

9. Select the One-Step Migration option, and choose the Next button.

10. Select the options based on your needs (see Table 8.5).

Table 8.5 One-Step Migration Options

Option	Description
Information to Create Mailboxes	Creates mailboxes for the selected users in the user list file.
Personal E-Mail Messages	Copies all messages and folders from the selected user's mailbox and server-based MMF. You can select all or set a date range.
Shared Folders	Select this check box to copy all shared folders to the public folder server of this server.
Personal Address Books	When selected, PAB entries in MMFs are copied and put into the selected user's inbox in a special message.
Schedule Information	Calendar files are copied from the CAL directory on the post office to a special message in the selected user's inbox.

11. Choose the Next button.

12. In the Select Which Accounts You Would Like to Migrate box, choose the mailboxes you want to migrate.

    or

    Choose the Select All button to select all mailboxes.

13. Choose the Next button.

14. In the Enter a Server Name box, type the name of the destination Microsoft Exchange Server computer. Choose the Next button.

15. Select the directory container for the new mailboxes.

N O T E You cannot move a mailbox from one directory container to another after the mailbox has been created. ■

16. Choose the Next button.

17. Choose one of the options in For Users That Don't Have Windows NT Accounts (see Table 8.6).

18. In the Choose a Windows NT Domain for New Accounts box, select the domain where the user's Windows NT accounts are located or to be created.

19. Choose the Next button to begin the migration process.

Table 8.6 One-Step Migration, Options for Users with No NT Accounts

Option	Description
Create Accounts and Generate Random passwords	Accounts are created with names that match the alias and random passwords. The passwords are written to the file BIMPORT.PSW in the working directory of the Migration Wizard. For users to log on to Windows NT, you need to distribute these passwords to them.
Create Accounts and Use Alias as Password	Accounts are created with names and passwords that match the alias.
Don't Create Windows NT Accounts	No accounts are created and the mailboxes can't be used by anyone until an account is assigned later.

Migrating MMFs

As explained earlier in the migration tools section of this chapter, MMFs can be migrated by the user to personal folder files, or by the Administrator to the private information store, depending on the location of the MMFs.

Network Errors

If there is a network failure during MMF migration, the client or Migration Wizard retries the network connection every ten minutes to reestablish a connection. An error message is displayed during this retry time.

Error Log

Any errors during client MMF migration are logged to a file in the client directory with a file name the same as the MMF name and an extension of .LOG. You can view them in NotePad or any other text editor.

To import an MMF file with the Windows NT or Windows 16 client, follow these steps:

1. From the File menu, choose Import.
2. In the Specify File to Import window, select the MMF file.
3. In the Import Mail Data window, type the password for this MMF file.

   Select the Import Messages check box to import all messages and folders.

   Select the Import Personal Address Book Entries check box to create a Microsoft Exchange PAB file.
4. Choose OK.

After Using the Migration Tool

Depending on your migration strategy, you need to delete the Microsoft Mail (PC) mailboxes or hide the post office. It is possible to make a full backup of the updated information store.

From Here...

Exchange's Migration tools give you powerful interoperability with existing MS Mail systems. After planning the steps and phases to migration, Administrators (with the help of tools like Migration Wizard), can create a smooth transition to Exchange, so they and their users can sooner get down to the business of information exchange.

- Chapter 7, "Planning Connections to Microsoft Mail Systems," gives you the information you need to have an MS Mail and Exchange system coexist.
- Chapter 11, "Migrating from External Systems," rounds out the discussion of how to move data from other kinds of mail systems.

Migrating from Lotus cc:Mail

Microsoft Exchange Connector for cc:Mail enables administrators to seamlessly integrate Exchange Server and cc:Mail systems, enabling them to exchange messages and synchronize directories. It supports both DB6 and DB8 and enables customers to take a phased approach to migration that causes minimal disruption within an organization.

Migration, or moving users from one messaging system to another, can also include mailboxes and attachments, addresses, and scheduling information from your existing system. We will discuss planning methods for interoperability and migrating users to Microsoft Exchange Server. Microsoft Exchange is packed with migration features that support multiple scenarios for interconnecting to other Mail systems. Tools like Migration Wizard simplify the migration process and ensure a smooth transition to Microsoft Exchange. ■

Planning, Architecture Overview

The minimal version of software required for the Microsoft Exchange cc:Mail Connector with cc:Mail is Lotus cc:Mail DB6, Post Office Database version 6.0, cc:Mail Import version 5.15, and Export Version 5.14. Support for cc:Mail DB8 requires Lotus cc:Mail Post Office Database version 8 and cc:Mail Import/Export version 6.0.

The Microsoft Exchange Connector for Lotus cc:Mail

The Microsoft Exchange Connector for Lotus cc:Mail enables administrators to seamlessly integrate Microsoft Exchange into cc:Mail environments. Once installed, Exchange Server and cc:Mail systems can exchange messages and synchronize directories. The cc:Mail Connector supports both DB6 and DB8 cc:Mail post offices. By introducing Exchange Server into a cc:Mail environment, cc:Mail users will benefit from Exchange Server's strong connectivity to the Internet and other systems. Also, customers can take a phased approach to migration that will cause minimal disruption within an organization.

The cc:Mail Connector has fast performance and offers more than just text—the cc:Mail Connector can transfer messages, attachments, embedded messages, OLE attachments, and file links. The Connector does not support all of the linking features in the Microsoft Exchange Client. A Microsoft Exchange Server system enables embedding objects into the message body, linking objects to the message body, inserting links to files, inserting shortcuts to Microsoft Exchange folders, and inserting shortcuts to Internet sites.

The cc:Mail Connector offers enhanced connectivity because you can connect cc:Mail systems to Microsoft Exchange Servers and immediately take advantage of Exchange's Internet Mail Service, which provides several times the message transfer of Lotus' SMTP gateway and MIME compatibility. Also, you can use any other Exchange Connector or MS Mail gateway through the cc:Mail Connector.

How the Connector Works

Microsoft Exchange Server uses the Connector and cc:Mail Import and Export programs to communicate with cc:Mail systems. The connector for cc:Mail is a Windows NT Service that transfers messages between Microsoft Exchange Server and cc:Mail. It also synchronizes some or all of the Microsoft Exchange global address lists (GAL) with the cc:Mail directory.

When a message is submitted to the Microsoft Exchange Server message transfer agent (MTA) for a cc:Mail recipient, it is transferred to the Microsoft Exchange Server information store. The Connector for cc:Mail Service retrieves the messages, converts it to ASCII file format, converts attachments as needed, and places the messages in the Connector Store. If the Import program can't deliver the message, a non-delivery report (NDR) is sent back to the sender. See Figure 9.1 for an overview of the components of the cc:Mail Connector.

FIG. 9.1

Architectural layout of
the cc:Mail Connector.

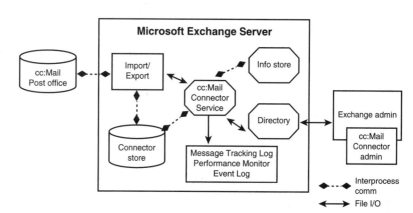

Directory Synchronization in cc:Mail is achieved as a scheduled, or on-demand, process that performs a full synchronization of the cc:Mail Directory with the Exchange directory. This process uses the Import and Export programs provided by cc:Mail.

The process of sending a message from a cc:Mail client to a Microsoft Exchange recipient is initiated by the cc:Mail Connector service. This service spawns the Export process, which places the requested information into a file in the Connector Store. This file is then retrieved by the cc:Mail Connector service and processed into an Import Container specified during the setup of the Connector. The Import Container can be any Exchange Recipients Container including the GAL.

When a message is sent from a Microsoft Exchange client to a cc:Mail recipient, the process is initiated by the cc:Mail Connector service as well. The service again spawns the Import process. Before this can take place, the IMPORT.EXE program must have data to import. The cc:Mail Connector service retrieves all Exchange recipient information from the Directory Service and that information is placed into a file in the Connector Store. These addresses are then imported into the cc:Mail Post Office.

Figure 9.2 shows the Connector for cc:Mail and the information required to connect to a post office. The configuration and setup for message transfer only requires a post office name, path, and password. No drilling down is necessary on different forms to get connected as with the cc:Mail MTA. Directory synchronization only requires a basic configuration of what you want to export and what you want to import.

FIG. 9.2

Post Office/Connector.
Information required for
the Connection to a
cc:Mail Post Office

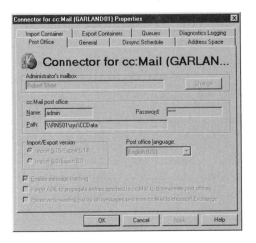

Using Multiple Connectors to cc:Mail

Directory synchronization is flexible and easy to configure. Synchronize only entries or types
of entries that you want between the two systems. You can synchronize cc:Mail mailing lists
and bulletin boards, as well as all types of Exchange recipients.

The Microsoft Exchange cc:Mail Connector is fully integrated with Windows NT. Performance
Monitor counters exhibit transfer rates, queue sizes, non-delivery occurrences, and directory-
synched entries. Events are logged to Windows NT Event Log in several different categories.
Read receipt and non-deliverable reports are generated for both systems to use link monitors
for determining if there is connectivity between your downstream post offices.

If you have many cc:Mail post offices within your organization or multiple cc:Mail post offices
spread over a large area, you can set up multiple connectors to link all cc:Mail and Microsoft
Exchange Servers. From the cc:Mail perspective, each Microsoft Exchange Server site
appears to be one large cc:Mail post office, regardless of the number of servers or recipients in
that site.

When planning multiple outgoing routes to one or more connectors to cc:Mail, consider the
following:

- Installing a connector on any or all Microsoft Exchange Server computers in your site,
  depending on your messaging traffic.

- Using identical address information in the Address Space property pages of two or more
  connectors to cc:Mail to route messages.

- Installing at least one Microsoft Exchange Server 5.0 in every site that indirectly
  communicates with cc:Mail. Microsoft Exchange Server 5.0 is required for cc:Mail
  address generation of Microsoft Exchange Server recipients.

Lotus cc:Mail Address Generation enables cc:Mail users to send mail to Microsoft Exchange
users—the Microsoft Exchange Server users must have an address of type CCMAIL.

Microsoft Exchange Server automatically generates a cc:Mail address for each recipient based on the site address. This enables a cc:Mail user to send mail to any Exchange user.

When the connector is initially in a site, the cc:Mail e-mail address generator creates an address of type CCMAIL (username at siteproxy) for every recipient, public folder, distribution list, and custom recipient in the site. The administrator configures the cc:Mail e-mail address format in the Site Addressing property page for the site.

Using the Migration Wizard

Once your Microsoft Exchange Server and Lotus cc:Mail systems are connected, it is easy to enable them to coexist or to migrate from cc:Mail to Microsoft Exchange. Microsoft Exchange Server offers a Migration Wizard to assist you with migrating. The cc:Mail Migration Tool is tightly integrated and enables you to upgrade custom recipients to mailboxes and retain former cc:Mail addresses so that old mail on both systems will be redirected to the new Exchange mailbox. The Migration Wizard also copies cc:Mail files to the recipient's Exchange mailbox and copies BBS (bulletin board systems) to Exchange public folders.

The Migration Wizard assists you with the creation of new NT accounts, and you can select how you want the Windows NT accounts for migrated users created (accounts can be created and given a random password). With the first method, you create Windows NT accounts for each mailbox and generate random passwords. The account name and passwords are written to the file ACCOUNT.PASSWORD in the working directory of the Migration Wizard. The second method is to create accounts and use an alias as the password. The final option is to not create Windows NT accounts that match the alias of a mailbox and create the mailbox without an associated Windows NT account with the method; no one will be able to access this mailbox until a Windows NT account is associated with it.

Figure 9.3 shows the options the wizard offers for creating Windows NT accounts during migration.

FIG. 9.3

The migration wizard is used to Extract users from cc:Mail and Import them into Microsoft Exchange.

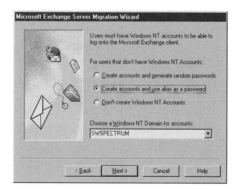

Migration Strategy and Planning

Microsoft Exchange Server has many migration tools to be used with Lotus cc:Mail. As you plan your migration, you will need to consider the following:

- What level of migration coexistence, mailbox migration, mailbox creation, or a combination of these will be best for your organization?
- Should all users be migrated, or only a subset of users?
- Do users have all the hardware necessary, or will migration occur in phases?
- What connectivity issues need to be addressed?
- Which users should migrate first?

Migration Levels from Full Migration to Coexistence

There are three levels of migration: coexistence, mailbox creation, and mailbox migration. The type you choose depends on how much data you want to move from your existing system to Microsoft Exchange, as follows:

- *Establish coexistence with an existing system.* This level enables users on both cc:Mail and Exchange to exchange mail. You have a chance to test connections between the two systems—addresses are extracted from the existing system and added as custom recipients in Microsoft Exchange. This provides a foundation for migrating users to Microsoft Exchange, usually before actual migration.
- *Create new Microsoft Exchange Server mailboxes without data.* At this level, only user account information is copied from the existing system. This creates empty mailboxes and, as an option, Windows NT accounts. This approach is used to migrate users without migrating their data, either with a plan to migrate their data later, or to skip migrating the data altogether.
- *Migrate mailbox contents.* At this level, mailbox contents are copied (not moved) from the cc:Mail to Microsoft Exchange Server mailboxes. The contents include messages, attachments, and calendars. This enables the user to use Microsoft Exchange without any data loss. This can follow coexistence and mailbox creation, or it can be combined with those steps for a quick migration.

You can use one of these three migration levels exclusively, or you can use all three as part of your migration plan. For example, after you install your first new Exchange server, you can migrate addresses from cc:Mail. For a test run, you can create new mailboxes without data. Once your testing is complete, you can migrate the mailbox contents to the new mailboxes and have the users upgrade their clients to Microsoft Exchange-based clients.

The following list describes issues associated with a migration from cc:Mail to Exchange:

- Migration testing shows that high volumes of data can take weeks or even months to migrate.
- Hardware used for the existing system needs to be freed up in early phases for redeployment during later phases.

■ Existing messaging applications are needed in some departments until they can be replaced with Microsoft Exchange public folders and custom form functionality.

■ Not all departments have the budget to upgrade at the same time.

■ Be sure your help desk group is able to handle the short spike of requests a quick migration is likely to create.

■ Investigate if departments have the hardware or system software to upgrade now.

■ Microsoft Exchange should be tested in a pilot with non-mission-critical users.

■ Keep in mind that Microsoft Exchange clients are not available for all platforms or networks.

Part

II

Ch

9

The following is a list of the types or levels of migration from cc:Mail to Exchange. You should choose the proper phase for your organization:

■ *Single-phase migration.* Gives users some of the enhanced features before migration while you are planning and testing the enterprise design.

■ *Multi-phase migration.* Gives all users a common user interface as you migrate mailboxes in stages.

■ *Multi-phase migration with dual access.* Enables users to retrieve mail from their old mailboxes after their mailboxes have been migrated to Microsoft Exchange Server.

Taking into consideration the previous two lists, you should be developing an idea of the migration strategy for your organization. As you plan your organization's new messaging infrastructure, you'll probably want to break down the project into steps. The major steps of the migration process can be divided as follows:

1. Connect Microsoft Exchange Client to existing systems.
2. Create directory and mailbox entries.
3. Extract and load accounts.
4. Set up directory synchronization.
5. Set up connectivity with the gateway.
6. Migrate server contents.
7. Move user's data.
8. Update the directory.

Now that you are aware of the issues, phases, and steps to migrating cc:Mail to Exchange, keep in mind the effect of these items on your organization. The next section takes the previous lists and applies them to an actual organization.

One-Step Migration

Depending on the size of your organization and your staff, you may be able to do a one-step migration. This can happen overnight, on a weekend, or on company shutdown time. If your organization can't tolerate the downtime or doesn't have the resources to migrate everyone in a weekend, phased migration is the best choice.

Instant migration may be better for your organization if the following applies:

- There is little or no existing data to move from the old system.
- You have enough people to migrate everyone in a night, weekend, or during a traditional downtime.
- All hardware and system software is in place.

One-step migration takes extra planning in the areas of:

- Replacing existing workflow applications.
- User and help desk training.
- Preparing for rollout and resource needs.
- Preparing for contingencies.

Should you choose to go with a single mail provider, such as Exchange Server, the single provider option provides for these scenarios:

- Every mailbox on the cc:Mail post office is migrated.
- Only some mailboxes on a post office migrate, and their addresses change.

Update the GAL and the directory. Mail sent to the old addresses from the personal address books and personal address lists will be returned as non-deliverable (if you delete the old mailbox) or pile up in the old mailbox.

With a multi-phase migration, you have two "providers:" cc:Mail Post office and Exchange Server, for instance. A dual provider provides for these scenarios:

- *All mailboxes are migrated and addresses are changed.* The users can still connect to the old post office and get mail that is sent to their old address, but as the GAL is updated, new messages sent to them are routed to their Microsoft Exchange Server mailbox.
- *Some mailboxes are migrated and addresses are not changed.* Routing on the Microsoft cc:Mail Connector is not updated, so mail sent to these users from Lotus cc:Mail users still arrives at their old mailbox, but messages sent from Microsoft Exchange Server users are delivered to the new mailbox. The users can now send mail from their Microsoft Exchange Server mailboxes and use Microsoft Exchange Server public folders.

The drawback of these options is that the profile must be edited three times: First, when the client is installed, again when the Microsoft Exchange Server provider is added, and again when the Lotus cc:Mail (PC) provider is removed.

When configured for dual providers, the use of the Microsoft cc:Mail provider should be limited to retrieving mail from the old mailbox. Mail addressed with the cc:Mail address book will be delivered and can be replied to. Choosing the Reply to All option on mail messages addressed to both Lotus cc:Mail mailboxes (not as Microsoft Exchange custom recipients) and Microsoft Exchange mailboxes will fail to reach the Microsoft Exchange mailboxes.

If the message is sent to Lotus cc:Mail mailboxes as custom recipients, the client transfers the message to the Microsoft Exchange Server. The Microsoft Exchange Server updates the

Microsoft Exchange mailbox address when it transfers the message to the Microsoft cc:Mail Connector, so they can be replied to by Lotus cc:Mail recipients.

Introduction to the Three-Phase Method

Large organizations might consider phased migrations, concentrating on more challenging sites prior to the major Exchange rollout. There also may be longer periods of coexistence with legacy mail. Smaller organizations, by contrast, would most likely be able to do a very quick migration—almost instantaneous.

If you belong to a large organization, your migration plan will probably take place in three basic phases:

1. Installing Exchange Server centrally.
2. Migrating users or branch offices and coexisting with legacy systems, like cc:Mail.
3. Completing migration in remote locations.

Sample Migration with the Three-Phase Method

A three-phased approach is used to simplify the task of migration. Inside each phase may be numerous individual tasks. On a high level, these three phases apply to any organization. The following sample walks you through the migration process for a larger organization.

Software Spectrum has its headquarters in Garland, Texas and offices in Los Angeles, Seattle, and Dublin (see Figure 9.4). The three American offices are connected over T1 lines. The headquarters and Dublin offices are connected over a wide-area X.25 network that uses X.400 services.

FIG. 9.4
Software Spectrum's
current cc:Mail system.

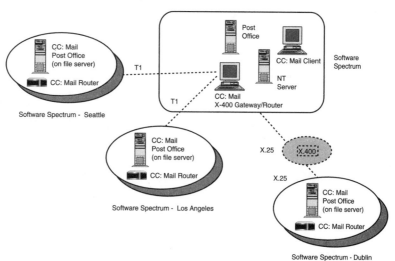

Its e-mail system consists of four Lotus cc:Mail Post Offices, with one in each office. In this example, all the PCs are using Lotus cc:Mail and Microsoft Windows 95.

Phase One: Migrating Headquarters to Microsoft Exchange

Garland installs a Windows NT and Microsoft Exchange Server on an existing Microsoft NT 4.0 network. Then, the cc:Mail Connector and X.400 are installed. The connector for Lotus cc:Mail is used to transfer messages between an Exchange organization and Lotus cc:Mail systems. It provides a method of directory synchronization between the two systems. An entire cc:Mail network can be connected to an Exchange organization using a single connector or multiple connectors.

You need to test each cc:Mail connector and both the cc:Mail and Microsoft Exchange clients. Before you send a test message from Microsoft Exchange client to a cc:Mail recipient, you need to create a custom recipient address for the mailbox you are sending the test message to. Once the address is created, the recipient appears in your personal address list. You must know the post office name and mailbox name for the recipient. You can use the cc:Mail Administrator program to find this information. Then to test the outbound side of the cc:Mail connector, you should send a test message from a Microsoft Exchange client to a cc:Mail recipient.

Next, send a test message from a cc:Mail client to a Microsoft Exchange recipient. This determines if the inbound side of the connector is functioning correctly. Once the address is created, the recipient appears in your address list. You must know the cc:Mail address for the Microsoft Exchange recipient. This information can be found in the Microsoft Exchange Server Administrator program. Before you send a test message from a cc:Mail client to a Microsoft Exchange recipient, you need to create a recipient address for the mailbox you are sending the test message to.

Using the built-in Migration tool, the company migrates its Lotus cc:Mail post office at headquarters to Microsoft Exchange. The Migration tool converts cc:Mail messages, attachments, embedded messages, and OLE attached file links. Scheduling data is converted to text and can be imported in Schedule+. The Migration Wizard also enables users of the new system to coexist productively with existing systems during and after the migration process.

At headquarters in Garland, they simultaneously start installing the Microsoft Exchange client on each of the Windows 95-based workstations and migrating mailboxes from the cc:Mail system to Microsoft Exchange Server. This gives those users access to the Microsoft Exchange Server. Those still using the Lotus cc:Mail client can continue to communicate with other users of Microsoft Exchange but without the enhanced functionality provided by Microsoft Exchange.

Installing Exchange Server consolidates the functions of three machines in the Garland office (the Lotus cc:Mail post office, cc:Mail Router, and X.400 gateway) onto one machine. Microsoft Exchange users can use cc:Mail gateways, and cc:Mail users can use the Microsoft Exchange gateways.

It also adds one-stop administration, connection monitoring, and performance monitoring. Windows NT Server Performance Monitor, which comes with NT, is a tool that can be used with Microsoft Exchange Server. It provides charting, alerting, and reporting capabilities that reflect current activity along with ongoing logging. You can also open log files at a later time for browsing and charting. Performance Monitor is located in the Administrative Tools group.

Monitoring involves viewing discrete components of the system. The connector for cc:Mail has ten performance counters associated with it.

After the Microsoft Exchange client is installed on all workstations, users in the Garland office have access to the complete functionality of Microsoft Exchange, including:

- Sending multiple messages to the same recipient
- Rich-text formatting and OLE
- Information-sharing capabilities through public folders
- Flexible views
- Easy-to-use forms
- Improved group scheduling and task management
- Searching tools to save time locating addresses and the like

Microsoft Exchange users in Garland can continue to communicate with their counterparts in Los Angeles, Seattle, and Dublin. This enables the company to migrate in stages while still enabling all users to perform the following:

- Exchange mail messages with attachments.
- View read and undeliverable receipts.
- Take advantage of improved group scheduling and task management capabilities.

Phase Two: Coexistence

Next, the company installs Microsoft Exchange Server in the Los Angeles office. The Exchange Server will be configured with cc:Mail and a Microsoft Exchange Site connector. The Microsoft Exchange Server in Garland will be configured with a site connector to Los Angeles. Seattle and Dublin are still using cc:Mail post offices. Using the Microsoft Exchange Server as an MTA between the Microsoft Exchange Servers and the cc:Mail post offices offers different advantages: In the future, after all cc:Mail post offices have been migrated to Microsoft Exchange Servers, load balancing can be enhanced by adding an additional site connector. The following are reasons for adding additional connectors:

- *Auto Routing.* The server automatically configures itself for efficient routing.
- *Load Balancing.* If one communication link fails, the MTA will automatically reconfigure itself to balance the load over the remaining communication links.
- *Least-cost routing.* Enables administrators to assign costs to communications lines so the MTAs can intelligently route information over the line with the lowest cost. Combined with load balancing, this provides the highest availability of lines at the lowest cost.

Software Spectrum also installs Microsoft Exchange clients on all PCs in Los Angeles to access the Microsoft Exchange Server. At the end of phase two, all users in Garland and Los Angeles have access to the complete functionality of the Microsoft Exchange system. They can also continue to exchange messages with users in Dublin via the X.400, and the cc:Mail Connector manages the directory exchange between Microsoft Exchange and cc:Mail during this coexistence phase.

Part

II

Ch

9

Phase Three: Completing the Migration

In the final migration phase, the Seattle and Dublin offices install Microsoft Exchange on both the server and on the Windows 95 workstations. This consolidates the cc:Mail post office and router/gateway onto one server at each site. Now, users across the enterprise have full use of Microsoft Exchange's rich functionality and are able to share information with everyone else in their organization at any time. At this time, all sites exchange e-mail on Microsoft Exchange Server using site connectors between sites in America and the X.400 connector to Dublin. The Lotus cc:Mail system has been completely migrated to Microsoft Exchange Server.

The company has realized the cost savings of consolidating the functions of eight machines into four and has condensed the administration for all four offices onto one Windows NT-based workstation. They have a consistent enterprise-wide messaging and information exchange system and can install additional Microsoft Exchange gateways to extend these capabilities beyond the enterprise.

Additional Tips—Implementing Microsoft Exchange Client

The migration of the Microsoft Exchange client comes after the foundation of the Microsoft Exchange Server is in place. The Microsoft Exchange Server requires the appropriate site connectors and cc:Mail connectors to enable communication and directory synchronization between Microsoft Exchange sites and cc:Mail systems. Once the Microsoft Exchange Server is installed at your site and all the necessary connectors to support your environment are configured and tested, it is time to migrate your clients.

Once the Microsoft Exchange Client is installed on the user workstation, the client's data needs to be migrated. Before migrating groups of users, it is always recommended to have users delete old messages. Schedule this over a period of a week or so to allow users to perform this task. In addition to the clients cleaning up the mailbox, administrators should perform their normal cc:Mail post office maintenance such as backups and reclaims.

The Microsoft Exchange Migration Wizard simplifies the migration process and ensures a smooth transition to Microsoft Exchange. When using the Microsoft Exchange Migration Wizard, you are prompted for information such as the path name for the migration files, the Exchange Server you want the mailboxes added to, the Recipient container for the new mailboxes, and the Windows NT domain you want the accounts added to. The Migration Wizard enables you to migrate large numbers of recipients; when doing so, you can select a template account that contains default restrictions and properties for created accounts. Additionally, information and screen shots of the Migration Wizard are discussed later in this chapter.

Implementing Server Migration

The cc:Mail Server or Exchange Server is the provider. A *single-provider option* is full migration from one messaging server to another. A *dual-provider strategy* is one where both messaging systems coexist and two servers or providers are used.

Upgrading to Microsoft Exchange—the Lotus cc:Mail Provider

Now that we have discussed the one method for migration to Exchange, we will now discuss migrating the cc:Mail files from cc:Mail into the Exchange format. Additionally, we will discuss issues associated with upgrading from Lotus Organizer clients to Exchange Schedule+ clients.

Migrating cc:Mail Files to the Microsoft Exchange Server   Microsoft Exchange client users must migrate their mail message files to a personal folder file. Again it is recommended to have users delete old messages, and it is a good idea to allow some time for users to perform this task. In addition to the clients cleaning up their mailboxes, administrators should perform their normal cc:Mail post office maintenance of backups and reclaims. The Migration Wizard does not delete the cc:Mail files when it creates the personal folder file; after their contents are migrated and the client has been tested, it is recommended to delete the old files.

Part
II
Ch
9

Currently scheduled data from Lotus Organizer is converted to text and then can be imported into Schedule+ or Outlook.

Migrating Partial Post Offices   Migrating everyone off of a post office at the same time is not always possible. When migrating partial post offices, the following considerations are necessary:

- Routing to old post offices must be maintained so that the remaining users continue to receive mail.

- Mail sent to migrated mailboxes that passes through Lotus cc:Mail gateway will be delivered to Lotus cc:Mail mailbox, or returned as undeliverable.

- Directories in Lotus cc:Mail and with Lotus cc:Mail gateway that have the old mailbox address have to be updated immediately—the old address is invalid.

- For users who are still on Lotus cc:Mail, any mail they received in the past from a migrated user can be replied to, but the reply will be delivered to the Lotus cc:Mail mailbox or returned as undeliverable.

- For users who are still on Lotus cc:Mail, any Personal Address Book or personal address list entries they have for migrated mailboxes are invalid.

N O T E   No routing changes are required or allowed when doing a partial post office migration. The mailboxes remaining on the post office need mail addressed to them in order to continue being delivered.

Part of your migration plan needs to include how many mailboxes at a time will migrate to Microsoft Exchange servers. As a general rule, migrating the whole post office (every mailbox) will be easier to plan for, implement, and maintain than migrating a partial post office. Migrating a partial post office is more likely to occur during a pilot or limited rollout, when the number of users is small and the issues are easier to solve or work around. The following section explains why this is so, and gives examples of each of these scenarios.

Migrating Whole Post Offices   If you migrate every mailbox on a post office, you can maintain original network/post office/Mailbox Lotus cc:Mail addresses for each old mailbox as one of the proxy or e-mail addresses of the new mailbox. This has many advantages:

- With limited routing changes, mail continues to be delivered without interruption.

- Mail sent to migration mailboxes that passes through Lotus cc:Mail gateways is delivered.

- Directories in Lotus cc:Mail post offices and foreign systems connected to them with Lotus cc:Mail gateways that have the old mailbox address do not have to be updated immediately—the old address is still valid.

- For users who are still on Lotus cc:Mail, any mail they received in the past from a migrated user can be replied to.

- For users who are still on Lotus cc:Mail, any Personal Address Book or personal address list entries they have for migrated mailboxes is still valid.

Mail Pass-Through   Retaining the original e-mail address provides for pass-through from Lotus cc:Mail gateways. The Microsoft cc:Mail Connector to the post office must have an access component for the gateway installed. Because the Lotus cc:Mail type addresses for migrated mailboxes have not changed, the mail will be routed from the gateway to the Microsoft cc:Mail Connector and from there to the Microsoft Exchange mailbox.

Personal Address Books for Users Who Haven't Migrated   Personal Address Books entries function similarly to replies. For cc:Mail users, their Personal Address Book addresses continue to work for migrated mailboxes, because the addresses are the same.

Migrated personal address book entries will work for cc:Mail mailboxes that have not migrated. This means that if you do not update your Personal Address Book with the new Exchange e-mail addresses, some e-mail will still be directed to cc:Mail mailboxes that no longer exist. Mail addressed to mailboxes that have since migrated will be routed to the Microsoft cc:Mail Connector. The Microsoft cc:Mail Connector does not have a post office configured with that address and will return the mail as undeliverable. This undeliverable mail can be re-addressed from the Microsoft Exchange server GAL and can be delivered.

There is no tool that updates the user's Personal Address Book entries as changes are made in the Microsoft Exchange server GAL. To prevent undeliverable mail, users should remove all personal entries referencing clients migrated from their Personal Address Book, after the cc:Mail client is migrated to Microsoft Exchange mailboxes.

The Migration Package Elements

The following sections cover the main elements of Microsoft Exchange's Migration package. This package enables you to implement Exchange into environments with legacy mail systems. These tools assist with the extraction of e-mail addresses from the legacy systems and import them into Exchange.

The Source Extractor   There is a Source Extractor for every system such as Microsoft Mail, Lotus cc:Mail, Novell GroupWise, and PROFS. The Source Extractor extracts users, inboxes, folders, and address books from the source mail systems.

The following list contains the components of the source extraction tool used to convert extracted addresses into the Exchange format and provide support information for the migration process.

- *The Migration Assistant.* Converts all extracted data from the source system to Microsoft Exchange.

- *The Migration Wizard.* Included in Microsoft Exchange to guide administrators through migration. There is an option included for one-step migration and two-step migrations.

Passthrough Connectivity   Microsoft Exchange Server offers group distribution list support and enables cc:Mail users to send messages to X.400 and SMTP environments through the Microsoft cc:Mail Connector. Messages sent from the cc:Mail users through the Microsoft Exchange Server computer could use the Microsoft Exchange X.400 connector and the Internet Mail Connector to interchange messages with these environments. Alternatively, Microsoft Exchange users can send messages through any of the Lotus cc:Mail gateways through the Microsoft cc:Mail Connector.

After Using the Migration Tool

Depending on your migration strategy, you will need to delete the cc:Mail mailboxes or hide the post office. It is possible to make a full backup of the updated information store.

From Here...

Exchange's Migration tools give you powerful interoperability with existing Microsoft Mail, Lotus cc:Mail, and Novell GroupWise systems. After planning the steps and phases to migration, administrators (with the help of tools like Migration Wizard) can create a smooth transition to Exchange so they and their users can get down to the business of information exchange sooner.

For more information, refer to the following chapters:

- Chapter 11, "Migrating from External Systems," rounds out the discussion of how to move data from other kinds of mail systems.

- Chapter 21, "Configuring X.400 Connections," explains messaging between Exchange and a foreign X.400 system.

- Chapter 22, "Setting Up SMTP Connections," shows how Exchange provides Internet electronic mail.

- Chapter 24, "Exchange Performance Tuning and Capacity Planning," for details on how to tune up Exchange after a major migration.

Part

II

Ch

9

CHAPTER 10

Installing Exchange in a Netware Environment

There are many issues you must confront when installing Exchange in a Netware environment. They range in nature from technical considerations to organizational concerns. You need to understand, support, and maintain both Microsoft's Domain Model and Novell's NetWare Directory Services as well as determine what additional services, software, and migration tools are needed to enable both to coexist. ◼

The History of Microsoft and Novell Product Integration

Before Microsoft's NT server and when LAN Manager wasn't selling, Novell's Netware captured the Local Area Networking market and Microsoft chose to go after the desktop market. In most environments, Microsoft and Novell products coexist under the same roof.

Server Considerations

Expertise with both Novell Netware and Windows NT server. Consider common protocols between Netware and Windows NT.

Client Considerations

Exchange security is tied to NT Domain security—create client accounts for each Exchange recipient.

Migration Considerations

What utilities are available to move client data? Where do clients store their e-mail data? Do they use separate passwords for Logon and e-mail?

Organizational Concerns

How many locations does your company have? How are the sites connected? How many users are at each site?

The History of Microsoft and Novell

Many years before Microsoft created Windows NT, their network operating system platform was a product called Microsoft LAN Manager. Without getting into the details, it didn't sell very well, and Novell captured the networking market with its Netware product line.

As Novell set up shop on corporate Local Area Network (LAN) servers, Microsoft chose to go after the desktop operating system market. Microsoft introduced its Windows 3.0 product. It ran on top of DOS, but was a revolutionary advancement in design and function from Microsoft's Windows 286 and Windows 386 environments. Its application software for Windows consisted of Word, Excel, PowerPoint, Mail, Schedule+, and Project. Microsoft also developed Dynamic Data Exchange (DDE) and Object Linking and Embedding (OLE) technology that tied its applications to one another and provided a robust desktop platform.

The two worlds remained separate. Developers of networking technologies continued to leverage NetWare's popularity by designing Netware Loadable Modules (NLMs) to run on top of the Netware servers. Many corporations continued to make heavy investments in Netware because it provided the best, most extensible, cost-effective networking solution on the market.

As a result of these two companies' abilities in different market segments, there were many Netware networks running with the Windows Operating System and Windows applications on the desktop. In fact, several organizations even executed Windows from the Netware server. This allowed administrators to manage users' Windows profiles and Windows application software configurations from any workstation, because all initialization files were kept on the server. Because Windows ran on top of DOS, all of the workstation network card and protocol drivers could be loaded in DOS, and a drive letter could be assigned to the Netware volume. Once the connectivity to the server was established, Windows and applications were loaded from the server.

In the past three or four years, however, things have changed. Microsoft introduced Windows NT as a network server solution, and Novell acquired WordPerfect and Borland's Quattro Pro spreadsheet. Novell then bundled these applications with its GroupWise e-mail and scheduling package to market a suite called PerfectOffice to compete with Microsoft Office. This was a 180 degree turn from the previous situation. Novell and Microsoft were trying to capture the piece of the business they did not have previously.

However, the Novell applications were not accepted by a large number of companies, with the exception of WordPerfect. Novell took a lot a criticism for losing focus on Netware and for not providing adequate support for its core product. Novell has since sold WordPerfect, and Quattro Pro; Novell is currently out of the applications business. During the time that Novell tested the application marketplace, they were also having problems with their first release of NetWare Directory Services (NDS) Netware 4.0. This encouraged people to start testing new networking platforms such as Windows NT Server. Microsoft began moving further ahead with NT and the applications software, which made it such a dominant player in the market.

The dominance of Microsoft Office applications and technologies such as OLE are the reasons why Exchange will be successful in any environment, including those with Novell servers. The

Exchange client components tie very closely with all the Microsoft products. Third-party companies write applications to the standard Application Programming Interfaces (APIs) that Microsoft incorporates into its products. The underlying networking technology and protocols should not sway you from implementing Exchange. Exchange's client-server model, integration with other Microsoft applications already use, and its open programming architecture will provide a solid foundation for your organization to build a global messaging architecture.

Exchange Installation Server Considerations

There are several things to consider on the server side when implementing Exchange. These consist of the following:

- Choosing a Network Protocol
- Migrating Users to the NT Servers
- Moving Existing Mail Data
- NT Server Expertise

Choosing a Network Protocol

The NT server that Exchange runs on can communicate over several protocols. The two real choices in the Netware environment are IPX and TCP/IP. NT supports both protocols out of the box, enabling your Netware clients to communicate seamlessly over the already existing network without modifying the client workstation protocols or adding new protocols to your routers.

This leads to an important point. You must have NetBIOS support enabled on all the NT Servers that will be acting as Exchange servers. The reason for this is that the clients look for Exchange servers across the network based on their NetBIOS names. NetBIOS is not required on the workstations but can be used if desired.

Migrating Users to NT Servers

Because most packages require you to create a separate account for mail, you already have systems in place for generating new accounts. In addition, users are already familiar with the interface; and you, the administrator, are already familiar with all the back-end utilities that go along with running the mail system. You already have backup procedures in place as well. All of this will have to change when you install Exchange. Although your clients will need minimal or no special configuration, the server side of things will be a bit different.

There are a few things you will have to keep in mind. One is that Exchange security is tied to NT domain security. This means that an NT domain login must be created for every account. This provides the user with powerful permissions features that allow users to delegate certain responsibilities to other users. For example, if you wanted your assistant to be able to access your appointment book, you could do it. You are able to get very granular as to what permissions are assigned to certain users.

Given the preceding, the biggest job you will have is importing all the current users and data from your current e-mail system. Although Microsoft provides a bindery migration utility, it imports only the Netware user names and group memberships. The problem with that is in most Netware environments, user names are based on a first initial, last name or first name, underscore, last name standard, because spaces are not allowed in Netware user names.

However, in most e-mail environments, the user's full name is listed in the e-mail directory. If you import a bindery from a Netware server, then run the NT User List to Exchange migration utility, you will wind up with a list of first initial, last name entries, rather than full names. This is unsatisfactory because you have to go back and re-key all the user names.

You can overcome this shortcoming by using one of the mail migration utilities that ships with Exchange or a third-party tool. For example, if you have Microsoft Mail post offices spread throughout your Netware network, you can run the Migration Utility and select MS-Mail and that will create the Exchange users with full names while migrating data. As the Exchange users are created, you can have the utility create the NT user accounts for you, thus making the transition seamless.

Moving Existing Data

When changing from a Netware-based e-mail system to Exchange, moving data is made easier by Microsoft and third-party data migration utilities.

Using Gateway Services for Netware   With Gateway Service for NetWare (Gateway Service), you can access file and print resources on NetWare servers from your computer. You can access resources on NetWare 4.x servers that use NDS and on NetWare servers that use bindery-style security. NT's Gateway Services for Netware enables the NT server running the Gateway Service to mount Netware volumes on the Netware server that the Gateway Service is connecting to. The purpose of this feature is to allow users on Microsoft NT networks to access volumes on a Novell server. The administrator of the NT server logs into the Novell server and mounts the disk as a logical drive. The NT server can then share this device with any NT server user. The same thing applies to printers on the network. You can associate a Netware print queue with an NT print queue and provide seamless access to authorized users on the NT server. While this may seem unconventional in a predominantly Netware environment, it does provide some interesting functionality. This tool can prove useful when using the Migration Wizard to move users from a Novell server-based e-mail package such as MS-Mail.

If the post office exists on Novell file server NOVELL001, on volume SYS1:, you can mount it on the NT server as drive D:, and just perform your import seamlessly. NT Server provides this functionality out of the box. Think of the alternative—you would have to copy all the associated post office files to a workstation and then copy them to an NT server.

Exchange Installation Client Considerations

There are many different ways a client workstation can be configured in a Netware network. For workstations using DOS/Windows 3.1 or DOS/Windows for Workgroups, 16-bit real mode drivers are used to access the Exchange server over IPX or TCP/IP.

In an IPX configuration, the IPXODI driver provides all the needed connectivity to the Exchange server. Through the use of the NWLink protocol on the Exchange server, the IPX client can seek out the Exchange server on the network. Once a connection to the server is established by the Exchange client software, all communication is handled through RPC.

When installing the Exchange client software on DOS, Windows 3.1, or Windows for Workgroups 3.11 machine, the installation program looks for a file called NETAPI.DLL. It then copies the appropriate RPC communication DLL based on the version of that file.

If you have TCP/IP running across your network already, and all the software is already installed on the workstation, you can have clients use TCP/IP to connect to the server. As long as the stack you use is Winsock compliant, the connection should be seamless.

For Windows 95 clients, using Microsoft's 32-bit IPX and TCP/IP drivers for your network card will provide robust connectivity. If you have these drivers already in place to access the Netware servers on your network, this same set of drivers will be used by the client to access the Exchange servers. One note is to make sure that if you are using the IPX protocol to communicate with Exchange, the Windows NT server will need to have the IPX protocol installed.

The client-server architecture of Exchange eliminates the need to actually mount any volumes of the server. The client communicates with the server via Remote Procedure Calls (RPCs) to provide seamless communication. For example, in the current cc:Mail and Microsoft Mail implementations, the user must provide a drive letter and path to the post office. That means they must be logged into the server and have the proper search paths and drive mappings established to communicate with the post office. With Exchange, all you have to do is configure the client to look for a certain server on the network. RPCs take care of the rest of the communications once the Exchange server is found on the network.

Exchange Migration Considerations

There are many sites that use Netware servers to house their shared file e-mail system. Users have different passwords for login and e-mail. The two systems are completely separate, with the exception of MHS-based systems like Novell's GroupWise, which ties into the bindery or NDS. For these organizations, there are real benefits to installing Exchange.

The movement away from the shared file system to client-server is a real boon to the administrators of those e-mail systems. Keeping database pointers in line, getting clean backups, and shutting down the system to make changes are all things these administrators have come to know all too well.

Part

II

Ch

10

There are several tools at your disposal to bring Netware users into the Exchange environment. You can use the Migration Tool that ships with Exchange or you can use the Bindery Import Tool that comes with Windows NT Server. The two solutions yield different results that are explained in the following sections. In addition, Gateway Services for Netware enables the NT server housing Exchange to access Netware volumes.

Using the Exchange Migration Tool

When you use this tool to give Netware users access to Exchange resources, that is all the Netware users will have. They are not given logons to the NT domain.

Think of your current LAN-based e-mail system, be it cc:Mail, MS-Mail, or POP. When you launch the client application on your PC or Macintosh, you are prompted for a login name and password, and the back end mail engine authenticates you. This same thing happens when you use the Migration Tool for Exchange.

Exchange can be thought of as an upgrade to your current mail system that will provide so much extra functionality. Microsoft has provided many tools that make Exchange an easy platform to implement regardless of your current server environment.

Although this system lacks the single log-on benefit that comes along with running NT Server, it is still very manageable and very robust.

Coexistence of Netware and Windows NT Server

Rather than migrating your existing Netware server-based e-mail system to Exchange, you might consider coexistence. Through Exchange's wide variety of bundled connectors, you can make the most of new technology while keeping your current system up and running. Consider the following real-world example.

ABC's Information Services Department uses Netware servers on the backbone of the campuswide network. The system has grown to over 5,000 users, all with Netware 3.12 accounts. ABC uses MS-Mail as their messaging platform.

Recently, the MS-Mail infrastructure has been showing signs of weakness because of the load being put on all the servers. The message databases have grown to over 500 megabytes, with thousands of Internet e-mail messages going through two gateways: one for students, one for everyone else.

At the same time, the need to perform database maintenance was becoming prohibitive. If the utilities weren't run every night, the database would get corrupted, causing the entire system to be shut down during peak hours. Additionally, data was being lost in the process. Also, the amount of storage needed to run the utilities was getting excessive, causing the need for the entire database to be moved to a separate server for the utilities to be effective. Needless to say, the system was breaking down.

This scenario lead ABC to explore the possibility of migrating the students over to Exchange because of its client-server platform. Rather than 3,000 students sharing one post office file on one Novell server, the company could move to the client-server model. However, they wanted to preserve their investment in Netware, but at the same time wanted to move to Exchange for messaging.

They set up an Exchange server for students to access mail, while still using the Netware server to load Windows 3.1 and house the Exchange client software. They used the Exchange Migration Tool to import the user data and accounts from the existing MS-Mail system so no data loss occurred.

They then called a Microsoft Solution Provider who installed the MS-Mail connector and set up the proper Directory Synchronization in the connector properties so that any new accounts created on the MS-Mail side would be reflected in the Exchange Global Address Book for the students. The Solution Provider gave ABC information on how to get hands-on Exchange training along with some basic Windows NT fundamentals.

Because IPX was the standard protocol loaded on the workstations, there were no workstation issues that needed to be addressed. The Exchange client software was loaded onto the Novell server, and a central program group was created and added to each user's PROGMAN.INI file using a batch file that ran upon log in to the Novell server. The users were provided with an on-line tutorial using the company's internal World Wide Web pages. These pages helped ease the transition from MS-Mail to Exchange for the users.

By implementing this solution, the company minimized the expertise needed on the Windows NT side of the house by using the migration tools that come with Exchange. Also, they continued to use their Novell server as a distribution medium, as well as a file repository. The log-in script capabilities of Netware were utilized in rolling out the client software to the workstations.

The one issue ABC must deal with is creating new users on the Novell server. They previously had the MS-Mail user accounts automatically generated through the same script they used to create Netware accounts. They edited this script to create the proper Exchange account information.

Can this be done, and how so? This implementation of coexisting systems can work in many environments. In addition, once the word spreads among the user community about how good the e-mail system can be, you can leverage this demand when proposing a full migration, as well as when deliberating the use of Exchange's more advanced groupware features.

Migrating from Netware to Windows NT Server

The introduction of Exchange by Microsoft may prompt the discussion of a complete migration from Netware to Windows NT Server. The reason for this is that for so many organizations, e-mail and group collaboration are the main reasons for having a network in the first place.

Combined with the introduction of Exchange are 32-Bit desktops, Windows 95 and Windows NT Workstation 4.0. As these 32-bit platforms roll out onto the desktop, migrating file and print services to Windows NT Server may be a more strategic decision. You may already have Microsoft application software. When you combine that with Exchange and then Windows NT

Part

II

Ch

10

Server and BackOffice, you have a completely integrated Microsoft networking solution. You should consult a Microsoft Solution Provider for more information about moving your organization off Netware and onto Windows NT Server.

The Role of Systems Integrators and Consultants

Many environments consist of nothing but Netware for file and print services. The organizations that operate in that environment choose Netware because it is very popular and there is a lot of third-party support for the platform. Choosing one platform leverages all the staff training across the organization.

Trying to roll out Windows NT servers to implement Exchange might seem like an impossibility in these environments; however, there are several benefits to using Exchange that have been described throughout this book, and not putting this technology into place due to the lack of expertise in the organization may be shortsighted.

You can turn to the following channels to get Exchange rolled out in your environment:

- Power Users
- Newsgroups and Web Pages
- Microsoft Solution Providers
- Microsoft Consulting Services

Power Users

These are the people in the organization who experiment with different technologies on their own time. You know who they are. These people are the ones who can train the other system administrators on NT concepts and work with the management to support an Exchange implementation.

Newsgroups and Web Pages

There are several newsgroups on the Internet that are related to Windows NT and groupware. They include such topics as administration, networking, hardware, services, compatibility, and advocacy. These groups are a great resource for getting in touch with people who run NT-based networks. In addition, there are Web pages solely dedicated to NT technologies that will definitely include Exchange. These sites include:

- **http://www.microsoft.com/Exchange**
- **http://www.swspectrum.com**
- **http://www. ExchangeServer.com/**

Microsoft Solution Providers

There are many consultant agencies and systems integrators that are certified by Microsoft as Solution Providers. Just as the Novell environment has the Certified Netware Engineer (CNE) program, Solution Providers must pass tests and spend a certain number of hours using the platform to be certified by Microsoft.

You can count on these professionals to assist you with your Microsoft Windows NT and Exchange projects, as they have the expertise and can assist in one or all phases of the project. They can be used in any phase of your project starting with development and deployment to the support and maintenance of your Exchange environment. Working with a Solution Provider delivers many benefits, including first-hand information and most importantly, knowledge transfer. Most also are very familiar with Netware servers and clients because many Windows NT shops migrated from Netware with the help of Microsoft Solution Providers. Contact Microsoft to get a list of Solution Providers in your area. You can find a list of Microsoft Solution Providers on Microsoft's Web site at **http:\\www.microsoft.com**.

Microsoft Consulting Services

For those organizations that will settle for nothing but the real article, Microsoft has a division to help you implement Microsoft technology solutions. These professionals provide the soup-to-nuts support with all the backing of Microsoft.

This group is a step up from the Solution Providers because they have access to all the resources of Microsoft including constant, up-to-date training and experience with the product. This is especially important in the case of Exchange. Many companies have been eagerly awaiting the delivery of Exchange 5.0, and Microsoft Consulting Services has the benefit of having gone through the beta testing of the product and all the knowledge gained from that testing. The beta program for Exchange 5.0 was offered to a select group of clients, some having recipients of up to 40,000. Others keep up-to-date accessing Microsoft's Exchange Web site. Microsoft's Web sites offer the public the opportunity to participate in many of Microsoft's product evaluations, and users can acquire product support and access to on-line knowledge bases.

Organizational Considerations

In addition to the networking and technical considerations involved when installing Exchange in a Netware environment, some organizations will have to undergo serious changes in their IS departments, especially in those shops running Netware servers, MS-Mail, and Microsoft applications like Excel, Word, and PowerPoint.

These organizations have made such a large investment in Microsoft technologies, but the network server platform has always been Netware. There may be great opposition in the organization to move to Exchange because it means that Windows NT server must be rolled out into the entire enterprise just to upgrade MS-Mail. Some managers will be harboring resentment toward Microsoft for painting them into a corner.

Breaking the Netware Culture

Novell, now rededicated and refocused on expanding its core technology competencies in networking, is strongly marketing and supporting its Netware 4.1 platform with Netware Directory Services (NDS), a global directory service and their 32-bit Intranet Client for Windows 95, Windows NT 3.51, and 4.0 workstations. This rededication has reassured many companies that their Netware investments are indeed safe.

Many Netware shops are starting to outgrow their LAN-based e-mail packages and are looking for more robust client-server solutions for e-mail and GroupWare. Exchange will function very well in Windows NT and Netware shops alike. Yes, the Exchange server must be an NT server; but as long as the connectivity is provided from the client to the server, there is no problem.

However, connectivity isn't the only problem. In many Netware-dominated shops, Windows NT is not a welcome solution. Because it isn't a Netware server, it takes no advantage of NDS trees already in place, although Microsoft is developing utilities that will enable Windows NT server to be managed as NDS objects.

Additionally, users must be migrated to the Exchange server and more importantly, staff has to be trained on NT Server because Exchange is so closely tied to the Microsoft operating system. This may be the biggest barrier to entry into Netware environments for Exchange. Many administrators might ask, "Why not use GroupWise for e-mail and groupware?"

Also, because the IBM acquisition of Lotus, Notes is being pushed very aggressively, as Lotus Notes offers Notes mail and Groupware solutions. Notes server can be run on a Novell server, thereby strengthening the resolve of some administrators to keep Windows NT out of their shops. It is advisable to keep in mind that Exchange will be heavily tied into the operating systems you will run on the desktop, along with the applications being run on the desktop. In the future, the server platform used to file and print services will become less important. What will become increasingly important are the applications that can be run on top of the server operating system.

Exchange ties-in very closely with Windows 95 operating system, as well as Windows NT Workstation 4.0. As your workstations change from DOS/Windows 3.1 to these newer 32-bit operating systems, Netware's dominance as the back end server will decline, because these new Microsoft desktop operating systems make it very easy to participate in NT domains and to use the resources within them.

Committing to an All-Microsoft Strategy

Many managers might be wary of committing to an all-Microsoft strategy. Not wanting to put all your eggs in one basket is a legitimate concern; however, you may want to consider the following points:

- Microsoft's Products are tightly integrated via OLE and MAPI.
- There is tremendous third-party support for NT and Exchange.
- Microsoft's Solution Provider program does not lock you into Microsoft for support.
- Microsoft solutions are competitively priced.

These points address many of the concerns of information technology managers. These concerns stem from the experience of IBM dominance of the mainframe market in the early days of mainframe computing. The solutions were very proprietary, very expensive, and hard to learn. The one thing to remember was that they worked. As long as you stuck with an all-IBM solution, you felt comfortable because everything worked together, and IBM engineers were familiar with the equipment.

Microsoft's product line of today has some of the same characteristics. It is well integrated, and there are many well-trained engineers who know the software.

However, unlike the old IBM, Microsoft has built an open architecture using the MAPI and OLE standards combined with the Win32 SDK to enable third-party vendors to extend the capabilities of the core products.

In addition, there are several channels of support which outlined previously that should allay the concerns of managers. You can feel secure that although you're committing to Microsoft products, you are not dependent on Microsoft for support and extensibility.

Migrating from Novell GroupWise

Migrating users from Novell GroupWise to Microsoft Exchange requires detailed planning; you will need to understand Windows NT and Microsoft Exchange architecture. Microsoft Exchange Server has many migration tools to be used with Novell GroupWise.

As you plan your migration you need to consider the following:

- What level of migration—coexistence, mailbox migration, mailbox creation, or a combination of these will be best for your organization?
- Should all users be migrated, or only a subset of users?
- Do users have all the hardware necessary or will migration occur in phases?
- What connectivity issues need to be addressed?
- Which users should migrate first?

The following tables show what mappings are supported during the coexistence of both Novell GroupWise and Microsoft Exchange in an environment and details folder mappings of migrated information.

Table 10.1   Content Mapping

GroupWise	Microsoft Exchange
Messages	Read Note
Note Request	Read Note (Textized)
Appointment Request	Read Note (Textized)
Task Request	Read Note (Textized)
Phone Request	Read Note (Textized)

continues

Table 10.1   Continued

GroupWise	Microsoft Exchange
Routing Slip	Read Note (Textized)
Calendar Data	Schedule+

Table 10.2   Folder Mapping

GroupWise	Microsoft Exchange
Inbox	Inbox
Inbox\UserName	Inbox
Inbox\Username\subfolder	Inbox\subfolder
OutBox	Sent Items
OutBox\Username	Sent Items
OutBox\Username\subfolder	Sent Items\subfolders
Trash	(not migrated)
Trash\Username	(not migrated)
Personal Folders	Personal Folders
Personal Folders\subfolder	Personal Folders\subfolder
Week View	Schedule+ Calendar

Migration strategies, coexistence, and full migration plans are detailed in both Chapter 8, "Migrating from Microsoft Mail Systems" and Chapter 9, "Migrating from Lotus cc:Mail." These chapters detail migration strategies from Microsoft MS-Mail and Lotus cc:Mail to Microsoft Exchange, and they can assist you with the planning, development, and deployment from Novell GroupWise to Microsoft NT and Microsoft Exchange.

Using the Migration Wizard

After your Microsoft Exchange Server and Novell GroupWise systems are connected, it is easy to enable them to coexist or to migrate from Novell GroupWise to Microsoft Exchange. Microsoft Exchange Server offers a Migration Wizard to assist you with migrating. The Migration wizard assists you with the creation of new Windows NT accounts and you can select how you want the Windows NT accounts for your migrated users created (accounts can be created and given a random password). Exchange mailboxes are not accessible until a Windows NT account is associated with it.

The Novell GroupWise migration tool is tightly integrated and enables you to extract data from Novell GroupWise systems to create mailboxes and import data. The Migration Wizard is the interface to the GroupWise Source Extractor, the source extractor takes information from a foreign system puts it in a neutral format and then imports it into Microsoft Exchange (see Figure 10.1). The Novell GroupWise Source Extractor will migrate user accounts, mail and Phone messages, Appointments, Notes, and Tasks. When migrating users from Novell GroupWise to Microsoft Exchange you have the option to migrate all Appointments, Notes, and Tasks, or select a start and ending date. There are a few prerequisites to running the

Novell GroupWise Source Extractor; all users that are to be migrated must grant migration ID access to Mail and Phone messages, Appointments, Notes, and Tasks before their data is exported.

FIG. 10.1

Novell's Groupwise 4.1 Source Extractor converts data to a neutral format that Exchange can use.

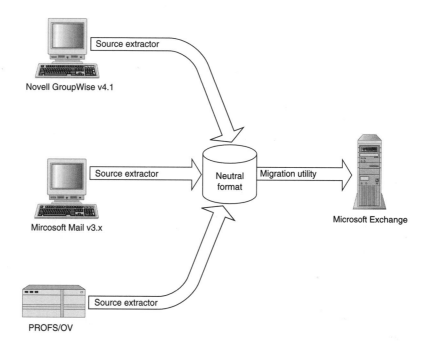

From Here...

As you can see, there are many issues you'll have to consider when installing Exchange in a Netware environment. Some obstacles you'll face are technical, some are organizational, but you'll find the robustness of Exchange will be a vast improvement over your existing file-sharing e-mail system.

The areas of concern are as follows:

- Networking Protocol
- User accounts and data migration
- Coexistence or Migration of Netware
- Back end administrator training

With the help of trained professionals, you will be able to work out all these issues and come up with an installation that makes the most sense for your organization. This chapter was intended to provide a starting point for any organization using Netware and to point out the relevant questions.

The following chapters contain more information on topics in this book:

■ See Chapter 4, "Integrating with Microsoft Windows NT Server," to get a more in-depth picture of what goes into creating Windows NT networks.

■ Chapter 7, "Planning Connections to Microsoft Mail Systems," gives you the information you need to have an MS-Mail and Exchange system coexist.

■ Chapter 8, "Migrating from Microsoft Mail Systems," provides the necessary steps to move users and data from an MS-Mail system to an Exchange server.

■ Chapter 9, "Migrating from Lotus cc:Mail," rounds out the discussion of how to move data from Lotus cc:Mail software.

Migrating from External Systems

This chapter's primary focus is on migration to Microsoft Exchange from host-based systems but also includes a brief overview of Migration strategies from SMTP mail and foreign X.400 messaging systems. This chapter covers both the use of Exchange as a gateway to these other systems and the process of transferring users to Exchange as the primary messaging system. ■

Migrating from a Host-Based System

Migrating from a legacy mail system such as PROFS.

Migrating from SMTP (Internet) Mail Systems

Exchange 5.0 can coexist with an SMTP mail system by using its Pop3 client. We provide a one-step plan to switch over to Exchange 5.0 from an SMTP Mail System by running the system in parallel.

Migrating from Foreign X.400 Messaging Systems

Exchange 5.0 enables you to share the X.400 address space with a foreign system to provide coexistence during the migration process.

Migrating from a Host-Based System to Microsoft Exchange Server

The first messaging systems were proprietary. For example, PROFS was the most popular proprietary messaging system established. There are about 6 million PROFS users today. Proprietary messaging systems such as PROFS were designed to provide messaging within organizations rather than between organizations. Also, with the advent of GUI interfaces, client/server architecture, open systems architecture, and the need for inter-LAN messaging, it is likely that first-generation tools like PROFS will be eclipsed by technologies such as Microsoft Exchange.

Let's quickly review the benefits of Exchange over a legacy host-system like PROFS:

- **APIs** Developed to establish interoperability, allowing one client interface and transparency toward different message stores, message transports, and directory implementations. Important architecturally for open architecture between disparate LAN systems. Exchange offers the recognized MAPI and CPC interface.

- **X.500** Recognized standard for distributed directory system.

- **Client/Server Architecture** Client/Server partitions responsibility between client and server, using a standard of remote access calls allowing the technology to become more efficient and taking advantage of the price/performance benefit of using distributed PCs, such as multi-processor RISC machines, rather than an expensive central host.

- **GUI Interface** Now with the preference of PC users, the popularity of the Windows interface has set the standard for user expectations with character-based interfaces such as PROFS increasingly likely to disappear.

In addition to the preceding advantages, new Exchange clients also get to enjoy the advantages of group scheduling, powerful enterprise-wide workgroup applications, and one-stop enterprise-wide administration. In summary, migrating from a host-based system such as IBM PROFS_ to Microsoft Exchange offers several significant advantages, including the potential for enormous cost savings, communication between organizations, and freed host resources.

Review the following for migration from host-based systems:

- Migration Planning considerations
- Migration steps
- Migration elements
- Sample migration
- Client migration
- Host to server migration
- Single versus dual-provider strategy
- Migrating partial versus whole post offices

NOTE Information that applies to IBM PROFS also applies to IBM OfficeVision/VM.

Migration Planning Considerations

The following list shows data that you can migrate from IBM PROFS by using Exchange's broad migration features:

- Calendars and reminders
- Nickname files
- Distribution lists
- Mailed documents

Introducing Migration Steps

When a large organization moves to a new messaging infrastructure, it's a good idea to break down the project into a series of steps. The major steps of migration can be divided as follows:

1. Use the MAPI driver (optional).
2. Create directory and mailbox entries.
3. Extract accounts, load accounts.
4. Set up connectivity (gateway).
5. Migrate the server contents.
6. Move the user data.
7. Set up directory synchronization.
8. Update the directory.

The Migration Elements

The following sections cover the main elements of Microsoft Exchange's Migration package. These tools and components of the Exchange system provide an easy and effective way to implement it in your environment. Additionally, the migration tools are used in a similar manner for each e-mail system migrated to Exchange.

Part

II

Ch

11

The Migration Tool

The following three tools are included with Exchange to provide an easy way for you to migrate from an existing e-mail system to Exchange. These tools extract the e-mail address information from the legacy system and guide you through the conversion and migration into Exchange.

- **The Source Extractor**—There is a Source Extractor for every system, such as MS Mail, PROFS, and so on. The Source Extractor extracts users, inboxes, folders, and address books from the source mail systems.

■ **The Migration Assistant**—The Migration Assistant converts all extracted data from the source system to Microsoft Exchange.

■ **The Migration Wizard**—Microsoft Exchange includes a Migration Wizard to guide administrators through the process. An option is included for one-step migration.

Connectors

The Connector is the main link between users of Exchange and external systems, such as SMTP/MIME/Internet connector for UNIX, X.400 connector, and of course, Microsoft Mail (PC) post offices.

Gateways

The Microsoft Exchange gateway for PROFS/OfficeVision provides seamless message transfer with Microsoft Exchange server. The gateway supports all the features of the existing Microsoft gateway for IBM PROFS version 3.4 but with tighter calendar and directory integration. The PROFS/OfficeVision gateway encapsulates Microsoft Exchange messages sent to other Microsoft Exchange users of a PROFS backbone to maintain data integrity.

Directory Exchange Agent   The Directory Exchange Agent (DXA) in Microsoft Exchange enhances directory synchronization with flexible scheduling, better time zone management, and update scheduling. Its multithreaded design improves throughput. Because the DXA includes multiple server support, the directory synchronization load is distributed across multiple "dirsync" servers for increased reliability and faster response. This setup reduces address list maintenance, increases security, and assures that updates occur more promptly. The DXA agent only can function if the proper connectivity exists between the e-mail systems. The DXA operates through the gateway to the legacy e-mail system.

Microsoft Schedule+ Free and Busy Gateway   Free and busy times are the times when people are available and unavailable. The connector processes users' free and busy information from MS Mail(PC) post offices and updates the information in Schedule+ Free Busy system folders. It then sends updates on free and busy information from Microsoft Exchange for MS-Mail PC Postoffices.

Schedule + 7.0 can access information from Schedule+ 1.0 users and access details about other Schedule+ 7.0 users. With the two together, Schedule+ 1 and Schedule+ 7 can do the following:

■ Add specific people to the meeting organizer.

■ Add people to a list of invitations and check their availability before scheduling a meeting.

However, because of the file formats of Schedule+ 1.0 and Schedule+ 7.0 differ, Schedule+ 1.0 users cannot access the detailed information of Schedule+ 7.0 users.

The Microsoft Exchange gateway for PROFS/OfficeVision does not currently support integration with Outlook. However, future versions of the gateway may offer this functionality.

Passthrough Connectivity

Microsoft Exchange Server offers hardy group distribution list support and enables MS-Mail users to send messages to X.400 and SMTP environments through the Microsoft Mail Connector. Messages sent from the MS Mail 3.x users through the Microsoft Exchange Server computer can use the Microsoft Exchange X.400 Connector and the Internet Mail Connector to interchange messages with these environments. Alternatively, Microsoft Exchange users can send messages through any Microsoft Mail gateway by using the Microsoft Mail Connector.

Using the Migration Wizard

You can use the Migration Wizard to migrate one or more mailboxes on a Microsoft Mail for PC Networks post office. When each mailbox on the post office is migrated, you have a choice of the information to migrate.

A Sample Migration

Software Spectrum is headquartered in Garland and has branch offices in London and Los Angeles. The headquarters has a mix of IBM PROFS and MS-Mail users. Both customer service and accounting departments need constant access to information on the host, communicating by way of the IBM PROFS system. Users in sales, marketing, and both consulting offices are all on MS-Mail post offices. Both consulting offices are connected to the headquarters by T1 lines. PROFS users are linked to Microsoft Mail users through the Microsoft Mail gateway to PROFS (see Figure 11.1).

Part
II

Ch
11

FIG. 11.1
Exchange has connector support for Profs via the Attachmate Zip office gateways for Exchange.

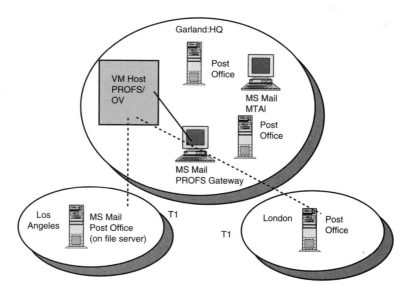

Phase One—Migrating to Microsoft Exchange Clients

First, the Microsoft Exchange client is installed on all workstations over time, both at head-quarters and in the branches. Microsoft Exchange clients that work with the Microsoft Mail post offices have the rich e-mail functionality in Microsoft Exchange and are still fully compatible with existing Mail clients. Exchange client talks to the PROFS host via the MS Mail Connector to PROFS.

Microsoft Exchange is then installed on the Windows NT-based server at the headquarters, and both PROFS users and MS-Mail post offices are migrated to the Microsoft Exchange Server. This action consolidates the PROFS gateway and two MS-Mail post offices on one Microsoft Exchange Server, combining the functions of three machines on one (see Figure 11.2). (The customer also can continue to use the Microsoft Mail-based PROFS gateway.)

The automated Migration Tool in Microsoft Exchange works with most common host-based systems as easily as it works with LAN-based systems to automatically extract data and convert it to the Microsoft Exchange system.

The following data is migrated from a host-based system to Microsoft Exchange: notes, notelogs, calendars, reminders, and address books (nicknames).

FIG. 11.2

Both PROFS users and MS Mail post offices are migrated to the Microsoft Exchange Server.

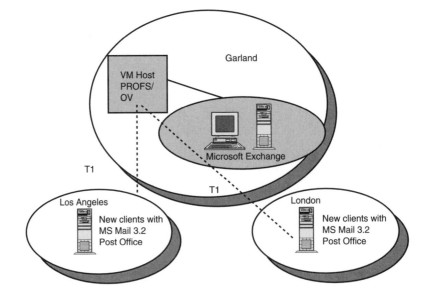

The following data is not migrated: personal address information, preferences and settings, and binary file attachments. After all headquarters users are migrated, they have access to the complete functionality of Microsoft Exchange. They also can exchange messages, attachments, OLE objects, and scheduling information with Microsoft Exchange clients who are working against the Microsoft Mail 3.x post offices in the branch offices.

Phase Two—Sending Microsoft Exchange Messages via a Microsoft Mail-Based Gateway

At the headquarters, before the Microsoft Exchange gateway to PROFS was installed, messages were routed to PROFS users from Microsoft Exchange users working against MS-Mail post offices through the Microsoft Mail gateway to PROFS. PROFS users also routed their messages back through the Microsoft Mail gateway.

Phase Three—Migrating the Branches to Microsoft Exchange Servers

Windows NT-based servers are added to the networks in both branches, and Microsoft Exchange is installed on each server (see Figure 11.3).

FIG. 11.3
The final configuration.

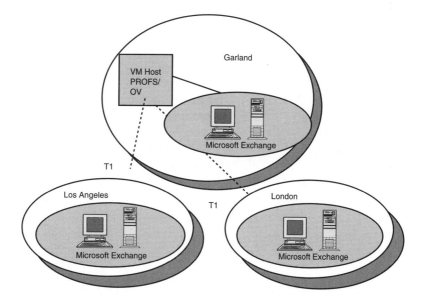

Now the power of Microsoft Exchange is unleashed across the enterprise. All users have access to rich text formatting of messages and exchanged documents, rules, public folders, forms, group scheduling, remote functionality, and more. Relevant customer service and accounting data from the host can be extracted and put in public folders that are available to all or specified users both at headquarters and at the regional offices. With immediate access to the same information, users across the enterprise can respond faster to market demands and make better-informed decisions.

In Figure 11.4, the message originates from PROFS and is routed by the PROFS gateway directly to the Connector post office in-queue and routed as are all other messages bound for Microsoft Exchange users.

FIG. 11.4

The message flow from
IBM PROFS users to
Exchange users.

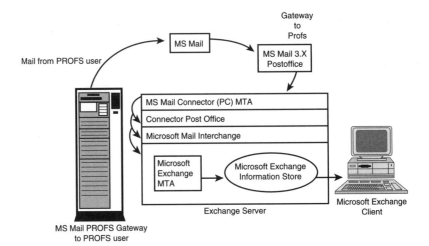

The Role of the Microsoft Mail Connector in Coexistence with PROFS

It's helpful to illustrate the message flow process. When using Microsoft Mail gateways with PROFS, it's a natural development to have Microsoft Mail gateways in coexistence with Exchange Server. The preceding diagram outlines the flow of a message that originates from PROFS and is routed to the MS-Mail user through the Microsoft Exchange gateway to PROFS. The message is passed through the PROFS gateway to the Microsoft Exchange Information Store. The gateway converts the PROFS message into a standard MAPI message.

When the message arrives in the Information Store, it follows the same message flow as if it originated as a Microsoft Exchange message. Going the other direction, a message from an MS-Mail user destined for a PROFS user takes the following route through the Microsoft Mail Connector.

Message Flow from Microsoft Exchange Users to IBM PROFS Users via Microsoft Mail-Based Gateway

In the reverse situation, a message originates from Microsoft Exchange and is routed through the Microsoft Mail Connector to the MS-Mail post office with a PROFS gateway installed.

In this case, the message from the Microsoft Exchange user is stored in the Microsoft Exchange Information Store, and is then sent by the Information Store to the Microsoft Exchange MTA. From there, it's routed by the MS-Mail Interchange to the Connector post office. The message then is routed from the Connector post office to its final PROFS destination directly by the Microsoft Mail PROFS gateway.

Going in the other direction, PROFS users who send messages to Microsoft Exchange users use the PROFS gateway in MS-Mail. The message from Microsoft Mail is picked up by the MS-Mail Connector (PC) MTA and placed in the Connector post office in-queue. Once there, the message is handled exactly the same as all other messages.

Using Client Providers for IBM PROFS

Using a PROFS MAPI client provider for the Microsoft Exchange Client is an alternative to or a variant of multiphased migration. Using Attachmate's ZIP! Office Client Connection product, the Microsoft Exchange Client can be used to connect to the IBM PROFS system, Microsoft Exchange Server, or both systems.

Having Users Drive Migration

With some programming, you can make a multiphased migration user-managed and user-driven. For example, the mailboxes for all users can be created in the Microsoft Exchange server computer but made hidden. When a user accesses his or her new mailbox and no longer needs the IBM PROFS system, he or she can send a special custom form. This form is already addressed to a mailbox. When the message is received, a program creates an account file with the sender's host account information, and then runs the source extractor. After the source extractor is finished, the files are copied to a network share and the Migration Wizard is started in batch mode. It imports the data into the empty mailbox and logs that this user has been migrated.

How the Source Extractor Works

The IBM PROFS source extractor is a multithreaded application when migrating messages. It runs in a specially defined MIGRATOR VM ID. Each thread takes the next VM ID from the list of VM IDs to be migrated and attempts to autolog on this VM ID. If successful, it invokes the MIGVIZ EXEC from a common mini-disk. This EXEC links to the MIGRATOR's 191 mini-disk, from which it can access the migration parameters and other migration programs. These programs extract the relevant data from notelogs, files, calendars, nickname files, and distribution lists and send the data to a file transfer VM ID. When it completes extracting all the data or when the maximum-wait time limit is reached, the thread goes on to the next unmigrated VM ID in the list.

Preparing to Migrate Data

Before installing the software, you need to create two VM IDs, MIGRATOR and MIGXFER, as described in the following sections. Create either a class B VM ID that can perform the autolog function or a class G VM ID that can perform this function. This ID must have the following:

■ A 191 mini-disk to store programs, accounts files, other required data tables, LOG, and STATUS files.

Part
II

Ch
11

■ A LINK to a mini-disk that contains the OFSUAD FILE or a LINK to xxxDBM 191 mini-disk.

■ A LINK to a mini-disk that contains the PROFS NICKNAME file and ADDRLIST files.

■ (Optional) Pre-ESA systems may need to provide a link to the VM DIRECTORY file, unless some other means exists to perform the AUTO LOGON of VM IDs from the MIGRATOR VM ID.

The following code shows a sample directory entry for the MIGRATOR VM ID:

```
USER MIGRATOR password 4M 8M B
ACCOUNT
IPL CMS
CONSOLE 009 3215
SPOOL   00C 2540 READER *
SPOOL   00D 2540 PUNCH O
SPOOL   00E 1403 A
MDISK   191 3380 ccc 016 vvvvvv MR readpw writepw
LINK    xxxDBM   191 395 RR
MIGXFER
```

This class G VM ID may be used to receive the files generated during the migration process from the reader to a mini-disk. This VM ID requires a mini-disk large enough to store all notelogs, calendars, mailed documents, and nickname information from the group of users participating in the migration run. Optionally, the Administrator may choose to designate the MIGRATOR VM ID to receive these files, rather than creating a second VM ID. The documentation assumes that there are two VM IDs. The following code shows a sample directory entry for the MIGXFER VM ID:

```
USER MIGXFER password 4M 8M B
ACCOUNT
IPL CMS
CONSOLE 009 3215
SPOOL   00C 2540 READER *
SPOOL   00D 2540 PUNCH O
SPOOL   00E 1403 A
MDISK   191 3380 ccc 100 vvvvvv MR readpw writepw
```

Installing the IBM PROFS Source Extractor

To install the Microsoft Exchange Server IBM PROFS source extractor with an MS-DOS 3270 Emulator, use the following procedures:

1. Log on as the MIGRATOR VM ID.

2. Insert the floppy disk with the PROFS Source extractor code into the A drive of the computer.

3. From the a:\ prompt, type **UPLOAD <path to terminal emulation software>** and press ENTER. Do not include a trailing backslash on the path.

4. Move the file MIGVIZ EXEC to a common mini-disk.

5. Repeat this process for the file transfer VM ID.

Installing the Microsoft Exchange Server IBM PROFS Source Extractor with a Windows 3270 Emulator

If you don't use terminal-emulation software, the files can be transferred to the MIGRATOR's 191 mini-disk with the sample RUNBATCH.EBM macro.

Customizing EXECs After Installation   You may need to customize the files MIGLOGON EXEC and MIGLINKP EXEC to work with your system. Before using MIGLOGON EXEC, you must change the variables rdpass and vmdir. Before using MIGLINKP, you may need to change the text for sysadmin.

Maintaining Directories   During a Multiphase Migration, you need to keep directories in both systems current. You can use the migration tools to export and import directory information, as described in the following sections.

Creating Addresses in Your Host System

If you don't have a directory synchronization requestor for your host system, then you need to handle the following:

- Export the mailbox and foreign system addresses from Microsoft Exchange Server with directory export.
- Change the format of the file.
- Import the addresses into your host system.
- Extract Custom Recipients from PROFS.

Mail sent in Microsoft Exchange Server computers and incoming mail from Microsoft Exchange Server gateways can be routed to the PROFS addresses. You can use this rather than using directory synchronization, but you have to repeat the process on a regular basis to update the Microsoft Exchange Server directory with changes in the existing system directory.

To create custom recipients, extract a file of IBM PROFS addresses. Move the file to the Microsoft Exchange Server computer. Import the IBM PROFS address file into Microsoft Exchange server with the Migration Wizard.

N O T E   The custom recipient information is created with PROFS target addresses. If mail sent from Microsoft Exchange Server mailboxes is routed through X.400 or SMTP to reach the PROFS host, you must modify the custom recipient data before importing it to have the proper address type and address. ■

1. On the computer where you installed the source extractor, log on as the MIGRATOR VM ID.

2. Type **MIGWIZRD** and press ENTER to start the source extractor. The screen displays the following code:

```
Source Extractor for IBM (R) PROFS (R) and OfficeVision (TM)
Microsoft Exchange Server Migration Wizard
```

```
The following parameters are specified in MIGPARMS DATA file.

You can change these parameters using this menu, or by using XEDIT.

OV/VM (PROFS) Nickname File: File name:        File type:
Accounts File:              File name:        File type:
PROFS Calendar MIGRATOR vmid (PROFS system only)
Notify VM id                                  : HOWARDS
File Transfer VM id                           : MIGXFER
Thread timeout (min)                          : 30
Spool Console required       (TRUE/FALSE) : FALSE
Number of migration threads                   : 05
Replace previously migrated accounts (TRUE/FALSE) : TRUE

 _ _ _ _ _ _ _ _ _ _ _ _ _ _ _ _ _ _ _ _ _ _ _ _ _ _ _ _

  << BACK     NEXT >>        FINISH              CANCEL      HELP
  F10/F22     F11/F23        F12/F24             F3/F15      F1/F13
```

3. (Optional) In the OV/VM (PROFS) Nickname File field, type the name and file type of the nickname file. If this field is not filled in, the source extractor uses OFSUAD FILE, if access to this file is available.

4. (Optional) In the Accounts File field, type the name and file type of the accounts file with a list of VM IDs for which you want to create custom recipients. If you plan to create custom recipients for all VM IDs, skip this step.

   Anywhere from one to all VM IDs can be specified in an account file. The account file has one VM ID on each line.

5. In the Notify VM ID field, type the VM ID to which alert messages are sent. This VM ID doesn't need to have administrator privileges.

6. In the File Transfer VM ID field, type the VM ID to which all the extractor data should be written.

7. Press the F11 key to continue. The screen displays the following:

```
Source Extractor for IBM (R) PROFS (R) and OfficeVision (TM)
Microsoft Exchange Server Migration Wizard

What information would you like to migrate?

Type Y to select option, or N to reject it.


Y Remote addresses creation information (REMADDR FILE)
N Mailbox creation information (MAILBOX FILE)
N Email messages (Notelogs and In-basket)
From: 1994/10/28 to 1995/10/28
N Schedule information (Calendars and Reminders)
From: 1995/10/28 to 1996/10/28
N Documents from OFSINDEX FILE
From: 1994/10/28 to 1995/10/28
N Personal Address Book (Nicknames and Distribution lists)

 _ _ _ _ _ _ _ _ _ _ _ _ _ _ _ _ _ _ _ _ _ _ _ _ _ _ _ _
```

```
<< BACK      NEXT >>       FINISH        CANCEL     HELP
F10/F22      F11/F23       F12/F24       F3/F15     F1/F13
```

8. Set the Remote Addresses Creation Information to Y. Set all other options to N.

9. To continue, press the F11 key. The screen displays the remote address file.

10. Edit the remote address file as needed to remove VM IDs for which you don't want Microsoft Exchange Server custom recipients, or to change the display names. The source extractor uses XEDIT as the editor, and all XEDIT commands and subcommands are available.

11. Press F12 to complete the process.

    This procedure creates REMADDR FILE on the MIGRATOR 191 mini-disk and sends REMADDR PRI and REMADDR PKL to the reader of the file transfer VM ID. The REMADDR PRI and REMADDR PKL files are in ASCII format.

Moving the REMADDR Address to the Microsoft Exchange Server   To move the REMADDR address to the Microsoft Exchange Server, take these steps:

1. Log on as the MIGXFER VM ID.

2. Type **MIGXFER** and press ENTER to start the transfer tool.

3. The transfer tool modifies the file named REMADDR FILE to the migration file format and transfers it from the reader to the mini-disk. The MIGXFER EXEC also creates MIGXFER BAT, MIGRATOR PKL, and MIGPURGE EXEC on the mini-disk.

4. Download the MIGXFER BAT file to the personal computer.

5. From the personal computer type the following:

   ```
   MIGXFER <path to your terminal emulation software>
   ```

   Transfer the REMADDR FILE and pack the list file to the personal computer as REMADDR.PRI and MIGRATOR.PKL.

6. On the host, type **MIGPURGE** to remove the files from the reader.

7. (Optional) Edit the REMADDR PRI file to remove addresses, modify display names, change the target address type, or add additional directory import fields and data. For example, if you want all the custom recipients to have telephone number data, you can add the field Telephone-Office1 to the end of the first line in the directory section, and then add telephone numbers to the end of each line of data.

The migration files now can be imported into Microsoft Exchange Server with the Migration Wizard. See the section, "Importing Migration Files," for the next step.

Creating Mailboxes

The procedure for creating mailboxes is exactly the same as creating custom recipients except that, in step 8 of the extracting process, set Mailbox Creation Information to Y. A MAILBOX file is created in place of the REMADDR file.

Migrating Data The process of migrating data creates secondary files and autologs onto the VM IDs that are being migrated. The VM IDs to migrate cannot be in use during the extracting process.

Extracting E-Mail Data To extract e-mail data, follow these steps:

1. Log on as the MIGRATOR VM ID.

2. Type **MIGWIZRD** and press ENTER to start the source extractor. The screen displays the following information:

```
Source Extractor for IBM (R) PROFS (R) and OfficeVision (TM)
Microsoft Exchange Server Migration Wizard

The following parameters are specified in MIGPARMS DATA file.

You can change these parameters using this menu, or by using XEDIT.

OV/VM (PROFS) Nickname File: File name:        File type:
Accounts File:              File name:        File type:
PROFS Calendar MIGRATOR vmid (PROFS system only)  :
Notify VM id                                 : HOWARDS
File Transfer VM id                          : MIGXFER
Thread timeout (min)                         : 30
Spool Console required          (TRUE/FALSE) : FALSE
Number of migration threads                  : 05
Replace previously migrated accounts (TRUE/FALSE) : TRUE


_ _ _ _ _ _ _ _ _ _ _ _ _ _ _ _ _ _ _ _ _ _ _ _ _ _ _ _ _ _ _ _ _


  << BACK     NEXT >>        FINISH           CANCEL     HELP
  F10/F22    F11/F23        F12/F24          F3/F15    F1/F13
```

3. (Optional) In the OV/VM (PROFS) Nickname File field, type the name and file type of the nickname file. If this field is not filled in, the extractor uses OFSUAD FILE.

> **TIP**
> If you are migrating only a few accounts, create an accounts or nickname file with these accounts in it, and set the appropriate field to point at the file.

4. (Optional) In the Accounts File field, type the name and file type of the accounts file with a list of VM IDs for which you want to create custom recipients.

5. (Optional) If you are migrating calendars from a PROFS system, enter the corresponding VM ID in the PROFS Calendar MIGRATOR VM ID field. Ignore this step if you are migrating calendars from OfficeVision.

6. In the Notify VM ID field, type the VM ID to which error messages are sent. This VM ID doesn't need to have administrator privileges.

7. In the File Transfer VM ID field, type the VM ID to which all the extractor data should be written.

8. In the Thread Timeout field, type the maximum number of minutes it should take to migrate each VM ID. When this time runs out, the MIGWIZRD EXEC reuses the thread.

9. In the Spool Console Required field, set the value to TRUE to send console updates to the MIGRATOR VM ID to monitor progress. Alternatively, set the value to FALSE so that the console updates are not sent.

10. In the Number of Migration Threads, set the number of VM IDs that will be migrated simultaneously. If you set this number too high, it can affect performance and resources on the host computer.

11. In the Replace Previously Migrated Accounts field, set the value to TRUE if you want to migrate data for VM IDs that previously were migrated.

    Alternatively, set the value to FALSE if you do not want to migrate previously migrated VM IDs.

12. Press the F11 key to continue. The screen displays the following information:

```
Source Extractor for IBM (R) PROFS (R) and OfficeVision (TM)
Microsoft Exchange Server Migration Wizard

What information would you like to migrate?

Type Y to select option, or N to reject it.

N Remote addresses creation information (REMADDR FILE)
N Mailbox creation information (MAILBOX FILE)
Y Email messages (Notelogs and In-basket)
From: 1994/10/28 to 1995/10/28
Y Schedule information (Calendars and Reminders)
From: 1995/10/28 to 1996/10/28
Y Documents from OFSINDEX FILE
From: 1994/10/28 to 1995/10/28
Y Personal Address Book (Nicknames and Distribution lists)

— — — — — — — — — — — — — — — — — — — — — — — — — — — — —

  << BACK    NEXT >>       FINISH          CANCEL    HELP
  F10/F22    F11/F23       F12/F24         F3/F15    F1/F13
```

13. Set the options to Y or N, based on the information you need to migrate. Also, update the date range for each type of information that is being migrated.

CAUTION

The date range doesn't dynamically update. To avoid not migrating recent items, set the To dates to a future date, in case you forget to update them.

14. Press F11 to continue. The screen displays the accounts file.

15. Edit the account file as needed to remove VM IDs that you do not want to migrate.

Part II Ch 11

The status field can have the following three possible values:

Init   Not migrated yet but will be migrated.

Timeout   Attempted to migrate VM ID, but reached the timeout limit before migration was finished. Will be migrated.

Done   Exported data from this VM ID in the past. Will be migrated only if Replace Previous Migrated Accounts field is set to TRUE.

16. (Optional) If you didn't create a small nickname file or accounts file with your list of VM IDs to be migrated, pare down the full list of users to only the ones you want to migrate.

17. Press F12 to start extracting data. The screen displays the following information:

```
Source Extractor for IBM (R) PROFS (R) and OfficeVision (TM)
Migrating mailbox information...
Migrating users...
Max_threads=05. Replace=1
N_input=63
AUTO SUFINE EXEC MIGRATE MIGRATOR READ
AUTO STGRAY EXEC MIGRATE MIGRATOR READ



RUNNING  MSVM7
```

18. When the MIGWIZRD EXEC is finished, type SHUT to end the program.

This process creates several items in the reader of the file transfer VM ID, depending on the options selected in the second screen, which are described in the following table:

Item Name	Description
MAILBOX FILE	Information to create mailboxes
<VM ID> PKL	Packing list for the migration files of the VM ID
<VM ID> PRI	Primary intermediate file for the migration files of the VM ID
<VM ID> SEC	Secondary intermediate file for the migration files of the VM ID

These files are stored in ASCII format and should not be edited. For each VM ID there can be multiple, primary/intermediate files.

Migrating Files to Microsoft Exchange Server   To move the migration files to Microsoft Exchange Server, follow these steps:

1. Log on as the MIGXFER VM ID.

2. Type **MIGXFER** and press ENTER to start the transfer tool. The screen displays the following information:

```
Source Extractor for IBM (R) PROFS (R) and OfficeVision (TM)

There are 180 K bytes available on A disk.
Total size of selected files is 1892 K.
Select a subset of files that can be transferred by editing this file.
```

```
User ID          File Size
00000 * * * Top of File * * *
00001 REMADDR          6080
00002 MAILBOX          4960
00003 EAST03           1328
00004 EAST02          36628
00005 EAST01          10064
00006 CENT01          98776
00007 CENT02         309728
00008 CENT03         282512
00009 CENT05           4344
00010 WEST01          16416
00011 WEST02          22004
00012 CENT04        1044180
— — — — — — — — — — — — — — — — — — — — — — — — — — —
FINISH               RECALCULATE            CANCEL
F12/F24              F10/F22                F3/F15
====>
```

3. (Optional) Select a subset of files to transfer by editing this list. If limited by space on the mini-disk, press F10 to recalculate the total size of selected files.

4. The transfer tool modifies the files to the migration file format and transfers them from the reader to the mini-disk. The MIGXFER EXEC also creates MIGXFER BAT, <VM ID> PKL, and MIGPURGE EXEC on the mini-disk.

5. Download the MIGXFER BAT file to the personal computer.

6. From the personal computer, type **MIGXFER** *<path to your terminal emulation software>* to transfer the migration files to the personal computer as *.PRI, *.SEC, and <VMID>.PKL. This step also consolidates all packing list files (PKLs) into one file.

7. On the host, type **MIGPURGE** to remove the files from the reader.

8. If you want, edit the MAILBOX.PRI file to modify information such as directory names or to add additional directory import fields and data. For example, if you want to migrate department information with each mailbox, you can add the field Department to the end of the first line of the directory header, and then add department names to the end of each line of data.

N O T E Important: If you need to change directory (common-name) names, do it before importing the migration files. After creating mailboxes, the directory name can be changed only by deleting the mailbox and creating a new one. ▪

Importing Migration Files

The Migration Wizard reads files created by the extractor and automates simple administrative tasks, such as creating mailboxes and custom recipients.

Import the migration files with the Migration Wizard. See Chapter 8, "Migrating from Microsoft Mail Systems," for steps on how to use the Migration Wizard.

Migrating from SMTP (Internet) Mail Systems

This section is relevant if your organization currently has a mail system with a proprietary gateway into the Internet or if you use an SMTP POP mail server connected directly to the Internet.

N O T E Any reference in this section about connecting to the Internet also applies to connections with other SMTP-based systems. ■

The Microsoft Exchange Internet Mail Service provides connectivity with any SMTP-based mail system. In the past, with a PC-based messaging system, it was necessary to connect a separate SMTP gateway PC to access the Internet or other SMTP system. Exchange is designed to talk to the Internet directly, and because of its other connectors and gateways, is well suited for use as a gateway for other systems.

You will encounter two types of migration when implementing Exchange in an SMTP (POP mail) environment, which are described in the following list:

- **System Migration**—Replacing existing SMTP gateways with Exchange servers
- **User Migration**—Transferring POP mail users to Exchange mailboxes

System Migration

You can use Exchange to replace the current SMTP Gateways in your organization. If you currently use the MS-DOS-based SMTP gateway for Microsoft Mail, you want to do this as soon as possible. Exchange provides a far more reliable and efficient method for bridging your organization into SMTP-based systems such as the Internet.

Migrating Users from POP Mail to Exchange

If your organization uses SMTP Mail (POP) mail servers for user accounts, consider the following points about migration to Exchange.

First, POP mail provides the flexibility to check messages from any point on the Internet with several commonly available mail clients (such as Qualcomm's Eudora, or even with an advanced World Wide Web browser, such as Netscape's Navigator). In Exchange 5.0, Microsoft has added a POP client giving it the same flexibility as all the other clients. This section provides some suggestions for migrating users to Exchange and beyond.

Building a Parallel SMTP System

Unlike the X.400 connector option of sharing address spaces with a foreign system, this isn't an option in the SMTP world. Therefore, it's not a practical method for gradual migration from a POP mail to Exchange. If you do happen to have a large number of POP Mail users that you want to migrate to Exchange, the best way probably will be to build all your accounts on parallel systems. Then, you have to "throw the switch" and redirect mail to your Exchange Server when it's all set up.

For example, for Software Spectrum, the Internet domain is SWSPECTRUM.com. We can temporarily set up an offline Exchange server to receive mail at **popmail@SWSPECTRUM.com** for testing. We create all the necessary user accounts on this parallel system, and test for proper routing to this address. Then at a specified time, we modify the entry in the DNS (Domain Name Server) to route all SWSPECTRUM.com mail to the machine previously designated as popmail@SWSPECTRUM.com.

If you have users that must retain a POP Mail account for some reason (for example, to check mail remotely without an Exchange client), then you can create two profiles on their client: one pointed at their Exchange server and the other pointed at the old server, thus giving them access to both areas.

Exchange offers excellent support for remote users, so use this method when a remote user does not have access to an Exchange client while on the road.

Migrating from Foreign X.400 Messaging Systems

The X.400 Connector for Microsoft Exchange provides all the connectivity needed for replacing a foreign X.400 system in your organization. This connectivity includes gateways for connecting to any system that uses X.400 standards.

As in connecting and migrating from SMTP mail, there are two kinds of migration, which are described in the following list:

- **User Migration**   Transferring foreign X.400 system users to Exchange mailboxes
- **System Migration**   Replacing existing X.400 gateways with Exchange servers

User Migration from Foreign X.400 Systems

When switching to Exchange from a foreign X.400 system, user migration will probably be a gradual process. During migration, there obviously will be some users on Exchange and others still using the foreign X.400 system simultaneously. Microsoft Exchange enables you to share the X.400 address space with a foreign system to provide coexistence during the migration process.

For example, the Sydney site is connected to the Los Angeles site through a public X.400 network. Originally, the messaging system in Sydney was a foreign X.400-based system, but now it is being migrated to Exchange. Suppose that 65 percent of the Sydney users were migrated (using the included migration tools) to Exchange. To maintain coexistence, you set up Exchange to share an address space with the foreign X.400 system (in the Site Addressing property page), which means that messages can arrive for users on both Exchange and the foreign X.400 at the same address.

The following list shows the message route in the preceding example:

1. A message from the public X.400 network enters through the Microsoft Exchange X.400 connector.

Part

II

Ch

11

2. If the user is an Exchange user (or a user on another system connected to Exchange through another connector), the message is delivered normally.

3. If the user isn't on the Exchange system, it will be routed to your foreign X.400 system and delivered to the user in that mailbox.

With this system, users can be migrated to Exchange at your pace, knowing that both systems will run side-by-side provided that you need them to do so. This approach also reduces the amount of non-deliverable messages often encountered when switching over to a new system.

System Migration

Another common system migration scenario is to replace your current MS-Mail X.400 gateways with a more robust Exchange server with both the X.400 and MS-Mail connectors.

In this scenario, Exchange receives incoming X.400 messages through the X.400 connector and routes them through, using the MS-Mail connector. Because there will not necessarily be any mail user on the Exchange servers, no user migration is needed. However, the next step is to migrate the users from MS-Mail to Microsoft Exchange, but this topic is covered in its entirety in Chapter 7, "Planning Connections to Microsoft Mail Systems."

From Here...

This chapter covers migrating from the PROFS, X.400, and Internet-based (SMTP) messaging systems. As shown, Exchange can serve as a gateway between itself and your current messaging systems, as well as provide a rich set of tools to smoothly migrate your users into Exchange.

■ Chapter 7, "Planning Connections to Microsoft Mail Systems," gives you the information you need to have an MS-Mail and Exchange system coexist and eventually migrate fully to Exchange.

■ Chapter 16, "Creating and Configuring Recipient," gives you methods for creating new recipients for migration to Exchange.

■ Chapter 21, "Configuring X.400 Connections," teaches you how to configure a connection to an X.400-based system.

■ Chapter 22, "Setting Up SMTP Connections," shows you how to configure the Internet Mail Service.

Exchange Administration and Configuration

CHAPTER 12

Using the Administrator Program

The Administrator program will become your familiar friend as you work with Exchange. From this program, you can manage an entire Exchange organization. Because Administrator is so versatile, it is also rather ominous-looking at first sight. The dozens of functions that are provided in menus and check boxes tend to be somewhat confusing initially. The primary goal of this chapter is to familiarize you with this application and assist you in navigating it comfortably. Administrator is the most useful tool for Exchange administrators, so learning its tricks now will alleviate many headaches for you in the future. ■

The Administrator Interface

Exchange's administrator was designed to be a single-seat view of the entire organization. Using this central program, you can manage all components (connectors, mailboxes, public folders, protocols, and so on) of your Exchange enterprise.

How to Navigate the Hierarchy Tree

Even though the administrator program is powerful enough to view your entire enterprise, it's organized in a very intuitive format. Like the tree-and-folder look of File Manager, you can easily navigate the tree.

How to Use the Administrator Menus

The administrator program has several pull-down menus. Some of these control creating new connectors, tracking messages, and importing users.

Starting the Administrator Program and Connecting to an Exchange Server

The first step is launching the Microsoft Exchange Administrator application from the TaskBar in Windows NT. You'll find it under Programs, Microsoft Exchange, Microsoft Exchange Administrator. After the initial splash screen, if you have not yet configured a default server, the Connect to Server dialog box appears (see Figure 12.1).

FIG. 12.1
Select your target
Exchange server;
then click OK.

This dialog box appears repeatedly when you work with Exchange, so you should be familiar with it. The dialog box asks you what server you want to connect to. In the text box, type the name of the server to which you want the administrator program. You must type the server name accurately.

N O T E You must have local machine administrator privileges on the server to which you are trying to connect. NT 4.0 requires this privilege to access the registry, which is where Exchange Administrator writes most of its changes. Previous versions of NT did not require local administrator access.

If you click the Browse button, you can view a graphical representation of the Exchange servers within your organization. From this window, you can choose the Exchange server you would like to administer.

The Set As Default check box allows you to designate the selected server as the default connection. The next time you launch the administrator program, you will not be prompted to choose a server; the default Exchange server's window appears. This check box is unavailable until you make an entry in the text box.

Click OK when you finish making your selections. The administrator program attempts to connect to the server. If you typed the name of an Exchange server that does not exist, or if the selected server or its connection is down for any reason, you get an error message and the option to attempt a different connection.

If you have already configured a default server, the connection is made and you see the Administrator interface, which is covered in the following section.

The Administrator Interface

You can use the Exchange Administrator to view your entire Exchange organization (see Figure 12.2). Like a satellite view of the earth from space, this window presents the big picture of your Exchange hierarchy. You have the option to zoom in as close as you want to view any object.

FIG. 12.2

The main Administrator window.

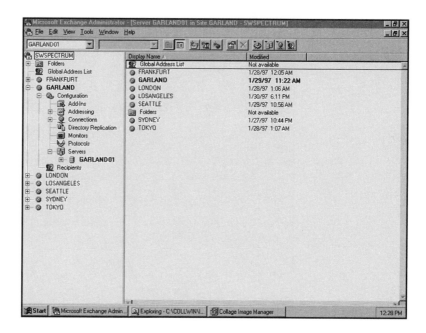

The left side of the window shows your Exchange hierarchy, displaying all the objects in your Exchange organization. The right side of the window displays the contents of the container object that is selected on the left side of the window.

The title bar of the window displays the server name, the site name, and the name of the object that is currently selected, in the following format:

Server *name* in Site *name*—Object *name*

Take some time to explore the Exchange hierarchy on the left side of the window, to get a feel for how the elements are organized.

Navigating the Hierarchy Tree

The Exchange site hierarchy window displays all of the components that make up your Exchange site in a treelike fashion. This includes recipients, servers, connectors, and any other Exchange component that you have installed. Navigating this window is much like navigating the directory hierarchy in File Manager or the Windows 95 Explorer. Many of the elements or objects in Exchange's hierarchy have multiple levels below them.

Part

III

Ch

12

A plus sign (+) to the left of an object indicates that the object has branches below it. Click the plus sign to display these branches. After you display the branches, the plus sign turns into a minus sign (–). When you click the minus sign, the branches disappear. Branches that have no plus or minus sign to the left of them are at the end of the tree. Clicking one of these branches displays its contents in the right window of the administrator program (see Figure 12.3).

FIG. 12.3

Object hierarchy tree.

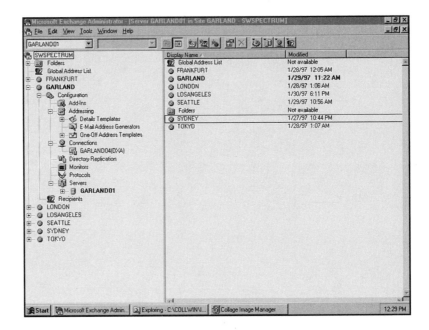

The top item of the site hierarchy tree is always the name of your organization. Double-click the name to collapse the entire tree view and start navigating from the top.

If you are setting up a new Exchange organization and have not yet established connections, you see only a small portion of local Exchange server elements in this default view. As new connectors and other objects are created, go through the Administrator window to see how these additional components have affected the overall Exchange hierarchy.

As you navigate the Microsoft Exchange hierarchy, you will notice that every object has an associated graphic icon. The following text shows the hierarchy tree and objects that are displayed in the Exchange Administrator program (refer to Figure 12.3 for an example of this structure).

Organization

The top or starting point of the Exchange server directory. All other directory objects are subordinate to this object. This is the directory name used in addressing and cannot be changed.

Folders

Public Folders

Public folders hold information that can be shared by various users. When a change is made in a public folder, that change is replicated to every replica of the folder throughout the organization.

Use this instance of public folders to view all the public folders and public folder replicas configured for Exchange.

System Folders

The system folders hold the Schedule+ Free/Busy information, offline address book, and EForms registry folder.

EFORMS REGISTRY

This holds all of the organization forms libraries that have been created in an organization.

Organization Forms Library

Organization forms libraries are public folders that store electronic forms. By default, any form saved to a public folder is available to all Exchange users.

OFFLINE ADDRESS BOOK

This address book contains lists of recipients that remote users can get information on about other users in the Exchange organization.

Offline Address Book

There is one offline address book per site listed here. By downloading this to their laptop, remote users can send mail to any recipient in the Exchange organization.

SCHEDULE+ FREE BUSY

This container holds one Schedule+ Free/Busy folder for each site. Every new mailbox that is created generates an entry in the Schedule+ Free/Busy Information public folder for the associated Windows NT account.

Offline Address Book

The first time a user logs onto Schedule+, an entry is created in the appropriate site folder. Also, every change in the user's schedule updates the appropriate folder. By setting restrictive permissions, users can prevent the publication of free/busy information and ultimately access to their schedule.

Global Address List

Lists all the mailboxes, distribution lists, public folders, and custom recipients that are contained within your Exchange organization.

Site

The name of a Microsoft Exchange Server computer's messaging site that is defined as a group of one or more Exchange servers connected together.

Part

III

Ch

12

Configuration

Contains configuration information about the site.

Add-Ins

The Add-Ins container holds optional third-party services that don't need a mailbox (Directory exchange, PC interchange, and AppleTalk interchange).

Extension

Contains property pages to a directory object. Common extensions are below.

Extension for MS Mail Connector

Extension for Schedule+ Free/Busy Gateway

Addressing

Details Templates

Localized (by language/country) templates that define the details that are displayed on recipient objects

English/USA

The default details template for American English

E-Mail Address Generator

This container holds the e-mail generators below, which automatically generate e-mail addresses for Exchange recipients.

cc:Mail E-mail Address Generator

Internet E-Mail Address Generator

Microsoft Mail Address Generator

X.400 E-Mail Address Generator

One-Off Address Templates

Localized (by language/country) templates that are used to determine what users input when they create new e-mail addresses from their Exchange Client for addressing mail messages to mailboxes not in the GAL or in the users' personal address book. These addresses are typically used once and then not used again.

English/USA

The default one-off address templates for American English

Connections

Contains all connectors that are used to link Exchange sites with other Exchange sites, with other MS Mail environments, or with other foreign e-mail systems.

cc:Mail Connector

Permits message exchange with Lotus cc:Mail networks

Internet Mail Service

Permits message exchange with Simple Mail Transport Protocol (SMTP) based e-mail systems.

MS Mail Connector

Permits message exchange with Microsoft Mail (PC), MS Mail (AppleTalk), and MS Mail (PC) gateways.

Site Connector

Creates a messaging bridge between two Microsoft Exchange sites on the same logical LAN.

X.400 Connector

Creates a messaging bridge between two Microsoft Exchange sites over an X.400 network or to a foreign X.400 system.

Microsoft Mail Connector for AppleTalk Networks (Quarterdeck Mail)

Permits message exchange with AppleTalk networks.

Dynamic RAS Connector

Creates a messaging bridge between two Microsoft Exchange sites over a Windows NT Remote Access link.

Directory Exchange Requestor

Sets up a Microsoft Exchange server to request directory information from MS Mail or other systems.

Directory Exchange Server

Sets up a Microsoft Exchange server to perform as a directory-synchronization server for external mail systems.

Dirsync Server

A dirsync server processes incoming updates from one or more directory requestors and incorporates the updates into the directory as custom recipient objects.

Remote Dirsync Requestor

Configures the internal representations of dirsync requestors that use this server. This internal information is used to authenticate and respond to requestors during directory exchange.

Directory Replication

Contains all directory replication connectors for Exchange. These connectors are bi-directional and enable replication of directory changes from one site to others.

Directory Replication Connector

An object that establishes recipient information sharing between sites.

Monitors

Contains monitoring tools that watch over an Exchange organization's servers and the links between them.

Server Monitor

Watches the status of a Microsoft Exchange Server's services and provides warnings or alerts if errors occur, such as service shuts down, server isn't on the network, and so on.

Link Monitor

Watches the status of messaging connections between Exchange servers by measuring the round-trip time of ping messages and alerting the Exchange administrator if the trip takes longer than expected.

Protocols (site defaults)

Holds all the Internet protocols that Exchange supports.

HTTP

HTTP protocol (Active Server Components) enables a user to mail messages from an Exchange server using an Internet browser from a UNIX, Macintosh, or Microsoft Windows-based computer.

LDAP

Lightweight, directory-access protocol (LDAP) is an Internet protocol that accesses the Exchange server directory. Clients with security permissions can use LDAP to browse, read, and search directory listings.

Use this to configure forms of authentication (clear text or SSL), anonymous access, searches, and closing idle connections.

NNTP

Configures network news transfer protocol (NNTP). Use this to configure site defaults, message content, and time-out options.

POP3

Post office protocol version 3 (POP3) enables users with POP3 clients to retrieve mail from their Exchange Inbox. Any third-party POP3 e-mail client can also access messages from an Exchange server.

Servers

Contain a list of the Exchange servers in this site and each of their core components.

Private Information Store

Stores all messaging data sent to individual mailboxes.

Logons

Use this to see information about users who have logged onto the information store.

Mailbox Resources

This shows resource information about mailboxes like the total amount of space a mailbox occupies.

Protocols (settings)

HTTP

HTTP protocol (Active Server Components) enables a user to access data mail messages from an Exchange server using an Internet browser from a UNIX, Macintosh, or Microsoft Windows-based computer.

LDAP

Lightweight, directory-access protocol (LDAP) is an Internet protocol that accesses the Exchange server directory. Clients with security permissions can use LDAP to browse, read, and search directory listings.

Use this to configure forms of authentication (clear text or SSL), anonymous access, searches, and closing idle connections.

NNTP

Configures network news transfer protocol (NNTP).

Use this to configure site defaults, message content, and time-out options.

POP3

Post office protocol version 3 (POP3) enables users with POP3 clients to retrieve mail from their Exchange Inbox. Any third-party POP3 e-mail client can also access messages from an Exchange server.

Public Information Store

Stores all messaging data posted to public folders.

Folder Replication Status

Use this to view the status of public folder replication within a site.

Logons

Use Logons to see who is currently logged onto a public folder.

Public Folder Resource

Use this to view information on resource usage.

Server Recipients

Contains all the recipients that call this server home.

Directory Service

Controls directory handling within a site.

Directory Synchronization

Also called Exchange DXA, this object controls general properties for Microsoft Exchange directory synchronization.

Part
III

Ch
12

Message Transfer Agent (MTA)

Transports messages from one server to another or to external connectors.

MTA Transport Stack

An MTA transport stack defines the transport used with a RAS or X.400 connector.

System Attendant

A core Microsoft Exchange service that manages log files and that is required to start other Exchange services.

DS Site Configuration

Holds general properties for directory services in an Exchange site.

Information Store Site Configuration

Holds general properties for all the Information Stores in a site.

MTA Site Configuration

Holds general properties for all the MTAs in a site.

Site Addressing

Holds general site-addressing data used in message routing.

Recipients

Contains a list of recipients for this Exchange site.

Mailbox

A private container for messaging data.

Distribution Lists

A group of individual recipients that can be addressed as a single recipient or e-mail address. This is similar in function to a listserver.

Custom Recipients

Foreign recipients whose mailboxes do not reside on a Microsoft Exchange server.

Public Folder

A receptacle where information that is stored can be shared among many users.

Microsoft Schedule+ Free/Busy Connector

A connector that receives Free/Busy scheduling information from Schedule+ for MS Mail.

Menu Overview

The Exchange Administrator program menus are as follows:

- *File.* Enables you to connect to other servers, create new connections and objects, and modify and view object properties.

- *Edit.* Enables you to execute standard Windows functions: Cut, copy, paste, delete, and so on.

- *View.* Enables you to choose the type of information displayed in the administrator window and how it is sorted; also allows you to set the aesthetic properties of the display (font, sizes, and columns).

- *Tools.* Enables you to perform various administrative tasks, such as tracking messages and importing Windows NT user lists.

- *Window.* Enables you to perform standard Windows appearance and arrangement functions, such as tiling, cascading, and switching between open windows.

- *Help.* Opens the Exchange online help system and provides Exchange version information.

Exchange Administrator Menus

The following sections describe the Exchange Administrator menus in detail.

File Menu

You will use the Administrator program's File menu (see Figure 12.4) to create the components that comprise an Exchange organization or site.

NOTE If you have two or more Exchange Server connections open at the same time, make sure that the correct window is in the foreground when you create components. ■

FIG. 12.4
The Administrator program's File menu.

Part
III

Ch
12

Connect to Server This menu item enables you to administrate a Microsoft Exchange server remotely, as though you were logged into it directly. Although the Administrator program enables you to view all the objects in your organization hierarchy, you cannot alter site connections, mailboxes, connectors, or site servers unless you are directly connected to a server in that remote site with the administrator program.

Close This menu item closes the active server connection window that you are using.

New Mailbox This menu item creates a new user mailbox. You must select a recipient container; otherwise, you are prompted to use the standard Exchange recipient container for that site.

New Distribution List   This menu item creates a new distribution-list recipient. (You must select a recipient container first.) You must then configure the properties for the distribution list.

New Custom Recipient   This menu item creates a recipient in a foreign mail system (cc:Mail, MacMail, MS Mail, SMTP, X.400, or the connected gateway).

New Other   This menu item displays the submenu shown in Figure 12.5, which allows you to create other types of Microsoft Exchange objects.

FIG. 12.5

The File–New Other submenu allows you to create many Exchange objects.

The items in this submenu are:

- *Server Monitor*. Creates a process that watches the operational condition of one or more servers in a site; can be configured to generate alerts when certain conditions (such as a stopped system service) occur.

- *Link Monitor*. Creates a process that monitors the state of messaging connections between Exchange sites and servers; the link monitors are configured to create alerts when errors occur.

- *Recipients Container*. Creates custom containers for certain object types. A good example is creating a specific Internet recipient's container that holds all custom recipients that have SMTP addresses.

- *Address Book View*. Configures the Address Book view.

- *Address Book View Container*. Modifies the configuration of the Address Book View Container.

- *MTA Transport Stack*. Defines underlying transport protocol for each X.400 or Dynamic RAS connector you create. Make sure that you have all necessary transport software set up properly in Windows NT (X.25 protocol); otherwise, you cannot proceed beyond this configuration point.

- *X.400 Connector*. Defines an X.400 connection to another Exchange site or foreign system. Before you select this item, you must define an MTA transport stack over which this connector is to communicate.

- *Dynamic RAS Connector.* Set up a part-time remote access link between servers. You can set up an RAS connection over modem, ISDN, or X.25 systems if you have the appropriate MTA transport stack installed.

- *Site Connector.* Sets up a connection between two Microsoft Exchange Server sites—typically, on the same logical LAN.

- *Directory Replication Connector.* Creates a directory-sharing relationship between two Microsoft Exchange sites.

- *Dirsync Requestor.* Configures a directory-synchronization requestor that is compatible with any messaging system that supports the Microsoft Mail 3.X directory-synchronization protocol. The Dirsync Requestor is most commonly used to request directory updates from a Microsoft Mail post office that is set up as a directory synchronization server.

- *Dirsync Server.* Configures a directory-synchronization server that is compatible with any messaging system that supports the Microsoft Mail 3.X directory-synchronization protocol.

- *Remote Dirsync Requestor.* The remote Dirsync Requestor allows a foreign system's Dirsync Requestor to connect to a Microsoft Exchange Dirsync Server.

- *Information Store.* Creates a public or private information store for an Exchange server. You can use this option only if a certain server does not currently have an information store of its own or if it has been deleted.

- *Newsfeed.* Use this wizard to setup a NNTP newsfeed. Be sure to have your provider's USENET site name, the names or IP addresses of your provider's host servers, the username and password your Exchange machine will use to log on to your provider's host computer (some providers do not require this), and your provider's "active file" ready.

- *Internet Mail Service.* With this wizard, you can setup the IMS to send and receive mail from the Internet or other SMTP systems.

Properties   This menu item enables you to view and edit settings for particular Exchange objects or containers. Double-clicking on the individual objects brings up the properties as well.

Duplicate   This menu item creates a new recipient object with properties exactly like an existing one. Selecting a distribution list and clicking Duplicate, for example, brings up a new distribution list with a blank name but with all the members of the original list. This option is the same as using copy and paste functionality in other Windows-based applications. This option is not available if you have not highlighted or selected a recipient.

Exit   This menu item closes all connections to Microsoft Exchange Servers and exits the Administrator program.

Edit Menu

The Exchange Administrator's Edit menu allows you to perform all the standard Windows Edit menu functions.

Part

III

Ch

12

Undo   This command works only with property text operations (cut, paste, and delete). Because you cannot access the Edit menu while a property page is open, this menu item is just about useless. Press Ctrl+Z instead to undo text commands.

Cut, Copy, and Paste   These menu items function as normal Windows-based commands for use with text entries. They perform the same functions as in Microsoft Word.

Delete   This menu item removes unwanted text entries or directory objects.

> **CAUTION**
> Delete operations on directory objects cannot be recovered without restoring from backup.

Select All   This command enables you to select an entire group of Microsoft Exchange objects in the Administrator program.

View Menu

The View menu (see Figure 12.6) is designed to filter or sort what information the Exchange Administrator program displays. Mainly, you can choose how to view recipients, thereby making a large global address list (GAL) a more manageable beast.

FIG. 12.6
The View menu filters
and sorts objects
displayed in the
Administrator window.

Mailboxes, Distribution Lists, Custom Recipients, and Public Folders   These menu items all filter the view for the list of Exchange recipients. A check mark appears next to the menu item that you are currently viewing. To view only a particular subset of the recipients, select an option other than the All option.

Hidden Recipients   This menu item is a filter that adds hidden recipients to any of the preceding viewing filters. Hidden recipients are recipients not seen in the GAL.

Columns   This menu item changes the columns of information that appear in the Administrator program's user interface. This item is available only while you are viewing a recipient container. After you click the Columns button, the dialog box shown in Figure 12.7 will appear.

FIG. 12.7

The Columns dialog box allows you to specify what object attributes are displayed.

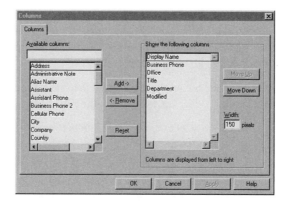

The left side of the dialog box shows all Exchange recipient attributes. The right column shows which ones are displayed in the administrator program.

To configure the displayed columns, follow these steps:

1. From the Available Columns list, select any additional attributes that you want to display; then click Add.

2. From the Show the Following Columns list, select any attribute that you do not want to display; then click Remove.

3. To change the order in which columns are displayed, select an attribute from the right list, and then click Move Up or Move Down.

N O T E Columns are displayed from left to right, even though you set their order from top to bottom. ▪

 T I P A better way to set column widths is to use your mouse. In the Administrator program's user interface, drag the mouse pointer over the dividing lines between each attribute column. When the pointer changes to a double-headed arrow, click and drag that column to the desired width.

4. To change the width of a particular column, select its attribute and edit the number of pixels it takes up on the Administrator program user interface window.

5. Click Apply to view your changes immediately on the background window.

6. Click OK to finalize your changes.

Sort By This menu item enables you to organize what you see in the Administrator program user interface. You can sort any Microsoft Exchange object, including recipients.

When you choose this menu item, a submenu appears, with two options:

▪ Sort by Display Name places the objects in alphabetical order by display name.

▪ Sort by Last Modified Date places the objects in order of the dates (and times) when they were last modified.

Part
III

Ch
12

Microsoft Exchange remembers every view setting for each object list in the Administrator program user interface. At the same time, you can choose to view your global address list sorted by display name and your connection sorted by date last modified, and you can have your local address list filtered to show only public folders.

Font   This menu item will open a Font dialog box that displays your currently installed system fonts. Select a font and then click OK to return to the Administrator program.

Move Splitbar   This menu item selects the dividing line between the Exchange site hierarchy and the objects corresponding to the hierarchy in the Administrator program. You can now adjust the window's partition. Use the mouse to drag the line to the desired position; then click to set the line.

TIP   Another way to organize the administrator program user interface is to drag your mouse over the line, and then click and drag it to the desired position.

Status Bar   This menu item turns the status bar on and off. The status bar displays useful help messages and shows the number of objects in the selected container.

Toolbar   This menu item turns the toolbar on and off. The toolbar displays certain menu items, such as creating a new mailbox, as buttons for easy access.

Tools Menu

The Tools menu provides access to various administrative utilities.

Directory Import   The Directory Import option allows you to read comma-delimited files and use them to create or modify recipients. These files may contain MS Mail recipients, Exchange recipients, or some other foreign e-mail system recipients. The files will need to be created either by using the Exchange migration tools or by using Directory export tools in the respective e-mail systems. The files contain recipient name and e-mail address information to be used in Microsoft Exchange.

The following is a list of the features you can perform using the Exchange Directory Import function.

- Import Directory information from another e-mail system or import.
- Add or change personal information for existing mailboxes and other recipients.
- Add members (in bulk) to distribution lists.

Microsoft Exchange includes some useful migration tools that provide similar functionality and are simpler to use. See Chapters 7 and 8 for more information on migrating from other mail systems and use of the migration tools.

Directory Export   This menu option creates text files of Microsoft Exchange directory information that can be imported into other messaging systems.

Extract Windows NT Account List This menu item selectively copies data from the Windows NT account list of a trusted domain. Files are stored in the CSV file format, which you can use with the Directory Import command to add and create Exchange recipients.

Extract NetWare Account List This menu item selectively copies user data from a Novell NetWare account list. Files are stored in the CSV file format, which you can then use to import into Exchange to create Exchange recipients and Windows NT user accounts.

Find Recipients This menu item allows you to search for recipients anywhere in your organization, based on a variety of criteria. When you choose Find Recipients, the dialog box shown in Figure 12.8 appears.

FIG. 12.8

The Find Recipients dialog box enables you to search for a recipient by any attribute.

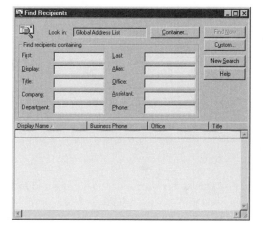

The top half of this dialog box allows you to specify search criteria; the bottom half displays the result of your searches.

To search for recipients, follow these steps:

1. The Look In box displays the recipient container in which a search will be executed. Click the Container button to display a global list of Exchange recipient containers in your organization; select one and then click OK.

   By default, the Look In box shows the primary recipients container of the server you are connected to.

2. In the Find Recipients Containing combo box, enter any distinguishing search criteria for the recipient.

3. To search by custom attributes, click the Custom button. A dialog box opens up, and you can enter your search parameters; then click OK to return to the Find Recipients dialog box.

4. Click Find Now when you finish entering search parameters. All matches of your search criteria are displayed at the bottom of the Find Recipients dialog box.

5. Double-click any listed recipient to view its Exchange properties.

Part

III

Ch

12

6. Click New Search to clear all search parameters.

7. Close the dialog box to return to the Administrator program.

Move Mailbox This menu item transfers a selected recipient to a different server within the same Microsoft Exchange site. When you choose Move Mailbox, the dialog box shown in Figure 12.9 appears.

FIG. 12.9

Transfer a mailbox
to another server in
the site.

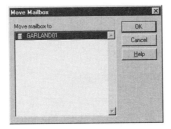

Select the Exchange server to which you want to move this recipient, and click OK. The mailbox is transferred to the new server's private information store.

N O T E This menu is unavailable unless you select a recipient from the recipient's container in the Exchange site hierarchy.

Add to Address Book View This menu item adds the highlighted recipient to an Address Book view. Remember, you must first create an Address Book view container (e.g., all Los Angeles Employees) before moving a recipient into it.

Clean Mailbox This menu item deletes messages in a particular user's mailbox, based on several criteria. This command can be useful when an unreasonable number of messages have piled up in a specific mailbox.

Select the criteria that you want to use to delete messages in this mailbox. A message must meet all the selected criteria to be deleted. The criteria are:

- *Age.* All mail older (in days) than the number in the All Messages Older Than (Days) will be deleted. All mail greater in size (in kilobytes) than the number in the All Messages Greater Than (K) box will be deleted.

- *Sensitivity.* All messages have a sensitivity attribute. You can select up to four sensitivity levels. All messages that have the selected sensitivity levels will be deleted.

- *Read Items.* This option is the read or unread status of the messages. You must select the status of messages to be deleted: Read, unread, or both.

- *Delete folder-associated information.* If cleared, no folder-associated information is deleted. If enabled, all information and messages associated with the selected folder are deleted.

- *Delete Items Immediately.* This item permanently removes messages from the mailbox.
- *Move Items to the Deleted Items Folder.* This item places the selected messages in that user's Deleted Items folder in the Exchange Client.

Start Monitor This menu item starts the selected server monitor or link monitor. This option is unavailable if a monitor is not selected.

Track Message This option launches the Message Tracking Center, which is a tool for following the delivery of messages through an organization.

Forms Administrator This menu item displays the Organization Forms Library Administrator, which enables you to manage the various forms created using the Forms Designer tool in the Exchange client software to meet specific messaging needs.

Save Connections on Exit This menu item is a toggle that can save information about your current server connections when you quit the Administrator program. The next time you open the Administrator program, it tries to reestablish the connections to those servers.

Save Connections Now The moment that you select this option, Exchange saves current Exchange Server connections. The next time you open the Administrator program, it tries to reestablish the connections to those servers.

Options This menu item displays two property pages that allow you to set options for Exchange mailboxes and other recipients. The property pages are:

- *Auto Naming.* Enables you to define a method for Display Name Generation and Alias Name Generation.
- *Permissions.* Enables you to set a default Windows NT domain where new mailbox accounts are to be created in addition to other object related permissions.

To set Auto Naming options, follow these steps:

1. Click the Auto Naming tab in the Options dialog box (see Figure 12.10).

Part

III

Ch

12

FIG. 12.10

The Auto Naming tab helps you generate mailbox display names.

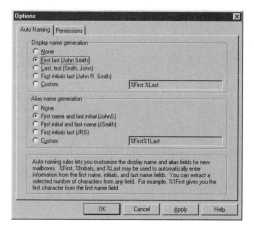

2. The Display Name Generation combo box allows you to define how the Administrator program generates display names when the e-mail system administrator is typing or importing new Exchange mailboxes. Choose None to always enter display names manually. Choose Custom to create a specialized entry type or template.

3. The Alias Name Generation combo box allows you to define how the Administrator program generates alias names when the e-mail system administrator is typing or importing new Exchange mailboxes. Choose None to always enter alias names manually. Choose Custom to create a specialized entry type.

4. Click Apply to set these properties and continue with the other properties.

5. When you finish making settings, click OK to return to the Administrator program.

To set Permissions options, follow these steps:

1. Click the Permissions tab in the Options dialog box.

2. Select the default Windows NT domain for all new mailboxes from the pull-down menu.

3. Choose Show Permissions page for All Objects if you want the permissions to be displayed in all the property pages of the objects that have them. By default, this box is not checked, and the permissions pages are hidden.

4. Choose Display rights for roles on Permissions Page to display the list of rights on the permissions page. *Roles* are sets of rights that define what type of access, and how much, a user or group has.

5. Choose Delete Primary Windows NT Account When Deleting Mailbox to delete the associated Windows NT account along with a mailbox. This box is not checked by default.

CAUTION

Proceed with caution; a deleted Windows NT user cannot log back into the domain.

6. Choose Try to Find Matching Windows NT account When Creating Mailbox to have the Administrator program search the Windows NT user list to find the matching account name. This box is checked by default.

7. Click Apply to set these properties and continue with the other properties on the permissions tab.

8. When you finish making settings, click OK to return to the Administrator program.

Window Menu

This menu is a standard Windows menu. You can create a new display window for a particular server. Cascade, Tile Horizontally or Vertically, and Arrange Icons function as normal. Refresh requests and update to all window information from the server.

Help Menu

This menu is a standard Windows help menu. The menu contains three standard options:

- *Microsoft Exchange Server Help Topics*. This option allows you to view standard help information on all Exchange interface settings.

- *Books Online*. This option allows you to read the official Microsoft Exchange Server documentation, with searchable indexes and tables of contents, online.

- *About Microsoft Exchange Server*. This option displays version and copyright information. It also displays a System Info button that runs NT diagnostics. NT diagnostics is very helpful in troubleshooting general purpose problems, displaying hardware information, and viewing the version of NT and the version of any installed Service Packs.

From Here...

See the following chapters for more information on topics related to the Exchange Administrator program:

- Chapter 13, "Directory and System Attendant Configuration," for managing core Exchange server components.

- Chapter 14, "Message Transfer Configuration," for managing the flow of messages between sites.

- Chapter 16, "Creating and Configuring Recipient," to build the global address list with all types of recipients.

- Chapter 18, "Using Directory Replication and Synchronization," to manage the directory synchronization process.

Part
III

Ch
12

Directory and System Attendant Configuration

With this section, we begin covering the details for configuring your Exchange server components. First, we will cover the steps to set up each Exchange site down to the server level. This will teach you to set site configuration properties as well as general settings for the core components of each Microsoft Exchange server. Subsequent chapters cover configuring additional components and using elements together to develop a complete Exchange organization.

In this chapter, you will learn the step-by-step process of configuring the core component properties. ■

Directory Service Site Configuration

Enables you to set preferences on Exchange site directory functions for all servers in the site from a single point.

Site Addressing

Configure site address properties that set default address values for X.400, cc:Mail, MS Mail, and SMTP for all new mailbox accounts in the site.

Server Configuration

General functions of the server are controlled and defined as custom to each server, as well as options to manage database inconsistencies on each server.

Directory Service

Control diagnostic information for the Directory Service for each server, as well as resolve possible out-of-synch conditions among servers in a site.

Directory Synchronization

Set up and manage the directory synchronization service between Exchange, MS Mail, cc:Mail, and other compatible foreign systems.

System Attendant

The master control of an Exchange server that enables other Exchange system services to run.

Configuring Directory Services

Directory Site (DS Site) configuration allows you to set preferences on Exchange site directory functions. Settings made to this object's properties affect an entire Microsoft Exchange site.

In this section, you learn how to do the following:

- Set tombstone lifetimes
- Set garbage collection intervals
- Generate and schedule the creation of offline address books
- Define the custom attribute for all recipients within an Exchange site
- Restrict access to site directory attributes and manage replication of directory objects

First, let us define some concepts essential to proper configuration of the Directory Service agent.

Tombstone Lifetime

A *tombstone* in Exchange directory terms is a marker representing a deleted directory object. At the moment when you delete a directory object, it is removed instantly from the local server only. All the other Exchange servers that participate in directory replication with this server do not become immediately aware of that object's deletion. Therefore, a tombstone marker is created that, when replicated to other servers, informs them of the original object's deletion. The tombstone lifetime dictates the number of days a tombstone marker exists before it expires and can be deleted from the system.

Here are some considerations for setting tombstone lifetimes:

- *Situation 1   Frequency of directory object deletion.* If you set the tombstone lifetime for an excessively long period of time and you frequently delete objects, there will be a large number of tombstone markers clogging your entire directory replication system.

- *Situation 2   Length of time a server could be down.* For example, you set the tombstone lifetime for a site at seven days. Let's say one server in your site is down for over a week. That downed server will not be notified of an object's deletion before the tombstone of some directory object is deleted. There will be some directory inconsistencies to correct as a result.

N O T E Tombstones cannot be used to undelete a previously deleted directory object.

Garbage Collection Interval

The *garbage collection interval* determines the number of hours between deletion of expired tombstone markers (referred to as *garbage*). Much like a traditional garbage collection service, this operation is a scheduled removal of expired directory "garbage." Once directory object tombstone markers have expired, they are ready ("placed on the curb") for deletion at the garbage collection interval.

Offline Address Book

Remote users can take advantage of Exchange address lists by downloading a current version of the offline address book. This address list is generated from the main address list, and the process is managed through these property pages. A remote user uses the offline address book like a standard recipient directory when disconnected from the network. The offline address book contains only the recipients or recipient groups specified by the Exchange administrator. The offline address book object itself is a hidden public folder held in the public information store of a designated Exchange server. There can be only one offline address book per site.

Custom Attributes

Custom attributes pertain specifically to recipients. They are added to represent any extra information you want to have entered when creating recipients. Where standard attributes are *city, state, zip, phone number,* a custom attribute can be anything from birthday, age, or hair color, to favorite music or bowling average.

Attributes

A new feature added in Exchange version 5.0 enables the administrator to select which site directory objects are accessible to certain classes of LDAP users and which objects are to be replicated to other Exchange sites.

Configuring DS Site Property Pages

In this section, you begin to configure the DS Site property pages. You will find that a wide variety of settings affect how directory functions are carried out in your Exchange site.

The General Page

Figure 13.1 shows the General property page and the various directory settings associated with it.

1. Select the General tab of the DS Site Configuration property pages. The General property page appears.
2. Enter a Display Name for this object as you want it to be displayed in the Exchange administrator program. By default, this name is DS Site Configuration. The alias name is set to Site-DSA-Config and cannot be modified.
3. Next to Tombstone Lifetime (Days), enter the length of time (in days) until a directory object's tombstone marker expires. By default, this value is set to 30 days.
4. Next to Garbage Collection Interval (Hours), enter the interval (in hours) between deletion of expired tombstone markers. See the preceding section for a more detailed description of the garbage collection interval. By default, this value is set to 12 hours.
5. Click Apply to set these properties and continue with other properties. If you are finished setting options, click OK to return to the administrator program.

Part
III

Ch

13

FIG. 13.1

General directory
settings for a site.

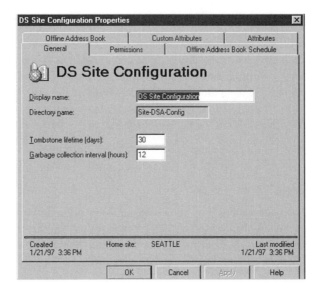

The Permissions Page

This property page allows you to define certain Windows NT user accounts that have rights to modify this directory object.

The Offline Address Book Schedule Page

This property page allows you to determine at what intervals a new offline address book will be generated.

1. Select the Offline Address Book Schedule tab of the DS Site Configuration properties pages. The property page in Figure 13.2 appears.

2. Click Always to continually re-generate updated versions of an offline address book. Once a cycle completes, a new one begins at the next system registry, defined as an "Always" interval, which by default is 15 minutes.

3. Click Selected Times, and use the time grid to set specific times when offline address book generation will begin.

   For example, if you know that your remote users connect first thing in the morning to update their offline address books, then set the schedule to begin several hours before you expect most of them to connect. That way, the whole generation cycle will be complete, and the address book they download will be as complete as possible.

4. Click Apply to set these properties and continue with other properties. If you are done setting all options, click OK to return to the administrator program.

FIG. 13.2
Set the schedule for
creating an offline
address book.

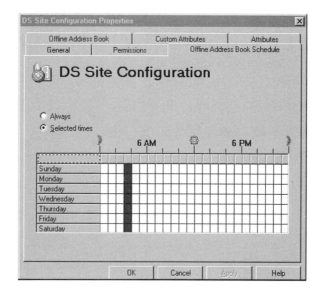

N O T E Generating an offline address book can often take several hours. If one cycle of offline address book generation carries into the next scheduled generation time, the generation will finish normally, then begin again at the next scheduled time after its completion. ▨

The Offline Address Book Page

This property page defines parameters on how the offline address book will be created. You choose what elements of the directory will be included. If you desire a highly customized list of recipients to be included in the offline address book, then consider creating a recipient container dedicated to offline address book generation.

1. Select the Offline Address Book tab of the DS Site Configuration Properties pages. The property page in Figure 13.3 appears.

2. Select the Offline Address Book Server by using the pull-down menu. This is the server that will actually generate the offline address book and from which a remote user will download the information. By default, this is the Microsoft Exchange server to which you are currently connected with the administrator program.

T I P Because the generation of a large offline address book can be a lengthy process, select a lower traffic and lower utilized server (if available) to perform this task.

3. Click Generate Offline Address Book Now to immediately begin the generation of a new offline address book.

Part
III

Ch
13

FIG. 13.3

Set offline address book creation and location options.

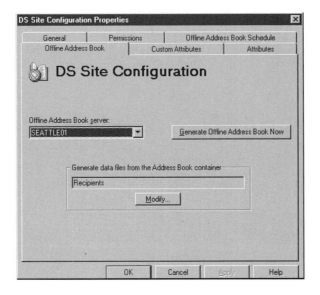

N O T E   Before an offline address book is available to remote users, it must first be generated. Note your generation schedule to see if the next scheduled cycle falls within an acceptable time frame. If necessary, click Generate Offline Address Book Now to create it immediately. ▨

4. The Generate Data Files from the Address Book Container box displays which recipient container is used to create the offline address book. Typically, you will want to use the global address list container in the offline address book for this site. Note that by default the selected container is the recipients from the local Exchange site, not the global address list. Click Modify to select a new recipient container.

   Choose the recipient container you want to use for the offline address book. Click OK to accept your choice.

5. Click Apply to set these properties and continue with other properties. If you are done setting options, click OK to return to the administrator program.

CAUTION

There must be only one offline address book per Microsoft Exchange site. Replicating the offline address book hidden public folder will create directory errors.

The Custom Attributes Page

This property page allows you to define characteristics that will appear on the Custom Attributes property page of each recipient only in the local site. The field can be defined to display any additional information for which you want to create a space.

To create custom attribute fields:

1. Select the Custom Attributes tab of the DS Site Configuration Properties page. The property page in Figure 13.4 appears.

2. Type in the names of Custom Attributes 1-10 in the spaces provided. By default, these entries are literally named Custom Attribute 1 through Custom Attribute 10.

3. Click Apply to set these properties and continue with other properties. If you are finished setting options, click OK to return to the administrator program.

FIG. 13.4
Set the custom attribute whose values you will set in the recipient's properties pages.

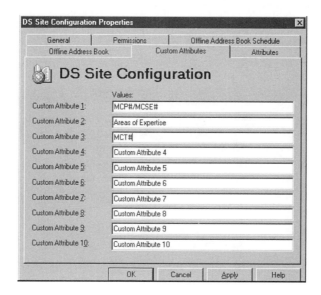

The Attributes Page

This property page is a new feature in Exchange version 5.0 that assists administrators in managing access for LDAP users and in directory replication of objects in the site directory. An example would be enabling authenticated users access to most mailbox attributes, such as "direct reports" or phone numbers, but denying access of these objects to anonymous users.

To reduce possible network traffic and system overhead associated with directory replication, additional options are provided to control inclusion of directory objects in Inter-site replication. Caution should be exercised when deselecting objects under the System attributes heading as it could affect directory operation.

Modifying attribute access options requires the following steps:

1. Select the Attributes tab of the DS Site Configuration Properties page. The property page in Figure 13.5 appears.

2. In the left-hand Configure list, select the requestor access type you want to modify.

Part

III

Ch

13

3. In the right-hand pull-down field, select the appropriate object you want to show access for in the display window immediately below. As the check boxes associated with the various objects are checked or unchecked, the data values for these objects become accessible to LDAP users or are included in directory replication to other sites.

It is important to note that in the case of custom attributes, only the data associated with the custom attribute is replicated, not the new label replacing the phrase Custom Attribute 1. This could result in one Exchange site relabeling their site's Custom Attribute 1 text to become Cube Number and then entering appropriate numeric values. Meanwhile, a different Exchange site might relabel its Custom Attribute 1 to Favorite Color with alpha values subsequently entered. When the two sites replicate data and the values of their respective Custom Attributes 1 are exchanged, the sites will see a mix of data types that makes no sense with the labels in their local sites!

FIG. 13.5

Attributes tab of the DS Site Configuration Properties page.

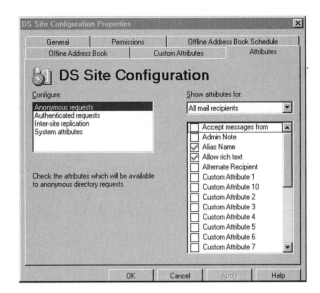

Configuring Site Addressing

These sets of property pages allow you to configure site properties that have to do with automatic creation of e-mail addresses, default site e-mail address values, and routing messages to their intended destination within an Exchange system. These options determine which servers will be used to calculate routing tables, and when to calculate those tables. Also, you can use these pages to get an overview of how messaging links are established in your organization.

The General Page

In this property page, you can edit this object's Display Name (see Figure 13.6) and also:

- Choose Routing Calculation Server. This server will be responsible for processing routing data for this server. The updated routing table will then be replicated to this server.

- Choose Share Address Space with Other X.400 Systems l. With this option selected, if an incoming X.400 message cannot find its intended Exchange recipient, it will be routed to the system sharing this address space. This option is helpful when running Exchange side-by-side with a foreign X.400 system (for example, during a migration to Exchange). By default, the X.400 address space is not shared.

FIG. 13.6

Set general site routing parameters.

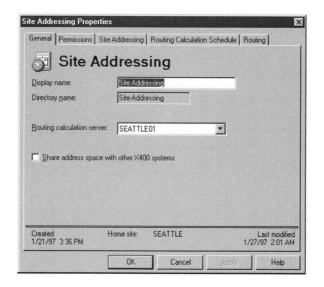

The Site Addressing Page

E-mail addresses are used by the various Exchange gateways and connectors to identify specific directory objects to other messaging systems (see Figure 13.7). In this case, these addresses affect all messages routed to this site. There are now four default addresses created each for MS Mail, SMTP, X.400, and now cc:Mail in Exchange version 5.0. If other connectors or gateways are installed, those addresses can be created by default as well.

An added feature in Exchange version 5.0 is the capability to select which address types will be automatically created when a new mailbox or public folder is created. This is controlled by simply checking or unchecking the box adjacent to the address type. Additionally, when a box is unchecked, the administrator is presented with the option to also remove this address from all currently installed mailboxes, if desired.

Just as in Exchange version 4.0, the default address values are editable. A common example for editing address values might be if your corporation elected to change the root DNS value for your SMTP addresses, such as swspectrum.com being changed to softwarespectrum.com.

FIG. 13.7
Set e-mail address entries for the entire site.

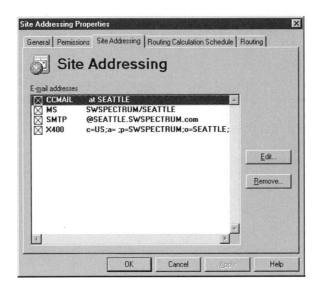

The Routing Calculation Schedule Page

When changes in site configuration are made, routing tables need to be rebuilt in order to maintain accurate message delivery information. By default, routing is calculated once per day at 4 a.m. local time (see Figure 13.8). Generally, the default settings will be more than adequate to maintain up-to-date routing tables in your site; use the manual override when immediate recalculation is necessary. If your site undergoes frequent changes in components (more servers, new connector types, and so on), you may want to increase the routing calculation frequency. Set the schedule in a standard schedule property page.

FIG. 13.8

Define a schedule when routing table calculations occur.

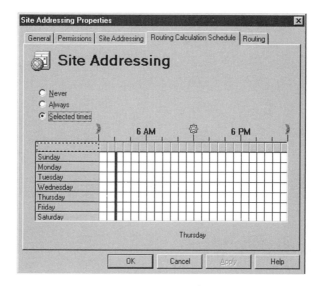

The Routing Page

Click a type of message destination and click Details to view the route of such a message. The dialog boxes in Figure 13.9 and Figure 13.10 appear.

FIG. 13.9

View the message routes available from this Exchange site.

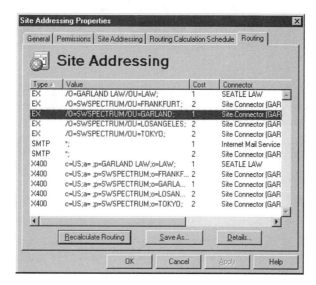

FIG. 13.10
View Routing Details for connector available from this site. Note the file extensions for this file type.

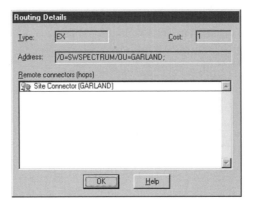

Server Property Pages

Each Microsoft Exchange server has its own set of property pages. Here, you can configure general functions that apply specifically to a single Exchange server.

The following are the property pages for server configuration:

- *General.* View server's directory name. No configuration options available.
- *Permissions.* Set access rights to this directory object.
- *Services.* Select which Microsoft Windows NT services that an Exchange server monitor will check by default when such monitor objects are created for this server.
- *Locales.* Set support for various foreign Exchange client language code page formats.
- *Database Paths.* Set the hard disk location for each information store.
- *IS Maintenance.* Schedule automatic information store upkeep and optimizing.
- *Advanced.* Toggle circular logging for the directory and information store, and configure information store inconsistency adjustment.
- *Diagnostics Logging.* A central location that defines what events associated with this server will be entered in the Windows NT Event Log.

To open the Server property page:

1. Navigate to your desired site with the Exchange administrator program.
2. Click the Configuration container of the selected site. All the site configuration objects appear in the administrator program's right window.
3. Open the Servers container. A list of Exchange servers in your site will be listed.
4. Click the server name on the Private Information Store you want to configure (see Figure 13.11). The following list of server objects is visible on the right display window of the Microsoft Exchange Administrator Program.
5. Open its property pages by selecting Properties from the administrator program file menu or by pressing Alt+Enter.

FIG. 13.11
Select the Exchange server to edit, then open its properties.

The General Page

This property page displays the server's directory name and has a space for an additional administrative note (see Figure 13.12). The server's directory name cannot be changed without reinstalling Microsoft Exchange.

FIG. 13.12
The server name cannot be changed after Exchange has been installed.

Part

III

Ch

13

The Permissions Page

This property page allows you to define certain Windows NT user accounts that have rights to modify this directory object. See Chapter 12, "Using the Administrator Program," for a detailed description on working with the standard Permissions property page.

The Services Page

This property page allows you to define what services will be checked by a Microsoft Exchange server monitor. The top display window shows all services currently installed on this Windows NT server. The bottom display window shows all the services by default currently monitored by Exchange.

Select a service from the top window and click Add to add it to the list of Monitored Services (see Figure 13.13).

Select a service from the bottom window and click Remove to take it off the list of Monitored Services.

Click Default to return to the basic services selected by Exchange Server.

FIG. 13.13

Select the services to be monitored by an Exchange server monitor.

The Locales Page

Locales determine how values (such as date or currency) are displayed in the Exchange client. International settings are determined by the Exchange client settings (see Chapter 30, "Using Outlook") and also affect default sorting order for lists. This property page allows you to activate certain locales from the list of installed locales.

The Installed Locales list box displays all the formats currently installed on this Exchange server. Click Add or Remove to edit the list of Selected Locales. The Selected Locales list box displays what formats are in use (see Figure 13.14).

FIG. 13.14
Use this dialog box to add or remove support for various foreign language Exchange clients.

The Database Paths Page

Database paths are pointers to the hard disk directories where Exchange actually stores information. This property page allows you to set the paths to the directory for placement of the public and private information store files on this server. The paths are set up when you initially install Exchange Server.

> **CAUTION**
>
> It is recommended that instead of manually editing the paths to the critical databases of the Exchange server that the administrator use the Exchange Optimizer Wizard to move these files and adjust the necessary directory and registry values automatically.

Part
III

Ch
13

The three main Exchange server databases are:

- Directory
- Private
- Public Information Store

Additional information files (see Figure 13.15) store additional Exchange data such as transaction logs.

T I P One basic way to improve Exchange performance is to spread the database files across several hard drives. The Microsoft Exchange Optimizer can assist with this process.

FIG. 13.15

Use this dialog box to view the physical location, such as the hard disk, for the various types of Exchange data.

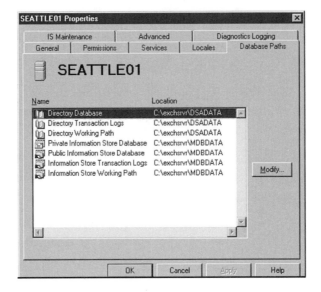

Click the Modify button to bring up a dialog box that enables you to browse through your system's file structure and select a location for the database information.

The IS Maintenance Page

Information Store Maintenance optimizes an Exchange server's operating speed. Basic maintenance includes disk defragmentation for improved hard disk performance and compression of the various database files by removing excessive "white space" left by deleted data (see Figure 13.16). Use this page to schedule maintenance for each Exchange server.

 T I P Maintenance tasks are taxing on hard drive and overall server performance. Always schedule them at the server's least busy period of the day.

The Advanced Page

This property page allows you to configure two advanced options:

- *Database Circular Logging.* Enabling these two check boxes allows Exchange to write over transaction log files after their data is saved to the database. Use this option to save drive space only if storage space availability is a serious consideration.

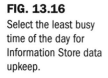

FIG. 13.16
Select the least busy
time of the day for
Information Store data
upkeep.

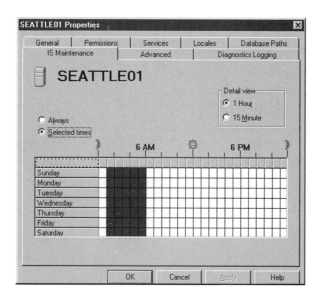

> **CAUTION**
>
> If the circular logging options are enabled, you will no longer be able to perform differential and incremental
> backups (see Chapter 25, "Maintaining Exchange").

■ *DS/IS Consistency Adjustment.* There are two components to each directory object saved
in a server's information store: the object itself and a corresponding entry in the
directory. Consistency adjustment corrects errors arising by mismatched information.
This feature will either add or delete a directory entry to match the existence or absence
of information store information.

This property page allows you to control at what point these inconsistencies are to be corrected. Select either the All inconsistencies to correct them immediately or select Inconsistencies more than *X* Days and enter the time an inconsistency can exist before it is automatically
corrected (see Figure 13.17).

Diagnostics Logging

This property page works in conjunction with the Windows NT Event Log to record various
"events" that occur within the many Exchange services. Various levels of logging determine
what constitutes an event and, therefore, what types of information are actually recorded in the
event log. For troubleshooting purposes, you would want a very detailed record of occurrences
and, hence, set a high logging level. However, normally you would want to log only events that
are critical, so set a lower logging level for everyday operation (see Figure 13.18). Individual
components (for example, Directory, MTA, and Information Store) also have diagnostic logging
pages for their individual service, but all services are available through this server property
page.

FIG. 13.17
Set general logging and inconsistency adjustment preferences.

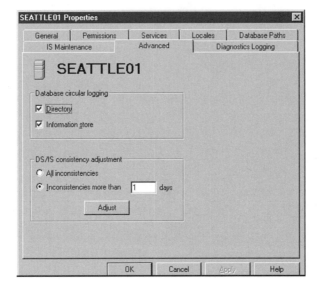

FIG. 13.18
Control log settings for all Exchange services running on this server.

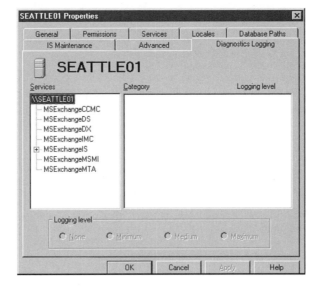

Configuring Directory Service

The Directory Service Properties pages are mainly used for configuring diagnostics information. However, there are two additional functions provided by this object that will be used more frequently during normal operation. These functions are:

- *Manually Synchronize Directory Information Within a Site*. This operation normally occurs every five minutes; but if changes have been made and you do not want to wait for automatic synchronization, then use this property page.

- *Manually Check Knowledge Consistency*. Knowledge consistency for this local server is its awareness of other Exchange servers within a site and other sites within your organization. This operation is run automatically once daily; but if Exchange servers or sites were added and the local server was not aware of those changes (for example, the local server was down during that time), then you may not want to wait for the automatic checking and do it manually.

Say, for example, that

Exchange Server SEATTLE01 is brought down for two hours for a memory upgrade. During the time of the upgrade, a new server, DUBLIN08, is added to the site. When SEATTLE01 is restored to proper functioning, it will not be aware of the existence of the new server until the Knowledge Consistency cycle is run at the end of the day. Knowing this, the administrator for SEATTLE01 runs the Knowledge Consistency cycle manually from the Directory Service Properties pages. SEATTLE01 is now aware of the new server's existence.

If an inconsistency is detected when checking manually, it is a good idea to manually execute all processes related to correcting inconsistencies. Use this sequence:

1. Check knowledge consistency from the Directory Service Properties pages and detect the error.
2. Manually update directory replication within the site by selecting Update Now also from the Directory Service Properties pages.
3. Open the Message Transfer Agent properties for this server and click Recalculate Routing from the General property page.

Although the preceding sequence is optional and will be automatically executed with a 24-hour period, performing the tasks immediately will reduce the possibility of other conflicts or errors.

Opening the Directory Service Properties Pages:

1. Use the Microsoft Exchange administrator program to navigate to the list of servers within the site to which you are connected.
2. Click an Exchange server within the site, and a list of configuration objects appears in the administrator program's right display window.
3. Select the Directory Service object and open its property pages.

The General Page

1. Select the General tab of the Directory Service Properties page (see Figure 13.19). The following property page appears.

Part
III

Ch

13

FIG. 13.19

Use these two controls to manually update the local site directory and check knowledge consistency.

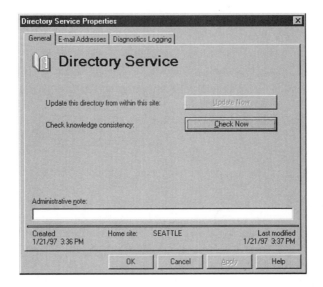

2. Click Update Now to request directory updates from all servers in the site. This process automatically runs every five minutes within an Exchange site.

3. Click Check Now to run a knowledge consistency check and detect any changes in servers in a site or sites in your organization. This process automatically runs once a day.

4. Enter any additional Administrative Note.

5. Click Apply to set these properties and continue with other properties. If you are finished setting options, click OK to return to the administrator program.

The E-Mail Addresses Page

E-mail addresses are used by the various Exchange gateways and connectors to identify specific directory objects to other messaging systems. There are four default addresses created each for MS Mail, SMTP, X.400, and now cc:Mail.

Setting public directory service e-mail addresses:

1. Click the E-Mail Addresses of the Directory Service Properties pages (see Figure 13.20). The following dialog box appears. The four default addresses (cc:Mail, MS Mail, SMTP, and X.400) are displayed.

2. Click New to add a specific e-mail address for this directory service. Select an existing address and click Edit to modify it, or click Remove to delete it.

3. Click Apply to set these properties and continue with other properties. If you are setting options, click OK to return to the administrator program.

FIG. 13.20
Define any additional
e-mail address for this
directory object.

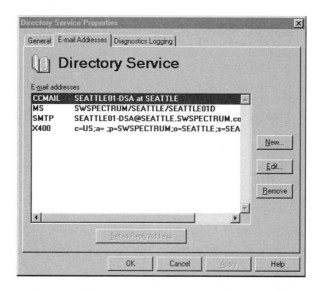

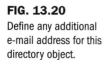

The Diagnostics Logging Page

This property page works in conjunction with the Windows NT Event Log to record various "events" that occur within the Directory Service (MSExchangeDS). Various levels of logging determine what constitutes an event and, therefore, what types of information are actually recorded. For troubleshooting purposes, you would want a very detailed record of occurrences within the Directory Service, and hence set a high logging level. However, normally you would want to log only events that are critical, so set a lower logging level for everyday operation (see Figure 13.21).

FIG. 13.21
This page controls
logging for the directory
synchronization service
only.

Configuring Directory Synchronization Service

These property pages allow for directory synchronization between Exchange, MS Mail, and other compatible foreign systems, which in Exchange Version 5.0 now includes direct support for cc:Mail. For further directory synchronization information see Chapter 18, "Using Directory Replication and Synchronization."

The following are the property pages available for configuration on the directory synchronization service:

- General
- E-mail Addresses
- Delivery Restrictions
- Incoming Templates
- Outgoing Templates
- Diagnostics Logging

To open the Directory Synchronization Service Properties Pages:

1. Navigate to your desired site with the Exchange administrator program.

2. Click the Configuration container of the selected site. All the site configuration objects appear in the administrator program's right window.

3. Open the Servers container. A list of Exchange servers in your site will be listed.

4. Click the server name on which you want to configure the directory synchronization service.

5. Click the Directory Synchronization object. Open its property pages.

The General Page

This property page allows you to view only the current server's name and enter an Administrative Note (see Figure 13.22). An Exchange server's name is set when the software is installed and cannot be changed after the fact.

FIG. 13.22
The name of this server cannot be altered.

The E-Mail Addresses Page

E-mail addresses are used by the various Exchange gateways and connectors to identify specific directory objects to other messaging systems. The directory synchronization service receives regular update messages sent to these addresses. There are four default addresses created each for cc:Mail, MS Mail, SMTP, and X.400.

The Delivery Restrictions Page

The Directory Synchronization service executes its functions by the transfer of messages between itself and other systems. This property page assures that only specific users can send messages to the directory synchronization service.

To configure delivery restrictions:

1. Select the Delivery Restrictions tab from the Directory Synchronization Properties page (see Figure 13.23). The following property page appears.

2. Use the dialog box to either restrict certain senders or to permit only certain senders.

3. Click Apply to set these properties and continue with other properties. If you are finished setting options, click OK to return to the administrator program.

FIG. 13.23

Use this page to prevent unnecessary messages from being sent to this service.

Part
III

Ch
13

The Incoming Templates Page

In this property page, you can define a template that will apply to all incoming directory synchronization messages (see Figure 13.24). See Chapter 18, "Using Directory Replication and Synchronization," for more details on this template and its use in directory synchronization.

The Outgoing Templates Page

In this property page you can define a template that will apply to all outgoing directory synchronization messages (see Figure 13.25). See Chapter 18 for more details on this template and its use in directory synchronization.

FIG. 13.24

Map standard MS Mail attributes to Exchange server recipients.

FIG. 13.25

Map Exchange server recipient attributes to the standard MS Mail directory template attributes.

The Diagnostics Logging Page

This property page works in conjunction with the Windows NT Event Log to record "events" that occur within the Directory Synchronization Service. Various levels of logging determine what constitutes an event and what types of information are actually recorded. For troubleshooting purposes, you want a very detailed record of occurrences within the Directory Synchronization Service, and hence set a high logging level. However, normally you would want to log only events that are critical, so set a lower logging level for everyday operation.

Configuring System Attendant

The System Attendant service must be running in order for most other Exchange system services to run. Stopping the System Attendant service, for example, will prompt the halting of several other Exchange services simultaneously.

Each Microsoft Exchange server within your organization can be configured with different properties. To configure the System Attendant Properties page:

1. Use the Microsoft Exchange administrator program to navigate to the list of servers within the site to which you are connected.

2. Click the server name whose System Attendant object you want to configure.

3. In the right display window, you will see a list of objects pertaining to that Exchange server (see Figure 13.26).

FIG. 13.26

The System Attendant is found in the individual Exchange server container.

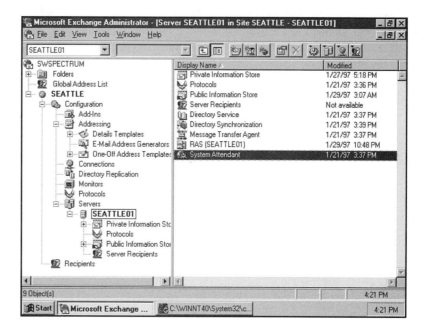

Part

III

Ch

13

Click the System Attendant object and open its property pages. The property page in Figure 13.27 appears.

FIG. 13.27

The System Attendant General property page.

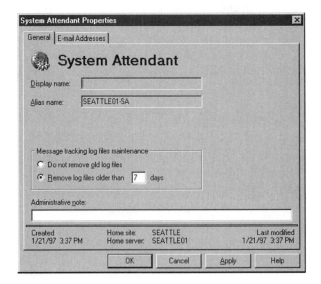

4. The General page is the first visible property page. The Display Name is set as System Attendant by default and cannot be changed. Likewise, the Alias Name for this object is set to <server name>-SA (for example, SEATTLE01-SA) and also cannot be changed.

   Under the Message Tracking Log Files Maintenance area: click Do Not Remove Old Log Files if you want the system attendant to keep such log files for an indefinite time.

5. Click Remove Log Files Older Than X Number of Days to have the system attendant on this server delete message tracking files after a specified number of days has elapsed. Enter the number of days in the box provided. By default, this option is selected, and the log files are deleted every seven days.

CAUTION

Opting to keep old log files on a server with a high volume of message traffic could easily take up many megabytes of storage space. If you do select Do Not Remove Old Log Files, make sure to keep track of log file sizes!

6. Enter any additional Administrative Note (such as reasons for keeping all old log files) in the box provided.

7. Click Apply to set these properties and continue with other properties. If you are finished setting options, click OK to return to the administrator program.

Setting E-Mail Addresses for the System Attendant

E-mail addresses are used by the various Exchange gateways and connectors to identify specific directory objects to other messaging systems. The System Attendant, though not capable of receiving messages, is a directory object just the same and has a set of e-mail addresses associated with it. There are four default addresses created each for cc:Mail, MS Mail, SMTP, and X.400.

1. Click the E-Mail Addresses of the System Attendant Properties page (see Figure 13.28). The four default addresses (cc:Mail, MS Mail, SMTP, and X.400) are displayed.

FIG. 13.28
The E-Mail Addresses page displays the three default address for this system attendant.

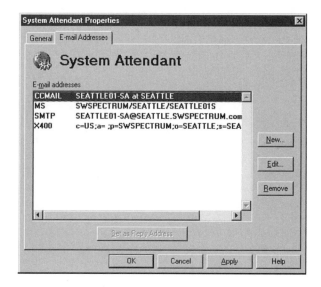

2. Click New to add a specific e-mail address for this system attendant. Select an existing address and click Edit to modify it, or click Remove to delete it.

3. Click Apply to set these properties and continue with other properties. If you are finished setting options, click OK to return to the administrator program.

All other functions of the System Attendant (such as checking directory replication inconsistencies and gathering information about other running Exchange services) are carried out without additional configuration by the administrator.

Part
III

Ch
13

From Here...

For more information on related items, see the following chapters:

■ Chapter 2, "Understanding Exchange's Organization Sites," contains additional information about how Exchange is structured.

■ Chapter 3, "Exchange's Integrated Server Components," details the fundamental components of Exchange.

- Chapter 18, "Using Directory Replication and Synchronization," covers the concepts and configuration of automated directory updating between Exchange and foreign systems.

- Chapter 28, "Troubleshooting Exchange with Diagnostic Tools," offers tips and assistance on solving and preventing problems with your Exchange configuration.

CHAPTER 14

Message Transfer Configuration

The Microsoft Exchange Message Transfer Agent (MTA) is the key component that provides addressing and routing information that delivers messages. Proper configuration of MTA settings is important to an efficient Exchange organization. As described in Chapter 3, "Exchange's Integrated Server Components," a message that originates in an Exchange mailbox reaches its destination in only two ways: The first—a message is addressed to a user on the same Exchange server and is delivered by the Information Store. The second—a message is addressed to a user on a different server or foreign system, and the MTA handles the message transmission.

Unless your organization consists primarily of one or two Exchange servers, the MTAs on various levels are the entities that are responsible for message routing and transmission. ■

Various Components of the Message Transfer Agent

Understanding undeliverable messages, Message Tracking, and Message Queues. Describe Messaging Defaults and MTA Overrides.

How to Perform the MTA Site Configuration Tasks

Start breaking into the General Tab area and begin to define your configurations.

How to Configure the Local MTA Properties

Configure and manage MTA services through property pages.

Understanding the Transfer Agent Components

The Microsoft Exchange Message Transfer Agent is primarily a Windows NT service running on each Exchange server in your organization. For connection to Microsoft Mail systems, an additional service called the MS Mail Connector (PC) MTA negotiates message transmission with MS Mail for PC networks.

Configuration of the primary Exchange MTA is handled through two sets of property pages:

- *MTA Site Configuration*. Defines overall settings for message transmission within the entire Exchange site.
- *Message Transfer Agent (for a specific Exchange server)*. Defines server-specific MTA settings, such as message size limits and logging levels.

Let's discuss some of the essential parameters involved in performing MTA Site Configuration.

Dead Letter

Any message that is defined as undeliverable by the Message Transfer Agent is classified as a *dead letter*. You can specify a dead-letter recipient (usually an administrator) from within the MTA site configuration property pages.

Message Tracking

To keep records of Message Transfer Agent activity within a Microsoft Exchange site, enable message tracking. A daily log file is generated and stored in the EXCHSRVR\TRACKING.LOG directory. Message tracking log files are in a text format. The full file name, to use the example, would be EXCHSRVR\TRACKING\970122.LOG. The individual log files are:

YYMMDD.log

Example

970122.log for MTA activity on Jan 22, 1997.

Message Queues

Each server has a list of messages that are waiting to be delivered by its MTA. The queues are distinguished as being either private or public Information Store messages. Messages are held in the queue until the MTA can successfully establish a connection with a remote MTA and transfer the messages or until the messages exceed their lifetimes (set in the messaging defaults).

Messaging Defaults

Settings for how (and how long) to transfer a message before certain time-outs occur are called *messaging defaults*. These values are set in the MTA Site Configuration properties and are used by all MTAs in the site unless a specific connection uses MTA override parameters.

MTA Overrides

Certain connectors—namely, the Dynamic RAS Connector and the X.400 connector—provide for object-specific MTA settings. Use the Override property page to change the default Microsoft Exchange Server MTA attributes when using a specific X.400 or dynamic RAS connector. Keep in mind their existence when you define messaging defaults in the MTA Site Configuration property page. Override property pages are there for developing flexibility in MTA configuration.

Performing MTA Site Configuration

To open the MTA Site Configuration property pages, follow these steps:

1. Navigate to your desired site with the Exchange Administrator program.

2. Click the Configuration container of the selected site (see Figure 14.1). All the site-configuration objects appear in the Administrator program's right window.

FIG. 14.1

The MTA Site Configuration is located in the Configuration container.

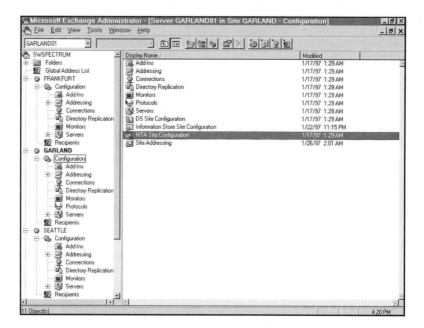

3. Select the MTA Site Configuration object from the list.

4. Open the MTA Site Configuration Object property pages by double-clicking the object.

At this point, you have three property pages to configure:

- *General.* Sets the MTA site configuration display name and the dead-letter recipient, and enables message tracking.
- *Permissions.* Sets security rights to the MTA Site Configuration object.
- *Messaging Defaults.* Defines connection and transmission parameters for the MTAs in your site.

The General Tab

To configure the General features, such as the display name of the MTA Site Configuration Object, follow these steps:

1. Click the General tab of the MTA Site Configuration Properties page (see Figure 14.2).

FIG. 14.2

The General MTA site configuration property page.

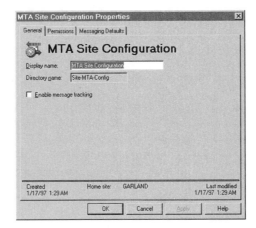

2. Type a new name in the Display Name box, if you want. The default name is MTA Site Configuration.

N O T E   By default, the Directory Name, Site-MTA-Config, cannot be changed. ■

3. In the Dead Letter Recipient section, click the None radio button if you want all nondeliverable messages to be deleted. By default, this option is selected.

4. Click the Modify button if you want to enter or change a name in the Dead Letter Recipient text box. The Exchange address list appears. Click the radio button next to the name in the box to designate that recipient as the dead-letter recipient.

5. Click the Enable Message Tracking check box to instruct the System Attendant to keep a daily log of all messages processed by the MTA. This check box corresponds to the Enable Message Tracking check box in the Information Store Site Configuration property page.

6. Click <u>A</u>pply to set these properties and continue with viewing/changing other properties.

7. When you finish making settings, click OK to return to the Administrator program.

The Permissions Tab

This property page allows you to define certain Windows NT user accounts that have rights to modify this directory object. See Chapter 11, "Migrating from External Systems," for a detailed description on working with the standard Permissions property page.

The Messaging Defaults Tab

To set the messaging default values for the MTA Site Configuration object, follow these steps:

1. Click the Messaging Defaults tab of the MTA Site Configuration Properties page (see Figure 14.3).

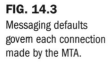 To return to the default Message Transfer Agent settings, click the Reset Default Values button.

2. Enter specific MTA configuration variables, as described in Table 14.1, which follows these steps.

   To the right of each item listed in the table is a box that contains a default numeric value. Replace any value with a number that will be used in establishing a connection through any MTA in the current site.

3. Click <u>A</u>pply to set these properties and continue with other properties.

4. When you finish making settings, click OK to return to the Administrator program.

FIG. 14.3

Messaging defaults govern each connection made by the MTA.

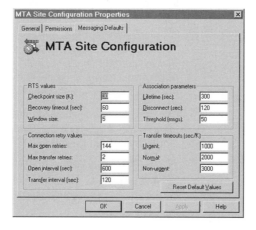

Table 14.1   MTA Site Configuration Parameter Values

Variable	Description
RTS Values	
Checkpoint Size (K)	The value (in kilobytes) used to verify packet transmission with returned checkpoints. By default, this value is 30.
Recovery Timeout (Sec)	The time delay (in seconds) before a broken transmission is retried. By default, the delay is 60 seconds.
Window Size	The number of checkpoints (in kilobytes) that can be transmitted without acknowledgment. By default, this value is 5.
Connection Retry Values	
Max Open Retries	The maximum number of consecutive failed attempts before the MTA ceases trying to open a communication channel with a remote MTA. By default, an MTA makes 144 attempts.
Max Transfer Retries	The maximum number of consecutive failed attempts before the MTA ceases trying to transfer a message packet. By default, the MTA makes two attempts.
Open Interval (Sec)	The delay (in seconds) between attempts to open a communication channel. By default, the delay is 600 seconds.
Transfer Interval (Sec)	The delay (in seconds) between attempts to retransmit a failed message packet. By default, this delay is 120 seconds.
Association Parameters	
Lifetime (Sec)	The maximum time that an idle connection between MTAs remains open. By default, an idle link is held open for 300 seconds after the last communication.
Disconnect (Sec)	The maximum time allowed for establishing or terminating a connection before the session is ended independently. By default, this time is 120 seconds.
Threshold (Msgs)	The number of messages that must be queued at this MTA before the MTA initiates a link to a remote MTA. By default, 50 messages must be awaiting transmission.
Transfer Timeouts (Sec/K)	
Urgent	The delay (in seconds per kilobyte of total message size) between retries of urgent messages. By default, this delay is 1,000 seconds. This is a time out value before messages are sent.

Variable	Description
Transfer Timeouts (Sec/K)	
Normal	The delay (in seconds per kilobyte of total message size) between retries of normal messages. By default, this delay is 2,000 seconds. The trend here is the less important the message, the longer you wait for a transmission.
Non-Urgent	The delay (in seconds per kilobyte of total message size) between retries of non-urgent messages. By default, this delay is 3,000 seconds.

N O T E   If you combine the default 144 Max Open Retries with the default 600-second Open Interval, Exchange waits 24 hours before returning a message as undeliverable. ▪

The following section discusses configuring Message Transfer Agent properties for each Microsoft Exchange Server.

Configuring Local MTA Properties

Each Microsoft Exchange Server has a Message Transfer Agent. The MTA property pages are designed to configure and manage this service.

First, you must select the MTA from the server within your site. Follow these steps:

1. Navigate to your desired site with the Exchange Administrator program.
2. Click the Configuration container of the selected site. All the site-configuration objects appear in the Administrator program's right window.
3. Open the Servers container by double-clicking it. A list of Exchange servers in your site appears.
4. Click the name of the server that houses the MTA that you want to configure (see Figure 14.4). The following list of server objects is visible on the right display window of the Microsoft Exchange Administrator program.
5. Click the Message Transfer Agent object, and open its property pages.

The following three property pages become available for you to configure:

- ▪ *General.* Sets local MTA name, password, and general message transmission preferences for this server.
- ▪ *Queues.* Lists messages awaiting transmission by the local MTA.
- ▪ *Diagnostics Logging.* Sets the level of events that are entered in the Windows NT event log.

Part
III

Ch
14

FIG. 14.4

The Message Transfer
Agent directory object is
located inside the server
container.

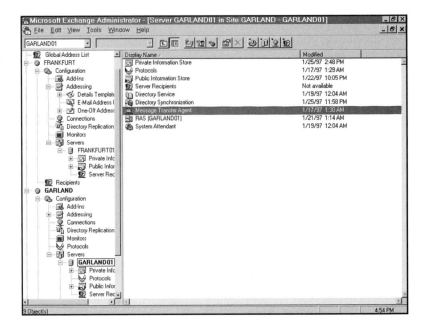

The General Tab

To set values for the local MTA name, password, and other general message transfer preferences for this server, follow these steps:

1. Click the General tab of the Message Transfer Agent Properties page (see Figure 14.5).

FIG. 14.5

The General Message
Transfer Agent property
page.

2. Type a name in the Local MTA Name box. This name will be used by remote MTAs (either on remote Exchange servers or foreign messaging systems) to identify this MTA. By default, this name is the name of the Exchange server on which the MTA is installed.

3. Type a password in the Local MTA Password box, if necessary. If you enter a password in this box, any remote MTA (either on remote Exchange servers or foreign messaging systems) must be configured to provide this password for authentication. By default, this box is blank, and no authentication is required of the remote MTA.

N O T E If you decide to change the Local MTA Name or to add or change the Local MTA Password, be sure to take into consideration any previously established MTA connections. All remote sites (and foreign systems, such as X.400) must be adjusted to reflect the new information. Authentication is never required between two MTAs in the same site. ▪

Use these settings as a filter to manage the messaging load for all traffic to and from this server. The upper-limit settings have precedence over message-size settings in individual connectors and recipient objects.

4. In the Message Size section, click the radio button that indicates how you want to restrict the passage of messages through this message transfer agent.

Click the No Limit radio button to allow this MTA to deliver messages of any size.

If you want to set a size limit, click the Maximum (K) radio button; then, in the text box, type an upper limit (in kilobytes) for messages that travel through this MTA. Any message that exceeds this size limit will be returned as undeliverable.

Rebuilding routing tables sometimes takes several minutes, so it is a good idea to go through each MTA property sheet, make all changes, and then recalculate routing.

5. Click the Recalculate Routing button to rebuild the routing tables for this MTA. (See Chapter 2, "Understanding Exchange's Organization Sites," for more information on routing tables.) New routing information for this MTA will propagate to all Exchange servers within the site automatically.

N O T E Routing tables are rebuilt once a day automatically. The routing table will rebuild when it detects a change in a new gateway or change in a connector configuration. ▪

6. Click the Expand Remote Distribution Lists Locally check box to force distribution lists created on remote sites to be expanded on this server. When a message is sent to a distribution list by a user on this server, the message is split into its component recipients locally. If this box is not checked, the distribution list is expanded in the remote site, following the configuration in the distribution list's own property pages. By default, this box is checked, and distribution lists are expanded locally.

Part

III

Ch

14

N O T E Consider both the physical locations of the majority of the distribution list's recipients and the messaging load on the local server. If you choose the default settings, make certain that the local server can handle the extra messaging traffic; expanding large distribution lists can be a considerable load on an already overburdened Exchange server. Also, if you know that the majority of the distribution list's recipients reside on Exchange servers on the remote site, consider allowing the list to be expanded there. ■

7. Click the Convert Incoming Messages to MS Exchange Contents check box to convert all messages to Exchange's MAPI-compliant format automatically. By default, this option is not selected, and messages are kept in the format in which they arrive at the MTA (such as standard X.400 format).

8. If you want, make an entry in the Administrative Note text box.

9. Click Apply to set these properties and continue with other properties.

10. When you finish making settings, click OK to return to the Administrator program.

The Queues Tab

The Queues tab of the Message Transfer Agent property pages lists messages that are awaiting delivery by the MTA. The two primary windows are Queue Name, which shows the queue that you are currently viewing, and Message List, which displays the messages in that queue. From the Message List window, you can view details about a specific message in the queue, change its priority for delivery, or delete it.

The Message List window has three columns that contain information about a particular message:

■ *Originator*: the original sender of the message

■ *Submit Time*: the time of the next transfer attempt for this message

■ *Size*: the size of the message, in kilobytes

To configure the Queues property page, follow these steps:

1. Click the Queues tab from the Message Transfer Agent properties page (see Figure 14.6).

2. From the Queue Name drop-down list, select the message queue to display. The list shows queues for the private and public information stores, as well as for any installed gateways.

N O T E The Internet Mail connector and Microsoft Mail connector have separate queues that you can access through their property pages. ■

3. Select a message, and click Details to view additional information about it.

The additional message information includes the message originator, submit time, message size, and priority. This button is dimmed if no messages are in the queue.

FIG. 14.6

Messages waiting to be delivered are held in the queue.

4. Click the Refresh button to update the Message List window with the latest list of messages in the MTA queue.

5. Click Priority to display the message's priority, and change the priority of the message, if you want. Priority can be low, medium, or high. Messages are sent in order of priority. A message's priority is set when a message is created.

6. To remove a message from the MTA queue, select a message and then click Delete.

7. Click Apply to set these properties and continue with other properties.

8. When you finish making settings, click OK to return to the Administrator program.

The Diagnostic Logging Tab

This property page works in conjunction with the Windows NT Event Log to record various "events" that occur within the message transfer agent. Various levels of logging determine what constitutes an event and, therefore, what types of information are actually recorded. For troubleshooting purposes, you would want a very detailed record of occurrences within the MTA; hence, you would set a high logging level. Normally, however, you want to log only critical events, so set a lower logging level for everyday operation.

From Here...

The Message Transfer Agent is the key component for routing and delivering messages to their destination. You administer MTA functions through two main sets of property pages:

1. MTA Site Configuration Settings for an entire Exchange site.

2. Message Transfer Agent Settings for an individual Exchange server's MTA service.

Part

III

Ch

14

See the following chapters for more information on topics related to the MTA:

- Chapter 3, "Exchange's Integrated Server Components," provides an overview of how the Message Transfer Agent integrates with other Exchange components.

- Chapter 16, "Creating and Configuring Recipient," Chapter 19, "Using the Microsoft Mail Connector for PC Networks," and Chapter 21, "Configuring X.400 Connections," all cover Exchange connections to other systems and explain how the MTA communicates with gateways and connectors.

- Chapter 28, "Troubleshooting Exchange with Diagnostic Tools," discusses troubleshooting the MTAs operation by using Diagnostic Logging.

CHAPTER 15

Information Store Configuration

The Microsoft Exchange Information Stores (public and private) are the databases that hold all Microsoft Exchange messaging information. In addition, the Information Store is the primary storage system for information relevant to users, including Messages, Server-based mailboxes and their contents; Public folders and their contents, Private folders that are stored on a server instead of on a user's computer; documents, forms, and user-defined items. ■

Information Store Site Configuration

Overall settings for the Information Stores of an entire Microsoft Exchange site can be modifed from a single location.

Private Information Store Server Configuration

Customize each server in the Exchange site with default global settings limiting each user's mailbox size. Additionally, set a related global default "trigger" level for warning messages to be sent to users as they approach their mailbox limit.

Public Information Store Server Configuration and Public Folder Replication

Each server in a site can maintain a local copy or replica of public folders and manage a replication process that keeps all replicas across the enterprise in sync.

Information Store Status

A new "short cut" in Exchange 5.0 enables the administrator to quickly see the status on key elements and functions of the Information Store, including current logons and mailbox resources used.

Important Information Store Concepts

The following concepts will be helpful to understand when proceeding through this chapter:

- **Top-Level Folder**   A public folder created at the highest point in the public folder directory tree. Usually only certain individuals in an Exchange organization are granted the right to create folders at the top of the hierarchy.

- **Public Folder Instance**   A replica of a public folder on a different site than it was created. Users can then connect to the local site's instance of the folder instead of crossing site boundaries (and adding to network traffic) and connecting to a remote site.

- **Public Folder Affinity**   When a user in a local site needs to connect to a public folder only available in a remote site, the choice of connection will be based on the costs assigned to that site containing replicas of that folder. A user will still need appropriate NT security rights to access the actual NT server in the remote site and will need access rights to the Exchange public folder itself.

- **Information Store Message Tracking**   The Information Store is responsible for message transfer between two users on the same Exchange server. To keep a record of Information Store message transfer activity within a Microsoft Exchange server, enable message tracking. A daily log file is generated and stored in the EXCHSRVR\TRACKING.LOG directory. The individual log files are named as follows:

  YYMMDD.log

  Example

  970611.log for Information Store activity on June 11, 1997.

Information Store Site Configuration

Settings made on the Information Store Site Configuration property pages affect all servers within an Exchange site. When first setting up an Exchange site, you should use these property pages.

To open the Site Configuration Properties pages, follow these steps:

1. Navigate to your desired site with the Exchange administrator program.
2. Click the Configuration container (see Figure 15.1) of the selected site. All the site configuration objects appear in the administrator program's right window.

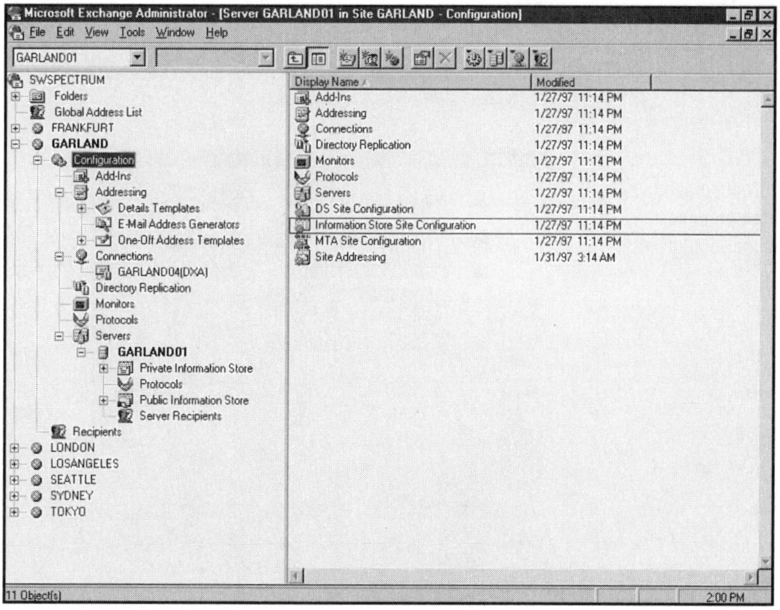

FIG. 15.1

The Configuration container holds all site configuration objects.

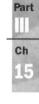

Part

III

Ch

15

Microsoft Exchange Administrator - [Server GARLAND01 in Site GARLAND - Configuration]

File   Edit   View   Tools   Window   Help

Display Name	Modified
Add-Ins	1/27/97 11:14 PM
Addressing	1/27/97 11:14 PM
Connections	1/27/97 11:14 PM
Directory Replication	1/27/97 11:14 PM
Monitors	1/27/97 11:14 PM
Protocols	1/27/97 11:14 PM
Servers	1/27/97 11:14 PM
DS Site Configuration	1/27/97 11:14 PM
Information Store Site Configuration	1/27/97 11:14 PM
MTA Site Configuration	1/27/97 11:14 PM
Site Addressing	1/31/97 3:14 AM

SWSPECTRUM
- Folders
- Global Address List
- FRANKFURT
- GARLAND
  - Configuration
    - Add-Ins
    - Addressing
      - Details Templates
      - E-Mail Address Generators
      - One-Off Address Templates
    - Connections
      - GARLAND04(DXA)
    - Directory Replication
    - Monitors
    - Protocols
    - Servers
      - GARLAND01
        - Private Information Store
        - Protocols
        - Public Information Store
        - Server Recipients
  - Recipients
- LONDON
- LOSANGELES
- SEATTLE
- SYDNEY
- TOKYO

11 Object(s)   2:00 PM

3. Select the Information Store Site Configuration object from the list.

4. Open its property pages.

At this point there will be five property pages to configure:

- General   Set display name, public folder container, and toggle message tracking.

- Permissions   Set access right to the Information Store Site Configuration directory object.

- TopLevel Folder Creation   Define which users are allowed to create public folders at the highest level of the public folder directory tree.

- Storage Warnings   Schedule when notification messages about exceeded storage space are sent to those users in violation of set restraints.

- Public Folder Affinity   Configure connections to public folders in remote sites.

The General Page

1. Select the General tab of the Information Store Site Configuration Properties page. The property page in Figure 15.2 appears.

FIG. 15.2

The Configuration container holds all site configuration objects.

2. If desired, type a new Display name as you want it to appear in the Microsoft Exchange Administrator program. By default this name is Information Store Site Configuration. The Directory name for this object is Site-MDB-Config by default, and it cannot be changed.

3. The Public folder container box displays the recipient container in which the Public Folders directory entries for this site are stored. By default, this box is blank, and Public Folders are stored in the standard recipients container. Click Modify to bring up a dialog box with a listing of all available recipient containers within this site. Select a container, then click OK.

4. Click the Enable message tracking checkbox to instruct the Information Store to keep a daily log file about all messages processed by the MTA. This button corresponds with the Enable Message Tracking checkbox on the MTA Site Configuration and enables usage of the Message Tracking tool in the Exchange Administrator program.

5. Click Apply to set these properties and continue with other properties. If you are done with all settings, click OK to return to the administrator program.

The Permissions Page

This property page allows you to define certain Windows NT user accounts that have rights to modify this directory object. See Chapter 12, "Using the Administrator Program," for a detailed description on working with the standard Permissions property page.

The Top-Level Folder Creation Page

This property page can either deny or allow certain users the capability to create public folders on the highest level of the public folder hierarchy.

N O T E Distribution lists can also be specified, and Exchange will use the members of that list to determine top-level folder creation permission. As the membership of the distribution list is modified, so are the permissions set here. ▪

To configure Top Level Folder Creation properties:

1. Select the Top Level Folder Creation tab from the Information Store Site Configuration Properties page. The property page in Figure 15.3 appears.

FIG. 15.3

Selectively assign Top Level Folder creation rights from this property page.

The Allowed to create top level folders box lists the recipients who are specifically given permission to create these folders. The Not allowed to create top level folders box lists the recipients specifically denied permission to create these folders.

2. Click the Modify button under either window if you wish to add or delete recipients from the lists. A standard address list dialog box appears. By default, All can create top-level folders and None are denied permission.

Click Apply to set these properties and continue with other properties. If you are done with all settings, click OK to return to the administrator program.

N O T E In most Exchange organizations, the default of allowing anyone to create top-level public folders is not preferred. The average Exchange administrator will want to limit top level creation to a select list or distribution list soon after creating a new site. ▪

The Storage Warnings Page

The actual storage limits are set in the following property pages for each corresponding recipient type:

- Mailboxes   Mailbox Advanced property page for each individual user, or a more global storage limit for all mailboxes on a particular server, in the private information store property page.

- Public Folders   Public Folder Advanced property page for each individual folder, or a more global storage limit for all public folders on a particular server, in the public information store property page.

The Storage Warning notification schedule actually initiates an automated process that evaluates the size of each message store object in the Information Store on each server in the site. If a server has a high number of mailboxes and public folders, this process can take up a fair amount of system resources as it runs.

Set the Storage Warning notification schedule by following these steps:

1. Select the Storage Warnings tab of the Information Store Site Configuration Properties page. The properties page in Figure 15.4 appears.

FIG. 15.4

Set the Storage Warnings notification schedule.

2. Select one of the three radio buttons that determine when recipients are notified.

   Never—This effectively disables storage warning notification.

   Always—A storage warning notification is executed immediately when a storage limit is exceeded.

   Selected times—Storage warning notifications are executed based upon the time slots selected on this property page.

T I P If you are using storage limits in a large organization, it is generally not a good idea to select A<u>l</u>ways and potentially overtax your servers during high-traffic times with a large number of scattered warning messages. It is better to schedule a time or times when messaging load is lower and have them all sent at once.

3. If you choose <u>S</u>elected times, the Detail view radio buttons become available. Select either the 1 Hou<u>r</u> or 15 <u>M</u>inute detail view, and the time grid will change its scale accordingly.

4. If you choose <u>S</u>elected times, pick the time blocks for connection. By default, storage warning notifications are scheduled once per day beginning at 8 p.m.

5. Click <u>A</u>pply to set these properties and continue with other properties. If you are done with all settings, click OK to return to the administrator program.

The Public Folder Affinity Page

This property page allows you to set up connection to public folders located in remote Exchange sites. To configure Public Folder Affinity:

1. Select the Public Folder Affinity tab of the Information Store Site Configuration Properties pages. The property page in Figure 15.5 appears.

The <u>S</u>ites window lists all the sites in your organization. The <u>P</u>ublic folder affinity window lists all the sites to where a connection may be established in order for a user to connect to a remote public folder. The Cost column displays the relative numeric value assigned to this site. Similar to message routing, the site with the lower cost will be used first.

FIG. 15.5

Define how a user connects to remote public folders.

2. To add a site, select it from the Sites window and click Add. To remove a site, select it from the Public Folder Affinity window and click Remove.

3. Enter the Connected site cost in the box at the lower right if the property page is 0. This site will always be used first if it is available. 1—99: Sites used in numerical sequence, with load on equally numbered sites being distributed evenly. 100: This site will be used only if no other site is available.

4. Click Set Value to save the cost associated with the selected site.

5. Click Apply to set these properties and continue with other properties. If you are done with all settings, click OK to return to the administrator program.

N O T E Exchange 5.0 adds a new option for public folder access within a single site called "location" as a part of an Exchange server's properties. Location specifically refers to physical location of servers on a high speed LAN or WAN where you can easily access any server with minimal network impact or bandwidth issues. As a user seeks access to a public folder, they are first connected to a server within the same Location as their home server. ■

Configuring Private Information Store

Now we will move on to configuring Private Information Store properties on an individual Microsoft Exchange server. The Private Information Store primarily holds data posted to user's mailboxes and private folders, in addition to mail associated to some Exchange connectors, such as the Internet Mail Service.

■ General   Set global mailbox storage limits; designate a public folder server

■ Logons   View a list of users' connections to the Private Information Store

■ Mailbox Resources   View general settings and amount of storage space used by each mailbox

■ Diagnostic Logging   Set logging levels for tracking down errors and debugging your organization

First you must select the Private Information Store from a server within your site:

1. Navigate to your desired site with the Exchange administrator program.

2. Click the Configuration container of the selected site. All the site configuration objects appear in the administrator program's right window.

3. Open the Servers container. A list of Exchange servers in your site will be listed.

4. Click the server name on which the Private Information Store you want to configure is located (see Figure 15.6). The following list of server objects is visible on the right display window of the Microsoft Exchange Administrator Program. New to Exchange 5.0 is a Private Information Store object as a sub-object under the server in the left window. Both display the same data.

5. Click the Private Information Store object. Open its property pages.

Part

III

Ch

15

FIG. 15.6

The Private Information Store holds all mailbox data of users on the local server.

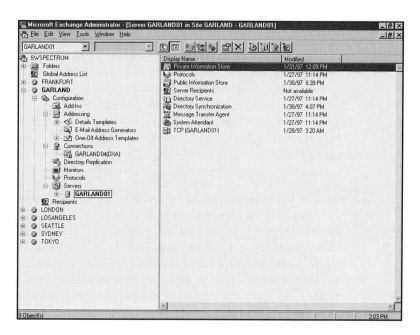

The General Page

This property page allows you to set global storage size limits for mailboxes on this server. Also, you can specify a different Exchange server to be responsible for the public folders created by users on this server.

To configure Private Information Store General properties:

1. Select the General tab of the Private Information Store Properties page. The property page in Figure 15.7 appears.

2. Select the Issue warning (K) checkbox and enter a value (in kilobytes) at which a mailbox owner will be warned of nearing storage limits. By default, there is no set value entered.

FIG. 15.7

The settings on this page apply to all mailboxes on this server.

3. Select the Prohibit send (K) checkbox and enter a value (in kilobytes) at which a mailbox owner will be prohibited from sending any additional outgoing messages until some stored message data is deleted. By default, there is no set value entered.

N O T E Issue warning and Prohibit send limits set on this property page are overridden by individual mailbox settings on each mailbox's Advanced property page.

4. Under Public folder server, select the Exchange server in your site on which will be stored public folders created by users with mailboxes on this local server. This is especially useful if a specific, dedicated public folder server has been setup in the site or location. By default, the public folder server used is the same one on which the folder was created—the current server.

N O T E If you select a server other than the local Exchange server, then you are effectively separating that server's public information and private information stores. Only select a different server if this complies with your overall load balancing plan for this Exchange site.

5. Click Apply to set these properties and continue with other properties. If you are done with all settings, click OK to return to the administrator program.

The message shown in Figure 15.8 is an example storage size warning message.

FIG. 15.8

This message is received when users exceed set storage limits for their mailboxes.

The Logons Page

This property page allows you to monitor the Microsoft Exchange users currently logged into a server. It consists of one main display window that shows all currently connected users. The window is broken down into various columns of information. The specific columns displayed are customizable both by information shown and width on the screen.

Here are the steps to follow for viewing Logon information:

1. Select the Logons tab of the Private Information Store Properties page. The property page in Figure 15.9 appears. The display window shows all users currently logged on to this Exchange server.

N O T E The Microsoft Exchange System Attendant is always listed in this window as well. ▓

2. Click the Refresh button to update the display window with the latest information.

FIG. 15.9

View currently logged on users.

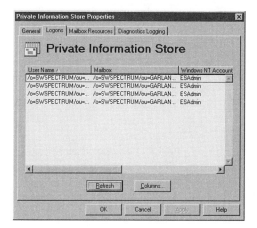

3. Click the Columns button to edit which columns are displayed and their width in pixels (see Figure 15.10). See the following for a description of each column heading and what type of information it can display.

4. Click Apply to set these properties and continue with other properties. If you are done with all settings, click OK to return to the administrator program.

Default Columns

▓ User Name   The name (display name) for the user logged on to this mailbox.

▓ Mailbox   The Exchange administrator program object display name for this mailbox.

■ Windows NT Account   The Windows NT account of the user currently logged on to this mailbox.

■ Logon Time   The date and time the user logged on to Microsoft Exchange.

Optional Columns

Several optional columns are available. A few useful columns to note are:

■ Full Mailbox Directory Name

■ Full User Directory Name

■ Logon Type

■ Open Attachments   The total number of attachments a particular user currently has open.

■ Open Folders   The total number of folders open within the user's Exchange client for this user.

■ Open Messages   The total number of messages a particular user currently has open.

FIG. 15.10
Display Columns available for the Logons property page.

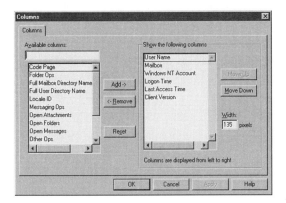

To save valuable time, a new option added in Exchange 5.0 is the capability to quickly view Logon information from the main Exchange hierarchy seen in the left window of the Exchange administrator program (see Figure 15.11).

FIG. 15.11

Logon information now available from the left window.

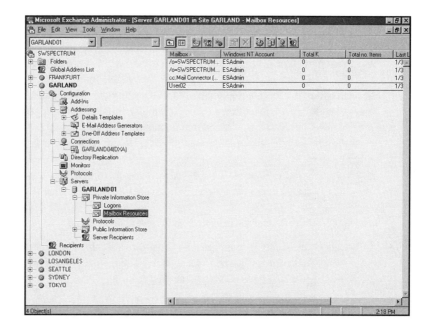

To access the Logon information using this new option, follow these steps:

1. Navigate to your desired site with the Exchange administrator program.

2. Click the small plus sign adjacent to the Configuration container of the selected site to further expand the hierarchy in the left-hand window.

3. Expand the Servers container in the left hand window. A list of Exchange servers in your site will be listed.

4. Click and expand the server name on which the Private Information Store you want to configure is located.

5. The displayed server objects now visible in the left display window of the Microsoft Exchange Administrator Program are identical in name and function to similar objects displayed in the right-hand window. Selecting properties of either the Private Information Store or Public Information Store displays the same data.

6. Expand the Private Information Store in the left window and click the Logons object to see the Logons information quickly displayed in the right window. The default columns shown in the right window can be added to by using the View menu and using the Columns option.

The Mailbox Resources Page

This property page enables you to view the physical resources, such as hard disk storage space, used by the Exchange mailboxes on the server. It consists of one main display window that shows the mailboxes on the current server, visible ultimately either through the properties window of the Private Information Store or using the new feature of Exchange 5.0 to allow quick access in the left window of the Exchange administrator program. The windows are broken down into various columns of information. The specific columns displayed are customizable both by information presented and width on the screen.

N O T E A mailbox will be displayed in this window only after the first time a user logs on to it. If the mailbox has never been used, it will not appear on Mailbox Resources property page.

Viewing Mailbox Resources information involves these steps:

1. Select the Mailbox Resources tab of the Private Information Store Properties page. The properties page in Figure 15.12 appears. The display window shows all the mailboxes on this server that have been used at least once.

FIG. 15.12

View server resource use on a per-mailbox basis.

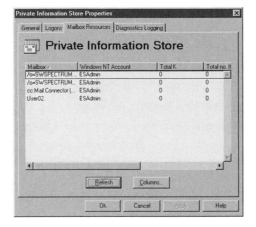

N O T E The Microsoft Exchange System Attendant and the Exchange account itself are always listed in this window as well.

2. Click the Refresh button to update the display window with the latest information.

3. Click the Columns button to edit which columns are displayed and their width in pixels (see Figure 15.13). See the following for a description of each column heading and what type of information it can display.

4. Click Apply to set these properties and continue with other properties. If you are done with all settings, click OK to return to the administrator program.

The Default Columns

- ▨ Mailbox   The Exchange administrator program object display name for this mailbox.

- ▨ Windows NT Account   The Windows NT account of the user currently logged on to this mailbox.

- ▨ Total K   The total amount of disk storage space (in kilobytes) taken up by the contents of this user's mailbox. This value includes any message attachments.

- ▨ Total Number of Items   The sum of all messages and attachments stored in a mailbox.

- ▨ Last Logon Time   The last time a user logged on to this mailbox.

- ▨ Last Logoff Time   The last time a user logged off from this mailbox.

FIG. 15.13

Display columns available for the Mailbox Resources property page.

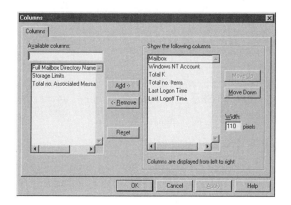

Optional Columns   This property page allows you to view the full e-mail address for the mailbox and the total number of associated messages in this mailbox.

- ▨ Full Mailbox Directory Name   The entire X.400 e-mail address for this mailbox.

- ▨ Storage Limits   Any storage limits imposed on mailbox, such as Prohibit Send.

- ▨ Total number of Associated Messages   The sum of stored views and deferred action messages (messages scheduled to be sent/processed at a later time) in this mailbox.

Similar to the previously noted Logon status screen, Exchange 5.0 offers the capability to quickly view Mailbox Resources information from the main Exchange hierarchy seen in the left window of the Exchange administrator program (see Figure 15.14).

To access the Mailbox Resources information using this new option, follow the steps here:

1. Navigate to your desired site with the Exchange administrator program.

2. Click the small plus sign adjacent to the Configuration container of the selected site to further expand the hierarchy in the left window.

3. Expand the Servers container in the left window. A list of Exchange servers in your site will be listed.

4. Click and expand the server name on which the Private Information Store you want to configure is located.

5. The displayed server objects now visible in the left display window of the Microsoft Exchange Administrator Program are identical in name and function to similar objects displayed in the right-hand window. Selecting properties of either the Private Information Store or Public Information Store displays the same data.

6. Expand the Private Information Store in the left window and click the Mailbox Resources object to see the Mailbox Resources information displayed in the right window. The default columns shown in the right window can be added to by using the View menu and using the Columns option.

The Private Logging Tab

This property page works in conjunction with the Windows NT Event Log to record various "events" that specifically occur within the Information Store. This property page is identical to that one found on the Public Information Store Properties pages. Various levels of logging determine what constitutes an event and therefore, what types of information are actually recorded. For troubleshooting purposes, you would want a very detailed record of occurrences within the Information Store and hence set a high logging level. However, normally you would want to log only events that are critical, so set a lower logging level for everyday operation.

FIG. 15.14

The new "shortcut" to quickly view Mailbox Resources.

Public Information Store/Public Folder Replication

The Public Information Store Properties pages are much more extensive than the Private Information Store due to the existence of public folder replication. To reiterate this concept, duplicates of public folders can be created to reside on Exchange Server in remote sites. Therefore, users based on the remote site can connect to the local copy of the public folder instead of crossing site boundaries to get to the information. This reduces network traffic between site boundaries. Replication can also be used to duplicate folders on other servers in the same local Exchange site to offer redundancy and load distribution across servers.

The following are the Public Information Store Properties pages available on each Microsoft Exchange server:

- General   Impose a global storage limit warning for all folders in this public information store.
- Instances   Select which public folders to replicate to the local server from remote sites.
- Replication Schedule   Set the times when public folders on the local server are replicated to the established remote instances.
- Age Limits   Set the lifetime of public folders or their contents.
- E-mail Addresses   Define and modify various e-mail addresses for the public information store directory object.
- Logons   View data about users currently connected to a public folder.
- Public Folder Resources   View data about quantity of server resources consumed by a particular public folder.
- Server Replication Status   Monitor each server's participation in public folder replication.
- Folder Replication Status   Monitor the replication of individual public folders.
- Advanced   Define the delay between replication cycles when Always is selected for the schedule. Also, define the maximum size of each individual replication message.
- Diagnostics Logging   Activate various levels of logging for troubleshooting purposes.

Just as with the Private Information Store, one of the new features of Exchange 5.0 offers quick access to the Status reports that previously could only be accessed through the properties of the Public Information Store. This Status information can now be seen in the Exchange hierarchy shown in the left-hand window of the administrator program.

The General Page

This property page has only the one option to set a global Issue warning (K) for all public folders on the local Exchange server (see Figure 15.15).

FIG. 15.15

Set a global (for all public folders on this server) public folder size warning.

Setting the General properties:

1. Select the General tab of the Public Information Store Properties page.

2. Click the Issue warning (K) checkbox and enter a folder data size (in kilobytes) at which a folder contact will be notified. By default, this option is unchecked. Warnings can also be set at the individual folder level on the public folder's Advanced property page, which overrides this global setting for the server.

3. Click Apply to set these properties and continue with other properties. If you are done with all settings, click OK to return to the administrator program.

The Instances Page

Use this property page to mark public folders for duplication to the local server. Such *instances* of public folders in the local site are actually created through the process of public folder replication (see Figure 15.16).

1. Select the Instances tab of the Public Information Store Properties pages. The following property page appears.

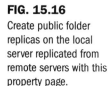

FIG. 15.16
Create public folder replicas on the local server replicated from remote servers with this property page.

The left, Public folders display window lists all the folders in the currently selected remote site. The right window Folders on this Information Store displays the list of both public folders on this server and other folders already designated for replication to this server.

2. Use the Site pull-down menu in the bottom left-hand corner to select a site in your organization. The public folders residing on that site are then listed in the left display window.

3. Select a public folder from the left window and click Add to mark that folder for replication to the local Exchange server.

4. To remove a public folder's instance from the local server, select it from the right display window, then click Remove.

N O T E You cannot remove a local public folder from the local Exchange server if it is the only copy of it in the local site. ■

5. Click Apply to set these properties and continue with other properties. If you are done with all settings, click OK to return to the administrator program.

The Replication Schedule Page

This property page allows you to set times when public folder replication messages are actually transferred. Take into consideration the potentially high volume of data that may need to be transferred from a large and heavily used public folder.

Setting the Replication Schedule:

1. Select the Replication Schedule tab of the Public Information Store Properties page. The dialog box in Figure 15.17 appears.

FIG. 15.17

Set public folder
replication times
for this server.

2. Select one of the three radio buttons that determine when this server initiates Public
   Folder replication.

   Never—This effectively disables public folder replication from this server.

   Always—Folder replication messages are sent every fifteen minutes. This time delay
   can be changed on this public information store's Advanced property page. By default,
   Always is selected.

   Selected times—Replication messages are transferred based upon the time grid on this
   property page.

3. If you choose Selected times, the Detail view radio buttons become available. Select
   either the 1 Hour or 15 Minute detail view and the time grid changes its scale accordingly.

4. If you choose Selected times, pick the time blocks for connection.

5. Click Apply to set these properties and continue with other properties. If you are done
   with all settings, click OK to return to the administrator program.

N O T E   Just a reminder that replication is not the same as simple duplication or copying.
Replication includes the concept of synchronization, which loosely translated means that
only the changes are sent to other replica "instances" around the enterprise. Sending only the changes
versus sending an entire copy of the folder not only saves time and bandwidth, it allows changes from
any instance to be added to all other instances. ■

The Age Limits Page

The Age Limits property page allows you to define when information in a public folder should
expire and be automatically deleted. This feature prevents public folders from becoming
bogged down with megabytes upon megabytes of outdated, useless information.

Example: You set up a CLASSIFIEDS folder. You set the age limits for posting in the folder for seven days. Once a message has been sitting in a folder for a week, it will then expire and be automatically deleted by the information store.

Setting Age Limits:

1. Select the Age Limits tab of the Public Information Store Properties page. The property page in Figure 15.18 appears.

FIG. 15.18

Set the amount of time a message can exist in a public folder before it is deleted.

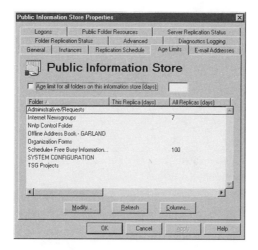

The main display window shows the columns of information about all the public folders on this server (including replicas). A description of the kind of information that is displayed by each column will be given later in this chapter.

2. To set an overall Age limit for all folders on this information store (days), select the checkbox and enter a number of days in which messages in all this server's public folders will expire.

N O T E You can override this setting on an individual public folder on that folder's Advanced property page.

3. Select a public folder from the list and click Modify to set individual age limits for this folder. The dialog box in Figure 15.19 appears.

Click the This replica (days) checkbox to set an age limit for a public folder's instance on this server only. Click the All replicas (days) checkbox to set an age limit set for all instances of a public folder throughout your organization. Click the Remove button to delete the selected public folder *instance* from the information store. Click OK to set your choices (see Figure 15.20).

FIG. 15.19

Set age limits on an individual folder basis.

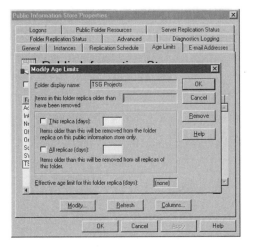

4. Click the Refresh button to update the display window with the latest information.

5. Click the Columns button to edit which columns are displayed and their width in pixels. More details on columns will follow.

6. Click Apply to set these properties and continue with other properties. If you are done with all settings, click OK to return to the administrator program.

FIG. 15.20

Display columns available for the Age Limits property page.

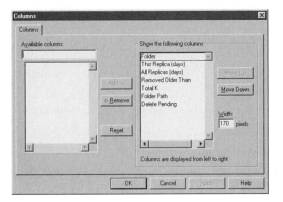

Default Columns

By default, all available columns are displayed:

- ■ Folder   The Exchange administrator object display name for the folder.
- ■ This Replica (days)   Age limit set for a public folder's instance on this server only.

- All Replicas (days)   Age limit set for all instances of a public folder throughout your organization.
- Removed Older Than   Notifies that messages older than the number of days displayed have been deleted.
- Total K   The sum of all messages in a public folder.
- Folder Path   The location of the public folder in the organization hierarchy (relative to this server or full X.400 address to another server).
- Delete Pending   Normally "false," this column shows "true" when a folder or messages with that folder are scheduled to be deleted.

The E-Mail Addresses Page

E-mail addresses are used by the various Exchange gateways and connectors to identify specific directory objects to other messaging systems. There are four default addresses created each for cc:Mail, MS-Mail, SMTP, and X.400.

Setting public folder E-mail Addresses:

1. Click the E-mail Addresses of the Public Information Store Properties page. The dialog box in Figure 15.21 appears and the four default addresses (cc:Mail, MS Mail, SMTP, and X.400) are displayed.

FIG. 15.21

Define e-mail addresses for this directory object.

2. Click New to add a specific e-mail address for this information store. Select an existing address and click Edit to modify it, or click Remove to delete it.

3. Click Apply to set these properties and continue with other properties. If you are done with all settings, click OK to return to the administrator program.

The Logons Page

Use this property page to monitor which users are currently connected to a public folder.

1. Select the Logons tab of the Public Information Store Properties page. The property page in Figure 15.22 appears.

FIG. 15.22

View users currently connected to public folders on this server. The main display window shows columns of information about connected users.

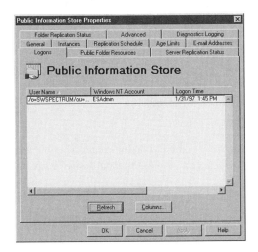

N O T E   The System Attendant is always shown as a public information store logon.

2. Click the Refresh button to update the display window with the latest information.

3. Click the Columns button to edit which columns are displayed and their width in pixels. See the following for a description of each column heading and what type of information it can display (see Figure 15.23).

FIG. 15.23

Display Columns available for the Logons property page.

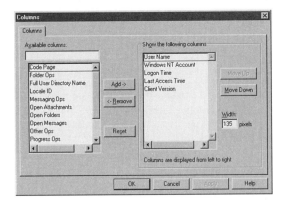

4. Click <u>A</u>pply to set these properties and continue with other properties. If you are done with all settings, click OK to return to the administrator program.

Default Columns

■ User Name   The name (display name) for the user logged on to this mailbox.

■ Windows NT Account   The Windows NT account of the user currently logged on to this mailbox.

■ Logon Time   The date and time the user logged on to Microsoft Exchange.

■ Last Access Time   The date and time the user last logged on and accessed the Public Information store.

■ Client Version   The version number of Exchange client used to access the server. This does not apply to users accessing folder information via the Internet and IIS with a browser.

Optional Columns

Several optional columns are available. A few useful columns of note are:

■ Full Mailbox Directory Name

■ Logon Type

■ Open Attachments   The total number of attachments a particular user currently has open.

■ Open Folders   The total number of folders open within the user's Exchange client for this user.

■ Open Messages   The total number of messages a particular user currently has open.

A new element added in Exchange 5.0 to save time is the capability to quickly view Logons information from the main Exchange hierarchy seen in the left window of the Exchange administrator program (Figure 15.24).

To access the Logon information using this new option, perform the following steps:

1. Navigate to your desired site with the Exchange administrator program.

2. Click the small plus sign adjacent to the Configuration container of the selected site to further expand the hierarchy in the left window.

3. Expand the Servers container in the left-hand window. A list of Exchange servers in your site is listed.

4. Click and expand the server name where the Private Information Store you want to configure is located.

FIG. 15.24

A valuable time-saving way to see Logon information.

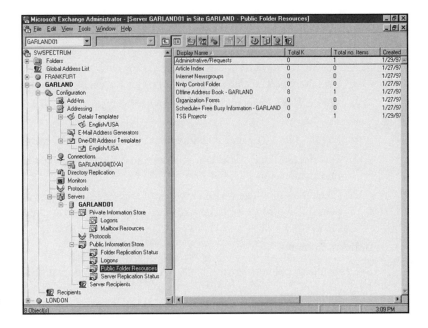

5. The displayed server objects now visible in the left display window of the Microsoft Exchange Administrator Program are identical in name and function to similar objects displayed in the right-hand window. Selecting properties of either the Private Information Store or Public Information Store displays the same data.

6. Expand the Public Information Store in the left window and click the Logon object to see the Logon information displayed in the right window. The default columns shown in the right window can be added to by using the View menu and then using the Columns option.

Public Folder Resources Page

This property page allows you to view the physical resources, such as hard disk storage space, used by the folders held on this public information store. It consists of one main display window that shows the public folders on the current server. The window is subdivided into various columns of information. The specific columns displayed are customizable both by information presented and width on the screen. Note that the Schedule+ Free Busy Information and the Offline Address Book are in essence public folders as well and are listed on the Public Folder Resources property page.

For viewing Public Folder Resources information, follow these steps:

1. Select the Public Folder Resources tab of the Public Information Store Properties page. The property page in Figure 15.25 appears. The display window shows all the public folders on this server.

FIG. 15.25

View server resources used by each public folder on this server.

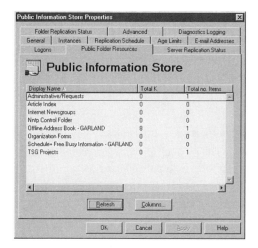

2. Click the Refresh button to update the display window with the latest information.

3. Click the Columns button to edit which columns are displayed and their width in pixels. See the following for a description of each column heading and what type of information it can display (see Figure 15.26).

4. Click Apply to set these properties and continue with other properties. If you are done with all settings, click OK to return to the administrator program.

Columns   Using this option, you can select which columns are to be displayed and their width in pixels.

FIG. 15.26

Display columns available for the Public Folder Resources property page.

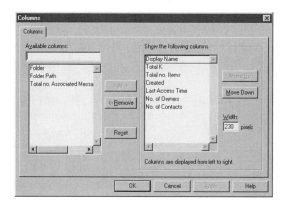

Default Columns   Using this option, you can view/set the default columns of information that will be displayed for the public folder.

■ Display Name   The Exchange administrator program object-display name for this public folder.

- ▓ Total K   The total amount of disk storage space (in kilobytes) taken up by the contents of this public folder. This value includes any message attachments.

- ▓ Total number Items   The sum of all messages and attachments stored in a mailbox.

- ▓ Created   The date and time this folder was created.

- ▓ Last Access Time   The last time a user logged on to this public folder.

- ▓ Number of Owners   The number of users designated as Owners of this public folder. See section on defining roles for a public folder.

- ▓ Number of Contacts   The number of users designated as contacts for this public folder. See section on defining roles for a public folder.

Optional Columns   Using this option, you can select the optional columns of information that will be displayed for the public folder.

- ▓ Folder   Folder name where messages are stored.

- ▓ Folder Path   The system file path to where this folder is stored.

- ▓ Total number Associated Messages   The sum of folder views and deferred action messages.

A new time-saving option added in Exchange 5.0 is the capability to quickly view Public Folder Resource information from the main Exchange hierarchy seen in the left window of the Exchange administrator program.

Here are the steps to access the Public Folder Resource information using this new option:

1. Navigate to your desired site with the Exchange administrator program.

2. Click the small plus sign adjacent to the Configuration container of the selected site to further expand the hierarchy in the left window.

3. Expand the Servers container in the left-hand window. A list of Exchange servers in your site is listed.

4. Click and expand the server name on which the Public Information Store you want to configure is located.

5. The displayed server objects now visible in the left display window of the Microsoft Exchange Administrator Program are identical in name and function to similar objects displayed in the right-hand window. Selecting properties of either the Private Information Store or Public Information Store displays the same data.

6. Expand the Public Information Store in the left window and click the Public Folder Resources object to see the Public Folder Resources information quickly displayed in the right window. The default columns shown in the right window can be added to by using the View menu and using the Columns option.

The Server Replication Status Page

This property page enables you to monitor the status of a public folder's replication to the current public information store on the server level. Exchange servers are individually configured for transmitting updated public folder information to other replicas in remote sites. This property page is primarily a single-display window with various columns of information. The columns to be displayed are modified by the Columns button. The information in this property page is used to not only verify that the selected remote public folders are indeed being replicated to this server but to monitor details about message transmission time.

To view Server Replication Status:

1. Select the Server Replication Status tab of the Public Information Store property page. The property page in Figure 15.27 appears.

FIG. 15.27

View the status of remote servers that replicate public folders to the local server.

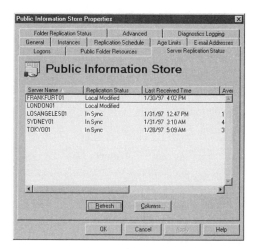

The display window shows all remote servers that replicate public folder data to this server.

2. Click the Refresh button to update the display window with the latest information.

3. Click the Columns button to edit which columns are displayed and their width in pixels. See the following for a description of each column heading and what type of information it can display (see Figure 15.28).

4. Click Apply to set these properties and continue with other properties. If you are done with all settings, click OK to return to the administrator program.

Default Columns

■ Server Name Name of the Microsoft Exchange server replication public folder data to this server.

■ Replication Status Notification of public folder replication status.

■ Last Received Time   The last date and time this information store received an update from the remote Exchange server.

FIG. 15.28

Display columns
available for the Server
Replication Status
property page.

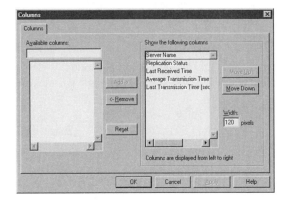

■ Average Transmission Time   The average length of time (in seconds) replication messages have taken to transmit to this server.

■ Last Transmission Time   The length of time (in seconds) that the last replication message took to transmit to this server.

Optional Columns

There are no optional display columns on this property page. By default, all the columns that can be displayed are displayed. Server Replication Status can now be viewed quickly without having to navigate too deeply into the various property tabs. Exchange 5.0 adds the capability to quickly view Server Replication Status information from the main Exchange hierarchy seen in the left window of the Exchange administrator program.

To access the Server Replication Status information using this new option, do the following:

1. Navigate to your desired site with the Exchange Administrator program.

2. Click the small plus sign adjacent to the Configuration container of the selected site to further expand the hierarchy in the left-hand window.

3. Expand the servers container in the left window. A list of Exchange servers in your site will be listed.

4. Click and expand the server name where the Public Information Store you want to configure is located.

5. The displayed server objects now visible in the left display window of the Microsoft Exchange Administrator Program are identical in name and function to similar objects displayed in the right-hand window. Selecting properties of either the Private Information Store or Public Information Store displays the same data.

6. Expand the Public Information Store in the left window and click the Server Replication Status object to see the status information quickly displayed in the right window. The default columns shown in the right window can be added to by using the View menu and using the Columns option.

The Folder Replication Status Page

This property page provides public information store monitoring capabilities on the individual folder level. This page is also one main display window whose information is displayed in columns.

Here is how you view Folder Replication Status:

1. Select the Folder Replication Status tab of the Public Information Store Properties page. The property page in Figure 15.29 appears. The display window shows all public folders involved in replication on this server's public information store.

FIG. 15.29

View the status of individual folders replicated from the local server and to the local server from remote sites.

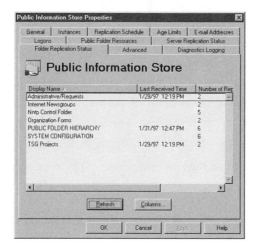

2. Click the Refresh button to update the display window with the latest information.
3. Click the Columns button to edit which columns are displayed and their width in pixels. See the following for a description of each column heading and what type of information it can display (see Figure 15.30).
4. Click Apply to set these properties and continue with other properties. If you are done with all settings, click OK to return to the administrator program.

Default Columns

- Display Name   The Exchange administrator display name for this directory object.
- Last Received Time   The last date and time this public folder received an updated replication message.

■ Number of Replicas   The sum of all instances of this folder throughout the local site.

■ Replication Status   Notification of public folder replication status.

FIG. 15.30
Display columns
available for the Folder
Replication Status
property page.

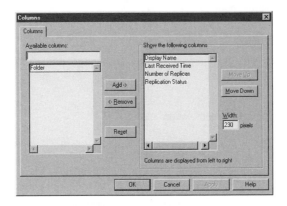

Optional Column

■ Folder   The public folder name.

The Status of Folder Replication can be accessed by leveraging features added to Exchange 5.0. From the main Exchange hierarchy the left window of the Exchange administrator program contains the Folder Replication Status object.

To access the Folder Replication Status information using this new option, follow these steps:

1. Navigate to your desired site with the Exchange administrator program.

2. Click the small plus sign adjacent to the Configuration container of the selected site to further expand the hierarchy in the left-hand window.

3. Expand the Servers container in the left-hand window. A list of Exchange servers in your site is listed.

4. Click and expand the server name on which the Public Information Store you want to configure is located.

5. The displayed server objects now visible in the left display window of the Microsoft Exchange Administrator Program are identical in name and function to similar objects displayed in the right-hand window. Selecting properties of either the Private Information Store or Public Information Store displays the same data.

   Expand the Public Information Store in the left window and click the Folder Replication Status object to see the Folder Replication Status information quickly displayed in the right window. The default columns shown in the right window can be added to by using the View menu and using the Columns option.

The Advanced Page

The Advanced property page allows you to customize some specialized settings involving public folder replication. When a folder is replicated to a remote site, the actual replication data broken up into messages addressed to the remote public information store. On this property page, you can set the upper limit for the size of the replication messages in order to better control messaging traffic.

1. Select the Advanced tab of the Public Information Store Properties page. The property page in Figure 15.31 appears.

FIG. 15.31

The Public Information Store Advanced property page.

2. In the Replicate always interval (minutes) box, enter the interval (in minutes) between outgoing replication messages when the Always radio button is selected in the Replication Schedule dialog box. By default, this interval is 15 minutes.

3. In the Replicate message size limit (K) box, enter the maximum message size (in kilobytes) of an outgoing replication message. By default, this maximum is set at 100K. Messages are grouped up to or subdivided to fit that size.

4. To reset the values of the two boxes to their default settings, click the Default button.

The Diagnostics Logging Page

This property page works in conjunction with the Windows NT Event Log to record various "events" that occur within the Information Store. This property page is identical to that one found on the Private Information Store Properties pages. Various levels of logging determine what constitutes an event and therefore, what types of information are actually recorded. For troubleshooting purposes, you would want a very detailed record of occurrences within the Information Store, and hence set a high logging level. However, normally you would want to log only events that are critical, so set a lower logging level for everyday operation.

From Here...

The information stores are the Exchange databases that hold all the messaging data in an Exchange organization. The private information store holds all the information in user mailboxes. The public information store holds public folders and also handles folder replication. Replication of public folders to other sites can reduce network traffic between sites across the LAN or WAN when a remote folder is used often. The information store configuration is handled through these property pages: Information Store Site configuration, Private Information Store, and Public Information Store.

For more information, please see the following chapters:

- Chapter 3, "Exchange's Integrated Server Components," provides a review of the information store and how it integrates into other Exchange components.
- Chapter 16, "Creating and Configuring Recipient," shows you how to set up the users' mailboxes held in the information store.
- Chapter 28, " Troubleshooting Exchange with Diagnostic Tools," for troubleshooting information store errors.
- Chapter 30, "Using Outlook," for creating public folders with the Exchange client software.

Creating and Configuring Recipient

A recipient is any directory object that is designed to receive information. This chapter explains the administrative process of creating and modifying these objects. Several tools are provided with Microsoft Exchange to assist administrators in creating user mailboxes. The Microsoft Exchange Migration tool and the import command in the Administrator Program enable you to import directory lists in bulk from external systems, such as Novell NetWare or Lotus CC: Mail.

Recipients are managed from the Administrator Program. This Program displays recipient objects when the user clicks their container within the exchange hierarchy. Microsoft Exchange Server defines four types of recipients:

How to Create and Configure a Mailbox

Learn how to create a mailbox. Create a mailbox that can be shared by more than one user.

How to Create and Configure a Custom Recipient

Find out how to create and configure a custom recipient. Learn how to send messages to MS Mail users, SMTP (Internet) users, and foreign X.400 users.

How to Create and Configure Distribution Lists

Learn how to create a group of many recipients. Find out how to forward a message to all the registered users of a group.

How to Create and Configure a Public Folder

Find out how to create public folders. Learn to Create public folders that can be receptacles of information for many users.

- Mailbox

  A mailbox is a container for messaging data. Generally, there is one user per mailbox. However, more than one user can sometimes share a mailbox.

- Custom Recipient

  A custom recipient is outside the main Microsoft Exchange Server messaging site. This usually pertains to users on the Internet, or another foreign messaging system.

- Distribution List

  A distribution list is a group of many recipients. A message sent to a distribution list is forwarded to all its registered users who are in that list.

- Public Folder

  A public folder is a container for information shared among many users.

Each recipient has multiple property sheets that hold its settings. This section demonstrates how to create and configure each of the four recipient types that the Microsoft Exchange Server defines.

N O T E Whenever you create a new recipient of any sort, you must first select the recipient container in which you want to store this new object. If none is selected, you will be notified that Recipients cannot be created in the parent container. ▦

Example:

Select New Mailbox from the Exchange Administrator file in the Garland site. You have not selected either the main Recipients container or any other custom container; therefore, the dialog box in Figure 16.1 appears.

FIG. 16.1

This notice displays when the proper container for the object has not been pre-selected.

Creating Mailboxes

The most common type of recipient is the mailbox. As mentioned previously, each mailbox generally has one user assigned to it. However, several users might share one mailbox. The term "mailbox" refers specifically to a Microsoft Exchange recipient on a Windows NT Server.

You can create a new mailbox using one of two methods:

1. Use the Windows NT User Manager to create an NT user account along with a mailbox.

2. Use the Microsoft Exchange Administrator program to create a mailbox for either a new or existing Windows NT account.

Creating a Mailbox with User Manager

Use the Windows NT User Manager to set up a new Windows NT account along with an Exchange mailbox. With the Microsoft Exchange Server installation you also get what is referred to as the Microsoft Exchange User Manager Extension (see Figure 16.2). This extension adds the menu *Exchange* to your Windows NT User Manager.

FIG. 16.2

The User Manager Extension lets you add and delete Exchange Mailboxes along with accounts in the Windows NT User Manager.

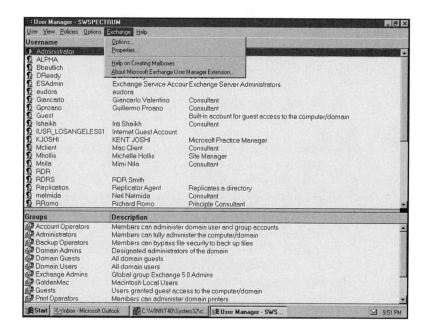

The *Exchange* menu enables you to view a user's mailbox properties without having to launch the Exchange Administration Program. More importantly, the *Exchange menu* integrates the creation of new Windows NT domain users with the creation of new Exchange mailboxes. You can use the following options to configure the Exchange User Manager Extension:

1. Select Options under the Exchange menu. The dialog box in Figure 16.3 appears.

2. The User Manager Extension can be configured to always create an Exchange mailbox when a new user account is created. The option `Always create an Exchange mailbox when creating Windows NT accounts` sets up the User Manager to contact your Exchange Server. This selection also makes a user mailbox every time you create a new NT user. If immediately after you create a new user you check this selection, the standard Exchange mailbox property sheets will be presented to you for configuration. By default, this option is checked when you install Exchange Server.

3. The User Manager Extension can be configured to always delete the mailbox when the user account is deleted. The option `Always delete the Exchange mailbox when deleting Windows NT accounts` sets up the User Manager to contact your Exchange Server and delete a user's mailbox. By default, this option is checked when you install Exchange Server.

FIG. 16.3

You can select from the Options dialog box to configure the User Manager Extension.

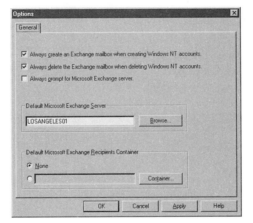

N O T E For the preceding option to function properly, you must be certain that the Microsoft Exchange Server is running properly. ■

4. Checking Always prompt for Microsoft Exchange server brings up the Exchange select Server dialog box every time the User Manager attempts a connection to Exchange. This option is not checked by default.

5. The Default Microsoft Exchange Server box displays the Exchange Server in which the User Manager Extension creates new user boxes. You can type in a new name. Alternatively, you can click Browse to select a different Server.

6. Click Container to select a custom recipient container. By default, None is selected. This means that all new mailboxes become part of the general recipient's container.

7. Click Apply to set these properties and continue with other properties. If you are done with all settings, click OK to return to the User Manager.

Creating Mailboxes in the Exchange Administrator

You will often want to create or administer several types of recipients. A more common way to do this would be to create a new user mailbox from within the Exchange Administrator program.

To create a new mailbox from within the Microsoft Exchange administrator, select the item **New Mailbox** from the administrator file menu. When the property pages for a new mailbox appear, you will be ready to proceed to the next step.

Configuring Mailbox Property Pages

No matter how the account is created, the property sheets associated with that mailbox are the same. The following is a list of property pages that we will cover in our discussion of mailboxes:

- General Information

  You use this to record basic mailbox information, such as name and location.

- Organizational Information

  For optional information about, for example, a company's organization. This might include a manager, or people who report to this mailbox owner.

- Phone/Notes

  You can use this to enter detailed telephone information and perhaps a long note about the user.

- Distribution Lists

  This category specifies the distribution lists to which this recipient belongs.

- E-Mail Addresses

  This page enables you to create, modify, and delete alternate addresses for this mailbox.

- Delivery Restrictions

  This defines from which addresses this mailbox will or will not accept messages.

- Delivery Options

  From here, you can give "send on behalf" permission and specify alternate recipients for messages sent to this mailbox.

- Custom Attributes

  This category enables you to add up to 10 administrator-defined fields used to keep additional information about the mailbox.

N O T E The field names are defined on the DS Site Configuration custom attributes page.

- Advanced

  This selection contains all settings relating to advanced administrator functions (trust levels, message sizes, storage sizes, text formatting, and hidden/not hidden status).

- Protocols

  This category specifies the available protocols to which this recipient belongs.

The General Page

You use the General Page to enter user data. The primary purpose of the General property page is to hold user information for a mailbox. In this place, you give the mailbox the name by which it will be known to all other users.

The key elements to a mailbox name are the Display Name and the Alias Name. Display Name is the name that appears in the Administrator window and in the Address Book. Alias Name is the string used to generate other addresses for this mailbox, such as Internet addresses.

For example, a suitable Microsoft Exchange Display Name could be Inti Shaikh with the Alias Name ISHAIKH. The Administrator Program and Address Book show the display name: Inti Shaikh. The SMTP address for this account, however, is formulated as *aliasname@domain* or: ISHAIKH@SWSPECTRUM.COM.

N O T E   A mailbox is often referred to by its user name, which is the same as its Display name.

The following explains how to set general properties for the mailbox:

1. Choose Recipients in the Exchange Server Administrator window. The list of mailboxes will appear on the right side of the window. Open the mailbox you want to configure.

N O T E   If you have just created a new mailbox, you can omit the preceding step. The reason is that the property pages appear immediately after you create a new mailbox.

2. Select the General tab. The dialog box in Figure 16.4 appears.

FIG. 16.4

General tab option lets you select the mailbox you want to configure.

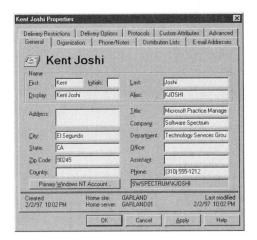

3. Enter the user's First name in the appropriate box.
4. Enter the user's middle initial in the Initials box.
5. Enter the user's Last name in the appropriate box.
6. Type an Alias that you will use to generate other e-mail addresses for this recipient.
7. Enter Postal information in the available Address boxes.
8. Enter appropriate Company and location (Department, Office) information for this user.
9. The Primary Windows NT Account sets the corresponding system account for this mailbox. The following section contains a more advanced description of this button.
10. Click Apply to set these properties and continue with other properties. If you are finished with all settings, click OK to return to the Administrator Program.

N O T E You can give a mailbox that is to be used by more than one person a generic name. A mailbox to be monitored by multiple people for purposes of technical support might be named Tech Support. ▪

T I P Microsoft Exchange Server can automatically generate a Display Name and Alias name when you type the user's first and last names.

Part
III

Ch
16

N O T E Display and Alias are the only two required fields in the general property page. ▪

Primary Windows NT Account Every Microsoft Exchange mailbox must have at least one associated Windows NT account. This is referred to as the primary Windows NT account. Logging into Windows NT gives your account full access to the Microsoft Exchange Mailbox for that user name. If you create an Exchange mailbox in the Windows NT User Manager, the primary Windows NT account name is that new account.

The following shows how to set a primary Windows NT account from the Exchange Administrator Program:

1. Select the General tab in the new mailbox property sheet.

2. Click the Primary Windows NT Account button.

3. Use Select an Existing Windows NT Account to browse through the Add Users and Groups dialog box. Select one. Then, click OK.

   Alternatively, you can use Create a New Windows NT Account to bring up the Create Windows NT account dialog box (see Figure 16.5).

FIG. 16.5

Create a Windows NT user account for an Exchange mailbox without using the User Manager.

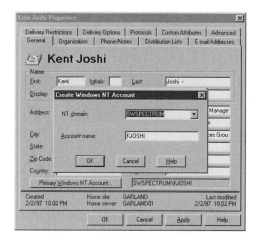

4. Pick the NT domain in which you want to create this account. Type a name in the Account Name box.

5. Click OK. The password for this newly created Windows NT account is the same as the mailbox's display name.

The Organization Page

This property page records data pertinent to how your company functions. The kind of information found in this place is names of individuals who report to this mailbox owner and the mailbox owner's manager. These individuals are all identified by their Exchange mailboxes. All this information is optional. The space is given to help you to be organized, however. It also provides for a specific definition of your organization with Exchange.

To set the Organization information, first specify the Manager of the mailbox owner:

1. Select the Organization tab. The dialog box in Figure 16.6 appears.

FIG. 16.6

The Organization properties let you define an executive hierarchy by Exchange mailboxes.

2. Click the Modify button under the Manager box. The address book displays. Select a recipient. Click OK. By default, the Manager space is blank.

3. To clear the Manager setting click the Clear button.

Next, specify a list of people who report to this mailbox owner:

1. Under the Direct reports box, click Modify.

2. On the left window select the appropriate mailboxes. Click Add to create a list on the right. Select and delete names manually in the right window to remove mailboxes from the list. Click OK to return to the Organization tab.

3. Click Apply to set these properties and continue with other properties. When you are finished with all settings, click OK to return to the Administrator Program.

The Phone/Notes Page

This property page gives you plenty of room to enter detailed telephone information concerning a mailbox user. There is also a large note space here to include any necessary comments. Once again, all these fields are optional.

The following explains how to configure the Phone/Notes property page:

1. Select the Phone/Notes tab of the Mailbox Property page. The dialog box in Figure 16.7 appears.

FIG. 16.7

Include any relevant telephone data or notes.

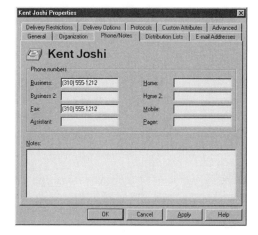

2. Enter all relevant phone numbers in their appropriate boxes.

3. If you need an administrative note, you can enter one in this place.

4. Click Apply to set these properties and continue with other properties. If you are finished with all settings, click OK to return to the Administrator Program.

The Distribution Lists Page

In this property page, you define this mailbox's membership to various distribution lists. Distribution lists are another type of recipient. The following discussion covers these lists in more detail.

You can add distribution list membership using the following steps:

1. Select the Distribution Lists tab in the user's mailbox. The dialog box in Figure 16.8 appears.

The dialog box contains the distribution lists of which the user is a member. By default, a new mailbox is not a member of any of the lists.

2. Click Modify to change group membership. An address book window appears. Using this window you can add or delete your desired distribution lists. Click OK.

N O T E   If no lists are available and you want to create some new ones, see the instructions later in this chapter. These instructions explain how to define those recipients.

3. Click Apply to set these properties and continue with other ones. If you are finished with all settings, click OK to return to the Administrator Program.

The Delivery Restrictions Page

Delivery restrictions screen incoming mail. Using the settings in this property page, you can define specific senders from which this mailbox will reject mail. Alternatively, you can define a list of addresses from which this mailbox will only accept messages. The two options are mutually exclusive. However, Exchange enables you to select senders in both lists.

The following explains how to set these options:

1. Select the Delivery Restrictions tab. The dialog box in Figure 16.9 appears.

    The left window lists only the senders that are permitted to send messages to this mailbox. Alternatively, the right window lists senders who will be rejected if they send messages to this mailbox. By default, they are both empty.

2. Click Modify under each window to add or delete senders. The address book dialog box will open. Type or select senders from the list. Alternatively, you can delete them in this window. Click OK when you are finished and want to return to the Delivery Restrictions property sheet.

FIG. 16.9

The Organization properties enable you to define an executive hierarchy by Exchange mailboxes.

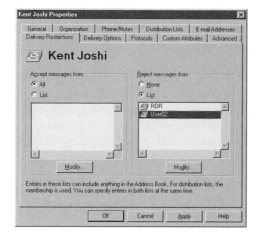

3. Click Apply to set these properties and continue with others. When you are finished with all settings, click OK to return to the Administrator Program.

The Delivery Options Page

A Microsoft Exchange Mailbox can be configured with special options that provide some interesting functions. You can set two different delivery options on this property page:

- Alternate Recipient for a Mailbox

   Another recipient can be set up to receive mail intended for this mailbox.

- Send On Behalf Permissions

   Gives other users the right to send messages as if they originated from the primary user.

Alternate Recipient   Occasionally, you will need to set alternate recipient for e-mail directed to a particular destination.

In our previous example, Jack will be going on vacation for two weeks. Instead of bouncing the messages back with an auto-reply, however, they can be redirected to an assistant's mailbox.

Use the following steps to set up alternate recipients:

1. Select the Delivery Options tab. The dialog box appears. The Alternate Recipient settings are in the lower-left corner of the dialog box. By default, the None radio button is selected and there is no entry in the box below it.

2. Under Alternate Recipient, click Modify. The address book dialog box appears. Select the recipient to whom you want all messages from this mailbox redirected. Click Add. Click OK to confirm your selection and return to the Delivery Option property page.

3. Select the And Alternate Recipient check box to both redirect a message to the alternate recipient and deliver it to the principal mailbox. This essentially delivers two messages. By default, this box is not checked.

Send On Behalf   This feature creates a situation in which one or many individuals are allowed to send mail "on behalf" of the primary mailbox. Authority is distributed across several users.

Example of using the "send mail on behalf" feature:

Michael Navarro, a 3-D graphics technical director in Los Angeles, has a team of animators. Michael is currently the lead on a *special effects* project with a major studio. The animators are allowed to communicate electronically with the effects supervisor at the studio. Each animator has been given Send On Behalf privileges on the Michael Navarro mailbox. Animator Richard d'Andrea sends a message requesting information from the effects supervisor. The messages received by the effects supervisor are titled as sent by:

Richard D'Andrea on behalf of Michael Navarro

Use the following steps to set up Send On Behalf privileges:

1. Select the Delivery Options tab.

   The Send On Behalf settings are found in the top half of the property page. The "Give Send On Behalf Of Permission To" window displays all the users that have been granted this right.

2. Click Modify to edit the user list. The address book appears. In the left window, choose the user to which you want to grant this permission. Click Add to add users. Alternatively, you can delete the names from the user list on the right window to remove them. Click OK to confirm your selection and return to the Delivery Options property page.

3. Click Apply to set these properties and continue with other ones. When you are finished with all settings, click OK to return to the Administrator Program.

The Custom Attributes Page

This property page lets you define up to ten extension fields for this mailbox.

Use the following steps to set up Custom Attributes:

1. Select the Custom Attributes tab. The dialog box in Figure 16.10 appears.

2. The dialog box lists all ten custom attributes on the left side of the box, and the user's values are entered on the right.

3. Type values for as many Custom Attributes as you want.

4. Click Apply to set these properties and continue with other properties. When you are finished with all settings, click OK to return to the Administrator Program.

FIG. 16.10

Set values for the
custom attributes
designated for this
site.

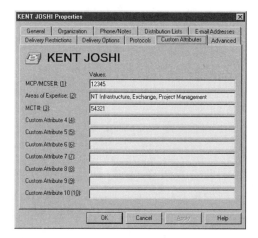

The Advanced Page

Advanced properties are mainly concerned with the attribute information of a mailbox's system. The following are the advanced properties:

■ Simple Display Name

This name will be used by systems that cannot interpret all the characters in a normal display name, such as spaces.

■ Directory Name

Read only field. The name by which this object is known within its context in the directory. This name is presented for information purposes only and cannot be changed in this property sheet.

■ Trust Level

The directory replication trust level determines whether a recipient is replicated to another site. If the trust level assigned to the recipient exceeds the trust level set for the connector during Directory Synchronization setup, then the mailbox will not be replicated. Chapter 2, "Understanding Exchange's Organization Sites," further discusses the application of trust levels.

■ Message Sizes

This property sets restrictions on maximum outgoing and incoming message sizes (in kilobytes) for this mailbox. Any message above the set limits in size are returned as nondeliverable.

■ Home Server

The Home Server is the Exchange Server on which this mailbox physically resides. The user must log on to the server listed to employ its client.

■ Information Store Storage Limits

You can set upper storage limits for this mailbox using this property. By default, a mailbox will use the values set on the Private Information Store property pages.

■ Container Name

This is the name of the recipients container in which this mailbox resides. This value is presented for information purposes only and cannot be changed in this property sheet.

■ Administrative Note

This note contains comments pertaining to settings on this page.

The following includes steps that help you configure Advanced Properties:

1. Select the Advanced tab. The dialog box in Figure 16.11 appears.

2. Enter a Simple Display name to be used by systems that cannot interpret all the characters in a normal display name.

3. Set the mailbox's Trust Level to the desired level.

FIG. 16.11

The Advanced property page gives you control over several mailbox functions related to the system.

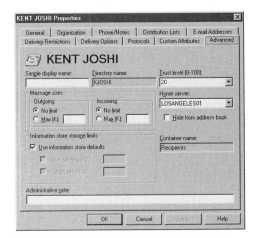

4. If you want to impose message transmission limits on this mailbox, click the appropriate Max (K) radio button. Enter the upper limit (in kilobytes) of message sizes you want to restrict.

5. If you want to change the serving on which the mailbox resides, select it from the Home Server pop-up menu. The entire contents of the mailboxes will be transferred to the new Server's information store.

N O T E   This has the same function as selecting Move Mailbox from the Administrator Tools menu. ■

6. Set mailbox specific `Information store storage limits` by clicking to remove the check in the Use information store defaults box. Type a storage size value (in kilobytes) in the Issue warning (K) at which users will be notified that their message storage is near capacity. Enter a value in the "Prohibit send (K)." When this maximum is reached, the user is blocked from sending mail from this mailbox. This will not, however, prohibit incoming mail. By default, these values are set in the Public Information Store properties for this Server. These values will affect this mailbox unless it is told otherwise.

7. Optional comments providing custom notes or instructions for a mailbox can be entered here (up to 1,024 characters). As an example, you can record the reasons for overriding information store defaults in this space.

8. Click Apply to set these properties and continue with other properties. When you are finished with all settings, click OK to return to the Administrator Program.

The Protocols Page

This property page displays the protocol list for the recipient. Select the Protocols tab. The dialog box in Figures 16.12 appears.

FIG. 16.12

This page lists available protocols for the recipient.

News groups, public folders on Exchange can be accessed by any client newsreader.

Creating Custom Recipients

Custom recipients are defined for sending messages to users outside the Microsoft Exchange organization global address list. Normally, these recipients are MS Mail users, SMTP users (Internet), or foreign X.400 system users. You can also create custom recipients for any other third-party connector or gateway. Once created, these recipients can be replicated across your organization as part of the global address list. They can receive messages from and send messages to a Microsoft Exchange Server. Custom recipient objects are identified by a globe icon in the Exchange Administrator program. Property pages for custom recipients are quite similar to those of standard Exchange mailboxes. The pages for custom recipients do not have as many advanced features as the latter.

The following steps help you to create a new custom recipient:

1. Select New Custom Recipient from the Administrator Program File menu. The New E-mail Address dialog box in Figure 16.13 appears.

FIG. 16.13

Address types for all installed connections and gateways are displayed in this dialog box.

2. Select an e-mail address type for your new custom recipient. All installed connector types are listed. Click OK.

3. In the preceding dialog box, enter the appropriate delivery information for the selected address type.

4. Click OK to set the address and proceed to the Exchange Custom Recipient Object property pages.

The following steps show you how to enter delivery addresses for specific custom recipients. Configuring a cc:Mail custom recipient is discussed below:

1. Enter the user's Display Name (see Figure 16.14).

FIG. 16.14

You need to specify delivery information for a cc:Mail post office recipient.

2. Enter the user's cc:Mail Mailbox name on the post office.

3. Enter the cc:Mail Post Office through which this user receives messages.

The following steps show you how to enter delivery addresses for specific custom recipients. Configuring an MS Mail custom recipient is discussed below:

1. Enter the correct name for this post office.

2. Enter the MS Mail Network name on which this user receives messages.

3. Enter the MS Mail Network name for the post office through which this user receives messages.

4. Enter the user's MS Mail Mailbox name on the preceding post office (see Figure 16.15).

FIG. 16.15
You need to specify delivery information for an MS Mail (PC) post office recipient.

5. Click OK to proceed to the Exchange custom recipient property pages.

The following steps explain how to enter a custom MS Mail for an AppleTalk address.

1. Enter the user's Display Name (see Figure 16.16).

FIG. 16.16
You need to specify delivery information for an MS Mail (AppleTalk) Server recipient.

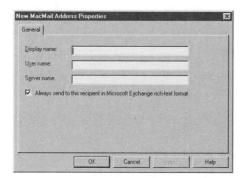

2. Enter the recipient's User Name as it appears on the Macintosh Server.

3. Enter the Macintosh Server name for this recipient.

4. Click Always Send to This Recipient in Microsoft Exchange Rich-Text Format to maintain special message formatting in messages transmitted to this recipient.

5. Click OK to proceed to the Exchange Custom Recipient property pages.

Follow these steps to enter a custom Internet or other SMTP address:

1. Enter an SMTP address in the single E-mail address box.

2. Click OK to proceed to the Exchange Custom Recipient property pages (see Figure 16.17).

FIG. 16.17

Entering an Internet address.

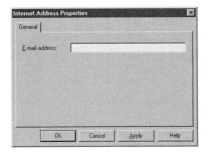

You must specify an Internet or other SMTP address in the window (must be in the user@domain format).

There are two property pages available to enter an X.400 address. The General page lets you define the specific address for a foreign X.400 recipient (see Figure 16.18). You can add more information for this recipient by using the Advanced page.

FIG. 16.18

This General property page defines a foreign X.400 recipient's delivery information.

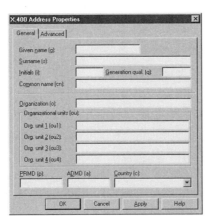

Configuring Properties for a Custom Recipient

After selecting the address type and entering delivery information for a custom recipient, you will be presented with the Exchange property pages for this recipient. You can also use this section as a reference for modifying custom recipient property pages after you have created the object.

The following explains how to complete the Exchange property pages for a recipient:

- General Information

  Records basic recipient information, such as name, location, title, and company. This section also enables you to change the e-mail address and its type for this custom recipient.

- Specifics About the Organization

  You can add optional information about your company's organization, such as a manager, and the people who report to this recipient.

- Phone Number and Notes

  In this place you can enter detailed telephone information and any additional notes about the user.

- Distribution Lists that Include the Recipient

  This page specifies the distribution lists to which this recipient belongs.

- E-mail Addresses

  This page enables you to create, modify, and delete alternate addresses for this recipient.

- Delivery Restrictions

  This page defines from which addresses this mailbox will or will not accept messages.

- Custom Attributes

  This page adds up to 10 administrator-defined fields that you can use to keep additional information about the recipient.

- Advanced Page

  This page contains all the settings concerned with advanced administrator functions, such as trust levels, message sizes, text formatting, and hidden/not hidden status.

The following sections explain the process of configuring custom recipient property pages. The specifics of each of the pages are discussed in depth.

Part
III

Ch
16

The General Page

Select the General property page (see Figure 16.19). This property page is almost identical to that of an Exchange mailbox. The main difference is the E-mail button in the bottom left corner of the window. When you click it, the dialog box in Figure 16.20 appears.

FIG. 16.19

The General property page gives you control over several system-related mailbox functions.

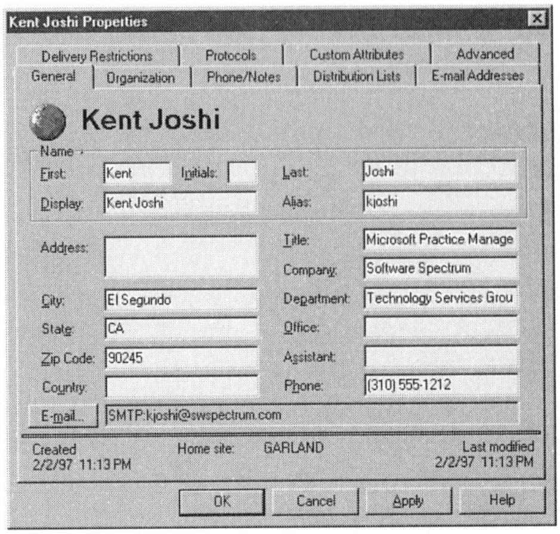

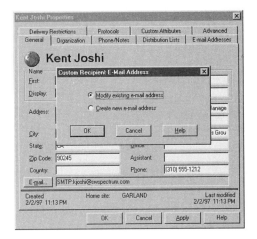

FIG. 16.20

Choose to edit the current e-mail address, or create a new one.

N O T E Notice the globe icon denoting a custom recipient.

Select `Modify existing e-mail address` to edit the recipient address in the appropriate dialog box for the current address type.

Select `Create new e-mail address` to create an entirely new address using the same process described previously.

A box to the right of the E-mail address button shows the current address type and value of this custom recipient. Address types are abbreviated in the following way:

MS: Microsoft Mail for PC networks

MSA: Microsoft Mail for AppleTalk networks

SMTP: Simple Mail Transfer Protocol addresses, for example, for the Internet

X.400: Foreign X.400 addressees

The Organization Page

If this custom recipient has one or more managers, and certain individuals must report to them, enter these names in the spaces provided. This property page is functionally equivalent to a standard Mailbox's Organization property page.

The Phone Number and Notes Page

On this page you can enter detailed phone number information for this custom recipient. This property page is functionally equivalent to a standard Mailbox's Phone Number and Notes property page.

The Distribution Lists Page

You can add Custom Recipients to distribution lists as any other recipient. This property page is functionally equivalent to a standard Mailbox's Distribution Lists property page.

The E-Mail Addresses Page

This page holds a list of e-mail addresses automatically created for this directory object. You can alter the recipient's principal from this window, so that it is the same as the one on the General property page. These addresses will be used when routing messages from other connected mail systems, such as MS Mail. This property page is functionally equivalent to a standard Mailbox's E-mail Addresses property page.

The Delivery Restrictions Page

You can define other users within the Exchange organization that will not be able to send messages to this custom recipient by using the Delivery Restrictions page. The Accept Messages From and Reject Messages From windows are functionally equivalent to a standard Mailbox's Delivery Restrictions property page.

The Custom Attributes Page

Enter additional custom recipient data in the appropriate fields. This property page is functionally equivalent to a standard Mailbox's Custom Attributes property page.

The Advanced Page

Use this property page to create a simple display name for this recipient, if required. You also use this page to set a trust level as needed for either directory replication and synchronization, or both. Also, set an upper limit for the size of messages addressed to this recipient. Similar to a mailbox, you can select to allow rich text formatting for messages to this recipient, or choose to hide it from being displayed in the address book.

When you select the Advanced tab, the dialog box in Figure 16.21 appears.

FIG. 16.21

You can set advanced properties for this recipient using the Advanced tab.

Because a custom recipient does not use storage space in a private information store, maximum storage options are removed from this page. Also, there is no option to change the home server for this recipient. The reason is that there are no messages being stored locally for this recipient.

The Protocols Page

Enter additional protocols data in the appropriate fields. This property page is functionally equivalent to a standard Mailbox's Protocols property page.

N O T E   Custom recipients do not have a Delivery Options property page. Therefore, you cannot specify alternate recipients. You also cannot give Send On Behalf privileges to that recipient. ▩

Creating Distribution Lists

The following describes the function of the property pages for a Distribution List:

▩   General Information

The General Information property page records basic recipient information, such as name, owner, and members. The General Information property page also allows you to select the expansion server for this list.

▩   Distribution Lists

The Distribution Lists property page specifies the distribution lists to which this distribution list belongs. Lists can be nested within each other to develop a hierarchy for message distribution.

■ E-mail Addresses

This page enables you to create, modify, and delete alternate addresses for this distribution list.

■ Delivery Restrictions

This page defines from which addresses this distribution list will or will not accept messages.

■ Custom Attributes

On this page you can add up to 10 administrator-defined fields that you use to keep additional information about the distribution list.

■ Advanced Page

All the settings concerned with advanced administrator functions are contained on this page, such as trust levels, message sizes, reporting options, and hidden/not hidden status.

The General Page

The following describes the function of the General Tab in the Distribution List property page:

1. Select the General tab in the Distribution List property page. The dialog box in Figure 16.22 appears.

FIG. 16.22

The General property page gives you control over several system-related mailbox functions.

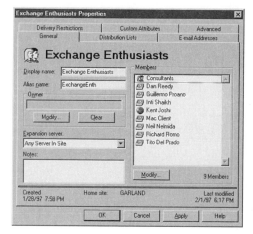

2. Enter a Display name for this distribution list as you want it to appear in the address book.

3. Enter an Alias name which will be used to generate other e-mail addresses for this distribution list.

4. The Owner box displays an Exchange user that has the right to modify a list's membership from within the Exchange client. Normally, only an administrator can modify a list's membership. Click Modify to open the address book. Select an owner from the list. Then, click OK. Use the Clear button to remove that user as the distribution list owner.

5. The Members box lists the current distribution list membership. Click Modify to bring up an address list. You can then click ADD to put new members on the list. Members can be mailboxes, custom recipients, or other distribution lists.

6. You can also select an Expansion Server for this list. By default, Any Server In Site is selected, and the distribution list will be expanded on the Server from which it was sent. Select a specific server from the menu and this distribution list will always be expanded there.

7. Enter any additional Notes in the box provided.

8. Click Apply to set these properties and continue with other ones. When you are finished with all settings, click OK to return to the Administrator Program.

The Distribution Lists Page

Lists can be nested by making them members of other lists. Click the Modify button to add or delete other distribution lists of which this list is a member.

The following illustrates how one list can be nested in another:

There are three new distribution lists in the SWSPECTRUM organization. The first two lists are named SWS LA and SWS Houston. Each distribution list has a membership of users, including mailboxes and custom recipients. The third address list created is named SWS Exchange Enthusiasts. This list only has five members. The members are the other distribution lists along with three additional recipients meant to receive messages intended for these groups. Visually, the hierarchy resembles the one in Figure 16.23.

FIG. 16.23

Nested distribution lists can facilitate list management.

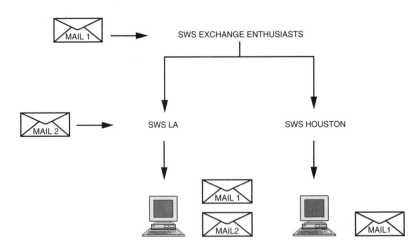

For comparison, examine the following three property sheets depicting this structure.

The SWS LA and SWS Houston Distribution Lists property sheets show the following membership information (see Figure 16.24).

The SWS Exchange Enthusiasts distribution list has both the SWS LA and SWS Houston and three additional recipients as its members. The property sheet for SWS Exchange Enthusiasts looks like Figure 16.25.

Recipients within SWS LA will now receive messages addressed to the Exchange Enthusiasts, as well. A similar result can be obtained by adding all the individual recipients to the Exchange Enthusiasts distribution list. However, you would then have two lists in which to keep track of individual members. Nesting lists facilitates management by placing recipients into smaller logical subdivisions.

Part
III

Ch
16

FIG. 16.24

A Distribution list can have distribution list membership, as well.

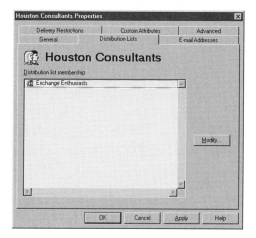

FIG. 16.25

Members of the top level distribution list hierarchy.

The E-Mail Addresses Page

Use this property page to establish alternate e-mail addresses for this distribution list. This property page is functionally equivalent to a standard Mailbox's E-mail Addresses property page (see Figure 16.26).

FIG. 16.26

The E-mail Addresses page displays alternate address data corresponding to all installed connectors and gateways.

For example, jsmith@corpor.com, an Internet mail user, can address a message to ExchangeEnth@GARLAND.SWSPECTRUM.COM. In effect, this user can send the message to over 50 members of this distribution list.

The Delivery Restrictions Page

You can define other users within the Exchange organization who will not be able to send messages to this distribution list. The Accept Messages From and Reject Messages From windows are functionally equivalent to a standard mailbox's or custom recipient's Delivery Restrictions property page.

The Custom Attributes Page

Using the Custom Attributes Page, you can enter additional custom recipient data in the appropriate fields. This property page is functionally equivalent to a standard mailbox's or custom recipient's Custom Attributes page.

The Advanced Page

The distribution list's Advanced property page (see Figure 16.27) is similar to Advanced property pages of other types of recipients. Simple display name, Directory name, Trust level, and Message size are the same settings found on the Advanced property pages of other types of recipients. The following are options specific to the Distribution List property page:

FIG. 16.27
The distribution list
Advanced property
page displays some
settings that are similar
to those of other
property pages.

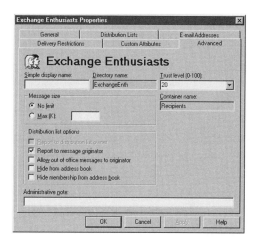

▓ Report to distribution list owner

When checked, this option sends a message to the distribution list owner when a
message that exceeds the specified size limit is sent to this list. By default, this is not
checked.

▓ Report to message originator

When checked, this option sends a message back to the message originator. By default,
this option is checked.

▓ Allow out of office messages to originator

When checked, this option responds with an Out of Office Message for any registered
user who is a member of the distribution. By default, this option is not checked.

▓ Hide distribution list from address book

As with other recipients, this prohibits the distribution list from appearing in the address
book. Users will need to know the name of the list to address it manually.

▓ Hide membership from address book

When checked, the distribution list name itself is displayed in the address book. Users
will be able to view the individual members of the list, however.

Creating and Configuring Public Folders

Public Folders are created and designed from within the Microsoft Exchange client. Then, they
are copied to a public information store. General configuration is handled through the Administrator Program. The following is an overview of the Public Folder property pages:

▓ General information on the folder

This page gives the folder's name and display name, age limits, and specific client
permissions.

- Replicas of the folder

  Add or remove copies of public folders on other severs within your organization.

- Folder replication status

  You can view and track the folder replication process for troubleshooting purposes using this page.

- Replication schedule

  This page helps you specify at which times information within public folders will replicate throughout your organization.

- Distribution lists

  A folder is a member of certain distribution lists. This page helps you specify to which lists it belongs. Any messages sent to the distribution list will also be stored in this public folder.

- E-mail Addresses

  This page enables you to create, modify, and delete alternate addresses for this public folder.

- Custom attributes

  This page lets you add up to 10 administrator-defined fields used to keep additional information about the mailbox.

- Advanced

  Contains all the settings concerned with advanced administrator functions, such as trust levels, message sizes, replication messages importance, storage limits, and hidden/not hidden status.

Configuring a Public Folder's Property Pages

Public folders are listed near the top of the Administrator's object hierarchy (see Figure 16.28). To view the public folder hierarchy in your organization, click the Public Folders object in the Administrator Program.

To edit a specific folder within your site, open its property pages. You will be able to set all the options presented in the preceding list. To edit a public folder's contents, you must use the Microsoft Exchange client program and have appropriate client permissions. Another section later in the chapter discusses assigning client permissions. The next section covers the options available on the Public Folder property pages.

FIG. 16.28

View the public folders within your organization in the Administrator's hierarchy window.

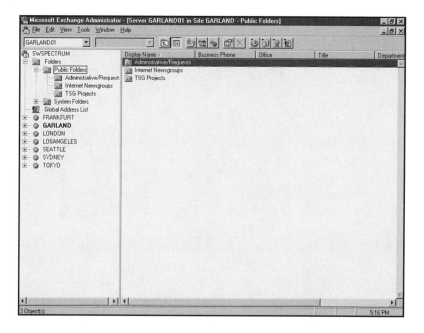

The General Page

The public folder is a unique recipient in that many different users can view and edit the information that it receives. As with other recipient types, the General property page enables you to set names for this object, as well as other general administrative notes. However, there are some very specific settings for this recipient type.

The following steps describe in detail how to set General properties for the public folders:

1. Select the General tab of the Public Folder property pages. The dialog box in Figure 16.29 appears.

2. You can change the Folder Name in the appropriate box. This name is first assigned when the folder was created in the Microsoft Exchange Client program.

3. If you want to give the public folder a different display name for the address book, click the radio button marked Use This Name: under the heading of Address Book Display Name. By default, the Same As Folder Name button is selected.

4. You must enter a required alias name used to generate additional e-mail addresses for this public folder.

Part
III

Ch
16

FIG. 16.29

General properties for
Public Folders are
somewhat different from
other recipient types.

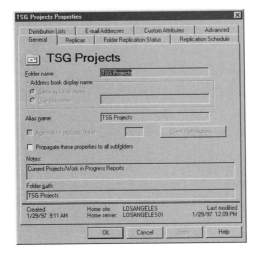

5. Click the `age limit for all replicas (days)` check box. On the right side of the
   check box, enter the number of days after which a message will be automatically deleted.
   By default, there are no set age limits for a public folder, unless predetermined by public
   information store settings (see the scenario later in this section).

6. Enter any additional Notes in the space provided.

7. The Folder Path box displays the hierarchy of subfolders that leads to this public folder.
   If this is a main level folder, and not a subfolder, then only this folder's name is displayed.

8. Click Apply to set these properties and continue with other properties. When you are
   finished with all the settings, click OK to return to the Administrator Program.

Two important additional properties are specific to a public folder:

- Age limits
- Client permissions

Age limits determine the number of days that a message can remain in a public folder before it
is deleted. This function helps to automatically purge the folder of outdated information. For
example, if you set a folder age limit to one day, once that 24-hour period has expired, the message is deleted.

N O T E The Public Information Store has a similar age limit setting used for all the public folders it
contains. The Public Information Store setting overrides any age limit set at the individual
folder level.

Example:

The Public Information Store on Garland has an age limit setting of seven days on all its contents. SW Projects, a public folder held on the GARLAND Public Information Store, is set with an age limit of 10 days. The public information will override any individual settings. Any message in the SW Projects folder will be deleted after seven days.

Client Permissions   These are the available Roles:

- Owner

   This role marks the user as folder owner. This role also gives the user complete permission on this folder.

- Publishing Editor

   This editor is given all create, edit, and delete permissions on a folder. This role also gives permission to create subfolders. It does not, however, mark the user as the owner.

- Editor

   This role gives all create, edit, and delete permissions.

- Publishing Author

   Permission to create subfolders is given to the publishing author. Also, gives create, edit, and delete permission only to their items.

- Author

   This role gives permission to create, edit, and delete only their items.

- Reviewer

   Permission to read items is given to the reviewer.

- Contributor

   The contributor is given permission to create (though not to read) items.

- None

   No permissions are given on this folder. This role is often used as a default to limit access to a specific public folder.

The following steps help you to set up permissions:

1. Click the Client Permissions button on the Public Folder General property page. The dialog box in Figure 16.30 appears.

FIG. 16.30

Client Permissions determine what level of access a user has on a public folder.

The Name: and Role: columns display current users and their roles (see Figure 16.31). The Default role applies to any user not shown on this list.

2. Click Add to bring up the address list and add members to the Client Permissions list. Click a name. Then, click Remove to delete it from the list. Again, click a name. Then, click Properties to bring up that user's property pages.

3. The Roles pull-down menu displays preset roles for certain types of users. Clicking the menu pulls down the following list:

FIG. 16.31

You can use the Roles pull-down menu to give customized properties to a user.

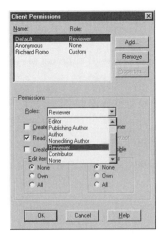

Select a role from the menu. Note that the check boxes and radio buttons reflect the change in access rights for each role.

4. Alternatively, you can customize a role by clicking the available radio buttons and check boxes. If by clicking, you set a configuration that matches one of the predefined roles, that role will be displayed in the Roles pop-up menu heading. For example, you select the Author permission from the menu. The boxes and buttons display the permissions for the user role Author. When you click the Create Sub-Folders button, the name in the Roles menu changes to Publishing Author.

5. Click OK to set these permissions and continue editing other public folder properties.

The following list details the check box definitions:

- Create Items

  This check box gives permission to post items to the folder.

- Read Items

  When you check this box, you are given permission to open any item in a folder.

- Create Subfolders

  Check this box to give permission to make a subfolder of the main public folder.

- Folder Owner

  All permissions are given with respect to this folder.

- Folder Contact

  A user with Folder Contact status receives automatic error or conflict messages from the folder, such as replication errors and oversize limit warnings. This user also receives users' requests for more access or other administrative tasks. Often, the owner and the contact are the same individual.

Radio buttons   The Radio buttons give users edit and delete permissions.

The following list outlines the scope of Edit permissions:

- None

  Users cannot make any modification to existing public folder items.

  Users cannot delete any folder items, even ones they have created themselves.

- Own

  The user can edit only items that they have created.

- All

  The user can edit any folder item, regardless of its creator.

The following list details the scope of Delete permissions:

- None

  Users cannot delete any folder item, even ones they have created themselves.

■ Own

Users can delete only items that they have created.

■ All

The user can delete any folder item, regardless of its creator.

The Replicas Page

This property page displays the destination servers to which a public folder will be replicated. You also can add or remove replicas throughout your organization using this window.

The following steps help you to configure replicas:

1. Select the Replicas tab from the public folder property sheets. The dialog box in Figure 16.32 appears.

FIG. 16.32

View the public folders within your organization in the Administrator's hierarchy window.

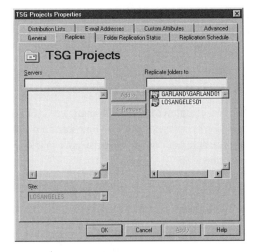

The left side of the screen labeled Servers lists all the public folders. The right side of the screen labeled Replicate folders lists all the Servers to which this folder is replicated.

2. Using the Site pull-down menu at the bottom of the property page, select the site of the destination Server. Click and highlight the desired Server from the list of Exchange Servers on the left side of the window.

3. Click Add to include that Server in the replication list.

4. To remove a Server from the replication process, click its name on the right window. Then, click Remove.

5. Click Apply to set these properties and continue with other properties. When you are finished with all settings, click OK to return to the Administrator Program.

The Replicate Folders To box should now list every Server to which you want this particular public folder replicated. If not, repeat the preceding steps until all desired Exchange Servers are selected.

From Here...

This chapter showed you how to create and configure a mailbox, how to create and configure a custom recipient, and how to create and configure distribution lists.

For related information, read the following chapters:

- Chapter 19, "Using the Microsoft Mail Connector for PC Networks," where you learn how the Microsoft Exchange can coexist or provide backbone support for MS Mail networks.

- Chapter 20, "Using the Microsoft Mail Connector for AppleTalk Networks" is about how to establish a messaging link between Microsoft Exchange and a Macintosh server running Microsoft Mail for AppleTalk networks.

- Chapter 21, "Configuring X.400 Connections" to learn how the Microsoft Exchange X.400 Connector is used to create a message route between two Exchange servers or between one Exchange server and another messaging system that complies with the X.400 standards.

CHAPTER 17

Setting Up the Site Connector and Dynamic RAS Connector

This chapter is the first in this book that is dedicated to the specifics of linking two or more Microsoft Exchange sites. By now, you should have learned enough to be able to select the most appropriate connector between the Exchange servers in your organization. This chapter deals with the two connectors designed only to link Microsoft Exchange servers. Other connectors, such as X.400 or Internet Mail Connector, can be used both to link Exchange servers and to provide a gateway to foreign mail systems. The two connectors used only between Exchange servers are:

- Site Connector—Full-time message link over high-bandwidth network links
- Dynamic RAS Connector—Part-time scheduled message transfer over low-bandwidth lines

    This chapter covers the basics of setting up a Site Connector and a Dynamic RAS Connector. Because a site can have any combination of connectors to a

How to Install a Site Connector to Link Two Exchange Sites over a High Bandwidth Connection

The site connector is probably one of the best connectors to link two Exchange sites together. Since no translation is needed (such as from a foreign messaging platform), you get high performance and a direct connection for moving messages.

How to Configure the Site Connector Property Pages

Set property page by accessing the available tabs. In addition to adjusting the tabs, you will learn how to delete a site connector.

How to Install a Dynamic RAS Connector and MTA Transport Stack

Set up RAS by configuring Message Transfer Agent. Install the RAS MTA Transport Stack and set properties through Tab controls.

How to Configure the Dynamic RAS Connector to Transfer Messages Between Sites

Install the Dynamic RAS Connector by configuring the phone book entry for Dial-Up Networking for remote access.

remote site, or even multiple connectors of a certain type, you will need to repeat the same steps outlined in this chapter each time you set up a new connector. ■

Understanding Site Connectors

The Microsoft Exchange Site Connector provides the most direct link between sites. Communication is handled through remote procedure calls between servers in each site. Messages do not need to be converted to a different format (such as X.400) to be transmitted to a different site.

You should be familiar with the following concepts before you attempt to set up and configure a Microsoft Exchange Site Connector:

- *Target servers*—The list of Exchange servers in the remote site that will be involved in transferring messages to and from the local site.

- *Routing costs*—A number assigned to each connection on a relative scale from 1 to 100. Messages are first routed to connections that have the lowest cost; message transfer is distributed evenly across all connections that have the same assigned cost. You can set routing costs for a site as a whole, as well as for individual Exchange servers.

- *Bridgehead server*—A specific Microsoft Exchange server in a site that is designated to establish communication with the remote site. Normally, the specific server that establishes this connection varies, depending on messaging traffic. Designating a bridgehead server is useful for controlling the message-transfer points between two sites.

Installing a New Site Connector

Installing a Site Connector to exchange messages between sites is a two-step process. First, you must set up a connector in the local site. The connector enables message traffic to the target site. Second, to receive messages from the remote site, you must install a corresponding Site Connector in the remote site. When you set up a new connection between sites, the Exchange Administrator program automatically prompts you to create the second Site Connector in the remote site. If you do not create a remote site (or cannot, due to access restriction in that site), you must coordinate your efforts with the remote site administrator to negotiate a successful connection between sites. The remote administrator must create a corresponding connector that links to your site.

Before you install a new Site Connector, make certain that the following conditions are met:

- The underlying network between two sites is properly configured and operational.

- All Microsoft Exchange services are running on both sites.

- You know the exact server at the remote site to which you want to connect.

- If you want to establish the corresponding Site Connector at the remote site, be sure that you have administrative access rights to the foreign Exchange server.

To create a new Site Connector, follow these steps:

1. Navigate through the Exchange Administrator program's hierarchy, and click the Connections object (see Figure 17.1). The right display window shows all the connections currently running within this site.

2. Pull down the File menu and choose New Other; then choose Site Connector from the New Other menu. The New Site Connector dialog box appears (see Figure 17.2).

FIG. 17.1

The Exchange Administrator program's display window shows all current site connections.

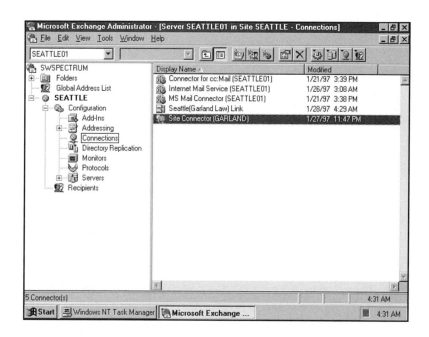

Part

III

Ch

17

3. In the text box, type the name of a specific Microsoft Exchange server at the remote site.

FIG. 17.2

Enter the name of an Exchange server at the remote site.

N O T E The server name that you enter is used to identify the remote site and does not necessarily mean that this server is the machine that will handle message traffic between sites. Conceptually, a Site Connector resides at the site, not on any particular Exchange server. ■

4. Click OK. The Administrator program attempts to locate and access that server on the network.

If you attempt to create a site connector at a site where such a connector already exists, you will be notified of the situation and will not be allowed to create another connector.

Configuring Site Connector Properties

After creating a new Site Connector, you will need to configure its properties. The property pages for the Exchange Site Connector are as follows:

- *General.* Enables you to set an overall routing cost for this connector and designate a bridgehead server, if appropriate.

- *Target Servers.* Enables you to select the specific servers in the remote site that will receive messages from the local site.

- *Address Space.* Allows you to assign various e-mail address types and associated routing costs for this site connector object.

- *Override.* Enables you to specify custom login information if a target server is outside the local Windows NT domain.

General Tab   The General tab is where you set Site Connector communication options. Primarily, you will define which site you are connecting to and which servers specifically will handle that connection. The following steps guide you through configuring the General tab:

1. Click the General tab of the Site Connector property pages (see Figure 17.3).

2. If you want, type a new name for this site connector in the Display Name box. The default display name is in the format Site Connector (site name).

FIG. 17.3
Use the General Site Connector property page primarily to define the site to which you are linking.

3. If you want, type a different directory name for this site connector in the Directory Name box. The default directory name is in the format Site Connector (site name).

4. The Target Site box shows the name of the remote site to which you are connecting. This data is provided for your information only. To change the target site at this point, you must click Cancel to exit the property pages and create a new Site Connector.

5. In the Cost box, enter a routing cost for the site connector. An Exchange server uses this cost to determine whether to use this connection over other available connections. By default, a new site connector has a routing cost of 1.

6. If you want, specify a bridgehead server that will handle communication with the remote site. By default, the Any Server option is selected, and communication will be handled by the combination of target servers specified in the remote site's connector. If you select a specific server, that one machine will process all message transfer through the Site Connector.

7. If you want, make an entry in the Administrative Note box.

8. Click Apply to set these properties and continue setting other properties.

9. When you finish making settings, click OK to return to the Administrator program.

Target Servers Tab   Use the Target Servers tab to set which remote Exchange servers will receive messages through this Site Connector. Servers that do not get listed are excluded from communication with the local site. Follow these steps:

1. Click the Target Servers tab of the Site Connector property pages (see Figure 17.4).

   The Site Servers list on the left side of the dialog box shows all the available servers at the remote site. The Target Servers list on the right side of the dialog box shows the

FIG. 17.4

Select the servers in the remote site to link through this Site Connector.

Part
III

Ch
17

Exchange servers at the remote site which communicate to the local site through this site connector.

2. Select a server from the Site Servers list and then click A<u>d</u>d to make it a target server for this site connector.

To remove a server from the <u>T</u>arget Servers list, select it and then click <u>R</u>emove.

3. The Target Server C<u>o</u>st section displays the routing costs for the selected target server. In the text box, type the desired routing cost for each server and then click Set <u>V</u>alue to store that value.

4. Click <u>A</u>pply to set these properties and continue setting other properties.

5. When you finish making settings, click OK to return to the Administrator program.

Address Space Tab   The Address Space tab is where you tell Exchange which messages are routed through this Site Connector. Without an appropriate entry, messages will not find their way to the remote site. Follow these steps:

1. Click the Address Space tab of the Site Connector property pages (see Figure 17.5).

2. Click one of the New address types (<u>G</u>eneral, <u>X</u>.400, <u>M</u>S Mail, <u>I</u>nternet) to add an address space entry for this connector. Select an existing address space entry and click <u>E</u>dit to modify it or click <u>R</u>emove to delete it.

FIG. 17.5
Add or modify address-space entries to define message routing for this connector.

3. Click <u>A</u>pply to set these properties and continue setting other properties.

4. When you finish making settings, click OK to return to the Administrator program.

Override Tab   If the site to which you want to connect is not within the same Windows NT domain (or within a trusted domain), you must specify logon information for this Site Connector. This property page allows you to enter such data. Use the following steps:

1. Click the Override tab of the Site Connector property pages (see Figure 17.6).

FIG. 17.6

Configure connector logon information to a remote Windows NT domain.

2. In the Windows NT Username box, type the name of the account that you want to use to log on.

3. In the Password box, type the password that is associated with that account.

4. In the Confirm Password box, type the password again.

5. In the Windows NT Domain Name box, type the domain in which the remote site resides.

6. Click Apply to set these properties and continue setting other properties.

7. When you finish making settings, click OK to return to the administrator program.

If a Site Connector is not set up in the remote site, the dialog box shown in Figure 17.7 appears. It prompts you to create one.

FIG. 17.7

Specify whether to create a corresponding site connector at the remote site.

Part **III**

Ch **17**

Click No if you do not want to create and configure the remote Site Connector at this time. If you do click No, realize that message transfer will not occur until you set up that remote Site Connector at some later time. Click Yes to create and configure a Site Connector for the remote site at this time. The property page for the second Site Connector appears (see Figure 17.8).

FIG. 17.8

General property page for the corresponding site connector at the remote site.

Configure this Site Connector following the procedure that you use to configure a local Site Connector. Keep in mind that the target servers now are Microsoft Exchange servers that were the local servers in the previous connector configuration.

After you create and configure a Site Connector between two sites, the remote site appears in your Exchange Administrator program's hierarchy view. You can view all the Exchange objects at the remote site, but you cannot make any changes unless you log on directly to an Exchange server at that site. To share address lists with the connected site, for example, you must set up a directory replication connector to that site. See Chapter 18, "Using Directory Replication and Synchronization," for setting up directory replication between sites.

Deleting a Site Connector

If you want to remove a Site Connector that services message traffic between two sites, you first must determine what other services depend on the existence of that Site Connector. If other connections (such as a directory replication connector) rely on the Site Connector as the only link for message transport, you cannot delete that Site Connector; you first must delete any other dependent connections and then delete the Site Connector. If you do not want to delete the other connections, you must supply another link between sites that can service the other connections.

To delete a Site Connector, follow these steps:

1. Navigate through the Administrator Program's site display, and click the Connections object.

2. Select the Site Connector that you want to delete.

3. Pull down the Edit menu and choose Delete, or press the Delete key on the keyboard.

N O T E To disable all message transfers between sites, you must remove connectors from both the local and the remote sites. Log on to the remote Exchange server and then remove the Site Connectors by using the process described in this section.

Using the Dynamic Remote Access (RAS) Connector

The Microsoft Exchange Dynamic RAS Connector uses existing Windows NT Remote Access Services to facilitate temporary, low-bandwidth messaging links. The Dynamic RAS Connector establishes a temporary scheduled link to a remote Exchange site via a modem or any other RAS-compatible transport (e.g., ISDN or X.25), transfers messaging data, and then disconnects. This section covers installing and configuring the Dynamic RAS Connector to link your messaging sites.

Before installing a Dynamic RAS Connector, you must do the following things:

■ Install the Windows NT Remote Access service on the Exchange server that will be establishing the connection.

■ Enter a RAS phonebook entry for the remote Exchange server. Use your Windows NT documentation or online help to guide you through this process.

■ Configure the hardware that is required for the remote access link (e.g., a modem or ISDN terminal adapter).

■ Know the name of the remote server with which you want to establish the link.

Installing a Dynamic RAS Connector involves these steps:

■ Install the RAS MTA transport stack. Because the MTA will use a transport that is not supported directly through Microsoft Exchange server, you must define an external (i.e., Windows NT Remote Access Service) transport stack to use in message transfer.

■ Install and configure the Dynamic RAS Connector itself. Follow the steps in the following sections.

Installing the RAS MTA Transport Stack

You add the RAS MTA Transport Stack from within the Administrator program. Follow these steps:

1. From the Administrator program, select New Other from the File menu and then select MTA Transport Stack from the submenu. The New MTA Transport Stack dialog box appears (see Figure 17.9).

FIG. 17.9

The New MTA Transport Stack window is used by the Dynamic RAS Connector (and the X.400 connector) to select an underlying transport for message transfer.

The Type section of the dialog box lists the available MTA transport stacks on this Exchange server.

N O T E Only the RAS MTA Transport Stack is used for the Dynamic RAS Connector.

The Server section of the dialog box lists all the servers at the current site.

2. Select RAS MTA Transport Stack from the list of available transports.

3. Select the server in your local site that will handle the remote-access connection. The transport stack will be installed on that server.

4. Click OK to accept the transport stack and Exchange server settings. The General tab of a new Dynamic RAS Connector appears (see Figure 17.10).

FIG. 17.10

The RAS MTA Transport Stack property pages.

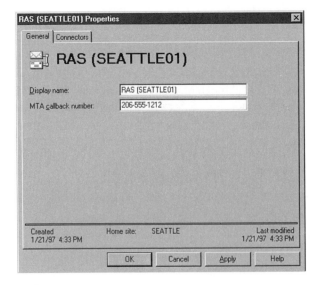

The MTA Transport Stack has only two property pages to configure: General and Connectors. Configuration usually is a one-time process unless you change the local MTA callback number. Refer to the Connector property page to view the Dynamic RAS Connectors that use this MTA Transport Stack.

Configuring MTA Transport Stack Property Pages

Settings in the MTA Transport Stack pages affect all Dynamic RAS Connectors that use it. The following section guides you through configuring the RAS Transport Stack. The process is similar to configuring MTA Transport Stack for X.25, TCP/IP, or TP4 connections as well.

General Tab The General tab lets you configure a display name and callback number for this RAS MTA Transport Stack.

1. In the Display Name box, type the name under which you want this transport stack to appear in the Exchange Administrator object display window. You cannot modify this name after you create it. By default, the stack is named in the RAS format (server name).

2. In the MTA Callback Number box, enter the phone (or other device) number of the local Microsoft Exchange server.

N O T E The Windows NT Remote Access service uses a callback number as a means of authentication. The remote server receives a call, gets the callback number, hangs up, and dials the originator to establish a RAS link. It may be necessary to insert a prefix of an outside line number before the callback number when you dial out from a business phone.

3. Click Apply to set these properties and continue setting other properties.

4. When you finish making settings, click OK to return to the Administrator program.

Connectors Tab

1. Click the Connectors tab of the RAS MTA Transport Stack dialog box (see Figure 17.11).

   The Connectors tab lists all the Dynamic RAS Connectors that use this transport stack. If you have set up the RAS MTA Transport Stack for the first time, the list is blank. After you set up at least one Dynamic RAS Connector, that connector is displayed in this tab; you can select it and then click Edit to modify its properties.

2. Click Apply to set these properties and continue setting other properties.

3. When you finish making settings, click OK to return to the Administrator program.

Part

III

Ch

17

FIG. 17.11
The RAS MTA Transport
Stack Connections tab
lists all current Dynamic
RAS Connectors.

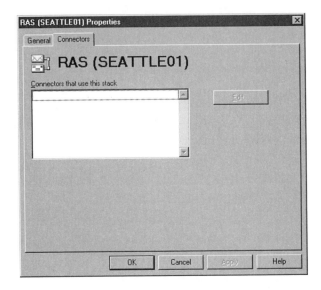

Installing and Configuring a Dynamic RAS Connector

You create a new Dynamic RAS Connector from the Microsoft Exchange Administrator program. If you have not yet installed the RAS MTA Transport Stack, you must do so before proceeding with the following sections.

Installing a New Dynamic RAS Connector

Use the following step to install a new Dynamic RAS Connector: Pull down the Exchange Administrator File menu and choose New Other; then choose Dynamic RAS Connector from the submenu. The tabs for the new connector appear.

Following are the tabs that you use to configure a Dynamic RAS Connector:

- *General*. Enables you to specify the name, remote server, MTA transport stack, maximum message size, and Windows NT RAS phonebook entry.
- *Schedule*. Enables you to set a connection schedule for this Dynamic RAS Connector.
- *RAS Override*. Enter alternative logon and RAS callback number information.
- *MTA Override*. Enables you to change the default MTA settings when you use this Dynamic RAS Connector.
- *Connected Sites*. Enables you to view, add, or modify addressing of the connected sites.
- *Address Space*. Enables you to define which messages pass through this connector.
- *Delivery Restrictions*. Enables you to specify which users can (and cannot) send messages to this Dynamic RAS Connector.

General Tab   The General tab lets you set the communication methods for this Dynamic RAS Connector. Part of this configuration requires you to enter the telephone number data for the remote site, so have that information available when configuring the following options.

1. Click the General tab of the Dynamic RAS Connector property pages (see Figure 17.12).

FIG. 17.12

Set general Dynamic RAS properties.

2. In the Display Name box, type the name that you want to appear in the Microsoft Exchange Administrator display window.

3. When you create a Dynamic RAS Connector, enter a name for it in the Directory Name box.

4. In the Remote Server Name box, type the name of the Microsoft Exchange server to which you are establishing a link.

5. From the MTA Transport Stack drop-down list, select the local Exchange server that will handle the remote access connection.

6. From the Phone Book entry, select the entry that dials into the remote server.

   If you have not yet created an appropriate entry:

   • Click Start at the bottom of your screen.

   • Open Accessories and click Dial-Up Networking.

   • Once you have highlighted the option of DUN, click the local Exchange server's Dial-Up Network entries. In our example connector (see Figure 17.13), this brings up the Windows NT RAS entry in the Dial-Up Network for Garland Law.

Part

III

Ch

17

FIG. 17.13

The Windows NT remote access service Dial-Up Network shows an entry that is set to dial into a remote Exchange server.

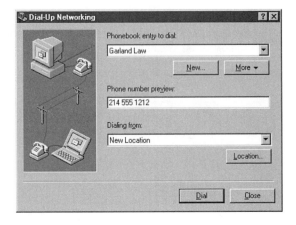

If you have not yet done so, create a Dial-Up Network entry, then close the RAS Dial-Up window.

 Setting an upper limit for message sizes often is a good idea. Particularly with a low-bandwidth link (e.g., a 28.8 Kbps modem), several large messages that have attachments could easily create a bottleneck through this connector.

7. If you want to set an upper limit for the size of messages that pass through this connector, click the Ma**x**imum (K) radio button, and in the text box, type the size limit (in kilobytes). A message that exceeds this maximum size will be returned as undeliverable. By default, the No **L**imit option is selected, and messages of any size can pass through the connector.

8. Make an entry in the Ad**m**inistrative Note box, if you want.

9. Click **A**pply to set these properties and continue setting with other properties.

10. When you finish making settings, click OK to return to the Administrator program.

Schedule Tab   Use the Schedule tab to control how often the Dynamic RAS Connector becomes active and initiates a connection. Follow these steps:

1. Click the Schedule tab of the Dynamic RAS Connector property pages (see Figure 17.14).

2. Click one of the following four options that determine when this Dynamic RAS Connector connects:

   • *Remote Initiated.* This option sends messages only when the remote MTA connects to this MTA. Both MTAs must have the two-way alternative option selected.

FIG. 17.14

Set connection times for this Dynamic RAS Connector.

CAUTION

Only one MTA can be configured to be remote-initiated. Otherwise, if both MTAs are waiting for the other to initiate the connection, the messages will never be delivered.

- *Never.* This option effectively disables this Dynamic RAS Connector.
- *Always.* This option provides a remote access connection whenever messages need to be transferred. By default, this option is selected.
- *Selected Times.* This option enables the Dynamic RAS Connector to initiate communication based on the time grid.

3. If you chose Selected Times in step 2, the Detail View radio buttons become available. Choose either 1 Hour or 15 Minute; the time grid changes its scale accordingly.

4. If you chose Selected Times in step 2, choose the time blocks that you want to use for the connection. In Figure 17.4, the Dynamic RAS Connector is set to initiate connections at 6 A.M. and 6 P.M. on weekdays, and at noon on weekends.

5. Click Apply to set these properties and continue setting other properties.

6. When you finish making settings, click OK to return to the Administrator program.

RAS Override Tab   The RAS Override tab is designed to supersede RAS settings for both logon information and callback numbers. The following steps guide you through these settings:

1. Click the RAS Override tab of the Dynamic RAS Connector property pages (see Figure 17.15).

FIG. 17.15

RAS Override allows you to configure custom logon information from this tab.

2. In the Windows NT Username box, type the name that you want to use to authenticate this Dynamic RAS Connector.

3. In the Password box, type the password.

4. In the Confirm Password box, type the password again.

5. In the Windows NT Domain Name box, type the name of the domain where the remote server resides.

6. In the Optional Phone Numbers combo box, type a phone number in the MTA Callback Number box.

7. Enter a different phone number in the Overriding Phone Number box.

8. Click Apply to set these properties and continue setting other properties.

9. When you finish making settings, click OK to return to the Administrator program.

MTA Override Tab   Because of the typically low-bandwidth links associated with a remote access connection, it often is a good idea to set a different MTA configuration specifically for messages transmitted through this Dynamic RAS Connector. You set the MTA default configuration through the Site MTA property pages. Any setting in the MTA Override property page supersedes default MTA settings when the Dynamic RAS Connector negotiates a connection (see Figure 17.16).

FIG. 17.16

Set specific override properties for the Message Transfer Agent.

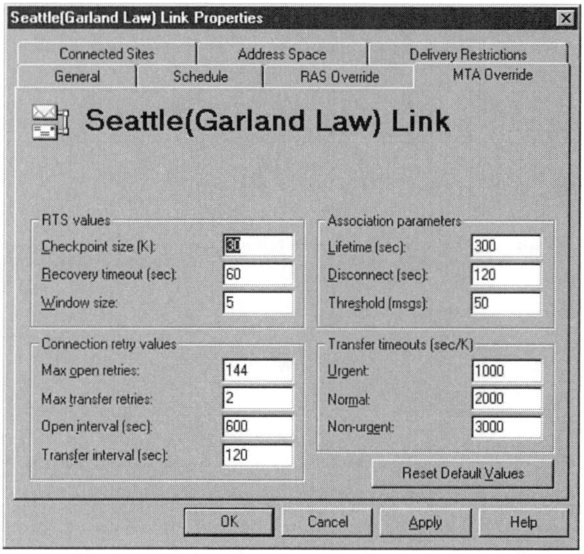

Connected Sites Tab This property page lets you view which sites are linked via the current RAS Connector. Figure 17.17 shows a Connected Sites property page listing linked sites (blank if none).

FIG. 17.17

View directly and indirectly connected Exchange sites.

Sites listed in the Connected Sites tab can receive messages from the local site via the current connector. If a site is not listed, it may be available to view other links established via other connectors.

Address Space Tab   The Address Space tab defines which recipients can be reached through this connector (see Figure 17.18). Only enough addressing data is provided to distinguish messages that should be sent through this connector.

FIG. 17.18

Identify routes to this connector by using Address Space entries.

Routing costs are entered along with each Address Space entry.

Delivery Restrictions Tab   The Delivery Restrictions tab specifies which users can and cannot send messages through this connector. This tab's options are as follows:

- *Accept Messages From.* Creates an exclusive list of recipients who have permission to send messages through this Dynamic RAS Connector.

- *Reject Messages From.* Lists specific recipients who are denied permission to send messages through this Dynamic RAS connector.

To set delivery restrictions, follow these steps:

1. Click the Delivery Restrictions tab of the Dynamic RAS Connector property pages (see Figure 17.19).

2. In the Accept Messages From or Reject Messages From combo boxes, click the List radio button.

3. Click the Modify button below each list to display the Microsoft Exchange address list.

4. Select the desired senders to include or exclude as per the above lists and then click OK.

FIG. 17.19

Delivery restrictions allow you to specify who can access the Dynamic RAS Connector.

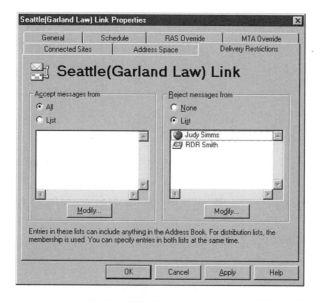

5. Click Apply to set these properties and continue setting other properties.

6. When you finish making settings, click OK to return to the Administrator program.

From Here...

This chapter showed you how to link together two or more Microsoft Exchange sites. For related information, read the following chapters:

- Chapter 5, "Designing Exchange Topology," for planning your site and considering remote-access connections.

- Chapter 14, "Message Transfer Configuration," for additional information on configuring MTA connection settings.

Part
III

Ch
17

Using Directory Replication and Synchronization

Chapter 2, "Understanding Exchange's Organization Sites," showed you general concepts about how directory replication and synchronization work in an Exchange organization. This section teaches you how to set up and configure directory replication and synchronization in Microsoft Exchange Server. ■

How to Configure Directory Replication

This section reviews replication, how and when it occurs within a site, between sites, and within the Exchange network, as well as outside the Exchange Network.

How to Configure Exchange Directory Synchronization Services

In this section, we configure the dirsync requestor or use the dirsync server. EDS is deployed with a MS Mail Connector using Microsoft Mail directory-synchronization protocol.

How to Configure Directory Synchronization with Microsoft Mail for Appletalk Networks

This section will define and configure directory Synchronization and show how to configure Microsoft Mail Clients on Appletalk networks by setting up an Apple Macintosh Requestor to the Exchange Server.

How to Configure the Directory Exchange Agent (DXA) to Handle Directory Synchronization on a Server

Performing setup tasks and controlling the DXA on Exchange servers by adjusting the six tabs that maintain DXA.

Understanding Exchange Replication

This chapter assumes you have a basic understanding of Microsoft Exchange's directory architecture, Microsoft Exchange Server is installed and running on at least two sites, and that the external system is functional (you can send and receive messages).

Just for a quick review, *directory replication* is the process by which Exchange Server renews and updates user directory data. This process occurs between servers in an Exchange site, as well as between servers in different sites throughout your organization. The following sections describe the steps you will use to set up replication between your Exchange servers.

Directory Replication Within a Site

Directory replication within a Microsoft Exchange Server site is automatic. The replication function is handled by the directory service and is always in operation while that service is running. This process requires no maintenance other than making certain that the servers in a site can exchange standard messaging information.

Mean time between replication requests is approximately five minutes, which means that a directory change effected on one server ripples through to each server in a site within five minutes. Network load and available bandwidth affect this process.

The following is an example of how a directory change propagates through an Exchange site:

- Administrator Richard creates a new mailbox recipient, Ron Smith, on the server SEATTLE01.
- Upon creation of the user, the new directory object is a legitimate candidate for directory replication.
- Within five minutes, user Kent on Microsoft Exchange Server GARLAND01 (a server at the same site as SEATTLE01) cannot only address Ron Smith as a recipient, but can also see his name in the Global Address List.

Directory replication within a site is automatic. If you do not want a specific recipient to be copied during replication, you must make it hidden.

Replication Between Sites

The replication of directory information between two Microsoft Exchange sites is the second logical step in maintaining a cohesive directory structure within your organization. This section covers replication between the following:

- Exchange sites on the same network (LAN)
- Exchange sites on different networks

Directory Replication Connector

The principal tool used to set up directory replication is the *directory replication connector*. It handles the exchange of all directory information. As the administrator, you need only provide the site names and the names of the appropriate bridgehead servers to establish a replication connector.

Setting up replication between two Microsoft Exchange sites involves three steps:

1. Create a directory replication connector for both sites.

2. Identify the bridgehead server at each site that is responsible for transferring directory updates.

3. Establish a replication schedule to determine how often directory updates will traverse a site link.

The following sections provide details on configuration for specific situations. The general steps for setting up directory replication, however, are the same for all types of networks.

Directory Replication Between Sites on the Same Network

This section describes the procedure for using directory replication between two Exchange sites physically connected on the same LAN. Typically, this means high-bandwidth links between groups of servers in close geographical proximity. In the real world, this can be two distinct corporate divisions in the same building, for example. Whatever the case, your Exchange servers will be able to communicate with each other over your standard network connections and will not require the use of any additional transport mechanism.

Part
III

Ch
18

The following is a list of requirements before setting up replication between sites on the same network:

■ The messaging link between both servers is fully functional (sending and receiving messages). Usually, you use a site connector to establish such a link between sites on the same network.

■ You have administrator permissions on each server with which you will be establishing a directory-replication relationship.

To set up directory replication between sites on the same network, follow these steps:

1. Open a New Directory Replication Connector from the Administrator program's File menu under New Other. The New Directory Replication Connector dialog box appears (see Figure 18.1).

2. From the Remote Site Name drop-down list, select the site to which you want to connect.

3. In the Server in Remote Site box, type the name of the remote server.

4. Click the radio button labeled Yes, the Remote Site Is Available on This Network.

FIG. 18.1

Use this dialog box to set New Directory Replication Connector options.

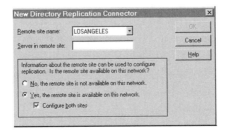

 You almost always choose this option when both sites are on the same LAN, because the option saves you time and reduces configuration errors. Only external situations, such as administrative security restriction within a company, might require separate configuration of such directory replication connectors. For example, an Admin on one site may not be given sufficient administrative privileges of the remote site to establish a connection alone.

---

5. Click the Configure Both Sites check box. This option automatically creates and configures a corresponding directory connector at the remote site.

6. Click OK to proceed to the Directory Replication Connector property pages.

N O T E   Because both servers are on the same LAN, Exchange can locate the site and communicate with the remote server via remote procedure calls. You need to specify only the remote site's name in the New Site Connector dialog box. ▨

To facilitate the interchange of directory data between sites, you must designate replication bridgehead servers. These servers process directory update requests from other bridgehead servers and also generate their own requests for updates. A one-to-one relationship must exist between bridgehead servers for sites that exchange directory information.

Following are a few example situations:

▨ Example 1: You want to establish directory replication between the sites GARLAND and SEATTLE. GARLAND01 and SEATTLE01 are the selected bridgehead servers. These servers will be the only replication point for Exchange directory information between the Garland and Seattle sites. You make no allowances for the use of multiple directory replication connectors to balance server load, link traffic, and so on.

In directory replication, you must designate a local bridgehead server and a remote bridgehead server when you set up a directory replication connector. *Local* and *remote* are relative terms. When you configure a directory replication connector between sites, the General tab of each connector shows different information for each end of the connection.

▨ Example 2: You want to establish a directory replication relationship between the sites GARLAND and SEATTLE.

The GARLAND Directory Replication Connector's General tab displays the following information:

Local bridgehead server   GARLAND01

Remote bridgehead server   SEATTLE01

The SEATTLE Directory Replication Connector's General tab displays the following information:

Remote bridgehead server   GARLAND01

Local bridgehead server   SEATTLE01

You can create multiple directory replication links to one site if they originate from different sites. Directory information can pass between two sites at only one point, however.

■ Example 3: This example discusses the use of multiple directory replication connectors in a site. In this case, GARLAND is the site that has multiple connectors. SEATTLE's bridgehead server (GARLAND01) replicates directory information with bridgehead server GARLAND01 (see Figure 18.2).

FIG. 18.2

Directory replication across multiple bridgehead servers.

Simultaneously, the LOSANGELES site replicates information to the GARLAND site. LOSANGELES01 is the bridgehead server for the LOSANGELES site. LOSANGELES01 links to a second bridgehead server at the GARLAND site: GARLAND02.

A smaller organization could manage by setting up multiple directory replication connectors on one server. This procedure is not generally recommended but is an option for sites that have few users, infrequent directory updates, or a limited number of servers. In this case, both SEATTLE01 and LOSANGELES01 can be bridgehead servers linked to GARLAND01 (see Figure 18.3).

In the preceding examples, directory information between the SEATTLE and LOSANGELES sites is synchronized automatically by the sites' common link, GARLAND.

You set up bridgehead servers in the Exchange Administrator program. To designate bridgehead servers, follow these steps:

1. Click the General tab of the Directory Replication Connector Properties page (see Figure 18.4).

2. From the Local Bridgehead Server drop-down list, select the local server that will handle incoming and outgoing directory update requests. The default selection is the name of the Exchange server on which you are currently logged in.

3. From the Remote Bridgehead Server drop-down list, select the server at the remote site that will receive and request updated directory information.

Part

III

Ch

18

FIG. 18.3
Setting up multiple
directory replication
connectors.

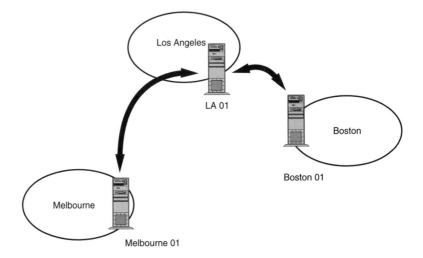

FIG. 18.4
The General tab of the
Directory Replication
Connector Properties
page.

After you establish a directory replication connector, you can change the local bridgehead
server for that connector, but make sure that you update the remote connector to reflect the
change. Usually it is best not to make such changes and to plan in advance for a situation that
might require you to change this information. If you must change the local bridgehead server,
this change will prompt Exchange to reinitiate the replication cycle.

Replicating Directory Information Between Sites
on Different Networks

Sites located on different logical LANs can share directory information almost as easily as sites
on the same LAN. Because you cannot use a site connector to link bridgehead servers, however, you must configure a custom connector to that site.

The following conditions must exist before you set up directory replication between sites on different LANs:

- The messaging link between both servers is fully functional (sending and receiving messages). This link can be set up with any available connector (Site, X.400, or Internet) that supports message transfer between sites.

- You know the e-mail address of the remote site bridgehead server's directory. The Exchange directory replication connector needs this address so that it knows where to direct replication messages. You must enter this information manually.

To set up directory replication between sites on different networks, follow these steps:

1. Open a New Directory Replication Connector from the Administrator program's File menu under New Other. The New Directory Replication Connector dialog box appears.

2. Click the radio button labeled No, the Remote Site Is Not Available on This Network. This will highlight the two input boxes below it.

3. In the Remote Site Name box, type the name of the remote site with which you are establishing replication.

4. In the Server in Remote Site, type the name of the remote bridgehead server.

5. Click OK to proceed to the Directory Replication Connector property pages.

Addressing Tab   When you configure replication between two sites that are not on the same network, you must supply the e-mail address of the bridgehead's server directory. Follow these steps:

1. Click the Addressing tab of the Directory Replication Connector Properties page. The Addressing dialog box appears.

2. In a new connector, you see a blank address space for the remote bridgehead's server directory. Click the Modify button. The New Entry dialog box appears.

3. Select the address type that you want to create. This type should be identical to the type of connector used to transmit normal messaging data between sites. GARLAND and SEATTLE, for example, are linked via a private X.400 link, so the address selection in the New Entry box should be X.400.

   The next dialog box will be different depending on what address type you selected in the preceding step.

Schedule Tab   Directory updates transmitted between bridgehead servers are executed according to an administrator-defined schedule. You need to evaluate the following elements before you decide on an appropriate replication schedule:

- Expected replication traffic
- Network bandwidth between sites

Part

III

Ch

18

■ Server load on bridgehead servers

■ Any scheduling constraints created by the type of messaging link

The first three items are related. If replication traffic is heavy between the two sites (if directory objects are frequently added, deleted, or modified, for example), this will affect available bandwidth. Sometimes, you have to have a frequent replication schedule to maintain an accurate global address list.

Scheduling constraints arise due to the type of site link used. This is especially the case when using part-time connections.

The site link between GARLAND and GARLAND LAW, for example, is established by a Dynamic RAS Connection. Three times a day, a modem connection to the GARLAND01 site is established; the connection is maintained for 30 minutes and then closed. You must configure the directory replication connector to transmit data when the network connection is up; otherwise, the connector may attempt to transfer directory updates through a nonexistent link.

To configure the replication schedule, follow these steps:

1. Click the Schedule tab of the Directory Replication Connector Properties page (see Figure 18.5).

FIG. 18.5

The Schedule tab of the Directory Replication Connector Properties page.

2. Click one of the three radio buttons in the top-left corner of the dialog box:

   • Never: disables directory replication.

   • Always: updates the replication schedule every 15 minutes.

   • Selected Times: allows you to specify the replication schedule manually.

3. If you chose Selected Times in step 2, click one of the Detail View radio buttons (1 Hour or 15 Minute) to view the time grid in different increments.

4. Select the block(s) of time during which you want replication to occur by clicking the schedule grid.

5. If you are done configuring all other tabs for this connector, click OK. Otherwise, click another tab to continue making adjustments.

Following are two general recommendations on scheduling replication time:

■ For international replication links, be sure to take into account the various time zones in which your site will operate. Off-peak hours for a server in London, for example, could fall in the middle of a high-message-volume time in Chicago.

■ For sites that have a large number of frequent directory updates, you should opt for frequent replication, keeping in mind the fact that increased message traffic affects network performance.

Viewing a Site's Directory Data

After you configure both directory replication connectors and establish directory replication between two sites, you can view all sites with which you are exchanging directory data. This is the case because the local site receives directory updates from the immediately connected remote site, as well as from every other remote site with which that site is replicating data.

To view inbound and outbound sites, click the Sites tab of the Directory Replication Connector dialog box. Inbound sites are those from which the local site receives directory updates. Outbound sites are those to which directory updates are sent.

In an example earlier, we created directory replication connectors to SEATTLE to GARLAND, SEATTLE to FRANKFORT and SEATTLE to TOKOYO. After the first successful replication request, you see the site names displayed in the Sites tab, as shown in Figure 18.6.

Part
III

Ch
18

FIG. 18.6

The Directory Replication Connector Sites Properties page shows which sites are sharing directory information.

GARLAND is displayed in the Inbound Sites list. TOKOYO, FRANKFORT also appears in the list because they are involved in the process as a whole. The Outbound Sites list displays only SEATTLE because it is the one site that sends directory updates directly.

You also can use the Sites tab to request directory updates from selected inbound sites. You might need to request a directory update in the following situations:

- Your replication schedule is set to occur nightly, but you are aware that many changes were made at a specific site (perhaps a new Exchange server was created, with several new users), and you need to update the system immediately.

- A remote server was down during its scheduled replication time, and you need to force replication to maintain an accurate address list.

To request a directory update, follow these steps:

1. Click the Sites tab of the Directory Replication Connector dialog box.

2. Select the site from which you want to request directory updates. (You can select multiple sites by Shift+clicking them.)

3. Click Request Now.

Directory Synchronization

The third logical step to maintaining an up-to-date address list is *directory synchronization (dirsync)*. Directory synchronization is the process by which a Microsoft Exchange server shares address information with other messaging systems. Dirsync in Exchange is based on the Microsoft Mail directory-synchronization protocol, which is widely supported by many messaging systems.

This section covers the setup and configuration of dirsync between Exchange and MS Mail, as well as between Exchange and foreign systems that support the MS Mail dirsync protocol.

Before you begin, you must verify the following information about your Exchange setup:

- All services that are required to run the Administrator program are up and running.

- A functional messaging link exists between your site and the systems with which you want to establish dirsync. A link is usually established by the MS Mail connector or by another specialized connector or gateway.

Following is a brief review of how directory synchronization works and of the tools that you use to set up dirsync in Microsoft Exchange.

The MS Mail dirsync protocol has two principal elements:

- Directory Synchronization Requestor: an agent that sends directory updates to, and receives updates from, a directory synchronization server.

- Directory Synchronization Server: an agent that collects local address updates from requestors, compiles the updates into a master list, and sends the resulting modifications back to the requestors.

Microsoft Exchange Server includes one principal component—the *Directory Synchronization Agent (DXA)*—that operates directory synchronization. The Exchange DXA can act as either a dirsync server or requestor. In standard MS Mail dirsync, the dirsync server maintains a server address list. Exchange uses the global address list to replace the server address list.

N O T E When Exchange receives external addresses that are imported during synchronization, the addresses are stored in the directory as custom recipients. ■

Directory Synchronization Requestor

A single Microsoft Exchange server can act as a requestor for multiple MS Mail dirsync servers. To avoid errors, make sure that you do not set up multiple dirsync requestors to connect to the same dirsync server.

CAUTION

Do not set up more than one dirsync requestor to the same dirsync server in your organization. Doing so can result in corruption of directory information, including duplicate entries when the two sites attempt to exchange updates.

Setting Up a Requestor in Microsoft Exchange

Part
III
Ch
18

Follow these steps to create a connection to MS Mail:

1. In the Administration window, select a site in your organization.
2. Click the Connections icon. Your list of current connection objects appear.
3. Double-click MS Mail Connector in the Interchange tab; select the administrator's mail box.
4. Click the Connection tab.
5. On the right side of the window there is a Create button. Click this button to create a connection to your MS Mail PO.
6. Fill in Organization, Postoffice, and full UNC to maildata. Make sure before you do this that the Maildata directory has been shared.

Follow these steps to create an Exchange requestor:

1. In the Administrator window, select a site in your organization.
2. Click the Connections icon. Your list of current connection objects appears.
3. Choose File, New Other, Directory Exchange Requestor. The New Requestor dialog box appears (see Figure 18.7).

FIG. 18.7

This is the new Directory Exchange Requestor dialog box.

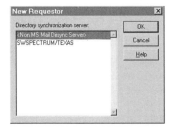

4. From the list of post offices defined in the MS Mail Connector, choose the dirsync server that you will use. If you are setting up a requestor for a non-MS Mail system, select <Non MS Mail Dirsync Server> (this procedure will be detailed in the "Requestor Configuration" section).

5. Click OK. The Properties page for your new requestor appears.

Now you must set up properties in each of the available tabs, as described in the following sections.

General Tab   The General tab allows you to name and configure the basic dirsync requestor properties. Follow these steps to configure from where to request directory updates and select the address types supported by this requestor:

1. Type the name of the requestor. You have 255 characters to give this requestor a name that should also identify the Exchange server site (see Figure 18.8). Check the Append to Imported Users' Display Name box to add the requestor name to each custom recipient that is created in the DXA process.

FIG. 18.8

The Dirsync Requestor General Properties page lets you set the basic options for a dirsync requestor.

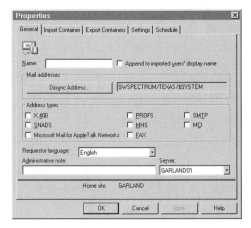

2. Click the Dirsync Address button to bring up the Exchange address list. From that list, select the custom recipient that pertains to your dirsync server.

N O T E   You must first create a Custom Recipient for the dirsync server with which this requestor will be exchanging dirsync messages. That custom recipient can be any MS Mail or compatible directory synchronization server in your organization. See Chapter 15 for information about creating custom recipients. ▪

3. In the Address Types section, check all the types that you want this requestor to obtain from the dirsync server. By default, MS Mail addresses are sent and received. If you choose an address type that the server cannot provide, the MS Mail default format (proxy) address is extracted instead.

4. The Requestor Language pull-down menu allows you to select the default address language template. Use the pull-down menu to choose a language template.

5. In the Administrative Note box, type any comments (up to 1,024 characters) that you feel are pertinent to this situation. The note is visible only in this tab.

6. The Server pull-down menu allows you to change the server at the local site that will handle this directory synchronization requestor. The default selection is the current server. Choose an Exchange server from the pull-down menu. A single Exchange server can be either a dirsync server or requestor, but not both. Also, only one requestor can be set up per Exchange server.

7. Click Apply to set these properties and continue setting other properties.

8. When you finish making settings, click OK to return to the Administrator program.

Import Container Tab   An *import container* is the recipient container that receives imported information from a dirsync server. This tab allows you to assign trust levels to the imported directory objects.

Because trust levels are exclusive to Microsoft Exchange Server, any imported recipients will not have trust levels assigned. The import container setting gives that object a trust level that Exchange uses to determine replication security. As in any other case of trust-level use, only objects that have a trust level equal to or lower to the trust level of the next site are replicated.

N O T E   If you are using multiple requestors to multiple dirsync servers but do not want directory information to be shared between those dirsync servers, you must create a separate container for each group that is imported. ▪

Suppose that you are using Exchange servers GARLAND01 and GARLAND02 as requestors to two Microsoft Mail network dirsync servers and that you do not want the MS Mail networks to share recipient information. You set each requestor to import to a different recipient container in the GARLAND site, each with different trust levels. When synchronization occurs, each list of recipients is imported into its own container (with its own trust level). The information is not mixed and is not synchronized to the other MS Mail server because of the trust level settings.

Part

III

Ch

18

The following steps describe how to configure the Import Container tab:

1. Click the Import Container tab of dirsync requestor property pages (see Figure 18.9). The Import Container page shows the current selected recipient. (The page is blank for a new setup.)

FIG. 18.9

The Import Container tab.

2. Click the Container button to display all container recipients. The Import Container Properties page appears (see Figure 18.10).

FIG. 18.10

Specify where you want incoming recipients to be stored.

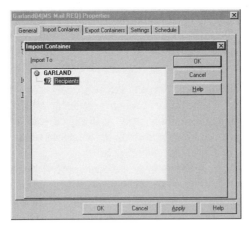

3. Select the recipient container in which you want all the custom recipients to be imported.

4. Click OK to return to the Import Container tab.

5. Enter a number in the Trust Level box. The default is 20.

6. Click Apply to set these properties and continue setting other properties.

7. When you finish making settings, click OK to return to the Administrator program.

CAUTION

After you choose a directory import container, you are stuck with it. The only way to alter where directory information is stored is to delete the requestor and set up a new one.

Export Containers Tab   An *export container* holds the directory data that an Exchange requestor sends out during synchronization. By default, a requestor does not send out any containers. If you need to export directory information via a requestor, follow this procedure:

1. Click the Export Containers tab of the dirsync requestor's Properties page (see Figure 18.11).

FIG. 18.11

The Export Containers tab.

2. To start exporting from a container, select it in the Recipient Containers list and then click Add.

    To remove an exported container, select it in the Export These Recipients list and then click Remove.

3. Use the Site pull-down menu to view recipient containers from other sites and select those for export (optional).

4. In the Trust Level box, set a general trust level for this export function. Individual objects within the selected container(s) are exported only if their trust-level settings are equal to or less than the settings in this box.

5. If you do not want to include custom Exchange recipients in the export procedure, click the Export Custom Recipients check box to clear it.

6. Click Apply to set these properties and continue setting other properties.

7. When you finish making settings, click OK to return to the Administrator program.

Settings Tab   The Settings tab allows you to set advanced properties for a directory synchronization connector.

To configure the Settings tab, follow these steps:

1. Click the Settings tab of the Directory Exchange Requestor Properties page (see Figure 18.12).

FIG. 18.12

The Settings tab.

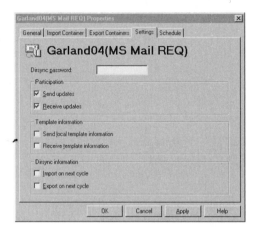

2. The Dirsync Password box allows you to give this requestor a password to use when it sends directory updates to a dirsync server. Enter a password if one is needed to access the desired dirsync server. The password is selected when you set up the dirsync server on the remote system. If a password is not needed to access the dirsync server, then leave this space blank.

3. The Participation check boxes let you define how this requestor is involved in synchronization. Click the appropriate check box for how you want this requestor to function:

   - Send Updates. The requestor will export directory information to a dirsync server.
   - Receive Updates. The requestor will import directory information from a dirsync server. By default, both boxes are checked. If neither is checked, then the requestor will not operate.

4. (Optional) Choose one of the following Template Information options:

   - Send Local Template Information. Exports address templates to the dirsync server.
   - Receive Template Information. Imports address templates from the dirsync server.

5. Choose one of the following Dirsync Information options, which forces the connector to import or export (or both) all appropriate information to the dirsync sever:

   - Import on Next Cycle. Requests every entry (of the selected address type) at the next dirsync sequence.
   - Export on Next Cycle. Sends addresses from the specified export containers to the dirsync server.

6. Click Apply to set these properties and continue setting other properties.

7. When you finish making settings, click OK to return to the Administrator program.

Schedule Tab   The Schedule tab allows you to set the time when update messages are transmitted to the directory synchronization sever.

> **N O T E** The verification messages or updates from the dirsync server are handled automatically. ▓

To set the requestor's schedule, follow these steps:

1. Click the Schedule tab of the dirsync requestor's Properties page (see Figure 18.13).

FIG. 18.13

The Schedule tab.

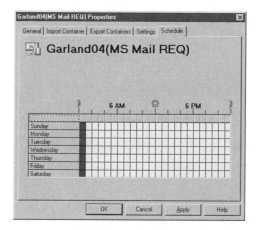

2. In the grid, click the boxes to select the time when you want directory update messages to be exchanges with the dirsync server. Update messages are sent at the beginning of the selected time. By default (if you don't select a specific time), dirsync messages are automatically scheduled for transmission at midnight.

3. Click Apply to set these properties and continue setting other properties.

4. When you finish making settings, click OK to return to the Administrator program.

This chapter has covered all the available options for configuring a Directory Exchange Requestor. You must now configure the MS Mail dirsync server to accept your new Exchange requestor. There are two primary settings to configure:

▓ *Password.* You must configure the MS Mail Directory Exchange server to recognize your new Microsoft Exchange requestor. If you selected a password in the Settings tab, remember to include it in your configuration. Your MS Mail for PC documentation will guide you through this process.

▓ *E-mail address.* When you configure your MS Mail dirsync server to recognize your new Exchange requestor, you need the MS Mail network and post office e-mail address of the local site. The local site's Site Addressing property pages contain this information.

Part

III

Ch

18

Using Exchange as a Directory Synchronization Server

Another way to integrate Microsoft Exchange into directory synchronization with MS Mail-compatible networks is to set up a directory *synchronization server* (also called a *dirsync server*) on Exchange. Then you can use standard MS Mail requestors on remote machines to partici-pate in directory synchronization.

Following are the general steps for setting up Exchange as a dirsync server:

1. In the Administrator program, create a directory synchronization server for the local Microsoft Exchange server site. Configure its properties.

N O T E   Although you can have multiple Exchange dirsync servers in your organization, you can have only one for each Microsoft Exchange site.

2. In the directory, define a remote directory exchange requestor object that corresponds to each requestor that will link to this server.

3. Configure each requestor on other systems that will use this server.

Creating and Configuring a Directory Exchange Server

When you create a new directory exchange server, it automatically gets an e-mail address based on the MS Mail address type for the local site. Because you can have only one directory exchange server per site, no addressing conflicts can exist.

To create a new directory exchange server in the Administrator program, choose File, New Other, Dirsync Server. If you have already set up another directory synchronization server in this site, the new Dirsync Server option is not available.

To configure an existing server from the Administrator program, follow these steps:

1. Click the Connections icon under the desired Exchange site.

2. From the list of connections icons, click the icon of your current dirsync server. By default, the name for this object is "DXA server."

3. Choose File, Properties to open the dirsync server property pages.

The following sections cover configuration of the dirsync server's property pages.

General Tab   To set general Properties, follow this procedure:

1. Click the General tab of the dirsync server's Properties page (see Figure 18.14).

2. In the Name box, type a unique name for this dirsync server. (You are allowed to use up to 64 characters.)

3. (Optional) Select a dirsync administrator that will receive dirsync status and error messages, and click the Dirsync Administrator button. The Exchange address List dialog box appears. Type or select a name (a user, public folder, or distribution list), and click OK. You return to the General tab.

FIG. 18.14

The General tab of the DXA Properties page.

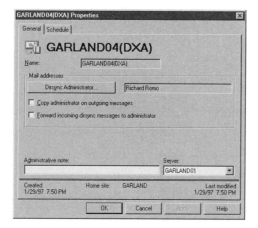

4. To send a copy of each outgoing update to the administrator, click the Copy Administrator on Outgoing Messages check box.

5. To view each incoming update message from each requestor, click the Forward Incoming Dirsync Messages to Administrator check box.

NOTE By default, neither Copy Administrator on Outgoing Messages nor Forward Incoming Dirsync Messages to Administrator is selected. Typically, you would choose these options only for troubleshooting purposes.

6. If you want, enter comments (up to 1,024 characters) in the Administrative Note box. The comments will be visible only in this tab.

7. Use the Server pull-down menu to select the Microsoft Exchange server computer that will host the directory synchronization process. By default, the current Exchange server is selected.

8. Click Apply to set these properties and continue setting other properties.

9. When you finish making settings, click OK to return to the Administrator program.

Schedule Tab   The Schedule tab defines when the directory synchronization server sends updates to its requestors. Server updates are independent of the schedule under which the requestors send their updates to the server. Directory updates are sent to requestors at the beginning of the scheduled hour.

To set the schedule, follow these steps:

1. Click the Schedule tab in the dirsync server property pages.

2. In the time grid, select the times when you want this dirsync server to send update messages to its requestors.

3. Click Apply to set these properties and continue setting other properties.

4. When you finish making settings, click OK to return to the Administrator program.

Part

III

Ch

18

Defining Remote Directory Synchronization Requestors

Just as you do with a standard MS Mail directory synchronization server, you must identify and define each remote requestor that will be communicating updates to the local Exchange dirsync server. Setting up each remote requestor involves two steps:

■ Define a remote dirsync requestor object in the Microsoft Exchange Server administrator program.

■ Establish the permissions that these containers will use when importing and exporting addressing data.

These two steps make your Exchange directory synchronization server aware of its requestors. Review the following section to verify that a remote requestor is properly configured and able to communicate with the local Exchange dirsync server.

Creating and Configuring a Remote Directory Synchronization Requestor

To create a new remote dirsync requestor, follow these steps:

1. In the Administrator program, choose File, New Other, Remote Dirsync Requestor. The property pages for a new remote dirsync requestor appear.

N O T E The New Remote Dirsync Requestor command is unavailable until you set up a Microsoft Exchange directory synchronization server. ▨

The following sections describe the tabs that you configure for a remote dirsync requestor.

General Tab   To set general properties, follow these steps:

1. Click the General tab of the Remote Dirsync Requestor Properties page.

2. Type a display name (up to 255 characters) for this remote dirsync requestor. This name is displayed as the directory exchange server object name in the Administrator program.

3. Check the Append to Created Users' Display Name check box to add the name of this requestor to each recipient created when synchronizing addresses with this requestor. This is useful for keeping track of a recipient's origin.

4. Click the Dirsync Address button to bring up the Exchange address list. From that list, select the custom recipient that pertains to the remote dirsync requestor.

N O T E You must first create a custom recipient for each remote dirsync requestor to provide address information about the requestor. ▨

5. Enter a password in the password box if your Exchange dirsync server requests one during synchronization. By default, this box is blank. If you do use a password for security, remember to set the same password on the remote MS Mail requestor to avoid authentication errors.

6. The Request Address Type box specifies the format in which address updates are set. MS (the default) is used by MS Mail (PC) and other compatible directory exchange requestors. Select MSA if you are synchronizing directories with a Microsoft Mail for AppleTalk network.

7. The Requestor Language pull-down menu allows you to change the default language template.

8. Click the Export on Next Cycle check box to send all address information to the remote requestor during the next synchronization session. By default, this option is not selected. Keep in mind that all directory information is exported automatically when you first configure a remote requestor.

9. If you want, enter comments (up to 1,024 characters) in the Administrative Note box. These comments will be visible only in this tab.

10. Click Apply to set these properties and continue setting other properties.

11. When you finish making settings, click OK to return to the Administrator program.

Import Container Tab   Much as you do in setting up directory exchange requestors, you use import containers to assign trust levels to objects that are being imported.

Because trust levels are exclusive to Microsoft Exchange Server, any imported recipients will not have trust levels assigned. The import container gives that object a trust level that you set in the Import Container tab. As in any other case of trust-level use, only objects that have a trust level equal to or lower than the next site's trust level are replicated. The following steps cover Import Container tab configuration:

1. Click the Import Container tab of the Remote Dirsync Requestor Properties page (see Figure 18.15).

Part

III

Ch

18

FIG. 18.15

Choose the container in which imported recipients will be stored.

2. The Import Container box shows the name of the recipient container that stores the imported addresses. By default, this box is blank. Click the Container button to select a recipient container. All current recipient containers appear in a dialog box. Select one container to hold directory imports and click OK to return to the Import Container tab.

3. In the Trust Level box, assign a trust level to the import container. (The default setting is 20.) Remember that only objects that have a trust level equal to or lower than the setting in this box will be updated during synchronization.

4. Click Apply to set these properties and continue setting other properties.

5. When you finish making settings, click OK to return to the Administrator program.

N O T E   You cannot modify import containers after you create them. If you must change where information is placed, you must delete the existing container and create a new one. ■

Export Containers Tab   The Export Containers tab specifies what information is sent out to the remote requestor during directory synchronization. By default, no information from the local site is exported. To configure data export, follow these steps:

1. Click the Export Containers tab in the Remote Dirsync Requestor Properties page (see Figure 18.16).

FIG. 18.16
The Export Containers tab.

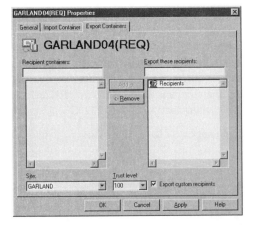

2. In the Export These Recipients list, select the container that you want to export, then click Add. To stop exporting a container, select it in the Export These Recipients list, then click Remove.

3. Use the Site pull-down menu to view other sites' containers, to which you can export recipients.

4. In the Trust Level box, set a trust level to limit replication of certain objects in the containers that you selected to export.

5. Click the Export Custom Recipients check box to include those recipients in synchronization. By default, this option is selected.

6. Click Apply to set these properties and continue setting other properties.

7. When you finish making settings, click OK to return to the Administrator program.

Configuring Remote Requestors

The final step in establishing directory synchronization between a Microsoft Exchange directory synchronization server and remote requestors is configuring the remote requestors on the MS Mail or compatible systems.

The following sections provide general recommendations on configuring directory synchronization requestors on the following types of remote systems:

- Microsoft Mail for PC networks
- Microsoft Mail for AppleTalk networks
- Other foreign mail systems

Directory Synchronization Requestor

The requestor that you are most likely to set up is one for a MS Mail for PC network. Standard MS Mail requestor programs connect to Exchange directory synchronization servers through the MS Mail connector as though the requestor were of the standard MS Mail type. You need to configure the requestor from within your MS Mail administrator program. Consult your Microsoft documentation for the procedure.

Before you configure the requestor, make sure that you have met all of the following conditions:

 T I P You can test the operation of a MS Mail connection by entering the address of your recipient manually in the "To" line of the Exchange client.

- Exchange and the Microsoft Mail connector are properly configured and running.
- The Microsoft Exchange directory synchronization server is installed and running.
- MS Mail for PC Networks is set up and running correctly on its own.
- If your Exchange server and the MS Mail post office are not on the same logical network, the MS Mail external or multitasking MTA program must be set up and running correctly.

Part
III

Ch
18

AppleTalk Networks

This section is dedicated to a discussion on address list sharing between Exchange and a Microsoft Mail for AppleTalk network. These solutions, though functional, are a poor substitute for the use of a Macintosh Exchange client directly. Primarily, these solutions will be used as a stop gap in preparation for an eventual complete migration to Exchange. Existing MS Mail AppleTalk servers can act as requestors to standard MS Mail (PC) dirsync servers. By pointing the Macintosh dirsync requestor to an Exchange dirsync server, your Mac servers can begin sharing address lists with your Exchange organization.

The Exchange Client for Mac 5.0 can act as a direct client to Exchange Server 5.0. Strategies are now different for the migration of Mac clients. However, it is important to understand how Exchange and Microsoft Mail for Apple Talk networks behave and are configured. Microsoft will continue to support the Macintosh Gateway by loading it on to the client CD which is Mac-friendly.

The first part of this section will cover the set up of a Directory Exchange Requestor in an MS Mail for AppleTalk network.

The directory synchronization requestor for MS Mail AppleTalk is installed with the Microsoft Exchange connection gateway.

Before you configure the MS Mail AppleTalk requestor, confirm the following situations:

■ Exchange and the Microsoft Mail connector are properly configured and running.

■ MSA (Microsoft Mail AppleTalk) is selected in the appropriate Exchange Remote Dirsync Requestor property pages. This setting is found under the General tab of this dirsync requestor.

> **CAUTION**
>
> If you do not set the requestor to receive messages in MSA format, duplicate entries are created in the MS Mail AppleTalk address list.

■ The Microsoft Exchange Connection gateway software is properly configured and running on the MS Mail AppleTalk server.

If you have met all the preceding conditions, you are ready to continue setting up the directory synchronization requestor. If you have been looking at a Windows screen layout all day, the following steps could be a nice change of pace.

Requestor Configuration

When you set up directory synchronization, you need to configure three principal requestor options. You must log in as the network manager on your MS Mail AppleTalk server to make all configuration and administrative functions available. The next sections describe how to set the following:

- Install General Requestor settings
- Identify the appropriate gateway
- Request the correct address types

General Requestor Settings   To set the General Requestor settings, follow these steps:

1. Open the Microsoft Exchange Connection folder on the Macintosh MS Mail server.

2. Click the Microsoft Exchange Connection Directory Exchange Requestor icon.

3. The first time you open a new requestor, a dialog box appears. Type your network manager password, and click OK.

4. The first time you set up a requestor, a configure dialog box appears. Subsequently, you must select Application from the Configure menu.

5. The Send Directory At box allows you to enter the time when directory updates are sent to the Microsoft Exchange dirsync server. Use the 24-hour format hh:mm. By default, this time is set to 4 a.m.

6. The Receive Updates At box allows you to enter the time when the requestor scans the Network Manager's inbox for directory updates.

7. In the Exchange Network box, enter the network name of the MS Mail connector.

8. In the Exchange PO box, enter the post office name of the MS Mail connector. This information is available on the Exchange MS Mail connector's Local Postoffice property page.

9. Use the Exchange Password box if you have also set a password in the corresponding Microsoft Exchange server remote dirsync requestor object. By default, this box is blank.

10. DXA Mailbox specifies the Exchange server mailbox to which the requestor will send update messages. By default, this is $SYSTEM. Normally you do not want to change this setting.

11. The Network Manager box defines the MS Mail AppleTalk account to receive address list updates from the Exchange dirsync server. By default, this mailbox is Network Manager. The Password field is for the account specified in the Network Manager box.

12. Requestor Name refers to the corresponding remote directory exchange requestor as set in the Exchange server directory.

13. The Fault Tolerance check box enables tracking of address updates. Synchronization numbers are created and used to recover address when an error occurs. This will avoid having to do manual directory import and export. By default, this is checked.

14. Include Server In Friendly Name sets all MS Mail AppleTalk addresses to display as `user@servername`. By default this is checked.

15. The Export World List check box, when not checked, will cease all updates being sent to the Exchange dirsync server. By default, this is checked.

Part
III

Ch
18

16. Click OK to save new settings and close the Configure dialog box. Click Revert to keep previous settings.

If you are configuring this requestor for the first time, the Gateway dialog box appears.

N O T E   If this not your first time configuring this requestor, then from the Configure menu choose Select Gateway. ■

In this dialog box, you must select a gateway. This is the passage through which messaging data will reach the Exchange server. By default, this is the connection gateway. Choose your preferred gateway and then click the Select button.

Address Filters   *Address filters* allow you to specify the address types that you want to receive from the Exchange server.

To configure address filtering, follow these steps:

1. Open the Address Filtering dialog box. If you just proceeded from gateway box, this is already open.
2. Check each address type you want to request from the Exchange dirsync server.
3. Click OK to save your settings and move on, or click Revert to return to the previous settings.

Starting the Requestor

To start the Requestor:

1. Open the Microsoft Exchange Connection folder in Macintosh Finder.
2. Double-click the MS Mail Appletalk directory exchange requestor icon to start it. The requestor starts, and a status dialog box appears. The status display refreshes when the system receives directory update messages.

If the requestor is not given the network manager name and password, or if you are not currently logged in as a Network Manager, then the request will run as a foreground application, locking the desktop and preventing you from running other applications. However, if you have given the password or are logged in as the Network Manager, then the application runs in the background.

To stop the requestor, choose File, Quit.

It is convenient to make the Macintosh dirsync requestor a startup item so you do not need to manually launch the application every time you restart the system. To make the requestor a startup item, follow these steps:

1. Make an alias of the directory exchange requestor. Do this by highlighting the requestor icon, then choose File, Make Alias.
2. Move the alias to the Startup Items folder inside the Macintosh System folder.

MS Mail AppleTalk Requestor

As network manager, you may want to execute a few maintenance tasks as part of administrating Exchange directory synchronization from the MS Mail AppleTalk end. Those tasks are importing a complete list of addresses, exporting a complete local address list, and re-synchronizing that information.

To import a complete list of known addresses, follow these steps:

1. Start the Exchange Connection Directory Exchange Requestor by double-clicking its icon in the Macintosh Finder.

2. Choose File, Import Directory. The Import Directory dialog box appears.

3. Choose Changes Since Last Update Only to immediately request the addresses that have changed since the last directory synchronization cycle.

   Alternatively, click the Complete Directory radio button and then click OK to import all available addresses of the selected type.

4. Click OK to finalize your settings.

> **N O T E** To verify that imports have proceeded correctly, you need to start MS Mail AppleTalk manually and choose Mail, Gateway Recipient. A dialog box appears that lists the new recipients. All requested information should be available in this list after you receive an import confirmation message from the dirsync server. ■

Part

III

Ch

18

Exporting Directory Information to Microsoft Exchange Server

The previous section described how to get MS Mail AppleTalk to receive addresses from Exchange. The following section describes how to update the Exchange address list with changes made on the MS Mail AppleTalk server. You will do this by telling the Exchange Connection software to export its contents to the Exchange dirsync server. The following steps describe the steps necessary to accomplish this:

1. Start the Exchange Connection Directory Exchange requestor by double-clicking its icon in the Macintosh Finder.

2. Choose File, Export Directory.

3. Choose Changes Since Last Update Only to immediately request the addresses that have changed since the last directory synchronization cycle.

   Alternatively, click the Complete Directory radio button to import all available addresses of the selected type.

4. Click OK to commence directory export.

After the Exchange server processes these update requests, it sends a confirmation message and a status report to the network manager's mailbox.

Another option is to export the local MS Mail AppleTalk addresses into a text-file format that the MS Mail (PC) import utility can read. Use this alternative when other methods are not operational.

To export the addresses (also called the *word list*) manually, follow these steps:

1. Start the Exchange Connection Directory Exchange Requestor by double-clicking its icon in the Macintosh Finder.

2. Choose Save to File from the File menu. A dialog box appears asking you for a location to save your exported information.

3. Select the folder in which you want to save your file.

4. In the Dump Work List Into box, type a file name. A unique identifiable name is recommended (perhaps including the date of the export for future reference).

5. Click OK to complete the export.

You can open the exported file with any text editor. All your addresses should be in that file, displayed in the following format:

> A 30_character_alias MSMAIL:address

(MS Mail is the address type of this entry.)

MS Mail AppleTalk or Exchange Server Addresses

Sometimes you need to remove all MS Mail for AppleTalk recipients from the Exchange address list, and vice versa. This situation occurs when MS Mail AppleTalk users become full-fledged Microsoft Exchange clients.

To remove MS Mail AppleTalk recipients from the Exchange server address list, follow this procedure:

1. Start the Exchange Connection Directory Exchange Requestor by double-clicking its icon in the Macintosh Finder.

2. Choose Remove Mac Names from Exchange from the File menu. A confirmation dialog box appears to verify that you actually want to do this.

3. Click OK. Every MS Mail AppleTalk and gateway recipient is removed from the Exchange global address list.

N O T E   If you suddenly realize that you really needed the addresses, you have to import them to restore the entries. Subsequent directory synchronization cycles do not replace deleted entries. ▨

Removing Exchange Recipients from the MS Mail AppleTalk Local Address List

Follow this procedure to delete Exchange recipients from MS Mail AppleTalk:

1. Start the Exchange Connection Directory Exchange Requestor by double-clicking its icon in the Macintosh Finder.

2. Choose Remove Exchange Names from Mac from the File menu. A confirmation dialog box appears to verify that you actually want to do this.

3. Click OK. Every Microsoft Exchange recipient in the local directory is deleted from the MS Mail AppleTalk word list.

Resynchronizing Address Information

As directory synchronization occurs, updates are exchanged, and the network manager receives periodic messages confirming that the process is operational and that changes have been incorporated.

Sometimes this process does not operate smoothly. In such cases, the requestor gives you the option of forcing resynchronization of the entire system manually.

If you believe that your system is out of sync, follow these steps:

1. Log on as network manager.

2. Start the Exchange connection directory exchange requestor by double-clicking its icon in the Macintosh Finder.

3. Choose Resync Cycle from the File menu. The Directory Exchange Requestor proceeds to restart its synchronization cycle.

The requestor receives the global address list from the Exchange server and resets the send/receive cycle.

If you get a message stating that the directory synchronization cycle is out of phase, you should initiate a complete directory refresh (import and export) between both systems. As described in the preceding sections, you should import the Exchange global address list and export the local address list to the Exchange dirsync server.

The MS Mail AppleTalk directory exchange requestor keeps a log of all its activities. This log is a text file stored inside the Preferences folder (in the System folder). Any standard text editor displays this file.

Part III

Ch 18

N O T E   This file logs all directory Exchange requestor activities, so the file could be very large if it is heavily used. Make sure that you delete or clear the file on a periodic basis. Confirming that synchronization is functional before you delete any log entries is a good idea.

Configuring Foreign Directory Exchange Requestors

Any foreign system that conforms with Microsoft Mail 3.x directory synchronization protocol can connect to an Exchange dirsync server. You probably need to consult your appropriate documentation for the process, but here are some general recommendations to follow before you configure synchronization with foreign systems:

- Make sure that all Exchange server operations are working correctly.
- Install and configure the correct gateway for Exchange communication with the foreign system.
- Properly configure the Exchange directory synchronization server and the appropriate remote requestor.
- Install whatever gateway the foreign mail system requires to communicate with Microsoft Exchange.
- Test to see whether standard messages can be transferred between systems. Because directories are not in sync, you have to enter the addresses manually.

Configuring Microsoft Directory Exchange Agent (DXA) Settings

The *DXA* is the Exchange component that actually runs the dirsync server and requestor. By default, the DXA is configured to allow both server and requestor processes to run. You can modify general settings for the DXA, as described in the following sections. The DXA is configured through an object named Directory Synchronization on each Exchange server in your site.

See Chapter 12 for more information on configuring all directory services on Exchange.

Configuring the Directory Synchronization General Tab

The Directory Synchronization General tab allows you to choose the server that carries out the DXA functions. Any server at the site is eligible, but always take into consideration other functions that a server is performing. To choose a server, follow these steps:

1. In the Administrator program, select a site in your organization.
2. Click the Servers icon to list the Exchange servers in this site.
3. Select the Microsoft Exchange server that you want to configure.
4. Select the Directory Synchronization object.
5. Click the General tab in the Microsoft Directory Synchronization object.
6. Use the Administrator Note box and type any additional comments you may want to add.
7. Click Apply to set these properties and continue setting other properties.
8. When you finish making settings, click OK to return to the Administrator program.

E-Mail Addresses Tab

The e-mail addresses are used to send and receive synchronization update messages. You will need the E-mail Addresses Properties page to create, modify, or delete these addresses. By default, Microsoft Exchange server automatically generates MS Mail (PC), X.400, and SMTP addresses for each DXA. Several services, such as dirsync requestors and servers, use these addresses for communication with the DXA.

To create or modify Microsoft DXA addresses, follow this procedure:

1. Click the E-Mail Addresses tab.

2. To change an existing address, select it and then click Edit. The dialog box for its particular address type appears.

3. To create a new address for this DXA, click New. Select what type of e-mail address you want to add, then type in all necessary addressing information. Click OK to return to the E-Mail Addresses tab.

4. To delete an existing address, select it, click Remove, and click OK to confirm the deletion.

5. Click Apply to set these properties and continue setting other properties.

6. When you finish making settings, click OK to return to the Administrator program.

> **CAUTION**
>
> Many other Exchange services use these addresses. If you plan to change or delete them without appropriate consideration of such services, directory synchronization will fail.

Part

III

Ch

18

Delivery Restrictions Tab

This tab is useful because it prevents messages that are unrelated to directory synchronization from being sent to the DXA. You also can set up delivery restrictions to allow messages to be sent only by specified senders. In the Delivery Restriction tab, you select specific addresses from which the DXA will reject or allow messages. By default, the DXA accepts messages from all senders. Such an open "door" could cause errors and delays in proper directory synchronization.

To set delivery restrictions, follow these steps:

1. Click the Delivery Restrictions tab of the Microsoft DXA. The left side of the tab lists the specific senders who have permission to send messages to the DXA. The right side lists senders who are not allowed to send messages to this DXA.

T I P Entering specific accepted senders is the most fault-tolerant approach to this setup. Be aware, however, that if you set up a new requestor without modifying the tab, all of that requestor's messages will be rejected.

2. To accept messages only from specific senders or to reject messages from specific senders (the settings are mutually exclusive), select List and click Modify. The Microsoft Exchange Address Book appears.

3. Select the specific container from which you want to view recipients in the Show Names From The menu. The corresponding recipients are shown in the Type Name or Select From List box.

4. Type select or a name from the list. If you can't see or remember the name you are looking for, you can use the Find button. The Properties button will display standard recipient properties for your selection.

5. Once you have selected a name or multiple names on the left, click Add.

6. Click OK to return to the Delivery Restrictions property page.

7. Click Apply to set these properties and continue setting other properties. If you are done with all settings, click OK to return to the administrator program.

Incoming Templates Tab

Incoming templates are Address templates that take incoming address information and map it for specified Exchange server directory recipient attributes.

An address imported though synchronization with an MS Mail network, for example, could have the occupation and telephone attributes. For consistency, you would want to map the occupation tag to the Exchange Title attribute.

To map templates to Exchange server attributes, follow these steps:

1. Click the Incoming Templates tab of the Directory Synchronization Properties page (see Figure 18.17).

2. To modify an existing mapping, select it from the list and then click Edit. The Incoming Template Mapping dialog box appears.

   In the Map the String box, edit the template identifier string that MS Mail uses. In the To the Attribute box, edit the recipient attribute in which you want to store the incoming information. When you finish, click OK to return to the Incoming Templates tab.

N O T E All mapping strings must match the incoming strings.

3. To create a new mapping, click the New button. The Incoming Template Mapping dialog box appears. Type a string found in the incoming address information. Use the To the Attribute pull-down menu to select which Exchange attribute you want to associate with that string. Click OK to return to the Incoming Templates tab.

FIG. 18.17

Define incoming templates for synchronized addresses.

4. To delete an existing mapping, select it and then click Remove.

5. Click Apply to set these properties and continue setting other properties.

6. When you finish making settings, click OK to return to the Administrator program.

Outgoing Templates Tab

Outgoing template mappings are the inverse of the preceding function. You can map Microsoft Exchange server directory recipient attributes to outgoing MS Mail-compatible template information.

To map Exchange server attributes to an MS Mail template, follow these steps:

1. Click the Outgoing Templates tab of the Directory Synchronization Properties page (see Figure 18.18).

2. To modify an existing mapping, select it in the list and then click Edit. The Outgoing Template Mapping dialog box appears. In the Map the Attribute box, edit the recipient attribute that you want to map to the MS Mail template. In the To the String box, edit the MS Mail template identifier string in which you want to place outgoing-attribute information. When you finish, click OK to return to the Outgoing Templates tab.

3. To create a new mapping, click the New button. The Outgoing Template Mapping dialog box appears. Use the Map the Attribute pull-down menu to select which Exchange attribute you want to map to a string on the remote system. Type that string in the To the String box. Click OK to return to the Outgoing Templates tab.

4. To delete an existing mapping, select it and then click Remove.

5. Click Apply to set these properties and continue setting other properties.

6. When you finish making settings, click OK to return to the Administrator program.

Part
III

Ch

18

FIG. 18.18
Outgoing template
mappings translate
Exchange attributes to a
user-defined string.

As soon as you activate the directory exchange requestor for the first time, it exports a complete local address list to its Microsoft Exchange directory synchronization server. Also, the requestor sends out a request for entries in the Exchange address list. The Microsoft Exchange dirsync server returns a confirmation message, saying that it received the requestor's transmission; then that server sends all the data in the export container to the dirsync requestor.

Subsequent transmissions between dirsync requestor and server consist only of updates to the address lists. You can force the import or export of directory information manually, as well from the appropriate connector tabs.

Be aware that directory synchronization updates sent by the Exchange dirsync server are in the form of messages sent to the network manager's mailbox. From that mailbox, the messages are picked up by the Microsoft Exchange connection and synchronized into the local address list. These messages should not be modified or deleted; altering those messages interrupts the synchronization process and could produce data loss.

N O T E Large imports from the directory exchange server (several thousand entries) are known to take up to several hours. Be aware of such time requirements. Also be aware that during that time, no other messages will pass the Exchange connection gateway. ■

Starting Directory Synchronization

After you meet the preceding requirements, you can start the directory synchronization service. Follow these steps:

1. Open the Windows NT Services Control Panel (see Figure 18.19) for the server on which you want to begin synchronization.

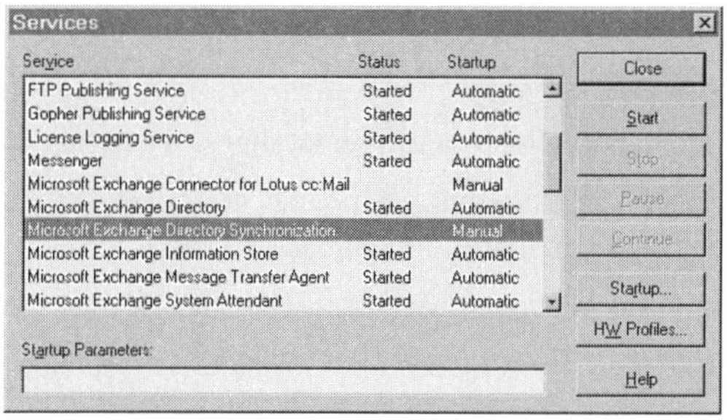

FIG. 18.19

Exchange services running under Windows NT.

2. Select the service name Microsoft Exchange Directory Synchronization.

3. Click Start. The service starts, and synchronization begins.

4. Close the Services window.

> **N O T E** If you set a specific time for directory synchronization that occurred while the service was stopped, a delay may occur until the first sync cycle actually begins. You can force immediate execution of a replication cycle in the property pages of the appropriate connector supporting synchronization. ▨

Stopping Replication Services

To stop replication services:

1. Open the Windows NT Services Control Panel.

2. Select the service name Microsoft Exchange Directory Synchronization.

3. Click Stop. The service stops, and synchronization stops.

4. Close the Services window.

> **N O T E** Remember from earlier discussions when the synchronization is shut off? We do not get any updates and changes of Exchange Servers Directory Services. So, it is a good idea to notify fellow administrators and users that the replication services has stopped. ▨

From Here...

This chapter guided you through the process of establishing directory-sharing relationships between Exchange sites and between Exchange and other messaging systems. With this information, you can begin to structure your own directory-sharing architecture. Remember that the goal in directory replication and synchronization is to have the most complete and useful address lists possible without overloading server processing or network bandwidth in the process.

Part

III

Ch

18

For more information, read the following chapters:

- Chapter 5, "Designing Exchange Topology," gives you a good understanding of the types of site connections that you need for efficient directory replication.

- Chapter 13, "Directory and System Attendant Configuration," guides you through configuring all settings pertinent to Exchange's directory system.

- Chapter 19, "Using the Microsoft Mail Connector for PC Networks," shows you how to configure the MS Mail connector—an essential element of directory synchronization with Exchange.

- Chapter 20, "Using the Microsoft Mail Connector for AppleTalk Networks," to learn about what is required to establish message traffic between Exchange and MS Mail (AppleTalk).

Using the Microsoft Mail Connector for PC Networks

As discussed earlier, MS Mail is a shared file system e-mail application. It relies on a series of flat configuration files to transfer data between the users on the post office. ■

The MS Mail Connector Components

The MS Mail Connector has several main components. In this chapter, we will describe MS Mail Connector Message Transfer Agent (MTA), Connector Post Office, MS Mail Interchange, Exchange MTA, and Exchange Information Store.

Setting Up the MS Mail Connector

MS Mail Connector can be connected in six steps. In this section, these steps will be described in detail.

Auditing the MS Mail Connector

To assist with debugging and routing between MS Mail and Exchange, we start to increase the level of auditing by adjusting the Diagnostic Logging tab.

Understanding the MS Mail Connector

The connection from Exchange to MS Mail requires several components. As discussed in Chapter 8, "Migrating from Microsoft Mail Systems," Exchange can coexist or provide backbone support for MS Mail networks. The MS Mail connector is the message transfer component included in the Exchange server. It provides the MS Mail External and post office functionality to Exchange. External is a message transfer application that runs in single threaded mode on DOS or as a multitasking application on OS/2. In the recent release of MS Mail version 3.5, a set of Multitasking Message Transfer Agent As were ported to run on Windows NT.

Figures 19.1 and 19.2 illustrate a visual comparison of the two message transfer agents.

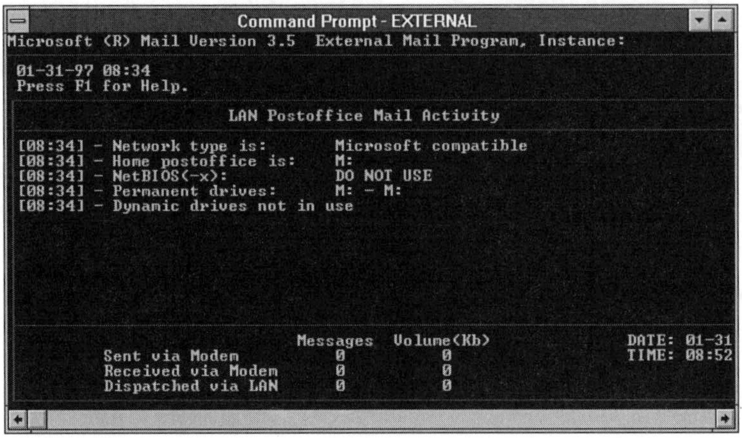

FIG. 19.1
The External application running on DOS.

```
─                        Command Prompt - EXTERNAL                    ▼ ▲
Microsoft (R) Mail Version 3.5  External Mail Program, Instance:
01-31-97 08:34
Press F1 for Help.

                      LAN Postoffice Mail Activity

[08:34] - Network type is:        Microsoft compatible
[08:34] - Home postoffice is:     M:
[08:34] - NetBIOS(-x):            DO NOT USE
[08:34] - Permanent drives:       M: - M:
[08:34] - Dynamic drives not in use




                                   Messages   Volume(Kb)        DATE: 01-31
                    Sent via Modem      0          0            TIME: 08:52
                    Received via Modem  0          0
                    Dispatched via LAN  0          0
←                                                                           →
```

N O T E   The Exchange MS Mail Connector has a rich GUI interface that provides many new features. ■

In order to connect to an MS Mail post office on the same WAN/LAN, you must configure an MTA to do the following:

- ■ Send and receive messages
- ■ Convert the messages to the native format
- ■ Deliver the messages to the destination post office and recipient

In Exchange, you configure the MS Mail Connector to receive messages from the Exchange MTA, convert the messages into the MS Mail format, and then deliver them to the target post office diagrammed in Figure 19.3.

FIG. 19.2

The Exchange MS Mail Connector.

FIG. 19.3

The Exchange to MS Mail Architecture.

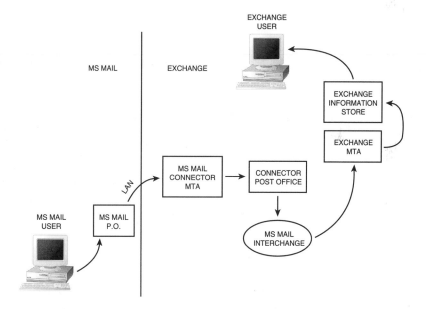

Exchange creates a local or "virtual" post office on the Exchange server. This post office models the MS Mail 3.x post office architecture. This post office becomes a shared file systems post office under the Exchange hierarchy. On the Exchange server, you have the information store, directory services, system attendant, and mail transfer agents. The Message Transfer Agent (MTA) communicates between the information stores and the different mail connectors. This includes the Internet Connector, the Connector, and the MS Mail Connector.

The core component of the connection from Exchange to MS Mail (PC) is the MS Mail Connector. It is used for the information transfer between Exchange and MS Mail sites and post offices. Once the Exchange server processes the data interchange, the MS Mail (PC) MTA can route the information to the MS Mail downstream post offices. Exchange serves as the hub post office for several clusters or spokes of MS Mail post offices.

Follow these steps to connect Exchange to MS Mail:

▪ Configure the MS Mail Connector interchange.

  1. Define a connection to the directly connected downstream MS Mail post office.

  2. Set up a single MS Mail Connector (PC) MTA service for the network service.

  3. Configure message routing to Exchange on each MS Mail post office.

  4. Add the network and post office names of each of the downstream MS Mail post offices to the Exchange address space of the direct connection MS Mail post office.

  5. Configure Directory Synchronization for the MS Mail post offices with the Exchange Directory Synchronization server.

N O T E   Once you migrate the hub and spoke architecture of MS Mail to Exchange, the Exchange servers become the mail hubs. The key benefit is that the same server that processes local mail or the information store can be the MTA for the existing MS Mail post offices. Exchange can easily incorporate into existing mail architectures. This includes existing MS Mail post offices running on Novell NetWare file servers. ▪

Exchange MS Mail Connector marries the functionality of a hub or gateway post office and the External application. The MS Mail Connector (PC) MTA component of the MS Mail Connector provides the functions of the MS Mail External and Multitasking MTA application. These include the following:

▪ Message delivery between MS Mail post offices and gateways

▪ Distribution of messages to recipients on MS Mail post offices on the same WAN/LAN

As you migrate from existing MS Mail shared file post offices, you may need to continue operating MS External and the Multitasking MTAs at the same time as the MS Mail Connector of Exchange. These older MTA applications do not provide the same rich feature set as the MS Mail Connector. The MS Mail Connector will allow you to integrate Exchange into any MS Mail environment using existing External or Multitasking MTA applications.

This example applies to all MTA connections including asynchronous modem connections and X.25 service.

N O T E   With the Exchange server running on Windows NT, you can take advantage of the built-in remote access services of the operating system. This way you can create a WAN environment without separate asynchronous connections. All the servers are networked together via a WAN/LAN. ▪

The MS Mail Connector contains the following Exchange components:

- *MS Mail Connector Interchange.* This is the Windows NT service which transfers and routes information between Exchange and the MS Mail Connector post office.

- *MS Mail Connector Post Office.* The important thing to remember is that the MS Mail Connector post office resides on the Exchange server as a virtual post office to provide the translation between the native MS Mail message store and the native Exchange information store. This is a temporary information store for messages.

- *MS Mail Connector (PC) Message Transfer Agent (MTA).* This is a Windows NT service that connects the MS Mail Connector post office with one or more MS Mail post offices. This MTA also handles the mail transfer between post offices.

The message route from Exchange to MS Mail (PC) is as follows:

1. Exchange user creates a message addressed to an MS Mail (PC) recipient and submits it.

2. Exchange information store forwards the message to Exchange MTA.

3. Exchange MS Mail interchange converts the message to MS Mail format and drops the message into the Connector post office.

4. Attachments, OLE objects, and rich text formatting are saved and converted onto the Connector post office.

5. The Connector (PC) MTA delivers the message to the destination MS Mail post office.

Setting Up the MS Mail Connector

As previously mentioned, the MS Mail Connector transfers information from Exchange and existing MS Mail (PC) post offices.

N O T E Each server in the organization can only run one instance of the MS Mail Connector. This instance can service more than one connection to MS Mail post offices and MS Mail gateways.

There are six key steps to setting up the MS Mail Connector:

1. Define the MS Mail Connector administrator mailbox.

2. Configure the general MS Mail Connector settings.

3. Connect to each MS Mail post office.

4. Configure the MS Mail Connector (PC) MTA for each post office communication. Protocol: asynchronous, LAN, or X.25.

Part
III

Ch
19

5. Launch the MS Mail Connector services.

6. Configure the directory services to include MS Mail post office recipients.

N O T E   This chapter assumes that the connectivity exists between Exchange and the MS Mail post
offices. If you need more information on connectivity between post offices, please see
Chapter 9, "Migrating from Lotus cc:Mail." ▨

There are two primary ways to connect to existing MS Mail post offices: LAN connectivity or
remote connectivity, which includes asynchronous and X.25 connections shown in Figures 19.4
and 19.5.

FIG. 19.4

Exchange to MS Mail
post office via LAN.

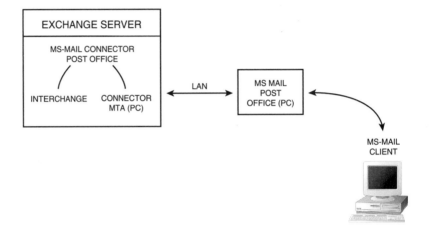

FIG. 19.5

Exchange to MS Mail
post office via
asynchronous or X.25
connections.

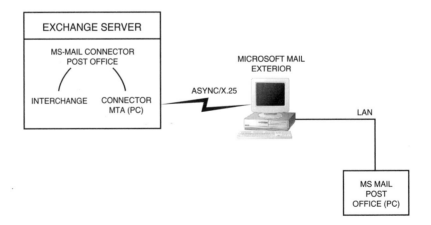

The main difference between connection methods is that with the remote connection, an additional instance of External must be running in order for the remote post office to transfer messages. This addition will require extra overhead for administration.

TIP If you have remote post offices with this configuration, you may want to either use NT Remote Access service to perform LAN based connections or migrate these post offices to Exchange ahead of other post offices.

Configuring the MS Mail Connector Interchange

The following steps configure the MS Mail Connector Interchange service:

1. Open the Exchange Administrator Application. This can be performed from the console on the Exchange server or from a workstation with connectivity to both the Exchange server and the MS Mail post office.

2. Choose the site from the organization list, the server name from the site, and the MS Mail Connector from the Connections list (see Figure 19.6).

3. Open the MS Mail Connector to configure the properties for the initial post office connection (see Figure 19.7).

   The Interchange tab allows you to select the "Administrator's Mailbox" which will receive system informational and alert messages from the Connector. These messages are typically due to nondelivery of mail (bounced mail) and failed messages.

FIG. 19.6

Select the MS Mail Connector.

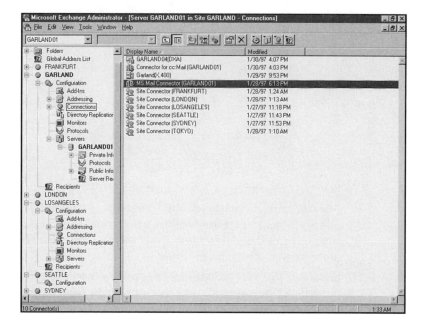

Part
III

Ch
19

4. Select the Administrator Account. This account can be a user, group, distribution list, or public folder (see Figure 19.8).

FIG. 19.7

The MS Mail Connector dialog box for (GAR-LAND01) with the Interchange tab selected.

FIG. 19.8

Configuring the Administrator Account for the Connector.

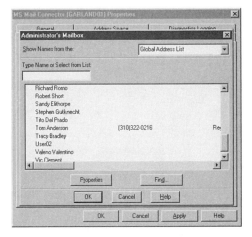

5. Select OK to return to the Interchange tab.

6. From the Interchange tab, select the primary language for the recipients. The selected primary language is used for interoperability with MS Mail clients using an alternate language. This is useful for International users of Exchange. The default value is prompted from the Exchange server.

7. Select the "Maximize MS Mail 3.x Compatibility" check box. This option is used for OLE compatibility in messages transferred between the older version used in MS Mail clients and the new version of Exchange clients.

   By selecting "Maximize MS Mail 3.x Compatibility," two versions of each OLE object are created. This option will increase or double the size of any OLE messages. If this option is not selected, MS Mail 3.x clients will not be able to view or save embedded objects originating from an Exchange client.

If you want to enable "Message Tracking" for the MS Mail Connector, select "Enable Message Tracking." This option will record message information into the tracking logs. It can also debug problems when messages do not appear to be routing properly or it can be used to locate potential lost messages. The default for this option is "disabled." For more information on message tracking, see Chapter 28, "Troubleshooting Exchange with Diagnostic Tools."

8. Click Apply to set these properties prior to defining the additional properties of the remaining tab menus.

N O T E The AppleTalk MTA Connector portion is discussed in Chapter 19, "Using the Microsoft Mail Connector for AppleTalk Networks." ■

MS Mail Connector

The following steps configure the MS Mail Connector Interchange service:

1. Select the General tab.

   This tab shows the server name (GARLAND01). The server name cannot be modified (see Figure 19.9).

FIG. 19.9

Use the General tab to set basic properties of the MS Mail Connector.

Part
III

Ch
19

2. Define "Maximum Message Size."

   You can define an upper limit for messages transferred through the Connector or accept the default value of "No Limit." This option is useful if you want to restrict the size of the attachment transferred between systems. Attachments can easily reach megabytes of data in size.

   To limit the size, enter a maximum value between 0 and 9999999 kilobytes.

3. Type an administrative note or comment with respect to the MS Mail Connector. Include the initials of the technician working on the service. This comment can only be viewed from this Property page.

4. Click "Apply" to set the properties and configure the remaining Property pages.

N O T E   You must first enter a value in the "Address Space" tab menu in order to define the MS Mail connection and close the connection property window. ▨

Defining Post Office Connections

The following steps are used to set up the connections for MS Mail (PC) post offices over LAN, asynchronous, or X.25 connections. Each connection method will be described individually.

Creating a LAN Connection   Use the Connections tab and Property page to create a LAN connection from Exchange to an MS Mail post office.

The following are steps to perform a LAN connection to an MS Mail post office:

1. Select the Connections tab.

N O T E   You may want to clear the "Confirm Before Connection Changes Are Applied" check box, if you do not want to have additional confirmation messages displayed before changes are set. ▨

This tab shows the organization and site name which is actively being configured (see Figure 19.10).

FIG. 19.10

Connections tab is used to define LAN connections.

2. Click the "Create" button to configure a new LAN connection post office (see Figure 19.11).

FIG. 19.11

Create Connection to
MS Mail post office.

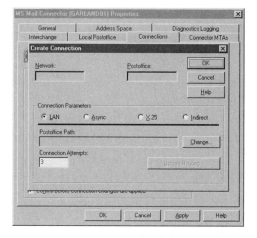

3. Select "LAN" under the Connection Parameters window.

4. Click the Change button to specify the path to the LAN-based MS Mail post office.

5. In the Post Office Path dialog box, enter the complete path to the server, file share, and directory containing the MS Mail post office in the "Path" box.

   Use the following format:

      Microsoft Networking: \\server\share\path

      Novell Networking: \\server\volume\path

6. Specify a Network or Domain log-on name and password in the "Connect As" and "Password" fields. You only need to complete these entries if any one of the following are true:

   • The post office is on a server with share-level security; no domain security.

   • The post office is in an untrusted domain, outside the domain model for the Exchange rollout.

   • The Exchange service account is not a valid user on the target server.

7. Click "OK" to confirm entries. If the connection is valid, the network and post office names will be entered into the appropriate fields on the Create Connection dialog box.

8. Define the number of connection retries for messages being sent to this post office. If this value is exceeded, the message is returned to the sender with an undelivered notification. The default value is 3.

   An optional setting is to configure the routing information about the downstream post office from the one created. To import this information, follow these steps:

   A. Click the "Upload Routing" button.

      A "Downstream Post Offices Summary" dialog box appears with the routing information of any post office or gateway indirectly connected through this post office. If this post office is a "hub" for other post offices, this information should be uploaded. If the post office is a downstream post office, you may want to skip over these steps.

Part
III

Ch
19

    B. Select any downstream post office you do not want to have uploaded. Choose the post office and click "Delete."

    C. Click "OK" to set the routing changes.

N O T E The information upload from this selection does not affect the configuration of the external options on the MS Mail post offices. ▪

  9. Click "OK" and return to the Connections Property page.

 10. Click "Apply" to set the changes for the connection.

Creating an Asynchronous Connection   Use the Connections tab and Property page to create an asynchronous connection from Exchange to an External MTA for an MS Mail post office (see Figure 19.12).

FIG. 19.12

Connections tab is used to define asynchronous connections.

Do the following to perform an asynchronous connection to an MS Mail post office:

  1. Select the Connections tab.

  2. Click the Create button to configure a new asynchronous connection (see Figure 19.13).

  3. Select the "Asynchronous" radio button.

  4. Type in the Network name and post office in the respective field for the Asynchronous connection post office.

N O T E Unlike the LAN connection, you must enter the information for these values. ▪

  5. In the Sign on ID field, enter the serial number for the remote post office. The Sign on ID format is: ##-#####.

FIG. 19.13

New Connections dialog box with Asynchronous selected.

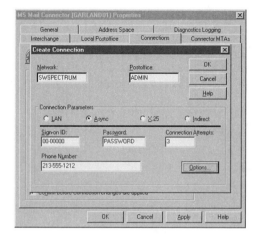

6. Enter the remote post office site password in the Password field.

7. Enter a value for the "Connections Attempts" box. The range is from 0 to 99. This value determines how many connection attempts Exchange will make to try to communicate with the remote post office, before returning the message to the original sender. The default value is 3.

8. Enter a phone number in the respective field. Make sure to add area code and any additional dialing prefixes. If you must dial a special digit (such as 9) to get an outside line, this must be included in the configuration. The phone number entered is the phone number for the remote post office MTA running the External application.

N O T E Make sure that the phone number you enter contains all prefixes. In addition, this number should direct Exchange to the remote MTA running the External application. ▪

9. Click the Options button to enter additional configurations for asynchronous connections.

10. Enter a value for "Maximum Message Size." The default is set to "No limit" (see Figure 19.14). If you want to limit the message size to be transferred over an asynchronous connection, enter a value between 0 and 9999 kilobytes in the respective field. This limits the size of attachment data, without limiting routing data.

11. Enter a value for "Failed Connection Retry For Urgent Mail." The value ranges from 1 to 99 minutes between connection attempts for messages defined as urgent. The default value is 10 minutes.

12. Enter a value for "Failed Connection Retry for Normal Mail." This value ranges from 1 to 999 minutes between attempts to reconnect for messages defined as normal. The default is 10 minutes.

13. Enter a value for "Dial Every." This value ranges from 1 to 999 minutes between connections for regular calls.

Part

III

Ch

19

FIG. 19.14

Advanced options for the asynchronous connections.

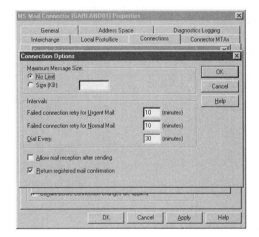

14. Check the box in order to select "Allow Mail Reception after Sending." This allows messages to be transferred in a bidirectional single connection. This option offers faster and more efficient message delivery. If this selection is not made, connections are made on an individual basis for "Sending" and "Receiving" messages.

15. Check the box to select "Return Registered Mail Confirmation." This will allow message confirmations to be transferred over the connection and between mail systems.

16. Click OK to set changes.

Creating an X.25 Connection   Use the Connections tab and Property page to create an X.25 connection from Exchange to an External MTA for an MS Mail post office. This connection is very similar to the Asynchronous connection. This section assumes that the X.25 protocol is already configured and running on this Windows NT server.

Do the following steps to perform an X.25 connection to an MS Mail post office:

1. Select the Connections tab (see Figure 19.15).

2. Click the Create button to configure a new X.25 connection.

3. Select the "X.25" radio button. This brings up the additional configuration for the X.25 parameters (see Figure 19.16).

4. Enter the Network and Post Office names in their respective fields.

5. Enter the sign-on serial ID in the format ##-#####.

6. Enter the remote post office password.

7. Define the number of connection attempts. The default is 3.

8. Define the X.121 address. This value should include the entire X.121 address, consisting of up to 16 digits. The format should be as follows:

   [Area][DNIC][DTE Address][sub-address]

FIG. 19.15
Connections tab is used to define X.25 connections.

FIG. 19.16
New Connection dialog box with X.25 selected.

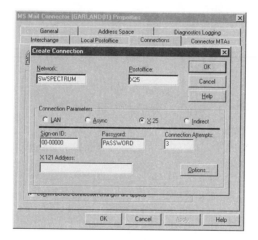

For more information on Exchange and X.25 support, refer to Chapter 20, "Using the Microsoft Mail Connector for AppleTalk Networks."

9. Click Apply to set the specifications.

N O T E   The "Options" dialog box for X.25 is identical to that for the Asynchronous connection.

Creating an Indirect Connection   You can use the MS Mail Connector to act as a hub post office. The hub post office can be specified to feed various spokes or indirect post offices.

Indirect connections are supported over the LAN or asynchronous or X.25 connections. They can be used to replace the External application running to service multiple downstream post offices.

Part
III

Ch
19

Do the following steps to perform an indirect connection to an MS Mail post office:

1. Select the Connections tab.

2. Select the hub post office and then click Create to configure the indirect post office.

3. From the Create Connection dialog box, select the hub post office from the "Indirect Via" drop-down list (see Figure 19.17).

FIG. 19.17

Connection tab is used to define indirect connections.

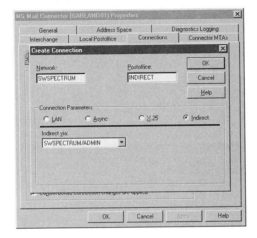

4. Click OK to set the configuration.

These are the four options for MS Mail connections provided with Exchange.

The message queue is the final component of the Connections tab menu. The queue lists messages awaiting delivery by the MS Mail Connector. Figure 19.18 shows an empty queue after all pending messages were delivered. Normally, you would use the queue window to monitor the message load passing through your MS Mail Connector.

FIG. 19.18

MS Mail Connector message queue.

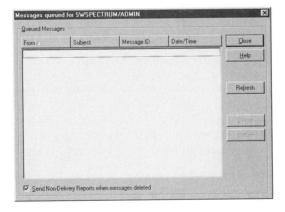

Configuring the Message Transfer Agent

The following steps are used to create the Message Transfer Agent services for connections over LAN, Asynchronous, or X.25. Each connection method will be described individually.

Creating an MS Mail Connector (PC) MTA   Use the Connector MTA's tab and Property page to create the MTA services to transfer messages from Exchange to an MS Mail post office. Follow these steps:

1. Select the Connector MTA's tab (see Figure 19.19).

2. Click "New" to create a new MTA service.

3. Enter a name for the MTA service (see Figure 19.20). This name is used by the Windows NT operating system to register the MTA Connector as a system service. Once the service is defined, you cannot modify the name. You would have to remove the service and re-create it.

   Because the MTA runs as a system service, there are several character string limitations:

   - up to 30 characters, maximum
   - letters a–z in lowercase format
   - letters A–Z in uppercase format
   - numbers 0–9
   - the <space bar>

   If you use any other character string, the service will not be able to register with the operating system.

Part
III

Ch
19

FIG. 19.20

MS Mail Connector
MTA's tab menu—New
Service.

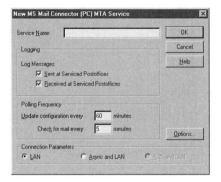

N O T E   Naming the convention is important with services. If you preface the MTAs with "MS Mail
Connector," they will interfere with the integrated Exchange Mail Windows NT services listed
in the Control Panel—Services. ▦

4. Select the "Log Messages Sent At Serviced Post Offices" check box. This option will set
up logging in order to record each message transferred to the MS Mail post office
environment.

5. Select the "Log Messages Received At Serviced Post Offices" check box. This option will
set up logging in order to record each message transferred from the MS Mail post office
environment.

6. Enter values for the "Update Configuration" field in minutes. This checks for updated
information based on the interval minutes entered into this field. The default is 60
minutes.

N O T E   If you enter a 0 in this field, you will stop the configuration from checking for messages. ▦

7. Enter a value for the "Check for Mail Every" field. This field accepts values from 0 to 999
minutes. This is the polling interval for how long the MTA waits before rechecking for
mail coming to the MS Mail Connector post office. The default value is 5 minutes.

   If you have multiple instances of the MTA service to service multiple MS Mail post
offices and gateways, you may want to stagger this time interval so that each instance
does not overlap. One service would check for mail every five minutes and the next
service would check every six minutes.

8. Select the LAN option in the "Connection Parameters" section.

9. Define the MTA Connector options by clicking the "Options" button.

   These options apply to both the LAN and the Asynchronous connection methods (see
Figure 19.21). The first selection is for "Maximum LAN Message Size." You can set an
upper limit for the size of messages transferred through this MTA. The values range
from 0 to 9999999 kilobytes and the default is "No Limit."

The next entry is used to define the "Close Post Office If" value. This value is used to close the destination post office connection when disk space utilization has reached whichever threshold point you designate from 0 to 999999999 kilobytes. Messages will queue up on the MTA until they are timed out or additional disk space is added on the destination post office.

In addition to closing the connection, you can set a value for "Open Post Office If" disk space that has been added or made available. This value ranges from 0 to 999999999 kilobytes. Disk-space availability must rise above this value in order for message transfer to restart.

FIG. 19.21

MS Mail Connector MTA's tab menu— New Service, Options dialog box.

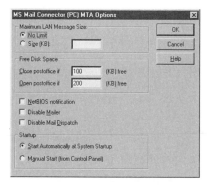

The next three check boxes are used for administrative notifications to the MS Mail LAN post office users. These have no impact for Exchange users. The first option is to check the "NetBIOS Notification" in order to have the MTA send a NetBIOS broadcast message.

The NetBIOS Broadcast will only work if the server and clients are running the NetBIOS protocol. In addition, you must start all the NT service MTAs prior to launching the External application on the destination post office for NetBIOS broadcasts to function properly. For more information, see the user manuals for the respective operating system to learn how to install NetBIOS.

Select "Disable Mailer" and "Disable Mail Dispatch" to stop mail notifications from being distributed via the External and Dispatch applications associated with the destination MS Mail post offices. These do not impact the Exchange users. For more information on the application, refer to your MS Mail Administrator Guide.

Select the "Startup" box to define the method that this NT MTA service will launch. The options are to have the MTA start automatically or manually.

Click OK to set these configurations.

10. Click OK followed by "Apply" to set all the configurations for this MTA service. If you modify these options for this service at a later point, you will need to stop and start the NT service in order to have the changes take effect.

To complete the MTA service, you need to define the post offices service by the MTA services.

Part
III

Ch
19

1. From the MS Mail Connector property sheet, click the "List" button. The Serviced LAN Post Offices dialog box appears.
2. In the "Serviced LAN Post Offices" dialog box, select the post office to be serviced from the right panel of "Available LAN Post offices."
3. Click the Add button in the middle and the selection becomes a "Serviced LAN Post office."
4. Click OK to set the configurations.

If you need an additional service for an Asynchronous connection, you will need to modify an existing MTA or create a new service. The following are the configuration differences for the Asynchronous connection:

1. Click Create to create a new MTA service or click Edit to modify an existing MTA.
2. On the Property page, select the "Async and LAN" option (see Figure 19.22).

FIG. 19.22

MS Mail Connector MTA's tab menu—New Service via Asynchronous or X.25 connection.

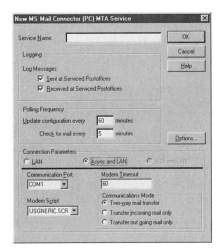

3. Enter the appropriate values for the following:

Communication Port   This is the server communication port to be used for the MTA service. The default value is "COM1."

Modem Script   This is used to define the initialization string for your particular modem.

N O T E   If you have an existing modem that requires a customized script file, you can copy this script to the following path on the Exchange server:

`<UX.NO>%Exchangeroot%\connect\msmcom\maildata\glb`

Modem Time-out   This is the value for the number of minutes the MTA will wait for a connection with the destination post office.

Communication Mode   This value defines whether the MTA will send and receive messages or only handle one-way message transfers.

4. Click OK to set the configuration settings.

   If this MTA has been modified, it will need to be stopped and restarted from the services control panel.

After you have configured all your MTA services and defined which post offices are serviced, you need to start the MTA NT services in order to begin message transfer. Do the following steps to start these services:

1. Open the control panel for the server services.

2. Locate the MTA service to be started, select the service, and click "Start" (see Figure 19.23). The service will start and you can begin transferring messages between mail systems.

FIG. 19.23
MS Mail Connector MTA
Windows NT service.

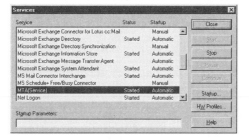

MS Mail Connector Address Space

The following steps are used to create the address space for the MS Mail post offices serviced by this MS Mail Connector.

Address space is used to properly route messages throughout the organization. If you have additional gateways installed, address space is important to ensure the proper message route.

1. Select the Address Space tab (see Figure 19.24).

2. Select the address space to be created. Your choice will depend on the type of gateway used to receive these message transfers. The address spaces are associated with a specific template for each connector. The template assists with entering the destination mail address. The options are:

   - New General   A blank template for creating a destination address when a template is not available. Typically each connector will provide an address template.

   - New Internet   A blank template to enter SMTP or Internet message routes.

   - New X.400   A blank template for creating an X.400 message route.

   - New MS Mail   A blank template to create an MS Mail message route. After the MS Mail Connector is configured to transfer messages through the associated MTA service, a message route is automatically generated in the MS Mail address space.

Part
III

Ch
19

FIG. 19.24

MS Mail Address Space
tab menu.

To configure the MS MAIL Address Space, access property pages on the MS Mail Connector.

1. To create or edit the MS Mail address space, select the address space in the connection window.

2. In the Property page for the MS Mail address space, you must enter the network and post office of the destination MS Mail post office.

N O T E   When you enter values for the address spaces, you can use wildcards. For example,

MS:SWSPECTRUM\ADMIN*

This address routes messages to all users on the destination post office. ▪

3. All the address spaces will create a message route from this MS Mail Connector to the destination or foreign mail system. For more information on routing and addressing, see Chapter 23, "Exchange Maintenance."

Configuring the Local Exchange Post Office

When you use the MS Mail Connector for MS Mail (PC), Exchange must create a local or "virtual" MS Mail post office. This is known as the local post office, which was created automatically when you installed the MS Mail Connector. It was first configured when you set up the MS Mail post office interchange in the first part of this chapter.

The local post office is a working MS Mail post office. Exchange uses this post office to transfer messages to MS Mail post offices. The message first goes into the MTA and then gets transferred and converted into the local post office before being transferred out to the destination post office.

To configure the local post office, follow these steps:

1. Select the Local Postoffice tab (see Figure 19.25).

FIG. 19.25

MS Mail Connector
local post office
configuration.

2. Enter the network and post office name for the local Exchange MS Mail post office interchange. These values can be changed. By default, Exchange enters the organization and site name into these fields.

3. Enter the password to be used by External MTA applications when you are connecting to and signing on to this local post office to transfer messages.

 N O T E This is a good time to note the local post office Sign on Serial ID. You will need this information when you are configuring External to communicate with this local post office. ▓

4. Click the "Regenerate" button under the MS Mail Connector Addresses heading. This selection will generate the proper addressing scheme to be used in routing messages through this local post office.

   If any changes are made to this local post office, you must execute the address regeneration. You will need to update the information on the remote External MTA, gateway, or post office as well. Additionally, if you change this information, you must stop and restart the NT MTA service and Connector interchange. A warning will appear to force you to confirm this action.

5. Click OK to accept configuration settings and apply them to the Connector.

MS Mail Connector Post Offices and Gateways in PC Mail

Once you have finished configuring the Exchange MS Mail Connector, you must configure each MS Mail PC post office to work with the settings in Exchange. Refer to the MS Mail Connector's local post office settings to create an External post office site in MS Mail 3.x.

Part
III

Ch
19

To configure the MS Mail post office, follow these steps:

1. Attach your Exchange server to the MS Mail post office with a network connection.

2. Launch the MS Mail Administration utility to configure the post office settings.

> **N O T E**   Once you have used the Exchange GUI interface, you will not want to have to go back to using the DOS character-based administration utility of MS Mail v3.x. ■

3. Toggle to the External-Admin Configuration menu item (see Figure 19.26).

FIG. 19.26

Use the MS Mail Administration utility to configure the post office.

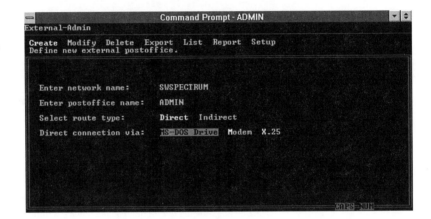

4. Select Create and define the network, post office, and route for the Exchange MS Mail Connector local post office.

   In this example, the MS Mail post office is called ADMIN on the SWSPECTRUM network. An External route has been added to the Exchange local post office called TEXAS on the same SWSPECTRUM network. The connection type is direct. The only time you would use indirect is if you were routing MS Mail through another MS Mail hub post office prior to transferring the message to Exchange.

5. Select Yes to create the route and then exit the Administration application.

Once you have modified the settings for the post offices, if you have any MS Mail 3.x gateways, you will have to modify those as well. Because there are many different types of MS Mail gateways, you will be unable to describe the process for each one. The key components to modify are the network and post office names, sign on ID, and post office password. Refer to your user's manual for more information on configuring the gateway.

Managing the NT Service for the MS Mail Connector

Now that the MS Mail Connector is completely configured, you must start the connection service to begin transferring messages between Exchange and MS Mail.

To start the MS Mail connection services, follow these steps:

1. Open the Windows NT control panel or Windows NT Server Manager and select the "Services" option.

2. Select the MS Mail Connector Interchange service (see Figure 19.27).

FIG. 19.27
Use the MS Mail Administration utility to configure the post office.

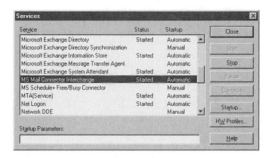

3. Click "Start" to launch the service.

N O T E The MS Mail Connector (PC) MTA is set to "disabled" because it is only used in the configuration of individual MS Mail MTA services. This service cannot be started. ■

4. Close the services window.

Testing the Connection Between Exchange and MS Mail

Now that all the services are running and messages are configured to route between Exchange and MS Mail, you should test the connection.

To test the message routing between Exchange and MS Mail, follow these steps:

1. Using the MS Exchange client software, create and send a message to a recipient with a destination on the MS Mail post office.

2. Verify in the MS Mail 3.x client software that the message has arrived.

3. Reverse this process to verify MS Mail to Exchange message routing.

4. If the messages do not arrive, the first place to begin diagnosis is in the Windows NT Server Event log for the Exchange server.

The MS Mail Connector interchange events is logged as "MSExchangeMSMI" for mail transfer between the Exchange information store and the MS Mail Connector local post office.

The MS Mail Connector (PC) MTA events are logged under the associated MS Mail MTA services names.

In Figure 19.28, you can see that the MTA has created a system message on the Exchange local post office with the respective name. In this example, the MTA service is called "MTA (service)" and the event would be logged with this name (see Figure 19.29). As you can see,

Part
III

Ch
19

the MTA server, ADMIN, has successfully started. When the MTA begins, we can use our Event Viewer to drill down on to event detail.

FIG. 19.28

Windows NT event log for MS Mail Connector entries.

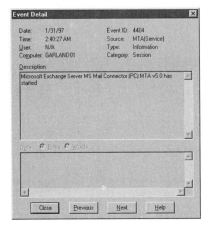

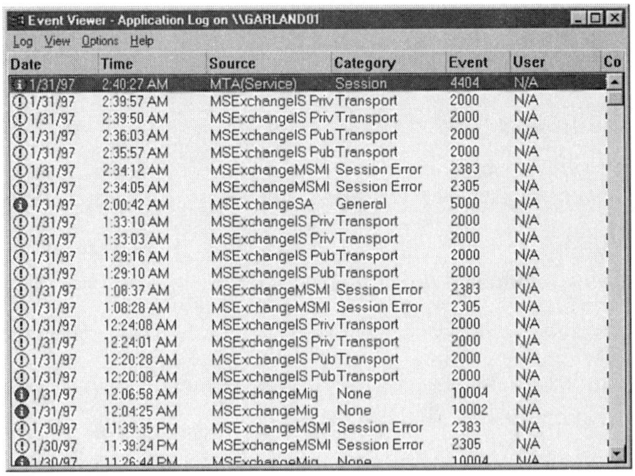

FIG. 19.29

The Windows NT event log will store a significant amount of events from the Exchange server. Each process has a unique service ID.

As you can see, Exchange provides numerous messages to the event log. If you have trouble with communication between Exchange and the MS Mail post office, you can adjust the sensitivity of the auditing levels. To assist with debugging and routing problems between Exchange and MS Mail, you may want to increase the level of auditing for the MS Mail Connector.

To adjust audit levels, follow these steps:

1. Open the MS Mail Connector Property page and select the tab for "Diagnostics Logging" (see Figure 19.30).

2. On the left panel are the services to be monitored and on the right are the category and logging levels. The service is the MS Mail Interchange Connector. The categories to adjust are MS Mail Interchange Connector, the MS Mail PC MTA, and the MS Mail AppleTalk MTA. (Note that the AppleTalk MTA will be discussed in the next chapter.)

   The levels indicate the level of granularity of information that you would like logged into the event viewer. The levels for the MS Mail Connector are None, Minimum, Medium, and Maximum. Typically, you will have Minimum selected for the categories of the service that you are using. If you are not going to use the AppleTalk MTA, there is no need to turn logging on.

   If problems do arise with the connections between Exchange and MS Mail, you can increase the logging levels while you are in the debug mode. Realize that increasing the logging levels can potentially overload your event logs with an abundance of information. The increase in logging should only be set while you are debugging a problem. Once the connection has stabilized, it is a good idea to reduce the logging levels.

FIG. 19.30

The MS Mail Connector tab menu for adjusting system auditing levels.

Part
III

Ch
19

If you are still having problems with MS Mail message routing and the event logs are not providing the information necessary to solve the problem, try the following:

1. Delete and then re-add the MS Mail Connector, including all the MTA services.

2. See Chapter 26, "Diagnostic and Troubleshooting Tools."

3. Contact Microsoft Product Support Services.

Directory Synchronization

The final component to configure is the Directory Synchronization between Exchange and MS Mail.

This section will assume that the Directory Synchronization server is already set up and running on Exchange. Each site can only run Directory Synchronization server. However, each server can support numerous directory requesters and remote directory requesters. In addition, this section will assume that Exchange and the MS Mail post office can both send and receive messages via the Interchange Connector and the PC MTA. Directory Synchronization was explained in detail in Chapter 17, "Setting Up Site Connector and Dynamic RAS Connector."

Once the Directory Synchronization server is set up and configured on the Exchange server, there are a few steps needed to ensure the MS Mail post offices are included in the synchronization process.

1. Make sure that the Exchange Site Directory Synchronization service is installed and running (see Figure 19.31). Check your Windows NT system service list to confirm this.

FIG. 19.31

The Exchange Directory Synchronization server properties.

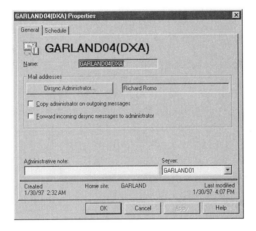

2. Install and configure a remote directory requester to synchronize the Exchange Global Address List (GAL) with the GAL on the MS Mail 3.x post office network (see Figure 19.32). The remote directory requester has all the information needed to communicate with the Exchange local post office prior to synchronizing with the connected MS Mail post office.

3. Open the MS Mail 3.x administration application and select the post office configuration options (see Figure 19.33). From this panel, you can configure the directory synchronization options, as well as the use of the global address for the local post office.

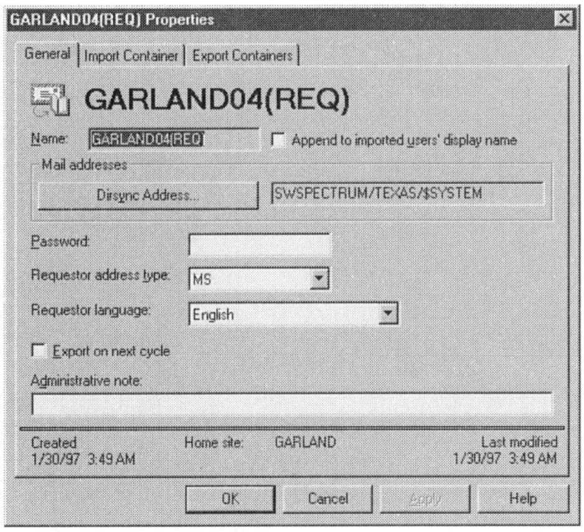

FIG. 19.32

The Exchange remote directory requester used to synchronize with foreign systems, including MS Mail 3.x.

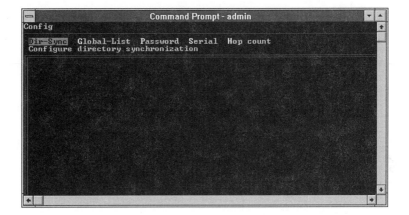

FIG. 19.33

Configuration options in the MS Mail administration program.

4. From the "Dir-sync" menu, toggle to the "registration" menu to configure the Directory Synchronization server information. The information for the Directory Synchronization server will be the same as the Exchange MS Mail local post office. From this panel, enter the network, post office, and password for the server (see Figure 19.34).

5. From the "Global Address" menu in the post office configuration options, you will need to specify for the MS Mail 3.x post office to use the global address list.

Once the MS Mail administration is completed, you should stop and restart the Exchange Directory Synchronization Server service. As well, stop and restart the MS Mail Connector Interchange.

As you can see, there are many components required to connect Exchange with MS Mail (PC) post offices. The message route includes the Exchange information store transferring messages to the Interchange Connector which converts the message to the local MS Mail post office, before the Exchange MTA transfers the message to the remote MS Mail Post office via a LAN connection or over an asynchronous or X.25 link.

Part
III

Ch
19

FIG. 19.34

Creating a Directory Synchronization requester in MS Mail.

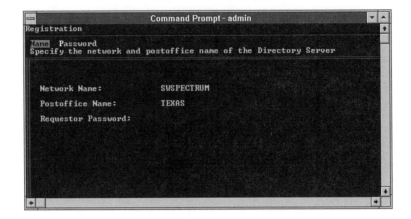

From Here...

This chapter has explained the connection between Exchange and MS Mail (PC) post offices. For more information, see the following chapters:

■ Chapter 7, "Planning Connections to Microsoft Mail Systems," will go into the steps associated with implementing the MS Mail Connector.

■ Chapter 20, "Using the Microsoft Mail Connector for Appletalk Networks," will help you configure Exchange to work in an AppleTalk environment.

■ Chapter 28, "Troubleshooting Exchange with Diagnostic Tools," will cover tracking messages and rebuilding the mail database.

Using the Microsoft Mail Connector for AppleTalk Networks

In this chapter, you learn how to establish a messaging link between Microsoft Exchange and a Macintosh server running Microsoft Mail for AppleTalk networks. Unlike a Microsoft Mail for PC network, Microsoft Mail (AppleTalk) does not use the post office paradigm. Therefore, the process for connecting to an Exchange server is somewhat different. With respect to the Macintosh side, the Macintosh server believes it is communicating with a standard Microsoft Mail (PC) post office. Microsoft Mail for AppleTalk uses a special gateway component to communicate with the Exchange Microsoft Mail Connector. With respect to the Exchange side, the Microsoft Mail Connector has specific configuration settings, and message queue for Microsoft Mail (AppleTalk) connections. Any configuration specifically pertaining to Exchange communicating with Microsoft Mail post offices is not applicable. ■

Establishing a Network Messaging Link Between Windows NT and Macintosh Server

To communicate between a Mac and NT, you need to set up services for Mac. Then you can set up a Microsoft Mail Connector to communicate between Exchange and Microsoft Mail for AppleTalk.

Configure the Exchange Microsoft Mail Connector to Communicate with Microsoft Mail (AppleTalk) Servers

After you share a volume and set up our network connection between Mac and Exchange, you need to configure a Microsoft Mail Connector.

How to Configure the Microsoft Exchange Connection on Microsoft Mail (AppleTalk) Servers

NT server running Macintosh services enables the Mac server and NT server to communicate. Now we need to configure the components for the Microsoft Mail AppleTalk Connector.

Introduction to the Microsoft Mail Connector

In this section, you learn about the connectors used to establish a link between Exchange and Microsoft Mail (AppleTalk) servers.

The two core Exchange Microsoft Mail Connector components are the same:

- Microsoft Mail Connector Interchange: The Exchange service that routes messages between the Exchange server and the Microsoft Mail Connector post office.

- Microsoft Mail Connector post office: This component is an Exchange emulation of a true Microsoft Mail post office. It stores messages in transit to and from Microsoft Mail (PC and AppleTalk).

Exchange also includes one additional component for communication with Microsoft Mail (AppleTalk) servers:

- Microsoft Mail Connector (AppleTalk) message transfer agent: A Windows NT service that routes messages between the Microsoft Mail Connector post office and the Microsoft Mail (AppleTalk) server.

The following details the procedure for connecting Exchange to a Microsoft Mail for AppleTalk network:

1. Set up all necessary network connections between systems.

2. Install and set up the Exchange Microsoft Mail Connector.

3. Place the Connector post office on a Macintosh accessible NTFS volume.

4. Configure the Exchange Microsoft Mail Connector to communicate with Microsoft Mail (AppleTalk) servers. This includes starting the Microsoft Mail (AppleTalk) MTA service.

5. Install and configure the Microsoft Exchange Connection software on the Microsoft Mail (AppleTalk) gateway server.

6. Enter address space entries for the MS (AppleTalk) server. Test for correct message routing between systems.

7. If you want additional Microsoft Mail (AppleTalk) servers to communicate indirectly with the Exchange server, install and configure the gateway access component on each Macintosh server.

8. Test transfer of messages to indirectly connected Microsoft Mail (AppleTalk) servers if applicable.

9. Once messages are routed properly to all servers, proceed to set up directory synchronization to maintain up-to-date address lists among systems.

Installing Services for Macintosh

The following steps help you to configure your Exchange server to support Microsoft Mail for AppleTalk networks. Windows NT Services for Macintosh enable your server to communicate over Apple's native AppleTalk protocol. You must have an NTFS partitioned hard disk to support Services for Macintosh:

N O T E The following steps are quick guidelines to help you set up NT services for Macintosh. Consult your Windows NT Server documentation for more advanced configuration information. ▨

1. Open the Control Panel and double-click the Networking icon (see Figure 20.1).

FIG. 20.1

The Windows NT Network is part of your Windows NT server.

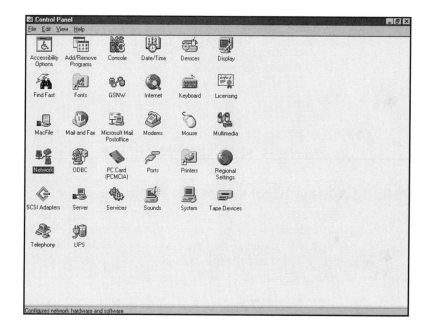

2. If Services for Macintosh is not listed in the Installed Network Software scroll box, it is not installed. Click Add Software. The Add Network Software dialog box appears (see Figure 20.2).

3. Select Services for Macintosh from the list of available Network Services. Click Add.

4. Type the directory path to your Windows NT server software—for example, CD-ROM, floppy disk, or server volume. Click Continue.

5. After the services are loaded from disk and installed, you will return to the Network Settings. Services for Macintosh should now be on the Installed Network Software list.

6. Click OK to complete service installation.

7. You will be prompted to restart your server to update the Network settings.

   Click Restart now, if this is appropriate. Alternatively, you can click Don't Restart Now to return to the Windows NT screen.

Part
III

Ch
20

FIG. 20.2

Select Services for Macintosh among the list of available components.

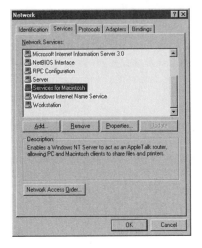

> **N O T E**   If you choose not to restart immediately, remember that you will have to do so before continuing with Exchange to Microsoft Mail (AppleTalk) configuration. ■

Creating a Macintosh Accessible Volume

A Macintosh Accessible Volume must be created so that your Microsoft Mail AppleTalk server is capable of seeing your Exchange server on the network. Then, the two systems can trade messaging data. The volume itself is a directory within the NTFS structure configured for connection from a Macintosh. The Macintosh server will be configured to automatically log on to this volume on start-up.

The following steps show you how to create and configure a Macintosh Accessible Volume:

> **N O T E**   For more information on Macintosh Accessible Volumes, refer to your Windows NT Server documentation. ■

1. Open the Windows NT Explorer.
2. From the explorer, you can find the following folder.

    C:\EXCHSRVR\CONNECT\MSCON\MAILDATA (assuming you've installed Exchange Drive C).

> **N O T E**   This assumes that you have named the main Exchange directory "EXCHSRVR" during installation. ■

3. From the MacFile menu, select Create Volume. The Create Macintosh-Accessible Volume dialog box appears (see Figure 20.3).
4. The Volume Name should be "MAILDATA."

FIG. 20.3

You can create a New Macintosh-Accessible Volume from the MacFile menu.

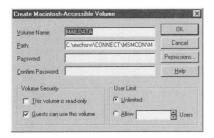

5. You can enter a Password once. Then, you can enter it again in Confirm Password. The Macintosh server must use this information to connect to this volume. By default, no volume password is entered.

6. For enhanced security, clear the Guests Can Use This Volume check box.

7. Confirm that this volume is a read-only remains unchecked.

8. Be sure that the Unlimited User Limit radio button is selected.

9. Click OK to create this volume and return to the explorer. Better yet, click the Permissions button to set access rights to this volume.

Configuring Macintosh-Accessible Volume Permissions

After creating a Macintosh-Accessible Volume you must define what users and groups have permission to access it. This is done in the Macintosh-Accessible Volume Permissions dialog box. This dialog box is almost identical to the Macintosh File Sharing dialog box. In this box, you select the Windows NT accounts that have access rights to this volume. The following steps will guide you in setting access rights to this volume:

1. There are two ways to open the permissions for a Macintosh-Accessible Volume. You can do this by clicking Permissions from the Create Macintosh-Accessible Volume dialog box. Alternatively, you can select the Volume from the Explorer. Then, select Permissions from the MacFile menu. The Macintosh View of Directory Permissions dialog box appears (see Figure 20.4).

2. Use the_(ellipses) buttons to configure an Owner and Primary Group for this volume. These determine who is able to connect to this volume through the Macintosh Chooser.

FIG. 20.4

You can set access permission for this volume.

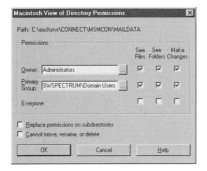

Part III

Ch 20

3. Confirm that See Files, See Folders, and Make Changes permissions remain checked for the Owner and Primary Group.

4. Clear the check boxes pertaining to Everyone. This prevents anyone, except those users contained in Owner and Primary Group, from using this volume. By default, the Everyone permissions are checked.

5. Select the Replace Permissions on Subdirectories check box. This gives all directories within the current one permission settings identical to the ones on this page. By default, this box is not checked.

6. Click OK to set these permissions and return to the explorer.

Testing Connection to the Macintosh-Accessible Volume

You have completed the Macintosh-Accessible Volume configuration. This directory is now available for connection through the Macintosh Chooser. To confirm accessibility, you can test a manual connection, using the following steps:

1. Open the Chooser application from your Macintosh's Apple menu.

2. Click the AppleShare icon in the Chooser. Then, select the AppleTalk Zone, if applicable, in which your Exchange server is located.

   The Exchange server should now be listed in the Select a File Server display window.

3. Click the server's name. Then click OK.

4. On the connect dialog box, make sure the Registered User radio button is selected. Enter the user Name and Password for this server. Then, click OK.

5. After you are authenticated, a list of available Macintosh-Accessible Volumes displays in the Select the Items You Want to Use: window.

   Your newly created "MAILDATA" (or whatever customized name you chose) volume should appear on the list.

6. If your Volume is not visible, repeat the preceding steps for creating and configuring a Macintosh-Accessible Volume. Otherwise, proceed to the following section.

Configuring the Microsoft Mail Connector for Use

Now that connectivity between Macintosh and Windows NT server has been established, the next step is to set up the Exchange Microsoft Mail Connector to send and receive messages with the Microsoft Mail (AppleTalk) server.

The following list details the property pages for the Exchange Microsoft Mail connector. This list also discusses how they are configured to work with AppleTalk networks.

- Interchange. This page helps you set up the Microsoft Mail Connector (AppleTalk) MTA.

- Local Postoffice. Using this page, you set the local information that a Microsoft Mail (AppleTalk) server uses to identify and connect to the Microsoft Mail connector. Any standard Microsoft Mail (PC) post office uses this data to connect, as well.

- Connections. You can view the AppleTalk MTA's message queue using this page. All other options are reserved for Microsoft Mail (PC) connections.

- Connector MTAs. This page is not used with respect to connecting to Microsoft Mail for AppleTalk networks. Normally, this page defines which Microsoft Mail (PC) Post offices are serviced by this Exchange server.

- General. You use this page for both PC and AppleTalk Microsoft Mail connections to set an upper limit for message sizes.

- Address Space. On this page, you define which messages will be routed through this Microsoft Mail connector to either type of Microsoft Mail system.

- Diagnostics Logging. You define logging levels for the Microsoft Mail (AppleTalk) MTA service on this page. You also configure logging for the Interchange activity and the Microsoft Mail (PC) MTA on this page.

Configuring Exchange Microsoft Mail Connector Properties

This section covers the installation of Microsoft Mail Connector properties primarily corresponding to communication with Microsoft Mail (AppleTalk) servers. For a complete guide to the Microsoft Mail connector, see Chapter 19, "Using the Microsoft Mail Connector for PC Networks."

Interchange Page

The following steps guide you through the Interchange configuration:

1. Open the Microsoft Mail Connector property pages.

2. Select the Interchange tab. The Microsoft Mail Connector (GARLAND01) Properties page appears (see Figure 20.5).

FIG. 20.5
You can designate mailboxes to be used by the Microsoft Mail Connector Interchange property page.

Part
III

Ch
20

3. You must set an administrator's mailbox if one has not already been defined. It will receive status notification from Microsoft Mail Connector. If one is not defined, click Change. Then, select a mailbox from the address list.

TIP   For a larger organization, it is a good idea to create a POSTMASTER account to receive the potentially large volume of status messages. This way, one administrator mailbox will not be burdened with an extra message load. Also, other administrators can view the delivery messages without logging on to a general administrator mailbox or somebody else's personal mail.

4. Select the Primary Language for Clients from the pull-down menu.

5. Check the Maximize Microsoft Mail 3.x Compatibility box to provide for OLE objects embedded in Exchange messages.

6. Unless you are currently using message tracking for troubleshooting purposes, make sure the Enable message tracking check box is cleared. For more information on message tracking for troubleshooting purposes, see Chapter 28, "Troubleshooting Exchange with Diagnostic Tools."

7. Configure the AppleTalk MTA settings. The following section discusses these settings.

Mail Connector AppleTalk MTA

You can open a messaging link between Exchange and Microsoft Mail (AppleTalk). To do this, you enable the Microsoft Mail Connector AppleTalk message transfer agent by following these steps:

1. Click the Configure button under the Microsoft Mail Connector (AppleTalk) MTA. The Microsoft Mail Connector (Apple Talk) MTA Options dialog box appears (see Figure 20.6).

2. Select the Enable Microsoft Mail Connector AppleTalk MTA radio button under the Set Status window.

N O T E   Enabling the AppleTalk MTA adds to the list of services in the Windows NT Services controller panel. ▨

3. Select the Start Automatically at System Startup radio button to configure this option. By default, this option is selected. Click OK to return to the Interchange property page.

N O T E   Normally, you will always set the AppleTalk MTA service for automatic startup. If, for example, you have a situation that requires some troubleshooting, and you want to have complete manual control over this service, select the Manual Start radio button. ▨

4. Click Apply to set these properties and continue with other ones. When you are finished with all settings, click OK to set them and to return to the Administrator Program.

FIG. 20.6

You can view and set Microsoft Mail (AppleTalk) MTA service status.

The Local Post Office Page

The Local Post office information identifies the Microsoft Mail Connector Post office to the Macintosh Microsoft Mail (AppleTalk) servers and any Microsoft Mail Post offices on the network.

1. Select the Local Post office tab from the Microsoft Mail connector property pages. The Microsoft Mail Connector (GARLAND01) Properties page appears (see Figure 20.7).

2. Enter the Microsoft Mail Network name for this post office. By default, this is the Microsoft Exchange organization name.

3. Enter a Post office used to identify this connector to other Microsoft Mail servers. By default, this is the Exchange server's name.

FIG. 20.7

You can configure the local Microsoft Mail Connector post office information.

4. Enter a Sign-on Password used to authenticate other mail systems. By default, this is set to PASSWORD. You should change it for security reasons.

5. If you make any changes to post office settings, click Regenerate to rebuild addressing data.

N O T E For Local Post office information changes to take effect immediately, you must restart the Connector Interchange service, as well as the Microsoft Mail MTAs. ▬

6. Click Apply to set these properties and continue with other ones. When you are finished with all settings, click OK to set them and return to the Administrator Program.

The Connections Page

The Connections property page only gives you the option of viewing the Microsoft Mail (AppleTalk) MTA message queue. The other options, such as Modify, Delete, and Create, are available only for Microsoft Mail (PC) connections. The MTA queue lists all outgoing messages awaiting transmission by the Microsoft Mail AppleTalk message transfer agent.

To view the Microsoft Mail (AppleTalk) MTA message queue, follow these steps:

1. Select the Connections tab from the Microsoft Mail Connector Properties page. The Microsoft Mail Connector (GARLAND01) Properties page appears (see Figure 20.8).

   The Connections display window shows all current Microsoft Mail connections.

FIG. 20.8

You use this page to view the Microsoft Mail connector AppleTalk message queue.

2. Click the AppleTalk Mail entry in the window. The Modify and Delete buttons will dim.

3. Click the Queue button to bring up the Messages queued for AppleTalk Mail dialog box (see Figure 20.9).

4. The Queued Messages window shows the current messages awaiting delivery by this MTA.

From	The message sender
Subject	The information on the message's subject line
Message ID	The Exchange message identification code
Date/Time	The time the message entered the queue

5. Click Refresh to update the message list.

TIP The queued message window is a listing of messages awaiting delivery at that moment. To get a more dynamic view of messages passing through the connector, you must repeatedly click the Refresh button. Clicking this button also gives you the latest updates.

FIG. 20.9
The Microsoft Mail (AppleTalk) message queue shows all the pertinent information on current messages.

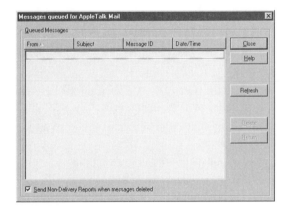

6. Select a message. Then, click Delete to remove it from the queue. If Send Non-Delivery Reports when messages deleted is checked, the message sender will be notified of the deletion.

7. Select a message. Then, click Return to remove a message from the queue and return it to the sender.

8. Click Close to return to the Connections property page.

Part

III

Ch

20

Macintosh Microsoft Mail (AppleTalk) Configuration

This section describes the configuration required on the Macintosh side of the Exchange/ Microsoft Mail (AppleTalk) connection.

The following are the Macintosh server configuration elements:

- Log in to the connector post office (Maildata volume).
- Log in to the Local Microsoft Mail (AppleTalk) server as Network Manager.

■ Install the Microsoft Exchange Connection Gateway.

■ Configure the Gateway with the Microsoft Mail client.

■ Install the Macintosh Directory Exchange Requestor (DER) (optional).

Follow these steps to log in to the connector post office:

1. Open the Chooser application from your Macintosh Apple menu.

2. Click the AppleShare icon in the Chooser. Then, select the AppleTalk Zone, if applicable, in which your Exchange server is located.

   The Exchange server should now be listed in the Select a File Server display window.

3. Click the server's name. Then click OK.

4. On the connect dialog box, make sure the Registered User radio button is selected. Enter the user Name and Password required to access this volume. Click OK.

5. After you are authenticated, a list of available Macintosh-Accessible Volumes displays in the Select the Items You Want to Use: window.

   The MAILDATA, or the customized name volume should appear on the list.

6. Select Maildata volume.

7. Select the check box to the right of the Maildata volume to have this volume automatically mounted every time the Macintosh server starts up.

   Select the Save My Name Only radio button to request your password when the volume attempts to mount at startup.

   Select Save My Name and Password to store your log-on data and then automatically authenticate your connection when the Macintosh starts up.

8. Click OK to mount the volume.

Installing the Microsoft Exchange Connection Gateway

The Exchange Connection Gateway is provided with your Microsoft Mail Connector software. Install it on your Macintosh Microsoft Mail server to allow it to connect to the Exchange connector post office.

The following section assumes you have Microsoft Mail for AppleTalk Networks installed and properly running on your Macintosh server.

The following steps guide you through installing the Connection Gateway on your Macintosh server.

1. Log on to your Microsoft Mail (AppleTalk) server as Network Manager.

2. Load the disk containing the Exchange Connection Installer. Open the installer application. The Connection Installer dialog box appears.

   If no previous gateways have been installed, the Gateways Installed on This Server: window appears blank.

3. Select Install Gateway from the Gateway menu.

4. Select the GW icon from the dialog box. Then, click Install. The dialog box appears.

5. Enter a unique Gateway ID. This identifier is used by the Microsoft Mail (AppleTalk) server to distinguish each gateway. By default, the ID for this gateway is NC.

6. Enter a Gateway name as it will be displayed in the gateway list. Click OK. The dialog box appears.

7. Select which gateway templates to install for this gateway. Choose only those that you can access through this gateway, for example, those you use in your Exchange organization. Click OK.

N O T E   A gateway template becomes available in your Microsoft Mail (AppleTalk) client to create custom recipients for other messaging systems. ▨

The Gateway is installed. Now, switch to your Microsoft Mail (AppleTalk) client, which should still be logged in as Network Manager.

Configuring the Exchange Connection

With the Microsoft Mail (AppleTalk) client, you now need to configure various gateway and post office connection options.

N O T E   You must be logged in as Network Manager to administer a Microsoft Mail (AppleTalk) server. ▨

Specify the post office location and general gateway configuration by following these steps:

1. Select Gateway. Then, select Configuration from the Mail menu.

   A dialog box prompts you to locate the Connection Store (MacGate) directory. Click OK.

2. Scroll through the MAILDATA volume and locate the MACGATE folder. Click Open.

3. Enter a Blocking Factor value. This value limits the number of messages that can be transferred with each gateway cycle.

4. Enter an Aging Factor value. This is the amount of time, in minutes, that a message can remain in the Microsoft Mail Connector post office before a notification message is sent to the Network Manager.

N O T E   Setting the Aging Factor to zero turns off notification. ▨

5. Set the Max Size value. Messages exceeding this size (including attachments) cannot pass through this gateway. By default, this size is 100 kilobytes.

6. Select a logging level for this gateway. Select one of the three radio buttons: Critical, Errors, or Details.

Part

III

Ch

20

Scheduling Gateway Connections

This screen is functionally similar to Exchange's schedule property pages. Use this dialog box to configure at what times during the day this gateway connects to the Microsoft Mail Connector post office. Your decision for the time of the day the gateway is to connect to the Microsoft Mail Connector post office should be based on factors particular to your situation. For most, bandwidth, server loads, and connection costs (for example, over leased lines, or ISDN) are the limiting factors in this decision. If bandwidth or line costs are not an issue in your case, set the connection times as frequently as you want.

To set connection times, follow these steps:

1. Select Gateway. Then, select Connect Times from the Mail menu. A schedule grid appears for you to set connection times.

2. Select the radio button that determines how frequently you want this gateway to initiate the connection.

   The Never button effectively deactivates the gateway.

   The Always button connects at the interval (in minutes) set at the bottom of this dialog box.

   The Times Selected in the Chart Below defines connection times by those that are highlighted in the time grid.

3. Select the Connect immediately when there is Outgoing Mail check box to initiate a gateway connection as soon as a message is sent to the gateway.

4. If you chose the Selected Times option, use the time grid to mark the specific time you want the gateway to connect and transfer messages.

Installing an Access Gateway

After you have installed and configured the Connection Gateway, you can install additional access gateways on your Microsoft Mail (AppleTalk) system. This enables other Macintosh Microsoft Mail servers to communicate with Exchange and all its gateways and connectors.

You install an Access Connection Gateway by following these two steps:

- Extract the Access gateway from the Exchange Connection gateway.
- Install the Access gateway on another Microsoft Mail (AppleTalk) server.

For step-by-step procedures for additional gateway installation, consult your gateway documentation.

From Here...

The information in this chapter bridged two distinct mail environments (Exchange and Microsoft Mail for AppleTalk) with some external tools. However, most likely this will be just the first step in a full migration of Macintosh users onto Exchange. It is important to understand that Exchange Server 5.0 has a Macintosh Client that loads directly onto the Macintosh. This client has a profile just like the 95 client and can access an Exchange 5.0 server. The Macintosh client has an Inbox that sends and receives mail. It can also read and update public Exchange Folders. This chapter assumes that you want to have Microsoft Mail for AppleTalk Coexisting with the Exchange 5.0 system.

- Chapter 7, "Planning Connections to Microsoft Mail Systems," gives you an idea of how to connect a Microsoft Mail System to Exchange 5.0.

- Chapter 18, "Using Directory Replication and Synchronization," discusses configuring directory synchronization between Microsoft Mail (AppleTalk) and the Exchange server.

- Chapter 19, "Using the Microsoft Mail Connector for PC Networks," gives you additional information on using the Microsoft Mail Connector.

- Chapter 29, "Installing and Configuring Outlook," gives you a better understanding of an Outlook installation for any PC's that may be in your environment.

- Chapter 31, "Using Advanced Outlook Features," provides additional information on client profiles and information services.

Part
III

Ch
20

Configuring X.400 Connections

The Microsoft Exchange X.400 Connector is used to create a message route between two Exchange servers or between one Exchange server and another messaging system that complies with the X.400 standard. An X.400 connector is flexible due to its variety of available transport protocols. An Exchange site can utilize several X.400 connectors over various transport stacks, simultaneously providing multiple message routes as well as load balancing. ■

Install an MTA Transport Stack that Corresponds to Your Current Network Environment

The X.400 can communicate over several network transport protocols including: TCP/IP, TPO/X.25, and TP4/CLNP.

How to Install a new X.400 Connector—Establish Messaging Links Between Exchange Sites or Between One Exchange Site and a Foreign X.400 System

Configure the MTA Transport Stack and set up an X.400 connector between sites.

Configure the various X.400 Property Pages for Property Operation

An X.400 system is a collection of components that work together to transfer messages. The property pages configure these components to make a message-handling environment out of two systems that pass messages back and forth.

Test an X.400 Connector to Verify Proper Message Transmission

There are many parts built into the X.400 system. To test this system, one must test all its capabilities. These capabilities include: MAPI-based system, Multipart forms, Rich text formatting and attachments.

X.400 Supported Transport Protocols

The X.400 Connector can communicate over several network transport protocols. Out of the box, Exchange supports the use of the X.400 Connector with the following transport stacks:

- **TCP/IP**—Transmission Control Protocol/Internet Protocol. Uses the Windows NT TCP/IP services to establish communication over TCP/IP networks.

- **TP0/X.25 with the Eicon port adapter**—Transport Protocol 0/X.25. Both dial-up and direct connection over X.25 networks using the Eicon software and hardware solution. You may use multiple X.25 port adapters on each server, and each must have its own MTA Transport Stack (and appropriate hardware).

- **TP4/CLNP**—Transport Class 4/Connectionless Network Protocol. Exchange includes a setup driver that enables it to work with the TP4 interface on Windows NT.

Before you can install a new X.400 connection, you must do the following:

- Make sure that the Exchange server has a necessary network transport protocol. For example, you must have the Windows NT TCP/IP protocols running and configured to successfully set up an X.400 connector with a TCP/IP Transport Stack.

- Configure and test all necessary networking hardware to confirm that a link exists. In the TCP/IP example, you can use the PING IP ADDRESS statement from the Windows NT command line to test this link.

- Know the exact X.400 address of the remote site or foreign system.

X.400 Connector Installation and Configuration

Whether installing an X.400 connection to another Microsoft Exchange server or foreign system, there are four primary steps to follow:

1. Install an appropriate MTA transport stack.
2. Install and configure a local X.400 connector.
3. Configure the X.400 connection on the remote Exchange site or foreign system.
4. Test the connection for message receipt and formatting consistency.

Installing an MTA Transport Stack

When you are certain that all applicable network software and hardware is installed on the Windows NT server that will be handling the connection, you are ready to proceed with installing an MTA Transport Stack. This section will first cover how to install the MTA Transport Stack and then how to configure the Property pages for each one.

The installation procedure is as follows:

1. From the Exchange administrator program File menu, select New Other, then select MTA Transport Stack. The New MTA Transport Stack dialog box appears (see Figure 21.1).

The Type section of the dialog box lists the available MTA Transport Stacks on this Exchange server.

FIG. 21.1

The New MTA Transport Stack is used by the X.400 Connector (and also the Dynamic RAS Connector) to select an underlying transport for message transfer.

NOTE The RAS MTA Transport Stack is not used for X.400 connections. ▓

The Server section of the dialog box lists all the servers in the current site.

2. Click MTA Transport Stack. Select the server in your local site that will handle that type of connection. The transport stack will be installed on that server.

3. Click OK to accept the transport stack and Exchange server settings. The Properties page for the appropriate transport stack appears.

NOTE If all the necessary hardware/software for the network transport is not installed, you will get an error message stating that the required components are not ready. The MTA Transport Stack cannot be installed until these conditions are met. ▓

Configuring MTA Transport Stack Property Pages

Each MTA Transport Stack has two corresponding Property pages: a General page that identifies specific local addressing data, and a Connections page that lists all the X.400 connectors using this transport stack for communication.

This section includes steps to set up a new TCP/IP transport stack. If you are not using TCP/IP as a network transport, then skip this section.

General Tab The General tab fulfills two functions for a new TCP/IP MTA Transport Stack. First, you can give it a name for display in the administrator program. Second, you can enter specific OSI address information if your network environment requires that you distinguish between applications that use the TCP/IP network transport. Follow these steps:

1. Select the General tab in the TCP/IP MTA Transport Stack Properties page (see Figure 21.2).

Part

III

Ch

21

FIG. 21.2

Set the name and local transport information in this Property page.

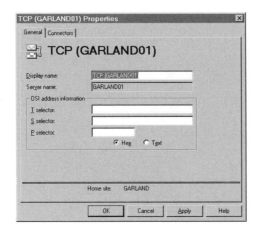

2. Enter a Name for this MTA Transport Stack as you want it to appear in the administrator program's display window. By default, this transport is named as TCP (server name). You can only change it when you are creating a new transport stack.

3. The Server Name box displays the Exchange server on which this MTA Transport Stack is installed. The server cannot be changed at this point. To use a different server, you must Cancel out of these Properties pages and install a new MTA Transport Stack.

4. Under OSI Address Information, enter numbers required to distinguish Exchange from other services or applications using the TCP/IP Transport Stack. There is one box for each of the following three network layers:

   T selector: Transport Service Access Point (TSAP)
   S selector: Session Service Access Point (SSAP)
   P selector: Presentation Service Access Point (PSAP)

5. Select either the Hex or Text radio button, depending on the type of data you enter in the preceding boxes.

6. Click Apply to set these properties and continue with other properties. If you are done with all the settings, click OK to return to the administrator program.

Connectors Tab   The Connectors Property page displays a list of every Microsoft Exchange X.400 connector that uses this TCP/IP MTA Transport Stack. You can open the Property pages for each listed X.400 connector from this page as well. Follow these steps:

1. Select the Connectors tab on the TCP/IP MTA Transport's Properties page (see Figure 21.3). All X.400 connectors using this MTA Transport Stack are listed in the Connectors That Use This Stack list box.

2. Select an X.400 connector name from the list (if any are available), and click Edit so that its Properties page appear.

3. Click Apply to set these properties and continue with other properties. If you are done with all the settings, click OK to return to the administrator program.

FIG. 21.3

A listing of X.400 connectors using this MTA Transport Stack (blank if no connectors are set up).

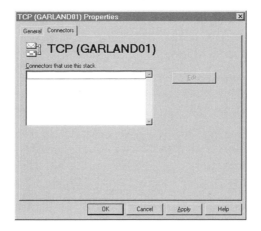

X.25 Transport Stack

This section includes steps to set up a new X.25 transport stack. If you are not using X.25 as a network transport, then skip this section. Follow these steps:

General Tab   The General tab fulfills two functions for a new X.25 MTA Transport Stack. First, you can give it a name for display in the administrator program. Second, you can enter specific OSI address information if your network environment requires that you distinguish between applications that use the X.25 network transport. Follow these steps:

1. Select the General tab in the X.25 MTA Transport Stack Properties page.

2. Enter a Name for this MTA Transport Stack as you want it to appear in the administrator program's display window. By default, this transport stack is named as Eicon X.25 (server name). This name can only be changed when creating a new transport stack.

3. Enter the Call User Data as provided by your X.25 network provider. This can be up to 256 characters.

4. Enter the local X.121 Address as specified in the X.25 network set up under Windows NT.

5. Under OSI Address Information, enter numbers required to distinguish Exchange from other services or applications using the X.25 Transport Stack. There is one box for each of the following three network layers:

   T selector: Transport Service Access Point (TSAP)

   S selector: Session Service Access Point (SSAP)

   P selector: Presentation Service Access Point (PSAP)

6. Select either the Hex or Text radio button, depending on the type of data you enter in the preceding boxes.

7. Select the radio button that corresponds to your type of X.25 connection—Async Phone Line (Dial-up X.25) or Leased Line.

Part

III

Ch

21

8. If you select Leased Line, enter the I/O port on which your Eicon adapter is installed.

9. Click Apply to set these properties and continue with other properties. If you are done with all the settings, click OK to return to the administrator program.

Connectors Tab   The Connectors Properties page displays a list of every Microsoft Exchange X.400 Connector that uses this X.25 MTA Transport Stack. You can open the Properties page for each listed X.400 connector from this page as well.

Use this Properties page to view which Microsoft Exchange X.400 connectors use this X.25 MTA Transport Stack. Follow these steps to view the list of connectors and open the Properties page for connectors on the list:

1. Select the Connectors tab on the X.25 MTA Transport's Properties page. All X.400 connectors using this MTA Transport Stack are listed in the Connectors That Use This Stack list box.

2. Select an X.400 connector name from the list (if any are available), and click Edit so that its Properties page appear.

3. Click Apply to set these properties and continue with other properties. If you are done with all the settings, click OK to return to the administrator program.

TP4 Transport Stack

This section includes steps to set up a new TP4 transport stack. If you are not using TP4 as a network transport, then skip this section.

General Tab   The General tab fulfills two functions for a new TP4 MTA Transport Stack. First, you can give it a name for display in the administrator program. Second, you can enter specific OSI address information if your network environment requires that you distinguish between applications that use the TP4 network transport. Follow these steps:

1. Select the General tab in the TP4 MTA Transport Stack Properties page.

2. Enter a Name for this MTA Transport Stack as you want it to appear in the administrator program's display window. By default, this transport stack is named as TP4 (server name). You can only change this name when you are creating a new transport stack.

3. Under OSI Address Information, enter numbers required to distinguish Exchange from other services or applications using the TP4 Transport Stack. There is one box for each of the following three network layers:

   T selector: Transport Service Access Point (TSAP)
   S selector: Session Service Access Point (SSAP)
   P selector: Presentation Service Access Point (PSAP)

4. Select either the Hex or Text radio button, depending on the type of data you enter in the preceding boxes.

5. Click Apply to set these properties and continue with other properties. If you are done with all the settings, click OK to return to the administrator program.

Connectors Tab The Connectors Properties page displays a list of every Microsoft Exchange X.400 connector that uses this TP4 MTA Transport Stack. You can open the Properties page for each listed X.400 connector from this page as well. Follow these steps:

1. Select the Connectors tab on the TP4 MTA Transport's Properties page. All X.400 connectors using this MTA Transport Stack are listed in the Connectors That Use This Stack list box.

2. Select an X.400 connector name from the list (if any are available), and click Edit so that its Properties page appears.

3. Click Apply to set these properties and continue with other properties. If you are done with all the settings, click OK to return to the administrator program.

Installing and Configuring an X.400 Connector

When you have properly installed all the needed MTA Transport Stacks, you can create the actual X.400 connector that will transfer messages over that transport. You must have the following information in order to proceed in setting up a new X.400 connector:

■ **A unique name for this connector**

For identification in the Exchange administrator program.

■ **Remote MTA name**

String identifying the Message Transfer Agent on the remote Exchange site or foreign system.

■ **Remote MTA password**

String used to authenticate an X.400 messaging link (only needed if the remote MTA requires password authentication).

■ **Stack address**

The unique identifying address for the local X.400 connector.

■ **Address space**

Any address entry that will uniquely identify a message's route through this X.400 connector to a remote site or foreign system.

N O T E For an X.400 connection to be established, a connector must be set up on both sides of the link. For a Microsoft Exchange server, this means setting up a corresponding Exchange X.400 connector. For a foreign X.400 system, this involves using that system's administrative tools and entering appropriate addressing data for the Exchange server. (See guidelines near the end of this chapter.) ■

Part
III

Ch
21

Creating a New X.400 Connector

From the administrator program File menu, select New Other, X.400 Connector. The New X.400 Connector dialog box is displayed (see Figure 21.4).

FIG. 21.4

Select an MTA Transport Stack for this X.400 connector.

The New X.400 Connector Type dialog box lists all the currently installed MTA Transport Stacks. Select one from the list and click OK. The X.400 property sheets open.

N O T E   If you have not yet configured an MTA Transport Stack, you cannot continue from this point. Follow the instructions in the previous section to set up the underlying transport stack. ▦

Configuring an X.400 Connector

The X.400 Connector property pages allow you to configure any X.400 connection, whether it is between two Exchange sites, or to a foreign X.400 system. The following is an overview of the X.400 property pages and the functions of each:

- **General**

  Sets connector names, transport stack, and general X.400 message preferences.

- **Schedule**

  Sets times when a local MTA will initiate communication with the remote site.

- **Stack**

  Sets connection parameters for establishing a link to the remote Exchange server or foreign system. A different Stack page will be displayed, depending on which transport was selected for this X.400 connector.

- **Override**

  Changes the default MTA attributes for messages routed through a specific X.400 connector.

- **Connected sites**

  Lists sites directly and indirectly connected to Exchange. Can also be used to set up indirect connection to sites.

- **Address space**

  Enters enough information to specify a message route through this connector.

- **Delivery restrictions**

  Defines specific senders who will be allowed or denied permission to transmit messages through this connector.

- **Advanced**

  Sets detailed X.400 communications specifications for this connector.

General Tab Use the X.400 General tab to set the principal communication options for a new connector. The following steps guide you through configuring the X.400 connector General tab:

1. Select the General tab of the X.400 Connector Properties page (see Figure 21.5).

FIG. 21.5

Select an MTA Transport Stack for this X.400 connector.

2. Enter a Display Name for this connector as you want it to appear in the Exchange administrator display window.

3. Enter a Directory Name used for addressing purposes.

4. Enter the Remote MTA Name in the box provided.

5. If required, enter a Remote MTA Password for the preceding remote MTA.

6. MTA Transport Stack displays the currently selected transport for this X.400 connector. You can change the MTA Transport Stack with the drop-down list box.

7. Under Message Text Word-Wrap you can force a carriage return in all the outgoing messages by clicking the At Column button and entering the column number. By default, this is set to Never.

8. If your X.400 connection is to a foreign messaging system that does not support MAPI, clear the Remote Clients Support MAPI checkbox. All rich-text and other MAPI characteristics are removed from outgoing messages.

9. Enter any additional Administrative Note.

Schedule Tab Use the Schedule Properties page to control how often the X.400 Connector becomes active and initiates a connection. Follow these steps:

1. Select the Schedule tab in the X.400 Connector Properties Page (see Figure 21.6).

2. Select one of the four radio buttons that determine when this X.400 Connector connects.

Part
III

Ch
21

FIG. 21.6

Set connection times for this connector.

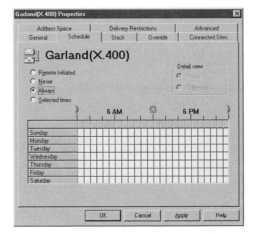

Remote Initiated—Send messages only when the remote MTA connects to this MTA. Both MTAs must have the two-way alternate option selected in the Advanced Properties page.

CAUTION

Only one MTA can be configured to be remote-initiated. Otherwise, if both MTAs are waiting for the other to initiate the connection, the messages will never be delivered.

Never—A connection is never established. This option effectively disables this X.400 Connector.

Always—An MTA connection is established whenever messages need to be transferred. By default, this option is selected.

Selected Times—The X.400 Connector initiates communication based on the time grid on this Properties page.

3. If you choose Selected Times, the Detail View radio buttons become available. Select either the 1 Hour or 15 Minute detail view and the time grid will change its scale accordingly.

4. If you choose Selected Times, pick the time blocks for connection.

5. Click Apply to set these properties and continue with other properties. If you are done with all the settings, click OK to return to the administrator program.

Stack Tab   Each MTA Transport Stack has a different Stack page, primarily because each transport uses different addressing conventions. This section first covers the top section of the Stack Properties page which is unique to each transport. The second part of the page covers entering OSI information to identify a particular X.400 connector with the transport stack. The

OSI information is common to all Stack Properties pages and is covered only once following the address information section.

The X.400 Stack Properties Page   Follow these steps:

1. Select the Stack tab in the X.400 Connector Properties page (see Figure 21.7).

FIG. 21.7

Enter the TCP/IP addressing data for the remote MTA.

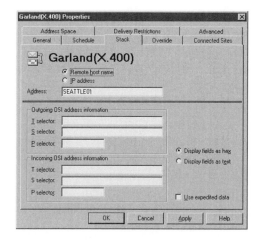

2. Select the appropriate radio button for the remote site's address. Use Remote Host Name if the remote server can be identified either through the Domain Name Service (DNS) or the Windows Internet Naming Service (WINS). Use IP Address if a host name is not available.

TIP Using an IP address will make for a slightly faster connection time to the remote system. However, using the IP address numbers may be too cryptic for administration purposes (that is, more difficult to remember and identify at first glance).

3. Enter the host name or IP address in the Address box.

4. Proceed to the "Outgoing and Incoming OSI Information" section later in this chapter.

X.25 Stack Properties Page   Follow these steps:

1. Select the Stack tab in the X.400 Connector Properties page. The X.25 Transport version of the Stack Properties page appears.

2. Enter your Call User Data as given by your X.25 provider.

3. Enter Facilities Data as specified by your X.25 provider. This contains a comma-delimited list of additional connection parameters.

4. Enter the X.121 Address of the remote server. This information can be obtained from the remote server's X.25 transport information.

5. Proceed to the "Outgoing and Incoming OSI Information" section later in this chapter.

Part
III

Ch
21

TP4 Stack Properties Page   Follow these steps:

1. Select the Stack tab in the X.400 Connector Properties page. The TP4 Transport version of the Stack Properties page appears.

2. Enter the network service access point (NSAP) or the address of the remote X.40 system.

3. Proceed to the "Outgoing and Incoming OSI Information" section that follows.

Outgoing and Incoming OSI Information   The Outgoing and Incoming OSI information combo box in the Stack Properties page, shown in Figure 21.7, is the same for all transports that were previously covered. The following steps will cover how to configure the various outgoing and incoming information:

1. Under Outgoing OSI Address Information and Incoming OSI Address Information, enter numbers required to distinguish this X.400 connector from other services or applications using this transport stack. There is one box for each of the following three network layers:

   T selector: Transport Service Access Point (TSAP)
   S selector: Session Service Access Point (SSAP)
   P selector: Presentation Service Access Point (PSAP)

2. Select either the Display Fields as Hex or Display Fields as Text radio button depending on the type of data you enter in the preceding boxes.

3. Select the Use Expedited Data checkbox if your network recognizes data packets identified for accelerated transfer. Some networks require the use of expedited data. Refer to your transport and network documentation for more information.

4. Click Apply to set these properties and continue with other properties. If you are done with all the settings, click OK to return to the administrator program.

Override Tab   With the Override Properties page, shown in Figure 21.8, you can set the connector-specific MTA. These settings only affect MTA links established through this X.400 connector.

Enter a different Local MTA Name if the foreign X.400 system cannot accept the Microsoft Exchange server name. Sometimes the server name may be too long or contain characters (for example, spaces) that a foreign X.400 MTA cannot accept.

Enter the Local MTA Password to require authentication when establishing communication from a remote system.

Enter specific MTA configuration variables. The following table lists each variable and its function within the MTA (see Table 21.1).

FIG. 21.8

Enter MTA override settings for this connector.

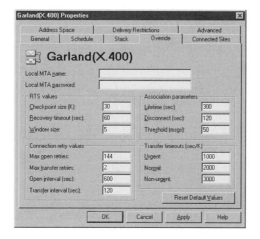

Table 21.1 MTA Variables and Functions

Variable	Function
RTS Values	
Checkpoint size (K):	The value used to verify packet transmission with returned checkpoints. By default, this is 30K.
Recovery timeout (sec):	The time delay before retrying a broken transmission. By default, the delay is 60 seconds.
Window size:	The maximum number of checkpoints that can be transmitted without acknowledgment. By default, this value is 5K.
Connection Retry Values	
Max open retries:	The maximum number of consecutive failed attempts before the MTA stops trying to open a communication channel with a remote MTA. By default, an MTA makes 144 attempts.
Max transfer retries:	The maximum number of consecutive failed attempts before the MTA stops trying to transfer a message packet. By default, the MTA makes two attempts.
Open interval (sec):	The delay (in seconds) between attempts to open a communication channel. By default, this delay is 600 seconds.
Transfer interval (sec):	The delay (in seconds) between attempts to retransmit a failed message packet. By default, this delay is 120 seconds.
Association Parameters	
Lifetime (sec):	The maximum time that an idle connection between MTAs remains open. By default, an idle link is held open for 300 seconds after the last communication.

Part

III

Ch

21

continues

Table 21.1 Continued

Variable	Function
Association Parameters	
Disconnect (sec):	The maximum time allowed when establishing or terminating a connection before the session is ended independently. By default, this is 120 seconds.
Threshold (msgs):	The number of messages that must be queued at this MTA for it to initiate a link to a remote MTA. By default, 50 messages must be awaiting transmission.
Transfer Timeouts (sec/K)	
Urgent:	The delay (in seconds per kilobyte of total message size) between retries of urgent messages. By default, this delay is 1,000 seconds. This is the time-out value before messages are sent. An Urgent message is set by the user when composing a message.
Normal:	The delay (in seconds per kilobyte of total message size) between retries of normal messages. By default, this delay is 2,000 seconds. The trend here is the less important the message, the longer the wait in sending the message again.
Non-urgent:	The delay (in seconds per kilobyte of total message size) between retries of non-urgent messages. By default, this delay is 3,000 seconds.

N O T E If you combine the default 144 Max open retries with the default 600 second Open interval, it adds up to a total of 24 hours before a message is returned as undeliverable. ▣

Each item has a box to its right with a default numeric value. Replace any value with a number that will be used when establishing a connection through this X.400 connector. To return to the default Message Transfer Agent settings, click Reset Default Values.

Connected Sites Tab   This Properties page lists other Microsoft Exchange sites that are available via this X.400 connector. This includes sites that are indirectly linked through this connector.

Here is an example of when to use this feature. Exchange site Seattle is linked to site Frankfort via a public X.400 network. Seattle, in turn, is linked to Garland through a high bandwidth line using a site connector.

When data replication between sites occurs, information about indirectly connected sites appears in the Connected Sites window.

In this case, the indirectly connected sites are Garland and Los Angeles. A message sent from Frankfort to Los Angeles is sent to the first site it is connected to and then forwarded to the next site, and so on, until Los Angeles is reached (see Figure 21.9).

FIG. 21.9

Indirect link sites: The mail will appear in Los Angeles after it hops through Seattle and Garland.

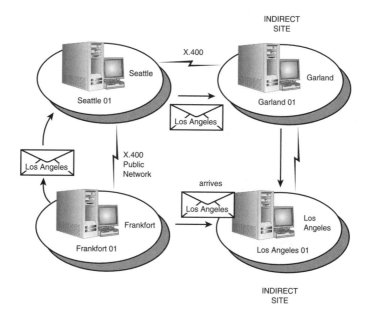

Manually Modifying Indirectly Connected Sites

You may also manually insert an address entry for an indirectly connected site. This is done from the Connected Sites Properties page as well. This page may also be used to modify an existing route.

N O T E If you are using an X.400 connector to link to a foreign X.400 system, you can skip this section.

The following steps are used to add or modify connected site entries:

1. To create a new entry, click the New button on the Connected Sites Properties page. To change an existing entry, select it from the list and click Edit on the Connected Sites Properties page. The General page appears first. Click the Routing Address Properties page.

2. Enter the Organization name in which the remote Exchange server exists. By default, your current organization is displayed.

3. Enter the name of the Microsoft Exchange Site in which the remote server exists. By default, this entry is left blank.

The following steps are to specify a routing address for an indirectly connected site.

1. Click the Routing Address tab (see Figure 21.10).

FIG. 21.10
Manually enter
connected site
information.

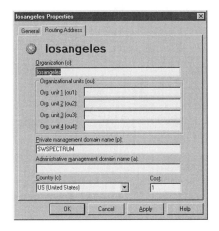

2. By default, the Organization name displayed is the site name you entered in the preceding General Properties page.

3. Enter X.400 routing information needed to connect to the remote server. The following is a list and description of the routing information required:

- Organizational Units   Identify the Exchange servers via their valid X.400 names.

- Private Management   Enter the PRMD of the remote Domain Name (PMDN) server.

- Administrative   Enter the PRMD of the remote Management Name (ARMD) Domain server.

- Country   An X.400 value that identifies the country of the server.

- Cost   Standard Microsoft Exchange routing cost value. By default, this cost is 1.

To delete a connected site entry, select the site address entry from the Connected Sites Properties page and click Remove. That remote site will no longer be available through this X.400 connector.

Address Space Tab   This Properties page defines the messages that are routed through this connector. Only enough addressing data is provided to distinguish messages that should be sent through this connector. Routing costs are also entered along with each address space entry.

Delivery Restrictions Tab   This Properties page filters the individuals that can or cannot send messages through this connector. There are two easy-to-understand delivery options (see Figure 21.11):

■ Accept Messages From: Creates an exclusive list of recipients with permission to send messages through this X.400 connector.

■ Reject Messages From: Lists specific recipients that are denied permission to send messages through this X.400 connector.

FIG. 21.11

Enter a routing address for the indirectly connected site.

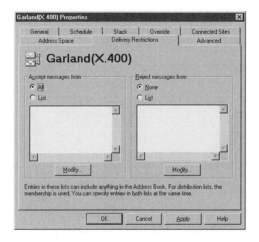

The following steps show how to set up the different delivery options:

1. Select the Delivery Restrictions tab in the X.400 Connector Properties page.

2. Click the List radio button under either Accept Messages From or Reject Messages From.

3. Click the Modify button underneath each list so that the Microsoft Exchange address list appears. Select the desired recipients to include or exclude from X.400 message transfer through this connector.

4. Click Apply to set these properties and continue with other properties. If you are done with all the settings, click OK to return to the administrator program.

Advanced Tab   The Advanced tab is where you can control some of the finer points of X.400 connectivity with Exchange Server. You will define which X.400 standard to utilize, and how various elements of the messages are transferred through the system. Follow these steps:

1. Select the Advanced tab from the X.400 Properties page (see Figure 21.12).

2. Under MTA Conformance, select the radio button pertaining to the correct X.400 standard you will be using. Exchange supports all the latest X.400 standards, but you must select the setting that conforms to what your provider uses. These are your three options:

1984
1988 X.410 mode
1988 normal mode

> **CAUTION**
>
> To avoid message transmission errors, be sure to select the standard supported by your X.400 carrier and the remote X.400 system.

FIG. 21.12

Delivery restrictions limit who can access this X.400 connector.

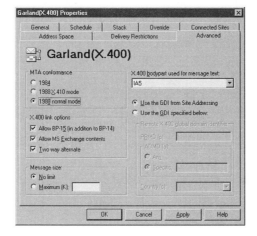

3. Under X.400 Link Options select all the checkboxes pertaining to features you want in this link.

   Allow BP-15 (in addition to BP-14) is only available if 1988 MTA conformance is selected. Use the BP-15 extension standard for message attachments.

   Allow MS Exchange Contents should be used only when the remote system is a Microsoft Exchange server. It permits the transmission of MAPI message properties as an object of the X.400 message using the Message Database Encoding Format (MDBEF).

   Two-Way Alternate permits both to take turns sending and receiving message data. Use when the remote MTA supports this functionality.

4. Under Message Size, click Maximum (K) and enter a value (in kilobytes) if you want to set a maximum for message transmission. By default, No Limit is selected and messages of any size can pass through this connector.

5. Under X.400 Bodypart Used for Message Text, use the drop-down list box to select the body part type used for the content of an outbound message. It must be supported by the foreign system. These settings do not affect inbound messages.

6. Select the Use the GDI from Site Addressing radio button to use the Global Domain Identifier from the Site Addressing page to prevent message transfer loops.

7. Select Use the GDI Specified Below radio button and enter the foreign system's GDI in the space provided. Obtain this information from the foreign system's configuration settings.

8. Click Apply to set these properties and continue with other properties. If you are done with all the settings, click OK to return to the administrator program.

Configuring a Foreign X.400 System

The specifics to configuring a foreign X.400 system vary from system to system. The following are general guidelines to follow when setting up a foreign X.400 system to communicate with a Microsoft Exchange server X.400 connector:

■ Microsoft Exchange server supports a wide variety of X.400 content and body part types. It is a good idea to attempt to match X.400 capabilities exactly with a foreign system's settings whenever possible.

■ If the local Microsoft Exchange X.400 connector is configured first, use the settings in the administrator program X.400 Properties page to retrieve settings for the foreign system.

■ If the foreign system is configured first, obtain all the necessary settings for the local Exchange server.

Verifying Connections

When both ends of an X.400 link are configured, you must proceed to test the connection. Because X.400 performs message format conversions during transmission, you must not only make sure that a message is properly received, but that its contents are correctly formatted.

Messages sent to a remote Exchange site via an X.400 connector should be received in the exact same format as they were transmitted. This includes the transmission of all the attachments as well. All MAPI information should be preserved in the conversion and transmission process.

Here is a sequence you can use to test your X.400 link between sites:

1. Create and send a message to a remote site using the Exchange client. Include the following in the message:

Rich text formatting (various colors, font sizes, and so on)

An attached file (of any sort)

An embedded OLE object (word processing document, spreadsheet, and so on)

2. Verify that the intended recipient receives the message in his or her inbox.

3. Check the message contents (including attachments and embedded objects) for data integrity.

4. Repeat the preceding steps by sending a message from the remote site to the local site.

Part
III

Ch
21

When testing message transmissions to foreign X.400 systems, here are some important test steps to follow:

1. Create a message as previously described, with rich text formatting and attachments.

2. Verify that the message is delivered to the intended recipient.

3. Check the message for data integrity. A foreign system with a MAPI-based client should preserve all rich text formatting and attachments. A foreign system with a non-MAPI-based client should receive the message in plain text. Any attachments should be preserved and there should be an additional attachment that contains all the information this client cannot display.

4. Create and send a message from within the foreign system's X.400 client, addressed to a local Microsoft Exchange mailbox.

5. Verify that the local user receives all messaging data (including attachments).

From Here...

In this chapter, you covered the following elements:

- Installing and configuring an X.400 MTA Transport Stack

- Installing and configuring an X.400 connector, using each type of MTA Transport Stack

- Guidelines for configuring a foreign X.400 system to communicate with a Microsoft Exchange server

- Testing X.400 links between Exchange servers and between an Exchange server and a foreign X.400 system for message data integrity

The following chapters provide more information on several of the items discussed in this chapter:

- Chapter 14, "Message Transfer Configuration," explains about setting general Message Transfer Agent options that affect message transmission over an X.400 Connector.

- Chapter 18, "Using Directory Replication and Synchronization," shows you how to set up directory replication between Exchange sites after they have a suitable messaging link system.

CHAPTER 22

Setting Up SMTP Connections

Today, the latest craze is the Internet. Exchange provides Internet electronic mail through the use of a robust Simple Mail Transfer Protocol (SMTP) connector service. The Internet Mail Service(IMS) Wizard is a new feature to Exchange 5.0 that automates the Internet Mail Service (IMS) configuration and enables Exchange clients to send and receive messages to and from people across the Internet. Clients do not need to be directly connected to the Internet to use this functionality.

This IMS is one of the core components of the Exchange server: It integrates directly with the rest of the mail services. You can configure the IMS as a stand-alone solution or use it as the backbone connectivity protocol. ■

Learning the Exchange Internet Mail Service Wizard

In the previous version, setting up Exchange for Internet messaging was a little complicated. Now, Exchange 5.0 uses a Wizard that guides you and makes the installation process painless.

Managing Simple Mail Transfer Protocol (SMTP) Messages

Once IMS is configured, you can track messages or even fine tune the logging level to solve difficult problems.

Configuring Advanced Options for the Internet Mail Service Connector

You can configure IMS to set transfer modes, connection limitations, and retry intervals, as well as several other IMS controls.

Learning the Internet Mail Service (IMS) Wizard

The Internet Mail Service Wizard helps you to navigate graphically through the configuration of the Internet Mail Service (IMS) that relies on industry standards to enable seamless integration with Exchange and existing SMTP mail systems. The IMS provides message transferring with any other system that uses the SMTP protocol. When you first start the Internet Mail Wizard (IMS) you must have Domain Name Service (DNS) already on your computer. The components of DNS are Hostname, Domain Name, Domain Name Computer's IP Address. It is also good to put the domain name (for example, swspectrum.com) into the domain suffix search order. When this is complete and you have rebooted the computer, you then must configure the A record and the MX record in the DNS Manager. The A record stands for Authority Record—this is an IP starting point of navigation through the vast Internet pathways. The MX record is a pointer to your exchange server so that you can be found by your ISP for mail delivery from the Internet. You can obtain the exact configurations for these components from your ISP. Once the above things mentioned are working correctly you can then continue with the installation of the IMS through the Internet Mail Wizard.

N O T E   If you have two WINS servers in your environment, set each of the WINS servers to point to
their own IP Address, for the primary as well as the secondary addresses. The reason this is
done as if one WINS server is faster than the other WINS server on your network it will try to register
itself with the faster WINS server, which causes an endless loop to occur that in turn could cause other
unknown problems.

Learning the Internet Mail Service (IMS)

The IMS is very versatile because it relies on industry standards to allow seamless integration with Exchange and existing SMTP mail systems. The IMS provides message transferring with any other system that uses the SMTP protocol.

Internet Standards on the IMS

The IMS is a new feature in 5.0 that enhances the Exchange architecture. Users from single or multiple Exchange or MS-Mail 3.x sites can communicate with the Internet via the IMS.

N O T E   Client workstations do not need to have an Internet connection to use the IMS.

The functionality provided with the IMS complies with Internet standards. The IMS relies on a set of standards that have been ratified over the past 30 years. These standards are a set of published documents known as Requests for Comment (RFCs). These are the guidebooks for developing applications to be used on the Internet. Following is a list of the key standards to which the Internet Mail IMS adheres:

  - *RFC 821.* This RFC is the Simple Mail Transfer Protocol (SMTP) standard. RFC 821 describes the message definitions for passing or transferring mail from one computer system to another.

- *RFC 822.* This RFC, which is the continuation of RFC 821, describes the message format and structure of the data in the message. The standard covers the header information (To, From, Subject, and message body data). This RFC deals with non-text attachments by decoding the data with uuencode and uudecode encoding. If you have an attachment, the IMS converts the attachment to text and populates the body of the message with the encoded data.

- *RFC 1521.* This RFC, which defines the standard for sending attachments over the SMTP protocol, is called Multipurpose Internet Mail Extensions (MIME). This RFC breaks down the components of a message and allows different portions to be sent in separate fields. With MIME, you can attach a variety of data types (such as Microsoft Word documents, video clips, and audio files) and transmit the data without conversion. This provides ease of use for sending data between sites.

- *RFC 1554.* This RFC defines the protocol used by the legacy Microsoft SMTP gateway for MS Mail 3.x. RFC 1554 defines the message format that is created when a message is transferred through the MS SMTP gateway. This RFC is similar to RFC 822, which provides for encoding attachments into the body of the message as text.

These RFCs allow for seamless integration with other SMTP mail systems across public and private Internet networks.

IMS Uses

Exchange supports a variety of connection methods, using IMS as the message connector. The following are different ways to use IMS in a production environment:

- SMTP gateway to an MS Mail Network of post offices (see Figure 22.1).

FIG. 22.1
MS Mail users can leverage the gateway in Exchange to provide Internet connectivity.

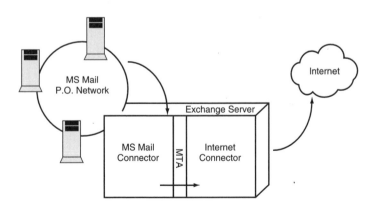

As described in Chapter 19, "Using the Microsoft Mail Connector for PC Networks," MS Mail 3.x users can send and receive Internet messages through the MS Mail Connector on Exchange. In this example, Exchange acts as an Internet SMTP gateway. Exchange converts the messages to MS Mail 3.x format, using the MS Mail Connector interchange, and then transfers the messages to the MS Mail 3.x post offices with the MS Exchange MTA services.

■ SMTP connector to an Exchange Network of post offices (see Figure 22.2). This example is similar to MS Mail 3.*x* use of the IMS , providing SMTP connectivity from the native mail-system client to the remote SMTP mail-system recipient. This functionality is seamless to users. The advantage of having all Exchange clients using the IMS is the fact that this architecture reduces the need for data-format conversions. At the same time that the IMS services Exchange clients, it can service existing MS Mail clients. This example extends the preceding example by providing additional support for Exchange clients.

FIG. 22.2

The IMS integrates directly with the Exchange server.

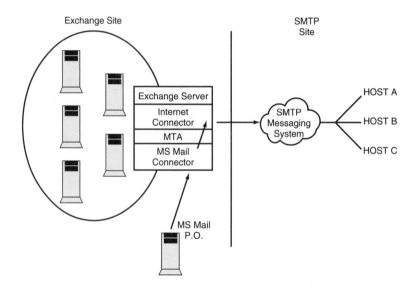

FIG. 22.3

The IMS can be used to link multiple Exchange sites.

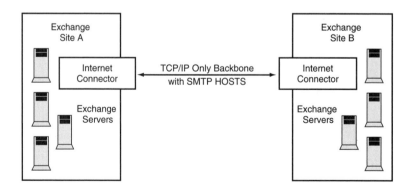

■ Using the IMS to link Exchange sites (backbone) (see Figure 22.3)   In this example, the IMS is used to link two Exchange sites. SMTP messaging is the backbone between the sites. Both Exchange sites need to be running the IMS locally. The IMS then communicates with the destination IMS.

This is especially useful in organizations where IMS is geographically distributed. Each location can maintain its own Exchange messaging services and still provide connectivity with the other sites. Using the IMS to backbone sites puts additional overhead on the IMS, which now is handling directory synchronization, folder replication, and message transfer through a single link.

Using the IMS in this manner preserves the Exchange functionality of rich text-formatted messages, OLE objects, and public folder postings. This solution is a manageable solution for linking Exchange sites.

■ Exchange server connecting to MS Mail 3.x with the IMS (see Figure 22.4). This example follows the backbone model. Instead of connecting with another Exchange site, however, the IMS is used to create a backbone with an MS Mail site. The MS Mail site will be using the Microsoft SMTP gateway.

FIG. 22.4

The IMS can be used to enable MS Mail 3.*x* to communicate with Exchange sites.

This solution permits immediate transmission of messages between Exchange and MS Mail sites. You do not have to configure the MS Mail Connector interchange, configure MTA IMSs, or set up remote directory synchronization.

The MS Mail 3.x gateway product does not support many Exchange features, including OLE v2.0 objects, MIME attachments, directory synchronization through the MS Mail gateway, and multiple-host connections. The MS Mail gateway can communicate with only a single SMTP host, whereas the Exchange IMS can have unlimited SMTP-host connections.

■ Windows 95 client connecting to Exchange server over the Internet (see Figure 22.5). This example focuses on the client connection with Exchange. A Windows 95 client with Exchange client software installed can access the Internet through a local service provider. After getting connected to the Internet, the client can transmit and receive messages through an Exchange Internet Mail IMS.

FIG. 22.5
The IMS can send and receive messages to Windows 95 client workstations.

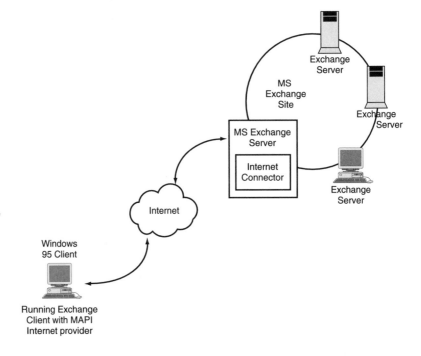

Understanding the Internet Mail IMS Components

The Internet Mail IMS has many new features that are not available in the MS Mail 3.x SMTP gateway. These new features offer a balance of power and flexibility to route messages over SMTP networks. As described in the preceding section, you can use the IMS's rich feature set in many ways.

After it is configured, the IMS transfers messages to remote SMTP mail systems by initiating a connection. When the connection is made, the messages are transferred across systems.

For incoming messages, the IMS listens to a TCP/IP port for connection requests. In similar fashion, once the remote system establishes its connection with IMS, messages and data are transferred into Exchange.

Inside the Exchange site, the IMS converts the message to an Exchange-format message and routes it to the Exchange recipient. The user will not notice any difference between an SMTP message and a normal Exchange message.

Setting Up Internet Mail IMS Components

Before you configure and run the Internet Mail IMS, you need to meet these requirements:

■ TCP/IP must be installed and properly configured on the Exchange Windows NT server that is running the IMS.

The server should have a static (nondynamic) Internet Protocol (IP) address. If you are using Dynamic Host Configuration Protocol (DHCP), you should exclude the IMS server's IP address from the pool of IP addresses used by DHCP. DHCP assigns IP addresses to TCP/IP clients automatically.

The reason for specifying a static IP address is that you are required to have a fully qualified Internet domain name. These values do not change dynamically with IP addresses; they are manually configured, and you would need to update them daily for the name to match the server's address.

■ In the TCP/IP section of the NT server configuration, you need to enable Domain Name Server (DNS) lookups. The DNS matches common domain names (such as yourcompany.com) into a specific numeric IP address.

You need to enter the host name and domain name of the IMS server (see Figure 22.6). In addition, you have to enter at least one value for the IP address of the DNS server. For more information on installing TCP/IP on an NT server, refer to your Windows NT user manual.

FIG. 22.6

These are the TCP/IP settings that enable DNS lookups on the Exchange server running the IMS.

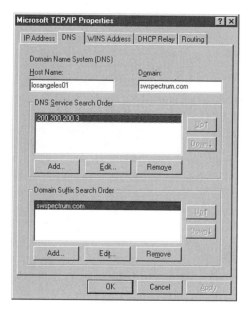

■ Add the IP address, host, domain, and Mail Exchange (MX) entries in the DNS server. Use the IP address and the host and domain information from the Windows NT TCP/IP configuration to enter into the DNS. Adding these values to the DNS allows for name resolution. The DNS provides the function of mapping a "friendly" name to an IP address. This way, when a user enters a friendly name, such as LosAngeles01. swspectrum.com, the DNS maps this name to its actual numeric IP address.

Figure 22.7 shows an entry for a server name and then an associated IP address. In addition to the host name and IP address, add an address space entry in the IMS configuration for Internet bound Exchange messages to pass through the IMS. This entry is called the Mail Exchange entry, or MX.

FIG. 22.7
The DNS entries for server LosAngeles01 in the domain swspectrum.com.

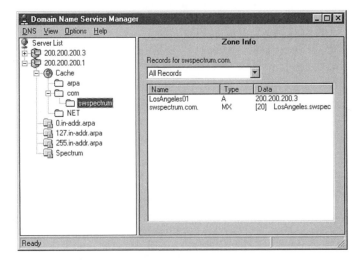

MX records associate SMTP mail messages with a routed destination host name and IP address. In Figure 22.7, you see an MX record for mail destined for msmail.swspectrum.com to be routed to server LosAngeles01.swspectrum.com. This way, when remote SMTP systems need to know where to send messages, they can look in the DNS records for the destination IP address of the mail messages. For more information on DNS entries and configuration, consult any related documentation for those products. There is also a wealth of information available on Internet Web sites and newsgroups to help you learn more.

Setting Up the IMS

After you meet the initial requirements for the IMS , you can begin to configure the IMS. Following is a list of procedures to use as you configure the IMS :

■ Define an administrative message account

■ Configure the address space serviced by the IMS

■ Specify the site address

■ Configure connection options

- Define message-content options
- Set interoperability options
- Set specific IMS message restrictions
- Management of SMTP messages
- Additional features of the IMS
- Test the IMS

You can configure all options from the Exchange Administrator program—select the Internet Mail IMS from the Connections section of the site hierarchy (see Figure 22.8).

FIG. 22.8

Selecting the IMS from the Exchange Administrator program.

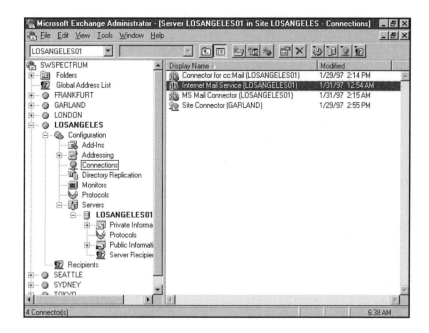

> **N O T E** The IMS is very complicated and has a multitude of options. Prepare yourself by setting aside a few solid hours to set up the IMS. ▪

Defining an Administrative Message Account

You must select an Exchange mailbox that will receive notification regarding the function of the IMS. This mailbox can be an administrator one or special account created for this purpose. Whichever option you choose, just make sure that the mailbox is checked periodically to catch important notification messages sent by the IMS.

1. Open the IMS property pages (see Figure 22.9) for the server that you want to configure.

2. Click the Change button to the right of the Administrator's Mailbox box. The dialog box shown in Figure 22.10 appears.

FIG. 22.9

A blank IMS tab.

FIG. 22.10

Select the administrator message account.

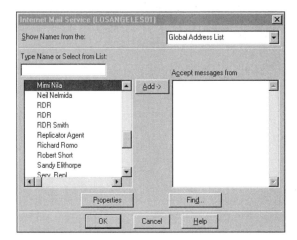

The administrator message account is used to send notices of events associated with the IMS and is similar to the postmaster account on the sendmail system for UNIX. This account is the default account for message errors, bounced mail, problems with the IMS, and other administrative notifications.

3. Define the notifications to be sent to the administrator message account (see Figure 22.11). From an administrative standpoint, selecting all the notifications is beneficial. If the volume of the notices is too excessive, change the administrator account to a public folder for the Exchange administrator group's use, or try to troubleshoot the cause for the notices before decreasing the notification settings.

FIG. 22.11
Define the notifications to be sent to the administrator message account.

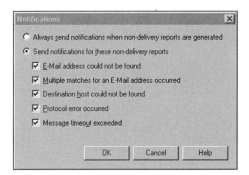

Configuring the Address Space Serviced by the IMS

The address space entries for the IMS define which message are routed through it. You must make at least one entry in this page to activate message routing through the IMS. The following steps guide you through creating and editing address space entries.

1. From the IMS property page, select the Address Space tab (see Figure 22.12).

FIG. 22.12
This Properties page displays Address Space entries for the IMS.

2. Click the New Internet address space button. The dialog box in Figure 22.13 appears.

   In the Address Space property page, you can enter multiple Internet domain names, MS Mail server names, X.400 names, or other IMS names to route messages through this IMS.

3. Click OK to set the configuration.

FIG. 22.13

Create a new Internet address space for the IMS.

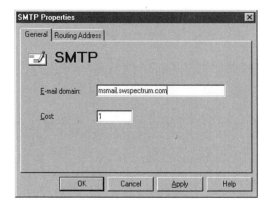

Specifying the Site Address

1. From the IMS property sheet, click Apply to set all the configuration settings. You see a reminder that you have to stop and restart the IMS.

2. Open the control panel services and locate the Exchange IMS (see Figure 22.14). If the IMS is already running, stop the service, then restart it for your new setting to take effect.

FIG. 22.14

NT service for the IMS.

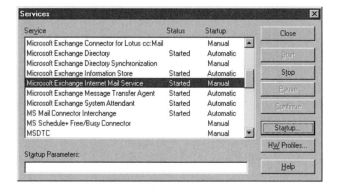

3. Select the "Site Addressing" icon in the Administrator program's display window and open its property pages.

4. Click the Site Addressing tab. The IMS dialog box appears (see Figure 22.15).

5. The addresses in the IMS dialog box are the global settings for all recipients at this particular site. Make sure that the recipient address for the IMS is the same as what is entered in the MX record of the DNS.

At this point, the IMS should be up and running. The IMS should be listening to port 25 of the TCP/IP protocol stack on the server—the port specified in RFC 822 for SMTP mail transferring. Now you can proceed to configure the additional options of the IMS.

FIG. 22.15

Global site-addressing properties.

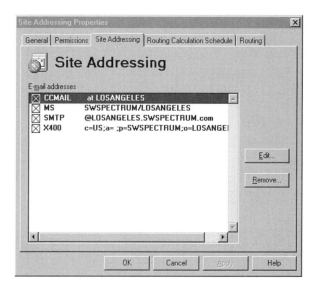

Configuring Connection Options

You can modify the settings for inbound and outbound transfer modes, connection limitations, delivery options, and message queues. Follow these steps:

1. From the IMS property pages, select the Connections tab (see Figure 22.16).

FIG. 22.16

Configure the IMS connections properties.

N O T E   The None option is a great tool to use in debugging the IMS. When this option is selected, you can keep the IMS running but restrict messages from being transferred from the site. Users will not notice any difference in their work, because messages will just queue up on the server until the transfer mode is reestablished. ■

2. In the Transfer Mode section, click a radio button to indicate whether messages will be incoming, outgoing, both, or neither.

3. Click the Advanced button to set the following options (see Figure 22.17):

   These options can be set based on the resources in your environment.

FIG. 22.17

Configure the advanced settings for the Transfer mode.

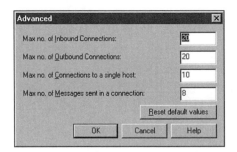

4. Configure the message delivery settings.

   The IMS allows you to use the DNS to resolve SMTP Mail message routes or use a single SMTP relay host. If you choose the DNS option, the IMS attempts to connect with the various destination SMTP mail systems directly. If you do not want to have Exchange perform the actual message transfer to the remote hosts for performance or security reasons, you can specify an SMTP relay host. Exchange is not a relay host. A relay host has the capability to receive SMTP mail, look at the header destination information, and then perform the message transfer to the remote host. Typically, the smart host functionality is run on a UNIX server. The process is known as sendmail. The DNS option removes the need to have a UNIX server running sendmail just to relay messages to remote hosts.

   An additional option is to configure the message-delivery options based on domain. Message delivery can be based on Domain Name Service (DNS) lookup. The IMS can perform a DNS request before forwarding messages to the appropriate destination. With the MS Mail 3.*x* SMTP gateway, you were forced to point the gateway to an existing SMTP relay host, which would actually deliver the mail to the final destination. The MS Mail 3.*x* SMTP gateway forced users to manage two servers to transfer Internet mail (see Figure 22.18).

   This is useful if it appears the IMS is having a difficult time transferring messages to a particular remote host. You can configure an individual entry for that specific domain causing message transfer problems. Entries can be in the form of domain, subdomains, and IP addresses. You can use wild cards as well.

FIG. 22.18

Configure the advanced settings for the SMTP message delivery.

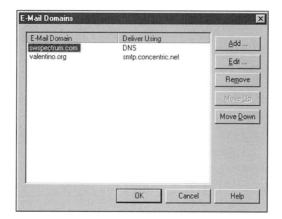

5. Define inbound connections.

You can configure the IMS to receive messages from all incoming hosts or reject remote hosts based on your input (see Figure 22.19).

FIG. 22.19

Configure the incoming connection to be accepted by the IMS.

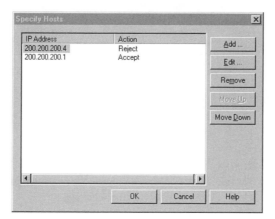

You can specify entries only in the form of IP addresses and subnet mask of the remote host to be rejected or accepted. This is useful when remote hosts are having a difficult time communicating with the IMS or when a particular remote host has a history of transferring junk messages or corrupt data.

N O T E Typically, as your users subscribe to Internet listserv mailing groups, a wide variety of mail systems will attempt to communicate and transfer mail into the system. Some of these remote systems do not adhere to the RFCs such as the IMS. This can cause communication problems between the systems. Suppose that I speak English and am from the West Coast, and that my business partner speaks English and is from the East Coast. Both of us speak English, but we may not always be able to communicate if our accents affect our speaking abilities. ■

6. Define the IMS message queue retry intervals.

   This option is used to define the retry attempt interval for the IMS, if it encounters a host to which it cannot transfer a mail message. The reason for the retry is that the remote host is too busy to process another communication request or is otherwise unavailable. The IMS queues up the message and waits until the retry interval expires before trying to transfer the message to the remote host. The default setting retries the first time in 60 minutes; the subsequent retries are made at 150 percent of the set time interval.

   If you use the default setting—the initial retry at 60 minutes—subsequent retries occur at 1 hour, 1.5 hours, 2.25 hours, 3.4 hours, 5 hours, 7.5 hours, and so on, for a total of 8 retries over 72 hours.

   Select the message time-outs button to configure more specific retry intervals (see Figure 22.20).

FIG. 22.20

Configure the message time-out settings to drop remote connections from the IMS.

Notice the granularity of the message queue retries. You can configure a specific retry interval based on the priority level of the mail message.

Make sure to apply your configuration changes before you move to another configuration tab. Remember that you have to stop and restart the IMS after you complete your configurations.

Defining Message Content Options

This section explains how to configure the default message content format, Exchange rich text formatting options, and message formats for individual domains.

To configure the options for inbound and outbound messages, follow these steps:

1. From the IMS property pages, select the Internet Mail tab.

2. The first option is to select the message content type for attachments. You have the option of configuring the IMS to send and receive messages via MIME or UUENCODE.

MIME provides support for a variety of file formats, which do not get broken up or encoded into the mail message as in uuencode. MIME support separates the attachments from the text portion of the message, retaining the original format.

3. Choose the MIME character set translation standard (see Figure 22.21). The default option is to use the ISO 8859-1 standard for MIME outbound mail messages.

FIG. 22.21

Configure the MIME Character Set Translation.

4. Use the pull-down menu to select the Non-MIME character set translation. The default option for uuencode messages is US ASCII for both inbound and outbound messages.

N O T E To send message content to the MS Mail 3.x SMTP gateway, make sure that you are using uuencode. The MS Mail 3.x SMTP gateway does not support MIME attachments. ▪

5. Click the E-mail Domain button. The E-mail Domains dialog box appears (see Figure 22.22). This dialog box enables you to configure specific character sets, message content formats, and maximum message size for messages transferred through the IMS.

6. Click Add to create additional e-mail domain entries, Edit to change an existing one, or Remove to delete one. When you are done with these settings, click OK to return to the Internet Mail property pages. Figure 22.23 shows the Edit E-mail Domain dialog box after you click the Add button.

FIG. 22.22

Use this dialog box to specify message content by e-mail domain.

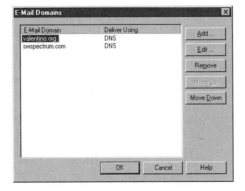

FIG. 22.23

Dialog box for creating a new e-mail domain configuration with message content options.

7. Click a site then click the server's icon for that site and select protocols. From the menu select properties and the MIME Types tab to define attachment formats.

   From this property page, you can configure the MIME types (see Figure 22.24). MIME types include support for Microsoft Word documents, video files, audio files, HTML documents, binary executables, and other format types.

8. Click the New button to create an additional MIME type. The New MIME Type dialog box appears.

   For the Microsoft Word Application, enter the MIME content type and the Associated extension in the dialog box (see Figure 22.25). The Microsoft Word MIME type is application/msword and the associated extension is .doc. When done, click OK to set the change and activate this new content type.

FIG. 22.24
Configure MIME
attachment formats.

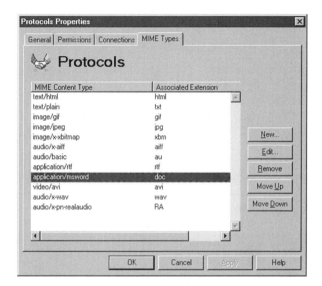

FIG. 22.25
Create a new MIME type
or edit an existing type.
You can configure for
document formats,
multimedia formats, or
even application binary
formats.

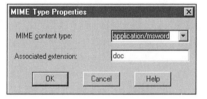

Setting Interoperability Options

Interoperability defines how display names are sent with outbound messages and how to set the maximum number of characters per line for outbound messages.

To set up the interoperability options for the IMS, follow these steps:

1. From the IMS property page, select the Internet Mail tab.

2. Click the Interoperability button in the Message Content information section of the Internet Mail tab. The Interoperability dialog box appears (see Figure 22.26).

   The IMS sends outbound messages with the display name of the sender/creator and the sender's alias. The display name typically is the sender's full name, first and last. If you have a user named Fred Rodriguez, for example, his alias might be fredro and his display name, Fred Rodriguez. Use the interoperability settings to maintain uniformity.

   You can set the following options to maintain interoperability: Message text word wrap, disable out of office response, disable automatic replies, and disable sending display names to the SMTP hosts.

FIG. 22.26
Define the inter-
operability options for
the IMS.

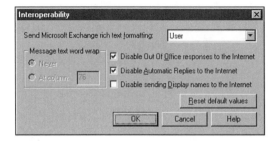

In the preceding example, you should check the box to make sure to send the display names in the outbound messages. In addition, you choose when to use MS Rich text formatting in messages (see Figure 22.27).

FIG. 22.27
Listed are the
options of when to
send RTF formatting
in outbound
messages.

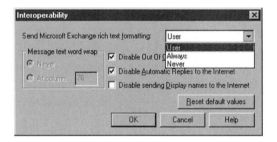

The options enable the user to select when they wish to send RTF data, always send RTF data, or never send RTF data. If this IMS only communicates with an MS Mail 3.x SMTP gateway, you should select the option to never send RTF data as the MS Mail SMTP gateway will not be able to understand this information.

3. Set the maximum number of characters per line. Also, if you choose the uuencode type in the Attachment section, the next window will give you the option to define the text word wrap. The default is set to 76 characters.

N O T E   The MS Mail 3.x SMTP gateway expects to see 76 characters in incoming messages.

4. Define the Message size limit.

5. Open the General tab (see Figure 22.28). This option enables you to configure message limitations for the IMS.

FIG. 22.28

The General tab enables you to set the maximum message size.

Defining IMS Message Restrictions

These settings deal with the actual message settings for the IMS.

1. From the IMS Properties sheet, select the Advanced tab (see Figure 22.29). From this tab menu, you can define the Message parameters, Maximum message transfer times (min), and the Message transfer quotas.

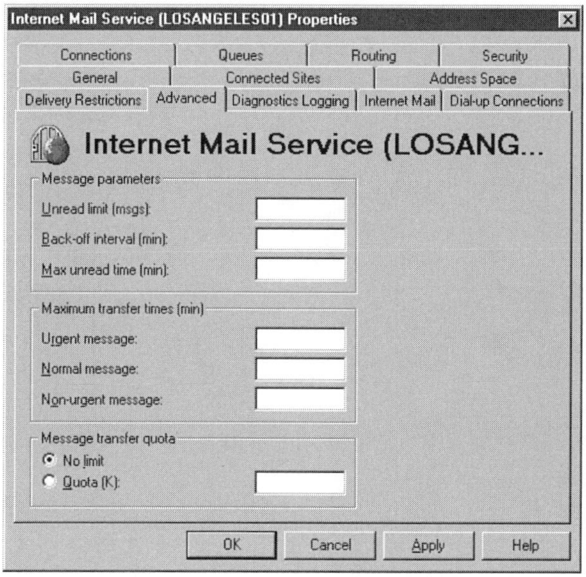

FIG. 22.29

The Advanced tab enables you to configure message transfer parameters.

Message parameters are used to limit the number of unread messages, to set the time to back off from message transfer, and to set a maximum unread message time. The values are set in the number of messages, and in the number of minutes.

The second portion of the Advanced tab menu defines the maximum transfer times broken down by urgent, normal, and non-urgent messages. These values are set in minutes and can be used to close connections that would otherwise be held open for long periods of time. This quota helps to reduce the amount of traffic to single hosts.

The last set of values is used to set upper limits for the size of messages transferred from the IMS to the remote hosts.

2. Click Apply when done modifying these entries to set your new values.

3. Next select the Delivery Restrictions tab menu (see Figure 22.30). Use this tab to restrict message delivery to certain users or to restrict those users from sending outbound SMTP mail through this IMS.

You have the option to either grant users access to the IMS or deny users access to the IMS. On the left panel you can manage the usage by adding users who can connect. On the right panel, you choose who cannot connect. Figure 22.31 shows the two windows of the IMS's Delivery Restrictions property page.

FIG. 22.30

Users can be granted access rights to use the IMS or restricted access to the IMS.

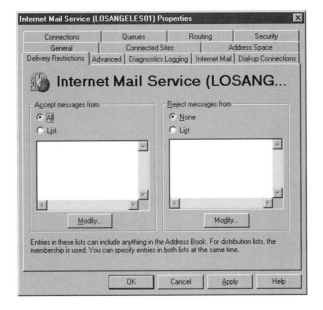

FIG. 22.31

You can manage access down to the user level.

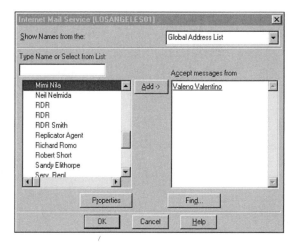

In addition to individual mailboxes, you can set delivery restrictions to distribution lists and custom recipients as well.

Managing SMTP Messages

After you configure the IMS and have the NT service running, you can configure the following additional features to assist you in managing the IMS.

1. From the IMS property pages, select the Internet Mail tab.

2. Your first option is to check the "Enable message tracking" field. This will log information about the daily IMS transactions to a common log that can be browsed to find transmission data on a particular message.

3. Your next option is on the Queues tab (see Figure 22.32). In this tab, you can get real-time statistics on the current processing of IMS data. If you check the queue and see that several messages are waiting to be processed or transferred to another system, you can begin to diagnose where you may have a problem.

4. Select the Diagnostics Logging tab (see Figure 22.33). Logged information gets written to the common NT event logs. On the left panel, the IMS (known as MSExchangeIMC in the event log) is listed. The right panel lists the actual log category options. These include:

   ■ Initialization/Termination monitors that the IMS starts and stops.

   ■ Content conversion is the process of converting message data from native SMTP into Exchange native format and vice-versa.

   ■ Addressing monitors the resolution of e-mail addresses with display names and foreign names.

- Message Transfer is the process that communicates with the remote hosts and transfers message from one system to the other.
- SMTP Interface Events refers to the core application IMS operation.
- Internal Processing is the service that routes the data inside of the IMS .
- SMTP Protocol Log records all events having an impact from the protocol stack or network communication.
- Message Archival processes the IMS temporary data while connections are being restored.

FIG. 22.32

This tab provides real-time data about the status of messages in the IMS queue.

Typical configuration of auditing or logging is to keep each active process set to the minimum log level. In the event that the IMS queue begins to back up, you may want to increase the logging level. Turning the logging on to maximum will flood the event log with many additional messages for you to sort through. Once you have solved the problem, I would suggest returning your logging levels back to the minimum level.

FIG. 22.33

From this tab, you can specify what level of service logging you need for the IMS.

5. Select the Connected Sites tab for the option to view the Exchange sites reached through this IMS. To configure routing to an additional site, click the New button at the bottom of the tab (see Figure 22.34).

   Adding a connected site creates additional routes for messages. Additional Exchange sites, as well as MS Mail 3.x post offices, can be routed to take advantage of the IMS.

FIG. 22.34

This option shows the additional sites connected to the IMS.

6. Enter the organization and site of the additional routed post offices when adding a connected site (see Figure 22.35).

FIG. 22.35

Enter a value for the organization and the site.

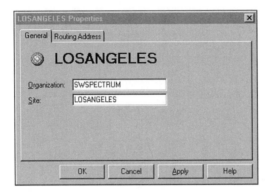

7. After you enter the site name, click the Routing Address tab to complete the new message route. The Properties dialog box, shown in Figure 22.36, appears.

FIG. 22.36

Complete the message route with a message type and post office.

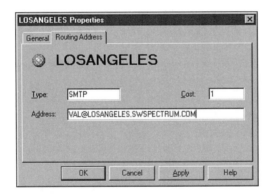

8. Enter a Type of mail connection. You can add an SMTP type and include the destination mailbox Address.

Defining Additional IMSs within a Site

The IMS runs as a single NT service per server. Typically, you have one IMS per organization to service the public Internet connection. Additional connections may be needed if you are going to use an SMTP backbone to move messages throughout the organization. The IMS is robust and can handle several thousand users. To balance the load, you can set up additional IMSs to distribute the processing.

To allow coexistence between two or more IMSs you must perform the following adjustments:

1. In the Address Space tab, modify the entries for existing IMS to accommodate the address space of the new IMS.

2. In the Connections tab, modify the maximum inbound and outbound sessions, along with what is specified in any new IMS.

3. Finally, for the new IMS to resolve properly in the DNS, you must modify the DNS or host file to reflect a new IMS's IP address.

Following are special routing suggestions for sites that have multiple IMSs:

- If your organization has multiple domains within the SMTP mail system, consider having each IMS handle messages for one specific domain.

- If your site has relatively balanced incoming and outgoing SMTP messages, consider configuring one IMS to receive SMTP mail and the other to send SMTP mail.

Testing the IMS

When the configuration of the service is complete, the last thing to do (after you stop and restart the service) is test the connection. Use the following steps to test your Internet mail connection.

1. First, send a message from an Exchange client on your site to a remote SMTP server. Verify that the message was properly received.

2. Examine the body of the message to make sure that any attachments came through without a problem.

3. From the remote host, send a message back to the IMS. Verify that the message was properly routed to the appropriate mailbox. If the message is delayed or does not reach the destination mailbox, you must track it down by using Exchange's troubleshooting tools. Refer to Chapter 24, "Exchange Performance Tuning and Capacity Planning," for more information of such tools. A good place to start verifying the working state of the IMS is first the IMS Queues tab and then the Windows NT Event Viewer for any alert messages.

From Here...

The IMS is a full-featured SMTP Internet Mail. The IMS offers numerous configuration selections to give the administrator full control of the service. In addition to being a service, the IMS architecture is scalable to include MS Mail post offices, Exchange sites, and Internet access clients. The IMS extends Exchange into the Internet.

This chapter explained the connection between Exchange and remote SMTP mail systems. For more information, see the following chapters:

- Chapter 11, "Migrating from External Systems," explains the steps associated with migrating from external systems.

- Chapter 26, "Monitoring Your Organization," helps you manage key Exchange components.

- Chapter 28, " Troubleshooting Exchange with Diagnostic Tools," helps you to debug connectivity and message routing problems.

CHAPTER 23

Setting Up NNTP

As you may already know, Exchange has robust Internet e-mail connectivity that enables any Exchange client to communicate with just about anyone on the Internet. But sometimes e-mail isn't enough. Sometimes, people need to communicate in an electronic discussion, like an on-line meeting or group discussion. Other times, people just want to get information out to thousands of people. Using e-mail for these tasks can be difficult. Thus, Internet newsgroups were created to do this task. In the 5.0 release, Exchange now enables any Exchange user to participate in these newsgroups using Exchange's Internet News Service (INS). INS uses a special application protocol called Network News Transfer Protocol (NNTP). Like newsgroups, NNTP was created for the Internet. In the Exchange product, the INS and NNTP technologies are so closely tied together that their terms will be used interchangeably in this chapter. When needed for clarity, this chapter highlights any differences.

To provide a complete picture, this chapter goes over the history of newsgroups before diving into the actual configuration of the NNTP and INS functions in Exchange. ■

The History of USENET and NNTP

Before you can understand how to use NNTP with Exchange, you'll need some history on USENET and the NNTP protocol. Specifically, you'll learn how USENET'S popularity brought about the creation of NNTP.

Understanding USENET

A short synopsis of how USENET is structured.

Understanding Newsfeeds

A definition of newsfeed and the differences between push and pull newsfeeds.

Installing a Newsfeed Connector by Using the Newsfeed Configuration Wizard

Learn how to set up a newsfeed and establish a newsfeed connection.

Configuring a Push (Outbound) and Pull (Inbound) Newsfeed from or to your Newsfeed Provider

Configure the newsfeed for a Push newsfeed and a Pull newsfeed.

Configuring the Various NNTP Property Pages for Operation of the Connector

Learn how to control NNTP protocol by setting up the property pages.

Historical Overview

Tom Truscott and James Ellis invented a system to pass information between UNIX systems. This system, called UNIX-to-UNIX CoPy or UUCP, was used to pass files from a server at Duke to a server at the University of North Carolina and vice versa. As the technology matured, the software was rewritten to handle a larger volume of data. The original version could only manage a limited amount of articles per newsgroup each day. Today, the system is called USENET and is estimated at over 250,000 sites worldwide hosting an estimated 18,000 newsgroups. However, USENET had its share of problems. Luckily, several systems and solutions were created to address these problems.

First, there was a need to develop an efficient way to distribute the news to non-UNIX clients. Many people began to realize there was valuable information in the newsgroups and they wanted to access them from non-UNIX desktops. Other users needed a newsreader that would help format the screen and take care of SMTP-like transmissions for the newsfeed. Still other users found the current versions of the newsreader software too cryptic to use. Also, this system needed more intelligence. It needed a built-in method that knew what to send and when to send it, as well as to record the condition of the server's last transmission. It also needed everything needed to run on top of a streaming protocol like TCP/IP. In February of 1986, an RFC appeared that established a higher-level Internetwork protocol that would fulfill the preceding requirements. It was called NNTP and it became the natural choice for sites using the Internet to transfer articles. It also has been chosen by Microsoft to run its Exchange 5.0 Internet News Service.

N O T E   A plain Exchange Server site is not the same as a USENET site. A USENET site is either a Backbone Server or an Intermediate server organized into an internetwork to pass data from one site to the next. ▪

Understanding Newsgroups

The basic building block of USENET is a newsgroup. As mentioned earlier, newsgroups are an online discussion group that are a many-to-many communication where e-mail is one-to-one.

The newsgroups are organized by subject into directories and sub-directories in the Backbone Sites (a key USENET site that processes a large amount of USENET traffic). These newsgroups (directories) are categorized by subject, area, and place. Examples of this are as follows:

Examples of Subject:

- Comp.   Computers
- Sci.   Science and technology
- Rec.   Recreation Arts and Leisure

- News.   News on the USENET itself
- Sco.   Society, social issue

Examples of Area:

- na.   North America
- ca.   State (California)
- ba.   Local (San Francisco)

Examples of Place:

- Att.   AT&T
- Well.   Site-specific (The WELL conference)

Part
III
Ch
23

Each category of the newsgroup has one or more sub-categories. A fictitious example may be the category cartoons, which may be called "cart." The cartoon area could have several categories under it. One category may be loon (short for Looneytimes). Under the loon category, there may be a subject called Rat. The newsgroup name would be cart.loon.rat. It could be broken down even further specifically into different interests. At the leaf node, people can send messages and start strings of conversations about their favorite topics using newsreader software. A leaf node is a USENET site that originates and reads USENET news. It does not relay any USENET traffic like a Backbone site. The newsreader software will aid in pulling these articles from the leaf node machine. However, it is important to note that you could send and read the newsgroup articles from Backbone and Intermediate sites, although this may not be practical considering the design of these sites.

Understanding USENET's Flow

When you post an article, it is spooled into a specific area where it is stored until another server contacts this server and queries for newsgroups. Then it is passed to the requesting server. This happens with all servers sharing newsgroups until all machines on USENET are updated. This is automatically done many, many times a day at predetermined times. Finally, the last server that receives information sends a message back to the parent server that it will not pass news. There are three categories of servers that participate in this flow:

- Backbone Site servers, which are the core of the USENET system.
- Intermediate servers, which pass news to leaf nodes and are usually the large ISPs and Universities.
- Leaf node servers, which do not have the ability to send information forward.

See Figure 23.1 for more information.

FIG. 23.1
The flow of information within USENET.

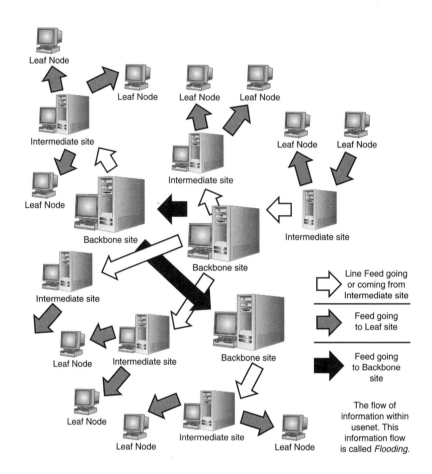

Understanding Newsfeeds

The flow from one USENET site to another is called newsfeed. Each USENET site receiving a newsfeed can be configured to accept and generate an NNTP connection and newsfeed to an outside source like Exchange Server. Exchange processes this flow of information and converts it into an Exchange format. Typically, you will connect your Exchange server to a provider or host machine offering a newsfeeds and an NNTP connection

Keep in mind that once you configure Exchange to accept an incoming newsfeed and Exchange is also moving information back out to other USENET sites, you are effectively including your Exchange Server site "in the USENET loop." Also, Exchange can accept multiple newsfeeds from different providers, but be careful that the information doesn't overlap (two feeds from different sources streaming in the same information).

Exchange has different types of newsfeeds. The basic difference is who initiates the newsfeed. With a push feed, your newsfeed provider intiates the newsfeed and essentially controls which newgroups you receive. Obviously, you will tell your provider which newsgroups your company needs, but from a configuration standpoint, the provider is in the driver's seat. The advantage of this feed is that it handles large newsfeeds better.

Pull feeds work well for smaller newsfeeds and are better suited for dial-up connections. Here, you configure the connection and choose which newsgroups your company needs. Then, Exchange initiates the newsfeed and retrieves any new messages.

Now, let's define two more terms before we talk about inbound and outbound newsfeeds. Typically, a USENET provider will have two hosts in one of two roles: an inbound host and an outbound host. These names can be somewhat confusing because the flow of information is the reverse of the host type. An inbound host is the host that provides a newsfeed into Exchange. An outbound host is the host that accepts a newsfeed from your Exchange server. The inbound and outbound host roles can be on the same machine, but for the purposes of this example, we've placed the roles on separate machines.

So, to put everything together, you can use a pull feed to pull messages from your provider's inbound host. Using a push feed, the inbound host initiates the connection and pushes the newsfeed messages to your Exchange server. Both of these transfers are called inbound newsfeeds.

Alternatively, you can use a push feed to send or push messages from Exchange to your provider's outbound host. You can also use a pull feed where the outbound host will receive messages from Exchange. Both of these transfers are called outbound newsfeeds.

The NNTP protocol works with either push or pull feeds to get or receive a conversation group. The communication between servers is governed by a set of rules built into NNTP. So, while the push and pull feeds are dynamically working, the NNTP protocol is communicating on a different level of the internetwork protocol stack in achieving control of the desired amount of the message flow coming in or out of the servers.

Planning for the Internet News Service (INS)

When planning to roll-out INS in your organization, consider the huge amount of resources that newsgroups can consume in your environment. Answering the following questions will make the actual installation and configuring of NNTP much easier.

1. What is the Fully Qualified Domain Name or Internet Protocol (IP) address of the Microsoft Exchange Server computer that is running the Internet News Service?

2. Do you plan to use a pull or push newsfeed for inbound messages or outbound messages?

3. Optionally, the ISP for your newsfeed service may need to know the inbound host account and password. However, this is optional and needed if you want to make your system more secure.

4. Will you use a dial-up (via DUN) or direct LAN connection to receive news from your provider? If you are going to connect using your LAN, consider using a push newsfeed. The LAN connection has a large bandwidth and can afford the excess traffic. For pull

newsfeeds, consider using a Dial-Up Network because of the small bandwidth associated with this type of communication.

Questions you will ask when you contact your ISP provider that subscribes to USENET newsfeed are as follows:

1. Specifically, ask your USENET site administrator for your FQDN (Fully Qualified Domain Name).

2. How will you receive your active file? As mentioned previously, an active file is a container that houses all of your newsgroup subscriptions. There are several ways to obtain this file from your provider. They can e-mail or FTP (File Transfer Protocol) it to you.

3. If you're planning to push feeds, you must send your newsfeed provider the list of newsgroups to which you want to subscribe.

Configuring NNTP

To install an NNTP connection to another Microsoft Exchange Server or foreign system, there are five primary steps to follow:

1. Gather the appropriate information from your newsfeed provider using the questions mentioned earlier. Be prepared to give your provider the appropriate technical information about your site.

2. Install the appropriate networking equipment and protocols. This equipment could include modems, CSU/DSU, and so on.

3. Install and configure a local NNTP connector.

4. Configure the NNTP connection on the remote Exchange site or foreign system.

5. Test the connection for message receipt and formatting consistency.

Installing an NNTP Newsfeed

When the applicable network software and hardware are installed on the Windows NT server that will be handling the connection, you are ready to proceed with running the Newsfeed Configuration Wizard. In running the Newsfeed Configuration Wizard, you must supply answers to several questions that were covered earlier in this section. It will ask you for:

- The USENET site name of the newsfeed provider that is supplying the newsfeed. Newsfeed is similar to mail messages, in that there is a path header for newsgroup messages. This could be helpful in understanding the origin of your feed. Typically, the name is the Fully Qualified Domain Name (FQDN) of your Backbone Site that has the USENET feed (such as server.ginco.com).

- The name of the administrator who will have the power to manipulate the system. This is someone with administrative rights over Exchange.

- The name and location of your active file if it is not going to be downloaded.

The Configuration procedure for the NNTP connection runs through a series of setup Wizard screens that will guide you.

From the Exchange administrator program File menu, select New Other, then select NNTP Newsfeed. The NNTP Configuration Wizard appears (see Figure 23.2).

The first screen reminds you to contact your NNTP newsfeed service provider for the information above in configuring NNTP.

N O T E The Dial-Up Network has to have an entry for the NNTP remote site's phone number to answer the Wizards question concerning who is your USENET provider if you are using Dial-Up Networking. ▪

FIG. 23.2

The new Newsfeed Configuration Wizard will take you through NNTP connector setup.

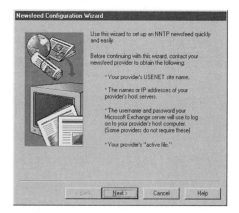

With the information from contacting our USENET service provider at your side, you can fill in the USENET site name with your Fully Qualified Domain Name. The "server to install on" is automatically selected. You can choose to install this connector on any server in the organization providing that you have proper permissions and administrative rights. Choose the next button on the bottom of the screen. It is important to understand that you are configuring a newsfeed that will come through a connection that has been configured with NNTP.

Here note that NNTP is a component that moves news across an internetwork, between sites, and into public folders. Then the client can read and post replies into the public folder and those messages eventually will be posted to the appropriate newsgroup.

It is necessary to configure whether you are going to pull or push with a newsfeed from the USENET provider. A pull newsfeed is associated with inbound newsfeed or an upstream newsfeed. An inbound pull newsfeed refers to the Exchange server initiating the call to the newsfeed provider.

It is NNTP that controls the conversation and it ends when the sender hangs up. The news articles that NNTP distributed on the Exchange server will be handled by public folders.

Push feeds are associated with inbound and outbound newsfeeds. When a Push inbound connection is established, the Host initiates the call to the Exchange server. Then the Exchange server is configured to accept the inbound push newsfeed. The newsfeed is filtered through an active file. Further, you must establish a push outboud newsfeed at your newsfeed provider and the security issues that go with the outbound feed. (See Figure 23.3 for an example of the Newsfeed Configuration Wizard.)

FIG. 23.3
This is where you need
to have FQDN for your
Newsfeed server.

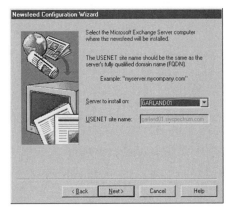

The NNTP Configuration Wizard provides three choices:

1. Inbound and outbound (typical).

2. Inbound only.

3. Outbond only (see Figure 23.4).

The Newsfeed Configuration Wizard begins to check on your network protocol. The network is either a LAN or Dial-Up Network (DUN). The network should be configured before using the Wizard. The phone book should have an entry for the Newsfeed Service provider. If there are no DUN phone book entries, the Wizard will flash a warning message informing the user that there are no phone book entries. The connection using DUN will be grayed out. If there is a phone book entry, it will appear in the box and you can select the appropriate site. If there is further authentication needed for your USENET host, there are entries for Account and Password. (See Figure 23.5.)

FIG. 23.4
Decide on what type of
newsfeed to create.

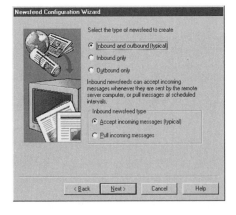

FIG. 23.5

Decide on the network type and if necessary enter USENET HOST Account and Password.

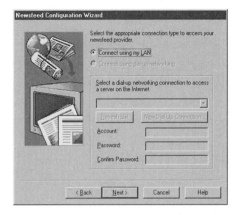

On this screen the Wizard program sets up a connection schedule that determines how often the Microsoft Exchange Server computer will connect to your newsfeed provider. The pull-down menu has intervals of 15 minutes, 1 hour, 3 hours, 6 hours, 12 hours, and 24 hours. From the Exchange Wizard program, select Next (see Figure 23.6).

FIG. 23.6

Setting up the time intervals for the newsfeed connection.

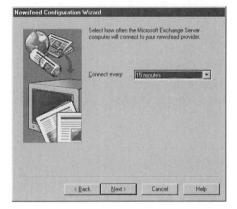

The USENET site name is entered in this box (see Figure 23.7).

The Wizard provides space to enter the host's name or IP address (see Figure 23.8). There is additional area for an alternative host name.

The Newsfeed Configuration Wizard sets up a secure connection to the provider (see Figure 23.9). A combo box provides authentication type. Ask the newsfeed provider which type of authentication works best. If your provider doesn't require this security, skip it. By selecting the next button, you will be ready to install your Internet news server.

FIG. 23.7
This is where your site name for your newsfeed provider is entered.

FIG. 23.8
An IP address or host name for the inbound host.

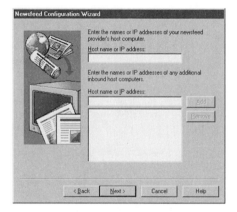

FIG. 23.9
Security for your Internet provider if it is required.

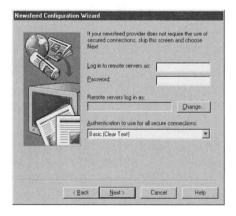

The Microsoft Newsfeed service is ready to be installed. However, at this point in the installation there isn't any newsgroup that we have selected. The Wizard indicates that there still must be a newsgroup selected. One reason that the Wizard hasn't asked for a newsgroup up to this point is that it needs the road map to all newsgroups, which is called the Active File. However, the Newsfeed needs to connect to the host so that it can download this file (see Figure 23.10).

FIG. 23.10

The Wizard needs to connect before downloading the active file.

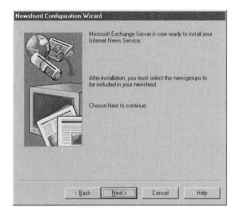

The administrator is chosen to delete and create all the public folders. Choose a person with administrator rights (see Figure 23.11).

FIG. 23.11

Choose an administrator with administrator rights.

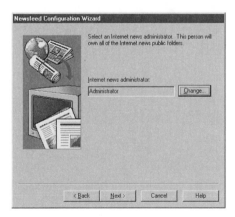

Exchange Server has made the connection with the host computer through NNTP. The Wizard wants to download the active file, which is a road map to newsgroups or conversations throughout the world. The Wizard gives three options:

1. Import a new active file for updates.

2. Download a file.

3. Access it later if there is a problem. (See Figure 23.12.)

Part

III

Ch

23

FIG. 23.12

For inbound connec-
tions the Active file is a
road map to the world's
newsgroups.

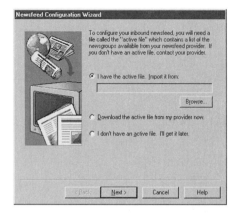

The Wizard is complete and ready to start accepting newsfeed. However, now it is time to call
your provider and decide what newsgroup you would like to subscribe. The installation is complete by clicking the finish button. (See Figure 23.13.)

FIG. 23.13

The Wizard that
configures Microsoft
Internet News Service is
done.

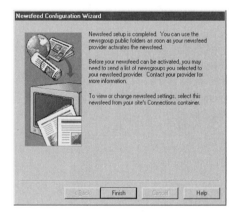

Configuring an NNTP Connection

The NNTP Connector property pages allow you to configure any NNTP newsfeed, whether it is
between two Exchange sites, or to a foreign NNTP system. The following is an overview of the
NNTP Newsfeed property pages and the functions of each:

■ **General**

Set connector names and general NNTP information preferences.

■ **Messages**

Set the maximum incoming and outgoing messages size and your newsfeed.

■ **Hosts**

Set connection parameters for establishing a link to the remote Hosts server, which is your newsfeed server. Set IP address of USENET host computers.

■ **Connection**

Use dedicated or dial-up connections to your hosts.

■ **Security**

Set authentication so that the Exchange Server can log on to the USENET Host computers and USENET Host computers can log on to Exchange.

■ **Schedule**

Specify when your Microsoft Exchange computer will connect to the remote USENET site to send and retrieve new information.

■ **Inbound**

Add newsgroup to your inbound newsfeed.

■ **Outbound**

Add newsgroup to your outbound newsfeed.

■ **Advanced**

Flush out news queues.

General Tab   Use the NNTP General tab to set the principal communication options for a new newsfeed. The following steps guide you through configuring the NNTP Newsfeed General tab.

1. Select the General tab of the NNTP Newsfeed Properties page (see Figure 23.14).

2. Enter a Display Name for this Newsfeed as you want it to appear in the Exchange administrator display window.

FIG. 23.14

Enable newsfeed.

3. Directory Name is defined during installation and can't be changed.

4. Change the name of the Administrator mailbox that was entered during Wizard installation (optional).

Messages Tab   Use the Messages property page to specify the maximum incoming and outgoing message size in your newsfeed.

1. Select the Messages tab in the NNTP Newsfeed Properties page (see Figure 23.15).

2. Under Outgoing message size or Incoming message size, select an option.

No limit   There is no size limit for the message.

Maximum (K)   Select and type a number representing the largest amount
                                of space this message can occupy.

FIG. 23.15

Enter the message size
of incoming and
outgoing messages.

Hosts Tab

1. Select the Hosts tab in the NNTP Newsfeed Properties page (see Figure 23.16).

2. Enter your USENET site name if your server initiates connections. You must connect the newsfeed to your remote USENET site by specifying the node name.

3. Enter the IP address or USENET Host computer name that is providing you your newsfeed. This name must be a Fully Qualified Domain Name if on the Internet.

4. Enter any additional inbound host computers. This depends on your USENET site and if they have additional servers. Always make sure that there isn't any overlap of newsgroup subjects.

5. When you want to remove an inbound connection. Select the remote host name or IP address you want to remove. Choose Remove.

FIG. 23.16

Enter the remote site and host name.

Connection

1. Select the Connection tab in the NNTP Newsfeed Properties page (see Figure 23.17).

2. Select the connection using Local Area Network (LAN).

Refresh list	Updates current connections.
New connections	Will add a new dial-up connection to the list of connections, then you must Refresh to update.
Account	Account name of dial-up connections.
Password	The password for the dial-up connection. This is an optional setting.
Confirm password	Verify the password is correct.

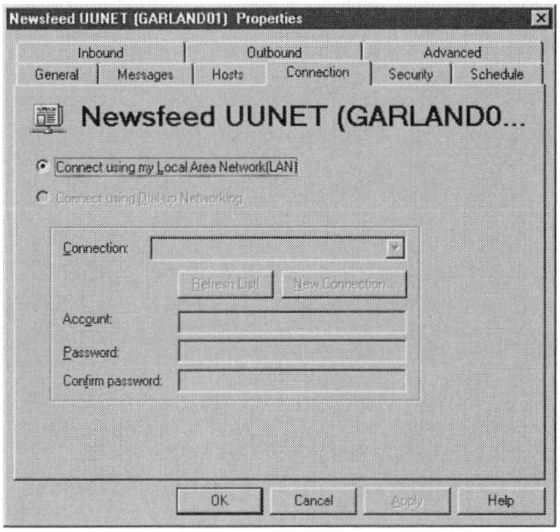

FIG. 23.17

Select either Local Area Network or Dial-Up Networking.

Security Tab   Security is optional and applies to both inbound and outbound feeds.

An inbound feed is a push to the newsfeed server. An outbound feed is a pull to the newsfeed server or vice versa. Security is set up in consideration of newsfeed server calling an Exchange Server or Exchange Server calling your newsfeed provider.

1. Select Authentication to use for all connections. There are three choices:

   Basic Authentication: Clear text unencrypted sent over the network. Most NNTP servers support this technique.
   Windows NT Challenge/Response: Account names and passwords are encrypted. However, the message stream is unencrypted.
   Secure Socket Layer: All data is encrypted. Optionally, password and account could be encrypted.

2. Set up security for outbound connections by selecting "Log in to remote servers as:". You are setting up a pull feed and need information from remote hosts. You are connecting to our newsfeed server. They must supply you with a password to enter into the password box.

3. Set up security for inbound connection by selecting "Remote servers log in as:". You are setting up a push feed and you need to supply information to the remote host so that your newsfeed provider can log on and push a feed to you (see Figure 23.18).

FIG. 23.18
Enter security data that will allow inbound or outbound feed.

Schedule Tab   Use the Schedule Properties page to control how often the NNTP Newsfeed becomes active and initiates a connection.

1. Select the Schedule tab in the NNTP Newsfeed Properties Page (see Figure 23.19).

2. Select one of the three radio buttons that determine when this NNTP Newsfeed connects.

3. If you selected times under Detail view, select a view for the schedule grid.

Never	Disables connections.
Always	Starts connections every 5 minutes.
Selected times	Assigns specific connection times in the Schedule grid.
1 Hour	Displays the schedule grid in one-hour increments.
15 Min.	Displays the schedule grid in 15-minute increments.

FIG. 23.19
Set connection times
for this connector.

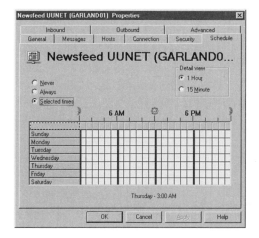

Inbound Newsfeed Tab Inbound newsfeed is usually a push feed from your USENET host. The inbound newsfeed can also be set up as an inbound newsfeed pull feed. This depends on the Configuration Wizard and, consequently, your newsfeed that was configured. You can select your newsgroups on this property page, which will reflect the active file that the Configuration Wizard downloaded.

1. Select Inbound tab from the property page of the Newsfeed property page.

2. Set up an Inbound pull feed by selecting the newsgroups that you want and pushing the button to "Include."

3. You can remove a newsgroup by selecting it and pressing "Exclude."

4. Select Inbound tab from the property page of the Newsfeed property page (see Figure 23.20).

5. If the Inbound push newsfeed was set up for this kind of newsfeed, choose the newsgroups' folders that you are subscribing to by using the Accept button.

At any time, you have the option of excluding (by using the reject button in Figure 23.20) a particular newsgroup from populating your public folders. You can exclude whether you're using a push or pull feed. Both feeds are inbound feeds.

FIG. 23.20

Inbound Message Feed for either push or pull, depending on what you set up with your Newsfeed Configuration Wizard.

You can create a news public folder from an existing newsgroup folder by selecting the Create Newsgroup Folder button. To create a new folder for a newsgroup, select from the folders that are being subscribed to from your provider.

Specifying a New Active file for an Inbound Push Feed   The active file is a file that has the road map to the USENET and when the USENET grows, it is wise to refresh this file to reflect the changes in the USENET.

1. Select the inbound tab.

2. Choose Create Newsgroup Folders.

3. Choose New Active File.

See Table 23.1 for options.

TABLE 23.1 The Option for Feed

The Option for Feed

Option	Description
Download from the newsfeed provider, via NNTP	If selected, the active file is imported from your newsfeed provider's host computer.
Import from a file	If selected, a dialog box appears promoting you to select an active file to import into your newsfeed.

Configuring Outbound Newsfeeds   Outbound Newsfeeds are feeds associated with sending messages and posting them in a newsgroup at your provider's computer. If a host computer needs to pull messages from your Microsoft Exchange server, you need to configure only

NNTP client support on your computer. Your host computer can then pull messages acting as though it was an NNTP newsreader. You must configure your outbound newsfeed (see Figure 23.21).

1. Select the outbound tab.

2. Select the public folder that contains the newsgroup you want to add to your list of newsgroup folders.

3. Choose include and choose OK.

4. Removing a newsgroup from an outbound newsfeed is very straightforward.

   Select the public folder that contains the newsgroup that you want to remove from the newsfeed.

5. Choose Exclude.

FIG. 23.21
Configuring your
outbound feed.

Newsgroup Hierarchies

Newsgroup Hierarchies are folders built with USENET public folders from newsfeed. Selecting a parent folder from an existing public folder enables this folder to be rearranged by user preference. Exchange 5.0 enables the organization to build its own order of folders from its newsfeed (see Figure 23.22).

1. From the Tools menu choose "Newsgroup Hierarchies."

2. Select the public folder that you want to designate as a hierarchy parent newsgroup public folder.

3. Choose OK.

4. You can remove the parent folder by choosing "Newsgroup Hierarchies." Select the public folder you want to delete from the hierarchy. Choose "Remove."

FIG. 23.22

Add or remove newsgroups to make your own network hierarchy.

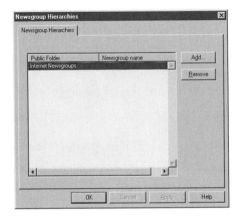

NNTP Protocol Properties

Now we'll turn our attention to the Network News Transfer Protocol (NNTP). We can adjust a few settings from the NNTP protocol property page. Then we can set properties for the NNTP object at the site and server level. Here's an overview of some key tabs :

- General Properties tab. Define display name and Directory name (see Figure 23.23).
- Anonymous tab. The anonymous tabs enable you to assign this right for NNTP protocol.
- Newsfeed tab. View newsfeed property pages.

FIG. 23.23

Set the server site defaults.

Use the general page to set the defaults for your site or server NNTP object.

1. In the Administrator window, choose a site or server, and then choose Protocols.

2. Double-click NNTP (News) SITE Defaults for the site: NNTP (News) for the site, NNTP (News) settings for the server.

3. Select the General tab.

4. Display name is a name that can be 256 characters long. This display name is not provided for by the system.

Note, the Directory is not adjustable, and is named during installation.

Enabling Anonymous Access

The user can be given permissions on an NNTP object. You can give permissions to a user who doesn't have to provide a unique login ID. The permissions limit the access that this type of user can have on this object.

1. Select the Anonymous tab on the NNTP property page (see Figure 23.24).

2. Select the box "Allow anonymous access."

FIG. 23.24
The Anonymous tab.

Properties for a Newsfeed

The Newsfeed properties page enables you to view the property page. The properties have been configured by the Newsfeed Wizard. Pressing the properties button will give you the option to review your settings. Questions are often asked about your newsfeed. The properties button is a fast and easy way to reference the configuration. See Figure 23.25 to configure your newsfeed properties.

FIG. 23.25

Highlight the newsfeed and choose properties.

Message Format

Message Format properties cover formats like MIME, UUENCODE, and multipart forms. Messages come into Exchange in foreign formats that need to be converted on the site object or on the NNTP server object. This applies to both incoming and outgoing messages. Exchange Server messages are converted when an NNTP client retrieves them. Messages that are sent by an Internet user are not converted and they are retrieved by an NNTP client the way the message was originally sent. The Message Format Properties pages can be set to convert these message formats. You can also control the message queue. We cover:

▨ Message format tab. MIME, UUENCODE, and multipart forms are covered here.

▨ Control message tab. Controlling the queues for newsfeed.

▨ Authentication tab. Specifies the type of authentication an NNTP Client has when logging in for a connection.

NNTP Messages coming from the Internet are often retrieved by NNTP clients and are unreadable. This applies to NNTP messages arriving and leaving. On the NNTP object protocol we can set encoding methods to convert the newsfeed in a readable format.

1. In the Administrator window, choose a site or server and then choose Protocols.

2. Double-click NNTP (News) Site Defaults for the site or NNTP (News) setting for the server.

3. Select the Message format options (see Figure 23.26). You have to select one or two of the message formats:

MIME:

▨ MIME is a standard that will help translate a message coming from the Internet. It complies with RFC 1521 and 1522. It will allow for multiple attachments like plain text, binary file data, graphics image data, and video data. If a non-MIME-aware client gets a MIME message, the message will not be readable.

Send message body as plain text:

A MIME body part is generated for the messages, because it is plain text. If the HTML text is selected, then a multipart plain text is generated.

Send Message body as HTML:

An HTML MIME body part is generated for the message. If sent, the message body part is plain text and is also selected, an HTML MIME body part is generated. HTML is an Internet standard that enables rich text formatting, such as bold italic color to appear in the message. If the HTML text is selected, then multipart plain text is generated, because HTML is plain text with codes called tags which give it the rich looking characters.

UUENCODE:

■ The UUENCODE format is a simple 7-bit ASCII format that encodes a binary file along with control information to assist in decoding the file.

BinHex (for Macintosh attachments):

This takes the message body as text with any attachments encoded by the BinHex method. A common method used by Macintosh operating systems.

Part

III

Ch

23

FIG. 23.26
Select message
format tab.

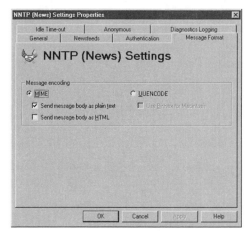

Control Messages Properties

Microsoft Exchange Server has a way it can control messages. Exchange can queue messages until you decide to use the messages. This can be helpful in many different ways. One possible use is that NNTP host computers use control messages to communicate with each other. Control messages are used to create and delete newsgroups and cancel messages that have already been posted through an inbound newsfeed. When Microsoft Exchange Server receives a control message to delete or add a newsgroup it, queues the control messages until you decide to reject or accept these new newsgroups. Exchange can control these messages through the Control Messages tab (see Figure 23.27).

1. Select the control message tab.

2. Select the queued control message you want to process.

3. Select Accept or Delete.

FIG. 23.27

Manipulate the control message by deleting or accepting the command.

Authentication

Authentication happens when a client logs on to the server and password and account information are compared and authenticated. The authentication process provides a user with certain permissions that provide access to resources. The problem with authentication is that people can intercept the password and account. After they have access to your accounts, they have access to your computer. With Exchange Server there are three options available for authentication: Basic Clear-Text, Windows NT Challenge/Response, and SSL Encryption.

1. In the Administrative window, choose site or server and select protocols.

2. Double-click NNTP (News) Site Defaults to configure site NNTP default or NNTP (News) Setting to configure server NNTP setting.

3. Select Authentication tab (see Figure 23.28). NNTP client uses authentication to log on to access the server. The client computer needs to authenticate one of the security methods.

Basic Clear-Text	A user name and password sent through the line without any encryption.
NT Challenge/Response	Enable authentication through Windows NT. The Challenge and Response is through the NT accounts. The Internet News Clients Mailbox or custom recipient cannot be used for this type of security.

SSL Encryption

This open Internet security standard is supported by Exchange. It can secure your system by securing encrypting the Newsfeed line, the password, and account ID.

FIG. 23.28
Choose the authentication you need.

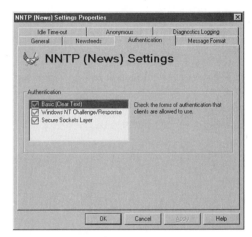

No discussion would be complete without a client. We can configure a client two ways through an existing mailbox or through a Custom Recipient Address. Authentication must be enabled at the server and at the mailbox or custom recipient. The client cannot connect if NNTP is disabled at the mailbox or custom recipient (see Figure 23.29).

■ Set up an NNTP client from a mailbox or from a custom recipient and set up clients.

FIG. 23.29
Enable the NNTP recipient.

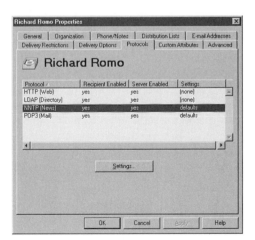

From Here...

This chapter has addressed the topic of newsfeeds and NNTP connections. For more information, refer to the following:

- Chapter 22, "Setting Up SMTP Connections," provides information on configuring your connection to the Internet.
- Chapter 27, "Monitoring Exchange Sites," will help in clearing up steps to setting up advanced security.
- Chapter 31, "Using Advanced Outlook Features," discusses setting up Outlook, its profiles, and services.

Exchange Performance Tuning and Capacity Planning

I'm sure every system administrator has had this temptation: to launch the network server from the company's roof in order to make it go faster.

You find your temptation increasing when users catch you in the hall complaining about poor performance. However, you can find an alternative to the dramatic option preceding by discovering why Exchange is slow, then take more positive action.

In particular, this chapter discusses what situations can cause Exchange to operate sluggishly. This is important, because poor performance costs money in lost time and productivity. The sections in this chapter give you tools to solve your problems. You also learn some answers to that simple question, "How many users can Exchange support?" This chapter also touches on capacity planning so that your server and network can stay ahead of their workload. ■

Define Important Optimizing Concepts and Key Phrases

You must understand key concepts when optimizing Exchange. The load placed on a server by a user opening a mail message is different than replicating public folder information.

How to Use Performance Tuning Tools with Exchange

Use Performance Optimizer, Performance Monitor, and LoadSim to tune Exchange. These tools automatically tune or provide information so you can manually tune Exchange.

Detect and Remedy the Most Common Bottlenecks

Using performance tuning tools, you can detect and minimize bottlenecks in the memory, network card, processor, and system bus.

General Recommendations for Exchange Server Roles

Separate Exchange's functions onto different servers for better performance and fault tolerance.

Answers to "How Many Users Can Exchange Support?"

Use LoadSim to simulate the load of thousands of users and graph your server's response time. Adjust the test's variables and hardware resources and graph a better curve.

N O T E   The examples presented in this chapter might not completely match your environment. It is extremely important you recognize your environment's unique elements and move forward with the most appropriate tuning strategy. ▓

The Art of Performance Tuning

As you may have heard before, tuning is more of an art than a science. There are no mystic techniques that detect and tune all Exchange servers in all situations. A majority of the time, you'll find yourself learning how individual system components work together producing a result. Then, you must consider the trade-off between the different results. For example, you may want to adjust your system components to provide more stability at the cost of slower performance.

Defining Users

Before you can answer the question, "How many users can an Exchange server support?" you need to understand the types of Exchange users in your organization.

Their usage patterns can range from reading and generating a few messages each week to hundreds every day. A small percentage of the user population, therefore, can be responsible for a majority of usage. It's a bit like driving in the left lane on the highway when you encounter some traffic. There's always one slowpoke who seems to cause the traffic to slow down. Overall, you must understand the different types of users (light, medium, or heavy) within your organization, as well as their daily tasks.

Defining Servers

Obviously, each organization purchases hardware specifically for its business needs. Consider a centralized company with one main location, and several warehouses and sales offices distributed throughout the country. The firm might house most of its computing power in corporate headquarters in the form of high-end servers. The company then places cheaper, low-end machines in the remote offices. The high-end servers meet the needs of power users in headquarters, while remote field personnel are satisfied with low- end machines to dial into and receive e-mail.

Another company might have several independent business units throughout the country. In this firm, mid-range servers are used to provide computing power as close to the customer as possible. Therefore, each business unit can provide the fastest service.

You need to understand your company's use of server resources, as well as distinguish between low- and high-end machines (CPU speed and RAM) as defined by your organization.

Defining Load

When monitoring a server, you will notice its workload rising as more users connect and begin to work on it. In addition, you might notice other remote servers connecting to the server (through Exchange's connectors), therefore generating even more load. However, the remote servers have users connecting and asking their local servers to perform remote tasks. These remote user requests ultimately are generating some load on your local server. All server load, therefore, is ultimately generated by users' requests.

Direct versus Background Requests

When users ask the server to open an unread message, they cause the server to perform that task as a direct result of the users' request. As such, a server's workload rises in direct proportion to the number of users working directly with it. On an Exchange server that is only serving users, direct requests make up most of the load. Direct requests are also synchronous in nature.

Background requests occur when a server is performing a task related to or on behalf of a user's request. Some examples of these tasks include replicating public folders and directory service information, expanding distribution lists, performing background maintenance, and transferring and delivering mail messages. Similar to direct requests, the load due to background requests is still proportional to the number of users directly connected. However, background requests occur asynchronously. Users, therefore, do not need to be directly connected to initiate this work.

In the context of background requests, delivering mail places most of the load on the server. The resources consumed for message delivery are directly proportional to the volume of mail generated by your users. Therefore, accurately determining what types of "users" are within your organization is key to tuning Exchange.

Remember, direct and background requests create different types of load on the server. You can measure this with the tools that this chapter describes.

How Many Users Can Exchange Support?

When a user initiates a request, the server uses one or more of its hardware resources to complete the task. The main resources are the CPU, Memory, Mass Storage (disk drives), and the Network Card. Suppose a request requires one second of CPU time and two seconds of disk time—and that these cannot overlap. Assume also there is no other process that will interfere with this request's execution. The disk, therefore, is the "bottleneck" of the operation as it is the resource that expends the most time during a request's execution.

For example, two users issue the same request. Requests arrive at the server spaced three seconds apart. Each will be serviced and each user will not notice any unusual delays (other than the typical three-second response).

If the second request arrives one second earlier, however, a bottleneck momentarily forms as the server is placed under a slightly heavier load and begins to form a queue. Consequently, the second user notices a slightly longer (one second), delay in response time.

Once users begin to connect, and requests begin to queue up, the bottleneck becomes more pronounced. The server will slow down, and there will be some unhappy users. The point at which server load increases and response time becomes unacceptable is when you've reached the number of users that Exchange, given the hardware, can support.

Three variables exist that will affect response time:

- User requests
- Number of users on one server
- Capacity of server hardware

As the number of user requests grows, so does response time. The same relationship is true for users per server. Hardware capacity has the opposite relationship: As it increases, so does its capability to handle more users and requests, therefore decreasing response time.

The next section shows you how to make your operation more efficient by tuning existing resources and planning for your users' demands.

Using Exchange's Performance Tuning Tools

Three tools exist that can help you tune your server, reduce response time, and make your operation more efficient.

- Performance Optimizer—this tool ships with Exchange and optimizes a server's configuration (such as threads for the Information Store or the MTA) after asking a series of usage questions—for example, total number of users. It also analyzes hard drive space and performance to recommend placement of databases and logs. This tool is the easiest to use and can be run immediately after Exchange's setup.
- Performance Monitor—this handy utility ships with Windows NT Server and provides several graphical views on Exchange and the way it utilizes hardware resources. During installation of the Exchange Administrator program, pre-defined monitors are added to the desktop window.
- LoadSim—this program ships with Exchange and can generate the load of hundreds of virtual clients from one physical computer. You can configure the type of user, such as, light (perhaps 10 messages a day) to heavy (with more than 50 messages plus attachments). LoadSim determines the possible response time given your current server hardware and software configuration.

N O T E For best results, use LoadSim after employing Performance Optimizer and Performance Monitor. ▓

Using the Performance Optimizer

The Performance Optimizer automatically analyzes and optimizes key hardware for the best performance with Exchange.

The Optimizer first analyzes the server's logical drives. Then, it determines the most effective location for the MTA, information store, directory, and transaction log files. Specifically, the Optimizer locates the logical drive with the quickest sequential access time, and uses it for the transaction log files. It does this because the transaction logs are written sequentially for maximum performance. The Optimizer then locates the logical drive with the fastest random access and uses it for the server's particular role. For example, a dedicated backbone server moving messages to other sites reserves its swiftest random access drive for MTA files. A public folder-only server will use its hard drive for the public information store files. Keep in mind that the Performance Optimizer can only examine a drive down to the logical, not the physical, level. If you have divided your physical hard drive into sections or you have partitioned a RAID array into multiple logical drives, the Performance Optimizer cannot provide a drive configuration that will give you increased performance.

The Performance Optimizer also analyzes the total amount of physical RAM and determines the necessary amount of memory for the directory and information store. You are also given the option of limiting the amount of RAM that Exchange uses. This is especially useful if there is another application running on the server that needs a sizable amount of RAM such as SQL Server.

Although you can and should run the Performance Optimizer immediately after setup, you should consider running it again *after* the following changes:

- Adding or removing a connector

- Changing a server's role within a site, for example, when a backbone server becomes a public folder server

- Changing or upgrading any major hardware component, such as RAM, CPU, hard drives, or network adapter. If you double the amount of memory in your Exchange server, it will not be recognized until you run Performance Optimizer.

- Migrating a large number of users from a non-Exchange system (MS Mail, cc:Mail, and so on).

The Optimizer is especially useful in its capability to automatically move the various databases and work queues from one drive location to another, while also changing any necessary NT registry values, as well as Exchange values. An example might be if drive space for the Public Folder database (PUB.EDB) becomes constrained and a new multi-gigabyte RAID is added. The optimizer can be configured to easily shift the PRIV.EDB to the new drive space and make all the needed changes.

Using the Performance Monitor

An Exchange system should be structured so its resources are used efficiently and distributed fairly among the users. Performance Monitor (Perfmon) monitors specific system resources so you can meet your system structure goals.

Many times, you might be motivated to solve all problems the instant they appear. In fact, you might find your motivation dramatically increasing when users loudly display their unhappiness. To be prepared for such problems, you should first review Perfmon before moving too quickly in one direction. This can be accomplished by using the set of overview counters. Presented later in the chapter, these counters will keep you from plunging too quickly and deeply into a dilemma only to discover that you've missed the problem. When your system is under a load you want to monitor, bring up all the overview counters in Perfmon. Then, you can determine which resource is being overworked.

Perfmon is powerful enough to be used as a console that runs 24 hours a day and includes thresholds for the various key counters. If a threshold is broken, the monitor might send a net broadcast or spawn a pager process to let an administrator know that attention is needed. This type of scenario helps to proactively solve problems before they affect end users too greatly.

Each section that follows has been listed in order of influence to Exchange's performance. Within each section, each counter is listed in the format Object: Counter. This will help you locate the particular counter within the Performance Monitor.

N O T E   You might be wondering what is a good figure for *Server*: Bytes Total/sec or for *MSExchangeMTA*: Messages/sec. The truth is that there is no simple answer. The reason is that your network has far too many variables.

Next, you might be wondering what are the maximum values. Again, there are no simple answers. For example, how could you find how fast your car can go? You can probably discover this by driving as fast as possible. But notice all the variables that will affect your maximum speed. Do you test drive the car up or down a hill, at sea level, or at 10,000 feet? Whether you test drive on a cold or a hot day will affect the result. For example, cold air is denser and provides a performance boost, especially for turbo and supercharged engines.

The best approach is to drive your system through many conditions until you get a feel for its normal ranges or personality. To assist you in this process, you can use LoadSim, which creates a synthetic load of hundreds of users on your system. While running your simulation, crank up Perfmon to monitor the load.

How to Detect Disk Subsystem Bottlenecks

With most Exchange systems, the disk subsystem has the most influence on performance. The primary consideration with the disk subsystem is not size but the capability to handle multiple random reads and writes quickly. For example, when Exchange users open their inboxes, the set of properties in the default folder view must be read for approximately the first 20 messages. If the property information is not in the cache, it must be read from the information store on disk. Likewise, a message transferred from one server to another must be written to disk before the receiving server acknowledges receipt of the message. This is a safety measure to prevent message loss during power outages. Now imagine the read and write activity of 300 heavy e-mail users on one server. Their combined requests would generate a multitude of random traffic on the disk subsystem.

> **CAUTION**
>
> Sometimes, you see extremely high %Disk Times and think that your disk subsystem is bottlenecked. However, you want to examine other overview counters before going in one direction. For example, when available memory drops to critical levels, NT will begin to page or write unused data or code to the hard drive to make room for more active programs. With extreme RAM resource starvation, your disk subsystem can be reading and writing furiously and appear to be bottlenecked. Looking at other general disk counters in Perfmon will validate this illusion.
>
> However, when you examine both memory and disk subsystem counters, you'll notice that during prolonged memory paging, disk activity increases. The solution is to add more memory, not to increase your disk subsystem capacity.

Physical Disk: % Disk Time

Disk Time is the percentage of elapsed time that the selected disk drive is busy servicing read or write requests. In other words, this counter provides an indication of how busy your disk subsystem is over the time period you're measuring in Perfmon. A consistent average over 95 percent indicates significant disk activity.

Physical Disk: Disk Queue Length

This counter measures the number of requests that are waiting to use disk subsystem. This counter should average less than two percent for good performance. Use the Disk Queue Length counter combined with the % Disk Time counter, to give you an exceptional overview of your disk subsystem's workload.

Both counters can monitor either your server's physically installed disk spindles or RAID bundles.

Addressing Disk Subsystem Bottlenecks

Separate All Transaction Logs

The public and private information stores both utilize a transaction log that is written sequentially to disk. If possible, place the logs into separate physical spindles, preferably with the private store on the fastest drive with a dedicated controller on a FAT partition.

Install Additional Hard Disks

You can separate Windows NT processes (such as paging file), and Exchange processes (such as message tracking logs) to enhance performance. You can also separate the public and private information stores transaction logs to separate disks or arrays for even more performance.

Overall, if you have a RAID subsystem, installing more drives coupled with a large RAM cache on the RAID controller yields faster throughput.

Install Faster Hard Disks and Drive Controllers

Choose a disk with the lowest seek time available, which means the time required to move the disk drive's heads from one track of data to another. The ratio of time spent seeking as opposed to time spent transferring data is usually 10 to 1.

Determine whether the controller card does 8-bit, 16-bit, 32-bit, and now 64-bit transfers. The more bits in the transfer operation, the faster the controller moves data. The latest Ultra-SCSI technology offers the best combination of these features.

Use RAID Disk Striping to Increase Performance

Use RAID 0 (disk striping) to increase overall capacity for random reads and writes. You will need at least two physical drives for RAID 0. Use RAID 5 (disk striping with parity) for slightly less performance, but more fault tolerance. You will need at least three physical drives for RAID 5. If you implement RAID at the hardware level, choose a controller card with a large (4 megabytes) on-board cache. Several vendors offer complete solutions of this type.

Memory Requirements in Exchange

When Exchange runs, it only keeps portions of data needed, referred to as pages, in memory at any one time. When it needs a page of data that is not in RAM (page fault), NT will load that page into physical memory from a peripheral, which is usually the hard drive. The average instruction in memory executes in nanoseconds, which is one-billionth of a second, and hard drive seek and access times are in milliseconds. Therefore, NT must run 100,000 times slower than normal to retrieve a page from disk.

Keep in mind that Exchange needs a minimum of 32MB of RAM and experience has shown that 64MB is a much more realistic level, given all that an NT server and Exchange need to do quickly in RAM.

How to Detect Memory Bottlenecks

The following sections will assist you in detecting detrimental system performance caused by improper use of RAM. Also, you will learn some techniques to better handle memory usage on your Exchange servers.

Overview counter—Memory: Pages/sec

Pages/sec reports the number of pages read or written to a disk to resolve page faults. You can turn this on when your system is under a typical load. If this counter averages above 5, a memory bottleneck is starting to form, and your disk subsystem is beginning to take a beating.

Addressing Memory Bottlenecks

Add Memory

You will want to add more memory until paging stops or occurs minimally. Afterwards, be sure to run Performance Optimizer to adjust Exchange's memory caches.

Use Multiple Paging Files

If your disk subsystem supports concurrent I/O requests, using multiple paging files usually improves system performance. Be sure to place the paging file on your fastest hard drive, and experiment with separating NT's paging file from Exchange's transaction log files.

Remove Unnecessary Services

Disable any unneeded NT services, protocols, and device drivers. Even idle components consume some memory and contribute to general system overhead.

Part
III

Ch
24

How to Detect Network Bottlenecks

A network by its heterogeneous nature is full of potential performance bottlenecks. A company full of servers and clients talking in different protocols can often cause poor performance with Exchange. The following sections will help you detect poor network performance with Exchange and help you improve it.

When a network bottleneck forms, one of the following three scenarios can result:

- Server Overload

  The server doesn't respond within a reasonable time to users' requests given its current capacity. Sometimes this is due to an overload of another resource; for example, the disk subsystem.

- Network Overload

  The network doesn't respond within a reasonable time. The reason is that the load of the users' requests has exceeded the capacity of the physical medium. In other words, the network has run out of Net Available Bandwidth (NAB).

  Although the counters presented in the following section will indicate that the network or a specific link is overloaded, you will want to use Microsoft's SMS product or a packet sniffer to be certain.

- Network Corruption

  The network is periodically transmitting corrupt data. In this case, the load is on both the server and the network due to the fact that each bad transmission requires a retransmission.

How to Detect Client Side Bottlenecks

The following counters are available to clients running NT:

> *NWLink*: Bytes Total/sec (IPX/SPX)
>
> *Network Interface*: Bytes Total/sec (TCP/IP)
>
> *NetBEUI*: Bytes Total/sec

If you want to measure a client's workload, use the appropriate counter for your protocol. When your overview counters are generally idle, but your network counters are high, you can usually infer that your network has a bottleneck on the client end. This means that your client is doing most of its work gabbing with the network.

This counter also gives you an indication of how much load this client is placing on the network.

Redirector: Network Errors/sec

This counts serious network errors between the redirector and one or more servers. It applies to any protocol running on the client station, and shows if you have a network corruption problem. Each error is logged in detail in NT's Event Log.

This counter should normally be zero.

How to Detect—Server Side Bottlenecks

Server: Bytes Total/sec

This counter measures most of the meaningful server activity, and provides an insight into the server's load. It also provides an insight into how much load this server is contributing to the network's overall load.

Server: Sessions Errored Out

This counter measures the number of client sessions that are closed due to unexpected network errors. If this counter rises on one server, you might have a faulty network card. If the counter increases on several servers, check into the LAN infrastructure itself, such as routers, hubs, bridges, physical cabling, or connections to determine whether you have a more serious network corruption issue.

This counter should normally be zero.

Apply Faster Hardware on Heavy Traffic Links

For the most leverage, you should apply hardware upgrades to machines generating the most traffic, as well as servers on the heaviest traffic links. This will provide a system-wide balance for your Exchange environment.

You can use a combination of the counters mentioned in the previous sections to determine which machine is generating traffic. A product such as Network Monitor (included as a tool with Microsoft SMS) or a standard network "sniffer" can determine which network links experience the greatest load.

Segment Your Network

If the Server: Bytes Total/sec or corresponding client counter begins to reach the maximum bandwidth of the network link to which your server is connected, you should consider segmenting your network. On an Ethernet segment, this value is approximately 1.2 megabits per second, once you include the overhead of the network.

Part
III

Ch
24

Match the Network Card to the System Bus

If your client or server has a 32-bit or 64-bit bus, use a 32-bit or 64-bit adapter card. Overall, you should use the fastest network card and matching bus available.

Increase Your Bandwidth

If you determine your network is overloaded, increase its bandwidth by upgrading to faster network link technology, for example, Fast Ethernet, FDDI, or ATM.

How to Detect Processor Bottlenecks

Exchange is tightly integrated with NT. Therefore, it can take full advantage of a more advanced processor or multiple processors. You should eliminate all other bottlenecks before investigating the processor. *Processor*: Percent Processor Time or System: Percent Total Processor Time.

Either one of these counters will determine whether your CPU is overloaded. These counters measure the total time your system is executing programs (non-idle threads). If either counter averages over 95 percent, your CPU is probably experiencing a bottleneck. The System counter is useful for multiprocessor systems. The reason is that it averages the processor use for all installed processors.

Upgrade your Processor

You can upgrade to the fastest processor available. If this has been done, add additional processors if your hardware supports symmetrical multiprocessing. Keep in mind that NT Supports Power PC and Alpha, as well as Intel processors.

Overall, the addition of another CPU will typically give a better performance increase than upgrading to a faster single processor. The reason is that the multithreaded design of all Microsoft BackOffice products enables superior performance in a multiple processor environment. An example might be a server with two 90 MHz CPUs that outperforms a server with a single 200 MHz CPU because NT's symmetric multi-processor (SMP) functions allow many more threads to be active.

Off-Peak Scheduling for the Processor

You might also consider scheduling processor intensive activities to off-peak hours. Such processor-intensive functions might be a generation of the Offline Address Book, Routing Table updates, or the creation and sending of storage limits warnings to users.

How to Detect System Bus Bottlenecks

If you have a Pentium or Pentium Pro system, use the p5ctrs from the NT Resource Kit to detect any bus bottlenecks. You'll have to take an extra step of running pperf to configure which Pentium counters you want to see.

Pentium: Bus Utilization (clks/sec)

Pentium: % Code Cache misses

Pentium: % Data Cache misses

If you see a high bus utilization for your system and a high percentage of code and data cache misses, your bus may be forming a bottleneck.

Use Larger CPU Caches   If there are a lot of cache misses, upgrade to the next largest or largest L2 cache available.

Off-Peak Scheduling for the Processor   Like the recommendation for processor bottlenecks, you might also consider scheduling processor intensive activities to off-peak hours. Such processor intensive functions might be generation of the Offline Address Book, Routing Table updates, or the creation and sending of storage limits warnings to users.

Also, investigate and relocate any non-Exchange services that can be executed on a separate machine.

Exchange Specific Counters

N O T E   All of the following Exchange counters are available in Perfmon after you have installed Exchange. ▪

The counters below provide Exchange-specific monitoring information. If you are just beginning with Exchange or are new to monitoring, stick with the hardware specific counters above. They provide an accurate, high level view. When you are ready to drill down on specific Exchange components, use the counters below for detailed bottleneck detection.

Trend Counters

For best results, track trend counters with Performance Monitor's log. This allows you to average out the day-to-day spikes that can lead you down the wrong road. The average also sets a baseline of typical loads for your server.

Of course, you're also welcome to view these counters for an immediate snapshot of your server, but bear in mind that the numbers will be fairly meaningless unless you have a baseline to measure it against.

MSExchangeMTA: Messages/sec

Messages/sec monitors the number of messages the MTA sends and receives every second. In other words, it measures the traffic generated by message flow. This is a quick way to focus on message traffic sent to other servers. For more specific information on message traffic, refer to the message tracking logs.

MSExchangeMTA: Messages Bytes/sec

Similar to the preceding counter, this counts the sums of the number of bytes in each message the MTA sends and receives each second. In other words, it reports the amount of message traffic measured in bytes.

MSExchangeISPublic: Messages Submitted/min, Message Recipients Delivered/min

These counters go measure the rate of messages being submitted and delivered to the Public store. Keep in mind, the delivered counter will generally be higher since messages usually have multiple recipients.

MSExchangeISPrivate: Messages Submitted/min, Message Recipients Delivered/min

These counters measure the rate of messages being submitted and delivered to the Private store.

Part
III

Ch
24

MSExchangeDS: Reads/sec

This counter measures the amount of traffic generated by directory synchronizations.

Service Time Counters

For best results, you should also track these counters with Performance Monitor's log. However, these counters are better suited for on-the-spot monitoring and evaluation, especially those counters that should be zero for the best throughput.

MSExchangeIS Private: Send Queue Size

MSExchangeIS Public: Send Queue Size

MSExchangeMTA: Work Queue Length

These tell you if the components are keeping up with the submitted load. The queues may be non-zero at peak traffic times, but it shouldn't stay there consistently, especially during slow times.

MSExchangeIS Private: Average Time for Delivery

MSExchangeIS Public: Average Time for Delivery

These counters indicate how long it takes the Store to deliver messages.

Optimizing Dedicated Exchange Servers

This section is for advanced Exchange administrators who want to divide Exchange's functionality onto separate servers for even more performance. Each server's hardware will be used differently depending on the dedicated role it's fulfilling for Exchange. After determining which hardware resource will be in demand, use the monitoring information and recommendations mentioned earlier to optimize the server for its role.

Optimizing Messaging Servers

Exchange servers that just facilitate user requests spend most of their time accessing the Information Store (IS) log and database. Because both of these components have different personalities, create a disk environment that is tailored for maximum throughput for the appropriate IS need.

The IS log is stored on the hard drive, so use the fastest hard drive possible. Because the log is written sequentially, consider isolating it on a dedicated drive or even a dedicated, cached controller and drive.

The IS database should also be on the fastest hard drive possible. Choose one with the lowest possible seek time because the database is accessed randomly. For best results, combine drives with low seek times in a RAID-5 array. Typically, the controller will have an on-board cache. The striping should speed up things considerably.

Beyond the disk, the next common bottleneck on dedicated user servers is the CPU. Use the processor counters and recommendations earlier to detect and eliminate any bottlenecks. Next, network and memory resources should be monitored. Again, use the counters and recommendations earlier.

Optimizing Connector Servers

A dedicated connector server uses one of Exchange's connectors (X.400, cc:Mail, IMS, site, or cc:Mail) to interface with other messaging platforms. Typically, the server will also serve non-Exchange clients using POP3, HTTP, NNTP and so on.

The key Exchange component in action is the MTA. Like the IS database, it uses the hard drive in a non-sequential (random) manner. You can use the IS database recommendation for disk bottlenecks on a connector server.

The next resource to monitor is the network interface. Review the network bottleneck section in this chapter. If any WAN links are involved, review Chapter 5, "Designing Exchange Topology," especially the network links section to ensure your WAN is adequate.

Finally, you'll want to look at the CPU. Connector servers can do an extraordinary amount of message translation when talking to non-Exchange messaging systems. This translation tends to be CPU intensive at times, so examine your processor counters and take the most appropriate action.

Optimizing Public Folder Servers

You'll have a more difficult time discovering bottlenecks on dedicated public folder servers. Because public folders are so versatile, its usage and resulting load on hardware resources varies across a wide spectrum. For example, one company may use the folders to distribute a department status each week even though there isn't any posting of replies back into the folder. This kind of use is much different from a company that pulls and pushes gigabytes of newsgroups using Exchange's NNTP functionality.

The best approach here is to use the general purpose Perfmon counters to get an overview for your particular company. You may want to track these counters over time to ensure your on-the-spot checks aren't missing the big picture. When you have discovered the hardware resource that's consistently bottlenecked on average, you can step in to alleviate things.

Typically, if your company is a heavy public folder user, you'll want to consider splitting the IS public database and logs to separate disks. Specifically, if there is more reading from the folders than writing, tune your disk subsystem for the IS database (non-sequential disk access). For heavy writing, focus on the IS logs (sequential disk access). Typically, companies with a strong appetite for using NNTP for Internet newsgroups will fall into the latter category.

Optimizing Servers with Shared Roles

In smaller shops, Exchange often shares the server's resources with other non-Exchange functions (logon validation, SQL, print serving). If dedicating Exchange isn't an option, use the set of Perfmon overview counters to profile your particular system and determine how your particular mix is affecting the server. If you're planning on deploying Exchange to a server with other responsibilities (such as a Primary Domain Controller), take the time to use LoadSim to determine if the server's current hardware will handle the additional load from Exchange.

Real World Answers to "How Many Users Can Exchange Support?"

LoadSim can help you measure response times using an artificially generated server load. LoadSim can also measure "user acceptability" by weighting certain actions that are perceived as more important by the user like opening versus sending. Most users expect mail to open quickly, but are comfortable with a slight delay when sending.

Calculating Acceptable Server Response Times

LoadSim measures two items with respect to an Exchange server: response time and "acceptability." To measure response time, LoadSim uses the 95th percentile. If the 95th percentile for a set of actions is one second, 95 percent of the response times are at or below one second. Only five percent (one in twenty) of the response times exceeded one second. To compare, the maximum response time is the 100th percentile. In other words, 100 percent of the response times are at or below the maximum.

To measure acceptability, LoadSim places a heavier weight on simulated actions that are perceived as more important to a real user. For example, most users expect quick responses when opening or deleting messages. They aren't, however, as affected by a small delay when sending mail. The actual actions and weights are categorized on the following table.

Table 24.1   LoadSim Can Give You Weight Values

Action	Weight
Read	10
Delete	2
Send	1
Reply	1
Reply All	1
Forward	1
Move	1

N O T E   LsLog is a LoadSim tool that enables you to change the default percentile (95) and the weighted values for any action. For more information, refer to the LoadSim documentation and online help. ▪

To arrive at the final number, LoadSim multiplies each percentile value by the corresponding weight. Then, LoadSim adds the results, and divides by the sum of all weights. This final number is referred to as the score and represents the response time experienced by a simulated user.

The following list includes client requirements and recommendations that might make your LoadSim experience more productive:

- The test clients should have NT 3.51 or higher, a Pentium 60 MHz chip or faster, at least 32M of RAM, and a paging file of 100MB or more. If you want to simulate 200 or more users on one client, you'll need at least 64M of RAM.

- Avoid simulating more than 300 users per client. The DLLs responsible for client-to-server communication will fail to scale, and your test results will not be realistic. In other words, the response time for 500 simulated clients will not be accurate for 500 actual clients on separate machines.

- For best results, you should allow six hours per simulation to gather enough data for reliable, reproducible results. Only analyze the last four hours of the simulation. This enables the server to stabilize after all simulated users have logged on. Of course, you are free to develop your own standards. However, remember to allow enough testing time, especially when simulating fewer than 100 users.

- Run your initial tests on an isolated network which removes real-world traffic. Then, after gathering enough lab data, you might want to run some tests with a network load on the wire to determine whether your environment's network load will affect response time.

- LoadSim cannot perfectly simulate the network traffic of real users. Although 200 LoadSim users create 200 logical server connections, there is only one network card and physical wire. Therefore, simulated network overhead (as measured by Perfmon) will be lower compared to using separate client machines.

- LoadSim doesn't simulate all Exchange features, such as rules and PST-based users. Review the LoadSim documentation for a complete updated listing of simulated tasks.

- LoadSim isn't a perfect simulation of your environment. Its numbers are only good estimates. Despite this, you will still find LoadSim's data extremely useful.

Capacity Planning with LoadSim

ON THE WEB

At the time of this writing, the author team for this book had the most current code base of Exchange (RC1). Unfortunately, it had not been fully optimized for accurate testing

Thus any LOADSIM scores would be extremely distorted and not reflect real-world findings. When Microsoft releases a fully optimized beta version or the final version, an errata will be posted on the Que Web site with the test statistics and graph illustrating simulated users and their response times.

You will find this and other updates at **http://www.quecorp.com/seexchgs5**.

Part III

Ch

24

From Here...

You now know which components to measure and how to use optimization tools. You also know the answer to the question, "How many users can Exchange support?" This knowledge will help you solve the largest performance problems within your organization.

This chapter addresses the topic of performance tuning and capacity planning. For more information, refer to the following chapters:

- Chapter 25, "Maintaining Exchange," for additional information about tools and techniques for optimizing your Exchange servers.

- Chapter 26, "Monitoring Your Organization," for information on additional utilities that assist you in watching over the servers and messaging links in your Exchange organization.

- Chapter 28, " Troubleshooting Exchange with Diagnostic Tools," which explains the tools and techniques you'll use when troubleshooting Exchange.

CHAPTER 25

Maintaining Exchange

After you plan and lay out your Exchange organization, the next step will be to establish the maintenance strategy for your organization. No matter how solid your design and implementation of the Exchange architecture, some tasks must be performed daily to maintain optimum performance and smooth operation.

This section will assist you in performing the routine tasks that will prevent messaging errors, help you fine-tune performance, and recover lost data when the worst happens. ■

Adding, removing, and transferring users

Learn how to add, remove, and transfer users. Learn the techniques to transfer recipients created on one Exchange server to a different machine.

Creating templates to facilitate creating new mailboxes

Learn how to create templates to automate your routine Exchange maintenance.

Monitoring mailbox and public folder usage

Information store is the central storage facility for all Exchange messaging data. Learn how to effectively manage the public and private folders throughout your organization.

Rebuilding routing tables

Learn how to manually update the routing table. Find out how often it is automatically updated.

Get an insight on MTA (Message Transfer Agent) Queues

Learn how to configure these queues step by step.

Creating Different Server Recipients

During normal Exchange organization operation, there will be times when recipients created on one Exchange server need to be transferred to different machines.

Some common circumstances for relocating recipients are these:

■ Internal reorganization: A user moves to a department in the company that is serviced by a different Exchange server.

■ A server is down: A server must be taken offline for an extensive period of time.

■ Optimum performance: After reviewing usage, you decide that for better performance, you need to switch a user's home server (or site).

Distribution lists and custom recipients are server-independent objects. They belong to a site as a whole, not to a specific Exchange server, and therefore, do not need to be transferred among servers in a site.

Moving Exchange Mailboxes

Mailboxes are the most common types of recipients. Moving a mailbox will also transfer its entire private information store contents (including attachments) to the destination server.

Because the Exchange information store uses intelligent storage for handling attachments addressed to multiple recipients on the same server, keep in mind that additional space is required to split these files. Consider the following example.

User A and User B on server GARLAND01 both receive a message with a 1-megabyte file attachment. The total storage space used on GARLAND01 to hold this file is 1 megabyte. Both users are referencing the same instance of the file.

Suppose you transfer User A to server GARLAND05. The user's entire mailbox message contents and attachments are moved to GARLAND05's private information store. This means the 1-megabyte file now exists on both servers.

To move mailboxes to another server in the same site:

1. Use the Exchange administrator program and first select and expand the site desired and then the server within that site where the mailboxes currently reside.

2. Select the mailboxes you wish to relocate. You can select a series of them by using Shift+click or a scattered assortment by using Ctrl+click.

3. When all desired mailboxes are highlighted, select Move mailbox from the administrator program's Tools menu. The following dialog box shown in Figure 25.1 will appear.

4. Select the destination server from the Move mailbox to server list. Click OK.

5. The mailboxes will be transferred immediately.

6. View the destination server's recipient container to confirm that the mailboxes now exist on the new server.

FIG. 25.1

Select the destination server in the Move Mailbox dialog box.

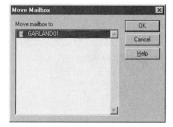

Messages in transit to a mailbox when it is moved to another server will be delayed until the appropriate routing information is properly updated.

To transfer a mailbox to a different site, you must use the Import/Export utility provided in the Exchange administrator program's Tools menu.

N O T E There is currently no automated method for moving users from one site to another. The user's mail could be moved to a personal folder on the user's local desktop or file server home directory while a new mail account is created in the new site. The mail could then be placed back on the server in the new mailbox. ▦

Moving Public Folders

Normally, you will accommodate a wide number of public folder users by creating replicas of folders across your organization. Then, according to the replication schedule, the folders will update each other with changes.

One method to create a public folder replica:

1. Using the Exchange administrator program, select the site where the public folders reside.
2. Select the Recipients container for that site.

N O T E Select Hidden Recipients from the View menu if your public folders are hidden in the administrator program display window. ▦

3. Select the public folder you wish to replicate and open its property pages to begin replication configuration.

For more information, see Chapter 15, "Information Store Configuration."

Public Folder Replicas

Chapter 16, "Creating and Configuring Recipient," goes into more detail about configuring all aspects of the public folder recipient type. This section describes the Replicas property page for a public folder.

Part III

Ch 25

1. Select the Replicas tab of the public folder's property pages. The property page shown in Figure 25.2 appears.

FIG. 25.2

Select the destination server for this public folder.

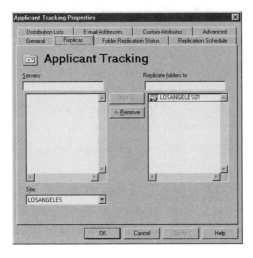

The Servers display window lists all Exchange servers in the site selected in the Site pull-down menu found in the lower-left corner.

The Replicate folders to display window lists the Exchange servers currently selected as destinations for folder replicas.

2. Select a Site from your organization with the pull-down menu.

3. Select or type the name of the destination Exchange server within that site. Click Add.

4. To remove a destination server, select it from the right display window and click Remove.

5. Click Apply to set these properties and continue with other properties. If you are done with all settings, click OK to return to the administrator program.

CAUTION

Do not replicate the Offline address book public folder to any other server in your site. There must only be one instance of that folder in each site.

Moving a Public Folder with the Exchange Client Software

The Exchange Client (on Windows or Windows NT) can also be used to move public folders. You must have sufficient permissions on a specific folder in order to move it to a new location. Assuming you have the necessary permissions, to move a public folder with the Exchange Client software, do the following:

1. Expand the Public Folders object from the Exchange Client display window.

2. Locate the public folder you wish to move.

3. Click and drag it to its new location. You will see a progress box as the information store data is relocated.

Moving a folder from an Exchange client is not the same as replicating. The contents of the folder are actually moved based on the location of the target folder's physical location. If the target folder is on a server in a remote site, the contents will be copied via the client PC to the remote server. This could be very time-intensive, depending on the amount of content in the folder being moved.

Creating Mailbox Templates

A principal part of Exchange maintenance will be adding and deleting mailbox users. When adding a large group of recipients, you can avoid having to enter similar information (such as department or address) by using a mailbox template. You create a template mailbox by creating a dummy mailbox account (one not intended to receive messages) that will be copied when creating new users.

To create a mailbox template, do the following:

1. Using the Exchange administrator program, select a home site for this template mailbox in your organization.

2. Select New mailbox from the administrator program File menu, and the new mailbox property pages appear.

3. Give the new mailbox a Display name that will help you identify it as a template. (e.g., Import Template 1).

   Enter all additional mailbox attributes that you want to include in the new group of mailboxes such as department name, city, state, fax numbers, and so on.

4. Do not assign the new account association with an NT account in order to prevent someone from trying to use the account for mail purposes.

 T I P Check the Hide From Address Book setting on the mailbox template's Advanced property page to prevent it from receiving mail. Then, temporarily make it visible when using it to import new users (unless you want all your newly created mailboxes to be hidden as well).

To use your template when creating a new user mailbox, follow this procedure:

1. Using the Exchange administrator program, select a home server for the new mailbox to be created.

2. If the template mailbox is hidden, select Hidden Recipients from the administrator program View menu. Then select the Mailbox Template as previously defined.

3. Select Duplicate from the Exchange administrator program File menu.

4. Enter the relevant user information for the new mailbox such as name, phone numbers, and so on.

Part
III

Ch
25

By using the Directory Import option from the Tools menu, it is possible to create a large number of mailboxes with basic information by using a template, just like the mailbox was created earlier.

Performing Information Store Maintenance

The *information store* is the central storage facility for all Exchange messaging data. An information store can consume considerable disk space, depending on the size of your organization and the distribution of users per Exchange server.

The following property pages are important to maintaining the information stores:

- Private Information Store: Mailbox Resources: View Mailbox storage usage.
- Public Information Store: Public Folder Resources: View Public Folder storage usage.
- Exchange Server: Information Store Maintenance property page: Schedule hard drive optimizing for an Exchange server's information store.

Exchange 5.0 offers a few new "shortcuts" to make access to these status screens quicker from the left window of the administrator program versus having to drill down through to the property pages as noted earlier. See additional information as follows about these options.

Private Information Store Property Page

The Private Information Store property page allows you to view the physical resources used by each mailbox on a particular server. This property page lets you evaluate hard disk space usage and determine storage limits.

First, you must select the Private Information Store from a server within your site:

1. Navigate to your desired site with the Exchange administrator program.
2. Click the Configuration container of the selected site. All the site configuration objects appear in the administrator program's right window.
3. Open the Servers container. A list of Exchange servers in your site will be listed.
4. Click the server name on the Private Information Store you want to configure. The list of server objects is visible on the right display window of the Microsoft Exchange Administrator Program (see Figure 25.3).
5. Click the Private Information Store object. Open its property pages.

Mailbox Resources Property Page   The Mailbox Resources property page allows you to view the physical resources (e.g., hard disk storage space) used by the Exchange mailboxes on a server. It consists of one main display window that shows the mailboxes on the current server. The window is divided into columns of information. The specific columns displayed are customizable both by information presented and width on the screen.

FIG. 25.3

Select the Private Information Store object from among all the other server objects.

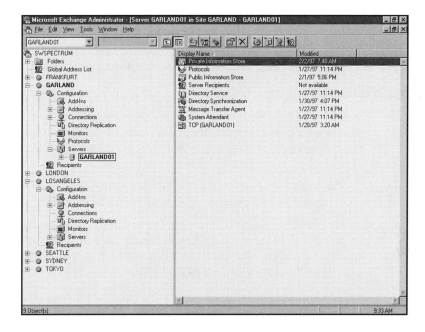

N O T E A mailbox will only be displayed in this window after the first time a user logs on to it. If the mailbox has never been used, it will not appear on the Mailbox Resources property page. ▓

To view Mailbox Resources information, do the following:

1. Select the Mailbox Resources tab of the Private Information Store Properties pages. The following property page shown in Figure 25.4 appears.

FIG. 25.4

Monitor mailbox storage requirements.

Part

III

Ch

25

The display window shows all the mailboxes on this server that have been used at least once.

N O T E   The Microsoft Exchange System Attendant and the Exchange account itself are always listed in this window as well. ▓

2. Click the Refresh button to update the display window with the latest information.

3. Click the Columns button to edit which columns are displayed and their width in pixels. (See below for a description of each column heading and what type of information it can display.)

4. Click Apply to set these properties and continue with other properties. When you are done with all settings, click OK to return to the administrator program.

Default Columns   Columns define what type of information is displayed in the standard dialog box. Default columns are preconfigured to display the most commonly needed information. Optional columns provide more detailed information that may be useful in troubleshooting errors. The following is a list of default columns:

■ Mailbox: The Exchange administrator program object display name for this mailbox

■ Windows NT Account: The Windows NT account of the user currently logged in to this mailbox

■ Total K: The total amount of disk storage space (in kilobytes) taken up by the contents of this user's mailbox (this value includes any message attachments)

■ Storage Limits: Any storage limits imposed on mailbox (e.g., Prohibit Send)

■ Total number Items: The sum of all messages and attachments stored in a mailbox

■ Last Logon Time: The last time a user logged in to this mailbox

■ Last Logoff Time: The last time a user logged off from this mailbox

Optional Columns   The following is a list of the optional columns to display in the dialog box:

■ Full Mailbox Directory Name: The entire X.400 e-mail address for this mailbox

■ Total number Associated Messages: The sum of stored views and deferred action messages (messages scheduled to be sent/processed at a later time) in this mailbox

A new time-saving option added in Exchange 5.0 is the ability to quickly view Mailbox Resources information from the main Exchange hierarchy seen in the left window of the Exchange administrator program (see Figure 25.5).

To access the Mailbox Resources information using this new option:

1. Navigate to your desired site with the Exchange administrator program.

2. Click the small plus sign adjacent to the Configuration container of the selected site to further expand the hierarchy in the left-hand window.

3. Expand the Servers container in the left-hand window. A list of Exchange servers in your site will be listed.

FIG. 25.5

Mailbox Resources information view.

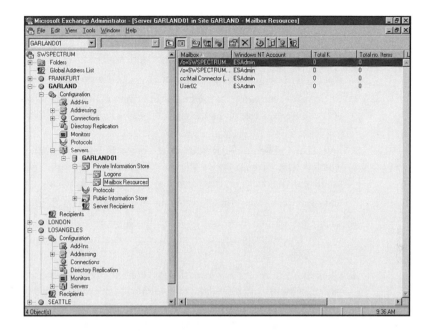

4. Click and expand the server name on which the Private Information Store you want to configure is located.

5. The displayed server objects now visible in the left display window of the Microsoft Exchange Administrator Program are identical in name and function to similar objects displayed in the right-hand window. Selecting properties of either the Private Information Store or Public Information Store displays the same data.

6. Expand the Private Information Store in the left window and click the Mailbox Resources object to see the status information quickly displayed in the right window. The default columns shown in the right window can be added to by using the View menu and using the Columns option.

Public Information Store Property Page

The Public Information Store property page allows you to view the physical resources (e.g., hard disk storage space) used by the folders held on an Exchange public information store. It consists of one main display window that shows the public folders on the current server. The window is subdivided into various columns of information. The specific columns displayed are customizable both by information presented and width on the screen.

The Schedule+ Free Busy Information and the Offline address book are in essence public folders as well and are listed in the public folder resources property page.

The Public Folder Resources Page The public folder resources page allows you to monitor what quantity of system resources are exhausted by the use of public folders on your system. First, you must select the Public Information Store from a server within your site as follows:

Part

III

Ch

25

1. Navigate to your desired site with the Exchange administrator program.

2. Click the Configuration container of the selected site. All the site configuration objects appear in the administrator program's right window.

3. Open the Servers container. A list of Exchange servers in your site will be listed.

4. Click the server name on the Public Information Store you want to configure. The list of server objects is visible on the right display window of the Microsoft Exchange Administrator Program.

5. Select the Public Folder Resources tab of the Public Information Store Properties pages. The following property page shown in Figure 25.6 appears. The display window shows all the public folders on this server, including those replicated from other servers.

6. Click the Refresh button to update the display window with the latest information.

7. Click the Columns button to edit which columns are displayed and their width in pixels. See the following for a description of each column heading and what type of information it can display.

8. Click Apply to set these properties and continue with other properties. If you are done with all settings, click OK to return to the administrator program.

FIG. 25.6

View resources utilized by each public folder on this server.

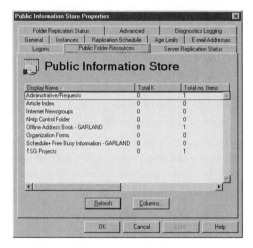

Default Columns   Columns define what type of information is displayed in the standard dialog box. Default columns are preconfigured to display the most commonly needed information. Optional columns provide more detailed information that may be useful in troubleshooting errors. The following is a list of default columns:

- Display Name: The Exchange administrator program object display name for this public folder

- Total K: The total amount of disk storage space (in kilobytes) taken up by the contents of this public folder (this value includes any message attachments)

- Total number Items: The sum of all messages and attachments stored in a mailbox
- Created: The date and time this folder was created
- Last Access Time: The last time a user logged in to this public folder
- Number of Owners: The number of users designated as Owners of this public folder (see section on defining roles for a public folder)
- Number of Contacts: The number of users designated as contacts for this public folder (see section on defining roles for a public folder)

Optional Columns   The following is a list of optional columns that can be used to display additional information about server resources:

- Folder: Folder name where messages are stored
- Folder Path: The system file path to where this folder is stored
- Total number Associated Messages: The sum of folder views and deferred action messages

A new time-saving option added in Exchange 5.0 is the capability to quickly view Public Folder Resources information from the main Exchange hierarchy seen in the left window of the Exchange administrator program (see Figure 25.7).

FIG. 25.7

Public Folder Resources information view.

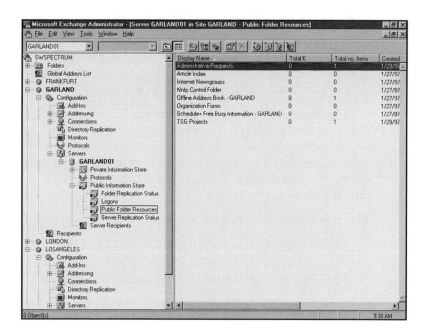

Part **III**

Ch **25**

To access the Public Folder Resources information using this new option:

1. Navigate to your desired site with the Exchange administrator program.

2. Click the small plus sign adjacent to the Configuration container of the selected site to further expand the hierarchy in the left-hand window.

3. Expand the Servers container in the left-hand window. A list of Exchange servers in your site will be listed.

4. Click and expand the server name on which the Public Information Store you want to configure is located.

5. The displayed server objects now visible in the left-display window of the Microsoft Exchange Administrator Program are identical in name and function to similar objects displayed in the right-hand window. Selecting properties of either the Private Information Store or Public Information Store displays the same data.

6. Expand the Public Information Store in the left window and click the Public Folder Resources object to see the status information quickly displayed in the right window. The default columns shown in the right window can be added by using the View menu and using the Columns option.

Defragmenting and Compacting Information Stores Offline

Exchange automatically addresses most defragmentation and compaction issues, but there are times when a manual execution is required. This involves using the Exchange EDBUTIL utility to defragment and optimize disk space allocation for an information store. It is important that you schedule this procedure at a time when message traffic is low or even nonexistent, because it involves stopping the information store service entirely.

The following command-line entry will defragment and compact the `priv.edb` file (Exchange Private Information Store) and automatically create a backup file. The EDBUTIL actually performs its work on the backup file and once satisfactorily completed, renames the backup to replace the original. This method minimizes possible further corruption of introduction of errors into the current production file. You will need enough disk space to hold both your current EDB file and the backup.

Here is an example command that includes a backup:

```
edbutil /d /ispriv
```

where `/ispriv` indicates the work is to be performed on the private information store. The general procedure for information store compacting is as follows:

1. Open the Windows NT services control panel and stop the Microsoft Exchange Information Store service (MSEXCHANGEIS).

2. Open a Windows NT command prompt window (or use the Run command from the Program Manager File menu).

3. Enter the `EDBUTIL` command using the following syntax

```
EDBUTIL [/d] [/information store type]
```

where /d indicates that switch options are present

Table 25.1 lists the available switch options for the EDBUTIL command.

Table 25.1 EDBUTIL.EXE Switch Options

Option	Description
/ds	Directory.
/ispriv	Private Information Store.
/ispub	Public Information Store.
/b	Makes a backup of the original file in the indicated location.
/r	Defragment and repair. Defragments the database as usual, but if errors are encountered, it attempts to correct the problem or removes the error. The end result is a problem-free database, but essential data may be missing.
/c	Performs a read-only database consistency check without making a copy. It does not repair or affect the database. It simply creates a report.
/t filename	Renames the newly compacted database to a specified filename.

4. Press Enter (or click OK if using the Run command from Program Manager) to start compacting.

N O T E Compacting a large information store could take a reasonable amount of time. So make sure to plan accordingly. ▓

5. After the compacting process finishes, restart the information store service.

6. Test the information store for proper functioning by logging into it with an Exchange client and trying to view messages or connect to a public folder.

7. If the information store is functional, you may remove the backup (.bak) file.

N O T E While the information store service is stopped, all message transfer attempts to the store are refused. Also, server mailbox users will not be able to open the store through their client. ▓

Maintaining Message Transfer Agents

The routing table is used by each Message Transfer Agent (MTA) in a site to calculate delivery paths for each message. Whenever a change is made that affects routing (e.g., modifying address spaces for a connector), it will not take effect until the site routing table has been rebuilt.

Normally, the routing table is rebuilt once per day unless the Routing Calculation Schedule has been modified. For more information on changing the Routing Calculation Schedule,

Part
III

Ch
25

see Chapter 3, "Exchange's Integrated Server Components." You can also opt to rebuild the table manually, this way:

1. Select the General property page of the Message Transfer Agent property pages. The property page shown in Figure 25.8 appears.

2. Click the Recalculate Routing button to begin rebuilding the routing table.

3. Click OK to return to the administrator program.

The MTA retrieves updated routing information from the routing table every 15 minutes. Therefore, it could take up to 15 minutes for routing updates to be utilized by the MTA.

FIG. 25.8

Use the General Message Transfer Agent Properties page to recalculate MTA routing.

MTA Message Queues

The Queues property page lists messages awaiting delivery by the MTA. There are two primary windows in this property page. The Queue name window shows which queue you are currently viewing and the Message list box displays the messages in that queue. From this, you can view details about a specific message in the queue, change its priority for delivery, or delete it entirely.

Within the Message list window, there are three columns that contain information about a particular message:

- Originator: The original sender of the message
- Submit time: The time the message entered the queue
- Size: The size of the message in kilobytes

To configure the Queues property page, do this:

1. Select the Queues property page from the Message Transfer Agent property pages. The following Queues property page shown in Figure 25.9 appears.

2. Use the Queue name pull-down menu to select which message queue to display. There are queues for the private and public information stores and any installed gateways.

FIG. 25.9

The message queue. It is blank because all pending messages have been delivered.

N O T E The Internet Mail connector and Microsoft Mail connector have separate queues that can also be accessed through their respective property pages. ■

3. Select a message and click Details to view additional information about it.

The additional message information includes message originator, submit time, message size, and priority. This button is dimmed if no messages are in the queue.

4. Click the Refresh button to update the message list window with the latest list of messages in the MTA queue.

5. Click Priority to display the message's priority.

Change the priority of a message if desired. It can be low, medium, or high. Messages are sent in order of this priority. A message's priority is set when a message is created, but can be adjusted for the purposes of this queue by changing values here.

6. Select a message and click Delete to remove a message from the MTA queue.

7. Click Apply to set these properties and continue with other properties. If you are done with all settings, click OK to return to the administrator program.

When dealing with MTA queue dialog boxes (or any other Exchange queue box), the messages you see on the list are a freeze frame of all queued messages at one point in time. To get a more dynamic view or to "catch" a message as it passes through the queue, you must continually press the Refresh button to get the latest updates.

MTA Diagnostic Logging

Logging falls mainly in the realm of troubleshooting. MTA logs can perhaps be used for other purposes, such as billing and accounting for number of messages transferred.

Maintaining Microsoft Mail Connector

The Microsoft Mail Connector has its own temporary message store called the MS Mail Connector post office. This gives the MS Mail Connector its own message queue property page from which to monitor message queue status.

To open the MS Mail Connector message queue window, do the following:

1. Navigate through the administrator program to the site desired, then locate and open the MS Mail Connector within the Connectors container to view its property pages.

2. Select the Connections tab (see Figure 25.10).

FIG. 25.10

View Connections.

3. Select from the Connections window the MS Mail connection you wish to monitor.

4. Click the Queue button. The MS Mail Connector message queue property page appears.

5. Select a sort order for the messages by clicking one of the categories on the top line of the Queued Messages window (see Figure 25.11).

   Information displayed in the queue:

   From the original message sender
   Subject   the data on the message's subject line
   Message ID   the message identifier
   Date/Time   the time when the message entered the queue

6. To remove a message, select it and then click Delete.

   If Send Non-Delivery Reports when messages deleted is checked, the original sender will be notified if his or her message was deleted from the queue. If it is clear, no notification will be sent when a message is deleted.

7. To return a message to its original sender, select it and then click Return.

8. Click Close to return to the MS Mail Connector Connections property page. Then, click OK to return to the administrator program.

FIG. 25.11

Monitor messages in Queued Messages box.

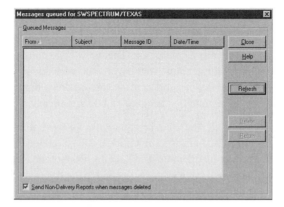

N O T E   As in the MTA queues property page, the view of queued messages is static. To update the display you must click the Refresh button. ■

Maintaining Directories

There are two components to each directory object saved in a server's information store: the object itself and a corresponding entry in the directory. Consistency adjustment corrects errors arising by mismatched directory information. This feature will either add or delete a directory entry to match the existence or absence of information store data.

The property page enables you to control at what point these inconsistencies are to be corrected. Figure 25.12 shows Advanced tab of the server Properties page where you configure directory inconsistency adjustment.

FIG. 25.12

This property page lets you adjust directory inconsistencies.

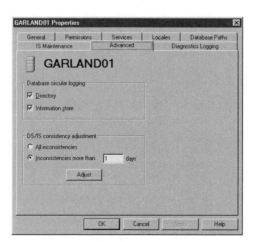

Select either All inconsistencies to correct them immediately or select Inconsistencies more than _X days and enter the time an inconsistency can exist before it is automatically corrected.

Understanding Knowledge Consistency

Knowledge consistency for the local server is its awareness of other Exchange servers within a site and at other sites within your organization. The knowledge consistency operation is run automatically once daily, but if Exchange servers or sites were added and the local was not aware of those changes' servers (e.g., the local server was down during that time), then you may not want to wait for the automatic checking and do it manually.

Suppose Exchange server GARLAND01 is brought down for two hours for a memory upgrade. During the time of the upgrade, a new server, GARLAND08, is added to the site. When GAR-LAND01 is restored to proper functioning, it will not be aware of the existence of the new server until the knowledge consistency cycle is run at the end of the day. Knowing this, the administrator for GARLAND01 runs the knowledge consistency cycle manually from the Directory Service property pages to make GARLAND01 aware of the new server's existence. (See Chapter 3, "Exchange's Integrated Server Components," for additional details on server properties.)

Resynchronizing Replicated Directory Information

If a directory inconsistency is detected when checking manually, it is a good idea to manually execute all processes related to correcting inconsistencies. Use this sequence:

1. Check knowledge consistency from the directory service property pages and detect the error.

2. Manually update directory replication within the site by running Update Now also from the Directory Service property pages.

3. It might also be a good idea to open the Message Transfer Agent properties for this server and click Recalculate Routing from the General property page.

Although this sequence is optional and will be automatically executed within a 24-hour period, performing the tasks immediately will reduce the possibility of conflicts or errors.

Defragmenting and Compacting Directory Information

Much like the information store, the Exchange directory can benefit greatly from offline defragmentation and compacting. The Microsoft Exchange directory service continually performs online compacting during its normal operation, but a dedicated, periodic, offline compacting will provide a more significant increase in performance. Not only will directory-accessing speed improve after compacting, but also hard disk space wasted through inefficient storage will be freed for use. Offline directory defragmentation and compacting requires stopping the Exchange Directory and Directory Synchronization services.

The following command-line entry will compact the dir.edb file (Exchange Directory database) and automatically back up the original to a file named dir.bak. As with the aforementioned use of EDBUITL with the PRIV.EDB and PUB.EDB, there must be sufficient disk space available to make a complete copy of the current DIR.EDB. Here is an example command:

```
EDBUTIL /d /ds
```

where /ds notes that the process is to run against the directory.

The procedure for compacting a directory is as follows:

1. Open the Windows NT services control panel and stop the Microsoft Exchange Directory service (MSEXCHANGEDSA) and the Directory Synchronization service (MSEXCHANGEDXA).

2. Open a Windows NT command prompt window (or use the Run command from the Program Manager File menu).

3. Enter the EDBUTIL command using the following syntax

```
EDBUTIL [/d] [/information store type]
```

where /d indicates that switch options are present. Please refer to Table 25.1 for the appropriate switch options.

4. Press Enter (or click OK if using the Run command from the Program Manager) to start compacting.

N O T E Compacting a large directory file could take a large amount of time, so make sure to plan accordingly. For a thousand users, for example, this process will possibly take an hour. ▪

5. After the compacting process finishes, restart the Exchange Directory and Directory Synchronization services.

6. Test the directory for proper functioning by accessing into the local address list with an Exchange client.

7. If the directory is functional, you may proceed to remove the backup (.bak) files.

Working with Directory Event Logs

Part of maintaining a healthy Exchange Organization is working with the Windows NT Event Log. It is important to keep track of Event Log sizes (to set upper size limits and expiration dates for log entries) so as to not let the Event Log become too large, but it should be allowed to grow large enough to hold many days worth of log entries. The two Directory Services to watch are these:

- ▪ MSExchangeDS: The directory service and directory replication process
- ▪ MSExchangeDX: Directory Synchronization

Logging levels for each service are set in the Diagnostic Logging property page. See Chapter 28, "Troubleshooting Exchange with Diagnostic Tools," for tips on using the Diagnostic Logging property pages for each service.

Part
III

Ch

25

Backing Up Your Exchange Server

Probably the most important maintenance procedure for Microsoft Exchange organization is backup of information store and directory information. Few things on a user's computer are as important to him or her as his or her e-mail. Implementing a good backup strategy is well worth the effort. This section will provide a general conceptual guide to Exchange backup. For more detail in using the Exchange Backup utility, refer to your Microsoft Exchange server documentation or the documentation of your Exchange "aware" NT backup solution.

Windows NT provides built-in tape backup and restore utilities that are supplemented by extensions installed with Exchange server. These utilities provide the basics for an adequate Exchange backup, but a full-featured backup software package would provide additional functionality and versatility. See Chapter 32, "Implementing Third-Party Integration Tools," on third-party integration for information about products that facilitate backup beyond what comes with the basic Exchange and NT package.

This section describes backup and restore procedures directly relevant to maintaining Exchange information. For full NT server backups, refer to your Windows NT or third-party backup software documentation.

The version of Backup included with Microsoft Exchange is aware of the servers in your organization and allows you to do backups for a single server, server group, sites, or even an entire organization if necessary.

The main Exchange information you will want to back up is located in the following paths:

\EXCHSRVR\MDBDATA

and

\EXCHSRVR\DSADATA

Important Exchange files to be backed up are these:

- Information store databases: SYSTEM.EDB, PRIV.EDB, PUB.EDB
- Information store logs: EDB.LOG
- Directory database: SYSTEM.EDB (separate from the information store SYSTEM.EDB file), DIR.EDB
- Directory logs: EDB.LOG (separate from the information store EDB.LOG files)

When restoring lost data, the log files are played back to reconstitute the databases to the point of the last backup.

A proper Exchange aware backup sequence can be completed without any downtime of the server, but performance is impacted for potentially connected users. As backup is performed, the transaction logs associated with the main information databases of Exchange (DIR, PRIV, and PUB) are reset to reflect that a backup has been made.

If a "non-Exchange aware" backup tool is used, the Exchange services will need to be stopped in order to release file locks on open files and databases. Once backup is complete, the transaction log files will need to be manually reset.

From Here...

This chapter showed you how to establish a maintenance strategy designed to ensure optimum performance and smooth operation. For related information, read the following chapters:

- Chapter 13, "Directory and System Attendant Configuration," provides more information on setting up and maintaining Exchange Directory services.
- Chapter 14, "Message Transfer Configuration," describes configuring messaging communication across your enterprise.
- Chapter 15, "Information Store Configuration," illuminates ways of working with both the private and public information store databases.
- Chapter 16, "Creating and Configuring Recipient," provides details about working with mailboxes and public folders.
- Chapter 26, "Monitoring Your Organization," discusses ways to monitor your systems and catch problems before they get out of hand.
- Chapter 28, "Troubleshooting Exchange with Diagnostic Tools," describes tracking down errors in an Exchange organization.

Part
III

Ch
25

Monitoring Your Organization

Many corporations do not realize that e-mail can become one of their most mission-critical applications. Literally, everyone in your company will use and come to depend on your messaging system. Like most systems, it's only as strong as your weakest link. Thus, Exchange Server incorpates several utilities to verify that your links are up and your servers are responding. The strength of these two basic components are the greatest factors in having a reliable Exchange System.

▬ **Important Terminology for Monitoring Your Exchange Organization**

Terms that help define test parameters for monitoring the Exchange Organization.

▬ **Set Up and Configure Link Monitors to Verify Messaging Connections**

Exchange has tests for the messaging system called link monitors. Link monitors test two points within an organization for message connections.

▬ **Set Up and Configure Server Monitors to Verify Proper Operation of Various System Services**

A server monitor watches a selected list of Windows NT services and tests whether they are running or not.

▬ **How to Use Monitor Status Windows to Read Monitor Data**

The server monitor window can monitor a server within the organization. Viewing this window can monitor many servers in the organization.

Understanding Exchange Monitoring Terms

Monitoring is the art of watching over your Exchange organization to identify and correct malfunctions before they become serious problems. An Exchange system consists fundamentally of Windows NT servers and links between them. Included with Microsoft Exchange server are two monitoring tools that service both components. They will be your eyes 24 hours a day to alert you when something goes wrong.

Exchange server includes two types of monitoring tools:

- Link monitor: Test messaging connections between Exchange servers in your organization.
- Server monitor: Test the status of Windows NT services on designated Exchange server.

The following terms are pertinent to using Exchange monitoring tools:

- Polling interval: The amount of time between system tests (time between ping messages sent or time between checking system service status).
- Warning state: A condition indicating that there potentially is a problem with a server or messaging link.
- Alert state: A condition indicating that a serious problem exists within the server or messaging link.
- Escalation path: The list of people, in order of notification priority, who receive alerts from a monitor.
- Notification: The process of alerting a system administrator that a specific server or messaging link is functioning abnormally.

Creating a Link Monitor

As an Exchange administrator, there are two fundamental ways that you may be notified of a downed messaging link:

- A user will try to send a message, it will come back undelivered, and you will receive an e-mail message from the user describing this fact.
- You can configure a link monitor to continuously watch that specific messaging connections are active and to detect unusual delays in message transmissions.

Link monitors watch for successful message connections between two points in an Exchange organization. They can also be configured to test connections to foreign messaging systems. Link monitors accomplish this by sending out a test message, called a *ping message*, and timing the round trip of that message.

A ping message sent by a link monitor is sent to test messaging connections. At the polling interval, a ping message is sent to every Exchange server and foreign system listed on the link monitor's servers property page.

To create a new link monitor, follow this procedure:

1. In the Exchange administrator program, select a site in your organization.
2. Open the Configuration container within the selected site.
3. Select the Monitors container; the right administrator program display window will show all the existing monitors (both link and server) in this site (see Figure 26.1).

FIG. 26.1
The Monitor container shows all monitors in the selected site. In our example, monitors can be made and executed anywhere in the organization with proper permissions.

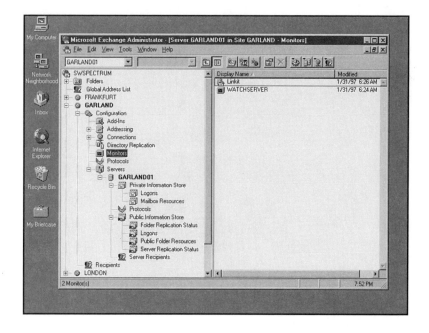

4. Select New Other, and then select Link monitor. The Link Monitor property pages appear.

Link Monitor Property Pages

The link monitor has several property pages:

- General: Name the monitor, set the polling interval, and optionally select a log file location.
- Notification: Specify how and to whom warning and alert messages are sent.
- Servers: Specify the local and remote Exchange servers and foreign messaging systems that will receive ping messages.

Part

III

Ch

26

■ Recipients: Configure ping messages to foreign messaging systems.

■ Bounce: Enter time delay before a server enters a warning or alert state due to a non-returned ping message.

The General Property Page

1. Select the General tab of the Linkit Properties page. The property page shown in Figure 26.2 appears.

2. Enter a Directory name for this link monitor. (The directory name cannot be changed for a link monitor after it has been created.)

3. Enter a Display name as you want it to be shown in the administrator display window.

FIG. 26.2

The Linkit Properties page lets you define a polling interval for this monitor.

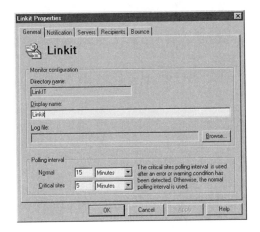

4. The Log File window shows the file name where monitor logs are being stored. Click Browse to select the file name and location.

N O T E Logging for link monitor activity is optional, so you need not specify a Log File location. ■

5. In the Polling Interval window, enter the units and time interval for Normal operation.

6. In the Polling Interval window, enter the units and time interval for Critical Sites.

7. Click Apply to set these properties and continue with other properties. When you are done with all settings, click OK to return to the administrator program.

The Notification Property Page

The Notification property page allows you to configure what happens when abnormal message link functioning is detected by a server monitor. There are three main types of notification:

■ Launch a process: Load an external application. This option is often used in conjunction with paging software.

- Mail message: Automatically sends an e-mail message to a selected recipient describing the situation.

- Windows NT Alert: Use the Windows NT Messenger service to notify a certain user or group of users.

The Notification property page is primarily one main display window list where all notification objects are displayed (see Figure 26.3). By default, this window is blank, and no notification is specific.

FIG. 26.3

The link monitor Notification property page shows who to contact in case of malfunctions.

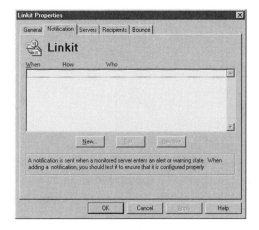

Click New to define a new notification object. Select the type of notification (see Figure 26.4).

FIG. 26.4

Select a Notification type.

Launching a Notification Process Configuring an external notification application is as easy as choosing the application and setting the time delay for notification. You must configure that external process for the specific type of notification it provides. All Exchange does is launch the process and pass along any additional required parameters (see Figure 26.5).

To configure the Launch Process Notification properties, do the following:

1. In the Time delay box, enter a numeric value and the time units (seconds, minutes, hours) from the pull-down menu.

2. Clear the Alert only check box if you want this notification process to occur when the server is in a warning state as well. Otherwise, the notification process will only launch in an alert state after the time delay is exceeded.

3. Click the File button and navigate your directory hierarchy to locate the process you want to launch in this notification. The Launch process box will display this file once selected.

4. Enter any additional command-line parameters you want to pass to the notification process once it is launched.

5. Select the Append notification text to parameter list check box in order to attach the actual notification text to the above command-line parameters during the process launch.

FIG. 26.5

Configure the parameters for the notification process.

> **N O T E**   If the external notification application is already configured, you may now use the Test button to verify property functioning. ▪

6. Click OK to complete these settings and return to the Notification property page.

You can change a Notification by selecting it from the Notification list and clicking Edit. You can delete a notification by selecting it from the list and clicking Remove.

Using Mail Message Notification   Mail notification will alert an administrator via e-mail that a server has entered an alert state (or warning state) due to excessive delays between message return.

To configure Mail Message Notification properties, follow this procedure (see Figure 26.6):

FIG. 26.6

Configure mail message Notification properties.

1. In the Time delay box, enter a numeric value and the time units (seconds, minutes, hours) from the pull-down menu.

2. Clear the Alert only check box if you want this notification process to occur when the server is in a warning state as well. Otherwise, the notification mail message will only be sent in an alert state after the time delay has been exceeded.

3. Click the Recipient button and navigate the Exchange address lists to select a recipient for the mail notification.

4. Click the Test button to verify proper notification functioning. Check the destination address to verify message delivery.

5. Click OK to complete these settings and return to the Notification property page.

Using Windows NT Alerts   Notification by Windows NT Alert (see Figure 26.7) is only useful if the recipient computer is turned on and a user is logged in to it. These alerts are transmitted via the Windows NT Message service and are displayed on-screen to a user.

FIG. 26.7
Define Windows NT
Alert parameters.

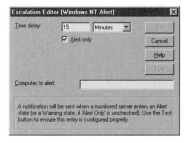

To configure notification properties for Windows NT Alert:

1. In the Time delay box, enter a numeric value and the time units (seconds, minutes, hours) from the pull-down menu.

2. Clear the Alert only check box if you want this notification process to occur when the server is in a warning state as well. Otherwise, the alert message will only be sent in an alert state after the time delay has been exceeded.

3. Enter the name of the Computer to alert in the box provided. Use the Windows NT server name (Exchange server name) for that computer.

4. Click the Test button to verify proper notification functioning. Check the destination computer to verify alert message delivery.

5. Click OK to complete these settings and return to the Notification property page.

The Servers Property Page

The Servers property page lets you determine which Exchange servers will be sent ping messages by the link monitor.

1. Select the Servers property tab from the link monitor's property page. The property page shown in Figure 26.8 appears.

   The left display window lists the Microsoft Exchange server in the site selected in the lower left pull-down menu. The right display window shows which servers will receive ping messages from this server.

2. Use the Site pull-down menu to select a site in your organization. The servers in that site will be listed in the left display window.

FIG. 26.8
Select which Exchange servers will receive ping messages.

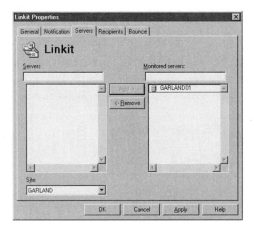

3. Select an Exchange server from the Servers window and click Add to enable monitoring for it.

4. To stop monitoring, click a server from the right display window and click Remove.

5. Click Apply to set these properties and continue with other properties. When you are done with all settings, click OK to return to the administrator program.

The Recipients Property Page

The Recipients property page allows you to configure ping message recipients in foreign messaging systems. At each polling interval, selected foreign recipients will receive a ping message. You must configure each recipient as a custom recipient in the Exchange administrator program. The link monitor will look at the returned ping message subject line for confirmation of message integrity. Alternatively, you can have the link monitor look at the returned message's body.

For link monitoring, ping messages must be returned by a foreign system. You must write a script that will return the ping message. Another common solution is to send a message to a nonexistent address on that system; the system then returns the nondeliverable message to the link monitor.

N O T E Some systems do not automatically return messages sent to nonexistent addresses; they redirect them into a default mailbox. Make sure the foreign system is configured to bounce back messages sent to nonexistent addresses. ▪

 T I P Create a separate container to hold the custom recipients created for foreign system link monitoring. Also, set the Hide from address book option for each recipient, so they will not accidentally be sent messages by others in your organization.

1. Select the Recipients tab from the link monitor property pages. The Recipients property page appears.

2. In the left display window, click Modify and select the custom recipients you have created to get ping messages from this link monitor. The monitor will check the subject line of the returned message for confirmation of link status.

3. In the right display window, click Modify and select the custom recipients you have created to get ping messages from this link monitor. The monitor will check the body text of the returned message for confirmation of link status. Use this option usually when sending ping messages to a nonexistent address (when the subject line is not normally preserved).

4. Click Apply to set these properties and continue with other properties. If you are done with all settings, click OK to return to the administrator program.

The Bounce Property Page

The Bounce property page allows you the maximum allowable round-trips before a server enters a warning or alert state.

To define bounce times, follow this procedure:

1. Select the Bounce tab from the link monitor property pages. The property page shown in Figure 26.9 appears (see Figure 26.9).

2. Enter the number and select the time units (seconds, minutes, hours) to wait for a return message before entering a warning state. The default time is 30 minutes.

3. Enter the number and select the time units (seconds, minutes, hours) to wait for a return message before entering an alert state. The default time is 60 minutes.

4. Click Apply to set these properties and continue with other properties. When you are done with all settings, click OK to return to the administrator program.

After configuring all Link Monitor property pages, you must start the link monitor for it to carry out its functions. See "Starting and Using a Monitor" later in this chapter.

FIG. 26.9

Use this page to define threshold time before entering warning and alert states.

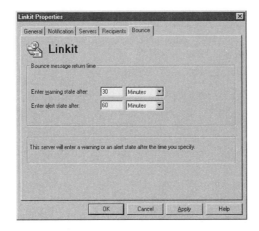

Creating a Server Monitor

A server monitor watches a selected list of Windows NT services for proper functioning. At each polling interval, the server monitor will check to see that the server is running by connecting to that server via a remote procedure call. The server's status is displayed in the server monitor's display window. You can also control (i.e., start, stop, pause) services via the server monitor display windows.

Additionally, these monitors can be used to monitor services that are not directly pertinent to Exchange if desired.

To create a new server monitor, follow this procedure:

1. In the Exchange administrator program, select a site in your organization.
2. Open the Configuration container within the selected site.
3. Select the Monitors container, the right administrator program display window will show all the existing monitors (both link and server) in this site.
4. Select New Other, then select Server Monitor. The Server Monitor property pages appear.

Server Monitor Property Pages

The server monitor has several property pages:

- General: Give the monitor a display name, set the polling interval, and select a log file location.
- Notification: Select alert type and delay times.
- Servers: Select which servers to monitor.
- Actions: Define procedure executed in case of malfunction.
- Clock: Set acceptable variations between system clocks.

If your organization includes different people who need to be notified of servers' malfunction, you must create separate server monitors. Also, if you want to set a different polling interval for a specific group of servers, you must create unique server monitors.

The General Page

The General property page allows you to name the server monitor and determine the polling interval and determine the location for a log file if one is desired.

To configure general settings for the server monitor, follow this procedure:

1. Select the General tab of the server monitor property pages. The property page shown in Figure 26.10 appears.

FIG. 26.10

Name this monitor and set its polling interval.

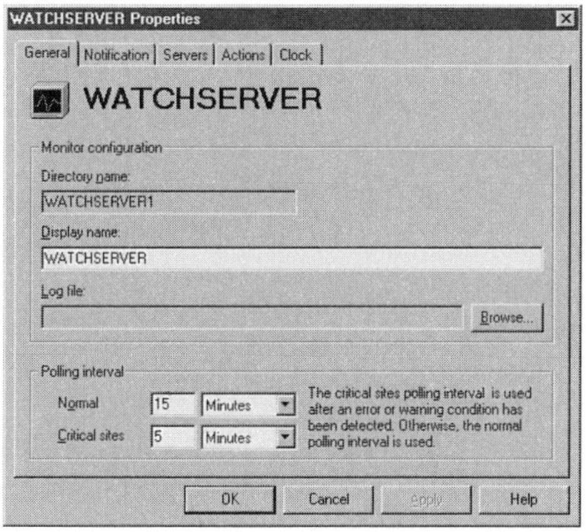

2. Enter a Directory name for this server monitor. (The directory name cannot be changed for a server monitor after it has been created.)

3. Enter a Display name as you want it to be shown in the administrator display window.

4. The Log File window shows the file name where monitor logs are being stored. Click Browse to select the file name and location.

5. In the Polling Interval window, enter the units and time interval for Normal operation.

6. In the Polling Interval window, enter the units and time interval for Critical Sites.

7. Click Apply to set these properties and continue with other properties. If you are done with all settings, click OK to return to the administrator program.

The Notification Property Page

The Notification property page allows you to configure what happens when a server monitor detects abnormal functioning. There are three main types of notification:

- Launch a process: Load an external application. (This option is often used in conjunction with paging software.)

Part

III

Ch

26

- Mail message: Automatically sends an e-mail message to a selected recipient describing the situation.

- Windows NT Alert: Use the Windows NT Messenger service to notify a certain user or group of users.

The Notification property page is primarily one main display window where all notification objects are displayed. By default, this property page is blank.

Click New to define a new notification object. Select the type of notification.

Launching a Notification Process   Configuring an external notification application is as easy as choosing the application and setting the time delay for notification. You must configure that external process for the specific type of notification it provides. All Exchange does is launch the process and pass along any additional required parameters.

To configure Launch Process Notification properties, follow this procedure:

1. In the Time delay box, enter a numeric value and the time units (seconds, minutes, hours) from the pull-down menu.

2. Clear the Alert only check box if you want this notification process to occur when the server is in a warning state. Otherwise, the notification process will only launch in an alert state after the time delay is exceeded.

3. Click the File button and navigate your directory hierarchy to locate the process you want to launch in this notification. The Launch process box will display this file once selected.

4. Enter any additional command-line parameters you want to pass along to the notification process once it is launched.

5. Select the Append notification text to parameter list check box in order to attach the actual notification text to the above command-line parameters during the process launch.

N O T E   If the external notification application is already configured, you may now use the Test button to verify property functioning.

6. Click OK to complete these settings and return to the Notification property page.

You can change a Notification by selecting it from the Notification list and clicking Edit. You can delete a notification by selecting it from the list and clicking Remove.

Using Mail Message Notification   Mail message notification will alert an administrator via e-mail that a server has entered an alert state (or Warning state as well, if desired).

To configure Mail Notification properties, follow this procedure:

1. In the Time delay box, enter a numeric value and the time units (seconds, minutes, hours) from the pull-down menu.

2. Clear the Alert only check box if you want this notification process to occur when the server is in a warning state. Otherwise, the notification mail message will only be sent in an alert state after the time delay has been exceeded.

3. Click the Recipient button and navigate the Exchange address lists to select a recipient for the mail notification.

4. Click the Test button to verify proper notification functioning. Check the destination address to verify message delivery.

5. Click OK to complete these settings and return to the Notification property page.

Using Windows NT Alerts   Notification by Windows NT Alert is only useful if the recipient computer is turned on and a user is logged in to it. These alerts are transmitted via the Windows NT Message service and are displayed on-screen to the specific user.

To configure notification properties for Windows NT Alert:

1. In the Time delay box, enter a numeric value and the time units (seconds, minutes, hours) from the pull-down menu.

2. Clear the Alert only check box if you want this notification process to occur when the server is in a warning state. Otherwise, the alert message will only be sent in an alert state after the time delay has been exceeded.

3. Enter the name of the Computer to alert in the box provided. Use the Windows NT server name (Exchange server name) for that computer.

4. Click the Test button to verify proper notification functioning. Check the destination computer to verify alert message delivery.

5. Click OK to complete these settings and return to the Notification property page.

The Servers Property Page

The Servers property page lets you determine what servers the server monitor is monitoring.

1. Select the Servers property page from the server monitor's property page. Select server tab from the property page shown in Figure 26.11.

   The left display window lists the Microsoft Exchange server in the site selected in the lower left pull-down menu.

   The right display window shows which servers are being monitored.

2. Use the Site pull-down menu to select a site in your organization. The servers in that site will be listed in the left display window.

3. Select an Exchange server from the Servers windows, and click Add to enable monitoring for it.

4. To stop monitoring, click a server from the right display window and click Remove.

5. To define specifically which services are monitored on each server, use the Services button. (See the procedure in the next section.)

Part

III

Ch

26

FIG. 26.11

Select which servers this monitor will watch.

Configuring Monitored Services   You can determine specific services to be monitored for each selected Exchange server. By default, only the core Microsoft Exchange services (Directory, Information Store, and MTA) are configured for monitoring. Monitored services can also be configured on the property pages for each individual Exchange server.

To configure monitored services with the server monitor, follow this procedure:

1. On the Servers tab of the Server monitor property pages, select a server to configure. Click the Services tab. The dialog box shown in Figure 26.12 appears.

   The Installed services window shows all the system services running on this Windows NT server. The Monitored services window shows the system services currently being watched.

N O T E   This dialog box is identical to the Services tab in an individual server's property pages. ▨

2. Scroll through the list of installed Windows NT services and select which one to monitor. Click Add.

3. To remove a service from the Monitored services list, select it and click Remove.

4. Click None to remove all services from the monitored service list.

5. Click Default to keep only the Microsoft Exchange Directory, Information Store, and Message Transfer Agent services on the monitored list.

6. Click All to include every Windows NT service in the Monitored services window (this is usually not a good idea, except under very special circumstances).

7. Click Apply to set these properties and continue with other properties. If you are done with all settings, click OK to return to the Server Monitor's Servers property page.

FIG. 26.12

Add or remove services to be monitored.

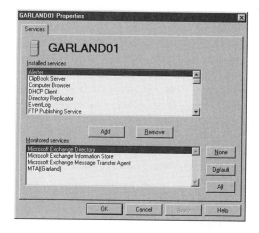

Configuring Monitored Services from Exchange Server Property Pages To open Server property pages, follow this procedure:

1. Navigate to your desired site with the Exchange administrator program.

2. Click the Configuration container of the selected site. All the site configuration objects appear in the administrator program's right window.

3. Open the Servers container. A list of Exchange servers in your site will be listed.

4. Click the server name on which the Private Information Store you want to configure is located. The list of server objects is visible on the right display window of the Microsoft Exchange administrator program.

5. Open its property pages by selecting Properties from the administrator program file menu or by pressing Alt+Enter.

6. Select the Services tab.

The Services Property Page

The Services property page enables you to define what services a Microsoft Exchange server monitor will check. It is identical to the page found on the server monitor Servers page. The top display window shows all services currently installed on this Windows NT server; the bottom display window shows the monitored services. Follow these steps:

1. Select a service from the top window and click Add to add it to the list of Monitored Services.

2. Select a service from the bottom window and click Remove to take it off the list of Monitored Services.

3. Click Default to return to the basic services selected by Exchange Server.

4. Click None to remove all services from the monitored lists.

Part
III

Ch
26

The Actions Property Page

Use the Actions property page to define what steps are to be taken when a monitored service ceases to function. By default, no action is taken when a service goes down (except notification). Settings on this dialog box apply to all Exchange servers selected on the Servers property page. If you want to define different actions for different servers, you must create additional server monitors. There are three action choices to configure:

- Take no action: Literally, to do nothing in response to a stopped service. (Normal notification functions will still occur.)
- Restart the service: Initiate a service restart command.
- Restart the computer: Initiate a server restart command.

First attempt actions are executed the first time a service is polled and found to be in a warning or alert state. Second attempt is after the second, and subsequent attempts are any time after the first two.

To configure Actions, follow this procedure:

1. Select the Actions tab from the Server monitor property pages. The property page shown in Figure 26.13 appears.

N O T E Actions defined in this property page are performed in addition to any notification action. ■

2. Next to First attempt, use the pull-down menu to select an appropriate action. By default, Take no action is chosen.

FIG. 26.13

Define what actions the server monitor should take upon detecting a service malfunction.

3. Next to Second attempt, use the pull-down menu to select an appropriate action. By default, Take no action is chosen.

4. Next to Subsequent attempts, use the pull-down menu to select an appropriate action. By default, Take no action is chosen.

5. Enter a Restart delay (in seconds) that the server will wait before initiating a restart command. By default, this value is 60 seconds.

6. Type Restart message that will be displayed by the server when a restart server action is initiated.

7. Click Apply to set these properties and continue with other properties. When you are done with all settings, click OK to return to the administrator program.

The Clock Property Page

The Clock property page configures system clock monitoring. Proper system clock synchronization is essential to running an efficient Exchange organization. So many connectors, gateways, and general maintenance processes depend on system-clock-based schedules that incorrect time setting could create many problems. The monitoring computer will generate an alert if both computers' system clocks are off by the predetermined number of seconds.

To set clock monitoring, follow this procedure:

1. Select the Clock tab of the Server Monitor property pages. The dialog box shown in Figure 26.14 appears.

FIG. 26.14

Make sure clocks in your organization are properly synchronized.

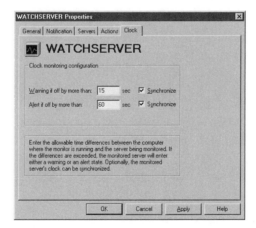

Part

III

Ch

26

2. In Warning if off by more than, type the maximum amount of time (in seconds) that the two clocks can differ before entering a warning state.

3. In Alert if off by more than, type the maximum amount of time (in seconds) that the two clocks can differ before entering an alert state.

4. Clear the Synchronize check boxes to prevent the clock from adjusting to the monitoring computer's clock. By default, this option is selected.

5. Click Apply to set these properties and continue with other properties. When you are done with all settings, click OK to return to the administrator program.

Starting and Using a Monitor

After creating a monitor, you must start it in order for it to perform its functions. You can start a monitor manually from the administrator program or automatically from the command line. The monitor's window must be open at all times when running (minimized is OK).

Automatically Starting a Server Monitor

You can configure a server monitor for automatic startup by creating a program item for it in the Program Manager Startup group. The following sequence automatically starts the administrator program and designated monitors when logging in to Windows NT.

1. In the Windows NT Program Manager, open the Startup program group.

2. Select New from the Program Manager File menu.

3. Select Program Item from the New Program Object dialog box. Click OK.

4. Enter a Description for this startup item.

5. Enter a command line following this format: **path\admin.exe / msitename\monitorname\server**

   Example command-line entry:

   ```
   E:\exchange\bin\admin.exe /mGARLAND\WATCHSERVER\GARLAND01
   ```

   Optionally, multiple monitors can be started with this command-line entry by adding an extra /m and identifying the monitor.

   Example:

   ```
   E:\exchange\bin\admin.exe /mGARLAND\WATCHSERVER\GARLAND01 /
   mGARLAND\LinkIT\GARLAND01
   ```

Manually Starting a Server Monitor

We can start a monitor from another server in the organization. In the following examples, the monitors where constructed and started at the Garland site. Note that the monitors exist in Los Angeles as well. To start a monitor manually from the administrator program, follow this procedure:

1. Using the Exchange administrator program, select the site in which the desired server monitor resides.

2. Open the Configuration container for the selected site.

3. Click the Monitors container for this site. The right administrator display window will show all the monitors you have created in your site (whether started or not).

4. Select the server monitor of your choice. From the administrator program Tools menu, select Start Monitor (see Figure 26.15).

5. In the Connect to server dialog box, select which server to connect to as a home server. Click OK to start the monitor. The server monitor's display window appears.

N O T E You must connect to a specific server in order to execute server-based operations (e.g., sending mail). ▓

FIG. 26.15
The administrator program's Start Monitor command.

Using Monitor Status Windows

Monitor status windows are your portal through which you view the current condition of monitored links and servers. The status windows periodically update and display data on their operation. With enough strategically placed monitors, you can get an overall feel of your organization's messaging conditions from a single machine in your enterprise.

Reading the Link Monitor Window

The Link Monitor window displays the condition of monitored links. Each line in the display represents one link. You can sort the display using the Column heading buttons. You can also change the width of the columns to make the display easier to read (see Figure 26.16).

FIG. 26.16
A functioning Link Monitor window.

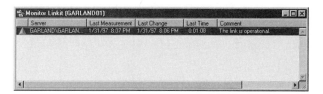

The Columns indicate the following things:

▓ Icon: Visually represents the link status

Up	Link is operational
Down	Link is not operational
Exclamation point	Warning state
Question mark	Link not yet monitored

■ Server: The Server that sent the ping message and to which it is expected to return

■ Last Measurement: The time the last ping message was sent

■ Last Change: Time that the status of the link changed

■ Last Time: The round-trip time of the last ping message sent from the sending server

■ Comment: A description of the monitored link condition

Reading the Server Monitor Window

The Server Monitor window displays one line for each server being monitored. The status of the server, as represented by the icon, reflects the status of all server components. If any component is down, the server is considered to be down (see Figure 26.17).

FIG. 26.17

A functioning Server Monitor window.

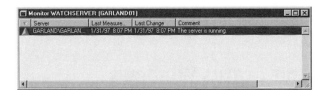

The Columns indicate the following things:

■ Icon: Visually represents a server's status

UpServer is operational

DownServer is not operational

Exclamation point (!) Warning state

Question mark (?) Server not yet monitored

■ Server: The name of the server being monitored

■ Last measure: Time the last Remote Procedure Call was sent to test the status of Windows NT services

■ Last change: Time the condition of service on a server changed

Double-clicking a status message in either a link or server monitor will bring up property pages with status information. See Chapter 28, "Troubleshooting Exchange with Diagnostic Tools," for an explanation of these property pages.

Stopping a Monitor for Maintenance

When bringing an Exchange server down for maintenance, consider the effects on monitors watching the server. Any server monitors will notice the halted services, initiate notifications, and enter an alert state. Any link monitors watching messaging connection through this server will enter alert mode and send out applicable notifications as well.

To prevent these problems, you can put a server into maintenance mode. When a monitor polls a server in this mode, it knows not to go through the normal alerts and warnings routine.

The command to specify a maintenance mode for a server is as follows:

```
ADMIN /t
```

After this command is executed, each monitor learns of the server's maintenance status at the next server poll. Keep in mind, each monitor's polling interval to be sure that all monitors are notified before you bring a server down.

The command can be modified with these additional switches:

-n	halts notification processes on a monitor, but keeps monitor initiated repairs
-r	keeps monitor-initiated notifications, but halts repair processes on a monitor
-nr	halts both notification and repair processes
-t	resets the monitor to normal mode

To confirm that a monitor has received a maintenance notification, open a link or a server entry in the monitor and select its Maintenance property page. The check boxes will give you this information.

From Here...

In this chapter, we have covered the two types of Exchange monitors. You will use these tools as your virtual eyes and ears watching over your Exchange servers and messaging links. Various notification options can be configured to alert you in the event a malfunction or aberration in standard performance occurs. However, these monitors are just additional tools at your disposal, not substitutes for good site and link planning and implementation.

- Chapter 13, "Directory and System Attendant Configuration," describes in detail ways of using the Server property pages to configure monitored services.
- Chapter 28, "Troubleshooting Exchange with Diagnostic Tools," provides more information on using monitors to diagnose problems.

Part
III

Ch
26

CHAPTER 27

Exchange Security

Exchange relies on the C2-level security included within Windows NT for a portion of its structure. C2-level security is a U.S. Department of Defense rating defined. It provides for discretionary access control (users, groups, and so on), object reuse protection (protecting deleted data), mandatory logon, and auditing of security related events. Windows NT can provide user authentication, resource access, and auditing. Each of these areas is described in this chapter. Exchange increases security with digital signatures and message encryption. ∎

Understanding Elements of NT security

Learn about NT accounts, groups, and permissions.

Understanding the Elements of Exchange's Security

Discover roles of key security components.

Installing and Managing the Key Management Server

This chapter explains Advanced security, person to person key exchange, and more.

Understanding NT Authentication

Every user, process, and service is required to enter a unique login name and password to gain access to the system. The operating system's interactive two-step security process of checking the login name with the password is known as *authentication*.

Microsoft Exchange Server enables the operating system to ascertain the identity and handle the validation of users and processes. The *identity* is the username and the *validation* is the user password. The operating system then will establish the security context, which explains and controls what kind of access will be granted to the user or process.

When a user or process logs on to the Windows NT server, there is no need for any other usernames or passwords to achieve access to Microsoft Exchange Server. This feature is unlike other types of message-system security features.

For example, a LAN Administrator on a Novell NetWare 3.1x is located on Server1 and the Microsoft Mail 3.x post offices and utilities are located on Server2. The administrator is required to enter a username and password for initial access to Server1. An additional username and password is needed for access to the directory structure on Server2. Moreover, a third username and password is needed to finally access the Admin program. Other message systems, such as Lotus cc:Mail, have similar security policies.

Defining NT Domain Architecture

Each user or resource within a single location, such as the Microsoft Exchange server, is a member of a particular *domain*. A domain is either a single Microsoft Windows NT server or multiple Windows NT servers that use the same security scheme and user-account database. Only one username and password is required to recognize, authenticate, and establish a connection to all the Windows NT servers and their resources in the domain.

Multiple domains or separate domain remote sites can connect by way of a *trust relationship*. This connection between the domains allows users on one domain the capability to access resources within the other domain. When the domains are in a trusted relationship, one domain (*trusting domain*) trusts the other (*trusted domain*). Any user located in the trusted domain can gain access to objects within the other domain.

For example, a user at Software Spectrum located in Garland who logs on to Domain A wants access to a resource on Domain B. Because Domain B located in Los Angeles has a trusted relationship with Domain A, the Domain B resources are available to this user. This situation is known as *passthrough authentication*, which allows having only one user account on one domain and the capability to access resources on the other.

The Types of NT Accounts

Windows NT accounts are the principal structure upon which authentication is based. Accounts consist of the two main elements: the user ID and the associated password. These two fundamental bits of information provide the key to access various services. There are two main types of Windows NT accounts:

- User accounts
- Service accounts

User Accounts

Single and multiple user accounts can be associated with a Microsoft Exchange server mailbox. The user attempting to establish a connection with a Microsoft Exchange server must be located within the same domain as the Microsoft Exchange server to which the user is trying to connect. If the user and the Microsoft Exchange server are located on different domains, the domains must be in a trusted relationship.

As another example, a user on Domain A at Software Spectrum in Garland wants to acquire access to a Microsoft Exchange server located on Domain B in Los Angeles; but in this case, Domain A and Domain B do not have a trusted relationship. The user on Domain A cannot establish a connection with the Microsoft Exchange server located on Domain B.

Service Accounts

On the Microsoft Windows NT server, an assortment of services is initiated when the system goes through its startup process. The Microsoft Exchange Server information store service and MTA established connections are good examples of services that run on a Microsoft Windows NT Server. These services, through a user account known as a *service account*, log on to the system and start up automatically.

The service account is an important feature to the Microsoft Exchange server. Create this account before beginning the installation of Microsoft Exchange server. This account affects the installation of and communication establishment between other Microsoft Exchange servers. When you install and join a new Microsoft Exchange server to a site with an existing Microsoft Exchange server, the service account is requested to complete the installation. The service account must be the same on all servers within a site. Without this account, Microsoft Exchange servers in the same site will not be able to communicate with each other. If a site extends over multiple domains, only one service account is needed, provided that a trust relationship exists between domains.

Part
III

Ch
27

Introduction to NT's Access Control

When a user logs on to a Microsoft Windows NT server, the security features of the operating system look to the security context (covered previously in this chapter) for information determining the permissions to access specific network resources. A *permission* controls access to individual objects located in the system that use specific authorization information. Each object is different and, subsequently, has different levels of permissions.

The following list shows the variety of permissions to control access that Microsoft Exchange Server offers:

- Mailbox
- Public folder
- Directory
- Group

Each of the permissions is discussed in the detail in the following sections of this chapter.

Mailbox Permissions

The Administrator program is the application used to grant permissions to log on and gain access to a Microsoft Exchange server mailbox. One mailbox can have either one or multiple user accounts with the user permission set for it.

Microsoft Exchange Server reviews all user accounts for the user permission when a logon is attempted. After the review completes, it verifies whether or not the user attempting to log on has this permission.

Public Folder Permissions

Using the Microsoft Exchange client, the owner of a public folder can grant permission to the following areas to access it:

- Mailboxes
- Distribution lists
- Public folders

As stated previously, different objects have different levels of permissions. The owner of a public folder can grant others the following permissions:

- Create items
- Read items
- Edit items
- Delete items

The public folder, similar to other Windows NT resources, reviews the user accounts for permissions for this resource. Then, the folder verifies that the object trying to access it has the appropriate permissions.

As an example, Software Spectrum has created two differing distribution lists within a Financial public folder on the Microsoft Exchange Server Accounting and Accounting Managers. The permissions can be modified on the Financial public folder so that members of the Accounting group have Read access, and the Accounting Managers may have Read and Write permissions.

Directory Permissions

Applying permissions to directories is different than applying permissions to public folders. With directories, the permissions are granted directly to the user's account database. Within the administrator application—although all users can see the directory listed—unless the users have the correct permissions, they cannot view the data inside the directory. A good example of a directory permission is *Add Child*. With this permission on the Recipient Container, a user can create mailboxes.

Roles are another way of making administrative tasks easier. Roles consist of built-in groups of certain kinds of similar permissions. For example, the following list shows the built-in permissions for the Admin role:

- Add child
- Modify user attributes
- Delete
- Logon

Organizing NT Groups and Permissions

Sets of user accounts with similar network resource needs can be placed into a *group*. This action simplifies the administrative task of adding permissions to individual users. If a group named MIS is created, all members of this group automatically have the permissions that are granted to the group, and these permissions are applied to the individual user. Any users accounts that are created after the group was created, or existing users who become additional members of this group, will have the same group permissions applied. Likewise, if the permissions of the group are modified, all members of the group will have their permissions changed. Microsoft Windows NT Server offers built-in *local* and *global groups* with the capability to also create local and global groups. When possible, use groups. Using groups diminishes the amount of time spent dealing with administrative tasks.

Part

III

Ch

27

Local Groups

Only the domain where the local group exists will contain the definition of resource permissions for this group. Additionally, no matter which domain the local group is located in, permissions can be granted only to that particular domain's resources. Local groups may contain the following:

- Other users
- Global groups from the same domain
- Users from trusted domains
- Global groups from trusted domains

N O T E Local groups cannot contain other local groups from the same domain. ■

Global Groups

Groups that can use resources within other domains are known as global groups. Global groups consist of a group of user accounts that was given access to permissions and rights for the following:

- The global group's own domain
- Servers and clients of the domain
- Any trusting domains

Global groups also can be members of local domain groups.

In essence, the creation of global groups allows for sets of users from within a particular domain and the available use of network resources, from both inside and outside the domain.

Using NT's Auditing Capabilities

Microsoft Windows NT has built-in auditing capabilities that allow the operating system to track events that occur within the system to detect security breaches. This tracking is an advantage for the Microsoft Exchange Server system. As discussed previously, the operating system handles the identity and validation of users for Microsoft Exchange Server. Moreover, the Microsoft Windows NT Server operating system can be modified to audit the Microsoft Exchange Server event services and directory objects. These events show up in the Windows NT event log.

N O T E Microsoft Exchange Server Administrators do not require permissions to administer to the Microsoft Windows NT Server. ■

Using Exchange's Advanced Security

As mentioned previously, Exchange uses several of NT's built-in C2-level security features. To augment this security, Exchange adds digital signatures and message encryption. To enable these advanced security features, you must designate one server within your organization that manages a special security database. This server is known as the Key Management (KM)

Server. Before discussing how the KM Server works with digital signatures and message encryption, make sure that you understand keys, tokens, certificates, and Exchange's revocation list.

Keys

Each mailbox created within Microsoft Exchange Server is given two pairs of electronic keys. One key pair, used for signing and verifying actions, is created by the Microsoft Exchange client. The other pair, used for encrypting and decrypting operations, is generated by the KM Server. The *private key* is known only by the user, and a *public key* is known by the public (it can be accessed by other mail users). This key-type of security features is known as *public/private key technology*, a data-encryption industry standard.

The Microsoft Exchange client, located on the user's local hard disk, stores the private keys in an encrypted security file (with the extension .EPF) within the client's local directory structure. The private encryption key is used for decrypting messages destined for the user's mailbox. The private signing key is used for signing messages when they are sent.

For every message recipient, each of his or her public encryption keys is used when the original message composer sends an encrypted message. The multiple public encryption keys are used to complete the encryption process. When each recipient receives the encrypted message, his or her public signing key is used to verify the identity of the message sender or composer.

Another key used by the Microsoft Exchange server is the *bulk encryption key*. This key is used in conjunction with both the public and private encryption keys. The bulk encryption key is used to encrypt the original message. The key then is placed into a *lockbox*, where it is kept to protect the key during transit. If the message has multiple recipients, a lockbox is attached to the message for each of the recipients. When the message is received at the recipient's location, the bulk encryption key is extracted from the lockbox and used to decrypt the original message.

Certificates

The Certificate Authority (CA) is the Key Management Server component that generates signing and encrypting certificates. *Certificates* bind the user's public key to the user's mailbox. The CA certifies the genuineness of those public keys created for users. Users have two kinds of certificates—an encryption certificate and a signing certificate. The *encryption certificate* is an attribute of the mailbox and contains the user's public encryption key. The *signing certificate* is contained in the user's security file on the local hard disk drive. It holds the user's public signing key.

The certificate also contains the following information:

- A unique serial number, generated by the CA for each certificate
- The CA's directory name (DN)
- The user's directory name (DN)
- The expiration date of the user's public key

Part
III

Ch

27

Exchange also supports the revocation of security certificates. This action permanently deactivates the security certificate for a mailbox. This should be done only when you are absolutely sure that you do not need to recover the security keys in the future. When the security certificate is revoked for a mailbox, anyone attempting to open an encrypted message previously sent from this mailbox is prompted with a warning, informing him or her that the message was secured with a revoked security certificate.

The revocation list contains the serial number and expiration date of all revoked certificates. This makes sure that the revoked user's mail account cannot be used by unauthorized personnel. The user then can be reconfigured for advanced security and another certificate issued. Reconfiguration will issue another token, and also another certificate serial number and expiration date.

You may want to consider revoking advanced security when the following situations exist:

- Users feel their security was compromised because it appears that someone is signing messages on their behalf or because someone has gained access to their security files and passwords.

  For example, a Software Spectrum salesperson's laptop was stolen in the field. You should revoke this salesperson's certificate to ensure that that person's security certificates are in the relocation list. Then you should reconfigure the user for Exchange's advanced security, generating a new security certificate for the user.

- An employee leaves your organization, and you want to ensure that the digital signatures and encrypted messages from this user are identified as invalid.

All revoked certificates originate in the KM Server database and are distributed to all the clients. Each client caches the original list and receives a daily update from the KM Server. For performance reasons, revoke users judiciously. When a message reaches its recipient and the signature is verified, it must be checked against the list before the message can be decrypted. The more certificates that are contained in the list, the more advanced security and performance of the client will degrade.

Tokens

When a mail administrator activates advanced security for a user, a temporary security *token* is generated. This random eight-digit code not only enables digital signing and data encryption, but also can be recovered if lost. The token should be loaded on the local workstation. Tokens are used only once, to secure a connection with the KM server and complete the advanced security setup for Microsoft Exchange Server advanced security users.

Key Management Server

One Microsoft Exchange Server integrated component is the Key Management Server, which is the central point for advanced security within the system. The Key Management Server provides the following services:

- Certifies public signing and encryption keys
- Creates public and private encryption keys
- Maintains backups of private encryption keys and public signing keys
- Generates tokens
- Maintains the original copy of the revocation list

All private encryption keys, public signing keys, and the revocation list are stored in the key management database. For additional security, the KM Server database itself is encrypted.

Each user that you want to use advanced security must be configured after the KM Server is configured. The users are given a temporary token to allow access to the KM Server so that the advanced security features setup can be completed.

When the Key Management Server is properly set up and advanced security is activated, users can take advantage of Exchange's digital signatures and message encryption.

Digital Signatures

Microsoft Exchange Server provides end-to-end authentication and data integrity through the use of *digital signatures*, which are based on a user's signing keys. Two processes, signing and verifying, are involved.

When a message is to be sent, the sender selects Digitally Sign Message. It then will have a "signature" placed on it. The signature, or *signing key*, claims that the message was derived from the indicated source. The name on the header is matched with the sender's name. This matching prevents forgeries. Before the recipient can receive the message, the destination verifies the signature on the message.

After the message is signed, it is transformed to *message hashes*, which are a unique representation of a message. Moreover, the hashes are then encrypted. The original message and the encrypted hash message are then sent with the signing certificate to the destination. The signing certificate contains the sender's signing key.

When the message reaches its recipient, the message is verified when user chooses Read Digital Signature from the toolbar. First, the sender's certificate is checked against the revocation list. If it is on the list, the recipient is notified that this user was revoked from the system. Next, the original message is hashed as the encrypted hash message is decrypted. These two messages, both in hashed states, now can be compared to each other. If the hashes don't match, the message has been modified in transit and the user is notified. This feature allows for built-in data integrity verification. See Figure 27.1 for an illustration of how messages are sent and received by using digital signatures.

Part
III

Ch
27

FIG. 27.1
Sending and receiving a
message with a digital
signature.

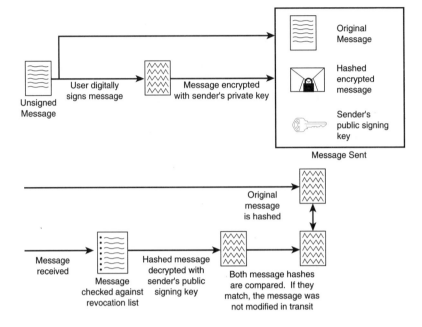

Introduction to Data Encryption

Microsoft Exchange Server provides confidentiality by encrypting the destined message.
When the message is sent, the data-encryption security feature scrambles the message. If you
viewed the message in this scrambled state, it would resemble a bunch of random alphanumeric characters. When the message is received at its destination, it is decrypted and put back
together in the original format.

Microsoft Exchange Server supports the following two standards to complete this security
task:

- CAST encryption algorithms
- Data Encryption Standard (DES)

N O T E The Data Encryption Standard (DES) is available with Microsoft Windows NT Server
software in Canada and the United States. ▪

When a user chooses Secure Message with Encryption from the toolbar, all of the recipients'
certificates are retrieved from the directory. Next, a bulk encryption key is created to encrypt
the message. Finally, the user's public encryption key is extracted from the certificate and
placed in a lockbox. This action prevents the encryption key from being used while the
decrypted message is in transit. The lockbox and the encryption key are then sent to the
recipient.

When the recipient receives and opens the message, the encryption key is used to decrypt the lockbox and the bulk encryption key from within the lockbox is used to decrypt the message (see Figure 27.2).

FIG. 27.2
Sending and receiving an encrypted message.

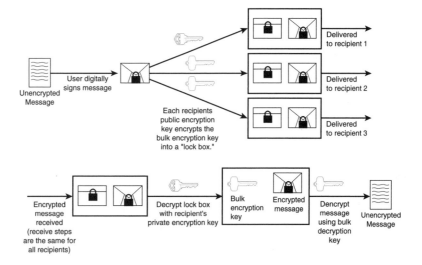

Using Key Management Server

The Key Management Server, which is a component of Microsoft Exchange Server, is the central point for advanced security. The following steps show what is involved to set up and maintain Microsoft Exchange Server advanced security:

- Selecting the server to manage the key management database
- Installing the Key Management component software and enabling individual users to take advantage of advanced security features
- Configuring remote sites to use advanced security
- Verifying that the Key Management component is functioning correctly
- Viewing security logs for errors or attempted breaches, and periodically clearing the logs of unneeded information
- Backing up and maintaining the key management database

Selecting the Server to Manage the Key Management Database

Only one Microsoft Windows NT server in the organization that is running Microsoft Exchange Server can become the Key Management Server (KM Server) and manage the Key Management advanced security database. Having multiple KM Servers can cause authentication and encryption errors. When deciding which Microsoft Exchange server to use as the KM Server, keep the following important points in mind:

■ Advanced security administration can be done only from within the site where the KM Server is located.

■ The server should be physically secure, such as placed in a locked room or area with restricted access.

■ The Key Management database should be backed up regularly.

■ The server must be using the NTFS file system for maximum security.

Installing the Key Management Component Software

In order to install the Key Management component software, the setup process asks for two passwords. One password is copied to a floppy disk. This option can be deselected on the property page during the beginning of the setup. If the copy is deselected, the setup process displays the password on-screen. It's recommended to write down this password.

Do the following steps to install your Key Management component software:

1. Launch SETUP.EXE from the Microsoft Exchange Server CD-ROM for your appropriate CPU (\SETUP\i386\EXCHKM for Intel processors).

2. Choose Continue to bypass the Welcome screen.

3. Enter Full Name and Organization information, and then choose OK to continue.

4. Confirm Full Name and Organization information.

5. Choose OK to bypass the Product ID information.

6. Setup shows a screen with the default directory (C:\SECURITY). If the default directory is OK, press Continue and skip to step 10.

7. Click the Change Folder icon to change the directory to which setup will install the files.

8. Select the directory in which install needs to install the files.

9. If directory doesn't exist, choose OK to confirm its creation.

10. Choose OK to continue.

11. Click the Typical button to execute the installation. KM Server then installs with all options.

12. The next screen asks about the Country Code selection and the creation of KM Server Startup Floppy Disk. Accept defaults, choose OK, and skip to step 15.

13. If you need to change the country code, select the correct country code.

14. If the decision is made to go with a diskless setup, deselect (clear the check box) the box beside the option. Choose OK to continue.

N O T E If there is not a KM Server Startup floppy disk created, the password for the Key Management Server Service is displayed on the screen.

Important: Please write this password down somewhere. This password cannot be changed with reinstalling the component. This password is needed by the KM Server Service to start up. This is the password that would otherwise be placed on the floppy disk. ■

15. If defaults were accepted from step 12, a request to insert a blank floppy disk in drive A appears. Insert the blank floppy disk and choose OK.

16. To complete a successful setup, click OK.

Starting the Key Management Server Service

The Key Management Server Service must be started to enable and configure advanced security for individual users.

NOTE If a KM Server Startup Floppy Disk wasn't created, the password that was displayed on-screen during the setup process must be input within the startup parameters for the KM Server service. ▦

Follow these steps:

1. Log on to Microsoft Windows NT Server as Administrator.

2. Select the Main program group, Control Panel, and then Services.

3. Locate the Key Management Server service entry, highlight it, and click the Start button. Refer to the preceding Note regarding diskless KM Server setups.

4. After displaying a message about starting the services, the Key Management Service status changes to Started.

5. Close the Services applet and exit Control Panel.

Changing Your Advanced Security Administrative Password

The Key Management Server requires an Advanced Security Administrator's password to modify any security-related items. This password is separate from any other passwords, which were explained in previous chapters. This password is specific for security-related administrative tasks.

If this is a new installation or if the advanced security password has never been changed, take the following steps:

1. Launch Microsoft Exchange Server Administrator program.

2. Connect to a Microsoft Exchange Server.

3. Click the Configuration container.

4. Choose the Encryption object and open its property pages.

5. Click the Security tab.

6. Choose Key Management Administrators.

7. Enter the Advanced Security Administrator password.

NOTE If the password has never been changed for any reason, the default password is *password*. ▦

Part

III

Ch

27

8. Click Change Password, type the old password into the Old Password box, and then type your new password in the New Password box. You then are asked to verify the new password.

9. Choose OK to save the changes.

Enabling Advanced Security Features for Individual Users

To allow users to digitally sign and encrypt messages, advanced security must be enabled for each recipient. With the KM Server in production, after the advanced security setup process for a user is initiated, an RPC call is made to the KM Server, which generates and returns a token.

Using Person to Person Key Exchange

Exchange 5.0 clients can individually exchange security keys and certificates, even between different organizations. This allows them to exchange signed and encrypted messages, even over the Internet. In previous versions, this function was limited to other Exchange users inside your organization.

Before you can send someone encrypted keys, or verify their digital signature, you must first obtain a trusted copy of their "public security keys." For users inside your organization, these keys are stored in the global address list for easy access. Exchange users outside of your organization must send you their public keys that can then be stored in your Personal Address Book for future use.

To send public security keys to a user in another organization, follow these steps:

1. Click Tools.

2. Choose Options and select Security.

3. Click the Send Security Keys button. A special e-form will be launched, which has details from your Global Address Book entry automatically filled out.

4. Type the Internet e-mail address of the person you want to send your keys to.

5. Press Send. The e-form will be sent through the Internet to the recipient whose name you typed.

On the receiving end the following happens:

1. The recipient opens the e-form in his or her Exchange client.

2. Click the Add to PAB button. This creates an entry in his or her Personal Address Book, including the sender's public security keys.

They can now verify the sender's digital signature and send encrypted mail. In turn, they can also send you their public security keys to enable full two-way secure e-mail.

Both the sender and receiver have a Verify Security Keys button on their e-form. This button provides a way for the receiver to ensure that the public keys the person sent are in fact the same public keys received. By calling the sender on the phone and asking him or her to press the Verify Security Keys button on the form sent (in the Sent Mail folder), he or she can read you the numbers from his or her screen, which form a unique "fingerprint" that identifies his or her keys. The receiver can do the same on the copy of the keys received. If the numbers match, you can be sure that the keys were not tampered with while traveling over the public Internet.

Configuring Remote Sites to Use Advanced Security

Users located in remote sites cannot be directly set up for advanced security because the KM Server uses RPC calls, but the users still can be set up for advanced security in an indirect manner. The Key Management Administrator can input the names of the users located at remote sites from a site that contains the KM Server. The tokens are generated for the individual users in the same manner that users located in the local site are generated. Then, the tokens must be securely transferred to the individual users for final setup of the client. Such transfers of token information are done "out of band" by a phone call, fax, or alternative means of communication.

Verifying that the Key Management Component Is Functioning Correctly

The Microsoft Windows NT Server logs information about the Key Management Server in the application's Event Viewer, which includes information regarding the KM Server functions and duties. If the option is used when launching the KM Server (this is done in the Control Panel's Services icon, within the startup parameters option), the events also will be shown in the KM Server command box.

Follow these steps:

1. Navigate to Administrative Tools.
2. Launch the Event Viewer.
3. From the Log menu, select Applications.

All log information regarding the Key Management Server that is being recorded in the Event Viewer is identified by an MSexchangeKM entry in the source column.

Viewing Security Logs for Errors or Attempted Breaches

Events that are generated by the Key Management Server are related to granting and revoking of permissions, security violations, and the internal operation of the KM Server. All events logged can be viewed in the Event Viewer.

Backing Up and Maintaining the Key Management Database

All advanced security data is stored in the SECURITY\MGRENT folder. This directory structure should be backed up on a regular basis. Any Microsoft Windows NT-compatible backup application can be used to archive the advanced security directory structure.

Part

III

Ch

27

The two services that must be running at the start time of the backup are the Information Store service and Directory service.

From Here...

This chapter described the rich security features available within NT and Exchange. With proper use, you can guarantee your users a robust messaging system while maintaining message integrity and system security.

For related information, see the following chapters:

- Chapter 24, "Exchange Performance Tuning and Capacity Planning," describes how to tune Exchange after applying security.

- Chapter 25, "Maintaining Exchange," discusses the day-to-day activities needed to keep Exchange running in top shape.

- Chapter 26, "Monitoring Your Organization," provides the tools to monitor all changes to your Exchange system before and after applying security.

- Chapter 28, "Troubleshooting Exchange with Diagnostic Tools," details several problem situations and their solutions.

Troubleshooting Exchange with Diagnostic Tools

Message Tracking

A powerful way to find link malfunctions.

MTACHECK

A method to scan the database for damaged objects, remove them, and rebuild the queue.

ISINTEG

A utility that performs diagnostics and repairs functions on the IS databases.

Diagnostic Logging/Windows NT Event Viewer

A program used to track system events by displaying log information of three types: Application, Security, and System logs.

Microsoft Exchange Server is an intricate product that consists of many components, so it is important in any pilot or installation that you set aside enough time for planning and installation. Many tools exist that can help you plan and analyze a Microsoft Exchange Server installation. This chapter familiarizes you with some of the tools Microsoft Exchange provides for diagnosing and troubleshooting various components of Microsoft Exchange within your organization. ■

Tracking Exchange Messages

Tracking a message through a Microsoft Exchange system can be a powerful way of finding link malfunctions. Message tracking can assist support professionals in pinpointing the exact servers or links at fault. It can also be used to determine the quality of service of the Microsoft Exchange system in areas such as performance, round trips between two servers, alternate route setup, and usage and reliability issues such as lost mail. Exchange provides tools to follow a message through its journey to verify transmissions at certain points of your organization. Here are some common uses for Exchange message tracking:

- Analyzing a message's path through the system to test for proper routing

- Determine the time delay for messages to pass through each connector in their path

- Finding mail that was not appropriately delivered (also called "lost" mail)

All message tracking information is stored by the system attendant on each server when tracking is enabled. The Exchange Server component that actually writes the entries to the log file is the System Attendant.

The location of this log is

> *driveletter*:\EXCHSRVR\TRACKING.LOG

Tracking logs are kept for an entire day and a new log is created the next day. Tracking must be enabled on each component through which the message flows occur.

For example, to track a message to a remote site connected via the Internet, you would need to enable MTA tracking on both Exchange sites and the Internet mail connector used at each site.

As explained earlier, Message tracking is a powerful tool to debug any problems with the Exchange System. Following is a discussion of how to enable Message Tracking on various Exchange Components:

- *Message Transfer Agent*. To enable tracking for every MTA in a site, select the Enable Message Tracking check box on the MTA Site Configuration General property page.

- *Information Store*. To enable tracking for every information store in a site, click the Enable Message Tracking check box on the Information Store Site Configuration General property page.

- *Microsoft Mail Connector*. To enable tracking for an MS Mail connector, click the Enable Message Tracking check box on the MS Mail Connector Interchange property page. You must enable tracking individually for each MS Mail connector in each site.

- *Internet Mail Connector*. To enable tracking for an Internet Mail Connector, click the Enable Message Tracking check box on the Internet Mail Connector Internet Mail property page. You must enable tracking individually for each Internet Mail Connector in each site.

Message tracking allows support professionals to view, sort, and filter the information collected by each individual server or the messages sent, received, and delivered by the server. Here is how you would use the Message tracking tools from the Exchange administrator program (see Figure 28.1).

FIG. 28.1

Open the tracking tools from the Exchange Administrator program.

1. Choose Tools, Track Message from the administrator program menu. The Connect to Server dialog box appears.

2. Choose a server in your site to connect to. Preferably, connect to a server with either the sender or recipient of the message you want to track in its address list. The Select Message to Track dialog box appears.

3. In the Select Message to Track dialog box, find the message you want to track. You are given the option to search for messages either by sender or recipients. (In this search tool, the sender or recipients must be listed in the address lists available to this Exchange server.)

   If the recipients you need are not listed in the address book, or if you already have a Message ID to use for tracking, click cancel on this page and proceed to the advanced search page (see Figure 28.2).

You can track a particular message identified in step 3 by using the Select Message to Track dialog box. This dialog box allows you to search for a message by either sender or recipient and can display the details of the message:

1. If you want to search for a message by its sender, click the From button and select a sender from the address book. If you want to search for a message by its recipients, click the Sent To button and select a recipient (or group of recipients) from the address book.

2. In the Look Back box, enter the number of previous days you want to search for messages. Keep in mind that message tracking must have been enabled on those days for a log to have been created.

3. To connect to a different Exchange server use the Browse button.

Part

III

Ch

28

FIG. 28.2

Search for message either via sender or recipients (must be visible in the address book).

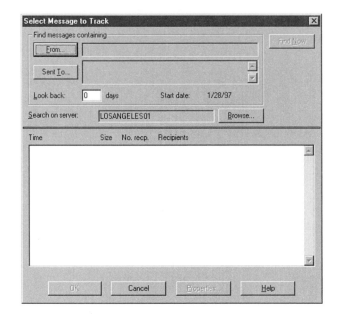

4. When all of your parameters are set, click the Find Now button. All tracking logs for the number of days selected will be searched sequentially. The results are displayed in the bottom window (see Figure 28.3).

5. Select a found message from the list and click Properties to view further property details about it (see Figure 28.4). Click Close when you are done viewing the message's details to return to the Select Message to Track dialog box.

FIG. 28.3

A successful search displays the message matching your criteria in the bottom display window.

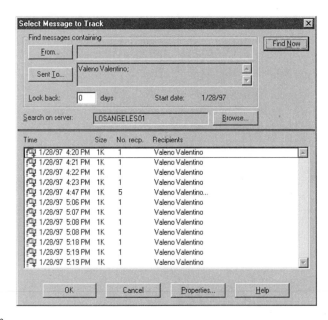

FIG. 28.4

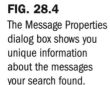

The Message Properties dialog box shows you unique information about the messages your search found.

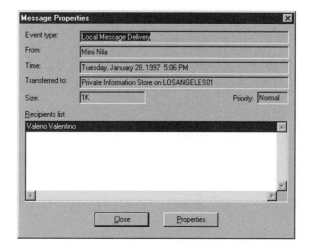

6. Click OK to return to the Message Tracking Center dialog box. In the Message Tracking Center dialog box, the Message ID field is now filled in with the appropriate information from the selected message and the Track button is now available.

Using the Message Tracking Center

The Message Tracking Center windows can trace a message (that is found in the search windows from the previous steps) through its path. It executes searches on all the message logs of the Exchange servers that handled it. This includes from the point it originated on an Exchange server (or entered the network through a connector or gateway) to the point it was delivered (or left the network).

Clicking the Track button in the Message Center dialog box (see Figure 28.5) performs the actual track on the message and fills in the information in the Tracking History box. The Tracking History box displays the steps taken in the process of delivering the message, including the action performed and the Exchange Server involved. A message's Tracking History is the sequence of steps taken to reach a destination.

There are two parts to the Message Tracking Center: the message search utilities that also display message details, and the Tracking tools for those messages. Once a message has been tracked, two additional buttons become available in the Message Tracking Center dialog. This button can search for messages and display message details:

1. The Message Tracking Search Parameters window displays the current message resulting from the search (blank if none). Click Search to bring up the Select a Message to Track dialog box.

Part
III

Ch
28

FIG. 28.5

The Message Tracking Center lets you search for a message in various ways, then trace its route once it is found.

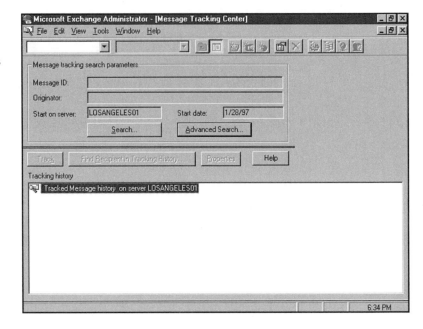

2. Click Advanced Search to find a message based on different parameters. The dialog box in Figure 28.6 appears.

FIG. 28.6

Search for a message using more advanced parameters.

Sent by Microsoft Exchange Server

Selecting Sent by Microsoft Exchange Server from the Advanced Search dialog box brings up the Select System Message to Track dialog box (see Figure 28.7), which helps you find messages originating from core Microsoft Exchange components. Typically, these are warning and status messages from the Exchange server to an administrator.

1. To search on a different Exchange server, use the Browse button (see Figure 28.8).

2. Use the From pull-down menu to choose which Exchange component (Directory, Information Store, System Attendant, Directory Synchronization Agent) to scan for as the message originator.

FIG. 28.7
Search for a message by using more advanced parameters.

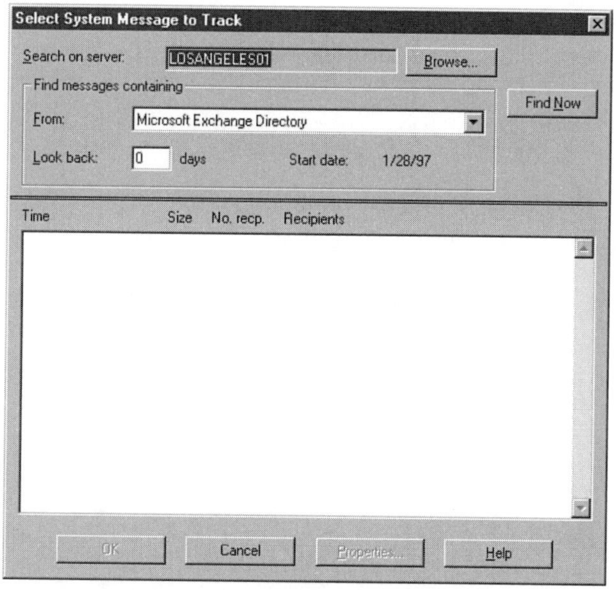

FIG. 28.8
Select an Exchange component that could have originated the message.

3. In the Look Back box, enter the number of previous days you want to search for messages. Keep in mind that message tracking must have been enabled on those days for a log to have been created.

4. When all of your parameters are set, click the Find Now button. All tracking logs for the number of days selected will be searched sequentially. The results are displayed in the bottom window.

5. Click OK to accept the found messages and return to the Message Tracking Center.

Transferred into this Site

Choosing this search option from the Advanced Dialog Box lets you search for a message that originated outside your Exchange organization (see Figure 28.9). You can filter this search by selecting the connector or gateway that a message passed through to enter the system.

FIG. 28.9

Find a message originating outside the organization.

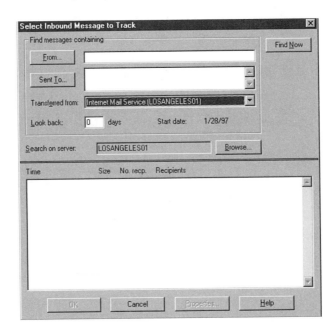

1. If you want to search for a message by its sender, click the From button and select a sender from the address book. Normally, you will not use this option if the sender is not a custom recipient in the address list.

   If you want to search for a message by its recipients, click the Sent To button and select a recipient (or group of recipients) from the address book.

2. Use the Transferred From pull-down menu to select a connector in your site as the inbound gateway for the message you are searching for.

3. In the Look Back box, enter the number of previous days you want to search for messages. Keep in mind that message tracking must have been enabled on those days for a log to have been created.

4. To connect to a different Exchange server use the Browse button.

5. When all of your parameters are set, click the Find Now button. All tracking logs for the number of days selected will be searched sequentially. The results are displayed in the bottom window.

6. Click OK to accept the found messages and return to the Message Tracking Center.

By Message ID

If you know the message ID for a particular message, you can find it by selecting this option. A message ID can be found in various Exchange logs, message queues, and also in the Microsoft Exchange client (see Figure 28.10).

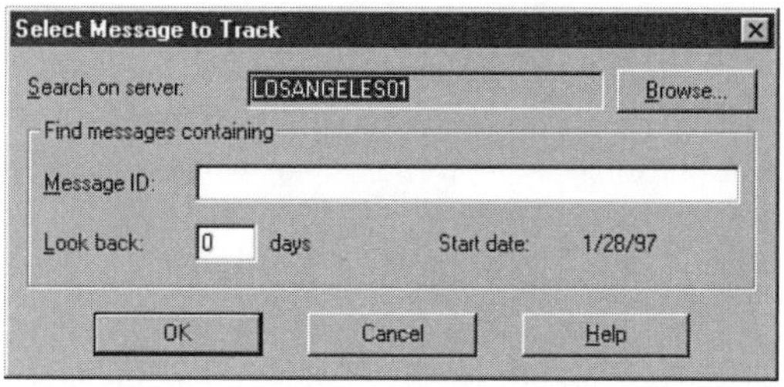

FIG. 28.10

Search for a message by its Exchange Message ID.

1. Click Browse to select an Exchange server on your site on which to search for the message.

2. Type (or paste if you've copied the message ID from a log file) the message ID into the Message ID text box.

3. Enter a number of days to Look Back into a log file. Start Date will display the first day to start looking for a message.

4. Click OK to search for the selected message and return to the Message Tracking Center.

Tracking a Message

After finding the message that meets your criteria, click Track from the Message Tracking Center dialog box. Assuming all the necessary tracking check boxes were activated, the display window will show you the path of the selected message from the first instant it entered the Exchange organization, to when it was delivered (or left the organization through a connector or gateway).

You can view details about the message route by clicking and expanding the message view in the display window.

Part
III

Ch
28

Additional Exchange Core Component Troubleshooting Tools

Following is a discussion of some of the Core Troubleshooting Tools to diagnose problems with MS Exchange. These are: MTACHECK and ISInteg. *MTACheck* is a support tool that assists the administrators in diagnosing the MTA queues. *ISInteg* is a support tool run on an offline information store that checks the consistency of the information store.

If the MTA queues become corrupt or unable to process a message, it is possible for the MTA to be unable to start. In these situations, a utility called MTACHECK.EXE that can be found in the \exchsrvr\bin directory can be used to repair the problem.

MTACHECK.EXE will check the consistency of the MTA queues, check the integrity of all objects, and if necessary, delete corrupt objects. Under most circumstances, the MTACHECK.EXE program will resolve any issues with a problematic MTA.

MTACHECK

A message transfer agent uses message queues to store messages. The queues are in essence databases that store messages awaiting delivery to their intended destinations. Occasionally, parts of these databases can become corrupt and cause message transfer errors. MTACHECK scans the queue database for damaged objects, removes them from the queue, and then rebuilds the message queue for correct operation.

MTACHECK can be used primarily in two types of situations:

- Routine tests of MTA queue databases for message integrity.
- Troubleshooting an MTA that has spontaneously stopped and will not properly restart. Running MTACHECK may clear the problem and enable the MTA to restart.

MTACHECK places removed data in a directory called MTACHECK.OUT. The MTACHECK.OUT directory is created in the path:

\EXCHSRVR\MTADATA\MTACHECK.OUT

The data files are created in that directory and given the name: DB*.DAT. MTACHECK creates one file for each damaged piece of data removed.

> **CAUTION**
>
> When removing damaged message files from the queue, MTACHECK may remove messages that cannot be recovered.

MTACHECK is run from the Windows NT command line of the Exchange server you want to scan. The executable is located in the directory:

driveletter:\EXCHSRVR\BIN\MTACHECK.EXE

First, you must manually stop the Message Transfer Agent Service before running this utility (MTACHECK will remind you if you forget). Then, delete the current contents of the MTACHECK.OUT directory. If it is the first time MTACHECK is run, the MTACHECK.OUT is not yet in existence.

N O T E The MTACHECK.OUT directory is automatically created when MTACHECK.EXE is run. ■

Use the following procedure to run MTACHECK on an Exchange server:

1. Stop the Message Transfer Agent service.
2. Remove or delete the contents of the MTACHECK.OUT directory.
3. Run MTACHECK.EXE from the Windows NT command line.
4. Analyze the results and restart the MTA service when appropriate.

Optional Switches   Use these switches to modify the MTACHECK execution:

/v	Start verbose display. Displays progress messages more frequently and in more detail.
/f	file name Saves progress messages to the specified file name.
/rd	Stands for Repair Database. This can be a very useful tool when data integrity is in danger.
/rp	Stands for Repair Postoffice. This switch is similar to rd but it specializes in repairing corrupted postoffices. This option is used specifically to repair the database and can be used to save critical data if in fact it can be saved. This can repair user data, mailboxes, and addresses.

MTACHECK /v /f MTACHECK.LOG is an example of a command that uses both of these switches. It enables the verbose status display, and it stores that display in a file called MTACHECK.LOG.

ISINTEG

The ISINTEG utility performs diagnostic and repair functions on the Exchange Information Store databases. This is a function similar to that performed by the MTACHECK utility.

Situations that would warrant use of this utility are as follows:

■ The Information Store service will not start properly.

■ After recovering an information store database with software other than the built-in Windows NT backup utility.

There are three main modes of operation for the ISINTEG:

- *Test Mode*. Runs diagnostic scan of the Information Store databases to detect errors.
- *Test Mode and Fix*. Runs the same diagnostics as normal, but proceeds to fix whatever it can in the process.
- *Patch Mode*. Used when recovering an information store database with a software other than the built-in Windows NT backup utility.

ISINSTEG is run from the Windows NT command line of the Exchange server you want to scan. The executable is located in the directory:

driveletter.\EXCHSRVR\BIN\ISINTEG.EXE

Optional Switches   Use these switches to modify the ISINTEG execution.

Switch	Description
-?	Displays this options list
-pri	Runs diagnostics on the private information store; by default, this is the test that will run
-pub	Runs diagnostics on the public information store
-fix	Runs diagnostics and corrects any errors that it can (also called Check & Correct)
-verbose	Displays more detailed diagnostic information
-l (*filename*)	Stores log information under a different file name; by default, INISTEG.PRI and INISTEG.PUB are the log files
-test *testname*,...	Runs a specific ISINTEG test; all available tests can be viewed with the -? switch

Using Diagnostic Logging

Diagnostic logging is a tool that lets you zero in on messaging problems that plague your system. These logging settings are set in the Diagnostic Logging property page for each component. Diagnostics are logged into the Windows NT event logs, which can then be viewed with the NT Event Viewer.

The following Exchange components have a diagnostic logging property page for their pertinent system services:

Directory Service

Directory Synchronization

Internet Mail Connector

Information store (both public and private)

Microsoft Mail Connector

Message Transfer Agent

 TIP The Diagnostic Logging property page for each Exchange server shows a unified list of that server's logging settings.

Subcomponents and Categories

Categories are the various functions of each Exchange service. You specify various levels of logging on a per-category basis. Different categories within a service (or subcomponent of that service) can be logged separately to track a problem to a specific function.

Some services (for example the Information store) also have subcomponents. Subcomponents are logging subdivisions beneath each Exchange service. Each Subcomponent also has a set of categories that can be logged individually.

For example, the Information Store service (MSExchangeIS) has three subcomponents. Each subcomponent (System, Public, and Private) pertains to roles of that service. Each subcomponent also has a set of categories pertaining to its specific functioning. The three categories of the Public subcomponent are

Replication Status Updates

Incoming Messages

Outgoing Messages

You would set a logging level for each category depending on the type of problem you are encountering.

Logging Levels

Each Exchange component enables you to set various levels of logging. These levels determine what type and how critical an event must be before it is recorded. Every logging level includes events from the level above it. The following are the logging levels available for all Exchange components:

None (level 0)	Log only critical events or error events. By default, this is set for every Exchange component.
Minimum (level 1)	Log only very-high-level events.
Medium (level 2)	Log important sequences of events.
Maximum (level 5)	Log everything. This will log the complete operation of the service and even include certain lines of code from a service. Use only when you have narrowed the problem down to a couple of categories.

The level numbers pertain to what Windows NT defines the event to be.

Part

III

Ch

28

Your decision to change logging levels should be based on tracking down a problem to a particular service and category. If you have a suspicion that a certain component is the culprit for a certain error, then start increasing logging levels gradually for a fewer number of categories.

For example, say that you are not properly receiving Internet mail anymore, yet all other types of messaging data are delivered without any problems. This would naturally suggest that you should increase the logging levels on all the categories of the Internet Mail Connector and not initially on the MTA or Information store. Then you proceed to narrow down the list of categories and increase the logging levels as you get closer to the source of the problem.

N O T E   Use the high logging levels (maximum and medium) sparingly and only when you have narrowed down the problem to a few categories. These settings generate a large amount of events and tend to fill logging space quickly. ▪

Using Windows NT Event Viewer

For review, an *event* is any notable incident within the Windows NT operating environment. Critical events will trigger an immediate on-screen notification to the administrator. However, the more run-of-the-mill events are only logged. These need not necessarily be errors, just occurrences worth recording. Windows NT logs three main types of events:

- ▪ *System events*. Status of system services and other system operations
- ▪ *Security events*. Logons and permission auditing
- ▪ *Application events*. Operational errors

Which events are actually logged is determined by the logging levels set for each Exchange component.

Keep in mind that Event Viewer is a general-purpose diagnostic tool. Many of the errors generated for Exchange are sometimes vague to provide a solid solution. You should use the other tools in this chapter to gather information before taking any troubleshooting action.

From Here...

This chapter familiarizes you with some of the tools Microsoft Exchange provides for diagnosing and troubleshooting various components of Microsoft Exchange in your organization.

For more information, read the following chapters:

- ▪ Chapter 24, "Exchange Performance Tuning and Capacity Planning," gives you the necessary tools to reshape your Exchange environment. Tuning your Exchange server is a logical step after you have applied the diagnostic and troubleshooting tools you have just learned.
- ▪ Chapter 26, "Monitoring Your Organization," tells you how to implement a monitoring scheme to help you detect common errors before they become serious problems.

The Exchange Client

CHAPTER 29

Installing and Configuring Outlook

Before Installing Outlook
Understand what type of environment Outlook can run in.

Installing Outlook
Learn how to install Outlook.

Configuring Outlook
Learn how to set up profiles and offline folders.

Outlook is your personal information manager. It enhances the features available in the Exchange Client and Schedule+. Not only can you manage your messages and appointments under Outlook, but you can also keep track of your activities, contacts, and documents. But Outlook doesn't stop there. In your Exchange organization, you can set up Outlook to share information with others and let others manage your information as well. This chapter will cover how to get Outlook up and running, and how to provide the proper foundation for your company to get truly organized. ■

Preparing to Install Outlook

Before running the setup program, there are a few questions to consider that will affect your client installation strategy.

- Do you want your installation to be server based, or do you want all the executables to reside on the client?

- Do you want to install from the CD or over the network?

- Would you like the administrator to preconfigure client options or have the users choose their own settings?

The answers to these questions will determine your approach to setting up Outlook.

Each of these areas will be covered in detail to make the answers to these questions a little more clear.

Installing Using an Installation Share

An installation share allows you to run the setup files directly off a hard drive without using a CD-ROM. An installation point to run setup can be located on a server or on the local machine. After loading all of the files, you then, in the case of a file server, share the directory with an appropriate title.

Follow these steps to install Outlook using an installation share:

1. You first need to copy the Outlook source file from the CD-ROM onto your hard drive.

2. To run an installation from the server, find the SETUP.EXE file and execute it.

3. The setup application will run as normal from that point on.

Weighing Server-Based Installation Advantages and Disadvantages

With a server-based installation, all users use a server-based copy of Outlook. There are advantages and disadvantages to this scenario:

- *Pros*—Less configuration on the clients. All settings can be maintained on the server. More change control over the installations.

- *Cons*—More LAN traffic; each time a user loads the Outlook, it must run across the network. Users may see a dramatic decrease in performance. Outlook cannot function while the server or network is down. Does not take advantage of the client/server model efficiently.

Outlook System Requirements

The following are the minimum requirements for your computer to run Outlook.

Hardware:

- 486 or Higher Processor
- 8M of RAM for Windows 95, 16M of RAM for Windows NT
- 24M of hard-disk space for Outlook files, 31M required for a typical installation
- VGA or higher-resolution video adapter
- Mouse or compatible pointing device

Software:

- Windows 95
- Windows NT Workstation 3.51 Service Pack 5
- Windows NT Workstation 4.0 Service Pack 2

Saving Your Personalized Information

Outlook can be configured to use the personalized files you had under the following clients: Exchange Client in Windows 95, Windows Messaging in Windows NT, or the updated Exchange Client from Exchange Server 4.0.

In the following list, you'll find the default extensions for a user's personal files.

- *.PST*   The file where all of your personal folders and messages are stored.
- *.PAB*   The file where all of your Personal Address Book entries are stored.
- *.SCD*   The file where all of your Schedule+ information is stored.

N O T E   If you are upgrading your client from Microsoft Mail 3.x, you will need to save your *.MMF and *.SCH files. These files contain your mail folders, messages, and Schedule+ information. They will be used to migrate all of your information into Outlook.

Installing Outlook

The entire install or setup process is very easy. All you have to do is follow the dialog boxes instructions. Ample help and various tips are available as you follow the setup screens.

The first step in the Microsoft Outlook procedure is to select the directory or folder you want the client to be installed into (see Figure 29.1). You can either go with the default, which is C:\Program Files\Microsoft Office, or you may change that by selecting Change Folder.

FIG. 29.1

Select the Destination Folder in which to store your messages.

Choosing an Installation Type

At the next screen, you are presented with two choices. (see Figure 29.2)

- *Typical* takes the most commonly used settings and installs them.

- *Custom* gives you the opportunity to pick and choose the components you require.

FIG. 29.2

Choose the type of Outlook setup.

Choose the installation method that fits your needs. If you are the adventurous sort and want to see all of the options available, go down the custom path. This option enables you to pick only the options that fit your requirements.

Table 29.1 Typical Outlook Installation

Option	Installed?
Microsoft Outlook Program Files	Yes
Office Assistant	Yes
Microsoft Exchange Server Support	No
Visuals for Forms Design	No
Find Fast	Yes

Option	Installed?
Holidays and Forms	Yes
Lotus Organizer Converters	No
Microsoft Outlook Help	Yes
Schedule+ Support Files	Yes
MS Info	Yes
Spelling Checker	No

At this point, you have two options (see Figure 29.3):

- *Change Option* allows you to go deeper into the highlighted choice.

- *Select All* does just what it says; it picks all of the options available.

FIG. 29.3
Outlook Options available during setup.

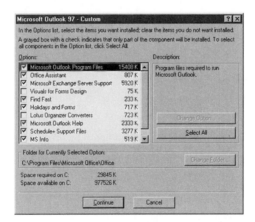

At this screen, you can specify what components of Outlook you wish to load.

After you have made all of the selections you want to use during setup, you can choose Continue to install the Outlook files. At this point, you see the setup progress bar and the various screens introducing the latest features. When you see the Completed Successfully screen (see Figure 29.4), hit OK and you return to your desktop display.

FIG. 29.4
Click OK.

Configuring Outlook

Now that you have installed Outlook, you need to configure it to work with your messaging environment. Start by installing some of the most common services to see how this is done. If you have any other Messaging Application Programming Interface (MAPI)-compliant messaging services, the configuration will be essentially the same.

Knowing Your Messaging Services

Before you start configuring Outlook, take a few minutes to inventory what messaging services you will want to access. Due to Outlook's many capabilities, you can receive messages from many sources besides the Exchange Server. One can also choose:

- Internet Mail (POP3 Server)
- Microsoft Fax
- Netscape Internet Transport
- Lotus Notes Mail
- Microsoft Network Online Service
- CompuServe Online Service
- Other MAPI-Compliant Mail Packages

Creating Your Outlook Profile

Your profile tells Outlook what services you are going to be using as well as where your personal files are located.

Before starting Outlook, you need to setup your profile.

1. From Control Panel, double-click the Mail icon.
2. Select Add to configure a new profile. The next screen you see is the Setup Wizard dialog box (see Figure 29.5).
3. Place check marks next to the information services you wish to use. You also have the choice of manually configuring the information services. This option enables you to answer questions in a nonwizard style manner. The preferred method is to check the boxes and press the Next button.
4. In the next screen, you must enter a profile name. You should choose a name other than MS Exchange Settings. After you enter a profile name, click Next (see Figure 29.6).
5. Enter the name of your Exchange Server. You do not have to enter the normal backslashes.
6. Enter the Mailbox Name. This is set up on the Exchange Server and is usually either a common name or a company standard.

FIG . 29.5
Information services
available to add to your
profile.

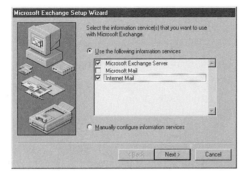

FIG. 29.6
Where you enter your
Exchange server and
mailbox name.

7. You are now asked if you will be traveling with this computer (see Figure 29.7). Your options are:

■ *Yes*—You will not be hassled about being offline when you are not connected to the network.

■ *No*—If you are using a computer that will normally be connected to a network. This will bypass some of the offline, mail-related issues.

FIG. 29.7
Will you be working
offline?

8. If at the last screen you chose yes, you will travel with this computer, you are then asked how you will connect to the Internet Mail server (see Figure 29.8). The best way to answer this question is to consider your normal mode of usage:

■ *Modem*—If you dial in from home or are on the road a lot and use your modem to connect to your server.

■ *Network*—If you have a network interface card in your mobile computer and this is the way you connect to your server while in the office.

FIG. 29.8

Are you going to be using Dial-Up Networking?

When you select Modem for your access method to the Internet mail server, you will be given the choice of connections. If you have Dial Up Connections already defined, the Wizard will let you choose from a drop-down list box. If you don't have predefined Dial Up Connections, or want to use another existing Dial Up Connection, choose New. This will allow you to create a new connection profile.

The next screen asks you to enter the name or IP address of your Internet Mail server (see Figure 29.9). This is the server on which you have an Internet or SMTP style mail account.

FIG. 29.9

Enter the name or IP address for the Internet Mail server.

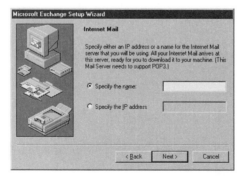

The server from which you would like to receive your Internet mail needs to support POP3 mail. This is a standard that allows other servers to interface and receive mail as a proxy service.

The next screen gives us the option of either choosing Offline or Automatic.

■ *Offline*—Will use the Remote Mail feature of Outlook. This feature enables you to view the headers and sizes of messages before downloading them.

N O T E This option is especially nice when you are on the road with a slow modem and someone tries to send you a 10M PowerPoint presentation. ■

■ *Automatic*—Downloads all incoming messages (regardless of size) and sends all outgoing mail. This method is fine if you have a fast modem and adequate space.

The next screen asks you to enter your account and name (see Figure 29.10). Your e-mail address is either the account or alias defined on the POP3 server. This will be in the normal Internet mail format of *username@domain*. Your name may already be entered from a previous setup or you may enter it now.

FIG. 29.10

This screen holds your Internet mail account information.

N O T E The name you enter will be displayed as the sender on all of your Internet mail, so put in a nickname if that is what you prefer. ■

Now you are at the point of entering your actual Internet mail account information. The Mailbox name is the account on the POP3 server. The Password is the password for this account (see Figure 29.11).

FIG. 29.11

Your Internet mail (POP) account information.

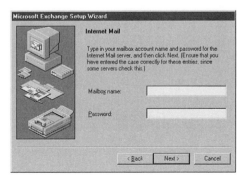

N O T E   Ensure that you enter the account name and password correctly (including case-sensitivity) due to most POP3 servers being located on UNIX servers. The UNIX operating system is case-sensitive in all fields. ▓

Now you are given the chance of either using a preexisting Personal Address Book or creating a new one (see Figure 29.12). You can either enter the path to your old Personal Address Book if you have one, or Browse for it. If you do not have a Personal Address Book, as is the case of a new install, you can choose Next and one will be created for you in the default location.

FIG. 29.12

Enter name for Personal Address Book.

N O T E   If you want to keep your Personal Address Book in another directory, you may enter it here. This is a good idea if you store all data files in a certain place for backup or security reasons. ▓

The next-to-the-last screen enables you to specify whether you want Outlook to start up when you first log on to your computer.

Congratulations! You have made it to the wrap-up screen (see Figure 29.13). All you have to do now is select Finish to start using Outlook with all of the services you selected and configured. (see next page) By configuring Outlook, a new profile has been created.

FIG. 29.13

This screen lists all your Mail profiles.

If you are not connected to the network, you may receive the option to Work Offline. If you will be connecting to the network, choose Connect; otherwise, choose Work Offline and use Remote Mail to send and receive your messages with your Exchange Server.

You are now ready to run Outlook. All you have to do is double-click your Outlook icon, and you are on your way to utilizing the full power of this versatile tool.

Configuring Offline Folders

If you expect to use Outlook while you are away from your local network, you need to configure an offline folder on your local hard drive. This folder must be created before you can work offline. To Create an Offline Folder:

1. From Control Panel, double-click the Mail icon.
2. Select the profile you want to configure with the offline folder.
3. Under the Services tab, select Microsoft Exchange Server, then click Properties.
4. Under the Advanced tab, click Offline Folder File Settings.
5. In the File box, type in the pathname of the offline folder. Make sure that the extension for the folder is .OST (see Figure 29.14). When you are finished, click OK.

FIG. 29.14

Enter file name for Offline Folder.

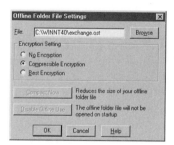

6. You may be notified that the file does not exist. Click Yes to create the new folder.
7. Save the changes made to the profile by clicking OK in the Microsoft Exchange Server window and clicking OK in your profile properties window.

From Here...

This chapter has covered the installation and configuration options of Outlook. The steps in this chapter were:

- Planning the Outlook rollout to meet your organizational needs.
- Installing Outlook on your platform.
- Configuring Outlook to work in your messaging environment.

Installing and configuring Outlook takes planning and some knowledge of your messaging environment. You will find a wealth of information in other related chapters in this book.

■ Chapter 30, "Using Outlook," to learn about handling e-mail, utilizing a calendar, and keeping a list of contacts.

■ Chapter 31, "Using Advanced Outlook Features," to see other features of Outlook and using it with your Exchange server to share Outlook information.

Using Outlook

This chapter will cover the basic features of Outlook. Whether you are using Outlook just an as e-mail client or as the tool to organize your company, you will find Outlook very powerful, but surprisingly easy to use. Furthermore, if you are familiar with using the Exchange Client and Schedule+, you will find Outlook has integrated these functions into one package. ■

Configuring Outlook

Understanding Outlook views and how to change them.

Using the Office Assistant

Meet the assistant that will answer your questions about Outlook.

Using the Inbox

Learn how to effectively communicate with others via e-mail.

Using the Calendar

Learn how the Outlook Calendar will keep you up to date with all of your appointments.

Managing your Contacts

This is your new address book where you can literally record everything you need to know about your contact.

Integrating with Office 97

Learn how Outlook and Office 97 work together.

Securing your Server Applications

Learn some of the tricks used to ensure that private information stored on the server cannot be viewed by others.

Configuring Outlook Views

The Outlook screen contains two main windows (see Figure 30.1). The left window is the Outlook Bar that looks like a vertical toolbar with icons to your favorite items sorted in Outlook groups. The right window is called the Information Viewer. When you choose an icon from the Outlook Bar, the contents of that folder are displayed here.

FIG. 30.1

Outlook Main View.

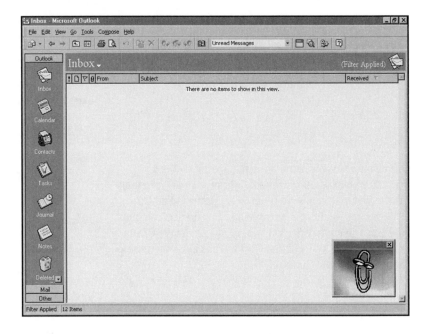

On the Outlook Bar, you will find three default groups when you first run Outlook: the Outlook Group, the Mail Group, and the Other Group. In Tables 30.1, 30.2, and 30.3, you will see which folders have been created in each group. The Outlook Group contains the set of folders that are the main features of Outlook (see Table 30.1).

Table 30.1   Outlook Group

Icon	Action
Inbox	Allows you to view the contents of your Inbox folder.
Calendar	Allows you to view your calendar. The calendar can be viewed in Day, Week, or Month format.
Contacts	Permits you to view the contact list in the Address Card View and other predefined views.

Icon	Action
Tasks	Opens your tasks list. Here, you can view details such as the person to whom a task was assigned, whether the task is active or overdue, and more.
Journal	Opens your Journal. You can manually add journal entries or view entries grouped in various ways. Contact activities like e-mail, faxes, meeting requests, phone calls, and usage of Microsoft Office documents can be automatically tracked.
Notes	Works like regular sticky notes. Allows you to post small, miscellaneous notes in the Notes folder.

The Mail Group contains the set of folders pertaining to e-mail (see Table 30.2).

Table 30.2   Mail Group

Icon	Action
Inbox	Enables you to view your incoming mail.
Sent Items	Enables you to view copies of outgoing mail.
Outbox	Enables you to view outgoing mail waiting to be picked up.
Deleted Items	Enables you to view mail and other items waiting to be deleted.

The Other Group is a group of folders that help you navigate around your computer system (see Table 30.3). This group is similar to Windows Explorer in Windows 95 and NT 4.0.

Table 30.3   Other Group

Icon	Action
My Computer	Accesses your computer's hard drives, floppy drives, mapped network drives, folders, and other files on your computer.
My Documents	Opens your folder for documents created using Microsoft Office and other Microsoft products.
Favorites	Displays your shortcuts to Internet links and other items.

Adding New Folders

You can add new folders to the Outlook Bar like adding shortcuts to your desktop in Windows 95 and NT 4.0 by performing the following steps:

1. Choose the group you want to add the new folder to.
2. Right-click and choose Add to Outlook Bar.

3. In the Look In drop-down box, there are two choices. Outlook points to your Outlook, Personal, and Public folders. File System points to your desktop, just like Windows Explorer. After finding the correct folder, click OK.

4. A new icon should appear in the group.

Adding New Groups

You can add new groups to your Outlook Bar with the following steps:

1. Right-click the Outlook Bar and choose Add New Group.

2. A new group bar appears and you can change the title of the group by typing over the highlighted title.

Using the Office Assistant

When you open Outlook for the first time, you will see the Office Assistant (see Figure 30.2). The Office Assistant is an animated character that is helpful in several ways. It can search for an answer to any question you may have about Outlook. Also, it can provide shortcuts that you may not be aware of or recommendations on how to make your work a little easier. You can hide the Office Assistant by clicking the x in the toolbar above it. You can display the Office Assistant by clicking the Office Assistant button on the toolbar.

FIG. 30.2

The Office Assistant.

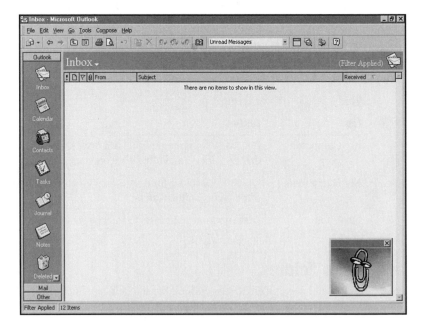

Configuring View Permissions over Exchange

One of the best features in Outlook, when used in an Exchange organization, is the capability to set view permissions for your main Outlook folders: Inbox, Calendar, Contacts, Tasks, Journal, and Notes. With this capability, Outlook moves from being a stand-alone product to a powerful information manager for you and your organization. However, you don't need to be worried that someone else could be monitoring your Outlook folders. Initially, all of these folders can only be viewed by you, the account holder.

By setting the proper permissions, you unlock a world of possibilities. At first, you can allow others to view your schedule to see when you are free or busy. Soon afterwards, you can delegate authority to others to manage your schedule and other Outlook features as well.

Part

IV

Ch

30

Follow this procedure to set permissions on your Outlook folders:

1. Open Outlook.
2. In the Outlook Bar, open the Outlook Group.
3. Right-click the folder you want to set view permissions and click Properties.
4. Click the Permissions tab (see Figure 30.3).
5. You can add users or groups you permit to view this folder by clicking Add and choosing names on the list.
6. Click the name in the Name/Role box to highlight it.
7. In the box next to Roles, use the drop-down list box to choose the role for that name. Table 30.4 provides information on the type of permissions available.
8. When you are finished configuring permissions for all of the names, click OK.

FIG. 30.3

View Permissions on Calendar folder.

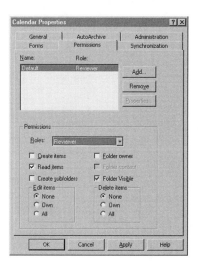

Table 30.4   Permissions

Role	Permissions Granted
Owner	All
Publishing Editor	Create, read, edit, and delete any items, and create subfolders.
Editor	Create, read, edit, and delete any items.
Publishing Author	Create, read, edit, and delete own items, and create subfolders.
Author	Create, read, edit, and delete own items.
Nonediting Author	Create and read items, but not edit items.
Reviewer	Read items.
Contributor	Create items.
None	No permissions in the folder. Use this as the default permission to prevent unauthorized users from accessing the folder.

Using the Inbox

The Inbox folder is the most important feature in Outlook for helping you communicate with others. From here, you can send and receive electronic messages. These messages can be as simple as a memo to as complex as a formatted message with attachments or electronic forms. In the Inbox, you can sort your messages either manually or automatically. This is great for users who are tired of clutter, and don't need another thing on the desktop in total disarray.

A great place to start is to understand the type of views available to you before your Inbox gets completely out of hand. You can adjust these views as needed to get the look of your Inbox that is most pleasing and functional to you (see Figure 30.4).

Table 30.5 lists the predefined views on how your messages are displayed.

Table 30.5   Inbox Views

View	Display Results
Messages	A list of messages.
Messages with AutoPreview	A list of messages with a preview of the first three lines of each message.
By Message Flag	Grouped by message flag.
Last Seven Days	Only those messages received during that past seven days are shown.
Flagged for Next Seven Days	Only those messages flagged for follow-up during the next seven days are shown.

View	Display Results
By Conversation Topic	Messages are grouped by subject.
By Sender	Messages are grouped by sender.
Unread Messages	Only those messages that have not been read yet are shown.
Sent To	The message recipients are shown rather than the sender.
Message Timeline	Icons arranged by date sent on a timeline are shown.

Part
IV

Ch
30

FIG. 30.4

Various Messages in your Inbox.

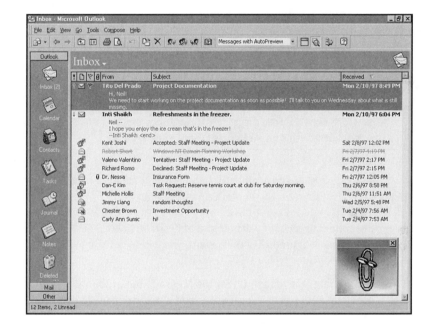

Creating Messages

In Outlook, you can create a new message using the following steps. The screen that appears while composing messages is actually a Mail form. This form is a guide to help you get your message out to the appropriate recipient.

To start creating a new message:

1. Open your Inbox from the Outlook Bar.

2. On the Standard toolbar, click the Mail Message icon to open a new mail form (see Figure 30.5).

FIG. 30.5

Message Tab of the Mail Form.

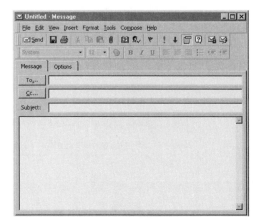

 TIP You can start a new mail message in a variety of ways. One way was described earlier. Also, pressing CTRL+SHIFT+M from anywhere in Outlook will bring up a new mail form. A third method is to right-click the Information Viewer and choose New Mail Message from the menu. Be aware that all other Outlook folders have the same set of shortcuts to open a new item.

N O T E A message only needs a valid name or distribution list in the To, Cc, or Bcc box for it to be deliverable. All other fields are optional.

The following sections will help you understand how to create and track your message. After you have configured all of the options, you can send the message by clicking the Send button on the toolbar or typing CTRL+ENTER.

Configuring Information Under the Message Tab of Your Message You have many options to configure before sending out a message. First, you need to decide who will get your message.

To add an address in the To field,

1. Click To.
2. Select one of the following from the drop-down menu:
    - Global Address list (if you are part of an Exchange organization)
    - Personal Address Book (from a previous version of the Exchange Client)
    - Contacts from your Outlook Address Book
    - Valid Internet/SMTP address

To add an address in the Cc or Bcc fields, follow the same steps as in the To field.

 TIP By default, the Bcc field is not shown when you compose a message. You can activate (or view) it or other fields such as the From: by selecting it from the View menu.

In the Subject box, you can type in a subject for this message.

In the Message Area, you can start creating your message. Outlook supports rich text so your message text can range from plain black text to something creative with color, different fonts, and attachments.

N O T E You need to know what type of e-mail client your recipients are using. By default, Outlook uses RTF (rich text format). If your recipients cannot handle this type of format, you may need to keep the message text as plain as possible. What you may consider hard work and creativity will show up as garbage to the recipient of your message.

Options Tab   In Outlook, you can control many characteristics of your message. Under the Options tab, you can set various details about your message.

General Options   The General Options sections helps you set notifications about your messages. You can alert the recipient of the importance of your message. You can also control any replies you are expecting from the recipient about your message. The following options are available:

- Importance—You can alert the recipient of the importance of your message. The available options are Low, Normal, and High. By default, all messages are Normal.

- Sensitivity—When you set the sensitivity of a message, a tag is added in the message notifying the recipient on how to treat the message.

- Use voting buttons—You can create a message where the reply to that message is a predefined choice. That choice appears in the Subject box, where you can later track those responses.

- Have replies sent to—If you think someone else would be interested in the reply to your message, you can set that option here.

- Save sent message to—By default, your outgoing messages are saved in your Sent Items folder in your mailbox. You can change the location of where your sent message are saved by clicking the Browse button and choosing a folder available to you.

Delivery Options   You can set options on when to deliver a message and how that message is handled after a particular day.

- Do not deliver before—You can create the message now and have it wait for the actual day and time you want the message delivered.

- Expires after—You can set a message to expire after a certain day and time. This is great for messages that will be meaningless after the expiration date. The message will then be "grayed out" in the recipient's mailbox.

Part
IV

Ch
30

Tracking Options   You can set options to be notified when your message was delivered and read. This option works best when you send messages within your Exchange organization.

■ Tell me when this message has been delivered—By selecting this option, you will receive a message that your message has been delivered.

■ Tell me when this message has been read—You will receive a message when your message has been read by the recipient.

Message Flag   In Outlook, you can enhance a message by inserting a message flag. Suppose you really want to stress the importance of the message without the recipient having to read through the whole message. The message flag is a great tool to help you notify the recipient of the importance of the message. A flag appears in the recipient's Inbox and a brief description of the reason for the flag appears under the message tab when the recipient opens the message. You can add your own flag to any messages you send out by clicking the message flag button on the toolbar. In the Flag Message dialog box, you can use the predefined flags or type in your own flag. You can also set the day and time when your message must be acted upon.

Reading Messages

In Outlook, reading and sorting messages can be an overwhelming responsibility if you don't manage your Inbox efficiently. Messages that appear in your Inbox may not be ordinary messages. Some messages have higher importance than others. Some may need special attention that require you to respond immediately to an appointment, meeting, or task request. And other messages may be important to you because they may be responses to requests you sent out previously. You have many tools available in Inbox to help you keep track of all of these events.

You can open a message by double-clicking the message you want to read. Depending on the message options set by the sender, you may see a note about the message in the comment area above the message header.

Responding to Messages   If you need to take further action concerning a message, you have three options:

■ Reply—You can reply only to the sender of the message. This is helpful if you want to keep your response private from other recipients that have this message.

■ Reply to All—If you choose Reply to All, your response is sent to everyone in the To and Cc line.

■ Forward—You can send the current message to someone else without notifying the sender.

In all of the previous options, you can still edit the message as if you are creating a new message. Responding to a message saves you the hassle of typing in the correct e-mail address.

Sorting Messages: Arrow or Groups   You can sort messages in many ways, depending on what you feel is most useful to you. There are two options on how to organize your messages.

Arrow   You can choose to sort message by field using the arrow. The arrow appears when you choose a field. Depending on the field you choose, messages can be sorted in ascending or descending order. In a field involving text, such as the Subject field, an ascending sort (also called the up arrow) sorts information from A to Z. A descending sort (also called the down arrow) will sort from Z to A. In a field such as the Received field, the up arrow indicates messages sorted from oldest message to newest message. The down arrow indicates messages sorted from most to least recent.

Groups   You can sort your messages by groups by following these steps:

1. Under the View menu, click Group By Box.
2. Drag the column header to the Drag a column header here to group by that column box.
3. Under the View menu, click Sort.
4. You can choose the way you want to sort this information here. Click OK to confirm the sort order you choose.

Using the Calendar

When you open Calendar for the first time, you see three sections in your Information view: your schedule for the current day, called the *Appointment area*; a calendar with a view of the current month and next month, called the *Date Navigator*; and your taskpad (see Figure 30.6). You can adjust the current view in several ways. You can change the width of your schedule for the current day by dragging the vertical bar that separates it from the other two sections to the left or right. By moving this bar, you increase or decrease the number of calendar months you can see, plus adjust the size of your taskpad. You can also move the horizontal bar above the taskpad to change the overall view.

Adding an Appointment to Your Calendar

In the Appointment area, you can instantly type in an appointment, without going into detail:

1. In the Appointment area, click the start time of your appointment.
2. Type in a short description of the appointment.
3. Drag the bottom bar for the appointment to the approximate ending time for it, then press Enter to set the appointment.

After you have set the appointment, you see a couple of default settings. The appointment is marked as Busy, represented by the blue bar. Also, a bell appears in your appointment, indicating that you will be reminded 15 minutes before the start of it.

FIG. 30.6

Calendar main view.

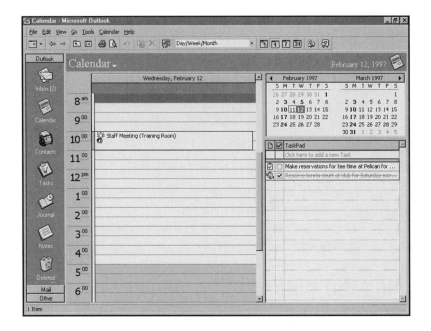

Adding a Detailed Appointment to Your Calendar

In Outlook, appointments can be more detailed and involve more than just a quick reminder to yourself of something that needs to be completed at a particular time. You may need to schedule a meeting with associates in your Exchange organization. Calendar is available to help you set a meeting time, send out requests to all attendees involved, and allocate resources that are required for the meeting.

To create a detailed appointment, here is a step-by-step example:

1. Open your calendar.

2. Select New Appointment from the Calendar menu (see Figure 30.7).

3. In the Subject text box, enter the topic for this appointment. When you are finished setting up the whole appointment, it will be saved as that subject.

4. In the Location text box, enter the location for the appointment. The drop-down list box will be available to you if you have set other appointments and want to use a previous location.

5. In the Start Time text boxes, enter the date and time of the appointment. Repeat this step for the End Time text boxes. If the appointment runs through the whole day, select the All Day Event option.

6. If you want to be reminded of the appointment, set the amount of time prior to the start of the appointment in the box next to Reminder. If you do not need a reminder, deselect the check box next to Reminder.

FIG. 30.7
Blank Appointment form.

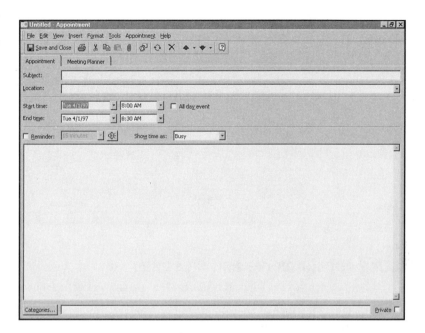

Part
IV

Ch

30

7. In the Show Time As box, use the drop-down list box to set your availability through the duration of the appointment.

8. The final section is the Notes area, where you can enter any miscellaneous notes for the appointment.

At this point, you have just finished setting up a detailed appointment. If your appointment involves only yourself, you can click Save and Close to complete the steps. However, if your appointment requires the attendance of your associates or a resource such as a conference room, you need to notify all parties involved.

Organizing a Meeting

This section guides you through making a meeting with other people in your company.

1. Create or open an existing appointment.

2. Click the Meeting Planner tab.

3. Under the Meeting Planner tab, notice that your name is the first required attendee in the All Attendees box. To start adding attendees or resources, select Invite Others. This displays the Select Attendees and Resources dialog box.

4. From here, you have three options to configure: Required Attendees, Optional Attendees, and Resources. After you have configured all of the necessary options, click OK. This returns you to the Meeting Planner tab.

5. You can now see an updated list of all attendees and their availability (see Figure 30.8).

FIG. 30.8

Viewing meeting attendees under meeting planner.

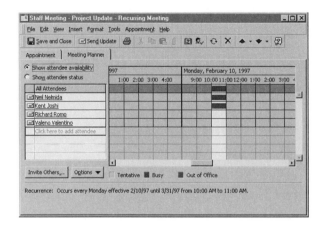

Editing Appointments and Meetings

In Calendar, you can adjust the details of an appointment or meeting quite easily.

Changing the Time of an Appointment or Meeting   You can change the starting and ending times of a meeting or appointment in various ways. In the Appointment area, you can drag the horizontal bar of either the starting time or ending time, or both to the updated times. A second method is to double-click the appointment and change the time directly on the appropriate time box.

Moving an Appointment or Meeting   If your appointment or meeting needs to be moved to a different day, you have two options available.

- First, you can drag and drop the appointment or meeting to the correct day. Make sure that the appointment or meeting appears in the Appointment area. Next, make sure the date that you want to move it to appears in the Date Navigator. Finally, you can click and hold down the appointment and drag it to the appropriate date in the Date Navigator.

- The second method is to double-click the appointment or meeting and change the date directly on the appropriate time box.

Recurring Appointments   Recurring or regularly scheduled appointments can be set automatically. Using the Recurrence feature, you can plan your schedule more efficiently (see Figure 30.9).

On the toolbar, click the Recurrence button. You can also select Recurrence from the Appointment menu. In the Appointment Recurrence dialog box, you need to complete all of the required information for the recurrence to be set correctly.

FIG. 30.9
Configuring Appointment
Recurrence dialog box.

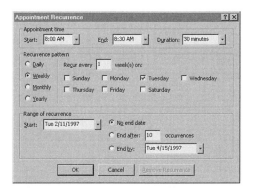

1. Appointment Time section—You need to type in the starting and ending times. Be sure to verify that the information in the Duration box is correct. You can set an appointment that lasts for more than one day.

2. Recurrence Pattern section—You can set various options pertaining to the frequency of the recurrence.

3. Range of Recurrence section—Set the start and end dates for the recurrence.

Adding Events

You can add special events such as a convention or anniversary to your calendar. The difference between an event and an appointment is that an event lasts the whole day.

Time Zone Issues

If your Exchange organization spans multiple time zones, there are a few things to consider when dealing with your calendar.

Setting Up Meetings over Different Time Zones   Suppose you are in Los Angeles and you need to set up a conference call with someone in your Exchange organization in New York. You want to make sure that both have the correct time information about that meeting. Outlook and the Exchange Server work together in getting meeting times correct. If the meeting is set for 9 AM Pacific Time in Los Angeles, the meeting time should and will appear as 12 PM Eastern Time in New York.

Traveling in Multiple Time Zones   Suppose you are traveling with your computer and your destination is in a different time zone. Outlook has a special feature to handle moving to a different time zone. The following steps demonstrate how to use this feature.

1. From the Tools menu, click Options.

2. Under the Options dialog box, click the Calendar tab.

3. To adjust the time zone, click the Time Zone button.

4. You will see the current time zone that you are in. You can add an additional time zone, by selecting Show an Additional Time Zone and adjusting the time zone displayed.

5. When you select the Swap Time Zones button, the additional time zone will be your current time zone.

6. Click OK to accept the changes.

Managing Your Contacts

The Contacts folder in Outlook provides a great way for you to store and organize all of the information you have about your associates and friends. It is more than a personal address book; it helps you track activities you have with your contact. Plus, you can define a view of your contacts that are most productive and meaningful to you (see Figure 30.10).

FIG. 30.10

Contacts Main View.

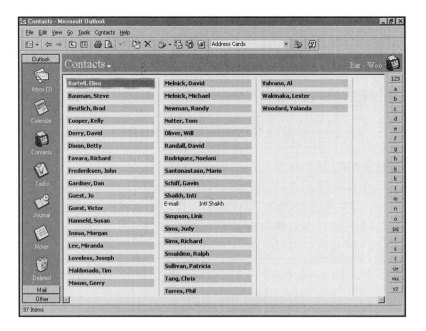

Adding Contacts

To add a contact, select Contacts on the toolbar and click New Contact. In the Contact dialog box, there are four tabs in which you can add information about your contact: General, Details, Journal, and All Fields (see Figure 30.11).

The General Tab   Under the General tab, you can type in some common information about your contact.

FIG. 30.11

Filling out the Contacts form.

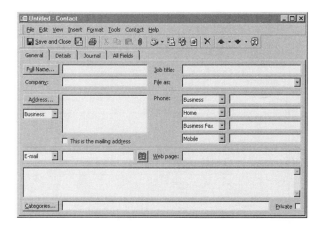

In the Full Name box, you can type in the name of your contact. You can also click the Full Name button to add more details about your contact's name such as Title and Suffix.

If your contact works for a particular company, you can enter it in the Company box, along with the position that person holds in the company in the Job title box. This information can be useful if you plan on grouping your contacts by company. Also, this affects the File as box, because you will have more options available to file your contact.

In the Address text box, you can type in the business, home, or other address of your contact. As when you click the Full Name button, you have the option to fill in the address, in greater detail, for your contact.

In the Phone text box, you have up to four available phone numbers you can enter and save for your contact. Also, you can specify what type of phone number each one represents, such as business, fax, home, cellular, pager, and so on.

If your contact is available through the Internet, via e-mail or a Web page, you can also save that information on the Contact dialog box.

Finally, you have the common features found throughout Outlook, such as a Notes area, the capability to put your contact in certain predefined categories, and to store your contact as private, hiding details of your contact from those who have to delegate access to your contacts.

The Details Tab   Under the Details tab, you have the option to add extra information about your contact such as department, office, profession, assistant's name, manager's name, birthday, anniversary, nickname, and spouse's name (see Figure 30.12).

The Journal Tab   Under the Journal tab, you can start recording journal entries for your contact and view particular entries made for your contact (see Figure 30.13).

FIG. 30.12
Viewing the Details tab.

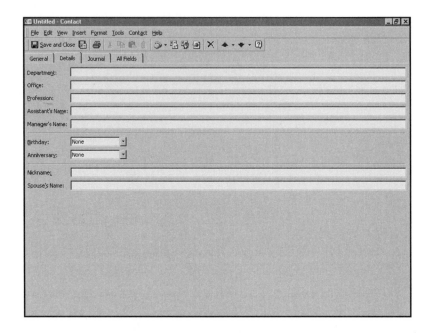

FIG. 30.13
Viewing all journal
entries for your contact.

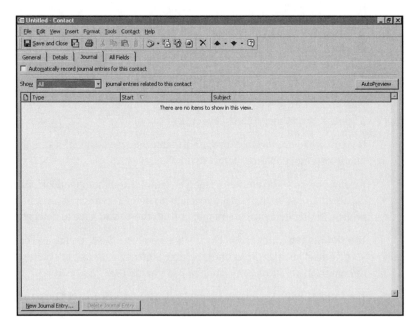

The All Fields Tab Under the All Fields tab, you have the ability to add even more information about your contact (see Figure 30.14). You can select from many fields and even add a few of your own.

FIG. 30.14
Frequently used fields of
your contact.

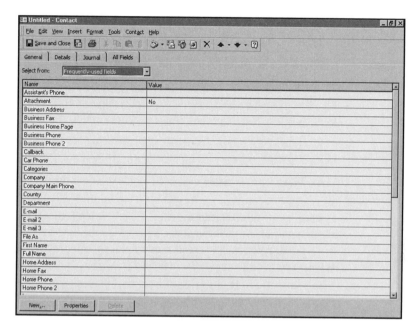

After you have configured all of the important and useful information for yourself, be sure to click Save and Close to finish adding in your new contact.

Viewing Contacts

Now that you have entered the appropriate information about your contact, you need to start organizing your contacts in such a way that you can find them when you need them.

Table 30.6 displays a list of predefined views to see your contact's information.

Table 30.6   Contacts

View	Display Results
Address Cards	Individual cards with primary mailing address and important phone numbers such as business, home, and fax.
Detailed Address Cards	Same as Address Cards, with secondary points of contact.
Phone List	Table that includes business, fax, home, and mobile numbers.
By Category	Grouped by category and sorted by contact name.
By Company	Grouped by company with job details.
By Location	Grouped by country.

Defining Custom Fields for Contacts View   Suppose you want to change the way you view your contacts. You may need to see information that is not set in the default views available. The following steps guide you through defining a view that is more useful.

1. In the View Menu, click Define Views.

2. In the Define Views for Contacts dialog box, click New.

3. In the Name of New View box, enter the name of this new view.

4. In the Type of View box, choose the type of display you want to see this new view.

5. In the Can Be Used On box, choose who and when this view can be displayed.

6. In the View Settings dialog box, click Fields to adjust the fields for the new view.

7. You can add fields from the Available Fields list to the Show these fields in this order list by clicking the desired field and then click Add. If a field is not displayed in the Available Fields, you can use the drop-down menu under the Select Available Fields From to select more fields. If you want to create a new field, choose the New Field button type in the appropriate information for the new field.

8. In the Show These Fields In This Order box, you can change the order of the fields displayed by clicking the field and then clicking the Move Up or Move Down button, to change the order of importance of that field.

9. When you are finished configuring all views, click OK.

Importing Contacts from Personal Address Book

If you worked with the Exchange client (Windows 95, Windows NT 4.0, Exchange Client 4.0) prior to moving to Outlook, you can import your old Personal Address Book into your new Contacts folder.

1. Under the File menu, click Import and Export.

2. In the Import and Export Wizard dialog box, highlight Import from Schedule+ or another program or file, and click Next (see Figure 30.15).

3. In the box under Select file type to import from, click Personal Address Book and then click Next.

4. In the box under Select destination folder, click Contacts and then click Next.

5. Click Finish to start importing data.

FIG. 30.15
Import and Export
Wizard dialog box.

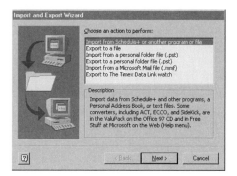

Integrating with Office 97

Outlook works seamlessly with applications and documents created in Office 97. Some of the features available are:

- Using Word 97 and WordMail features for Outlook e-mail.
- Integration of the Outlook Contact Manager and Word Mail Merge.
- Attaching Office files to appointments, tasks, or e-mail in Outlook.
- Using the Outlook Journal to keep track of when Office documents are revised.
- Creating tasks in Word, Excel, or PowerPoint.
- Using Import and Export Wizard to bring data from Microsoft Access, Excel, or Schedule+ into your Outlook folders.

From Here...

By now you have seen Outlook as a wonderful tool to help you communicate effectively with others and to keep you informed of your daily routine. But you have only seen a part of what Outlook can do to help you organize your work. Outlook has other excellent built-in features to help you keep track of everything that is important to you and you will see them in the following chapters.

- See Chapter 16, "Creating and Configuring Recipient," to set up accounts to be used with Auto Assistants.
- See Chapter 29, "Installing and Configuring Outlook," for explanations on how to configure other Outlook components.
- See Chapter 31, "Using Advanced Outlook Features," to see other features of Outlook and using it with your Exchange server to share Outlook information.
- See Chapter 32, "Implementing Third-Party Integration Tools," to see how applications from third-party companies can be used to enhance your environment.
- See Chapter 34, "Developing Exchange Forms," to learn more about the integration of forms in Exchange.

CHAPTER 31

Using Advanced Outlook Features

By now, we have discussed Outlook in terms of being a replacement for the Microsoft Exchange Client and Schedule+. But Outlook doesn't stop there. It has three other features to help you manage your activities and get through your schedule without a hitch. Plus, Outlook has made some updates on previously available features that are now much more easier to handle. ■

Utilizing Auto Assistants

Learn how to manage and organize your mail automatically by using auto assistants.

Managing Projects with Tasks

Understand how to manage tasks you have assigned to yourself and others.

Using the Journal

Keeping track of what is most important in your daily life.

Using Notes

Leaving simple reminders for yourself.

Other Outlook Features

Learn how to use Outlook features for you and your organization's advantage.

Web Outlook View

Discover how to access your mailbox and public folders on your Exchange Server from a frames-enabled Web browser.

Utilizing Auto Assistants

Auto Assistants help you manage your incoming mail by handling messages as they arrive in your Inbox. These actions include responding to, filing, and routing items. The Auto Assistant checks to see if the message meets specific conditions. The two Auto Assistants are the following:

- Inbox Assistant—Manages the mail coming into your Inbox on a daily basis
- Out of Office Assistant—Manages your mail when you are out of the office

Both Assistants use the same basic principles. Both are configured to accomplish tasks by using rules. Each rule is applied to incoming mail and consists of two parts:

1. Conditions: The characteristics of the message or form
   - Who the message is from
   - Who it is being sent to
   - Words in the subject box
   - Words in the body of the message

2. Actions: What happens when the rule's conditions are met
   - Moving items to a particular folder
   - Copying items to a particular folder
   - Forwarding items to another person
   - Deleting items

All rules are processed on the Microsoft Exchange Server. This enables the Auto Assistant to continue running even if you have not started Outlook. If the rule's actions can be performed without user intervention, the rule is completed entirely in the Microsoft Exchange mailbox. Examples of this are receiving alerts or moving a message into a set of personal folders. Remember that the personal folders reside on your client.

N O T E If you set up more than one rule, they are performed in the order listed.

Adding a Rule to the Inbox Assistant

To show how easy it is to use the graphical interface of the Inbox Assistant, here is a step-by-step example.

N O T E You need to be connected to your Exchange Server before you can add or edit an Auto Assistant.

1. Start or open Outlook.
2. Select the Inbox Assistant from the Tools menu. The following dialog box appears (see Figure 31.1).

FIG. 31.1

The Inbox Assistant dialog box showing the currently defined rule (blank by default).

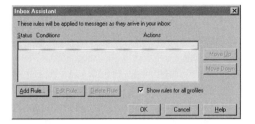

3. Click the Add Rule button. The Edit Rule dialog box appears (see Figure 31.2).

FIG. 31.2

Define rules to affect the messages in your Inbox.

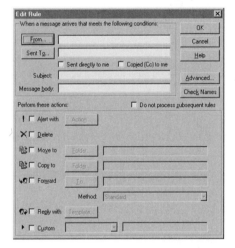

Part
IV

Ch
31

4. In the From box enter the name, or alias, of the person who will be sending the item.

5. In the Sent to box enter either your name or an account owned by you such as Sales, Tech. Support, or Administration.

6. If you would like to be notified if the message is either sent to you directly or copied (CC) to you, check the appropriate box.

N O T E You can check both boxes. The Assistant will also check for your name in distribution lists. ■

7. In the Subject box type a word or words with multiple strings separated by a semicolon (;) that you wish to include as a condition.

8. In the Message body box type a word or words, again with multiple strings separated by a semicolon (;) that you wish to include as a condition.

9. If you have something specific in mind, you can select the Advanced button, where you can specify additional search conditions.

    Example: You can locate messages that have attachments that are a particular size, or that do not meet the conditions you specify.

10. At this point, you can also click Check Names, which verifies names in the From and Sent To boxes by checking them against the address lists in your Address Book.

N O T E If a matching name is not found, or if there are multiple matches for the same name, the Check Names dialog box is displayed, where you can select the correct name or create a new one. ▦

11. You are now at the Perform these actions: box. Place a check in the Alert with box, which activates the Action button.

12. By clicking the Action button you are sent to the Alert actions dialog box. In this box, you can specify the text contained in the alert message and specify which sound will be played when the conditions are met.

13. Next on the list of actions is Delete.

N O T E This item is mutually exclusive. You cannot choose this item if you have chosen Alert, Copy, or Move. ▦

14. If you have not chosen to delete the item, you can now Move the item to one of your Personal Folders or to a Public Folder for which you have permission.

15. You may now Copy the item(s) to a folder.

    Example: You move the message to a Personal Folder and want to copy it to the bulletin board in a Public Folder.

16. Once you are done handling the item, you can choose to Forward it to one or many recipients.

17. If you are setting up an auto reply service, you can choose the Reply with button and specify a Template.

N O T E The Template can have additional recipients and attachments. ▦

18. The final option in the Edit Rule dialog box is Custom.

N O T E Custom actions are add-ons that are not provided by Outlook. ▦

19. Then select OK until you are back to Outlook.

20. The Inbox Auto Assistant is now ready to handle any messages meeting the criteria you specified.

Adding a Rule to the Out of Office Assistant

When the need arises, say a vacation or holiday, you can set up your Exchange Inbox to answer your mail with a friendly reminder that you are out. The following example configures the Out of Office Assistant to answer any messages while you are away.

1. Start or open your Exchange Inbox.

2. Select the Out of Office Assistant from the Tools menu. The Out of Office Assistant dialog box appears (see Figure 31.3).

FIG. 31.3

The Out of Office Assistant minds your mailbox automatically while you are away.

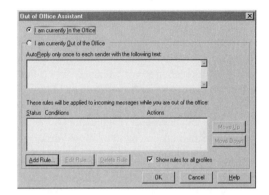

3. In the Out of Office Assistant dialog box, click the button that says you will be Out of the Office.

N O T E Clicking, "I am currently In the Office" will disable the Auto Assistant from replying to your messages. ▨

4. You may now type a message in the AutoReply box. This will send a reply only once to each sender.

N O T E This may be enough if you want a quick reminder. If you would like to handle the message in any other way, please continue. ▨

5. When you select Add Rule, you are presented with the same options that you are given during the Inbox Assistant.

6. In this case, select any messages Sent directly to you, or copied to you.

7. You can now Move or Copy the message into a predefined folder or leave it in your Inbox.

8. You can also Forward the messages to someone reading your mail while you are out.

9. Another option is to Forward the message to an address you can read while you are away, unless you are on vacation or something and don't want to think about work.

10. Probably the best feature for your needs, in this case, would be Reply with. You can send a message stating when you will be back and whether or not anyone will be replying to messages.

11. Click OK until you are back in Outlook.

Part

IV

Ch

31

N O T E   If there are any options that require more of an explanation, please refer to the steps in
Adding a Rule to the Inbox Assistant. ■

Using Remote Mail

You can use Remote Mail to view the headers of new items in your server Inbox. You then
select specific items to transfer to your off-line Inbox. Because you download only the items
you specify, this method can be faster than synchronizing your off-line Inbox, which downloads
all new items. For users that regularly receive large amounts of mail, these added levels of
control are very desirable because a single attachment in a message could take an hour or
more to download across a modem connection. When using Offline Folders, you have no control and are required to wait until all mail is delivered before working with individual messages.

You can also use Remote Mail to send mail you compose while offline. While working offline, it
is important that your computer and your Exchange configuration know how to authenticate
your Outlook client with your NT Domain and User account. Before attempting to automatically connect with Outlook, check your dial-up and log-in options under the properties of the
Exchange Server Service of your profile. Under the Dial-Up Networking tab, you must have
the correct log-in information.

N O T E   In the current shipping version of Outlook, it is not possible to have Offline Folders active
and be able to use Remote Mail. You will receive a warning telling you to disable Offline
Folders and you'll be directed on how to accomplish this. ■

Managing Projects with Tasks

In Outlook, Tasks can help you manage your daily responsibilities as well as keep track of all of
your future due dates on projects (see Figure 31.4).

Creating a New Task

The following steps help you create a new task.

1. Open Tasks from the Outlook Bar.
2. On the Standard toolbar, click the New Task Icon to open a new task form.
3. Under the Task tab, you have several options to configure before saving the new task
   (see Figure 31.5).

FIG. 31.4

Simple List view of Tasks.

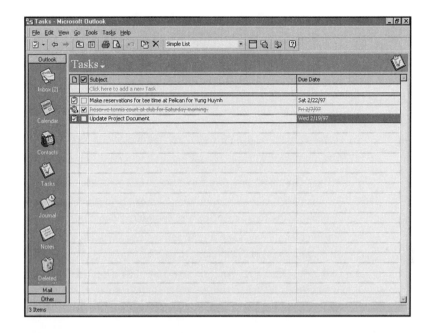

FIG. 31.5

Configuring information in the task form.

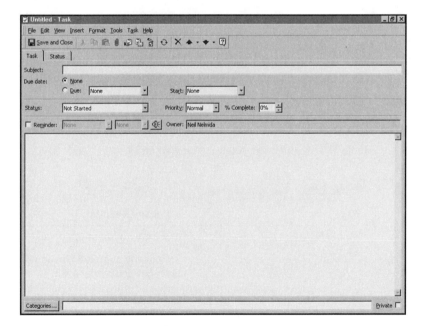

4. In the Subject box, type a description of the task you need to complete.

5. In the Due Date section, you have two options:
   - If the task has no due date, choose None.
   - If the task has a due date, use the drop-down menu in the Due box to pick the due date. If you want to record the start date of the task, enter that date in the Start box.

6. In the Status box, use the drop-down menu to choose the current status of the task.

7. In the Priority box, you can set the priority of the task from Low to High.

8. In the % Complete box, you can enter the percentage of the task completed at this time.

9. By default, a task has no reminder. You can be notified that your task is still incomplete by clicking the Reminder box and setting the date and time of the reminder.

10. For the Notes Area, Categories, and Private sections, you can add information similar to the appointment and contacts forms.

11. Under the Status tab, you can save information such as Date Completed, Total Work, Actual Work, Mileage, Billing Information, Contacts, and Companies.

12. When you are finished with the Tasks details, click Save and Close.

Editing

You can edit tasks in many ways. You can double-click a task to edit the whole task at once. Another method is to utilize the various views available to you. For example, you can edit a task in the Detailed List view by clicking the column you need to change and type over that informa-tion. In a column such as the Due Date, you can click the box and a drop-down menu with the Date Navigator appears.

Task views

Table 31.1 lists the ways you can view your tasks.

Table 31.1 Outlook Tasks

View	Display Results
Simple List	A list with minimum details.
Detailed List	Contains more information than the simple list, predefined by the user.
Active Tasks	Tasks that are not yet complete.

View	Display Results
Next Seven Days	Task due during the next seven days.
Overdue Tasks	Past due tasks.
By Category	Listed as groups, by category, sorted by creation date.
Assignment	Tasks assigned to associates in your organization, sorted by task owner and due date.
By Person Responsible	Listed as groups, sorted by owner and by due date.
Completed Tasks	A list of tasks that have been marked complete.
Task Timeline	Icons arranged by date on a timeline by start date. Tasks with start dates are arranged by due date.

Assigning Tasks to Others

You can assign a task to others in your organization, if the person you are assigning that task agrees to complete the task. When you try to assign a task, you must fill out a Task Request. This is similar to creating a new task for yourself, but it has a few options you need to configure before sending the request.

1. Under the Tasks menu, click New Task Request.

2. You will notice a few changes from the regular task form (see Figure 31.6).

3. In order for you to send this request, you must assign this task to at least one person. Enter that name in the To box. This is similar to addressing an e-mail message.

4. Notice that the reminder box is missing, but is replaced with two other options: Keep an updated copy of this Task on my Task List and Send me a status report when this Task is complete. You can choose how you want to be informed of the progress of the assigned task.

5. The rest of the New Task Request is the same as New Task.

6. When you are finished, click Send to send the task request.

FIG. 31.6
Task Request form
ready to be sent.

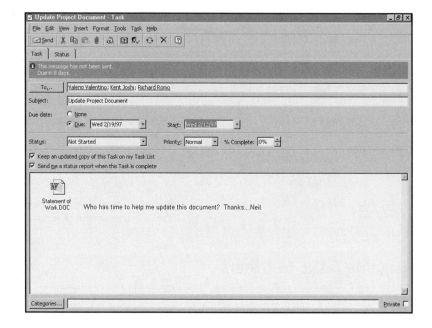

Recurring Tasks

You can have a recurring task and create it the same way you create a recurring appointment. Some examples of a recurring task include filling out a timesheet or backing up your server. You can automatically set these tasks in your task list. All you need to do is create or open a task, click the recurrence button on the toolbar, and set the recurrence pattern for your task.

Dragging a Task to Your Calendar

One of the many features in Outlook includes being able to drag a task from your tasklist to your calendar. This is a great way to remind yourself that you need to block out some time in your day to complete a task. Once a task is on your calendar, you can edit it like any other appointment.

Using the Journal

In Outlook, you can keep a record of your daily activities in your journal. You can manually add entries in your journal for miscellaneous activities. A key feature of Outlook is the ability to automatically record your activities that involve your contacts or any Microsoft documents that you worked on. This helps you organize your work, because if you need to locate a document or recall a meeting with a contact, the journal can be the best tool for you (see Figure 31.7).

FIG. 31.7
Viewing Journal
entries By Type.

FIG. 31.7
Viewing Journal
entries By Type.

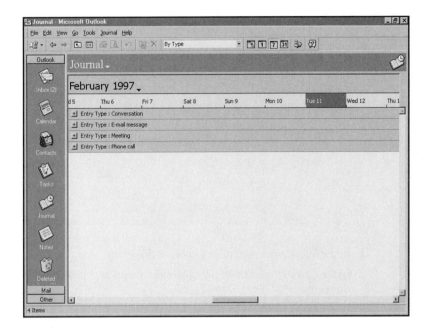

Part

IV

Ch

31

Table 31.2 provides a list of ways you can view journal entries.

Table 31.2 Outlook Journal

Views	Display Results
By Type	Grouped by type on a timeline.
By Contact	Grouped by contact name on a timeline.
By Category	Grouped by category on a timeline.
Entry List	All journal entries in a list.
Last Seven Days	Entries created during the last seven days.
Phone Calls	Entries recorded as phone calls.

Creating a Journal Entry

You can start recording a journal by following these steps:

1. Open your Journal from the Outlook bar.
2. On the Standard toolbar, click the Journal icon to open a new journal entry (see Figure 31.8).

FIG 31.8

Creating a new
journal entry.

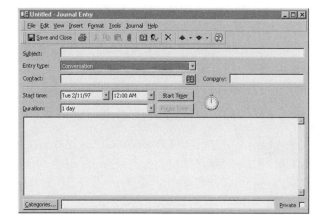

3. In the Subject box, enter the subject of this entry.

4. In the Entry type box, use the drop-down menu to choose the action performed for this entry.

5. In the Contact box, enter the name of the contact. You can add the company name in the Company box.

6. In the Start time section, you can enter the date and time.

7. In the Duration box, you can enter the amount of time spent on this subject.

8. The notes area, categories, and private boxes can be filled in the same way you filled out an appointment.

Using the Timer

The timer is available in Journal to keep track of the actual time the journal entry was open. This is useful if you want to keep track of the actual time spent in a meeting or on the phone.

Another feature in Outlook that will help you fill out a journal entry needing the timer is the AutoDate feature. Outlook can convert text descriptions such as *today* to the current date and *noon* to 12:00P.M. It can also decipher holidays such as New Year's Day and Independence Day.

The following example uses the AutoDate feature along with the journal to keep track of the actual minutes spent on an activity. Follow these steps:

1. Create a new journal entry.

2. In the Start time box, if the day is not correct, you can enter Today. This will automatically bring up the correct date.

3. In the box where the time is displayed, type Now. The current time will be displayed.

4. In the Duration box, type 0 for 0 minutes time elapsed.

5. Click Start Timer. The timer will run and the time box will update every minute.

6. Click Pause Timer to stop the timer.

7. You can fill out the rest of the journal entry and click Save and Close to save it.

Setting Journal Options

In Outlook, you can select which items can be automatically recorded in your journal. These items include contacts, Outlook items that involve contacts, and Microsoft products. To set an automatic journal entry, follow this procedure:

1. Under the Tools menu, click Options.

2. In the Options menu, select the Journal tab (see Figure 31.9).

FIG. 31.9

Configuring items and contacts to be automatically recorded in Journal.

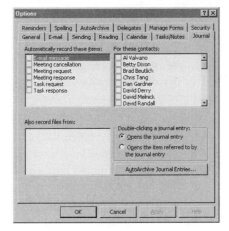

3. In the box under Automatically Record These Items, click the items you want automatically recorded for the contacts that you will choose.

4. In the box under For These Contacts, select the contacts that you want to record in your journal.

5. In the box under Also Record Files From, select the Microsoft products that you want to record in journal.

6. Click AutoArchive Journal Entries if you want to set the options for automatically archiving your journal entries after a specific duration (see Figure 31.10).

Part

IV

Ch

31

FIG. 31.10

Setting the amount of time to elapse before archiving journal entries.

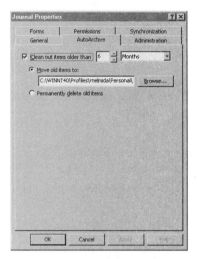

Using Notes

Notes can be very useful in helping you remember things. Just like the popular paper sticky notes, you can use Notes in Outlook to write down reminders for yourself, just as you would with paper.

To work with Notes in Outlook, click the Note button on the Outlook bar (see Figure 31.11). To create a new note, select Note, then click New Note. Optionally, you can press Ctrl+Shift+N from anywhere within Outlook. The Notes Information Viewer opens. You can now type in any quick reminders, questions, or ideas. The note will display over whatever part of Outlook you are currently in. Type your comments in the note and press Escape. Outlook will automatically save the note in your Notes folder. The next time you bring up Notes, your message appears.

By default, Notes are yellow, but you can change the color to blue, green, pink, or white to color-code your messages. To change the color of your note, right-click the Note you want to change. To change the color of a new note, click the icon at the top left corner of the note, and choose Color in the menu, and select the new color from the list displayed. Table 31.3 shows the different ways you can view notes.

Table 31.3 Outlook Notes

View	Display Results
Icons	Icons sorted from left to right by creation date.
Notes List	A list by creation date.

View	Display Results
Last Seven Days	Notes created during the last seven days.
By Category	Listed as groups, by category, sorted by creation date.
By Color	Listed as groups, by color, sorted by creation date.

FIG. 31.11

Sample notes in Notes folder.

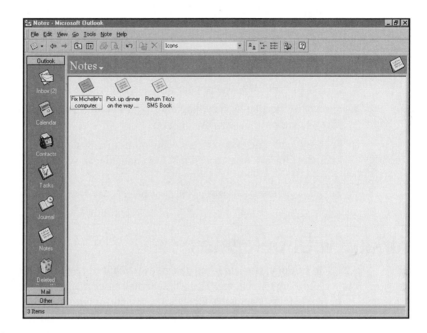

Profiles and Information Services

Outlook is very flexible. It can be used by more than one person or possess multiple configurations per user. This is accomplished with Profiles. Outlook can also be used to access multiple sources of information. This option is configured through a feature called Information Services.

Introduction to Profiles

Generally, the Profile that you create during installation is the only Profile you need, unless:

- More than one person uses the same computer; each person should have a Profile to keep mail private and secure.

- You need to work with a different set of services. You can create an additional Profile with those custom services.

N O T E You can start Outlook with the default Profile you have specified. You can also be prompted to select a Profile each time you start Outlook. ▪

 T I P Being prompted to select a Profile is a good idea when you use multiple Profiles, or when there are multiple users per computer.

Understanding Information Services

Information services provide great flexibility in the Exchange Client because they do the following:

- ▪ Control how your messaging applications address and route your mail.
- ▪ Enable you to modify where your mail and folders are stored.
- ▪ Specify the location for incoming mail, your Personal Address Book, and any sets of personal folders that you have created.
- ▪ Enable you to send faxes or connect to other mail systems such as Exchange, Microsoft Mail, the Internet, or a variety of MAPI-enabled mail systems.

Before you can use an information service, you must add it to your active Profile. ▪

Working with Delegates

N O T E In Outlook, you can setup delegates to manage resources such as conference rooms, office equipment, etc. These resources can be managed manually, making the delegate fully responsible for their availability, or automatically, depending on your organization's requirements. Since a resource cannot respond to any requests for its use, you can establish a delegate to take care of booking the resource for a particular meeting. To create a delegate, take the following steps:

1. Open Outlook using the profile set up for the resource account.
2. Under the Tools menu, click Options.
3. In the Options dialog box, click the Delegates tab.
4. Click Add to assign a delegate to the resource account.
5. In the Add Users dialog box, choose a delegate, then click OK.
6. The Delegate Permissions dialog box will appear and you can setup any additional permissions for the user.
7. Click OK when you are finished. This will bring you back to the Delegates tab.

8. In the Delegates tab, click the check box next to "Send meeting requests and responses only to my delegates, not to me."

9. Click OK to save these settings for the new delegate.

At this point, all meeting requests involving this resource will be automatically forwarded to the delegate.

You can also setup the resource account to be booked on a first-come, first-served basis. This would fully automate the process of booking a resource. However, to override any advanced bookings, you will need to contact the delegate or the administrator because they are the only ones with access to the resource account.

1. Open Outlook with the profile set up for the resource account.

2. Under the Tools menu, click Options.

3. In the Options dialog box, click the E-mail tab.

4. In the Settings for Automatic Processing of Mail section, make sure the Process Requests and Responses on Arrival box is selected.

5. In the Options dialog box, click the Calendar tab.

6. Under the Calendar tab, click the Advanced Scheduling tab.

7. In the Processing of Meeting Requests section, select the options that need to be handled automatically.

8. After selecting the appropriate options, click OK.

Working with Public Folders Offline

If your Exchange organization uses public folders, you can work with some or all of these folders while you are offline. This feature is very useful for organizations that keep documents on the server. This allows users who work with off-line folders to be continuously updated with information that is added to public folders. Also, this is a great way for you to make changes to documents while you are offline and have those changes automatically updated when you connect online.

Under public folders, you will find a folder called Favorites. You will store all of the public folders that you want to view offline here. To add these folders, follow these steps:

1. Under Public Folders, open All Public Folders.

2. Select the folder you want available when you are offline.

3. Under the File menu, choose Folder and click Add to Public Folder Favorites.

4. In the Add to Favorites dialog box, you can change the name of the folder. After choosing a name for this folder, click Add.

5. Under Public Folder Favorites, choose the folder you just added.

6. Under the File menu, choose Folder and click Properties.

Part
IV

Ch
31

7. In the Properties dialog box, click the Synchronization Tab.

8. In the This Folder is Available box, click When Offline or Online.

9. Click OK to confirm that this folder is now available to you offline.

Web Outlook View

The Web Outlook View is a very convenient feature available in Exchange Server 5.0 for users needing to attach to the server without having to use the full-featured Outlook client. This feature is very practical for someone who wants to use a computer with Internet access to quickly and efficiently check e-mail. Your organization can also utilize the Web Outlook View on computers that cannot run Outlook and need an alternative to attaching to the Exchange Server for secure access to mailboxes and public folders such as UNIX or Macintosh clients.

Messaging with Web Outlook View

In the Web Outlook View, you can access your mailbox on the Exchange Server to send messages and read messages in your Inbox. Contact your administrator for details on how to logon to your Exchange server from your Web browser. Once you pass the security setup by your network administrator, you will receive the log-on screen (see Figure 31.12).

FIG. 31.12

User logon to mailbox in Web Outlook View.

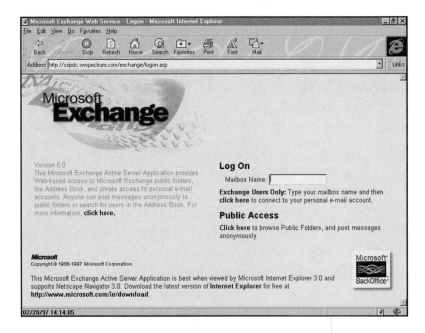

After successfully logging into your mailbox, you will see the current contents of your Inbox through the Web Outlook View (see Figure 31.13).

FIG. 31.13

Viewing the Inbox in
Web Outlook View.

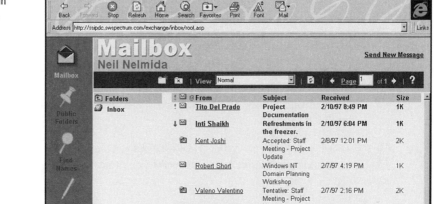

Creating Messages In the Action Area of the Web Outlook View, click Send New Message.
A New Message form will appear, which is similar to the Mail Form in Outlook (see Figure
31.14). You have several options to configure before sending the message:

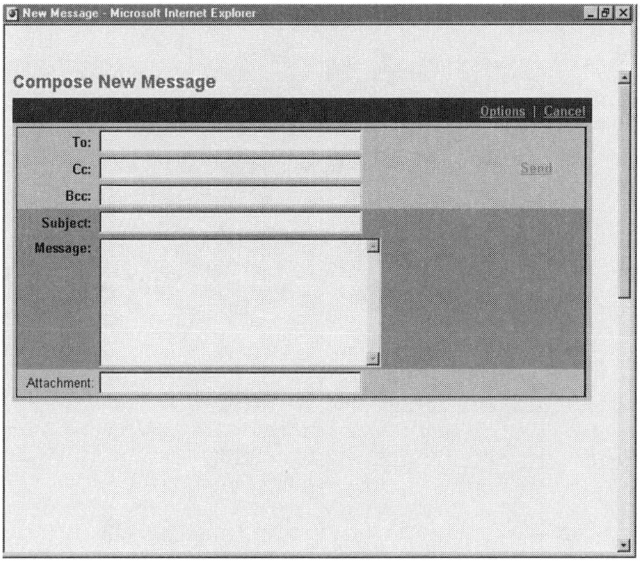

FIG. 31.14

New Message Form.

■ To:

This box contains a list of the main recipients of your message.

■ Cc:

Enter the recipients who need a carbon copy of the message.

■ Bcc:

This option lets you enter recipients who receive your message, but their names will not appear in the list of recipients in the To: or Cc: box. Also, Bcc: recipients are hidden from other Bcc: recipients.

N O T E When you enter a name in any of the above boxes, you can type in the Display Name of the recipient in your Exchange organization or the SMTP/Internet address for all other recipients. ▨

■ Subject:

You can add a brief description of your message here.

■ Message:

Type in your full text message here.

■ Attachment:

List of files you want to attach to this message.

■ Options

You can set several options for this message. These options include Importance, Read Receipt, Delivery Receipt, and Save a copy in the "Sent Items" Folder (see Figure 31.15).

FIG. 31.15
Configuring Message
Options.

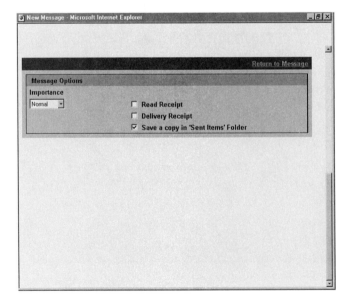

When you are finished filling out the form, you can send or cancel it.

Reading Messages You can open a message in your Inbox by clicking the sender in the From column (see Figure 31.16). After reading the message, you have several options to further handle this message:

FIG. 31.16

Reading a message from your Inbox.

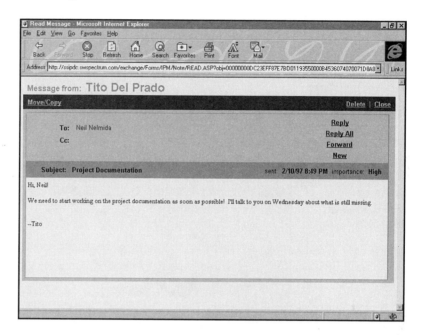

- Move

  You can move the current message to any folder available to you on the Exchange Server. You need to choose a folder, then verify that you want to move the message to that folder.

- Copy

  You can copy the current message to any folder available to you on the Exchange Server. Choose a folder, then verify that you want to copy the message to that folder.

- Delete

  This option deletes the message from your Inbox.

- Close

  This option closes the message and marks it as read.

- Reply

  When you choose this option, you only send a reply to the sender of the original message.

■ Reply All

This option is similar to Reply, but the reply is sent to all recipients that received this message.

■ Forward

You can forward this message to another recipient.

■ New

This option helps you create a new message.

Public Folders

You can access public folders as easily as your mailbox after you login to your Exchange Server over the Web Outlook View. Once you have been authenticated by the server, you can start posting and reading items stored in the public folders (see Figure 31.17). The following sections provide a basic guide for you to manipulate public folders.

FIG. 31.17
Web Outlook View of Public Folders.

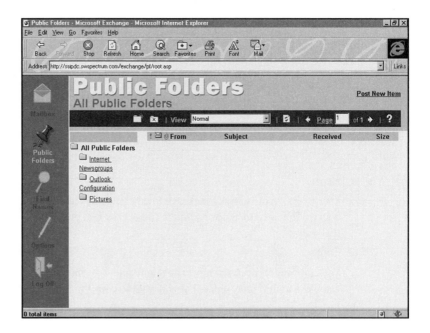

Post New Item   From your Web Outlook View, you can post a new item to a public folder. First, you need to select the correct public folder you want to post information (see Figure 31.18).

FIG. 31.18
Viewing posted
messages in a
public folder.

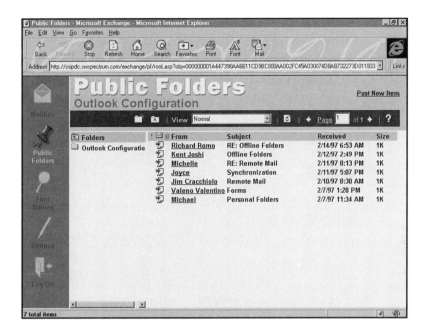

Then, in the Action Area of the Web Outlook View, click Post New Item. A New Post form appears and you have several options to configure before finally posting the item in the public folder (see Figure 31.19). They are as follows:

FIG 31.19
New Post Form.

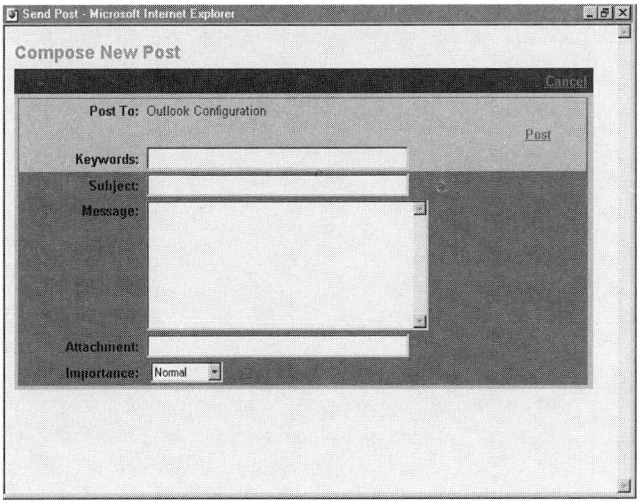

■ Keywords

You can add keywords to your post to help others determine whether your post is of some interest.

■ Subject

This is a brief description about your post.

■ Message

This is the body of the post. It contains the information you want to announce to the audience of this public folder.

■ Attachments

You can add files to your post to enhance it.

■ Importance

You can set the importance of your post as Low, Normal, or High.

■ Post

Select this option when you are ready to post your information to the public folder.

Reading and Responding to Posts   Posting information to a public folder is only part of what you can do over a Web browser. You can also read and respond to posts. To start reading posts, you need to select one from a public folder that interests you. After reading that post, you have three options to handle it and possibly continue the discussion.

■ Reply to Folder

This option enables you to post a reply to the post you just read. When you click this option, a Post Form appears with a copy of the old post in the Message Box. You can edit your reply and set the same options as a new post. Be sure to click Post to post the reply in the public folder.

■ Reply to Sender

This option enables you to send a new message to the author of the post. Because you are creating a new message, you can also send a copy of this post to other recipients.

■ Forward

You can forward this post to another recipient.

Find Names

The Find Names option allows you to search the Exchange Address Book. You can get detailed information about someone in your organization by typing in any information you know about that person. The available fields include Display Name, First Name, Last Name, Title, Alias Name, Company, Department, Office, and City (see Figure 31.20).

After typing in that information, click Find, and if there are matches to the request, a list appears. You can then select the name to get more information about that person. However, if you want to browse the Exchange Address Book, click Find with all fields left blank (see Figure 31.21).

FIG. 31.20
Using Find Names.

FIG. 31.21
Viewing the Exchange
Address Book.

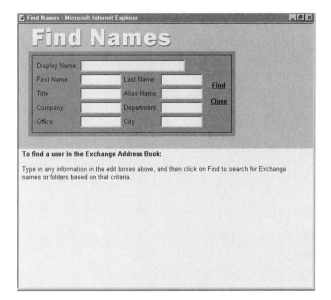

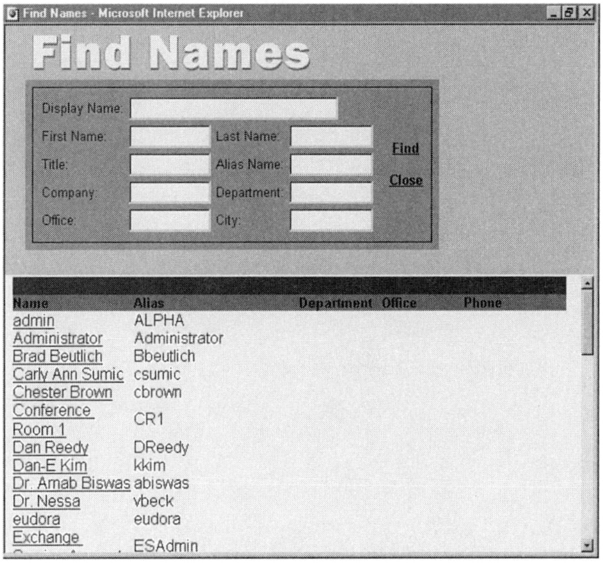

Options

Under Options in the Navigation Bar, you can set your Out of Office Assistant. You can indicate that you are In The Office. You can also select Out of the Office and have replies with a text message sent to each sender (see Figure 31.22).

FIG. 31.22
Reviewing Options
Screen.

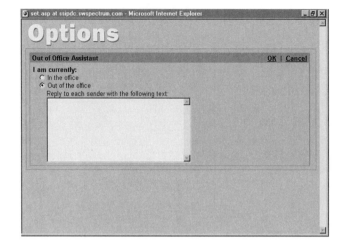

Logoff

By selecting Logoff in the Navigation Bar, you can logoff of Microsoft Exchange. You will receive a message reminding you to complete the log off process by closing the Web browser (see Figure 31.23). This is for your security, so that others cannot view your mailbox.

FIG. 31.23
Logoff message in Web
Outlook View.

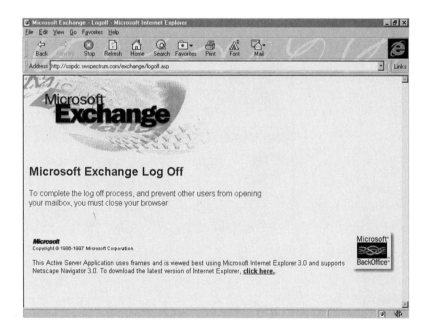

From Here...

As you can see, Outlook and the Web Outlook View are very powerful tools that can keep you and your Exchange organization very productive and well organized. The key to success is to develop a routine using these tools to keep everyone well informed and actively involved in your working environment.

- See Chapter 29, "Installing and Configuring Outlook," for explanations on how to configure other Outlook components.
- See Chapter 30, "Using Outlook," to learn more about the Inbox and Calendar.
- See Chapter 32, "Implementing Third-Party Integration Tools," to see how third-party applications can be used to enhance your environment.
- See Chapter 34, "Developing Exchange Forms," to learn more about the integration of forms in Exchange.

Part
IV

Ch
31

Third-Party Integration and Application Development

CHAPTER 32

Implementing Third-Party Integration Tools

By now, we have discussed all the core functions of Exchange provided in the shipped version. Although Microsoft has an extensive array of features built into the application, it cannot deliver all the features that end users need in their environment.

Third-party developers are essential resources in the deployment of Exchange in your environment. You saw that Exchange is more than just a messaging system. Exchange is an application framework. Third-party developers can extend the framework to provide a wide array of solutions on top of your core Exchange architecture. ■

Workflow Technologies

Do not confuse workflow with routing forms. Workflow is defined here as group collaboration guided by a strict set of rules.

Document Imaging Strategies

These company's products are centered around two areas: scanning in documents as images and managing data (images, videos, and so on). Each product ties in directly with Exchange.

Information-Sharing Resources

Information sharing or groupware is a key feature of Exchange. The products listed in this section considerably enhance Exchange's groupware functionality.

Information Providers

Utilizing the client/server architecture of Exchange, agents retrieve information requested by the user. While the agent is searching, the client is free to do other tasks.

Communications and Gateways to Extend Exchange

Paging, faxing, and voice mail services are communication services that can be integrated into Exchange. Using third-party gateways can extend Exchange's reach into legacy mail systems not supported by Exchange's standard set of gateways.

Using Workflow Technologies to Extend Exchange

Workflow sometimes is confused with electronic forms and forms routing. Workflow consists of a strict set of rules to a process. It extends the function of group collaboration.

Workflow is composed of several other key technologies: e-mail, document imaging, document management, and databases. The end result is that it should streamline business processes and reduce system costs by using workflow servers to perform tasks based on the business model (see Figure 32.1). These applications will be integrated with the Exchange client and will provide an agent running on the Exchange Server to process and manage the workflow.

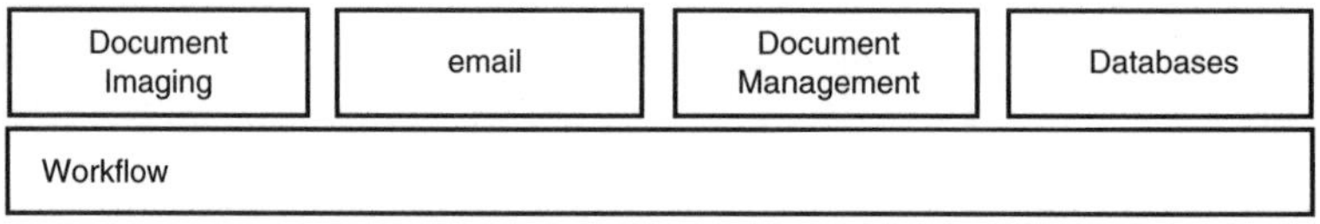

FIG. 32.1
Workflow framework
and technologies.

Document Imaging	email	Document Management	Databases
Workflow			

The following is a list of workflow technology solutions. Each product mentioned has a description of the components, as well as integration with Exchange. The products include Exchange client software integration and data routing to external database sources (see Figure 32.2).

- *Action Technology*—Action promotes its ActionWorkflow System. Together with Microsoft, it is working on the workflow API (WAPI). Action has numerous partners to include Watermark Imaging, Saros, PC Docs, and FileNet. Action is a leader of the Workflow Coalition. This organization is promoting a common framework for workflow-enabled applications. Action takes full advantage of Exchange's Groupware and Universal to provide an interface to the workflow of the business.

  Action uses the inbox in the Exchange client to start workflows and then receive status reports via e-mail. The Action Workflow Manager Server triggers the appropriate business rules with respect to the business model. The Workflow Manager can populate a database with the information or route a request by way of e-mail to a subsequent recipient. This takes advantage of the existing network.

  For more information:

  http://www.actiontech.com

- *FileNet*—FileNet also has a high-end workflow solution named Workflo. FileNet and Action both work together and are competitors. FileNet, however, positioned itself as the complete workflow solution. As mentioned previously, workflow includes e-mail, images, documents, and databases. FileNet has solutions to address all the components. The other components are discussed in following sections of this chapter.

  Both Action and FileNet are leaders in the Windows-based workflow market.

  For more information:

  http://www.filenet.com

    ■ *Axonet Information Center*—Axonet has a product named MegaFlow. This product is a simpler workflow manager. It doesn't have built-in support for the various workflow data types. However, it is extensible by way of OLE, and it supports RTF from the client side.

For more information:

http://www.tiac.net/users/axonet/

FIG. 32.2
Workflow business process.

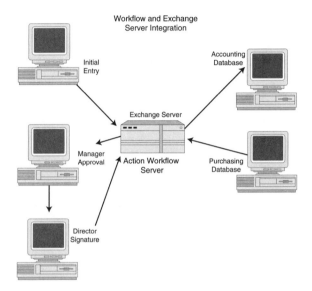

Document Imaging and Management with Exchange

Document imaging is the capability to take an object, scan it, and store the image for later use on the computer system.

Document management is the capability to take existing data in a variety of formats—including scanned images, audio and video files, word processing documents, and more. After the system has stored the object, the object is cataloged and managed for later use. This includes user-defined fields, object-file type conversions, object indexing, and security permissions.

Both of these technologies are complementary and separate. Document imaging involves capturing the object from an external source: paper, fax, and so on. The image must be processed and stored. You then would store the image into a document management system, which will contain more than just this one kind of data object (see Figure 32.3).

Part
V

Ch

32

FIG. 32.3

Document imaging and
document management
with Exchange.

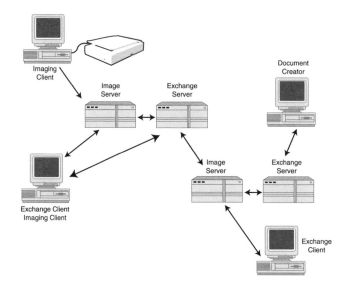

The following is a list of document imaging and management technology solutions. Each product mentioned has a description of the components, as well as integration with Exchange. The products include Exchange client software integration and server connections to external image repositories.

- *Watermark Imaging*—They are the primary NT-based, Exchange Server-enhanced, document-imaging solution. Watermark recently was acquired by FileNet to provide the complete workflow solution, as described in the previous section.

  Watermark can distribute scanned papers or faxes throughout the organization. This capability leverages the Exchange e-mail topology. Watermark provides the capability to e-mail a pointer into the storage system, to limit the amount of data transferred across the network, and to avoid duplicate copies.

  For more information, call (617) 229-2600.

- *Unisys*—Unisys recently has announced a solution integrated with Exchange's groupware function. The product is Unisys InfoImage Folder. The name indicates its positioning in the Exchange's universal inbox in the Exchange client. InfoImage Folder will compete with the Watermark imaging system.

  For more information:

  http://www.unisys.com

  or

  http://www.microsoft.com/exchange/

There are several document management solutions, which are described in the following list:

- *Saros*—Saros, recently acquired by FileNet, provides a document management solution, Saros Mezzanine. This product has a library metaphor for storing documents and data objects. The data objects are checked in and out. Mezzanine manages this procedure. Saros integrates with Exchange—a user can e-mail a document or object into the Saros library without having the client software installed on the PC. Users also can e-mail pointers to files inside of Saros without having to check out a document and e-mail the entire file to the recipients. This setup eliminates multiple copies of files. Saros has both the client e-mail integration and an NT server product as the library.

  For more information:

  http://www.saros.com

- *FileNet*—In addition to leveraging the acquisition of Saros, FileNet has acquired Greenbar Software to provide a Computer Output to Laser Disk (COLD) solution. FileNet will use this application as a tool for distributing printed reports. The reports will originate from their Workflo System, which provides FileNet two document management solutions, one for documents and one for system reporting.

  For more information:

  http://www.filenet.com

- *PC Docs*—PC Docs provides a set of electronic tools for publishing documents and accessing the information through the Exchange inbox in the Exchange client. From within Docs Open, you can publish a document to a public folder and then allow users to interact and discuss the document. Docs Interchange for Exchange consists of two agents, distribution and mail. The distribution agent will replicate by using the Exchange replication technology. It also allows for seamless integration between the Docs Open library and Exchange. Documents can easily be replicated into the Exchange folders. The mail agent allows Exchange client users to e-mail a query to the Docs Open library and access the Docs Open database. This doesn't require a user to have the Docs Open client on his or her workstation, just Exchange. Users can request documents be e-mailed back to them from the Docs Open library by way of the Docs Exchange Interchange.

  Watermark imaging is an imaging partner with PC Docs. From Watermark, you can send the scanned images into Docs Open.

  For more information:

  http://www.pcdocs.com

- *Common Ground*—Common Ground recently was acquired by Hummingbird Communications. Common Ground for Exchange provides a publishing and document management solution. Users can share access to documents by way of the Exchange network. Users can access the Common Ground Digital Papers directly from their Exchange client.

  For more information:

  http://www.commonground.com

Information Sharing

Information sharing is the capability to have group discussion forums with threaded conversations about a document, topic, or project. This capability is similar to an Internet News Group. This technology is the basis for groupware. Groupware provides a central repository for threaded conversation. The paradigm is activity that is classified as one-to-many. In this way, a user can write to one place, and then many people can access and comment on the information. Groupware is a base feature of Exchange (see Figure 32.4).

FIG. 32.4

Groupware: one-to-many conversations.

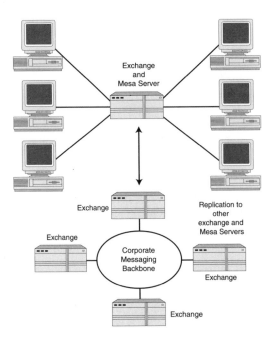

- *Mesa*—Mesa has a product named Conference Plus. This application is an add-in to the Exchange client. Another folder appears in the Universal inbox in the Exchange client, representing Mesa. After you click to open this folder, you can access the information with the threaded conversations.

  Mesa writes its information to the MAPI version 1.0 Exchange data structure. Mesa was one of the first third-party developers that worked on Exchange solutions by using MAPI. Its MAPI Message store runs as another Exchange service, taking full advantage of the rich administration and replication tools.

  From the client, Mesa allows direct access to Conference Plus folders by way of the Exchange inbox as a root-level folder. Mesa then provides an Exchange Interchange that provides two-way replication between Conference Plus folders and Exchange Mesa message stores to address existing users of Mesa. Finally, a migration utility is included to assist with converting folders from Conference Plus to the Exchange MAPI message store architecture.

Mesa is currently working on an Exchange Interchange for Internet News Groups, Lotus Notes, and other interchanges as needed in the marketplace.

For more information:

e-mail: **info@mesa.com**

Understanding Information Providers

Information providers comprise a content-driven focus of Exchange. Exchange is more than just an e-mail system. This technology demonstrates the power of this client-server application framework.

Several companies provide information agents, running on the Exchange Server to retrieve information of a given subject (see Figure 32.5). This technology can parallel what is known as a "Web crawler" on the Internet. These agents are given a specific topic and poll their respective information feeds.

This function is configured in a manner similar to other server-based rules on Exchange. The end user accesses the rules policy from the client workstation with the Exchange client and tells the agent what information to gather. At this point, the agent on the server executes the request and is not dependent on the client to be connected. The agent returns the information and resources to the user.

- *Fulcrum*—Fulcrum Search Server is a high-performance, text-indexing, and retrieval engine offering rapid access to vast amounts of corporate information stored in documents or databases. It supports ODBC connections to data sources. Users in a workgroup-computing environment have flexible access to large amounts of data.

  "Fulcrum Find" provides content-based indexing and retrieval of information in public folders, attachments, or e-form data. The server-based component is an Intuitive Searching engine, which is used to return specific subjects of content to the user. The search can be performed across multiple servers or on the desktop. The result set is a hierarchical list with the most number of hits at the top of the list. The user then can select the information source and read the content. Additionally, Fulcrum Find supports SQL statement calls to optimize the performance of a search query.

  For more information:

  http://www.fulcrum.com

698 | Chapter 32 Implementing Third-Party Integration Tools

FIG. 32.5

Information providers for Exchange Server.

Information Provider Architecture

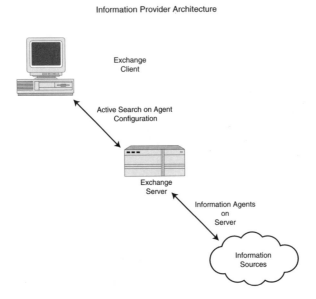

Exchange Client

Active Search on Agent Configuration

Exchange Server

Information Agents on Server

Information Sources

■ *Verity*—Verity Topic agents compete with Fulcrum. Verity goes beyond the corporation to provide a rich, integrated search and retrieval engine that can be directed to external data sources such as Reuters and the public Internet. Similar to Fulcrum, Verity has a server process that runs on the Exchange Server, which gets configured from the client PC running Exchange. The server automatically notifies the user when the information needed is located. The agents also can poll specific data sources and, when new information is found, automatically retrieve this data for the user.

The user can configure the agents remotely from the client or e-mail an agent or a query to be processed. The user can configure several agents to execute from the desktop or the server with the flexibility of the output format and location. Verity also can transmit the output of a query via fax, pager, e-mail, or public folder. Verity Topic can access data sources that include Exchange folders, attachments, ODBC data sources, Lotus Notes, and Acrobat Catalogs.

For more information:

http://www.verity.com

■ *Lexis/Nexis*—Lexis/Nexis is similar in features to Fulcrum Find and Verity Topic; however, it applies only to the Lexis/Nexis data services. Lexis/Nexis is an information-service bureau with thousands of new bits of information daily for the entertainment, legal, and medical professions.

The user agent is configured to connect with Lexis/Nexis, execute the query, and return the "hit-list" to the user. The user then can download the information that is needed. The product for Exchange is Tracker. Tracker searches across an index of 2,400 newspapers, with over 100,000 new articles each day. Users can customize Tracker as needed.

http://www.quecorp.com

Lexis/Nexis also has PubWatch, which is similar to the polling feature of Fulcrum and Verity. PubWatch polls Lexis/Nexis for new information on the subject entered by the user.

For more information:

http://www.lexis-nexis.com

- *SandPoint*—SandPoint Hoover is the final search and retrieval engine currently developed for Exchange. Hoover can search across data from multiple media, live news feeds, online databases, and corporate information in ODBC data sources or Exchange public folders.

  Hoover seems mainly targeted for its integration with external data sources. The user configures all queries from within the Universal inbox. The agent can search across over 5,200 data sources, including *The Wall Street Journal, Forbes, Dow Jones, Business Week*, and more.

  For more information, call (800) 775-4442.

Communications and Gateways for Exchange

Communications and gateways provide ways to extend Exchange in legacy systems or to provide new functionality. These technologies include wireless access to Exchange mail servers, X.25 support for international message transfer, and public and private network and systems. For Gateways, several third-party developers will extend Exchange with paging servers, fax servers, voice message servers, and connections into legacy mail systems, including Profs and All-in-One.

Part
V

Ch
32

Communication Support for Exchange

Communications gateways and service providers for Exchange provide the backbone for accessing the Exchange message stores by way of wireless networking protocols (see Figure 32.6) from a client PC or the technology to allow standards-based transmission of Exchange messages over X.400 and X.500.

The process follows this scenario: a request is made from the mobile user on its PC with the Exchange inbox. The request is encapsulated in a message and transferred by way of the wireless network to a server-based agent. The agent then de-encapsulates the messages and performs the action dictated in the message. At this point, it communicates with the Exchange Server to send or retrieve mail, change a server-based rule, or perform another Exchange task.

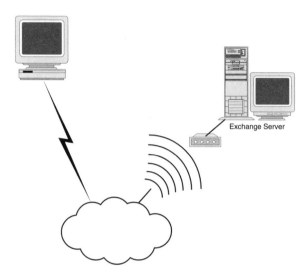

FIG. 32.6

Wireless Networking Services for Exchange Server.

Exchange Server

The key standards for wireless technology are ARDIS, CDPD, GSM, and Inmarsat. The following list breaks down the technologies and service providers for wireless communication.

■ *Inmarsat*—This is a standard satellite network provider with worldwide capability. Inmarsat is perhaps the largest provider worldwide, serving 50,000 users on land, on sea, and in the air. It provides both narrow-band and ISDN connections. It has worked closely with other wireless providers—AT&T, Vodafone, and Ardis—to create a set of standards for wireless networking. The goal was to split client and server functions from the network-layer transports.

Inmarsat (see Figure 32.7) developed a solution to give the user a common interface to messaging—Exchange client viewer. It extends the MAPI interface with a wireless interface to provide ease of future development efforts over wireless networking. The technology is known as Inmarsat Wireless Messaging. The technology is composed of enhancements to the client, a middle-layer agent, and a server component. The technology interpolates with other wireless networking standards—ARDIS, CDPD, and GSM.

The key elements to the user interface are remote copy of message headers, remote copy of messages, remote deletion of messages, remote forwarding of messages, and remote configuration of user rules and filters. The server request manager interfaces with the Exchange Server. The purpose is to process client-side requests from the mobile agent. It performs this process by using standard MAPI transport providers.

The mobile agent interfaces with the client and the server request manager. The mobile agent is responsible for interacting with Exchange on behalf of the mobile user. The agent handles authentication, server-based rules and filters, logging NT server events, and providing NT performance counters.

For more information:

http://www.worldserver.pipex.com

FIG. 32.7
Wireless networking
technology by Inmarsat.

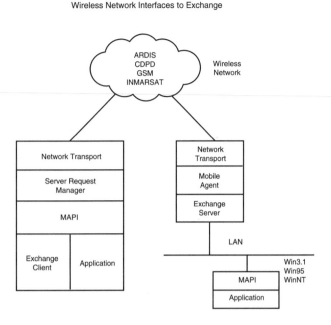

Wireless Network Interfaces to Exchange

- *Vodafone Group*—Vodafone and Paragon Software have an Exchange Middleware messaging solution for wireless networking. Vodafone follows Inmarsat's wireless messaging technology to provide users with wireless access to Exchange around the world. Vodafone has 40 GSM roaming agreements to provide worldwide coverage. GSM is an organization that provides a standard for wireless communication, which is growing at the rate of 10,000 new customers each day. Based on the number of GSM agreements, Vodafone is a leader in wireless communication.

  Paragon provides Precis Link, which is a MAPI-based remote access standard for Exchange. Precis Link provides similar functionality to Inmarsat, with offline message processing, to include rules, filters, forwarding, and deleting.

  Vodafone Networking uses advanced mobile communications of Short Message Server (SMS) and high-speed circuit switched data by way of its digital cellular networks. Precis link leverages these communication methods to allow users to access Exchange servers over satellite, digital cellular, and mobile-radio systems. Precis provides an easy interface for developers to leverage wireless networking, without needing full knowledge of the transport.

  For more information:

  http://www.vodafone.co.uk

- *AT&T*—AT&T wireless services provides wireless access for users into Exchange servers. AT&T relies on the communication standard, CDPD, or Cellular Digital Packet Data. Currently, CDPD is deployed only in the United States. CDPD makes wireless data communication ready for end users. It's based on the TPC/IP protocol. This offers easy

Part
V

Ch
32

integration with existing infrastructures. CDPD offers transfer rates of up to 19.2 KBPS, enhanced security, and the capability to support voice and data. Forty-seven of the top fifty cities in the U.S. already have CDPD service available. AT&T's service hopes to provide a cost-effective solution for the work-group model by allowing filed sales and support personnel to easily connect to resources.

Similar to Inmarsat and Vodafone, AT&T enables users to download headers before retrieving messages, remote administering rules and filters, and configure support for attachments. It provides server-based agents to perform tasks for the client.

The rough cost of the AT&T service depends on data transferred per month. A sample rate is 500K per month for $50. Please contact AT&T for current pricing information.

For more information:

http://www.airdata.com

■ *Eicon*—Eicon provides WAN services for the NT operating system. This is useful for the X.25 transport protocol support necessary for some X.400 and X.500 connections to value-added networking providers.

EiconCard for NT extends the TCP/IP stack included with NT over X.25, frame relay, and PPP and ISDN connections. It offers a high-capacity, robust implementation of X.25 for Exchange servers. As illustrated in Figure 32.8, NT now can be extended as a WAN IP router. EiconCard can take full advantage of the Microsoft back office remote access support.

For more information:

http://www.eicon.com

FIG. 32.8

WAN service for NT by Eicon.

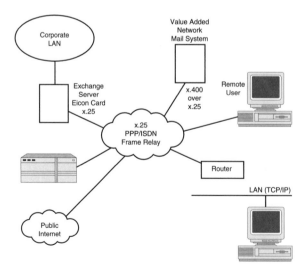

■ *Sprint*—Sprint provides Sprint Message Xchange service for Microsoft Exchange. SMX currently is used to link together various mail systems over Sprint's private network services. SMX now links Exchange LAN sites with other MS Mail, Lotus, and Exchange LAN sites. This method is effective to link LANs by outsourcing some of the messaging backbone to Sprint.

Sprint's network extends to 140 countries, which is a tremendous benefit if a company has both U.S. and European offices and wants to link together its Exchange LANs. Sprint acts as the Middleware network to support the connection, which is a huge cost savings to companies because they can connect to Sprint in native Exchange formats without maintaining extra X.400 gateways. Sprint provides addressing templates for recipients on X.400, the Internet, fax, and telex.

For more information:

http://www.sprint.com

Besides Sprint, several other value-added networking providers are working on supporting Exchange backbones. Services in the works will provide companies with links from Exchange into legacy systems, Profs, All-in-One, and Officevision; into other LAN mail systems such as Lotus and cc:Mail; and into other forms of messaging—EDI, fax, telex, CompuServe, X.400, and the Internet. A good way to think about these public and private networks is as a way to out-source gateways and address/message conversion processes. By supporting native Exchange formats, the providers can allow easy integration from the corporate LANs into trading and business partners.

Part

V

Ch

32

Gateway Support for Exchange

Gateways and connectors (see Figure 32.9) are used to extend Exchange into existing LAN-based mail systems or legacy host systems. They also can provide new types of functionality to enhance messaging within the organization. Besides new Exchange gateways, the existing MS Mail gateway is accessed from Exchange. You can access these through the MS Mail PC connector.

■ *Attachmate*—Attachmate is providing Profs and SNADS gateways for Exchange. These tools are used to extend Exchange into legacy SNA environments to link users with Profs and Officevision mail systems or use the SNA transport to communicate with other servers.

The gateways are known as Zip! Office gateways for Exchange. These gateways allow users on VM/CMS host systems to share messages with Exchange clients (see Figure 32.10). The gateway routes messages and status reports between Exchange and the host systems. Host users can use Profs, CMS Notes, or CMS Reader to read and create messages. This gateway also is used for processing SENDFILE or PUCH requests from VM to the LAN.

Exchange manages the in- and out-bound messages for the Zip gateway. Exchange stores the out-bound messages in its MTS Out folder. The Zip gateway polls this folder and, when it finds a message, processes the message. After the gateway has the message, it translates the message and attachment to be forwarded to the host system.

FIG. 32.9

The MS Mail gateways for Exchange Server.

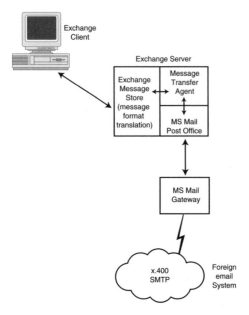

FIG. 32.10

ZIP! Office gateways for Exchange Server.

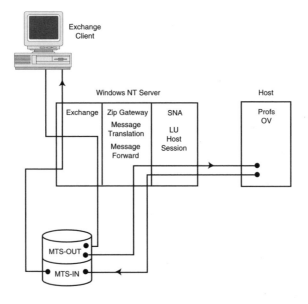

N O T E Due to message formats on the host systems, only one attachment can be sent in the body of a message. If multiple attachments must be sent to a host recipient, multiple messages must be used. ■

The Exchange Server with the Zip gateway running also must be able to connect to the host through an SNA gateway or be channel-attached to the host with SNA Server installed locally.

Besides the messaging gateway, Zip supports scheduling across systems (see Figure 32.11). Schedule Plus and Profs Calendar Users can be part of the same calendar network. The gateway routes calendar requests between the two systems, including scheduling meetings between platforms, viewing free/busy times, and logging appointment data in each system's calendar.

FIG. 32.11

The Zip! Office Calendar for Exchange Server.

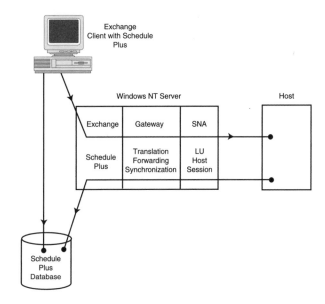

The calendar look-ups happen in real time. A request is made from the Schedule plus client and is communicated to Exchange. After the request is in Exchange, the Zip gateway translates the request into a native host format and forwards the schedule request to the host system.

The Zip gateway is an NT service and is integrated with the Event Log, Performance Counters, and Process Viewer. Multiple gateways can be installed on the same server hardware. This is similar to the MS Mail PC MTAs, which can run multiple instances of the MTA on a single NT server. The gateway also comes with its own configuration utility, to set the configuration information for delivery, message translation, nodes, address space, and queue status.

For more information:

http://www.attachmate.com

Part

V

Ch

32

- *RightFax*—RightFax has a fax gateway solution for Exchange. This gateway runs as an NT service for integration with the NT directory services and Exchange. The fax gateway consists of a client and server set of components.

  From the client, a user can create an e-mail message. When defining the recipients, the user can specify users to receive the same mail message by way of fax. The mail message doesn't need to be configured in any different manner. When the message is received by the Exchange Server and the recipient list is parsed, the server recognizes the fax recipient and routes the message through the fax gateway.

  On incoming faxes, RightFax supports DID lines for individual caller fax identifiers, which requires additional hardware to support phone-line trucks or direct connections to the phone systems coming in via T1 connections. One fax server can service over 700 DID lines. For a large organization, this capability enables every individual to have a direct fax line. When the fax server actually receives the incoming fax, it resolves the destination user recipient on the Exchange mail system by the DID identifier. The user receives faxes just as he or she does an e-mail message or other inbox application.

  The RightFax client becomes integrated with the Exchange inbox on the desktop. This client has numerous advanced features, including support for DTMF, OCR, Imaging letterhead, signatures, voice prompting, group send options, delayed transmissions, and support for complex graphics. Additionally, you can send document attachments by way of fax without doing the conversion on the client PC. The conversion is handled by the server gateway.

  For more information:

  e-mail: **dts@rightfax.xom**

- Icon Technology—Formerly Integra, recently purchased WinBeep Software. WinBeep provides an NT server-based pager gateway for Exchange. Similar to the fax gateway, from the Exchange client a user can send a message with a destination recipient through e-mail, fax, or pager by using the WinBeep Exchange pager gateway.

  The pager gateway is being developed by WinBeep at Integra technologies. The pager gateway will plug into Exchange just like any other gateway or connector. It will be administered from the Exchange administration utility.

  The pager gateway also can be used in conjunction with server-based rules. One example is if you use an alphanumeric pager, you can set up your e-mail to be forwarded to your pager when you are out of the office.

  Because the paging gateway is a rich, tightly integrated NT service, you can configure the SQL server to send reports and alerts by way of MAPI to the pager gateway to notify an administrator or manager of a situation.

  The Integra pager gateway works with several paging service providers: Ameritech, Comtech, MobileComm, PageMart, PageNet, Skytel, Southwestern Bell, Message Center, and USA Mobile. Additionally, it supports wireless communication through several protocols: ARDIS, DTMF, IXO, and TDP.

  For more information, call (800) 905-5062.

■ *Octel*—Octel developed a framework for voice messaging on top of the Exchange platform. The Unified Messaging Strategy consists of using the e-mail backbone for Exchange to connect to PDX phone switches and route voice mail directly to the desktop in the Exchange client inbox (see Figure 32.12).

Octel positions the phone systems as an extension to the messaging architecture of an organization. From within the inbox you may receive e-mail, faxes, documents, and now voice mail. Voice mail also can be accessed 24 hours a day by touch-tone phone. Voice mail has many of the same communication properties that e-mail uses. Voice-mail messages are stored and forwarded between users as needed. The messages also are routed by content or request.

Octel provides a client component to integrate with the inbox so that the voice-mail messages appear as e-mail messages. The users simply open the message to play the voice mail. The user also can reply to the original message or create a new voice message from the same interface. Exchange then handles the routing via mail or via the phone switches. The client also includes telephone dial-in support. The user dials into the Octel system to retrieve message information. The message information includes voice, fax, and e-mail messages. Voice messages can be easily played back over the telephone. Fax messages can be routed to an alternate fax number or forwarded to another user. E-mail messages can be read back to the user over the telephone via the text-to-speech hardware on the system.

FIG. 32.12

Sample office configuration-Octel Voice-Mail gateway for Exchange Server.

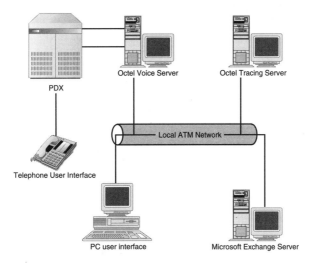

The Octel Server provides in- and out-bound voice functionality. It acts as a voice-mail gateway to external systems. The user can create a voice-mail message from the desktop and have Octel route the message to the destination to be played back for the user. This Octel system can take advantage of multimedia PCs but doesn't require them. If a user has sound capabilities on the PC, the voice-mail message can be played back from the PC. If the user doesn't have sound capabilities, when he or she opens the e-mail note that contains the Octel message, Octel dials the user's phone number from the PBX and plays the message back over the phone.

The key to this strategy is that Exchange and NT will handle all the directory services for the enterprise. The Exchange account that originates from the NT Domain account also will be used for the voice mail system. A component of the user account includes the voice-mail system information. However, all the voice-mail data is stored inside the Exchange message, in a compressed format. Octel also plans to include faxing as a functionality of this Unified Messaging Strategy.

The Octel server supports voice, fax, text-to-speech, and voice recognition. This includes support for DTMF, DID lines, PBX connectivity, and open computer-industry standards for customization. The server is based on Windows NT and takes full advantage of the user accounts, NT registry, Event Log, performance monitor, and all other NT management utilities. Octel provides additional management capabilities for the Octel server by way of Exchange's Administration utility and a separate administration application.

For more information:

http://www.octel.com

This section described many of the gateways, connectors, and communication protocols support by third-parties for the Exchange client and server.

Various ISV Solutions

Several companies have developed third-party enhancements to Exchange. These enhancements include electronic forms, Visual Basic reporting, directory service providers, security, and more. The following products continue to describe additional ways to leverage an investment in Exchange.

■ *Delrina*—Delrina offers its FormFlow electronic forms designer package for use with Exchange. The package offers forms and data routing, using the Exchange topology. This forms package offers database connectivity, multi-platform support, printing, and scalable architecture.

For more information:

http://www.delrina.com

■ *Crystal Reports*—Crystal reports announced a reporting tool for use with Exchange that enables easy integration and access to the Exchange MAPI information store. Crystal Reports provides access to Exchange reporting mechanisms and data exporting from the information store. This added capability enables the user to query, print, and modify data from the desktop. The amount of data within the information store is unlimited; it can be e-mail messages, e-forms data, system information, documents, voice mail, and more. Crystal Reports enables you to build interfaces to this information by using Exchange and Visual Basic. The information will be useful to both end users and system administrators.

For more information, call (800) 663-1244.

■ *Nortel Entrust*—Northern Telecom's Entrust security technology provides the software-based encryption and digital signatures services. Security is important because it provides a wrapper around confidential or sensitive data. The content of the message is guaranteed by a digital signature. The digital signature ensures the identity of the sender.

With Entrust's security in Exchange, Exchange can be used for electronic commerce, electronic transfer of funds, or database transactions. Nortel provides a solution for large-scale management of cryptographic keys. The automated key management is invisible to the end user, yet provides privacy into a distributed computing environment.

Entrust provides support for RSA, DSA, DES, and CAST security algorithms.

For more information:

http://www.entrust.com

■ *Hitachi*—Hitachi has announced a directory synchronization system, Syncware, for Exchange. Syncware synchronizes Exchange with all other e-mail systems in the environment. Syncware is the server component that will provide the directory services function. Additionally, there is **Agent@Exchange**, which is the directory services agent that runs on Exchange to export the directory information to Syncware.

Some features of Syncware include a streamlined user interface, enhanced rule mapping to convert names, and network monitoring and testing tools. A messaging administrator can tell at a glance the status of the synchronization throughout the enterprise. It integrates with cc:Mail, MS Mail, QuickMail, Lotus Notes, Groupwise, Beyond Mail, Davinci, Officevision, and SMTP mail.

The key benefit to this is the complex address translation that Hitachi has simplified for managing several directories. The conversion rules are built into the system, but can be modified for special use. The product consists of a server and agent model that is mail-enabled. Syncware agents are installed on each mail system, and the server is installed on a UNIX workstation. Each agent monitors which addresses get changed on the system. When a change occurs, it is forwarded via e-mail to the server. After the server is done processing the directory updates, it propagates the changes to the other mail systems. With this solution, Exchange can plan an active role in a mixed-mail enterprise environment.

For more information:

http://www.hitachi.com

Part V

Ch 32

N O T E Electronic data interchange is discussed in Chapter 33, "Using Electronic Data Interchange (EDI)." ■

We mentioned several third-party solutions for Exchange. This list is by no means complete. Please contact Microsoft for continued updates to the list of ISV's developing third-party application for Exchange at the following Web page:

http://www.microsoft.com/exchange

Exchange provides a robust messaging and groupware framework. Third-party developers are working to extend the framework with workflow, document imaging, document management, information sharing, information agents, communications connectors, gateways to external systems, and more. Microsoft provides the MAPI 1.0 application programming interface to allow additional developers to leverage the Exchange framework as needed. Beyond MAPI, Exchange SDKs (software development kits) are available for developing custom applications, external gateways, or integrated applications.

Consulting Solutions

Microsoft Consulting Services (MCS)—MCS is committed to assisting large customers to effectively design, deploy, and maintain all types of Exchange organizations. MCS also partners with Software Spectrum to conduct an Exchange Planning Workshop (EPW). More information on the EPW is presented below.

In addition to Exchange consulting, MCS also offers:

- Architecture and Design

  MCS provides solid architecture and design consulting using the Microsoft BackOffice family for your distributed computing environment.

- Line-of-Business Application Design

  Drawing upon its own expertise as the world's leading software developer, MCS has designed as well as managed the development of mission-critical client/server applications for several large companies, Using the Microsoft Solutions Framework (a proven methodology), all knowledge is transferred to fully empower your company.

- Project Management

  MCS can also serve in a project management role. Here, MCS guides your team through the enterprise-wide projects providing quality control, team management, and knowledge transfer to all involved.

- Enterprise Program Manager (EPM)

  The EPM program is designed for organizations who see value in a close, long-term relationship with MCS. A senior level consultant would work on-site for typically a one year commitment. This close relationship allows the consultant to fully understand your business and leverage MCS's expertise and resources to successfully design and deploy Microsoft technologies within your company.

For more information on Microsoft Consulting Services:

Visit **http://www.microsoft.com.**

Software Spectrum—For Exchange consulting solutions, contact Software Spectrum about their Exchange Planning Workshop. This three-day, comprehensive planning workshop on deploying Exchange is conducted by Microsoft Consulting Services and Software Spectrum's Technology Services Group (TSG). The workshops are held in several cities in the U.S. and Canada, and they're in a small, group environment where you work one-on-one with an Exchange expert who leads you through intensive planning exercises. After completing the workshop, you'll receive insight into:

- Physical Microsoft Exchange Site Architecture
- Logical, enterprise-wide Microsoft Exchange Organization Architecture
- Up-to-date inventory of your current mail infrastructure
- Microsoft Exchange Project Plan including the design, deployment, and testing phases of a pilot Exchange implementation
- Microsoft Exchange Total Cost of Ownership Report
- Estimated costs for your environment to migrate to Exchange
- Understanding of your Exchange support needs and estimated costs over three years
- And you'll receive all workshop materials and electronic tools used during the workshop

Software Spectrum also offers consulting world-wide in the following focus technologies: networking, application development, Internet/Intranet Services, Enterprise Management (Microsoft's Systems Management Server), and of course, Enterprise Messaging.

For more information on the Exchange Planning Workshop:

Phone: (800)624-2033 or visit **http://www.swspectrum.com.**

For more information on consulting:

Phone: (800)753-3266 or visit **http://www.swspectrum.com.**

From Here...

This chapter explained how Exchange can be extended by using third-party applications. For more information, see the following chapters:

- Chapter 1, "Overview of Microsoft Exchange," discusses key features of Exchange allowing you to determine where you may need third-party support or services.
- Chapter 33, "Using Electronic Data Interchange (EDI)," explains how to use the Exchange Server for Electronic Data Interchange transactions.

Using Electronic Data Interchange (EDI)

Exchange is a powerful electronic mail messaging platform. A new area where Exchange has been gaining momentum is in Electronic Data Interchange (EDI). Exchange enables Microsoft to enter this high-end commerce transaction system that runs most corporations around the world.

EDI is a strategic direction for Microsoft. EDI over Exchange complements Microsoft's Internet commerce strategy to provide a completely integrated solution. ■

What is EDI?

EDI is the communication standard for two companies to communicate with one another for the purpose of doing business. For example, a retail software outlet can use EDI to automatically order more copies of Exchange from a reseller.

Defining Exchange's Role in EDI

Microsoft sees EDI as a strategic direction for the Exchange product. Exchange was specifically designed with X.400 connectors and X.400 compliant MTAs, which enable Exchange to easily work with other X.400 systems, such as EDI.

Third-Party EDI Development

Exchange provides a flexible architecture for EDI add-ons. With products from independent software vendors (ISV's), Exchange is well positioned to compete in the high-end commerce arena of EDI.

What Is EDI?

EDI is an architecture for providing electronic commerce between trading partners. Trading partners are business organizations that wish to share commerce data via electronic means. One example is that a grocery store chain and a food manufacturer could be trading partners. Using EDI, when the store needs to order more food for the shelves, the products and amounts can be shipped directly to the manufacturer for order processing and shipment. In Figure 33.1, an example of an EDI data flow is displayed.

FIG. 33.1

This figure shows an EDI dataflow diagram.

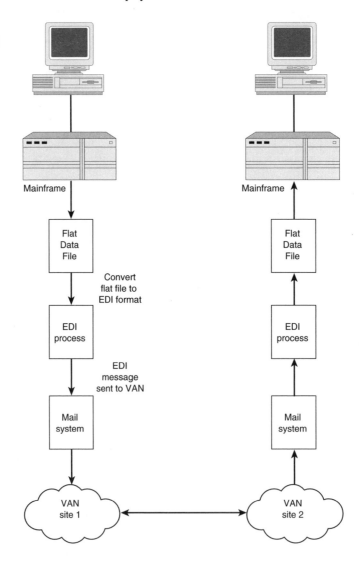

EDI is a complement to electronic mail as it promotes a paperless system. EDI applications today are complex, proprietary, archaic, and customized for specific systems and industries. Several standards have been drafted to define EDI in the marketplace. X.435 was specified in 1990. The X.435 standard is an extension to X.400, incorporating electronic commerce requirements. The original specification was to be used with X.400 P2 protocols which were standardized in 1984. X.435 today supports X.400 P22 protocols dated 1988.

N O T E Microsoft Exchange Server Message Transfer Agents (MTAs) are certified to this X.400 P22 protocol standard. This will ensure interoperability for customers. Only digital messaging MTAs have received this certification. ▓

Using EDI requires an application environment. A typical EDI architecture will have an e-mail client communicating with the mail server (see Figure 33.2)—in this case, an Exchange server. The mail server must support X.400 or SMTP addressing and connections. This is handled through the use of a gateway product running on the mail system. Exchange offers X.400 and SMTP connectors built into the server software package.

FIG. 33.2

This is an example of an EDI architecture.

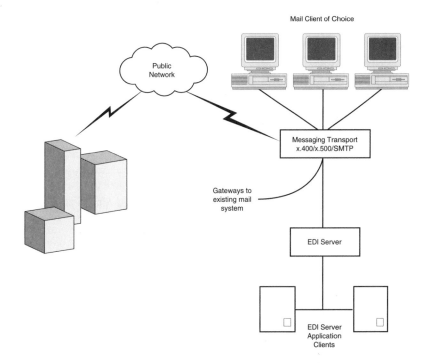

Mail Client of Choice

Public Network

Messaging Transport x.400/x.500/SMTP

Gateways to existing mail system

EDI Server

EDI Server Application Clients

Part **V**

Ch **33**

At the same time that mail is able to travel over X.400, EDI-enabled applications must generate EDI data files or preformatted EDI data packages. These packages are then sent over the same exact X.400 or SMTP connections. Depending on the final destination of the message, it may pass through an additional gateway to reach an existing mail system or traverse a Value Added

Network (VAN) to reach a trading partner. Between the EDI application and the X.400 connector is an EDI server. Third-party solutions are available to leverage Windows NT and Exchange to perform the function of EDI server. This EDI server is used to translate flat data files into EDI packages to be forwarded to the mail connectors. These products will be discussed later in this chapter.

The EDI Process

EDI starts with a trading partner agreement between you and your trading partner. This is an agreement between companies about the computer systems and technology to be used for the EDI dataflow. They must make a combined decision about the EDI standard to be used for the transactions, the information to be exchanged, the VAN, and scheduling of the information exchange.

The companies are ready to then create a document of an invoice in the business application and save the document in the system. The EDI translator automatically reformats the invoice into the agreed-upon EDI standard. The translator creates and wraps the document in an electronic envelope that has an ID for the target trading partner.

The communications portion can be part of the translation software or a separate gateway connector. In the case of Exchange, the EDI communication gateway begins to communicate on the network or over a dial-up line.

Once connected with the VAN, the envelope containing the document is then transmitted to the VAN messaging service. Several VANs today are beginning to support native Exchange formats to reduce the need for data format conversion. The VAN reads the ID on the envelope and distributes it to the correct mailbox.

The trading partner similarly communicates over its network or over a dial-up line and downloads all of the contents of the mailbox. The EDI translator opens the envelope and translates the data from the agreed upon EDI standard format to the format to be read by its application. The process is complete when the company's accounting department creates a check from the electronic invoice.

The key to EDI is to reuse the data by inputting the data only one time. The EDI and messaging systems handle the rest of the work. Data moves without intervention from the business application to the trading partner's application.

EDI Application and Translation

As you can see, EDI is a simple, yet extremely complex system. EDI translation software must integrate with EDI application software. It is important to rely upon industry standards to maintain this type of EDI relationship.

After defining the document in the business application, use an EDI mapper to create a map or relationship of the business document. With the mapper, you describe or associate the relationship between the datafields in your business application and the selected EDI standards. The mapper or association manager is an integral part of the complete EDI solution.

If both the EDI translator and business application are on the same type of computer, the data will move faster and more easily from one process to another.

EDI General Components

In an EDI deployment, several key elements are needed. The following list is an introduction into the key technology used in EDI:

- EDI translation management software manages the method in which data is communicated throughout the EDI dataflow.
- Mappers, association management implementations, and integration vary significantly from one translator to another. These mappers handle data mapping between fields in an EDI dataflow.
- Communications software is modular to the translator. Exchange and MAPI provide a programming tool that enables you to develop custom applications and make system calls to the communication protocols.
- Modem connectivity with a high baud rate provides more data throughput.
- VAN networking with Exchange partners provides the easy integration for EDI with a variety of worldwide trading partners.
- WAN networking is the notion of extending an existing WAN to link into trading partners' LANs.

EDI Glossary

The following is a list of the various terms used in the world of EDI. This list is an introduction to the basics of EDI. If you are considering using EDI to resolve business data management between you and a trading partner, please see **http://www.microsoft.com/exchange** for more information or contact your local Microsoft Solution Provider, Microsoft Consulting Services office, or Software Spectrum consulting office (see **http://www.swspectrum.com** for contact information) to discuss your implementation in detail.

Part
V

Ch
33

Common EDI terms:

ANSI. American National Standards Institute. A private, nonprofit membership organization that coordinates the development and approval of voluntary consensus standards in the United States.

ANSI ASC X.12. ANSI Accredited Standards Committee X.12. The committee was chartered by ANSI in 1979 to develop uniform standards for the electronic interchange of business documents.

DEX/UCS. Direct Exchange UCS.

DISA. Data Interchange Standards Association Secretariat for ANSI ASC X12.

DSD. Direct Store Delivery.

ECR. Efficient Consumer Response. Utilized in the grocery industry to determine consumer response to products, marketing, and promotions.

EDI. Electronic Data Interchange. A generic term for computer-to-computer transmission.

EDIA. Electronic Data Interchange Association. This group wrote the original UCS and WINS standards; they currently act as Secretariat for the Ocean, Rail, Motor, and Air EDI standards. They also host the annual Pan American EDI conference—one of the world's largest.

EDICA. Electronic Data Interchange Council of Australia. The Australian EDI administrative organization.

EDICC. Electronic Data Interchange Council of Canada. The Canadian EDI administrative organization.

EDIFACT. EDI for Administration, Commerce, and Trade. This is the International EDI Standard set by the U.N. and administered in the U.S. by DISA.

EFT. Electronic Funds Transfer. The electronic transfer of funds from payer to payee through the banking system.

Hub. Also known as sponsors, hubs are large companies active in EDI that strongly encourage their paper-based business partners to begin using EDI.

ISO. International Standards Organization.

JIT. Just-In-Time Manufacturing.

NEX/UCS. Network Exchange UCS.

NRF. National Retail Federation.

POS. Point-of-Sale.

Proprietary Standards. Industry-specific or company-specific data formats that do not comply with ASC X.12 standards.

Trading Partner. Vendor or other party with whom business is conducted.

Transaction Set. A complete business document—for example, an invoice, a purchase order, or a remittance advice.

VAN. Value Added Network.

The EDI Process

The EDI process is a very complex and integrated system to design, configure, deploy, and coordinate. Because of the proprietary computer systems, the integration with a value added network provider (VAN), and the coordination of standards with the trading partners, the process can be detailed.

The process can be broken down into two components: the sending system and the receiving system. The Sending system follows the data flow shown in Figure 33.3.

The following is a step-by-step breakdown of an EDI dataflow. You will see the main steps in an actual dataflow. This is a technical overview of these steps. These steps can be applied to any set of EDI trading partners.

1. Data is extracted from the corporate application in its native format. As the data is extracted, it is ordered into the message format. This file is saved on a record-based, user-constructed file. This file is called an Interface file.

2. The translation software processes parse through a table based on the message structure and Interface files specific for the EDI engagement. Translation software is the software that formats data into the specified EDI format. It is also used to extract data out of an EDI format. During the parsing process, data validation checks are made, codes are converted, partner profiles determined, and then the data is formatted based on the EDIFACT syntax specification.

3. This file, the Interchange file, containing the formatted data is ready to be transmitted via the messaging transport by X.400 into the VAN.

4. Before sending the Interchange file, the data file is encapsulated with an envelope defining the communication protocol and destination. The file is then transmitted. This process is called the Communications interface.

FIG. 33.3
This is a complete EDI data flow diagram.

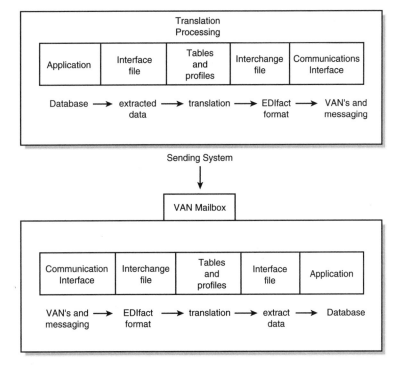

The Sending system adheres to the following dataflow:

1. The Interchange file can be received directly or via the VAN. From the VAN, the trading partner will connect to the VAN and retrieve the data from a predefined mailbox. This requires special software to enable the trading partner to access a VAN mailbox. This is also handled in the communication interface.

2. The Interchange file is downloaded and the data is extracted according to the message specification. Data validation is managed according to the known properties of the message. These are *mandatory, conditional, range*, and *radix*. The codes are then translated into a format used by the trading partner in-house.

3. The data sets are placed in an interface file for use in the in-house system. Additional data validation may be required in order to ensure data integrity.

4. The final step is to upload the data into the in-house system.

Exchange Integration with EDI

EDI typically relies on X.400 as the network transport and addressing scheme for conducting transactions. As discussed in earlier chapters, Exchange is based on X.400 standards and has the capability to communicate with other X.400 systems built right in. For X.400 support, Exchange can use X.25 protocols, run over TCP/IP, or connect with TP0 or TP4. One example would be to use X.400 addressing and connectivity over an IP-based network. In this case, Exchange server could communicate via X.400 over the public Internet. The X.400 support is bundled into Exchange server (see Figure 33.4). This does not require a third-party gateway.

Microsoft Exchange's role is to provide a secure messaging transport over X.400 for delivering EDI documents. On the client side, several third-party developers have EDI-enabled applications to work with MAPI and the Exchange client.

N O T E   Currently, X.500 directory standards exist; however, most organizations have not deployed X.500-based global directory services. X.500 is an elaborate directory standard. Most vendors have their own X.500 interpretation; this includes Exchange, Digital's Mail Bus, Novell's NDS, and more. The interface that these X.500 vendors provide is via X.400. To clarify, you would use X.400 to communicate with a proprietary X.500 directory. X.500 standards are the core logic for today's business enterprise messaging systems. ▒

The Exchange Message Transfer Agent is completely standards-based. It is certified for 1984 and 1988 X.400 standards. This will maintain interoperability for customers, VANs, and trading partners. With this level of certification, Microsoft was the first vendor to certify a product for both 1984 and 1988 standards. Future support for the proposed 1992 standard is planned.

FIG. 33.4
X.400 support in
Exchange is built into
the core product.

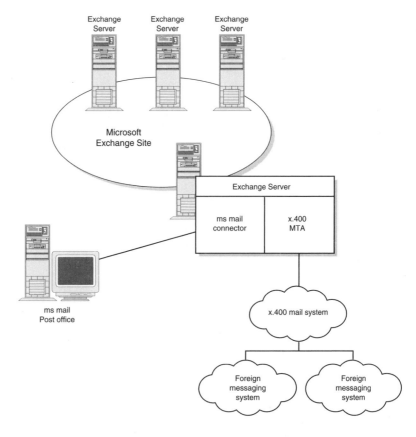

Exchange is a powerful EDI platform for several reasons:

- The public key encryption to validate data and sender information. Exchange provides several options for North American encryption of 56-bit and beyond and 40-bit export security algorithms to provide data encryption internationally. The key management is described in Chapter 26, "Monitoring Your Organization."
- Multiple protocol support
- Integration with the legacy application using MAPI 1.0
- Incorporation with NT operating system for c2 level security
- Integration with back office applications for SNA connectivity and for SQL data retrieval
- Supports a variety of messaging protocols and addressing formats

Third-Party EDI Application Support for Exchange

Several EDI software and service companies have developed Exchange EDI software tools to address data format translation from interface files to Interchange files. As well, there are EDI development toolkits available to build interfaces from legacy systems into Exchange.

Part
V

Ch
33

The following is a partial list of independent software vendors (ISV) with EDI solutions for Exchange. The companies provide X.400 messaging services, as well as EDI application development tools.

■ Mpact Immedia

Mpact has been a leader in electronic commerce software. It will offer transaction-based network services based on the Exchange server product. Mpact leverages the power of Exchange in addition to the native X.400 communication support. The product is called Interconnexions. This integrates Mpact's EDI system software with its VAN service to the Exchange messaging backbone.

Mpact also provides EDIkit. EDIkit enables developers to integrate EDI into a business application. EDIkit provides interface support for MAPI, which can be linked to any application using the "C" runtime environment to make EDI CMC calls in the application. The ease-of-use once integrated for the end-user is to have a print option. When the print option is selected, the data is extracted and translated into EDI and passed on to the messaging system.

JetForm Corporation, another company developing an electronic forms solution for Exchange, will integrate with EDIkit as well. The JetForm user interface will feed data into the business application. From there, the data is EDI accessible. Mpact provides an appellation development workbench with a set of APIs to use in application development.

For more information about any of these technologies, you can contact Mpact Immedia at **http://www.mpact.ca**.

■ EDISYS

EDISYS is the creator of VediX, Visual EDI for Microsoft Exchange Server. VediX allows for flexibility in application development to be able to EDI-enable a business application. This product uses Exchange to provide a robust and easy interface, multi-platform support, and multi-application integration. It is a state-of-the-art EDI translator that reads the interface file and performs the table and profile look-up to translate the file for a native data format into the EDIFACT standard data format. In addition, it provides easy setup and maintenance of trading partner profiles and translation maps for use in data mapping.

For more information, you can contact EDISYS at +44-0-1296-330011.

■ ISOCOR

Isocor provides the Isocor Messaging for NT Product line. The suite of applications is used for developing messaging servers, client tools for Microsoft MAPI on Windows 95, directory synchronization with Lotus and cc:Mail, and directory administration tools for X.500-based directories. It serves as a high-speed backbone for EDI on top of Exchange.

■ ISOTRADE is the product specifically for EDI-based applications including TSI and Sterling. MAPIWARE service modules for MAPI on Windows 95 are used to extend MAPI for use with X.400, X.500, EDI, and several security modules used with ISOTRADE.

ISOTRADE supports the global EDI standard X.435 messaging RFC. It installs directly onto the Exchange server running Windows NT. It will convert EDI transactions from X.12 and EDIFACT data formats to X.435 for electronic mail distribution using Exchange. The X.435 standard is encapsulated into the X.400 standard messages. Several VANs have already committed to supporting Exchange and EDI solutions. These are AT&T, GE, and SITA. This system can also route the EDI messaging over an X.400 connecting with TCP/IP. Many translation and business application developers support ISOCOR. These include American Business Computer, EDI/Able, EDS, Sterling, TSI, and others. From within one of these EDI applications, it can communicate with the ISOTRADE module running on the server.

ISOTRADE is a good model to illustrate how Microsoft Exchange is non-proprietary. It supports all of the EDI applications just listed. The leverage that it has is that relying on Exchange, it can pass EDI messages over X.25, TP4, or TCP/IP using X.435.

For more information, you can contact Isocor at **http://www.isocor.com**.

Exchange provides a robust messaging framework to build interfaces for EDI applications. As you have seen, several companies are providing EDI application software as well. VANs will provide native Exchange connectivity. EDI is a powerful way to extend and leverage the role of Exchange in the enterprise.

> **N O T E** EDI is a very difficult subject to cover in just one chapter. If you are interested in learning more about EDI, you might like to read some EDI text books, as well as research how EDI can be interfaced with your legacy business application. EDI solutions are generally very expensive and require special attention from application development through implementation. Make sure you discuss any EDI solution with the application development specialists from your department or a consulting service. ▦

Part
V

Ch
33

From Here...

This chapter has explained how Exchange can be used for EDI applications. For more information on extending Exchange services, see the following chapters:

- Chapter 5, "Designing Exchange Topology," discusses how to plan effectively for an Exchange deployment in your environment. After understanding EDI's role, you can tie key elements of it into an overall plan.

- Chapter 32, "Implementing Third-Party Integration Tools," presents several third-party products to provide additional leverage for Exchange in your business enterprise.

CHAPTER 34

Developing Exchange Forms

This chapter introduces you to the world of making custom Exchange applications without prior programming experience. However, if you're already familiar with Windows and Visual Basic, you'll have a very easy time using the Forms Designer interface.

The Exchange Forms Designer lets you lay out all the different fields on your form, link them to Exchange objects, and designate actions on events. Without any previous programming experience, you can create applications that will make your organization more productive. Many example applications are provided on the Exchange CD-ROM. You can use these predesigned forms, and modify them for your use. They are located in the \EXCHANGE\EFDFORMS directory of whatever drive you have installed the client applications. See the section "Installing the Forms Designer" for more information on installation.

Installing the Forms Designer Software

There are many factors to consider when installing the Forms Designer software. Remember where the Setup program for forms is located and the amount of hardware resources you need.

Explaining the Forms Environment

Before you dive into designing forms, understand how the pieces fit together. Learn about components such as forms libraries, views, and permissions.

Plan and Design Forms for your Organization

Exchange's structure provides for many different uses of the containers in the hierarchy. Design applications that leverage this flexibility. Two possible ways of using the Exchange framework are for discussion and reference purposes.

Use the Forms Designer to Build and Customize Forms

This section is a step-by-step tutorial on how to build and customize forms using the Forms Designer.

Extending Your forms with Visual Basic

Most of the shortcomings of the Forms Designer can be easily overcome with Visual Basic's 16-bit version or Visual C++.

The Forms Designer enables the creation of two types of forms:

■ Stand-alone forms

These forms are not associated with any particular folder. They facilitate the input of data with the intent to send it to an individual or group of users. These applications include message-taking, office supply requisitions, and vacation requests.

■ Folder forms

These forms facilitate the input of information into a public folder where permitted users can view it in an organized way. These applications include group discussions, bulletin boards, and enterprise-wide groupware databases. Filters can be applied to move data into sub-folders, and views can be applied to group or soft information.

Among the potential custom applications you can create are *electronic forms*. For example, in many organizations there are standard forms that are routed to specific individuals. Using the Forms Designer, you can create a travel-request form, time-off request form, or office-supply requisition. These applications take the work out of making simple requests. In addition, with the integration of *public folders*, the forms are easy to distribute throughout the organization. You no longer have to make sure that everyone has the most up-to-date form, and that they have enough copies. Distributing the forms electronically makes it easier for the user, and easier for the recipient who receives all the forms. He or she can easily organize and process all the requests in the universal inbox.

Another strong suit of the Forms Designer is to maximize the effectiveness of public folders. By designing an application, you can make it really easy to enter data into a public area. A great example of this use is for those organizations that post a lot of memos. Instead of printing out the memos and distributing them through the mailroom or by e-mail into everyone's inbox, you can just create a public folder called "Company Memos," and then write an application that lets the user enter the memo into some structured fields. Once the user executes the form, the memo is posted to an appropriate sub-folder under the main "Company Memos" folder. The sub-folder could be based on a field on your form that had a drop-down list of company departments. Using this system, everybody wins. The mailroom folks have less junk mail to route, the people in the copy room have less to copy (which saves toner), and most importantly, paper is saved, which is good for the environment as well as the bottom line. ■

Installation of the Forms Designer

As mentioned throughout this book, the Forms Designer is a *client application*. It is installed with Schedule+/ and the Exchange Client, as well as Outlook. However, you may not have installed it when you installed the other components. What follows is an installation procedure:

N O T E   Before you install the Exchange Forms Designer on your workstation, please consider using 48MB - 64MB of memory. This is espcially needed for application development that uses Visual Basic's 16-bit program to extend your applications.

These recommendations directly affect the capability of your development environment. ■

1. From the Client CD-ROM under either the Eng directory or the Frn directory, double click the EfdSetup directory and choose Setup.

2. Choosing the Complete/Custom from the menu, you see two options—Exchange Forms designer and Sample Applications. This option gives you a choice to install the Sample Applications or not. You may also choose Typical setup, which automatically installs the Forms Designer and the Sample Applications.

3. From the Complete/Custom window, choose Change Options.

4. In the Options box, select Forms Designer and Sample Applications, and choose OK.

5. Choose Continue.

6. Choose Continue.

If you had any previous version of the Forms Designer on your drive, Setup will detect it and display a screen asking you to reinstall, add/remove programs, or remove all. Any forms you create will not be overwritten by any new versions you may install.

Along with the application, all the different sources of help are installed. There are three different sources of help when you are designing applications: Cue Cards, On-line Help, and On-line Documentation.

These various sources of online help are a great supplement to this chapter. You will get the context-sensitive help you need, and at the same time you'll get more step-by-step tutorials to walk you through all the functions. The online manuals give you access at your fingertips. Most of the time, someone else has the manual when you need it.

Using Forms in Your Organization

Exchange's structure provides for many different uses of the containers in the hierarchy. You can design applications that leverage this flexibility. Two possible ways of using the Exchange framework are for discussion and reference purposes.

Discussion Applications

In many organizations, several different teams are working on different projects. As they get ideas, they usually send out an e-mail to all the people involved. As the weeks go by, everyone winds up with many e-mail and voice-mail messages that have no structure. Many are simply carbon copies, forwarded messages, or replies. It usually means going back and sifting through all the messages looking for information.

Some groups use a *bulletin board* or *internal newsgroup* to help centralize all the data. The only problem with this solution is that most e-mail packages that provide bulletin board capability have poor security. You can't control who can post, read, or modify. When using Usenet-style newsgroups, you can't control who can read and post very easily. You would either have to set up passwords, or host entries for each machine to read or post. It isn't very easy or robust.

Part
V

Ch
34

Using a custom Exchange application for discussion, you gain all the access control that is inherent in Exchange and NT Server. You can allow only members of the proper teams to access their information. In some cases, you would want to allow read-only access to people in other groups to promote team cooperation. Exchange's public folder structure is flexible enough to allow this.

Using a custom application can structure the data. The forms you create can contain certain fields, and also contain information about threads. The capability to structure information in different views gives the user the ability to choose a report sorted by date, author, or subject. You can also use structure subjects if you want to keep discussions along a certain topic.

Some of the most common uses of discussion applications are customer-support databases, brainstorming applications where team members can input ideas as they come to them, frequently asked questions lists, and meeting-summarization applications.

Reference Repositories

Exchange serves as a great repository of documents and objects as well as e-mail. You can easily write applications that provide easy access to all your standard documents throughout the enterprise. Many organizations have several standard documents such as policies and procedures manuals, style guides, and computer-usage guidelines. In addition, many organizations have standard Word document templates that they use. These objects can be placed in an Exchange public folder and made available right on the user's desktop.

Explaining the Form's Environment

A few pieces of the Forms environment need to be explained in the scope of the large Exchange picture. These components consist of

- Forms Libraries
- Views
- Rules
- Permissions
- Items

Forms Libraries

When you create a form, you save and install it into a folder forms Library. The properties of the forms saved into a particular folder are dependent on the properties of the folder. This includes access permissions. When the user chooses New Form on the Tools menu in the Exchange Client, he or she is presented with a list of forms available in the folder.

The Global Forms Library   The Global Forms Library houses all the forms that you want to make available to everyone in the enterprise. These forms could include vacation-request forms, corporate memos, or telephone message forms.

The Folder Library   Every folder, either public or private, has a forms library associated with it. You can save forms into one of your private folders, but they will only be shared with anyone to whom you have given access to your folders.

By putting forms into a public folder, you allow robust sharing based on the permissions of the folder, which are generally easy to change if the need arises. When new users are added to the Exchange system, their group memberships can determine which public folders they have access to.

For example, say you had a group called Directors that contained people at or above the level of director in your organization. You could create a folder that contained a form they could fill out that would make it easy to enter product data sheets, and store them in a public folder so that all people at that level or above could view and modify them. The folder you set up has the permission properties set to only enable members of the NT group Directors to view and modify.

The Personal Forms Library   This library is not shared with any other user. It contains the forms the person uses most often. If you have functions that you perform every day, and create a form to automate those tasks, you would place the form in your personal library. In addition, you can use these forms when working offline as long as your default information store resides on your local disk.

Views

Because forms reside in folders, it is pertinent to discuss folder views. Global views apply across all forms and folders, and folder views apply only to the selected form containing the view.

Think of views as the different reports generated off of a database. In the old days, you had to write different report specifications to get the data you wanted presented in the order you wanted.

Views allow you to order information and present it to the user the way he or she would like to see it. When you establish a form, you create structured fields within it that lend themselves very nicely to the four kinds of views:

- Filtering

  Using filtering gives you the ability to only view information that meets certain criteria. Let's go back to our Directors example. If you want, you can set a filter to only display product descriptions of a certain product line, rather than the whole line.

- Sorting

  This view enables you to sort on any field. In our example, you can easily sort by part number or department number if you like. Even better, you can sort by director name, which lets you easily see which director was responsible for which products.

- Grouping

  Grouping lets you use a hierarchical model like the Windows Explorer in Windows 95, or the File Manager in Windows NT. You can click a certain title or expand or collapse the information. You can group the items by product line, and then filter down to more specific product information for each product in that particular line.

■ Columns

You can format the data in your folder like a spreadsheet. This makes it very easy to read, and very familiar to a majority of users. You can place all your fields in any order you wish across the screen.

Views are created outside the form, in the Exchange Client. Once you install a form into a folder form library, all its fields are published to the library, allowing you to easily set up views later on in the Client.

Rules

Just as views are folder properties that apply to form, so too are rules. Rules are a powerful feature in Exchange that allow you to control what happens to an item once it is submitted to a folder.

Many e-mail packages have this functionality in some form. However, in most cases, you must be logged into your mail application for the rules to take effect. Also, most e-mail packages lack the ability to do this with bulletin board-type functionality.

With Exchange, an example of applying rules to a form entry would be that any item meeting certain criteria can be moved to a sub-folder, or e-mailed to someone else as a carbon copy, or even deleted if you so wish.

This functionality gives you much more control over the organization of your data, and even helps reduce redundant entries. It cuts down on administration because everything is automatic once the rules are established. For more information on rules see the section entitled, "Setting Folder Rules," later in this chapter.

Permissions

By establishing folder permissions, you control who has access to any of the forms contained in that folder's Library. You also control what the user can do in the folder. You can set options to allow read, write, and edit access. In addition, you can select pre-defined roles that allow the administrator to quickly establish a set of permissions for the user.

You can also delegate any user as an owner of a certain folder. This enables that user to give other users access permissions. This is analogous to Windows NT Server permissions that allow multiple users to be administrators for a certain domain. Giving someone else ownership permissions allows for multiple administrators and the delegation of responsibilities.

Items

An easy way to think of items is to think of database tables. In a database, tables consist of records, which consist of fields, which have values. Exchange forms work the same way. Folders contain items that contain fields that have values. It's very straightforward. An item is like a record in a database.

Explaining the Form's Components

If you are familiar with Visual Basic at all, this section will make a lot of sense and be refresher material. If you've never used Visual Basic, this section will provide very important information that will aid you in understanding the form design process.

The reason we mentioned Visual Basic is that Exchange forms are Visual Basic version 4 executable programs. They do not need to be run independently of Exchange, as the Exchange Client takes care of this process. Using forms is completely transparent to the user.

The Forms Designer serves as a front end to Visual Basic, so non-programmers can create robust applications using a simple tool without the advanced knowledge needed to use Visual Basic.

Using Visual Basic comes with some consequences. One thing is that non-Windows clients will not be able to use Exchange forms because there is machine-executed code involved, and non-Windows platforms cannot run this code.

On the flip side, however, companies that have in-house Visual Basic expertise can build robust, enterprise-caliber applications that take full advantage of object linking and embedding, as well as SQL Server access. For example, you could have an Exchange application that relies on the Global Address Book for addressing information, but at the same time writes fields to a SQL Server database somewhere on the network.

An Exchange form is made up of the following components:

- The Form Itself

  The form's appearance and behavior are set through its properties that will be discussed in the next section. You can use a form within a folder, as a part of another application, or as a stand-alone application.

  The form itself acts as a shell that encases its components. It is at the top level of the hierarchical structure of the form. Forms contain windows that contain fields.

- The Form Windows

  Forms can contain multiple windows that are used for different functions. One window might contain addressing information, while another might be an output window. Windows allow you to keep the screen neat and logically organized by function. Keep this in mind as you design your forms.

Part
V

Ch

34

By using multiple windows in the same form, as opposed to multiple forms, you keep greater control. It is easier to pass information between windows than between forms.

■ The Window Fields

Each window presents information as fields. You determine which fields will appear in which windows. You can either create new fields in each window, or carry over field values from other windows in the same form.

Fields are not limited to input and output. They can be menus and toolbars. They can initiate actions by having events assigned to them. The field's actions are governed by its properties.

Setting Properties of Form Components

Setting a form's properties is the most daunting task facing the form designer. It is through these properties that the application takes the desired effect. Properties sheets are the means by which the Forms Designer accomplishes its magic, without the need for writing code. Depending on the properties of each object, certain actions will bring about certain results.

As indicated by the title of the section, setting up the properties of each component is made easier because the properties are organized by Form, Window, and Field. The properties you can set for an item will vary with the item.

Form Properties

The general properties of forms consist of the display name, the icon the user will see, the version of the form, the item type associated with the form, and a brief description.

In addition to the general properties, the event properties control what happens when a user takes a certain action on the form. For example, if the user clicks a "Submit" button, you could have the form display a configuration window showing the value of all the current fields.

Window Properties

The general properties of a window are the name, tab order of the fields in the window, caption, and the WinHelp file name.

You can also control resizing options, borders, and colors of the window with the format properties.

Field Properties

In addition to the standard general properties like field name, caption, and location, fields allow you to set initialization values. This allows you to set default values to all the fields in your window. If you have a radio button in your window, for example, you can set whether it is selected by default or not.

All of these properties will be discussed in greater detail when we actually go through the design of a real form. Each property will be explained in detail. What is important at this stage is that you get the feel for what needs to be done when designing a form.

Installing Forms

Upon the creation of a form, a form project file with an .EFP extension is created. It is very similar to a Visual Basic project file.

When you choose the Install command from the Forms Designer, several things happen that are transparent to you. The form files are taken by the installation routine and Visual Basic project files are created. This enables you to use these .MAK files and use them within Visual Basic 4 to extend your applications at a later time.

Once that happens, the form is compiled into a .EXE file, just like when you use the "Make .EXE" command from the File menu in Visual Basic. In addition, a configuration file with a .CFG extension is created. This is used by the forms library for installation.

After that step is completed, the form gets installed into the forms library of your choice. You will now be able to access your form from the folder you chose.

Planning Your Exchange Form

You now have all the information you'll need to create an application. The information in this section will give you a general overview of the steps you will follow to create an application from beginning to end.

When designing a form, you should follow these simple steps:

■ Define the purpose of the application

This sounds very obvious, but this simple step will help you stay focused. By determining what the form will do, you'll give yourself information that will aid in the design. For example, if the application is a simple message-taking application that will be available to everyone in the organization, you may want to keep the design very simple, and you will know that the form will most likely wind up in the global forms library, so you might want to contact the administrator of the system to get permission to post it there.

■ Define the fields

Defining the purpose of your form will give you a good basis for what fields you should include on the form. To continue the example from above, you might want to include the time the person called, their name, company, the message, and whether to call them back or not.

Part
V

Ch
34

It is a good idea to come up with a logical structure of the field, which will help you lay them out on the screen and decide whether you need more than one window.

- Creating a folder for your application

- Create the form

   Using the Forms Designer, create the actual screen that will contain the fields. Drag and drop the objects onto the window on the form. This part of the Forms Designer feels very much like a drawing program. Make sure the form has a logical flow to it, and that all fields are appropriately marked.

- Set the properties of all objects

   Once you create the form, you need to go back and set the properties of all the objects on your form, including the form itself. Although some people like to set the properties of each object when it is created, doing it in two steps allows people to collaborate on the layout and confirm all the field choices and names before moving forward.

- Install the form

   Once you set properties on the objects on your form, you need to install it in order to test functionality of the application. If the application spans multiple forms, be sure that all the forms are installed in the folder. It's a good idea to keep the application in a personal folder so no one else can access it while it is being debugged and tested.

- Test the form

   In order to make sure your form performs all the functions you intended, in the way you intended, you need to test the form extensively. Things to look for are whether the screen layout is correct, required fields are in fact required, and that button groups work properly.

- Design the views

   As explained before, views let you order the data for your users. Once the form is installed, you need to establish the views that will better facilitate the purpose of the form. You can sort, group, filter, and make columns. Once you register your forms with the folder, users can access the views from the Exchange Client.

- Move or copy the form

   Once the views are designed, and further testing is performed, you can move or copy the form into its final destination folder. In your first step, if you remember, you knew who would be using the form, so you contacted the administrator to get permission to post the form into the proper public folder. You will now use that permission, and post the form. Planning ahead will save you a lot of time.

■ Set folder properties

Now that the form is in a public place, you can set the properties that will do such things as define a default view and whether or not the form is accessible. This is a good feature if you have not completely finished the testing process.

■ Set permissions

As stated throughout this chapter, you can set the permissions of the public folder that houses your forms. If you only want certain users to access your applications, or want the form to be read-only for certain people, you can set the permissions to reflect your wishes.

■ Set folder rules

You can set rules to specify actions for incoming data based on conditions. You could use this feature to eliminate duplicate data, generate carbon copies to certain recipients automatically, or move data to sub-folders.

You are now ready to create applications using the Microsoft Exchange Forms Designer. The next section will go into detail with a step-by-step tutorial. A sample form will be created from scratch, showing you how the outline above will help you design custom applications.

Creating the Web Site Button Form

You are now ready to design a form from scratch. We're going to try to follow the outline for designing forms described above as closely as possible.

■ Defining the purpose

Many organizations that have World Wide Web sites on the Internet choose to advertise their sites on other servers. These companies must come up with forms that enable the technical staff to communicate effectively and quickly with the media department that purchases the space on others' Web sites.

The form we're going to design facilitates that need. It makes it very easy to let the technical staff know exactly what's needed by the company housing the hypertext links.

■ Defining fields

You've already stated the purpose of the form rather clearly, so move on to defining the fields we'll use on the form.

Part
V

Ch
34

It is a good idea to collaborate with all the departments involved with the fields on the form at design time. They can provide a lot of key insights that will make the form much more useful to all the parties involved. For this form, the media, creative, and account departments need to be involved in the form-layout process.

The fields are shown in the following table:

Table 34.1 Web Site Button Form Field Names and Descriptions

Name of Field	Purpose
To	Addressee on the technical staff
Date	Date the note was sent
Subject	User definable subject field
Company	Company from whom you leased space
URL	Web site URL the button will reside on
OurURL	URL the button will point to
Size	Pixel size required by the company
StartDateEffective	Button start date
EndDateEffective	Button end date
Transport	Type of media required, if any
Address	E-mail address of company
Contact	Name of contact person
ContactPhone	Phone number of contact

This table is exactly what you should draw out before ever loading the Forms Designer. The field names will be used later in the field properties definitions. The purposes of each field will also help you and your colleagues better design the form and add fields later.

■ Deciding where the form will reside

You now have to determine where your form will reside. For this application, you will just store the form in a folder forms library. This is because there's a person in the media department who coordinates all the Web site space lease agreements and starts the routing of the form. He or she will use this form from a private folder. When trouble-shooting the form, it is much safer to keep the form in a private folder until it is ready.

You don't need to do anything special to use your Folder Forms Library. The form-installation procedure will do this for you. If you were using a public folder, you would have to obtain permission from the Exchange administrator to create the public folder and write items into it.

■ Creating the form

You are now ready to launch the Forms Designer and start drawing out your form. We will go through step-by-step. Figures will be used to walk you through each step. Each figure will be the result of the step before it. For example, step one will yield the figure immediately following it.

1. Double-click the Forms Designer icon. The Microsoft Exchange Forms Designer dialog box appears (see Figure 34.1).

FIG. 34.1
You can use the Wizard, open a template, or use an existing application.

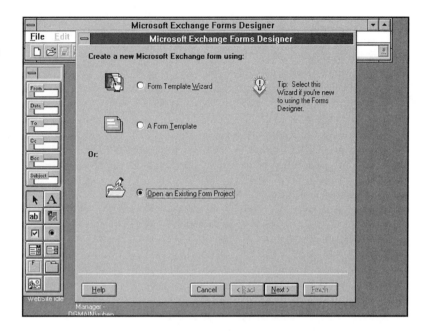

TIP You can use any of the sample forms provided to familiarize yourself with the different kinds of forms.

2. Choose the Form Template Wizard (see Figure 34.2) and click Next.

FIG. 34.2
The Wizard gives you the choice of using the form to send to another user or to post to a public folder.

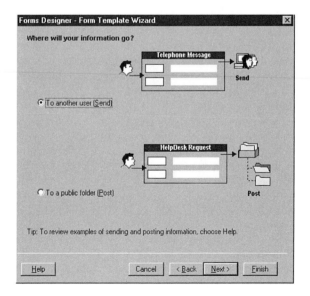

Part
V

Ch
34

   3. Select To Another User (send) and click Next.

   4. Select To Send info and click Next (see Figure 34.3).

FIG. 34.3
You can either use the
form to send info, or let
the user enter a
response to an existing
item.

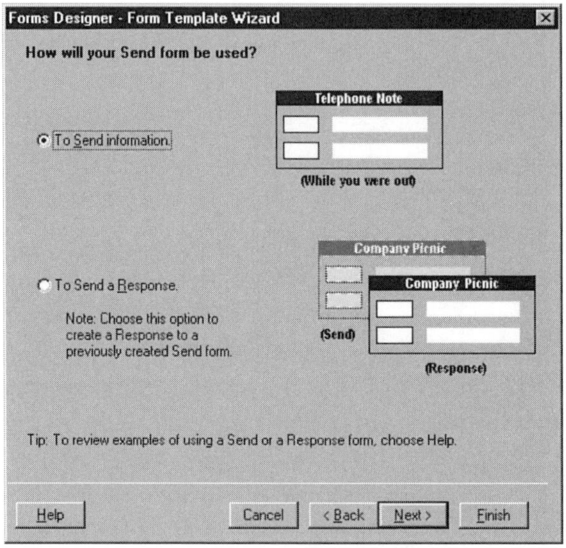

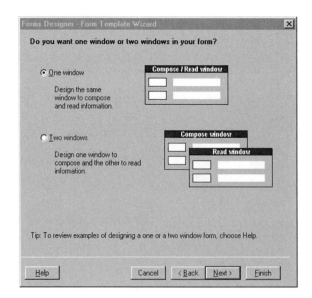

   5. Choose One Window and click Next (see Figure 34.4).

FIG. 34.4
The name and
description given to the
form will determine how
the user sees it in the
Viewer.

6. Type **Web site Button Form** in the Name field (see Figure 34.5), and **This form is used to send detailed information to the technical staff to expedite Website media buys** in the Description field .

FIG. 34.5

The Finish screen of the Wizard shows you the next steps you'll need to take when designing your form.

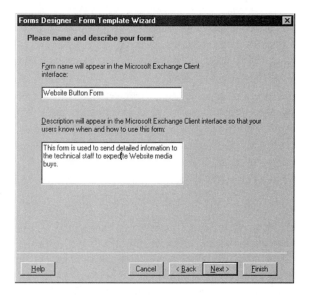

7. Click Finish (see Figure 34.6).

FIG. 34.6

Clicking Finish will lay out the default fields onto the form and bring up the screen where you can add fields to it.

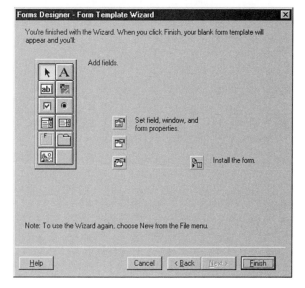

Part

V

Ch

34

8. Our form does not require a "cc" field. Click the middle of the field, and hit the DEL key.

9. We are now going to add the necessary fields to the form. First, select the Frame tool, and click the right side of the form as shown below. A frame will be created. This will house the StartDateEffective and EndEffectiveDate fields.

10. Now you'll create the text entry boxes for the fields that will go inside the frame. The frame is just an easy way to group fields. To create a text entry field, click the Entry Field tool, and drop the fields inside the frame. Then resize the fields as necessary by dragging on the border when the arrows appear.

    There are a couple of ways to create multiple fields. You can either create each one separately, or you can create one, size it, and copy and paste it. The final product will be what's shown below.

    You can replace the word Caption with the text describing the field. Just click in the box with the text of the caption and type over it.

11. We will now create a Listbox containing the name of the companies we usually deal with when we buy space. You can always add new companies easily.

N O T E You could use an Entry Field for this field, but for this example, it is good to try to experiment with the different field types. ▨

Select the Listbox tool from the toolbar. Drop it onto the left side of the form, and size it as shown below by using the same technique as before. In addition, type **Company** into the caption (see Figure 34.7).

N O T E The items that appear in the listbox will be input later when setting properties for each field. ▨

12. The next step is to add three more entry fields that will sit between the frame on the right, and the listbox on the left. They will contain the URL, OurURL, and Size fields. The result is shown below.

 T I P It is a good idea to save your form at this point. Select Save from the File menu, give your form the name WEBFORM, and click OK.

13. Let's now create the frame for the Transport field. This will consist of creating a frame with three radio buttons. The frame caption should read "Transport" and the three radio buttons should have the captions "America Online," "Compuserve," and "Internet," respectively.

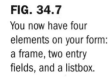

FIG. 34.7

You now have four elements on your form: a frame, two entry fields, and a listbox.

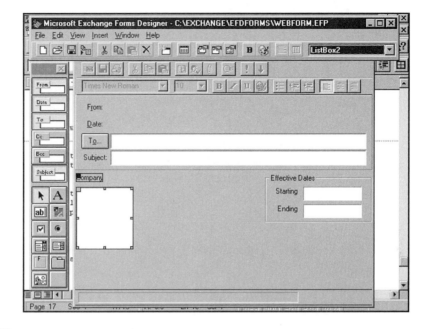

NOTE You'll notice that the listbox containing the company field has been extended. It is very easy to control the length of the box by just dragging on the border. ■

As a reminder, click within a caption to change the text, and drag the edges of the box to resize. To move boxes around, click somewhere inside the box when the cursor is an arrow and drag the item around the form. If you are familiar with Windows applications, this should be familiar to you.

14. You only need to create three more fields: entry fields that will hold the Address, Contact, and ContactPhone fields. They are shown in the Figure 34.8.

Setting the properties of all objects on the form

Now that the form has all the objects laid out on the screen, the next step is to make them actually perform functions. You do this through the use of properties. The various objects on the form, including the form itself, the windows, and the fields all have properties that define their use.

We'll first set the properties for all the fields on the form. The reason the fields come first is that each field is given a name in the properties field that will make it easier to reference when setting Window properties.

Part
V

Ch
34

FIG. 34.8
The form is now
completed.

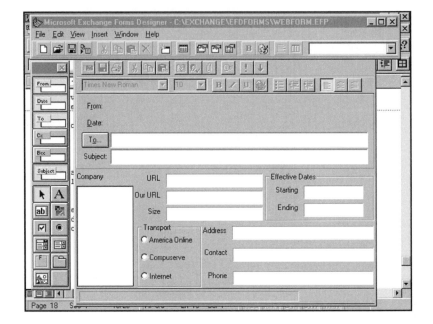

1. Double-click the Company field; the properties screen will appear as shown below. There are tabs of information: General, Format, and Initial Value.

 TIP You can select the field and press F4 instead of double-clicking the object. For fields in tight areas of the screen, this is the preferred method, because double-clicking these areas sometimes yields strange results such as the selection of text.

2. On the General tab, enter **Company** into the Reference Name field. The reference name is simply the variable name assigned to the field. You will use this when determining things like tab order.

3. Check the Required checkbox (see Figure 34.9). This field is required because without a company name, the rest of the fields cannot be complete. The purpose you established earlier will aid you in determining whether a field is required or not.

4. Click the Format tab. This tab controls the font, alignment, appearance, and style of the field value and the caption. The formatting defaults are correct for our purposes for this application.

5. Click the Initial Value tab (see Figure 34.10). This tab differs for each kind of field. Since we are using a listbox in this case, this tab gives you the opportunity to fill in the values in the list and select a default. Fill in the values according the figure shown below. These are the names of some popular Web sites that sell advertising space.

FIG. 34.9
The General Properties are complete for the Company field.

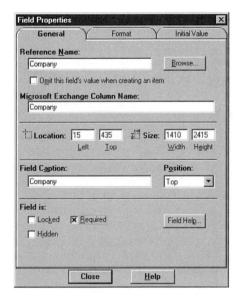

FIG. 34.10
Highlight any entry and click the Set selection to initial value button to make it the default.

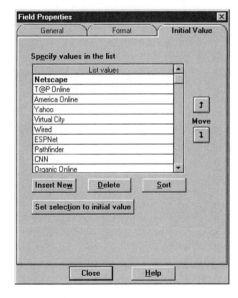

Part
V

Ch
34

6. Push the Close button.

7. Move the pointer over the URL field and double-click.

8. On the General tab (see Figure 34.11), type **URL** as the Reference Name.

9. Check the Required checkbox.

FIG. 34.11

The General tab contains the same information regardless of field type.

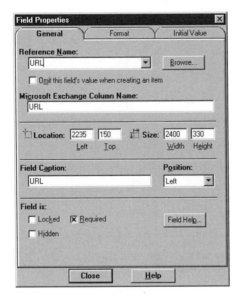

10. Complete the procedures in steps 7 through 9 for all the fields remaining on the form. The Reference Name will match the Caption in the General tab of all the fields (excluding spaces).

11. Double-click the Internet radio button in the Transport frame.

12. Click the Initial Value tab.

13. Click the selected radio button.

14. Select close.

You've now completed all the form properties required for this form. For other forms, you'll probably need to set other properties, and this example provides you with a good starting point.

Setting Window Properties

Forms contain fields and windows. Just as fields have properties, so do windows.

1. Select Window Properties from the View menu.

2. Type **WebButton** into the Window Name.

3. Type **Web Button Form** into the Window Caption field.

4. Establish the tab order by selecting fields and clicking the button marked. Follow Figure 34.12 for an example of the field order.

FIG. 34.12

The layout of the window is determined by its properties.

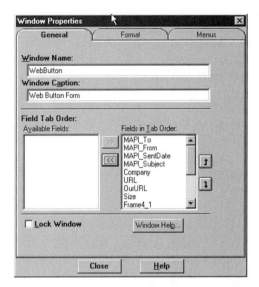

5. Click the Format tab (see Figure 34.13). This tab contains properties for window behavior. Things such as background color, window icon, and title-bar icons are set using this tab.

6. Click the Formatting toolbar checkbox in the Window Options section. Because all the necessary fonts are configured for each field, you don't need the Formatting toolbar for this specific application. It has been removed to show you the variations you can make to a form. (You can leave it if you wish.)

7. Change the Window Sizing Options drop-down box to Resizeable. Your properties sheet should be identical to the one below.

8. Click the Menus tab (see Figure 34.14). You can add and modify menu items here. For our form, we will not need to modify this at all. Refer to the on-line help and Microsoft documentation for more information on modifying menus.

9. Click the close button.

The Window Properties have now been set. This is the second tier of properties you need to set for your form. We will now move on to the third and final set of properties that will control how the form itself interacts with the user.

Setting form properties

We'll now set the form properties. We'll again follow the step-by-step model, using various figures to keep you on track.

Part

V

Ch

34

1. Select Form Properties from the View menu.

FIG. 34.13

Your Format properties are now complete.

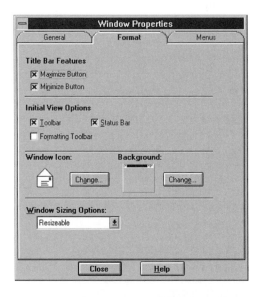

FIG. 34.14

The Menus tab gives you the opportunity to change the menus at the top of the screen.

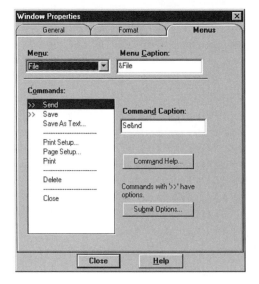

T I P You can also press Ctrl+F to get to the Form Properties.

This will bring up the properties that define your form. As you can see, the General tab (see Figure 34.15) contains the Form Display Name and Description you entered in the wizard. There are no other mandatory properties you need to set for this application.

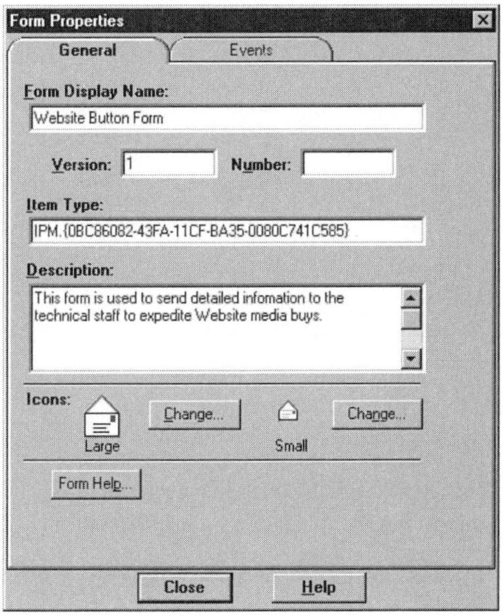

FIG. 34.15

You use the General tab to control how the user sees your form.

Form Properties

| General | Events |

Form Display Name:
Website Button Form

Version: 1   **Number:**

Item Type:
IPM.{0BC86082-43FA-11CF-BA35-0080C741C585}

Description:
This form is used to send detailed infomation to the technical staff to expedite Website media buys.

Icons:

Change...   Large   Change...   Small

Form Help...

Close   Help

N O T E Although the icon and help settings are set here, they are not modified for this application. Please refer to the Microsoft documentation and on-line help for more information on setting up help for your applications.

2. Click the Events tab (see Figure 34.16). You use this tab to define how the form will react to different events the user generates. This particular form requires no modification of these properties. See the Microsoft documentation and the on-line help for a full description of these fields.

3. Click the close button to return to the main editing window.

All of the needed properties are now complete for this form. From here, we'll continue on our list of steps that need to be followed when creating custom forms with Exchange.

Part
V

Ch
34

FIG. 34.16

The Events tab is used to control how the form will react when different events are triggered.

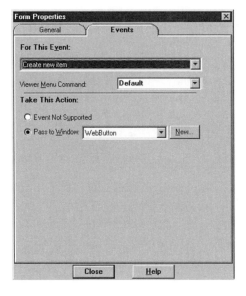

Installing the form

When you install a form, Visual Basic code is generated and an executable file is generated that Exchange will run when someone calls the form. This code can be called up within Visual Basic later on to add more functionality to the form or application.

1. In the Viewer, create a new private folder called **Website Buttons** (see Figure 34.17) in your Mailbox container.

2. Choose Install from the File menu. This will initiate the process of calling Visual Basic and compiling the form. After the computer finishes all those steps, a prompt will come up asking you where to install the form.

3. Click the Folder Forms Library radio button, and select Website Buttons from the list of folders. If the list doesn't appear, click the plus symbol to expand the tree of folders.

4. Click OK.

FIG. 34.17
The installation procedure does all the work for you. All you have to do is select where you want to reside.

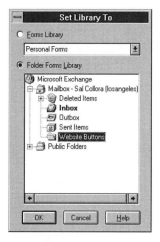

Testing the Form

You now need to run through the form to make sure everything works properly. This is really not a step-by-step process. Look for the following items:

- Required in the Field Properties are actually required to submit the form.
- Button groups only let you select one button.
- Form layout is correct.
- Fonts look appropriate at all resolutions.

To use the form, select New Website Button Form from the Compose menu in the Viewer.

Designing the Form Views

The Column Name property of each field becomes very important when designing views. You can group, sort, and display information by any one of the column names you defined in the design phase.

Our Website Button form (see Figure 34.18) is used to send structured data to another user. We've created a folder for the form and will now design a view. When the user receives a Button Form in his or her inbox, dragging into this folder will make the item conform to the default view.

1. From the Tools menu, choose Application Design, then Folder Designer.
2. Click the Views tab (see Figure 34.19).

Part
V

Ch
34

FIG. 34.18

Designing views is made easy by the Folder Designer.

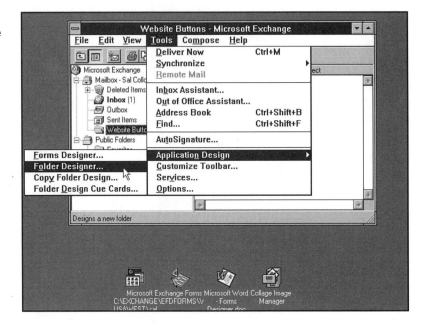

FIG. 34.19

The Views tab displays the views available, and provides a textual description of each.

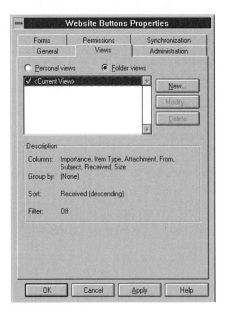

3. Click the New button.

4. Type **by Company** in the View name box.

5. Click the Columns button.

6. Highlight each of the entries in the Show the Following list and click the Remove button so the list is empty.

7. Click Company in the Available Columns list, and click the Add button.

8. Click Transport in the Available Columns list, and click the Add button.

9. Highlight Transport in the Show the Following list, and click the Move Down button.

10. Click Address in the Available Columns list, and click the Add button.

11. Highlight Address in the Show the Following list, and click the Move Down button.

12. Click Sent in the Available Columns list (see Figure 34.20), and click the Add button.

13. Highlight Sent in the Show the Following list, and click the Move Down button.

14. Click OK.

FIG. 34.20

The layout of the columns included in the view should look like this after steps 5-12 are completed.

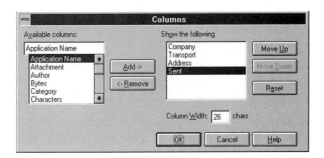

15. Click Sort.

16. Drop down the list, and select Sent.

17. Click the Descending radio button.

18. Click OK.

19. Click OK.

20. Double-click the by Company entry in the list to place the checkmark next to it. It is now the default view.

21. Click OK.

All the entries in this folder will now be displayed according to the view you created (see Figure 34.21).

Part
V

Ch

34

FIG. 34.21
Views determine how
the items appear in
the folder.

You have now completed all the necessary steps for the Website button form. The next steps are provided for demonstration only, because this form is a send form, which is intended to simplify sending structured information to a particular user.

You can, however, make the public folder the recipient of the message. This would enable a centralized repository of all the Website Button buys.

Copying the Form to a Public Folder

Your Website Button Form will only be used by a couple of people, so putting it into a public folder isn't really appropriate; however, for the purposes of illustration, we will go through the steps of copying a form into a public folder.

In some organizations, administration of these folders is centralized and information policy prevents the administrator from giving users permission to manipulate public folders. The user must pass the folder on to the administrator, and have the administrator perform the following steps.

In some cases, however, a new public folder will be created, and permission will be granted to the user to manipulate the folder and its forms library. The tutorial below assumes you have all the proper permissions.

1. Select the Website Button Form folder.
2. Choose Copy from the File menu.
3. In the Copy box, select the public folder you would like to copy the Website Buttons form into. In this case, it's the All Public Folders folder. Yours may vary.
4. Click OK.

Setting the Folder Properties

Now that the form has been moved to a public folder, you must now set the properties for that folder.

1. Right-click the Website Button folder and select Properties.
2. Select the Administration tab (see Figure 34.22).
3. Select by Company as the Initial view on folder. This will ensure that all items in that folder conform to the view we defined earlier.
4. Select Move/Copy in the Drag/Drop listbox.
5. Select the All users with permission radio button in the This folder is available to box.
6. Select the Forms tab.
7. Click the Only forms listed above radio button. This ensures that only the Website button form will be allowed in this folder. This protects against someone putting in some other kind of form, like a Vacation/Absence form in the Website Button folder.

FIG. 34.22
The Administration tab should now be completed as shown above.

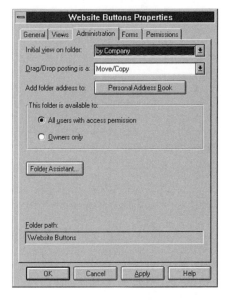

Setting Folder Permissions

1. Click the Permissions tab (see Figure 34.23).
2. Click the Default user and change the Role to None. These are the properties for all users. Changing the Role to None means that users have no privileges in the folder.

Part
V

Ch
34

The following table lists all the Roles and their associated permissions.

Table 34.2   Roles and Permissions

Role	Permission
Owner	All
Editor	Create Items Read Items Edit All Items Delete All Items
Author	Create Items Read Items Edit Own Items Delete Own Items
Publishing Editor	Create Items Read Items Edit All Items Delete All items Create Subfolders
Publishing Author	Create Items Read Items Edit Own Items Delete Own Items Create Subfolders
Reviewer	Create Items Read Items
Contributor	Create Items
None	No Permissions granted
Custom	Enables you to set permissions that do not match a predefined role

3. Click the Add button.

4. Select the users you want to have access to your folder and click the Add button.

5. Change the Role of each user you've added to Author. This allows them to Create and Read items in the folder. As you can see, each user can only edit and delete their own items.

FIG. 34.23
The Permissions tab enables you to control who has access to your form, and what operations each user can perform within the folder.

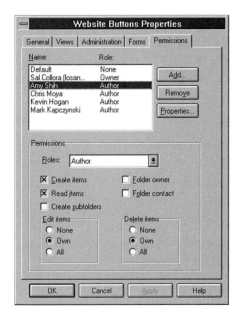

Setting Folder Rules

You can use rules for any folder, including the inbox. Rules process incoming items by running them through a series of criteria. The rule itself is the action to take upon the meeting of those specified criteria.

Some organizations have people with certain contacts or specialties. You can set up rules to copy messages to certain users with those specialties.

We're going to set a rule that will forward all Website Button requests for ESPNet to Ruben Perez because he processes all the ESPNet dealings. The user you choose will obviously depend on your own site.

1. Right-click the Website Button folder and select Properties.
2. Select the Administration tab.
3. Push the Folder Assistant button.
4. Click Add Rule.
5. Click the Advanced button.
6. Click the Folder: Website Buttons radio button in the Show properties of group.
7. Select the Company Checkbox.
8. Select ESPNet the listbox (see Figure 34.24).

Part
V

Ch
34

FIG. 34.24

The Advanced properties lets you select fields on the form as search criteria.

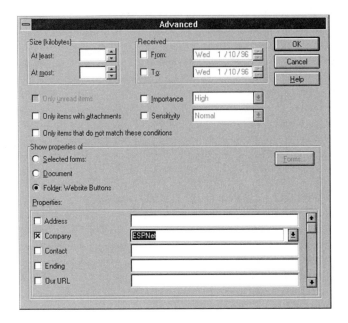

9. Click OK.

10. Click the Forward check box (see Figure 34.25).

11. Click the To button.

12. Select the proper user from the list and click the To button.

13. Click OK.

14. Click OK (see Figure 34.26).

15. Click OK again.

We've now completed all of the steps in the folder design process. Your form will now make it a lot easier to expedite Website Button requests. The purpose of using this kind of application was to show you how you automate any kind of process.

There are many examples of common office forms. Using what you have learned here, you can go about modifying those for your own purposes.

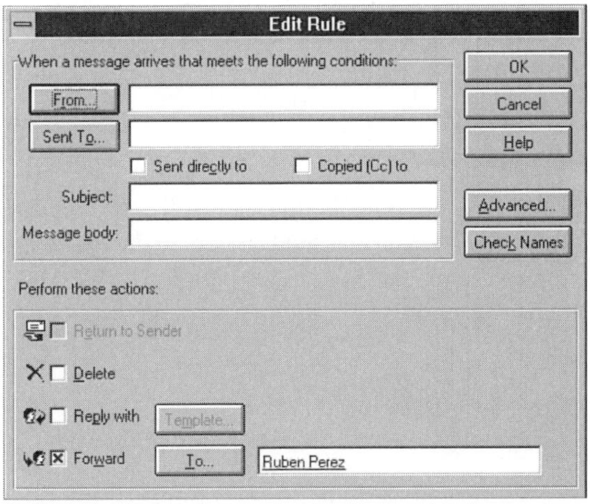

FIG. 34.25
You've now set up a complete rule. All ESPNet requests will be forwarded to the user

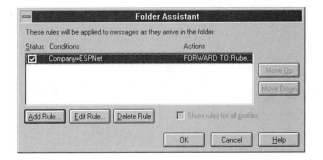

FIG. 34.26
The newly created rule is now added to the rule list in the Folder Assistant.

Using Your Form

Now that you've created a new form and placed it in a public folder, accessing it and using it are a snap.

Addressing to a Person

1. Select the Website Buttons Folder.
2. From the Compose menu, choose New Website Button Form. The form will pop up on your screen.
3. Fill out all the required fields.
4. Click the To button.
5. Select a recipient and click the To button.
6. Click OK.
7. Click the Send icon.

Part
V
Ch
34

Addressing to the Website Button Public Folder

1. Select the Website Buttons Folder.

2. Right-click, and select Properties.

3. Click the Administration tab.

4. Click the Personal Address Book button. This will copy the name of the folder to your Personal Address Book so you can send an item to the folder.

5. Click OK.

6. From the Compose menu, choose New Website Button Form. The form will pop up on your screen.

7. Fill out all the required fields.

8. Click the To button.

9. Select Personal Address Book from the Show Names from listbox (see Figure 34.27).

10. Select the Website Buttons entry.

11. Click the To button.

12. Click OK.

13. Click the Send icon.

FIG. 34.27

The Website Buttons folder is now in your Personal Address Book.

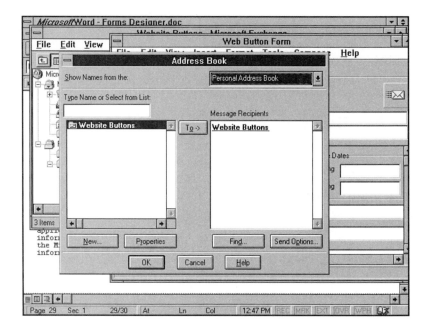

Extending Forms with Visual Basic

Since forms are Visual Basic applications, you can actually use Visual Basic to extend the functionality of forms beyond what the Forms Designer offers. The Forms Designer simply gives you a "No Programming" environment where you design very powerful applications without typing one line of code.

We will only be covering a brief overview of what you need, what goes into using Visual Basic to modify applications, and why you would want to. You can refer to the Microsoft documentation and Visual Basic documentation for specifics on using Visual Basic for MAPI and OLE applications.

Anyone who wants to use VB to extend an application created with the Forms Designer should be very experienced with Visual Basic, as well as MAPI and OLE. Forms are 16-bit applications, therefore, you can only use the Visual Basic for Exchange that gets installed when installing the Exchange Client and Forms Designer or 16-Bit Visual Basic 4.0.

Potential Uses of Visual Basic with Exchange Forms

You might be asking yourself, why would I want to use VB to extend forms? Here are just a couple of examples of how VB can improve your forms.

■ You can use a form to enter data into external databases. For example, if you have a form for ordering office supplies, you can extend the form so that once the purchasing supervisor reviews the requisition and approves it, the data gets entered into a Microsoft SQL Server database automatically and the purchase order generated with the daily run.

By using public folders, you can distribute the application throughout the Exchange network without actually copying the .EXE file on all the servers in your network for all your users to access. In addition, when the form gets modified, all the users on the network will get the most up-to-date version of the form automatically without the need to redistribute. All of that is controlled by the synchronization within Exchange.

■ You can include OLE controls in a form that can take data from OLE-compliant applications such as Excel. For example, if you want your form to grab the latest data from a spreadsheet and paste it into the form, you can write code that reads the contents of the OLE control into a file, and then reads the file into the form using OLE Messaging functions.

You can use this function to send hourly time sheets to a user in native Excel format. The form can contain a blank Excel worksheet that has the header cells filled in with the days of the month, and you just fill data right into the worksheet. The recipient can then either cut, copy, and paste the data, or save it directly as an Excel file.

Part
V

Ch

34

Modifying Applications

When you install a form using the Forms Designer, several files get created in a directory called <FORMNAME>.VB. These files are those used when extending forms with Visual Basic (see Figure 34.28).

FIG. 34.28

The WEBFORM.VB directory contains all the files used by Visual Basic.

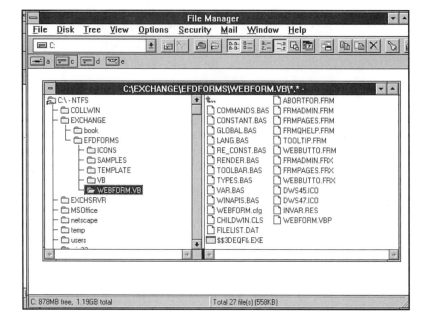

When using VB, only the <WINDOW NAME>.FRM files and the <FORM FILE>.CFG files are modified. Once you finish using Visual Basic to modify your form, you need to register all the new fields and properties in your form with Exchange. You will need to modify the .CFG file directly in Notepad or Wordpad to add all the objects and properties so they are recognized by Exchange.

N O T E   Before you can install the Forms Designer, the Exchange Microsoft client must be installed. In order to get the sample applications along with your installation, you can choose either Typical or Custom/Complete. Typical installs with most common files. Custom/Complete enables you to choose whether to install the sample applications or not. When you choose either of these installations you will have to reboot because during the installation system files will be changed.   ■

N O T E   When using forms with an NTFS partition you will not be able to use the custom forms in Microsoft Exchange if you are running Windows NT 3.51 Server or Workstation computer. To change this, you must use alter a specific registry key, and the registry key reads as follows:

HKEY_LOCAL_MACHINE\SYSTEM\CurrentControlSet\Control\FileSystem\NtfsDisable8dot3NameCreation = 0x1. To use custom forms, you must delete this key or set its value to 0. In a Windows NT 4.0 Workstation and Server environment, this particular registry key value is set to 0 by default.   ■

When you are planning to design forms, decide on a home directory for your work. This gives you a sense of structure from the beginning. If you don't establish structure from the beginning you won't know where the Forms Generator is keeping your files, which may lead to duplicate files in other directories all over your hard drive. When you pick a directory (such as c:\exchange\efdforms) the Electronic Forms Designer(EFD), it starts to store all your information in that folder. This is especially helpful when you extend your forms with Visual Basic's 16-bit version. The 32-bit version of Visual Basic 4.0 is not currently compatible with EFD at this time. When you install the form, you have finished. The EFD creates a folder with the same name as your efp file and a Visual Basic extension. Inside of this folder is the Visual Basic Project file (VFP).

Creating the Personnel Profile Information Application

In the following pages we create an application using both Form Designer and Visual Basic 16-bit version. This will demonstate a first look at extending your forms application with Visual Basic. Start the forms designer by clicking the Start button, and select Programs and then the Microsoft Exchange Folder. From there you will see an option for the Forms Designer. Click it to start it.

Creating The Personnel Information application may not cause your company's stock to rise, but it will teach you some useful tricks you can bring into the world of development using Microsoft Exchange's Development tools. In this section we take a look at using Send Forms in a folder, calling a hidden response form, using a rich edit field with the help of Visual Basic to enable file attachments in our form, and creating a custom response.

The Personnel Profile Information folder is a public folder that houses the forms you will be creating in this section. It will also contain different views you will create and the result of the information collected by our Personnel Information Application. A sample view of items submitted to the Personnel Profile Information folder is as shown here in Figure 34.29.

The Personnel Profile Information Request Form Its compose window, as shown in Figure 34.30, is used by a Manager to send a Personnel Information Request item to the user's Inbox. Its Read window is used by the members of the organization to read the request and open the Personnel Profile Information Response Form.

Part
V

Ch
34

FIG. 34.29

Sample View of Personnel Profile Information Folder.

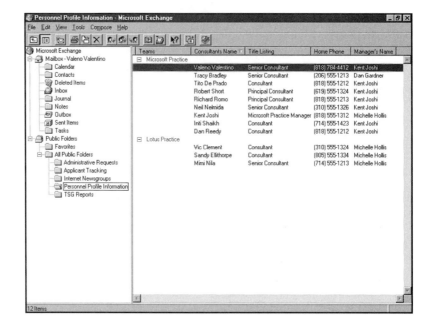

FIG. 34.30

Pre-addressing the Response Form.

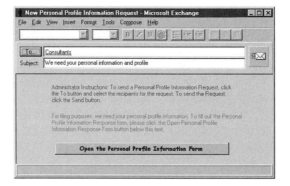

The Personnel Profile Information Response form—The Compose window, as shown in Figure 34.31, is pre-addressed to the Personnel Profile Information folder. When the user clicks the Send button, the item is automatically routed to that folder. The Read Window displays the information in the Personnel Profile Information Response item that the user submits to the Personnel Profile Information folder.

FIG. 34.31
Pre-Addressing the
Personnel Profile
Information Response
form.

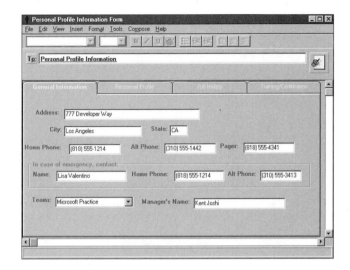

Creating the Personnel Profile Information Folder

To begin, you must login as yourself. If you don't, your profile will not reflect the location of your mailbox. Next, you need to create a public folder for storing the Personnel Information items. Where you create this folder is really up to you, but to make this application available to everyone you should use the All Public Folders folder as your starting point. To create the Personnel Information Folder, follow these steps:

1. In the set of public folders in the Microsoft Exchange Client, select All Public Folders.

2. Choose New Folder from the File menu, and, in the Folder Name box, type Personnel Profile Information.

3. Choose OK.

Restrict Folder Access

While you work on the folder, you want to restrict access to the folder so that you can design it without being interrupted. To restrict access, follow these steps:

1. Select the Personnel Information folder, and then choose Properties.

2. Select the Administration tab, and then select the Owners Only option button, as shown in Figure 34.32. Don't choose OK yet. You're not finished with the Administration tab.

FIG. 34.32
Using the Administratrion tab to select the Owners Only option.

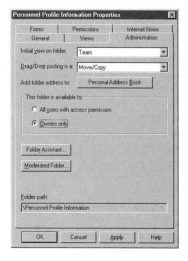

Make the Folder Address Available to Your Personnel Address Book

For this application, you will create a pre-addressed Response form. It's a lot like a pre-addressed envelope that you receive in the mail. In this case, the Response Information form is pre-addressed so that posting to the folder is automatic. We will now learn how to pre-address a folder. Before you can pre-address a form to a folder, the folder's address must be available to the address book.

To add a folder address to your Personal Address Book, do the following:

1. In the Administration tab, click the **Personnel** Address Book button to add the folder address to your **Personnel** Address Book. Although you won't get any confirmation, the address is added to your **Personnel** Address Book. If you look down at the bottom of the Administration tab you will see a backslash and the name of your folder in the folder path area.

2. Choose OK to return to the Microsoft Exchange Client.

Creating the Personnel Profile Information Request Form

The Forms Designer provides several generic pre-designed templates for you to begin using immediately. To get started with **Personnel** Profile Information Request form, you use the SNDR2WND.EFP template. This is a two-window Send Form similar to the one that you would use to send messages. It has To, From, and Subject fields, like a standard mail message.

Although you can use the Form Template Wizard to choose a template, it is faster to choose a template directly from the list of the file directory dialog box.

Before we open any files, create an application directory to house your files for this application.

1. Change directories to the following path C:\EXCHANGE\EFDFORMS.

2. Create two sub-folders. Call the first one PQINFO and the second PPINFO.

To open and use the SNDR2WND.EFP template follow these steps:

1. From the opening screen of the Forms Designer, select the *A Form Template.*

   If you are already running Forms Designer choose File, Open from the menu bar.

2. This is a read only file, so in order to edit it you must save it with another name in the PQINFO sub-folder. In the Exchange\Efdforms\Template folder, select the SNDR2WND.EFP file.

3. Click File from the menu and choose Save As.

4. Navigate through the directory structure to *C:\EXCHANGE\EFDFORMS\PQINFO*.

5. In the file name box type *pqinfo*.

Design the Compose Window

Figure 34.33 displays how the form will look when it is selected from the Compose (pull-down) menu. To run the Personnel Profile Information Request Form, choose new Personnel Profile Information Request from the Compose (pull-down) menu.

FIG. 34.33

Displays how the form will look when it is selected from the Compose (pull-down) menu.

The Personnel Profile Information Request window, shown in Figure 34.34 , is great for anyone who needs profile/personal information from a user or group of users in the company. You can use Figure 34.34 as a model to help customize this form.

Part
V

Ch
34

FIG. 34.34
Shows you how the Personnel Profile Information Request form will look in its final state.

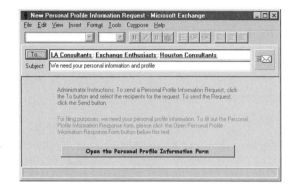

Set the Window Properties for the Compose Window

When you start designing forms you must always consider who will be using your form and how. On many occasions the Compose Window is different from the Read Window. The Personnel Profile Information Form is used to request information in a Compose Window. The end users see a form that looks similar to the one you sent, but they only see who sent the form to them and the date and time that it was sent. The Request form in the read window should include brief instructions to inform the recipient how to fill out the form.

Designing the Read Window

At run time, the Read Window of the form appears when the user double-clicks a Personnel Profile Information Request item in the user's Inbox. Figure 34.35 shows you an example of what the user will see in their Inbox.

Setting the Initial Value for the Subject Field

As a courtesy to the user, you can set the initial value to display in the subject field of the Read Window.

To set the initial value of the subject field, follow these steps:

1. Double-click the Subject field to view field properties, and then select the Initial value tab.

2. In the Subject box, type **We need your Personnel Profile Information**.

3. Then choose close.

FIG. 34.35

An example of what the user will see in their inbox when the Personnel Profile Information Request item has been delivered to them. The read window displays the Personnel Profile Information Request form and your instructions.

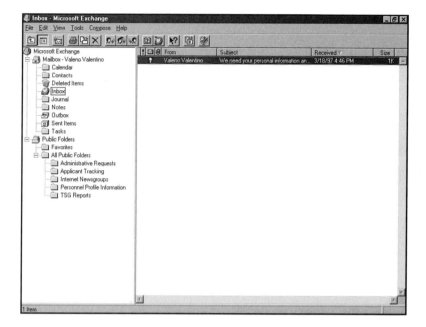

The title bar of the form window can also be defined in the Window Properties dialog box. As a general rule, it should begin with "New," followed by the name of the form. See Figure 34.36.

FIG. 34.36

Defining the title bar of the form.

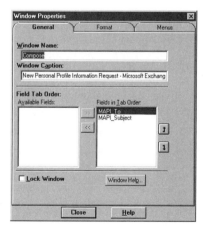

Part

V

Ch

34

To set the window caption, follow these steps:

1. Click View from the menu and select Window Properties.
2. In the General tab, change the Window caption to read *New Personnel Profile Information Request.*
3. Then click the Close button.

Copying the User Instructions Label Field to the Compose Window

In General practice, I usually create the information for the Compose Window first, then I copy that to the Read Window. Refer back to Figure 34.30 for an example of text to use as user and Administrator instructions.

To copy the user instructions, the following steps tell you how:

1. Click the user instructions label field.
2. Select Edit from the menu and choose Copy.
3. Select Window from the menu and choose Read.
4. Once again select Edit from the menu and choose Paste.

N O T E You add the Open Personnel Profile Information Form command button later in Visual Basic. ■

After opening the Read Window, remove the unnecessary fields from the form. You can do this by just selecting them and hitting the delete key on your keyboard.

To remove the To and Cc fields from the Read window, select each one and press the delete key on your keyboard. Now you can paste and reposition the user label field to your liking.

Resize the Read Window

The Read Window resizes just like any other window—just be sure you leave enough room for the button you will make later in Visual Basic.

Set the Window Properties for the Read Window

The window caption is the only property to set in the Window Properties dialog box. To set the window caption, follow these steps:

1. Select View from the menu and click *Window Properties.*
2. Click the General tab, then change the window caption to read *Personnel Profile Information Request*, and then choose Close.

Set the Form Properties for the Read Window

In the General tab of the Form Properties dialog box, change the display name and the item type for the form. To set the forms general properties:

1. Select View from the menu, and click Form Properties.

2. In the General tab, change the settings to reflect the table below.

Table 34.8   Setting Form Properties

Property	Setting
Form Display Name	Personnel Profile Information Request
Version	1.00
Number	PINFO7.1
Item Type	IPM.PersonnelProfileInformationRequest
Description	Use this form to send requests for Personnel and profile information in your company.

Events for the Request Form

The most common event is the Create New Item event. When you select View from the menu and click Forms properties. Then click the Events tab—you should see something similar to Figure 34.37.

FIG. 34.37
Viewing the Create
New Item event.

Every time the New Personnel Profile Information Request is chosen from the menu. The Create new item event executes. This event creates a new instance of The Personnel Profile

Information Request form. In other words, the Compose version of the Request form appears when the New Personnel Profile Information Request is chosen from the Compose menu. Figure 34.38 illustrates a new instance of the Personnel Profile Information item.

FIG. 34.38
Viewing the new instance of the Personnel Profile Information Request item from the Compose Menu.

Create a Custom Response

The first time people start working with custom responses, they ask themselves, "Why do I need two forms?" When you are sent a bill in the mail it usually includes a return envelope to make it more convient for you to pay your bill. The Read version of the request form is a request from you to the end user for information you need from him/her. On this form is a button which enables the end user to open another form so that they can enter the information you requested and return the form to the Personnel Profile folder for review.

We still have to set up a Custom Response event to launch the Personnel Profile Information Form. This creates a new Compose menu item each time it is executed. To do this use the Forms Properties events tab as shown in Figure 34.39.

1. Open the Form Properties Events tab.
2. Choose "Custom Response 1" in the For This Event field.
3. Select the Create Response radio button.
4. Browse to select the Response form (PQINFO.EFP); accept the default Response Form Item Type.

FIG. 34.39
Viewing a Custom Response already created in the Form's Properties Window.

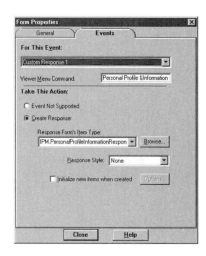

Save and Install the Form

The Forms Designer gives you a start in the design of forms, but the limited toolbox doesn't offer much depth. Most of the shortcomings of the Forms Designer can be easily overcome with Visual Basic or Visual C++. Before you can extend the functionally with Visual Basic, you must first install the form into the Personnel Profile Information folder. When you install this form the Visual Basic code is created for it automatically; this means a Visual Basic Project file and an CFG file are created. The CFG file will be used later by Inbox to install the Visual Basic Executable, so that the form with the new Visual Basic Code can run from the Inbox.

To install the Request Form, follow these steps:

1. Click the File menu and select install. If your file has not been saved before or changes are detected, the Forms Designer displays a message box informing you that changes to your form will be saved before continuing.

2. When the Folder Library appears, click Personnel Profile Information folder, as shown in Figure 34.40.

3. Click OK.

FIG. 34.40

Installing the Request Form in the Personnel Profile Information folder.

N O T E Always save the files with a name that relates to the contents of the file and is easy for you to remember. ∎

Creating the Personnel Profile Information Form

To get started with Personnel Profile Information form, you can use the SNDR2WND.EFP template. This is a two-window Send form used for creating response items. This file, however, is read only, so you must rename it before you can use it. The name I will be using throughout this chapter is ppinfo.

To Open and use the SNDR2WND.EFP template, follow these steps:

1. Select File from the menu and choose open.

2. This is a read only file, so in order to edit it you must save it with another name in the PPINFO sub-folder. In the Exchange\Efdforms\Template folder, select the SNDR2WND.EFP file.

3. Click File from the menu and choose Save As.

4. Navigate through the directory structure to *C:\ EXCHANGE\EFDFORMS \PPINFO*.

5. In the file name box type *ppinfo*.

To remove the Cc and Subject fields just select them and press delete.

From the toolbox, select the tab control and click your form. Resize the Tab control to fill the contents panel. To fill the reference name fields:

1. Name the tabs by double-clicking each one. The names I have chosen are as follows:

   * General Information
   * Personnel Profile
   * Job History
   * Training/Certification

Adding Fields to the Compose Window of the Response Form

Using the Designer toolbox, place the following fields on each respective tab, as illustrated in Figures 34.41—34.43.

FIG. 34.41

A picture of the first tab and the fields it contains.

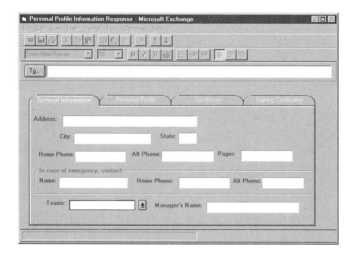

Table 34.3   Fields on first tab

Type of Field	Caption	Reference Name	Column Name
Entry	Address:	Address	Address
Entry	City:	City	City
Entry	Home Phone:	HomePhone	Home Phone
Entry	Alt Phone:	AltPhone	AltPhone
Entry	Pager:	Pager	Pager
Entry	In case of	Frame1 emergency,contact:	Frame1
Entry	Name:	Emergency ContactName	Emergency Contact Name
Entry	Home Phone:	Emergency HomePhone	Emergency HomePhone
Entry	Alt Phone:	Emergency AltPhone	Emergency AltPhone
ComboBox	Teams:	Teams	Teams
Entry	Manager's Name:	Manager's Name	Manager's Name

In addition to, or instead of a user typing in a Personal Statement, they can attach relevant files. To Attach a file to the Personnel Profile Information Form just select Insert from the Menu and click file. The file will automatically find the RichEntry field with the MAPI_Body_Custom type.

FIG. 34.42

A picture of the second tab and the fields it contains.

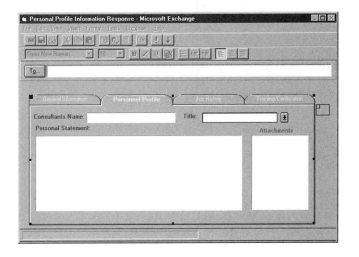

Table 34.4   Fields on second tab

Type of Field	Caption	Reference Name	Column Name
Entry	Consultant's Name:	Consultants Name	Consultants Name
ComboBox	Title:	Title	Title Listing
Entry	Personnel Statement:	Personnel Statement	Personnel Statement
RichEntry	Attachments:	Attachments	Attachments

FIG. 34.43

A picture of the third tab and the fields it contains.

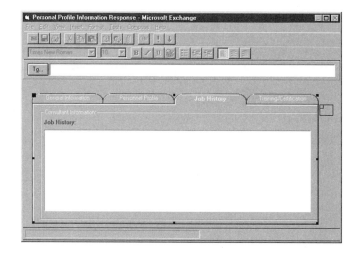

Table 34.5   Fields on third tab

Type of Field	Caption	Reference Name	Column Name
RichEntry	Job History:	JobHistory	Job History

FIG. 34.44
A picture of the fourth tab and the fields it contains.

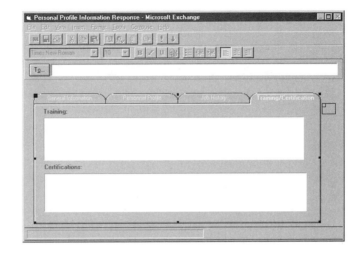

Table 34.6   Fields on fourth tab

Type of Field	Caption	Reference Name	Column Name
RichEntry	Training:	Training	Training
RichEntry	Certifications:	Certifications	Certifications

Set the Initial Value of the Teams Field

The initial value properties define the values that appear in a field at run time. In this case, you define the initial values for the Team ComboBox on the first tab. You can also choose a default value to appear at run time.

To set the initial value for the ComboBox field:

1. Double-click the Teams ComboBox, and select the initial value tab.

2. Type the values that appear in Figure 34.45

3. Select the field you want to be the default value and click the Set selection to initial value button.

Pre-address the Response Form

As I stated earlier, a pre-addressed form is like an envelope with a return address. You pre-address this form by setting the initial value of the To field to Personnel Profile Information folder.

Part
V

Ch

34

To predate the form:

1. Double-click the To field.

2. In the Initial Value tab, choose To, and then choose Personnel Address Book from the Show Names From The: drop-down box.

3. Select the Personnel Profile Information folder, choose To, and then choose OK.

4. Choose Close to return to the Forms Designer.

FIG. 34.45

Setting the intial values for the ComboBox field.

Set The Window Properties for the Response Compose Window

Now let's set the window caption and the field tab order. The window caption will appear in the title bar of the window. The field tab order is a property that controls the order in which the windows fields gain focus as the user presses the Tab key.

Setting the Window Caption:

1. From the View menu, click Window Properties.

2. In the Window Caption box in the General tab, change the current caption to *Personnel Profile Information Response.*

To set the tab order:

1. Select the field in the Available fields box, and then choose the Add arrow button or double-click the field to add the field to the Fields In Tab Order box.

   Leave MAPI-To as the first tab in the Fields In Tab Order box. Add the rest of the fields in the order they are listed in the previous table.

2. Now choose Close.

Copy Fields in the Compose Window to the Read Window

You can save design time by copying everything you've done so far in the Compose Window to the Read Window.

1. Select the Tab Control by clicking in an empty space anywhere on the tab control.
2. Choose Copy from the toolbar.
3. From the Window Menu select Read and then choose Paste from the toolbar.

Setting Window Properties for the Response Read Window

In the Window Properties dialog box, you will repeat the same procedures as were performed in the Compose Window to set the tab order and window caption name properties.

N O T E Leave the pre-assigned MAPI fields set, then order your fields in the same order of the Compose Window. ▨

Set Form Properties for the Response Read Window

Now we can name the form and give it a unique item type that matches the item type you specified for the Custom Response 1 event in the Request form.

To set the form display name, follow these steps:

1. On the Main window toolbar, click the Form Properties button.
2. In the Form Display Name box inside the General tab, type *Personnel Profile Information Response.*

To set the version, number, and item type:

1. In the Version box, change the number to 1.00.
2. In the Number box, type PINFO7.2
3. In the Item Type box, change the item type to IPM.PersonnelProfileInformationResponse.

Setting the form description:

1. In the Description box, type **Use this form to fill out and send Personnel profile and emergency information to the Personnel Profile Information folder.**
2. Now Choose Close.

Save and Install the Response Form

As stated earlier, when you choose install from the file menu in The Forms Designer, the Forms Designer tells you it will save the form before it installs it (Unless it is already saved). After a moment, the Folder Library appears. This enables you to save your form in a particular folder (such as the Personnel Profile Information folder).

Part
V

Ch
34

N O T E Always save the files with a name that is logical, descriptive, and easy to remember.

Creating the By Team View

The by Team View indicates which practice(s) the consultant is a member of.

The Team view consists of the following fields: Teams, Consultant's Name, Title Listing, Home Phone, and Manager's Name. Then the view groups these fields by team and sorts items in ascending order by Consultant's Name.

To create The Team View:

1. In the Exchange client, select the properties for the Personnel Profile Information folder.
2. From here, find the Views tab, and choose New.
3. Be sure to Remove any fields from the show the following columns box, so that it is empty when you start to add fields.
4. In the Available Columns box, select Teams and Consultant's Name, and then double-click them separately.
5. Set the column width of the fields

   Teams—36

   Consultant's Name—36
6. Choose OK.
7. In the Group Items By drop-down box, select teams, choose OK, and then choose OK again.

Setting Permissions

In the Permmissions tab, you define different levels of security for your folder.

To set permissions:

1. In the Personnel Profile Information Properties dialog box, select the Permissions tab, and then set permissions according to the following table.

Sometimes you might want to restrict users only to the items you want them to interact with. Figure 34.46 shows how to limit the forms a folder displays.

To restrict the types of items:

1. Select the Personnel Profile Information folder, and then choose Properties from the file menu.
2. In the Properties dialog box, select the Forms tab.
3. Select the Only Forms Listed Above option button, and then choose OK.

Testing the Application

The time has come to test the application. Once you are satisfied that it's working correctly, you can enhance its usability by giving it some extended capabilities in Visual Basic.

FIG. 34.46

Limiting the forms a folder displays.

To test the Request form in the Personnel Profile Information folder:

1. Select the Personnel Profile Information folder.
2. From the Compose menu, choose New Personnel Profile Information Request. The Request Form's Compose window appears.
3. In the To box, type your name, and then press Ctrl+K to resolve the address. Now click the Send Button.
4. Select the Inbox and double-click your new mail. The form will install (if it hasn't installed on your computer before) and display the read version of the Request form.

To test the Response form:

1. Select the Personnel Profile Information folder.
2. From the Compose menu, choose New Personnel Profile Information Response. The Response Form appears.
3. Fill out the appropriate information. Now click the Post button located at the right top of the Response form. This action will post the form to the Personnel Profile Information Folder.
4. Select the Personnel Profile Information Folder then make sure the view is set to teams. Click the plus symbol next to the appropriate team, and then double-click the consultant's name. This action displays the form with the information you requested. Tab through it and make sure that it is correct. Because it is posted in the Personnel Profile Information folder the information can always be changed.

Part
V

Ch

34

Adding a Button to the Form with Visual Basic

To modify a form generated using the Forms Designer, you must use the Visual Basic that comes with the Microsoft Exchange Client or the 16-bit compiler of Visual Basic version 4.0 or later.

To add a command button to the Compose Window, do the following steps:

1. In Visual Basic, from the file menu choose Open Project.
2. Here you will select pqinfo.vbp file, which is located in the directory path you created earlier in this chapter to house all of project files for this application.
3. The directory name will be PQINFO.vb
4. An example of this is the following:
   (C:\EXCHANGE\EFDFORMS\PQINFO.VB\pqinfo.vbp)

   After the project has been loaded, double-click the COMPOSE.FRM from the Project Window.

Adding the command button to the form:

1. If the toolbox is not visible, select toolbox from the view menu and it will appear.
2. Click the Command Button, and then add it to the Compose Form.
3. While the Command Button is still selected, press the F4 key on your keyboard. This will open up the Properties dialog box. Set the command button's Caption property to *Open & Personnel Profile Information Response Form*. Then set the Enabled property to False.

Cleaning up the Form Window

When the Forms Designer generates Visual Basic code for the form, it seems to scramble the components in the Compose and Read Windows. Fortunately, the generated code contains several procedures that arrange these components in the window at run time. To clean up the window, the first thing you should do is enlarge the window. Then hide the scroll bars by dragging them to the edges of the window. Next we hide the status bar by setting the Align property for the Status Bar Control to 0 –None. Now drag the status bar out of your work area as you did the scroll bars.

Increasing the Canvas Size

The form window canvas consists of a large picture control (Canvas_Ctrl) inside a much smaller canvas control (CanvasParent). To resize the canvas:

1. Before you can select the CanvasParent control to resize it, you must first reposition the Canvas_Ctrl inside the CanvasParent, as shown in Figure 34.47.
2. Select the CanvasParent Control, and then resize it until it looks like Figure 34.48.

FIG. 34.47

Increasing the size of the Canvas Ctrl.

FIG. 34.48

Visual representation of how the CanvasParent Control should look after resizing.

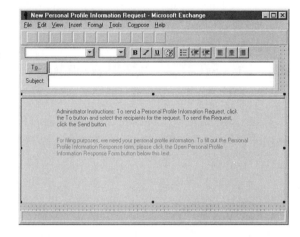

Adding Code to the Command Button

Double-click the command button, and add the code as shown below to the button click procedure.

```
Private Sub Command1_Click()
    Call menComposeCustomResponse_Click(0)
End Sub
```

This code calls the Click procedure for the Custom Response command and passes it an Index value of 0. This is the same value that the custom response menu command passes to the procedure. In our number system, when we count from 0 to 9 we have actually counted 10 numbers. The zero you passed the menComposeCustomResponse Sub Procedure represents the Custom Response 1 event you set up in the Forms Designer earlier in this chapter. If we were to pass a 1 to this procedure this would represent the Custom Response 2 event.

Part
V

Ch
34

Copying Command Button and Code Contents to the READ.FRM

1. Right-click the command button and choose copy.
2. Return to the Project window and double-click the READ.FRM. Repeat the steps to clean up this form as explained in the "Cleaning Up the Form Window" section.
3. Select the READ.FRM and paste the command button on the form.
4. Double-click the command button and insert the same code we inserted earlier in command button on the COMPOSE.FRM.
5. The next step is to save this project by selecting Save Project from the File Menu of Visual Basic.

Making an .EXE File

When you create a new executable (.EXE) file, you incorporate the changes that were made in Visual Basic. When you see the odd name of the executable that is generated, your first reaction will be to change it to something more readable. My advice is to leave it as is. When the Forms Designer creates an .EXE file for the form it also creates a .CFG file. If you were to change the name of the executable created by Visual Basic, you would have to update all the references made to it in the .CFG file. Frankly, it is more trouble than it is worth at this point.

Reinstalling the Personnel Information Request Form

When changes are made to a form in Visual Basic, you must use the Forms Manager in the Microsoft Exchange Client to install the form. Remember, only the person who created the folder can make these types of changes.

1. In the Microsoft Exchange Client select the Personnel Profile Information folder.
2. From the File menu, choose Properties, and then select the Forms tab.
3. Choose the Manage Button, and then click the install button.
4. Double-click the pqinfo.cfg file, which is located in the pqinfo.vb directory. If you are asked to overwrite an existing executable, choose yes.

To check and see if you have the right form, select the Personnel Profile Information folder once again and then select the request form from the menu.

From Here...

As stated earlier, we could devote an entire book to forms and application design under Exchange. We've tried to provide the information you need get your feet wet. You can always refer to the Microsoft documentation and the on-line Help for more information. Having read this chapter, you now should understand the following:

- Forms are ways of posting data to a folder or sending structured information to a user or users.
- Forms are Visual Basic executable files.
- The Forms Designer provides a non-programming interface for creating forms.
- Forms are stored in libraries.
- Forms are composed of windows and fields.
- Forms, windows, and fields all have properties that control their behavior.
- Placing forms in public folders gives users across the enterprise access to the forms and the data contained within them.
- Forms can be extended with Visual Basic.

It is always a good idea to tune your Exchange environment after making any major change. For tips on monitoring and tuning Exchange, read the following chapters:

- Chapter 24, "Exchange Performance Tuning and Capacity Planning," gives you the necessary tools to reshape your Exchange, especially after introducing a new change like a Form into your Exchange evironment.

- Chapter 26, "Monitoring Your Organization," tells you how to implement a monitoring scheme to help you detect common errors before they become serious problems.

Part
V

Ch
34

Index

Complete and Return this Card
for a *FREE* Computer Book Catalog

Thank you for purchasing this book! You have purchased a superior computer book written expressly for your needs. To continue to provide the kind of up-to-date, pertinent coverage you've come to expect from us, we need to hear from you. Please take a minute to complete and return this self-addressed, postage-paid form. In return, we'll send you a free catalog of all our computer books on topics ranging from word processing to programming and the internet.

r. ☐   Mrs. ☐   Ms. ☐   Dr. ☐

ame (first) [＿＿＿＿＿＿＿＿＿＿] (M.I.) [＿] (last) [＿＿＿＿＿＿＿＿＿＿＿]

ddress [＿＿＿＿＿＿＿＿＿＿＿＿＿＿＿＿＿＿＿＿＿]

[＿＿＿＿＿＿＿＿＿＿＿＿＿＿＿＿＿＿＿＿＿]

ty [＿＿＿＿＿＿＿＿＿＿＿] State [＿＿] Zip [＿＿＿＿] [＿＿＿]

one [＿] [＿＿＿] [＿＿＿＿] Fax [＿＿＿] [＿＿＿] [＿＿＿＿]

mpany Name [＿＿＿＿＿＿＿＿＿＿＿＿＿＿＿＿＿＿＿]

mail address [＿＿＿＿＿＿＿＿＿＿＿＿＿＿＿＿＿＿]

Please check at least (3) influencing factors for purchasing this book.

ont or back cover information on book .... ☐
ecial approach to the content .... ☐
mpleteness of content .... ☐
uthor's reputation .... ☐
blisher's reputation .... ☐
ok cover design or layout .... ☐
dex or table of contents of book .... ☐
ice of book .... ☐
ecial effects, graphics, illustrations .... ☐
her (Please specify): _____ ☐

How did you first learn about this book?

w in Macmillan Computer Publishing catalog .... ☐
commended by store personnel .... ☐
w the book on bookshelf at store .... ☐
commended by a friend .... ☐
ceived advertisement in the mail .... ☐
w an advertisement in: _____ ☐
ad book review in: _____ ☐
her (Please specify): _____ ☐

How many computer books have you purchased in the last six months?

is book only .... ☐   3 to 5 books .... ☐
ooks .... ☐   More than 5 .... ☐

4. Where did you purchase this book?

Bookstore .... ☐
Computer Store .... ☐
Consumer Electronics Store .... ☐
Department Store .... ☐
Office Club .... ☐
Warehouse Club .... ☐
Mail Order .... ☐
Direct from Publisher .... ☐
Internet site .... ☐
Other (Please specify): _____ ☐

5. How long have you been using a computer?

☐ Less than 6 months   ☐ 6 months to a year
☐ 1 to 3 years   ☐ More than 3 years

6. What is your level of experience with personal computers and with the subject of this book?

	With PCs	With subject of book
New	☐	☐
Casual	☐	☐
Accomplished	☐	☐
Expert	☐	☐

Source Code ISBN: 0-7897-1116-8

7. Which of the following best describes your job title?

Administrative Assistant ☐
Coordinator ☐
Manager/Supervisor ☐
Director ☐
Vice President ☐
President/CEO/COO ☐
Lawyer/Doctor/Medical Professional ☐
Teacher/Educator/Trainer ☐
Engineer/Technician ☐
Consultant ☐
Not employed/Student/Retired ☐
Other (Please specify): _____ ☐

8. Which of the following best describes the area of the company your job title falls under?

Accounting ☐
Engineering ☐
Manufacturing ☐
Operations ☐
Marketing ☐
Sales ☐
Other (Please specify): _____ ☐

9. What is your age?

Under 20 ☐
21-29 ☐
30-39 ☐
40-49 ☐
50-59 ☐
60-over ☐

10. Are you:

Male ☐
Female ☐

11. Which computer publications do you read regularly? (Please list)

_____
_____
_____
_____
_____
_____
_____
_____
_____
_____

Comments: _____
_____
_____

Fold here and scotch-tape to mail.

MACMILLAN COMPUTER PUBLISHING USA
A VIACOM COMPANY

Technical

Support:

If you need assistance with the information in this book or with a CD/Disk
accompanying the book, please access the Knowledge Base on our Web
site at **http://www.superlibrary.com/general/support**. Our most
Frequently Asked Questions are answered there. If you do not find the
answer to your questions on our Web site, you may contact Macmillan
Technical Support **(317) 581-3833** or e-mail us at **support@mcp.com**.